Danish Business Law

djøf FORLAG
JURIST- OG ØKONOMFORBUNDETS FORLAG
LYNGBYVEJ 17, POSTBOKS 2702
2100 KØBENHAVN Ø - TLF 39 13 55 00

Bent Iversen,
Lars Lindencrone Petersen
& Morten Wegener

Danish Business Law

English Translation by Hanne Grøn

DJØF Publishing Copenhagen
2004

Danish Business Law
3. edition

Print: Narayana Press, Gylling
Binding: Damm's Forlagsbogbinderi, Randers

Printed in Denmark 2004
ISBN 87-574-1054-2

DJØF Publishing
17, Lyngbyvej
P.O.Box 2702
DK-2100 Copenhagen
Denmark

Phone: +45 39 13 55 00
Fax: +45 39 13 55 55
E-mail: fl@djoef.dk
Homepage: www.djoef-forlag.dk

Contents

Preface

This book provides a general introduction to a number of central areas in Danish business law. The book is an English language translation of a Danish textbook whose latest edition dates from 2004. The translation aims at enabling foreign readers – whether seeking information on Danish law for practical purposes, in study contexts or for other purposes – to get a reasonably broad insight into various parts of Danish law of particular relevance to the business community by means of one single exposition in the field.

The account comprises both areas of purely national (Danish) law and areas in which an international influence has affected the Danish legal position. During recent decades the latter areas have increased in importance.Their frequent occurrence means that the foreign reader is likely to come across treatments of rules or sets of rules which are identical, in part or in full, with the rules in force in his/her own country. Most often the identical character of the rules is explained by the fact that the country in question and Denmark both participate, or have participated, in a certain international cooperation providing the basis for the national rules. The most conspicuous example of this nature is of course the comprehensive on-going process of making uniform laws in selected areas in a number of Western-European countries resulting from the cooperation within the European Communities (the European Union) which Denmark joined as a member in 1973. But also outside this special European cooperation Denmark has long participated, in the interests of international trade, in providing uniform national rules in important areas, or at least towards an approximization between the national legal orders of various countries. Thus Denmark acceded to important parts of the United Nations Convention for the International Sale of Goods (CISG) and to all the fundamental universal Conventions to protect intellectual and industrial rights. Further, Danish undertakings, operating on foreign markets, will to a considerable extent apply international models for draftings of contracts with their foreign contract partners as regards contractual contents, or they will include certain contract terms which may be available from international organizations within particular lines or trades, e.g. the terms originating from the International Chamber of Commerce, the so-called INCOTERMS.

As regards the areas of business law which are of either purely national character or where, despite international models, the national rules are diverging, we find it expedient already in this Preface to point to some recurrent characteristics of Danish law to provide the foreign reader with a general idea of the location of Danish law on the legal map. Therefore, we will outline a few general guidelines in that respect in the following.

First, it must be noted that in a large amount of areas – linguistic, economic, political, and cultural – Denmark has close historical ties to her Nothern neighbours (Finland, Iceland, Norway and Sweden). This is also reflected in the legal order. Thus, Danish legal development shows a striking similiarity to the development in the other Nordic countries with whose national legal orders Denmark holds close relations both as regards structure, methodical approach, and substantive content in important fields, including business law. Consequently, what is said about any Danish legal pecularities will to a great extent also apply to the rest of the Nordic countries.

Traditionally, the law of the Nordic countries is grouped with the so-called continental-European family of law (the Roman-German family of law, or "civil law" systems). In the main such categorization is tenable although it is necessary to bear in mind that there are quite important differences in relation to what is generally deemed to characterize continental European legal orders. Thus, Roman law influence on the legal development via court practice and legal scientific thinking was much less marked in the Nordic countries than in the main countries in continental Europe. This is illustrated e.g. by the fact that Roman law was never acknowledged in Denmark as a subsidiary *ius commune* to be applied. Second, neither Denmark nor the rest of the Nordic countries embarked on full-scale codifications of private law such as the French Code Civil and Code Commerce and the German Bürgerliches Gesetzbuch and Handelsgesetzbuch, indeed there is not even a clear dividing line between "civil" law (i.e. law applying to ordinary individuals) and commercial law. Important areas of private law in the Nordic countries – including central parts of contract and property law – are characterized by having developed and grown, to a far greater extent than on the rest of the Continent, in a pragmatic way on their own at a pace dictated by practical needs and thus by a certain lack of dogmatic points of departure.

As regards legal method, jurists and lawyers in Denmark and the rest of the Nordic countries will, like their counterparts in e.g. France and Germany, approach the legal system with the view that it represents a final and, in principle, complete entity where, in most cases, the point of departure will involve deducing from a legal rule fixed in a formal legislative setting what conslusion to apply to a concrete legal issue. Although the catalogue of possible source of law factors is in principle considered open – presumably to a greater extent in the Nordic countries that in the rest of the contiental European legal systems – there is no doubt that statue law made by the legislative power holds the principal place in this catalogue. Partly as a result of the lack of binding precedent power of court decisions the courts hold a weaker position when it comes to formation of law than is the case in Anglo-American law and legal orders based on that legal system.

The authors

CHAPTER 1

Introduction

by Morten Wegener

1. Business law as a branch of law

In a Danish legal context the term business law is not a particularly precise delimitation of an area of *law* but rather – except for taxation and duties' legislation – a term denoting the *legal rules* of particular relevance to the *exercise of business enterprise*. Thus the contents of the subject are not based on systematic considerations but are primarily determined by practical needs of providing a comprehensive account of the legal relationships of business entities.

In a society which is so thoroughly regulated as the present Danish society it is self-evident that the subject covers a very wide area of law indeed when the contents are described in this way. Undoubtedly, a substantial amount of the general rules of law in force is of particular relevance to the business community. Thus already from an expositional point of view the advisability of a sub-division into appropriate and fairly related contexts would seem to be indicated.

Such a division may be made on the basis of various considerations or criteria. In the present text we have chosen to give main emphasis to the *character of the common interests* underlying the legal rules (as they are manifested e.g. in legislation), i.e. to the delimitation of such interests into *public* ("community relevant") or *private* interests. With this delimitation as a starting point it is possible to make a rough and therefore not completely precise segregation of two major sub-areas, viz. the *business regulating* law and such parts of the law as are normally described as "property law". This term is very much wider in a Danish context than its common-law counterpart since it includes contract and tort as well.

The *business regulating law* deals with the regulation of business relationships which are governed by immediate *public* interests. This regulation may be manifested in the formulation of certain legal limits – or requirements in respect of the dispositions made by business enterprises when pursuing their activities in production, sale or other contexts. The observance of such limits or requirements is ensured by certain *public administrative authorities* acting on their own initiative by means of control, grantings of approvals, licences etc., and a violation of the rules may carry public sanctions, most often in the form of *criminal liability*. Statutory regulations of environmental protection, health security measures in production and sale, and regulatory measures to counteract restrictive trade practices are typical examples of this kind of legal regulation. However, the public authorities do not only apply the "rod" but also the "carrot" in the relationships with the business community. Thus, another important area of the business regulating law is concerned with public assistance or subsidy schemes in favour of business entities.

Where – as will have transpired – the business regulating law may be said to relate to certain business relationships towards public authorities in the latters' function of administrators of immediate public interests, the other sub-area, *property law,* deals with the legal regulation of relationships between citizens respectively and that area is therefore characterized by immediate *private* interests. In simplified terms the property law deals with the law relating to *assignable rights* – typically rights of an *economic value* – e.g. property rights in respect of real estate and chattels. The basic principle taken as a starting point here is the principle of the individual citizen's (or business undertaking's) *autonomy* and thus access to undertake or incur legal *obligations* towards others by *contract* or as a result of a commission of a *legal wrong* (e.g. a tort). In contrast to the legal regulation of business enterprises, the initiative of securing the observance of such obligations does not lie with a public body but with the party entitled under the individual obligation relationship (e.g. the contract). The remedies available in the event of violation of obligations typically take the form of *specific performance* and/or *compensation (damages).*

The area of property law of particular relevance to business enterprises is principally the legal rules governing the relationship of such business enterprises towards *customers* (in a broad sense of the word), towards *other partners* in a business co-operation (incl. lenders), towards *employees* and finally towards *third parties* affected by harmful acts originating from the exercise of a business enterprise. The individual areas of law corresponding to this part of property law are broadly speaking especially relating to the general rules governing: Formation and validity of contract, sale of goods and supply of services, statutory exclusive rights (e.g. patents), organisation of business entities (e.g. in sole proprietorships or in companies), financing and credit security, the importance of insolvency and other payment incapability, employment contracts of a broad description, tort and insurance law.

The main focus outside the introductory chapters will be placed on these subject matters. The business regulating law is only treated to a limited extent and only where linked to property law rules, e.g. as in Chapter 12 which deals with competition law.

2. The concept of legal rule

2.1. General substantive content

In this context a *rule* is defined as a *general linguistic* statement *prescribing* the appropriate *conduct* in certain situations or contexts of life. Thus, rules communicate *directives* as to what "must" or "ought to" be done or omitted.

Life in a human society is in every respect fenced in with rules. One example is the conduct in traffic situations where e.g. drivers' conduct is governed by the traffic rules. Other rules are concerned with more general human behaviour and are described in ethical and moral directives as to accepted conduct of life or thinking which are generally regarded as "correct" or "good".

Although in principle nothing prevents a person from making his own "private" rules – which is quite a common occurrence – by which he chooses to live, such rules are generally to be conceived as *social* phenomena: In more or less comprehensive contexts, guidelines for the relationship *between* human beings or for their social life are set up.

The rules which are described in Section 1 as legal rules and which are dealt with in the present account within a delimited area are, like other types of rule, codes in the sense just described. However, they have a number of special qualities of which at least one sets them out in a quite distinguishing manner from the other rules, viz. by the possible reaction to their non-observance. In the normal course of events, offensive conduct will be met by *disapproval* on the part of the surrounding world. Where a card player e.g. deliberately omits to follow suit in a card game he is usually blamed by his co-players who may extend their reaction to the infringement of the rule by interrupting the game and forbid the rule-breaker to participate in future games.

Where strictly moral rules are broken the same condemnation of the offensive party may result even to the extent of social ostracism for a period. As will be seen the disapproval of the surrounding world in these two examples takes the form of some *concrete* (non-formalised) reaction. Indeed, there are no other possibilities.

With the legal rules the situation is very much different.

The disapproval following in the wake of non-observance of obligations laid down by legal rules may be manifested in *formalised sanctions* (e.g.

punishment or compensation) imposed by certain authorities endowed – by virtue of other rules – with the power to impose such sanctions, especially courts of law. Such sanctions may ultimately be enforced by compulsion in the form of *physical application of constraint* via special bodies of authority (especially the police and bailiff's courts). The application of force is in other words monopolised. Traffic rules e.g. are legal rules. When an ordinary driver is caught by the police for disregarding traffic light signals he is liable to sanctions in the form of punishment, most often the imposition of a fine – and this sanction may, if necessary, be enforced by physical application of force.

As regards the property law rules the situation is in principle the same. Where a builder e.g. in the course of his work negligently causes harm to the neighbour's property or person, the general tort rules will provide the neighbour with a claim for damages in respect of the loss suffered by the negligent act. Where the parties cannot settle the matter among themselves the neighbour may bring an action in a court of law and obtain judgment against the builder. If the claim is successful, the neighbour may have the judgment enforced against the property of the builder with the assistance of the bailiff. Thus the judgment expresses the sanction available in the situation of non-observance of the obligation of the builder to act with care towards a third party's property or person which the common tort rules impose upon him.

Thus, briefly stated legal rules are codes, whose enforcement is the prerogative of special authorities, principally courts of law, whose agents may, if necessary, apply monopolised physical constraint in the enforcement process. There may well be an inter-action of legal rules and rules of another character, in particular moral rules. Drunk driving e.g. is a criminal offence. In addition the drunk driver is also met with extensive moral disapproval from the surrounding world. Such inter-action between legal and moral rules will generally act as an intensifier when it comes to controlling conduct, as will become apparent in the following section.

2.2. The legal system

All the rules of law in force at a certain time in a certain community, e.g. the present Danish society, are described as that community's *legal system* or *order*. The fact that the legal rules are of a general character, cf. the preceding Section, entails that they are aimed at an indefinite group of persons, typically in principle at all citizens and authorities within the geographical area governed by the legal system in question.

The prime function of the legal system is to *govern conduct*. In the legal regulation of various areas of life, contained in the legal rules, the aim is to lead human activities into certain directions under the common presumption – enhanced by the possibilities of compulsion just referred to – that the citizens act in accordance with the rules. Another function is to *solve conflicts*. Even the best arrangement and preparation of control attempts will fail to completely prevent disputes between individual citizens or between citizens and the authorities of a community. Therefore bodies must exist whose function is to solve such conflicts and it is necessary to have rules for their operation. Behind both the conduct-governing and the conflict-solving functions lies the general aim of ensuring peace and stability in the community in question. In spite of the compulsive character of the legal system it is therefore often referred to as a "peace" system. The legal system may also be said to make up a *certain arrangement* in which the individual rules are related to each other in a certain way, cf. the following Section.

Within any highly developed community, the legal system is – as already indicated – closely related to the state power. In such communities by far the majority of all legal rules are made by the state authority endowed with such power, cf. Chapter 2 for a review of the Danish sources. An obvious corollary to this is that one must be prepared for deviations – which under the circumstances may be quite substantial – in the various national systems of law and also in the operation of the legal decision process, cf. Chapter 3. The Danish legal system has a close affinity to the legal systems of the other Nordic countries, especially in the area of property law – whereas the differences are more marked when comparisons are made to the other West-European countries.

The difference in the legal systems is of course a major barrier to international business. But the importance is reduced, partly through the co-operation in the European Union and partly through other means of international co-operation, cf. Chapter 3 below.

3. Various Types of Legal Rule

3.1. Introduction

Naturally, the very large number of legal rules which are usually found in a modern community differ both in character and function. In this section a brief review is made of the various categories, normally made to distinguish the rules. A couple of other distinctions have already been touched upon, viz. the categorization according to substantive contents of the rules, i.e. on the basic matters of life under regulation (e.g. property law and business regulation law) and according to national or international origin.

3.2. Obligation rules and competence rules

A distinction may be made between obligation rules and competence rules according to the *function* of the rules in the legal system.

The function of an *obligation rule* is direct conduct control. The terms of the rule will express either a *prohibitory* injunction or a *mandatory* injunction ("command") reflecting whether the aim is to prevent certain acts or requiring a certain act to be made. Exceptions from prohibitory injunctions exist as "licences" and from mandatory injunctions as *"exemptions"*. The obligation rules are corner stones of the legal system. Their non-observance may result in a *legal liability*, typically consisting in a *judgment* imposing *specific performance, damages* or *penalty*, cf. also the preceding Section 2.1. Most of the various codes of conduct in the traffic rules are e.g. obligation rules.

However, obligation rules cannot exist on their own. It is necessary also to have rules regarding private individuals' and public bodies' *competence* (authority or capacity) to make legally relevant dispositions, e.g. to enter into contracts, make laws, pronounce judgments, assess taxes and charge duties etc. Such rules which may briefly be described as stating "*who* can do *what* and *how"* are referred to as *competence rules*. The result of the exercise of the act of competence is often called a *legal disposition* or *legal act*. Such acts may be general, where they are designed for an indefinite multitude of future applications (e.g. statutes) or specific, where they are aimed solely for application under certain circumstances of a case in point (e.g. a judgment or a contract of sale of specific goods).

Where competence rules are disregarded the direct result is that the act made will be *invalid*. The competence to legislate e.g. is shared between the head of state and the parliament (the Danish "Folketing") and an "Act" made by a Minister on his own is therefore invalid. Similarly the rules in respect of vitiating factors in contract listed in the Danish Contracts Act (s. 28 et seq) in respect of the effect of duress, fraud, undue influence etc. having existed at the formation of the contract) describe how a valid contract may be made. Therefore these provisions also contain competence rules.

3.3. Written and unwritten law

In communities such as the Danish the main contents of most law are in the form of *written* law which may be identified from certain texts, e.g. the statutes adopted by the Danish parliament, the Folketing. This does not imply that the rules in question are precise and immediately applicable, cf. 3.6 and 4 below. In certain areas, however, especially within property law there are also *unwritten* rules. Such unwritten law is identified, e.g. from the case law of court decisions, cf. Chapter 2, Section 5 below. One supreme example of such unwritten law is the ordinary rule of compensation in Danish law – the so-called culpa-rule (denoting fault liability) which has been developed in case law, cf. Chapter 5 for specific reference.

The distinction between written law/unwritten law mainly coincides with a distinction between the rules of law according to their *origin*. A distinction may be made here between "positively" created rules and rules without such foundation. The first category includes rules which have been made under a *definite formal procedure* in a body authorized to lay down rules. The other category mainly includes rules laid down by case law and established customs, cf. Chapter 2, Section 6 below for an account of the latter.

3.4. The hierarchy of rules

The legal rules differ in order of priority which implies a hierarchy under which a rule of *superior rank* will supersede a rule of *lower rank* where there is a conflict between two such rules.

As regards *written* rules of pure *Danish* origin, rules founded on the Danish Constitution (The Danish Act of Constitution 1953) rank above all other written rules. The power of the Folketing to make laws in co-operation with the Head of State is thus, as already mentioned, based on the Constitution and the Folketing would be barred from validly adopting legislation the rules of which go against provisions in the Constitution, such as illustrated a few years ago when the Supreme Court overruled ceratin parts of the co-called "lex Tvind" (designed to govern the controversial Tvind school system).

Similarly, provisions in statutory Orders made by Ministers, cf. Chapter 2, Section 4 below cannot supersede provisions of a statute adopted by the Folketing and assented to by the Head of State. This follows from the fact that ministerial powers to lay down such orders must normally be based on a legislative authority to such effect, i.e. the power must really derive from the Folketing.

There may also be conflicts between written Danish rules and rules of an *international basis*, e.g. EU-law, or rules of Conventions made by Denmark with other states. Where the conflict is with a so-called "EU-rule of direct applicability", e.g. most regulations issued by the Council of the European Union and from the European Commission, the EU rules take precedence over the purely national rules, cf. Chapter 3, Section 4.6.

Unwritten law may exist at all levels, including (though rarely) at the constitutional level. For such law it is more difficult to suggest a definite hierarchy if conflicts of ranking arise. Normally the conflicts need to be solved on a concrete assessment of the circumstances of the case creating doubt or conflict both where two unwritten rules conflict and where a written rule and an unwritten rule are at variance. In the assessment such factors as the character of the rules and their comparative age may be weighted.

3.5. Directory and Mandatory rules

The moulding of the pattern of behaviour aimed at in the legal rules may be more or less *intensive*. Thus some rules may be *deviated from by agreement* of the parties in that they make a different arrangement than the one a rule provides for. Thus the stated rule is only applicable where the parties have not agreed something else between them. Such rules may be referred to as "*non-mandatory*". They are especially common within the branch of property law relating to contracts, as e.g. the provision of the Danish Sale of Goods Act s. 1(1) which provides that most of the rules in the Act may be deviated from in the event of express agreement to such effect between the parties to the sale.

Rules which cannot be dispensed with or deviated from by agreement may be referred to as *mandatory*. The main body of the rules in the Danish legal system generally belongs to this category.

Whether a rule of law may be deviated from or not will, in the event of written law, appear from the text in which the rule is stated as the sale of goods example just showed. In other cases the question must be solved by construction of the rule. In the normal course of events it may be presumed that it is not possible to deviate from the arrangement established in the rule where such rule concerns immediate interests of the state or of third parties, or where the rule is dictated by considerations of protection in favour of a contract party. Consumers e.g. are often regarded as "weak" contract parties who should be protected, e.g. when entering contracts with business people, cf. the express reservation to that effect in the Sale of Goods Act s. 1(2) in combination with s. 4 a of the rules of the same Act under which a number of the rules of the Act cannot be dispensed with in a consumer sale to the prejudice of the (consumer) buyer.

The purpose of directory rules is to offer arrangements to contracting parties in specific contract relationships which they may apply in the absence of agreement to the contrary. Thus, in a contract of sale it is not necessary to stipulate the legal relationship of the parties in great detail as they may leave such content to be determined completely or partly on the basis of the Sale of Goods Act rules. Where the contract is silent, the Sale of Goods Act rules may be said to complement the contract by "*gap-filling*".

3.6. Precise and imprecise rules

The legal rules are also very different in regard to the degree of precision in the description of the circumstances to which the rules apply and/or the legal effects they bring about. The level of precision determines the degree of *freedom of choice/assessment* conferred upon the authorities responsible for applying the rules.

On a scale of precision, one extreme will be made up by rules of almost non-existing freedom of choice. The Danish Tort Liability Act s. 3 provides for compensation in respect of pain and suffering, operating prima facie on fixed amounts per day. Where liability is established with a tortfeasor, s. 3

does not leave any possibility of choice as regards the measure of damages. At the other extreme are rules, in which the restrictions binding the authorities are very modest, leaving ample room for the exercise of their own *discretion*. Under the Marketing Practices Act s. 2(1) a business enterprise may not use false, misleading or unreasonably incomplete statements calculated to affect the demand for or the supply of goods, real property or other property assets and services, including labour services – for possible direct effects of infringements, cf. ss. 13 of the Act (i.a. injunctions) and 22 (penalty). Almost all the limbs in the descriptions are vague, thus providing the possibility of a discretionary assessment in the application. The two examples also show that the issue of precision which was indicated at the beginning – may relate to the description in the rule of the factual circumstances which must prevail in order to apply the rule at all (The Marketing Act, s. 2) *or* to the description of the legal effects a certain given conduct will entail (Tort Liability Act, s. 3) *or* perhaps both – as an example may be quoted the provision in the Danish Product Liability Act s. 6(1) regarding producers' liability in respect of damage caused by defective products.

In a class of their own among imprecise rules are the so-called "*general clauses*". This term covers very broadly defined rules of very imprecise tenor – which relate to a more precise and detailed regulation – of certain factors of the same legislation, also covered by the broad provisions by virtue of their very generality. Thus the general clause acts as a kind of "sweeping-up" clause in relation to the detailed regulation elsewhere. An outstanding example is provided by the Contracts Act s. 36 which is i.a. also applicable to the invalidity situations described in the immediately preceding provisions of the same Act. Another important example is the provision in s. 1 of the Marketing Practices Act.

4. Sources of law and law source factors

In any confrontation with legal issues it is of course of paramount importance that the decision-maker or party attempting to evaluate the issue knows – or knows where to find – the relevant rules for resolving the issue and also the rules of construction underlying them.

This brings us to problems which are both important and complex. In the preceding two Sections the existence of the various rules of law was taken more or less for granted. In practice, however, it is not enough to reach for one's statute compilations and choose from a variety of ready-made rules much like the supermarket shopper choosing daily groceries from the shelves. Some effort is needed to extract the rules in a shape that will make them applicable to (i.e. operational on) the issues involved. First of all, they need to be *found and formulated.* The difficulties here have already been touched upon in the statements made above in 3.3. and 3.6. Where the rules involved are e.g. of unwritten nature – in that they are established in case law or based on customs – it is not possible to observe them immediately for closer study. Therefore some machinery must exist to make the rules visible. But which machinery and how does one go about the preparatory work involved? Similarly, imprecise rules based on legislation, often leave substantial doubt as to the possibilities of application. Is it possible to eliminate or at least reduce such doubt and, in the affirmative, how is it done?

Problems of this character are usually considered within the context of *sources of law.* This term is both in a direct and a figurative sense extremely apt. The substance which makes up the final rules derives from various "producers" (sources) in Denmark, especially from legislators, courts and administrative bodies. Most often the final rule will have derived content from more than one of these forces at a time. An example is again provided by the general clause in s. 36 of the Danish Contracts Act referred to in 3.6. The prima facie impression is of a highly imprecise rule whose possibilities of application within general contract law seem more or less without limit. But this impression does not hold when studying the practical application of the rule by the courts in cases before them. Thus it is always necessary also to include this source material – the court decisions – in an assessment of the content of the final rule and its possibilities of application.

If we were to define sources of law in more accurate terms they may be said to include all the factors influencing the authorities, applying the law, in their choice and/or formulation of rules to be applied in concrete legal issues. Chief representatives of authorities applying the law are the courts. In a community like the Danish, the courts will be the ultimate interpreters of law. It is not possible to give an exhaustive enumeration of the factors in question but the factors will certainly include legislation, administrative orders and regulations, court decisions, customs and the "flexible" element, most often described as "the circumstances of the case" (or alternatively, "cultural tradition"). As was mentioned above, the various factors often inter-act when formulating the relevant rules, and this inter-action should always be kept in mind. This also implies that it is not really possible to set up any binding hierarchy of the factors though the process of search should start in the existing legislative texts relating to the issue in point. Where such issue is within an area in which European Community law or other non-national sources, e.g. international customs, exist, such sources must of course be included in the research.

In practical work involving source of law factors it is essential to know where to find information relating to these factors. The development of the

Internet has meant that in a number of areas this medium provides the easiest acces s. to information on relevant issues of a Danish and an international character. In Chapters 2-3 reference is made to a number of electronical search facilities. If starting from scratch a useful place to begin a search would be the law site "Themis" (www.themis.dk/) or the website for Danish and international law" (www.thybo.dk/) providing a large number of links to various on-line services with a legal content.

5. The legal decision

In practice when approaching a factual issue with a view to evaluation of the issue under a rule of law found and formulated on the basis of the relevant source of law factors, and possibly interpreting, the final outcome is a *decision*, i.e. upon considerations of the factual and legal circumstances of the case a choice is made between two or more possible solutions. The thought process leading the decision-maker to this choice will almost always be characterized by a *balancing or assessment* of the factual and legal circumstances involved. It is important to keep this in mind to avoid the widespread misconception that a legal decision represents a deduction from one or more legal rules so that the result (the decision) is really dictated by the rule – and thereby logically compulsive – when the facts of the case are elucidated. The courts and other law applying authorities are not "slot machines" delivering defined decisions without an independent assessment. The same must of course apply to everyone else whose task is to present estimates on the legal evaluation of certain factual circumstances whether they relate to past or future matters, e.g. lawyers and commercial jurists.

CHAPTER 2

National Source of Law Factors

by Morten Wegener

1. Introduction

As was mentioned in Chapter 1, Section 4, sources of law refer to all the factors which influence the authorities applying the law (primarily courts of law) in their choice and/or formulation of rules applicable in the decision of concrete legal issues. This Chapter is devoted to the relevant factors of *Danish* origin which are treated separately. As was also mentioned in Chapter 1, it is important to remember that in practice the factors operate in an interaction so that more factors may simultaneously contribute to the formulation of the rule to be applied. The reference to relevant factors here signifies the materials the courts will generally be expected to turn to in their decision-making process. This does not signify that the courts are under a *duty* to consider all the factors presented here. Such duty on the courts will probably only exist in respect of rules, formulated in legislation, directly affecting the legal issue in point, and in respect of any case law practice (precedent) from the Supreme Court containing facts resembling those of the case in point.

2. The Constitution

The Constitution Act of 5 June 1953 contains rules especially on the composition of the supreme state organs (head of state, parliament (the Folketing), government, and courts of law) and on their ordinary powers and jurisdiction, including in this respect a number of important limitations (the socalled "freedom rights", cf. ss. 71 et seq.). The Constitution is far more difficult to amend than an ordinary piece of legislation. Section 88 prescribes that in order to amend the Constitution the bill proposing the change shall be adopted twice – in un-amended form – by the Folketing, the second time after a new general election has been held, and further approval is also required by referendum, under which a majority of the voters representing no less than 40 per cent of the electorate shall vote in its favour. Finally, the consent of the head of state in the form of "royal assent" is necessary.

The provision in s. 20 of the Constitution is very important in regard to the Danish participation in international co-operation implying delegation of so-called "sovereignty" from national to international authorities. Under the provision powers which are vested in the national authorities by the Constitution may – to a specified extent – be delegated by statute to international authorities set up by mutual agreement with other states in the furtherance of international law and justice and transnational co-operation.

For the adoption of bills relating to delegation of sovereignty, a majority of 5/6 of the members of the Folketing is required. If the bill is adopted, though not by the requisite majority, and the government upholds it, the fate of the bill will be decided by referendum, for further reference cf. especially s. 42(5) of the Danish Constitution Act.

In a national context the Constitution is the main foundation of the legal system. But constitutional interpretation and issues of application are rare in case law and so far the courts have displayed a great amount of reticence when reviewing whether an Act adopted by the Folketing is contrary to the Constitution. In more recent years a less reticent attitude may perhaps be found, cf. the example mentioned in Chapter 1, Section 3.4.

3. Legislation

3.1. The statutory process and the importance of legislation as a source of law

The term "legislation" refers to socalled "formal enactments", i.e. the general "directives" which have been given statutory status in the manner prescribed in the Constitution. The process normally involves introduction to the Folketing of the proposed legislation in the form of a bill which must undergo three stages of reading and adoption, followed by royal assent cf. especially ss. 21-22 and 41 of the Danish Constitution Act.

Acts must be *promulgated* (made public) in order to be enforced by the courts and administrative authorities, cf. the Danish Constitution Act s. 22.

Unless the individual Act otherwise directs, publication shall be made in the legal gazette "Lovtidende", which is an official paper published by the government (the Ministry of Justice, Legal Information Office), cf. Consolidating Act No. 842 of 16 December 1991 governing (the legal publications) Lovtidende and Ministerialtidende. S. 3 of this Act lays down the following provision regarding commencement dates of statutes: Where the individual Act does not make special provision for commencement date, the Act will take effect on the weekday following the date of publication in the "Lovtidende". Individual commencement dates are rather common.

The time stipulated for commencement is not necessarily co-inciding with the point in time from which factual circumstances bring about legal effects in accordance with the rules in the Act. There is no provision in the Constitution barring retrospective force being given to Acts and indeed such force is occasionally given.

As regards the importance of legislation as a source of law the first point to make is that there is an absolute presumption that the courts will consider existing legislation directly affecting the issue to be decided in a case, cf. the account in 1 above. Various factors will decide the extent to which the Act will be applied within its direct field of application, including especially whether the provisions of the Act may be dispensed with it or not (directory or mandatory provisions, cf. above, Chapter 1, Section 3.5) and the degree of precision of the rule applied, cf. Section 3.6. It is commonly believed that the more "finished" (precise and exhaustive) the individual legislative rules appear for application in defined cases, the stronger their force in relation to other source factors will be.

3.2. Reference places

As already mentioned, the texts of individual Acts are listed chronologically in the Lovtidende (Division A: Ordinary Acts) Division B: Finance Acts, Supplementary Appropriations Acts and Acts relating to government servants, and nationality Acts; Division C: International Agreements. An Index is made out for every year. In addition the statutory texts may be found in the publication "Love og anordninger" (Acts and Statutory Instruments) (corresponding to Lovtidende, Division A) in statute compilations, commented and un-commented (e.g. Karnov's Lovsamling – the Danish equivalent to "Halsbury's Statutes"), in special statute collections on specified areas and in commented editions of individual acts (e.g. the commented versions published by the Danish legal publishing house, Juristforbundets Forlag.

Naturally, the initial practical problem in applying the legislative texts consists in establishing whether any legislation exists in a given area and if so, the nature of such legislation. Currently the easiest, and probably safest, procedure is to consult one of the on-line services available, e.g. the data base "Retsinformation" (Legal Information) – under the Ministry of Justice, Legal Information Office – which i.a. contains the texts of all Acts in force (www.retsinfo.dk) or the website www.danmark.dk/ providing i.a. summaries of acts and bills with links to search the full texts of these. Traditional manual search sources include the publications "Danish Lovregister" (Danish Statute

Index) or "Schultz Lovnøgle" ("Statutory Key Index" published by the legal publishers Schultz) which both contain exhaustive indexes and head words.

3.3. Travaux préparatoires

Travaux préparatoires – the preparatory materials or "history" underlying enactments – including comments on proposed legislation and the parliamentary debates on it may be very important when the detailed content of a specific rule is to be determined. The issues which may arise in this context are treated in Section 8 under statutory interpretation.

4. Ministerial Orders and other statutory instruments

4.1. Origin and importance as a source of law

Like statutes, statutory instruments such as ministerial orders are general rules of law directed towards everybody. They are issued by a central administrative authority, usually by the Minister within whose province the regulation in question has been made. As the public administration is subject to a so-called *legality principle* which i.a. implies that administrative acts in relation to citizens must be authorised ("covered") by legislation a minister may not on his own lay down rules of law creating rights or obligations in respect of the citizens. The making of ministerial orders therefore requires a statutory *authorization* to such effect from the legislative power to the minister in question.

Ministerial orders and other statutory instruments are especially common for the making of detailed regulation in connection with existing legislation and occasionally also in areas in which a need for current adjustments of existing rules has been registered, e.g. in response to developments in pay and/ or prices in the community. To obtain enforceability, statutory instruments must be promulgated in the same way as statutes, i.e. by publication in the "Lovtidende".

The difference between "*Consolidated*" Acts and ordinary Acts is that the former "sweep up" existing piecemeal legislation, original and with subsequent amendments, so that the total legislation on the subject is presented in an updated form including all currently applicable provisions, as e.g. the Consolidated Act on Lovtidende referred to in 3.1.

In a sense the issuing of statutory instruments implies a delegation of legislative power (to make generally binding rules) to the administrative authorities which also implies that in principle such instruments have just the same legal force as sources of law as primary legislation. As regards the direct field of application it may thus be taken for granted that the courts will consider rules in statutory instruments – always provided, of course, that the issuing authority (the Minister) has kept within the authority conferred upon him.

4.2. Reference places

As already mentioned, the texts of existing statutory instruments are published in "Lovtidende" (Division A) and will also be available in the publication "Love og Anordninger" (Acts and Statutory Instruments") and in some of the common statutory compilations. Most special statutory compilations and commented editions of the statutory texts will also contain information on any statutory instruments applicable in the area in question. The indexes referred to in 3.2 on current ministerial orders etc. may also be valuable when seeking to determine the amount of statutory instruments existing in respect of a particular subject. Finally, the texts of existing instruments may also be found in the database "Retsinformation" (Legal Information).

5. Case law

5.1. Origin and importance as a source of law

Case law, in the context of source of law factors, refers to the importance of the contribution, decisions made by the courts in earlier cases on the same or related issues, may make for the assessment of a current case. Thus previous decisions act as precedents on the argument that the decisions already made and reflecting an established approach to certain legal problems should also be followed in the case now being tried. The legal terminology describes such earlier decisions as *judicial precedents* and the value of earlier decisions is reflected in their *value as such (binding) precedents*. This value is dependent on the room for general application allowed by an earlier decision.

In a source of law context there are some important differences between legislation and delegated legislation on the one hand and case law on the other hand. Where legislation aims at a general regulation of a particular area, the courts must necessarily take their point of departure in *actual* cases presented for decision. Prima facie, these cases are the only ones decided upon. Unlike the legislative power, the courts may not implement a general regulation of an area on their own initiative but are bound to await initiatives from the external world in the form of actions being brought before them. Consequently their role is of a more passive character. Nevertheless the importance of case law as a source of law is indisputable which to some extent is attributable to the fact that courts are generally expected to take earlier decisions into account where the same or at least similar issues arise in subsequent cases, especially where the earlier decisions have been made at the superior courts, cf. below.

Possible precedents applicable to the decisions of a given issue may be found primarily in the law reports available on the market, cf. 5.2 infra. The search will normally be based on the facts of the case currently to be decided and a preliminary estimate of the legal issues it contains. Attention is focused in the first place on finding previous decisions whose facts are as similar to those of the case in point as possible. The next step is to ascertain the legal rules the older decisions were based upon and the reasoning behind the judgments. Especially *the reasoning*, commonly expressed in the judgment's *ratio decidendi* is important in this respect. On an overall view it may be said that the more *general* the ratio, the more extensive application is permissible. Thus where the ratio in a case is completely based on the narrow context of the actual facts of the case, its value as a judicial precedent is normally limited.

Other factors also influence the authority of a court decision. Naturally, decisions from the *Supreme Court* (Højesteret), the highest court in the national hierarchy, enjoy highest authority. The lower courts (the two High Courts, the Maritime and Commercial Court and town/city courts, cf. Chapter 4, below) normally adapt their decision-practice to any existing Supreme Court decision in an area, and the Supreme Court itself will also take considerable account of its own previous decisions to ensure continuity in the development of law. Decisions from the High Courts and from the Maritime and Commercial Court generally leave more room for flexibility and town/city court decisions are generally only ranking as precedents if no practice may be established from the superior courts in the area involved. Since administrative decisions are subject to judicial review, cf the Constitutional Act s. 63, the administrative authorities will normally seek to adapt their practice to conform with the approach which may be expected to meet with approval by the ordinary courts of law.

A number of other factors may decide the source of law importance attached to court decisions, in particular the *age* of the earlier decision may be relevant. Very old judgments will only play a modest role if developments in society have changed materially in the area involved since the decision was made.

Case law as a source of law is probably most important when applied in direct interaction with legislation, e.g. as is often seen, when the scope of a provision in an Act is defined in more precise terms in a number of subsequent court decisions. But, as previously mentioned, it also happens that independent law may originate – or develop – from court decisions, cf. Chapter 1, Section 3.3 for the reference to the common compensation rule in Danish tort law. Sometimes such "judge-made" law is embodied ("codified") in subsequent legislation. Thus, central areas of the legislation in contract and property law, e.g. the Sale of Goods Act, express principles originally formulated in court decisions, and in customs, cf. Section 6, below, for reference to the latter.

5.2. Reference places

There is only one "official" series of law reports in Denmark viz. the "Ugeskrift for Retsvæsen" (Danish Weekly Law Reports). In these reports Supreme Court decisions and a selection of decisions from the High Courts and the Maritime and Commercial Court are reported. A number of indexes are made for each year, including subject indexes. The publication, which has been published since 1867, is normally to be found in major libraries. Decisions dating back to 1950 are available on cd. So far, compared to other Western countries, internet access to decisions from the Danish superior courts has been slow to develop, but this is changing via various initiatives, e.g. it is now possible to search for Supreme Court decisions from the most recent six months on the Court's homepage (www.hoejesteret.dk) .

Apart from the law reports etc., a number of special reports concerning particular areas of law are also available and there may be extensive reference to current relevant case law in commented statutory compilations or single act publications, often with summaries of cases included. Various special services on the Internet will (partly on a subscription basis) offer information on decisions in selected areas, e.g. the publishing house "Magnus" (www.magnus.dk). It is also possible – against payment – to gain on line access to the cd-edition of "Ugeskrift for Retsvæsen" (www.thomson.dk)

6. Other forms of "unwritten" practice

6.1. Legal customs and usage

The source of law commonly described as *"custom"* is not derived from the general rule-production of certain authorities (e.g. legislation) or decisions (e.g. judgments) but from certain established *patterns of behaviour within the population* or within particular groups of the population. Earlier there was a common distinction between two legally relevant patterns of this kind. Where 1) the conduct had been followed generally, for a long time and without interruption, and 2) under the assumption that there was a legal duty to act in such manner, a *legal custom* was said to exist. The authorities applying the law were deemed to be bound to take such conduct patterns into account. As opposed to this kind there were sets of established usage in certain *trade and commercial* relationships without the presumption of legal obligation referred to. Such usage may be described as "conventional" usage. In respect of the latter the authorities applying the law had a choice: They might include the usage in their considerations but were not legally bound to do so.

The modern accepted view is that case law does not recognise the two requirements referred to in order to determine the existence of a legal custom and it is also generally acknowledged that there is no reason to distinguish between cases in which certain conduct patterns *must* be taken into account and cases in which they *may* be taken into account. Whether conduct patterns are legally relevant – and in the affirmative to which extent they are relevant – is in modern case law decided on an assessment of all the circumstances of the case. Main distinctive factors will normally mainly include: how well-known and how wide-spread the conduct is, the period of time it has been practised, the life conditions it applies to and whether – from a social point of view it may be said to be "good" or "bad".

On this background it may be said for certain that an area in which legal relevance may be expected to be imputed to certain patterns of behaviour in practice is precisely within *commercial* relationships particularly in connection with *contracts* of sale and supply of goods and services. Thus in practice the area of the *mercantile usages* referred to above is of particular relevance. Their importance may occur where they are applied e.g. in *gap-fillings* of in-complete agreements, i.e. agreements in which the parties have failed to address themselves precisely to all relevant terms of the agreement. In important areas including in this respect sale of goods, the legislative rules are actually supersed by any trade usage, cf., e.g. the provision in the Sale of Goods Act s. 1 ("... follows from trade usage or other custom") and cf. further the account in Chapter 1, Section 3.5. Under case law there is no requirement that the parties have known the existence of the usage in order to apply it.

It is normally necessary to obtain comprehensive (expert) information to decide *whether* a certain pattern of behaviour exists among a certain group of persons which might be of legal relevance in the way described. For establishment of possible usages in trade relationships, the matter is normally referred to the Danish Chamber of Commerce (HTS Interesseorganisationen, www.handelskammeret.dk) who will give an opinion upon consulting experts in the line of business in question.

6.2. Codes and practices of specific lines of trade etc.

Professional organisations sometimes lay down general guidelines partly for the professional ethics desirable from the members in the exercise of their profession or business, and partly for the use of professional skill in their work. The organisation for Chartered Accountants e.g. has formulated a number of standards to be adhered to by the profession in the course of their business towards clients.

Such codes may represent usages within the line of business involved or may form the basis from which such usages develop, cf. the preceding Section. Even apart from this, the codes and practices may be of legal relevance, however, especially where it is to be decided whether a negligent professional conduct on the part of one of the members of the profession may result in civil or criminal liability. Where guidelines like the codes mentioned do exist, the point of departure in the assessment of the professional care or lack of it will most often be taken with reference to the standards described here. Information on the existence of ethical codes etc. is available from the organisation of the line of business in question. Such organisations may also often deliver persuasive opinions for use in legal actions as to whether a member of the profession may be deemed to have acted in a proper professional manner in a given context.

6.3. Administrative practice

As a matter of course, within property and contract law the importance of a particular administrative practice from a source of law point of view is normally only slight. One point only will suffice here: Since, as was mentioned in 5.1, the courts of law may test the validity of administrative decisions under their power of judicial review where such validity is doubtful, it is evident that in principle the courts' freedom of action as towards the legal approach manifested in a given administrative practice is supreme. An examination of the court decisions available does, however, reveal that a certain amount of consideration is taken for administrative practice and that the courts are perhaps allowing the administrative authorities a margin of error, albeit a modest one. Where two constructions of existing legislation could equally prevail, case law tends to choose the construction applied by the administrative authority.

Only by way of exception will cases of a pure or predominant contractual substance be tried by administrative authorities, this applies e.g. to the Consumers' Complaints Board, cf. Chapter 4, Section 7, below. The decisions made and the administrative practice expressed in them are no more binding on the ordinary courts of law than other administrative decisions.

Some of the central administrative authorities (ministries, boards etc.) regularly publish information on decisions involving general points of law or administrative practice in special publications. Another source of information is provided by the annual reports which are also issued. Reference to major decisions in the consumer area is e.g. made in the annual reports made by the Consumer Agency and may also be found on the Agency's homepage (www.forbrugerstyrelsen.dk). Ministerial circulars, circular papers, general guidances etc. are usually published in the publication "Ministerialtidende" or in the database "Retsinformation", cf. above Section 3.2. Search may also be made on the authorities' own websites (where such are provided) of which a list is given at the site: www.detoffentlige.dk/) .

6.4. Practice from private dispute-solving boards

Apart from the Consumers' Complaints Board (c.f. the preceding Section) there are various dispute-solving boards organised on a private basis outside the administrative authority field.

Their function is to try complaints from consumers in respect of traders in certain lines of trade or other delimited areas, cf. Chapter 4, Section 7, below. The president of such boards is often a judge. Among some of the important examples may be cited: The Banks' Complaints Board (www.pengeinstitut-ankenaevnet.dk) , The Insurance Complaints Board and the Mortgage Credit Complaints Board (www.ran.dk) The decisions made are not binding on the courts though the courts will be likely to consider an established board practice. Information on such practices is available in the annual reports issued by the individual boards.

6.5. Ombudsman's practice

Recommendations made by the Danish Parliamentary Ombudsman are also of slight importance within property and contract law which follows naturally from the confinement of the Ombudsman's jurisdiction to public administration only. Therefore, the general point to be made here is the same as the preceding sections: The courts have unlimited freedom of action as towards recommendations made by the Parliamentary Ombudsman which is also reflected in practice where court decisions contrary to recommendations made by the Ombudsman and decisions supporting his views may both be found.

Information on Ombudsman's practice may be found in the annual reports issued and published by the Ombudsman's institution and – for the most recent years – directly at the institution's own homepage: www.ombudsmanden.dk) or via "Retsinformation".

7. The circumstances of the case

7.1. General on the concept of circumstances of the case

Cases may arise in practice where no established source of law can be found as a legal basis and the judge is so to speak without resources as regards the legal basis to support the decision he must arrive at. For the courts must decide on the matters brought before them and the option of dismissing the case is not possible. Some solution must be found and a legal basis to support it must accordingly be produced.

The popular phraseology used for the basis of the decision in this kind of situation is a decision on the "circumstances of the case" (alternatively "nature of the case involved" or "cultural tradition"). In its pure form the situation most often arises when new conditions of life occur which have never been considered by the courts, nor has any provision been made for them in legislation. An example is provided by the number of un-solemnized co-habitation relationships ("common law marriages") which surged upwards from the late 1960s and caused a number of legal actions between the parties, especially regarding property disputes, on the termination of the co-habitation. No legislative provision had been made for this situation, nor were earlier court decisions or other sources of law available to rely upon. Decisions had to be made on the "circumstances of the case".

As a guideline for the judicial approach in formulating the legal basis of a "circumstances-of-the-case" decision it may be said that the judge should consider whether the rule he sets up (himself) could be applicable not only to the case in hand but also in future similar cases. Thus considerations about the *factual, general* consequences of the legal basis applied must be an important ingredient in the decision-making process. Apart from these considerations, in practice it will often be seen that emphasis is placed on whether the decision – on an overall view – may be deemed "*fair and reasonable*".

The circumstances of the case may also play an independent role – minor, but by no means negligible – especially when they interact with one or more of the other sources of law, in particular with legislative rules. When the courts e.g. are to determine the scope of a rule in a new legislative measure (interpret the rule, cf. the next Section) the situation may involve a choice between several possible constructions with no decisive indication of which to prefer. The choice may then be decided by the "circumstances of the case", so that e.g. considerations regarding effects will point to the construction to be adopted.

7.2. The possible importance of law and economics

Recent years have seen a debate, inspired in particular by the US and perhaps with a touch of a fashionable trend, regarding the possible role to confer on the socalled law and economics views, partly in a general assessment of the appropriateness of the legal state in a given area, partly in a concrete legal decision-making and in representations of the law in force. Law and economics is not a subject combining the two disciplines but a purely economic subject analysing and assessing parts of the legal order, e.g. (parts of) contract law and tort law, by means of traditional microeconomic tools. Efficiency parameters, e.g. in the form of maximisation of wealth without including aspects of distribution are crucial in the process. A starting premise is that the legal order via its function of conduct control will or may contribute to the creation of values in society and the argument is that parameters such as those mentioned are essential when assessing whether such creation is effected in a satisfactory manner.

As was mentioned above in Chapter 1, Section 4, source of law rules in force do not contain an exhaustive catalogue of the various factors which may be considered by the authorities in their application of law to concrete decision makings. Far from being oblivious of the outside world the discipline is, as a starting point, open and dynamic. Thus, analyses and arguments made by social sciences other than jurisprudence are not dismissed as long as such analyses and arguments are of a realistic character. Accordingly there is no formal impediment to taking views developed in connection with economic analyses of the law into consideration.

On the other hand it must be said that a number of substantial objections may be raised to giving such views more than marginal status – perhaps e.g. as an element of argument along "circumstances of the case" lines – when decisions on concrete law issues are to be made. The same applies for a representation of the law in force in a given area. In this context only the following will be emphasised: The premises attached to basic microeconomic theories and models based on these which are typically applied in analyses of law, e.g. conventional price theories, will imply that such theories/models must be said to relate to life in a Utopian society. Without challenging the scientific character of the theories they are therefore generally – also in a legal context – less suited for a description and explanation of an extremely multi-facetted and complex reality, let alone for producing relevant suggested solutions to problems from that real world (since they do not relate, as was said, to factors in practical existence but to "Nirvana" issues). In this context efficiency in one economic sense or other is not a parameter which may generally be given any substantial primary importance in the decision of legal issues, in particular when competing with deep-rooted legal values such as justice and legal certainty. In practice, the courts both in Denmark and in the rest of Europe, have been reluctant to apply considerations of a law and economics character to any noticeable extent.

8. Legislative Interpretation

8.1. The need to interpret legislation and the basis of interpretation

As mentioned in Chapter 1, Section 2.1, rules are general *linguistic* statements prescribing something. The fact that the rules are communicated to their addressees by means of language endows them with the uncertainty normally attached to such communication.

The uncertainty manifests itself in various ways. In illustration we may cite a common word like "place". When studying the so-called *lexical* meaning of the word, i.e. the linguistic applications available, it will be apparent that it is *ambiguous*. Various meanings are possible, e.g. a place defined as geographical area in a city which has not been built on, a place in a specific hierarchy or contest situation (1st place) etc. Sometimes the word is also *vague* in its exact meaning, i.e. there could be ambiguity as regards the actual facts referred to, e.g. the size of the area necessary to deserve the designation of "place".

Ambiguity and vagueness characterise a large number of words. But usually the meaning of words is not discussed separately outside the context in which they appear, i.e. on their lexical meaning alone, because such discussion will serve no sensible purpose. Only when the words are used in *definite statements or representations* – as carriers of definite *meanings* – will they be relevant in a communication between human beings. The context in which words appear will often present ample opportunity to reduce the uncertainty following from the ambiguity or vagueness. The *context* may be of a linguistic character, e.g. the entire sentence or section in which the word appears. For these purposes such linguistic context may be termed "*internal context*". Also extra-linguistic circumstances may affect the meaning, e.g. the group of people to whom the statement is addressed (the "audience"), the aim of making the statement, any special stresses being imposed, etc. That kind of circumstances may be described as "external" context or the "*situation*". In most cases the context will immediately indicate the sense in which a word is currently used.

The process involved in *determining the meaning of linguistic utterances* is called *interpretation* or *construction*. In the area of law such activity is needed in several respects, principally with regard to interpreting legislation and contracts. In the next Sections various interpretation questions concerning legislation are singled out for treatment. In this area, as in the source of law application, no common rules have been given on a legislative level as regards the process involved. Thus it is also true in this context that the practical application as manifested in court decisions will act as bases. Some general starting points may be given, as follows:

Any legal interpretation activity is a *context interpretation,* i.e. both (internal) context and situation (c.f. just above) will usually play a decisive role. Second, the purpose of interpretation will commonly be to establish a *practically reasonable interpretation*. The art of "devil's advocacy" is poorly estimated in the Danish court-rooms.

The aspect of context implies that words and word combinations may be used in another sense than the common one, i.e. it should be kept in mind that a *special legal sense* is applied here. Sometimes there will be an explanatory note to such effect in the legislation itself but this is by no means always the case. The word "place", as referred to above, is used without any explanation at all in the Danish Sale of Goods Act, s. 11. The section provides that if the seller is to see to the sending of the goods to any area within the limits of the "place", delivery shall not be deemed to be made before the goods are in the buyer's possession. None of the common senses of "place" really provides this rule with a reasonable content and place here is a special term of art in legal language. For the purposes of s. 11, "place" means the area within which goods of the particular kind are commonly supplied (brought out by the seller's own employees, cf. further in Chapter 10 (infra).

Finally it should be pointed out that the inter-relationship between the approach adopted in a source of law decision and the interpretation activity may be so close that in practice it is extremely difficult to separate the two processes. One major example of this will be seen where the assessment of the sense of a legislative rule (statutory interpretation) is affected by one or more of the court decisions (source of law factors) in which the issue in question has been decided. Another example is given at the end of Section 7.

8.2. Aids to interpretation

8.2.1. Introduction

Since any interpretation is context-bound, a number of factors commonly included in the interpretation process and functioning as bases for the interpretation preferable (i.e. canons of construction), will now be expounded on. Three of the most important factors of this kind, from a practical point of view, are treated in the following Sections. The canons of construction referred to must form the bases of making a choice between two or more possible interpretations. On an overall view, the choice is governed by the purpose of construction referred to above, viz. the aim of arriving at a practically reasonable construction.

8.2.2. Linguistic analysis

The construction process is usually initiated with a linguistic analysis of the statutory text with the purpose of ascertaining the linguistic meaning of the words applied. Even at this early stage the context, cf. 8.1 above, plays an important role. The context of a given statutory provision comprises as a minimum the entire statute in which the provision in question is contained (and often considerably more, cf. the following section). Vague provisions cannot be analysed in isolation but must naturally be viewed with regard to the place they occupy and the function they fulfil in the whole enactment.

A certain *presumption rule* may be set up for the result of the linguistic analysis which purports that there is a presumption that in order to be tenable, a construction must be *linguistically reasonable,* i.e. correspond with common language usage (perhaps common *legal* language usage). Thus to rebut the presumption the interpreter must show tenable grounds for his (contrary) interpretation.

8.2.3. The importance of travaux préparatoires

The term travaux préparatoires here denotes the materials made by the Folketing, government or on the latter's initiative in connection with the making of a statute (alternatively the designation statutory motives are used). The materials to consider will be the bill presented to the Folketing with the comments and recommendations attached, the parliamentary debates and any reports on the bill submitted by the permanent committees of the Folketing to which the bill has been referred upon the first reading in the Folketing. Other important preparatory materials may relate to advisory statements which have preceded the presentation of the bill. Among these the expert opinions are of a particular importance. Much new legislation is prepared in an expert commission, workgroup etc. set down by the relevant minister who will report back in writing to the minister. The bill prepared will commonly take its basis in the report and the report itself may even contain a proposed draft for a bill.

Preparatory materials in the sense described may often contribute to the interpretation of vague provisions in the Act adopted at a later stage. It is also indisputable that the courts to a large extent include preparatory materials in their considerations of the meaning of legislation. This does not imply, however, that the courts will necessarily follow the view expressed in the preparatory materials and there is also a ranking of priority of the travaux preparatoires themselves. Most attention is focused on comments on the bill, on reports from the parliamentary committee in question and on the expert expoundings referred to. In contrast, the parliamentary debates in the Folketing itself are only exceptionally given importance. It may be relevant how old the materials are so that the importance diminishes with age.

The Folketing also produces materials other than legislation, e.g. decisions, inquiry debates and questions to ministers and the replies given. The weight attached by the courts to these materials in terms of interpretation contribution is more doubtful. It has not been possible to find decisions indicating that such materials have been given *independent* weight.

The most important types of travaux préparatoires are available in a published form. Bills presented and comments attached are published on a current basis in the Folketingstidende Schedule A and reports from parliamentary committees in respect of bills in Division B of the same publication. In Schedule C bills that have been adopted and proposals for parliamentary decisions are entered. The presentation speeches of ministers and summaries of the oral debates are to be found in the main volume of the publication (Debates). To complete the total publication there is a survey volume with indexes of each parliamentary year. Information on travaux préparatoires in connection with parliamentary debates may also be found in the Yearbook of the Folketing. The database Legal Information (Retsinformation), cf. 3.2 above, which contains the full text of "Folketingtidende" from 1985-86 is a useful practical help, and it should also be noted that all legal instruments produced in connection with the legislative process for the parliamentary year 1997-98, 1st collection, may be found on the parliamentary website: www.folketinget.dk. Reports from expert commissions etc. are most often published in the series published by the State Information Service (published since 1951 and consecutively numbered.

8.2.4. The object of a legislative measure

The object or purpose of a given Act may appear expressly and with a reasonable amount of certainty in the Act itself or it may be evident from the travaux préparatoires of the Act. In that case, of course, an important construction basis is already present which the courts will apply in the determination of the meaning of a given rule in the Act in question.

In practice it often occurs that express purpose indications are not given and that a reasonably evident and unambiguous purpose cannot be deduced from either the Act or the travaux préparatoires. This leads to the question whether a certain purpose may be attributed to the Act for application in a subsequent interpretation process? Judging from case law the question must be answered in the negative. Such hypothetical purpose indications are not acknowledged as relevant interpretation reference factors.

8.3. When statutory provisions are contradictory

Even though the system of justice is in principle organised on national terms in which the various rules are categorised and their various functions defined (cf. Chapter 1) it may occur that two rules are contradictory to the extent that irreconcilable legal effects are related to the same factual circumstances. Where e.g. a certain conduct is prohibited and amounts to a criminal offence in one rule whereas another rule allows the conduct naturally the interpreter is faced with a real problem. The situation may arise both in cases in which the relevant (contradictory) rules are in the same Act and where they are in two different acts. The contradictory effect may be *total*, i.e. none of the rules may be applied without conflicting with the other or it may be *partial*, i.e. both rules – or one of them have/has a further application in which area no conflict arises. The latter situations are most common.

In practice the interpretation process will normally involve an attempt to construe the rule in a way which dispenses with the conflict itself, e.g. by attributing to one of the rules a less comprehensive area of application. Where this is not possible some principles for solving the conflict have been developed. Under the *principle of "the superior Act"* a rule of superior rank takes precedence over one of inferior rank if a conflict occurs (cf. Chapter 1, Section 3.4). Under the *principle of "the special act"* where conflicts arise between two contradictory rules, the special rule takes precedence over the ordinary rule. Finally, the *principle of "the younger Act"* leads to a preference for a recently passed act for an older one.

While it may be presumed with a great amount of certainty that the courts will in clear-cut cases follow the principle of the superior act, two other principles are more characterised by serving as *persuasive rules of presumption* to be used in the interpretation and thus it is not to be expected that the courts will follow them to the letter. The very generality of the rules will often make them difficult to apply, e.g. in the determination of a special rule as opposed to a another rule, or where the two last-mentioned principles will both be applicable in the same case.

8.4. Various types of interpretation results

8.4.1. Introduction

With an approach based prima facie on ordinary language usage (cf. 8.2.2, above) the result of the interpretation process may be viewed as a *defining,* a *narrow* or a *wide* construction. The first type of construction which occurs far more often than the others will only seek to specify the application possibilities of the rule in question within the limits made up by ordinary language usage. Thus it does not really present particular problems. With the other two types the points of construction reference data available and the assessment from a practical point of view have led to either a narrow or wide application in relation to the limit in question.

In the following two sections some comments are made on narrow and wide interpretation. It is important to keep in mind that what is being characterised is interpretation results and not factors which may *justify* a narrow or wide application of a rule. As already mentioned, such justification is ultimately to be sought in assessments based on what is prima facie a reasonable outcome from a practical point of view.

8.4.2. Narrow interpretation

In a narrow interpretation, assessments of the kind just referred to will lead to the non-application of a given rule in cases which from an ordinary language view would be covered by it. Thus the wording is dispensed with and the area of application is narrowed down.

The process of narrowing down cannot be described in general terms. An example has been given in section 8.3 (conflicting rules). Another typical situation will involve cases in which the purpose underlying the rule does not require its application to an extent corresponding to the express language content.

8.4.3. Wide interpretation

In a wide interpretation, the interpreter will disregard the wording in the opposite direction and apply the rule to cases which in ordinary language usage are evidently beyond the area of application. In practice, a fundamental requirement for extending the limits of application will normally be the presence of what is termed "*compatibility of causes*" between the inductable area of application for the rule and the area to which it is contemplated to apply it. The latter area must be comparable to the other and a similar need for the application of the rule must exist. Normally a further requirement is that there is a "*legal gap*" (uncovered issue both in case law and legislation), i.e. that the contemplated (extended) area of application must not be subject to other legal regulation.

It is not possible to give any further indication of instances in which a wide interpretation will be relevant. The construction type occurs fairly often within property and commercial law. Under the provision in s. 32(1) e.g. the wording only deals with the importance of misprints and other clerical errors whereby a statement has received a different content than the one contemplated. In practice, however, the rule is given a wide interpretation and is applied correspondingly to other types of mistake, e.g. mistake in the decision-making basis, cf. further Chapter 7.

An alternative term for wide interpretation is *analogous interpretation* or a certain rule may be said to be "applied analogously".

8.4.4. Contrary inference

Contrary inference (negative presumption rule) may occur where a certain rule is maintained (strictly) with its content as it is, thus the interpreter refuses to apply a wide interpretation (apply it analogously). This is not really an interpretation variety. The wording "inference" is perhaps also somewhat misleading. The same need for caution in the reference to justification for narrow/wide interpretation as was mentioned in 8.4.1 will apply to this sort of "negative presumption".

CHAPTER 3

EU law and other international source of law factors

by Morten Wegener

1. The EU law. Character of legal basis

As was mentioned in Chapter 1, Section 2.2, differences between individual national systems of law impede international trade in goods and the international supply of services. Uniformity and stability – and thus predictability – in the legal bases across borders stimulate international trade. Therefore it is no wonder that international co-operation goes a long way back especially between large or smaller groups of states with the purpose of achieving at least some uniformity between the various national rules.

One of the most comprehensive and so far most successful co-operations of this kind is the co-operation within the European Union (the EU). Its success is undoubtedly primarily attributable to the proximity of the participating countries, not only geographically but also – despite much ignorance, narrow-mindedness and naivety and the isolationism and provincialism attached to these characteristics, which have been marked not least in Denmark – also economically, politically and culturally.

The co-operation of which Denmark has been a member since 1973 currently comprises 15 states. Since 1998 a process with a view to extending the number of members to include a number of socalled candidate states has been going on and in 2002 agreement was reached on the inclusion of 10 of these states in the Union as from 1 May 2004 (they are: the three Baltic countries, Poland, Hungary, the Czech Republic, Slovakia, Slovenia, Cyprus and Malta). If the remaining part of the decision process in respect of the extension, including national referendums, proceeds without problems, the Union will comprise 25 states as from the date mentioned. In addition, Romania, Bulgaria and perhaps Turkey are still waiting in the wings.

The basis of the cooperation has so far consisted of a number of treaties (interstate agreements) made between the participating countries, including in particular the treaties on the European Coal and Steel Community and the European Atomic Energy Community (both originally dating from 1957). The Treaty on the Eupeoan Union (also called the "Maastricht Treaty", 1992), the Amsterdam Treaty (1997), and the Nice Treaty (2000). The last mentioned – which became effective as from 1 February 2003 – contains adaptations of the cooperation and its institutions in view of the enlargement of the Community which was envisaged at the time, cf. above.

> Special arrangements in respect of individual member states may imply that their commitment to participate in the cooperation may differ in certain areas. Thus Denmark does not participate fully in the extended cooperation established by the Union Treaty and the AmsterdamTreaty as a result of the concessions made to Denmark in the socalled Edinburg decision from 1992. The special arrangements for Denmark included her participation in the end-phase of the creation of an economic and monetary union (The "EURO") and a possibility of differences in common dispositions within the defence area (the socalled four "national reservations"). On the other hand the Amsterdam and Nice treaties also provided the access for Member States who wish to go further in the community than others to establish a socalled "strengthened co-operation" under certain conditions.

Following the negotiations on the Nice Treaty the European Council (cf. below 3.2) set up a *convent* in 2001 consistsing of i.a. representatives for the governments and national parliaments in the then Member States and candidate states with a view to considering the various fundamental questions in connection with the future development of the EU. The convent finished its work in 2003 by presenting an agreed draft European constitution to replace all the former Treaties, cf. above. The Draft keeps up the political areas already known but contains a statement of the ambitions and bases of value for the Union together with a number of simplifications and specifications of the former Treaties, e.g. an integration of the Charter on fundamental rights (so far in principle non-binding), cf. below 4.3.1. In addition, the Draft provides an extension of the access to make decisions in the European Council (below 3.3) with qualified majority, a certain strengthening of the powers of the European Parliament (below 3.5) and improved access for national parliaments to follow the work in the Council. It is established that entering and leaving the community is on a voluntary basis. The Draft has been placed on the aganda of a socalled government conference (initiated in October 2003) with participation of governemnt representatives in the former 15 Member states and the 10 accession states. The conference is to make a final decision on the further fate of the Draft "as soon as possible" including whether adoption should be sought in its present state or in an amended form. At the time of writing the result is not to hand and it is of course equally uncertain whether the Draft – even if agreed by the conference – will subsequently be ratified – possibly in referendums by the indiviudal member states. Therefore the following is necessarily based on the fundamental Treaties already adopted and will contain only a few further comments on the Draft Constitution Treaty.

The Treaties applying so far of which the Treaty on the European Economic Community (in the following called TEC) is by far the most important in practical terms have formed the main constitutional basis of the cooperation between the states in the community – or to put it another way- they have been the main pillars of the special legal order developed for the coperation. In an international context the law developing on the basis of the Treaties (often called secondary or derived EU law) has a quite unique character. Within some of the cooperation areas comprised by the Treaties the Member States have surrendered (or "lent") part of their freedom of action or socalled sovereignty to the EU authorities. In these areas the EU institutions may in principle act independently of the Member States and *enjoy special authority under the Treaties to make legal rules.* Rules validly agreed and laid down in these areas may *bind* the Member States, often even if a minority of the states have opposed the legal measure in question. Further some of these rules are *directly applicable* to the citizens of the individual Member State and may be enforced by the national courts. Where there is a conflict between a national rule and an EU rule, the EU law takes *precedence,* cf. further below in Section 4.6. This is the normal position under the cooperation governed by the oldest three Treaties, including the TEC.

In contrast, the cooperation under the Maastricht and Amsterdam Treaties regarding foreign and security policy issues is of ordinary international law character, cf. the immediately following, and the cooperation introduced by the same Treaty on "legal and internal affairs" normally requires consensus among the Member States. In accordance with this position the European Union is usually described as resting on three "pillars". Pillar 1 is made up by the cooperation under the TEC of the unique character mentioned above which is predominantly of an economic nature. Pillars 2 and 3 relate to the cooperation on a common foreign and security policy and to legal and internal matters both of which are, as mentioned, of a fundamentally different character.

Apart from this the Member States also cooperate in many fields other than the Treaty areas. The law created in this way is, however, of a fundamentally different character than the independently established EU-law in that it requires so to speak step-by-step that *special agreements* are entered into – and thus that consensus be achieved – between the countries in exactly the same way as common solutions for the Member States require agreement in other international organisations, e.g. the UN. A further difference is that such kind of agreement is normally only of direct importance at state level – and not directly applicable to the citizens. Therefore, co-operation between the member states outside the sphere of the EU-Treaties is of *quite ordinary international character*, or as it may alternatively be put, of a *public international law character*, cf. further in Section 6.

The following account of the central EU-bodies (the institutions) and the legal acts and instruments emanating from them is primarily based solely on the TEC and the relevant Article references also relate to that Treaty.

2. Some fundamental EU law principles

On the basis of the Treaties and/or the prevailing case law practice from the Court of Justice a number of fundamental legal principles governing the co-operation within the EU and the administration of the EU rules may be formulated. (These principles will also apply if the constitutional draft, cf. the preceding Section, is adopted.) First, the EU authorities are subject to a *principle of legality* which corresponds in nature to the equivalent principle in Danish law, cf. above Chapter 2, section 4.1. Under this principle decisions may only be made where the requisite sanction for them is present in the Treaties, and naturally, decisions made must not be contrary to EU law, in particular to Treaty terms. Second, EU membership requires the Member States to become subject to a *solidarity principle* under which the main obligation is for the Member States to loyally perform their duties under the Treaties and enter a loyal co-operation. Third, the aims of the EU dictate a *principle of non-discrimination.* Any discrimination exercised on the ground of nationality is as a predominant rule prohibited within the jurisdiction of the Treaties. Fourth, when applying the EU rules a *principle of proportionality* must be followed: Measures taken under EU law must be necessary in light of the object pursued, i.e. there must be a reasonable proportion between the objects pursued and the means applied in their pursuit. EU also acknowledges the *fundamental rights* guaranteed under the European Convention of Human Rights and the way these rights arise from the common constitutional traditions of the Member States. Finally a *subsidiarity principle* applies. Outside the areas in which the EU authorities have sole jurisdiction under the Treaties in relation to national authorities a measure from the EU ranks as subsidiary to a national solution, i.e. the EU measure will only be relevant where national measures are inadequate in the light of the common objective set up in respect of the activity in question.

3. The central EU institutions and their competence

3.1. The Community Institutions: General

The cooperation and the law-making within the EU take place in a number of central institutions in a process frequently presenting many complications under limits imposed by the Treaties and in which each institution has defined functions in an attempt to balance the various interests.

The most important institutions are the *European Council*, the *European Union Council*, the European Commission, the *European Parliament* and the *Court of Justice*. An obvious comparison may be made here to the distribution of powers in the Danish constitution, as manifested in the separation of the legislative, the executive and the judicial powers (the Folketing and Head of State, government and the courts) cf. the Constitution Act s. 3. Such a comparison leads to a listing of substantial differences. The most spectacular difference is that the institution whose members are chosen by the populations of the member states by direct election – the European Parliament – does not enjoy a monopoly of legislative competence like the Danish Folketing, indeed the Parliament has no possibility of actual legislative initiative. In these areas the European Parliament has only a certain limited co-decision power.

3.2. The European Council

The European Council consists of the heads of state and government in the member states, the chairman of the European Council with the assistance of the foreign ministers and one further member of the Commission, respecttively. The Council is required to meet at least twice a year. Under the Union Treaty, its tasks are to provide the Union with the impetus necessary for its progress and determine the general political guidelines in this respect. Thus the Council is primarily a forum for general political discussion in the EU on the highest political level and any decision-making attached hereto. The Council has developed into an independent institution from the institution referred to in the following Section:

So far the precidency of the European Council has followed a rotation practice between the Member States for periods of six months at a time. The Draft EU constitution, cf. above, suggests the introduction of a president of more permanency, viz. a president elected by the Council for a period of two and a half years and with a possibility of re-election once.

3.3. The Council of the European Union

This institution – commonly referred to as the "EU Council", the Council of Ministers", or simply "the Council" – consists of a representative from each Member State on Minister level who is authorised to commit the government of the state in question, cf. the provisions in Arts 202-210 in the Treaty. The office of president alternates between the Member States for periods of six months at a time. The minister to participate is decided by the individual Member State. Usually this depends on the issue to be dealt with so that the minister of the province in issue attends meetings concerning his/her specific area of competence whereas the foreign ministers will attend when issues of a more general nature are on the agenda.

Under the TEC the Council of Ministers has power to make rules on the most fundamental EU areas and the most important general regulations are indeed emanating from this institution. As far as possible consensus is sought among the members. Where it is necessary to take a vote, however, the main rule is that a simple majority is sufficient for the adoption of a given proposal with each Member State having one vote. This main rule is somewhat theoretical, however, since numerous provisions in the Treaty – including those of most vital importance – require a qualified majority or unanimity. From an overall point of view, an important consequence of these provisions is that the large countries cannot force their way through the voting system.

For decisions of qualified majority the votes of the individual Member States carry different weights. Denmark has been given three votes out of total of 87, cf. TEC Art 205. Under the Nice Treaty this will be changed as at 1 January 2005 to seven votes out of a total of 345 (with 25 Member States). A qualified majority requires at least 255 votes in favour of the decision in point and that a majority of the Member States representing no less than 62 per cent of the population in the EU adopts the measure. If the proposed Draft Constitution Treaty is implemented a certain simplification will occur in that a qualified majority would consist (as from 2009) in a majority of the Member States representing at least 60 per cent of the population in the Union.

3.4. The European Commission

So far, the European Commission (normally described only as "the Commission") has consisted of 20 members appointed by common accord by the Member State governments for 5-year periods, cf. Arts 211-219 of the TEC. Usually only the presidency of the Commission has been debated since the normal practice has been to appoint the members each country has suggested for the office. The composition is under normal practice made up of two members from each of the five largest countries and one from each of the small countries. With the enlargement of the Community by 10 new Member States in 2004 a continuation of this scheme would imply that the number of commissioners would be inappropriately high. Therefore the Nice Treaty provides that the Commission is to consist of one representative for each member State and that the countries which have applied for membership shall be entitled to a member of the Commission when they accede to the EU. As from 1 January 2005 shall surrender their second Commissioner and the Commission will subsequently consist of 25 members.Further the Nice Treaty provides that when the Community membership number reaches 27 a reduction of the number of Commissioners shall be negotiated and at the same a rotation scheme will be introduced whereby the countries accept not to have a member in alternate turns.

The president of the Commission and the total number of commisioners is subject to approval by the European Parliament. During the term of office dismissal of commissioners may only be made by the Court of Justice on the petition of the Council or Parliament. There is, however, an alternative. On a vote of censure in respect of the whole Commission by the European Parliament, the entire Commission will be forced to resign. While members of the Council represent the individual states' members of the Commission act independently of Member States. Indeed they are required to safeguard the common EU interests only. The Institution acts collectively, if necessary by voting on simple majority basis. However, the individual members are responsible in certain specified subject areas (agriculture, industry, environment etc.) and are in this respect comparable to Danish ministers.

The Commission has substantial and rather unique functions in the co-operation within the Communities and the law-making process. The functions may be divided into three broad categories.

In the first category, the Commission acts as a kind of dynamo and catalyst for the development of the various EU measures. As mentioned above, all important decisions made by the Council require prima facie preceding proposals put forward by the Commission. Compared to a Danish environment the Commission is thus formally the main initiator of legislation.

Secondly, the Commission acts as the EU executive power. When e.g. a Council decision has been made on a certain Community measure the implementation of such measure will normally lie with the Commission, e.g. acting on authority from the Council for the preparation of the necessary secondary legislation. Further the Commission is in charge of the administration of the EU revenue and expenditure under the Budget adopted.

In its third function, the Commission may be said to act as the EU watch dog in relation to the Member States, e.g. and in particular by its power to control the Member States' observance of their obligations under EU law and, where necessary, to take legal action against a Member State before the Court of Justice, cf. below Section 3.6.

Under the Draft Constitution it is proposed that the Commission is to consist of the president, a foreign minister for the EU (one of the vice-presidents of the Commission) and 13 socalled "Europe" Commissioners who shall be elected on the basis of equal rotation between all Member Sates. In addition the president will appoint commissioners without voting rights from all the other countries. It is not proposed to change the Commission's role in respect of the law making process and in the administration of EU matters fundamentally.

3.5. The European Parliament

The European Parliament (or simply the "Parliament) consists of a maximum of 732 members who are elected by direct election in the Member States for 5-year-periods, cf. Arts. 189-201 of the TEC. In Denmark 16 members have been elected so far (out of a maximum of 626). Under the Nice Treaty the number will be 13 as from 1 January 2004 with effect as from the 2004-2009 election period.

As already mentioned, even if its influence has been markedly increased by the latest amendments to the Treaties, the Parliament is no legislative forum in the usual democratic sense. The principal functions of the Parliament may be referred to two main categories, viz. a certain participation in the legislative and budgetary processes and a certain amount of control which it exercises over the Commission, i.a. the Parliament's ability to censure the entire Commission, as referred to above. One of the most controversial elements, presumably, of the Draft Constitution Treaty is the proposed strenghtening of Parliamentary participation in the procedures mentioned.

3.6. The European Court of Justice

The European Court of Justice (or simply the Court of Justice) which sits in Luxembourg, consists of one judge from each Member State. The term of office is 6 years with a possibility of re-appointment. The judges must be independent and further requirements are that they possess the qualifications required for appointment to the highest judicial office in their own countries or that they possess professional qualifications of generally acknowledged distinction, cf. Arts 220-245 of the TEC.

It was envisaged in the TEC and statute of the Court that the Court would sit in divisions or, in special cases, "large chambers" but in exceptional cases the full Court may also sit. To relieve the Court of Justice of some of its case load a Court of First Instance was set up in 1989 (the "small court", also composed of one judge from each Member State) which hears certain types of case, e.g. concerning the application of the competition rules of the Treaty, cf. now Art 225 of the TEC. Appeals against decisions made by the Court of First Instance may be made to the Court of Justice but only on a point of law, e.g. in regard to the application or interpretation of the community rules. Under Art 225 A special first-instance courts may be set up to hear issues deriving from special subject areas.

Under Art 220 of the TEC the Court's task is to ensure that in the interpretation and application of the Treaty, the law is observed. "Treaty" should not be taken too literally here since the jurisdiction of the Court is over community law generally, i.e. including derived (secondary) EU law, e.g. the rules validly adopted by the Council and the Commission. This also limits the jurisdiction of the Court of Justice: Only where judicial action is sanctioned in the TEC or other community law based on the TEC may the Court exercise its power, cf. the enumeration of various case categories in Art 226 et seq. Its action is also – like a national court of law – dependant on external initiative, i.e. from an authority or individual with a cause of action (c.f. above Chapter 2, Section 5.1). The most important types of cases heard by the Court comprise cases concerning *breaches of the Treaty,* judicial review of legal instruments and acts made by the other central EU bodies with a view to possible *annulation* and which are legally binding and concrete (c.f. the concept of legal instruments and acts, Chapter 2, section 3.2), and *preliminary issues*. The preliminary rulings are concerned with the interpretation of the community law and are given when such issues arise in actions at the national courts. A ruling from the Court of Justice – which is made upon reference from the national court concerned – will be binding on the national court.

The Court of Justice is no ordinary court of appeal in relation to the national courts in the sense that appeals against their decisions will lie to the Court of Justice. Its jurisdiction is limited to community law issues and there is a further restriction as regards the access of litigants to bring issues before the court. On the other hand within the jurisdiction defined the Court of Justice fulfils some very important functions partly in respect of ensuring that Member States and the EU bodies do not digress from their course (Treaty breaches, annulment cases), partly that the community law is interpreted and applied uniformly in the Member States (preliminary rulings).

4. EU Law as a Source of Law Factor

4.1. Introduction

From a Danish perspective, the source of law problems in relation to EU law are primarily concerned with its importance as a source of law factor for

Danish courts when actions involving a possible application of EU law in *Denmark* are brought before them. To clarify the position on this point it is necessary first to look at the factors of which the EU law is composed, cf Sections 4.2 and 4.3 for an account of the most important written and unwritten sources. The written sources are primarily made up of various forms of legal acts and instruments issued by the Council and the Commission, cf. the modest catalogue in Art 249 of the TEC, whereas the unwritten law is developed primarily from the case law of the Court of Justice. In Section 4.4 the interpretation of EU law is touched upon while Section 4.5 gives a brief account of where to find the law. Source of law problems of the category referred to above are treated in Section 4.6. They may be said to stem from the fact that the national systems of law and community law are not living separate lives, each in its own compartment. On the contrary, as was mentioned in Section 1, the EU rules are to a considerable extent components of national law as well and may be directly enforced at Danish courts of law in disputes between private individuals or between private individuals and public authorities.

4.2. Written Sources

4.2.1. The Treaty

Most Treaty provisions describe rules of competence concerning the authority of the EU institutions referred to in Section 2 but there are also various obligation rules applicable to citizens in the individual Member States, e.g. the prohibition against agreements in restraint of trade which may affect trade between Member States (as regards obligation rules and competence rules, cf. Chapter 1, Section 3.2).

4.2.2. Regulations

Under Art 249(2) of the TEC regulations are *general, universally binding and directly applicable in any Member State*. The "general" nature implies that – like Danish legislation – they regulate general conditions and are addressed to an undefined group of persons. The direct applicability implies that once they have been issued and promulgated they become legally valid in the Member States in the same way as national legal rules. Thus, a regulation issued by a EU institution is part of the Danish law in force in the same way as ordinary Danish acts and decrees without the need for national implementation. Incidentally, such acts and decrees are the closest Danish parallel to regulations.

Regulations are issued by the Council or the Commission. They are applied especially where a completely identical state of law in the Member States is aimed at. To become effective, Regulations must be published in the

"European Community Gazette" (in Danish: De Europæiske Fællesskabers Tidende or "EFT"). They normally come into force 20 days after publication.

4.2.3. Directives

As regards the *aims set out*, directives are binding on all *Member States* but they leave the choice of form and method of implementation to the national authorities, cf. Art 249(3) of the TEC. The immediate difference between regulations and directives is thus apparent in two aspects. First, the addressees of a directive are not everybody but only Member States. Second, in contrast to regulations, directives require an initiative from the Member States towards implementation of the rules stated in the directives in order to integrate them in the national systems of law. Directives must be *incorporated* or *implemented* – in the national laws by special measures on the part of the Member States themselves. In Denmark the implementation will usually be by way of new legislation incorporating the directive's obligations in respect of the Danish state.

No immediate parallel to directives can be found in Danish law. They are often used where the Treaty dictates a harmonisation of the law in the Member States in some area but national considerations make it desirable to make special allowances to a certain extent. Where a directive in accordance with these considerations merely stipulates a certain common minimum standard which the member States may deviate from in a positive direction at their own discretion the directive is usually described as a *"minimum directive"* and conversely, as a *"maximum directive"* (or "full harmonisation directive) where no deviations are allowed. Hybrids of the two basic forms may occur. Recent Danish legislation on product liability, mercantile agents and some aspects of trade mark law e.g. has been based on minimum directives.

Directives are issued by the Council or the Commission. They normally provide a certain timelimit for their implementation which is often disregarded by the Member States. They are communicated to the States to which they are directed and will be effective from that date. Though no special requirements are set up regarding public notification directives are published in the European Community Gazette.

Non-observance of directive provisions may give rise to Treaty violation cases before the Court of Justice, cf. above Section 3.6 and various other unpleasantness for the Member State in breach, cf. below Section 4.6.3.

4.2.4. Decisions

Under Art 249(4) of the TEC, decisions are binding in all details on the parties to whom they are addressed. They are normally issued from the Council or the Commission. The addressees may be individual citizens, groups of citizens, individual Member States or all Member States. It follows from this that decisions may be either specific or general. Specific decisions addressed to citizens correspond to the specific decisions made by national administrative authorities. General decisions addressed to Member States may sometimes have the same character as directives. General decisions of a directive-like character are published in the European Community Gazette for reasons of general information. The same applies to certain specific decisions containing principles of general interest.

4.2.5. Recommendations and opinions

Recommendations and opinions are not legally binding, cf. Art 249(5). Recommendations are normally made on the initiative of the EU body concerned (Council or Commission) whereas opinions are reactions to applications to that body. Apart from this there is no real difference between them.

4.2.6. Other types

In EU practice numerous other designations are used in respect of statements from the EU institutions. The term *order* is applied to legally binding statements without external addressees, e.g. in respect of organisation affairs. The term *resolution* may be used of Council decisions which are not legally binding but do contain political commitments. The term *"conclusion"* may be seen for a large variety of adoptions by the Council – ranging from absolutely non-binding statements to something which is most comparable to actual decisions, cf above. Further the Commission issues general guidelines on the administration in certain defined areas in socalled *communications*.

As will be apparent, many different designations for the legally relevant materials emanating from the EU authorities are applied. The language usage may be somewhat imprecise. Therefore, it is important to bear in mind that the label is not decisive for the legal effects. They must be based on the real contents of the legal acts in question.

In the Draft Constitution Treaty a ceratin simplification has been sought and the designatiom of the various legal acts is different. In the Draft terminology regulations and directives are called "European laws" and European "framework laws", respectively. The Draft also uses the designations "European consolidation statutes" (roughly corresponding to national consolidation acts) "European decisions" (corresponding to the former concrete decisions) and finally, the already known recommendations and opinions.

In certain instances the EU has authority to enter into *treaties* with third countries and with international organisations. Such treaties automatically become part of EU law and thus will be of legal importance in the Member States as well.

4.2.7. The hierarchy of rules. The language

Like national sources of law the EU sources may to a certain extent be divided into a hierarchy, cf. above, Chapter 1, Section 3.4. Rules based on the Treaty of course rank superior to rules established by the Council and the Commission. Within the latter, rules from the Commission rank lower than those of the Council though this only applies where the authority of the Commission has been derived from that of the Council, e.g. in the form of an authority issued by the Council. Apart from this it is impossible to say anything definite about the hierarchy of the rules among themselves. Conflicts, where such arise, must ultimately be solved by the Court of Justice.

As compared to written national law the user of EU law must be prepared for some rather considerable differences of drafting. The application of a so-called "preamble" (introduction or introductory speech) e.g. is not used currently in Danish legislation but is applied in EU law to state the *justification* of a given measure which under the Treaty must accompany Regulations, Directives, and Decisions. The contents of the preamble will therefore often be of considerable importance for interpretation purposes.

The official languages of all Member States are authentic legal languages of EU law. Legal acts which are published are therefore translated into all languages, including Danish.

4.3. Unwritten sources

4.3.1. Decisions by the Court of Justice

The most important implications of the decisions of the Court of Justice which have played, and still play, a considerable role as regards the interpretation of Eu law consist of the development of a wide variety of general legal doctrines or principles. In relation to national authorities this is especially true of the doctrine of direct effects of EU law and of its supremacy over national law, cf. further below in Section 4.6. In relation to EU law itself, principles have been developed which contain requirements in respect of its administration whether such administration is undertaken in the Member States or by EU bodies. The Court has e.g. presumed, as stated above in Section 2, that certain "fundamental rights" are part of the EU law. This has been possible through incorporation of the fundamental rights (freedom rights, i.a.) applying in each Member State and under the European

Convention of Human Rights into the EU law and by decreeing that EU measures contrary to such principles may not be accepted. This additional protection of individual citizens in the Member States developed through case law was incorporated ("codified") in Art. 6 of the Union Treaty and also prevailed in the EU Charter of 2000 on fundamental rights (so far of a "declaration of intention" character but in the Draft Constitution it is proposed to endow the principle with legally binding status)..

The Court may of course apply precedent-importance to earlier decisions of its own and will also do so to a great extent, e.g. when referring to previous decisions interpreting the Treaty provision which is in issue in a subsequent case. The same applies to decisions of the Court of First Instance which will of course also refer to previous Court of Justice decisions. It is also evident that the other EU institutions will seek to organise their practice along principles which previous decisions of the Court of Justice have acknowledged and which will therefore be likely to meet judicial approval again.

4.3.2. Other unwritten source of law factors

In principle, the existence of unwritten source of law factors other than the Court's decisions as parts of EU law, including customs and the "nature of the case" is acknowledged but their importance is slight. In relation to the application at the national courts their practical importance must be deemed to be nil. No national court would e.g. dare to decide an EU point of law solely on the basis of "nature of the case"-criteria without submitting the issue to the Court of Justice for a preliminary ruling.

4.4. Interpretation of EU law

As will have become apparent from the preceding Sections, interpretation of EU law is predominantly the province of the Court of Justice. Thus a student of the interpretation of EU law must first analyze the Court decisions both as regards the interpretation methods applied and as regards the results arrived at.

A comparison with the interpretation of the written national source of law factors (cf. Chapter 2, Section 8, above) will not reveal as much difference in principle, as regards the interpretation bases. The interpretation of EU law will also involve analysis of wording, context, preparatory materials and purposes though the Court of Justice will not include travaux preparatoires as an element of interpreting Treaty provisions. One special interpretation element is, as already mentioned, existing preambles. As regards wording, the analysis will not be restricted to the linguistic formulation of the rule in question in a single language version but will include the drafting in all the languages used. As mentioned in Section 4.3.1 reference is very often made to previous decisions in similar cases without implying, however, that considerable flexibility in response to changing needs may not be shown.

At the balancing of the interpretation data, the reader must be prepared to come against a much higher degree of consideration in respect of purpose deliberation than experienced with national courts of law, especially where the purpose statements are based upon fundamental aims in the Treaty terms, including those stated in its preamble. This also indicates the ratio decidendi which the Court of Justice will ultimately apply to the solution. There is a distinct tendency to prefer the interpretation which most effectively contributes to promote the purpose presumed to be achieved with the legislative measure in question with due consideration to the purpose provisions in the Treaty. Sometimes the integration purpose has been important in this respect – also to the extent that the Court has been open for the need of adaptation of the interpretation dictated by an integration process which is already under way or desired. Hence the Court has come to play a much more visibly political role than Danish courts of law.

4.5. Reference places for EU law

As already mentioned, a number of the most important legal acts are published in the European Community Gazette (Div. C: Proposals for legal acts and certain non-binding directions, Div. L: Binding (adopted) legal acts). A special issue contains the acts issued prior to the Danish entry and which were still in force in 1973. A survey of the total materials is available from the Index of current EU law published by the Commission twice a year. A commented compilation in Danish is also available in the EU-Karnov (latest edition 2002) published by the legislative publishing house, Karnovs Forlag, who also offer a disc version and and an on line version of the compilation. The decisions of the Court of Justice are available in an independent publication "Compilation of Decisions of the Court of Justice and of the Court of First Instance" which appears with a varying number of volumes every year. Finally, a large number of the EU bodies publish annual reports containing information of developments in the legal regulation and decisions establishing general points of law.

Direct access to the source materials is often more easily achieved via the Internet. The initial seach may be made at the EU common server (http://europa.eu.int/index-da.htm) which also provides links to the home-pages of the individual institutions and to various EU databases, especially EUR-Lex (free of charge) http://europa.eu.int/eur-lex) and Celex (against a fee): http://europa.int/celex). More recent decisions from the Court of Justice and from the Court of First Instance are available in full texts via the Court's homepage (http://www.curia.eu.int/da/ index.htm).

4.6. The supremacy of Community law and direct effect

4.6.1. The concepts of "direct applicability" and "direct effect"

To grasp the relationship of EU law to national law it is essential to understand the meaning of the two concepts in the headline. "Direct applicability" is used to describe the way a Community rule is to be *subject to national incorporation measures* in order to fully become part of national law, e.g. and especially, any legislation which transforms the Community rule to a national rule. Directly applicable EU rules are not subject to such a process and will thus become elements of national legal systems without more.

The concept of "direct effect" relates to the way in which EU rules may *justify rights and obligations in respect of citizens of Member States capable of being upheld at the national courts.* Under the Court's practice a main criterion is whether the provision is so clear and unconditional that it is capable of serving as a basis for rights and obligations of the nature in question. Most directly applicable EU provisions will also have direct effects but there is no absolute merger, e.g. a direct effect may be too imprecise or it may only be relevant to Member States. Conversely, it does happen that provisions which are clearly not directly applicable in the aforementioned sense are given a certain direct effect.

Direct effect may be relevant in both a *vertical* and a *horizontal* respect. In the former case, the EU provision is given effect in respect of the relationship between a Member State and its citizens. The horizontal relationships, on the other hand are relevant as between individuals of the Member States.

4.6.2. Which EU rules are directly applicable?

On a practical level, the question asked in the headline may be limited to general legal acts in the form of EU regulations and directives and the EU Treaties with third countries. As has appeared from the account in Sections 4.2.2 and 4.2.3 the position differs in this context between regulations and directives. Regulations do not require national incorporation measures and such measures are therefore normally not allowed under the Court's practice with a view to stressing their Community legal basis. Conversely, in order to become parts of national systems of law directives are required to undergo transformation or implementation measures (incorporation) of such nature as to ensure a complete and precise fulfilment of the obligations the directive in question places on the Member States. In other words, regulations are directly applicable whereas directives are not. Since Treaties entered into by the Community Institutions with third countries within the Treaty-jurisdiction of the EU automatically become parts of Community law, cf above Section 4.2.6, the same requirements as for regulations apply here.

4.6.3. Which parts of Community law have direct effects?

Under its decision practice, the Court of Justice has given direct-effect capability to *TEC Articles* both on a vertical and a horizontal level. The main requirements are to the effect that the Article in question is so clear and precise that it must be deemed appropriate for application at national courts and that the Article may be said to create an unconditional obligation which is complete in the sense that it leaves no room for the exercise of choice or discretion by the national authorities. Accordingly, the legal position of Treaty Articles is that where such criteria are satisfied Treaty Articles may give rise to rights and obligations for the citizens in the Member States which may be enforced at the national courts both in relationships between citizens (horizontal direct effect) and between citizens and national authorities (vertical direct effect).

Whether *Community regulations* are directly effective in the Member States depends, under the Court's decision practice – on the construction of the regulation in question on premises parallel to those referred to above under Treaty articles. By far the majority of regulations no doubt satisfy the criteria referred to and will thus be capable of both vertical and horizontal direct effects.

The situation is much more complicated as regards d*irectives.* As mentioned in Section 4.2.3 they are only addressed to the Member States and are in principle only binding on the Member State as regards the aims put forward in the directive. Where a Directive has not been implemented in time or where it has been incorrectly implemented the legal effects in respect of citizens of the Member States seem incapable of arising on such bases. The position is, however, slightly different under the Court's practice. Failure to implement – or a defective implementation – may give rise to rights to individuals of the Member state in question provided that the provisions of the directive satisfy the criteria referred to above under Treaty Articles (especially as to clarity and precision). Thus, in certain circumstances Directives may have a *vertical direct effect* as regards *rights* of individual citizens. The Court has based its view on the Member States' duty to faithfully comply with the obligations of a directive within the time limits set. But on the other hand on a *horisontal* level, the Court has *rejected* imposing *obligations* on individual citizens on the basis of non-implemented – or defectively implemented – directives. Where direct effect may not be deemed to apply it is, however, possible that the Member state which has breached its duties in the implementation of a directive may be held liable to citizens who have suffered loss as a consequence.

Decisions of a character resembling directives, cf. above Section 4.2.4 may be directly effective under the same criteria and to the same extent as directives. As regards *Treaties with third countries* the direct effect is first examined in the light of the extent to which the Treaty in question is addressed to the citizens. Where the Treaty is silent on such issue the Court has held that a construction of the Treaty (based on public international law) must determine whether it is appropriate to apply direct effect capability under the circumstances.

The question of direct effect of Community rules in the sense described here will always ultimately be in issue at the national courts. This does not imply, however, that the national courts are to decide whether direct effect applies or not. Where such effect is doubtful, the issue must be submitted to the Court of Justice for a preliminary ruling under the rules referred to in Section 3.6. As was mentioned in that Section, the national court will be obliged to follow the interpretation of the EU law and its status in the context in issue expressed in the Court's ruling.

4.6.4. Supremacy of EU law

As will be apparent from the preceding Sections various types of EU rules are of such character that they may or indeed must be applied by national courts in actions brought before them. This may bring about a situation in which an EU rule and a national rule are in conflict. Therefore guidelines for solving such conflicts must be developed.

Even though – from an EU law point of view – the Treaty contains no express provisions on the issue there is no doubt as to the end result: In the event of conflict the EU rule takes precedence over the national rule. Consequently, the national court will be obliged to disregard the national rule in favour of the EU rule. Under the Court's practice this solution is long established. On the principal level the central justification for this is also evident. With their entry into the EU the Member States have limited their freedom of action in favour of that of the Community and may thus be deemed to have relinquished their ability to issue (or uphold) rules which are at variance with EU law. The uniform and effective implementation of Community law would further be endangered if the national courts were not obligated in this way. In the Draft Constitution the supremacy principle is contained in Art 10(1). In national case law in the Member States the principle of supremacy must now be deemed to be generally established. The only area in which the solution may still be doubtful is where there is a conflict between EU rules and national rules at the highest ranking level. In such cases it should probably not be taken for granted that a national court will disregard its own constitutional law in favour of an EU rule. In a Supreme Court decision of 1998 (Ugeskrift for Retsvæsen 1998, p. 800) Denmark addressed the issue on a general point of law regarding the constitutionality of the Act on Denmark's Accession to the EC. In its grounds the Supreme Court held i.a. (ground 9.6) that "the courts cannot be deprived of the access to review the issue as to whether an EU legal act exceeds the limits of the sovereignty surrender made at the time of accession" and that "Danish courts (must) therefore consider an EC legal act inapplicable in Denmark if the extraordinary situation should arise that it may be established with requisite certainty that an EC legal act sustained by the European Court rests on an application of the Treaty which is beyond the surrender of sovereignty under the Accession Act. The same applies to Community rules and legal principles resting on the practice of the European Court". If the Draft constituion is implemented the specifications contained therein will presumably reduce the problem to one of a hypothetical character.

4.6.5. The duty to apply EU interpretational practice to national law interpretation

Within the judicial practice of the Court of Justice a principle has been developed under which national authorities and courts of law are under a duty to interpret and apply national rules in *conformity* with all parts of binding EU law, also in cases in which it is not directly effective. The principle which is primarily based on the loyalty obligations which the Member States are under in relation to the EU (the solidarity principle, cf. Section 2) is especially important as regards EU directives. There is a parallel principle in public international law, cf. below, Section 6.2.3 (interpretation and presumption rules).

5. Cooperation outside the EU scope

As mentioned in Section 1, there is also an extensive cooperation between the EU countries outside the Treaty areas. This cooperation has been manifested, e.g. in the making of *special treaties*, of which an important example is the Convention of 19 June 1980 in respect of the law applicable to Contractual Obligations, cf. Chapter 26, infra). Another example of practical importance is the Convention of 27 September 1968 regarding the jurisdiction of the courts and enforcement of judgments in civil cases (The Judgments Convention), cf. Chapter 22, below on both examples.

In contrast to the EU law referred to in the preceding Sections the provisions of such Treaties are of ordinary international character. They are based on the agreement made and not on an independent legal establishment from the EU authorities. Consequently, the Treaty provisions must be incorporated in the national legal orders to give them direct effectiveness as regards the citizens in the Member States. In other words, the procedure of public international law obligations must be followed, as reviewed in the following Section.

6. Other international source of law factors

6.1. Introduction

Outside the EU cooperation international source of law factors mainly occur in connection with agreements which Denmark has entered into with other states. The most important of these agreements are the results of Danish participation and membership in various international organisations, e.g. the UN, the Council of Europe, the International Employment Organisation etc. As mentioned in Section 1, the prevailing characteristic of such co-operation is that it is neither as profound nor extensive as the EU co-operation and that the authorities of such organisations are not endowed with an independent access of issuing general legal acts and instruments with binding effect in respect of the member states or of their citizens. The co-operation is, as was mentioned, of an *ordinary public international law character*. The source of law factors stemming from such co-operation which could be relevant are described in Section 6.2. In Section 6.3 the importance of any international customs (usages) is set out and Section 6.4 describes possible other international source of law factors.

The fundamental question relating to sources of law is the same as with the Community law, viz. what is the importance of such factors for decisions made by *Danish* courts of law and other *Danish* authorities?

6.2. Ordinary public international law

6.2.1. Subject matter and character of ordinary public international law

The public international law is concerned with the ordinary international legal order. Its core subject is the legal relationship *between states*. It differs from national law (and from central parts of EU law) in the first place by the way the legal rules are established. They are based almost exclusively on *agreement* or on *legal customs* between states, and not on general directions issued by central authorities empowered to such rule-making. Secondly, there are no rules in the public international law regarding the monopolised application of power to enforce compliance with the rules which characterises the national legal orders, i.e. there is also a fundamental difference in the enforcement of the law. This does not exclude the existence of various international conflict-solving organs of a court-resembling character, e.g. the socalled International Court in Hague or the European Court for Human Rights in Strasbourg. But the decisions made at such courts are not enforceable in the ordinary manner of speaking.

Common source of law relevance is primarily attached to that part of public international law which seeks to regulate the relationship between citizens or between citizens and public authorities. Since – as was mentioned above – the public international law only concerns the legal relationship between states this purpose can normally only be realised if the rules in question are *incorporated in the individual national legal orders.* A general requirement in public international law is that the states loyally perform their public international law commitments but as a main rule no requirements are made as to the manner of performance. Thus it is for the individual states to decide how to make rules of the public international law character referred to applicable within their own territories. In some countries, including Denmark, the starting point is that public international law rules are not applicable until a special national legal act has been issued to such effect, in practice this will involve the passing of national legislation giving legal force to the public international law in the country in question as described in the following Section. From a Danish point of view the public international law and legal order and the national legal order are in principle confined to two separate compartments, though with a communicating door between them, cf. on the opposite relationship as regards the EU law, Section 4.6. above.

Within business law the public international law customs are of no practical significance. Most often they will not be capable of direct effectiveness as towards the citizens, and they are therefore disregarded in the following. Public international law agreements on the other hand are certainly important. They are normally described as "treaties" or "conventions". Some are of global character, e.g. those related to the UN cooperation . Others are limited to the Western world, e.g. with their bases in the co-operation in the Council of Europe or in the European Union outside the EU law proper, cf. above Chapter 3, Section 5. The subject matters covered are wide, ranging from rules relating to the formation of certain types of agreement (as e.g. the important example of sale of goods) and the protection of certain rights, e.g. patents, to rules governing choice of law – the law applicable to certain legal relationships involving parties of who have their residence or place of business in different countries.

The procedure involved in the creation of the rules reflects that they are based on agreement (or contract). The basis of agreement is the result of negotiations – often extremely lengthy – between the governments of the states involved. When agreement has been reached, the next step is normally approval ("ratification") in the individual countries before the agreement can become effective. As already mentioned, the implementation in the individual countries further requires social national measures, cf. immediately below.

Treaties, conventions etc. to which Denmark has acceded, are published in "Lovtidende" (Div. C).

6.2.2. The incorporation of public international rules in Danish law

The action required to make public international law rules applicable in this country depends fundamentally on the substance of the rules in conjunction with the existing legal state of affairs.

The existing legal state of affairs may be deemed to correspond to the public international law rules already and where such presumption is tenable no further act will be required. Most often, however, the application of treaties, conventions etc. entered into will require new legislation or at least amendments to existing legislation. In that case, the consent of the Folketing is necessary for the entry into the agreement in question, cf the Danish Constitution Act s. 19(1). Further, the government must introduce a bill calling for implementation of the public international law rules in Denmark to the Folketing, i.e. see to their proper incorporation into Danish law.

It is possible to incorporate the public international law rules by *redrafting* them into (new) Danish legislation, cf. e.g. the Act referred to in Chapter 10 concerning choice of law in international sales of goods, implementing the socalled Hague Convention on international sales of goods. An alternative approach is to make a *"reference"*, i.e. incorporation of the public international law rules by retaining their original linguistic formulation and making express reference to them in a special Act passed for that purpose, cf. the important example of the legislation on implementation of the UN Convention of 1980 on contracts for the international sales of goods (CISG) referred to in Chapter 9. Incorporation by reference is now the most common method.

It will be seen that there are certain similarities to incorporation of directives from the EU bodies, cf. above Section 4.2.3. The decisive differences are – as will be remembered- to the effect that directives are not based on agreement, they are not to be ratified by the Folketing and in certain circumstances they have direct effect and finally, failure to implement them, or defective implementation, may attract liability for Treaty violation before the Court of Justice and also liability in damages towards the citizens who may have suffered a loss on that account.

Upon incorporation the public international law rules have become elements of current Danish law and are prima facie treated like rules of purely Danish origin, i.e. in a source of law context their rank is equal to that of Danish legislation. Some special interpretation questions may arise, however, cf. below Section 6.2.5.

6.2.3. Source of law importance of non-incorporated public international law

Where incorporation has not been made situations may arise involving conflicts between public international law rules and Danish rules. This situation may arise in cases where incorporation has not yet been managed or where the Danish rules were deemed already to conform with the rules of the public international law and that presumption subsequently proves to be wrong.

The starting point for the solution of such conflicts does not present problems. The non-incorporation rules are in-applicable if they are contrary to Danish rules and they are incapable of giving authority for decisions by Danish authorities where a statutory authority is necessary in the cases in question. On the basis of case law, however, it must be said that the courts seek to alleviate the consequences of this starting point to enable Denmark to perform her public international law commitments. This approach has been manifested with particular practical effect in two ways:

First the court may make use of the *"interpretation rule"*. This implies that national rules should always – as far as possible – be interpreted so as to conform with existing public international law commitments. In genreal, Danish courts are apparently willing to go a long way towards solving disputes in this way.

Alternatively, the courts may use the *"presumption rule"*. This implies that a presumption is set up under which the competent Danish authorities (primarily the legislative authorities) are deemed not to have wanted to act contrary to any public international law commitments which Denmark is bound by. Accordingly, national rules must be applied so as to avoid acts which are contrary to public international law.

The two rules are overlapping. However, the presumption rule has an independent content by covering instances in which conformity between the national rule and the public international law rule cannot be achieved by way of ordinary interpretation of the former. There are limits, however, to the judicial flexibility. Where there are material and distinct differences between the two rules this factor is recognised. In such cases the Danish rule will govern the issue in point and thus it is left to the legislative powers to bring about the necessary conformity.

6.2.4. Other conflicts between public international law and national law

A somewhat similar situation may arise where incorporation of the public international law rules has been made and conflicts prove to exist between them and the existing incorporated legislation. In practice, the situation will of course require that incorporation has been made by re-phrasing, cf. above Section 2.2. Existing discrepancies or conflicts are normally of a technical nature, especially in the form of imprecise or even incorrect translations.

Conflicts of such nature are solved, as far as practically possible, by applying an interpretation to the national rule which conforms to that of the public international law, cf. the similar situation in EU law in Section 4.6.5.

6.2.5. Interpretation of rules of a public international law background

Special interpretation problems arise when rules of a public international law background are to be interpreted, e.g. rules of a treaty which has been incorporated into Danish law.

At first sight, the interpretation data are in principle the same as when interpreting purely national rules, cf. above Chapter 2, Section 8, i.e. wording, context, any travaux preparatoires, and the purposes as expressed by the government in question. Nor is there any doubt that the general aim of the interpretation is the same as for interpretation of rules with a Danish background, i.e. the aim is to arrive at a practically reasonable result. The views underlying the interpretation and presumption rules referred to above in Section 6.2.3 may be helpful guiding principles in this context.

On the one hand, the special interpretation problems may appear at the purely linguistic interpretation. The original (and thus public international law applicable) versions of several treaties entered into by Denmark and incorporated in Danish law are not available in Danish but only in one of the main languages, especially English, French or German. Thus, the international Convention on Contracts for Sales of Goods (CISG), cf. below Chapter 9, has no original Danish text. In such cases it is abundantly evident that the linguistic analysis of the public international law provisions must follow the language rules applying to the language(s) used in the original text. Secondly, it is also evident that it is of paramount importance in the interpretation process whether the rules in question are of *international background* and are endowed with an *international scope*, i.e. whether a presumption of legal uniformity across borders may be entertained. Context and situation are not limited to Denmark and Danish considerations. This general view is aptly expressed in Art. 7(1) of CISG. Under this Article the interpretation process must take into account the international character of the rules, the need to promote a uniform application of its provisions and observance of good business usage in international trade. The ultimate choice of interpretation alternative, where several are possible, must accordingly be based on international trade interests.

6.3. International Customs

Just as in the national legal environment, certain patterns of conduct, developed by the citizens among themselves in respect of settlement of various conditions of life may be legally relevant to a court's decision when they occur in an international context (national law reference, cf. Chapter 2, Section 6.1). The importance of custom is almost exclusively limited to commercial matters and will be manifested primarily in *international customs* or usages of relevance between contract parties in different countries. Thus the customs are not really of public international law status, cf. above,

Section 2, which will apply to patterns of conduct between *states*, whereas the usages described here are relevant to immediate relationships between *citizens*.

The fundamental requirements of attaching legal importance to international usages are primarily of the same nature as the requirements of purely national ones. Thus, a first requirement is to substantiate that in a given area, e.g. within a certain line of business, a certain common pattern of conduct exists which is of such firm establishment that it is at all relevant to consider its possible legal status. The question may, if necessary, be referred to the opinion of experts, whether individuals or organisations, e.g. the International Chamber of commerce (ICC) in Denmark upon reference from the Danish Chamber of Commerce. In the affirmative, the problem of relevance must be considered, including the weight to be attached to the conduct in question. As was seen with national law, it is not possible to give simple directions as to the factors the courts will include in their deliberations. The decision will depend on an overall assessment taking into account a great variety of circumstances, cf. further Chapter 2, Section 6.1 for the most important of these, with the additional criterion in this context, however, that an evaluation of the "quality" of the usage (good or bad) must of course be made from an international perspective.

Where the usage is deemed to exist and *where* such usage is found to be legally relevant in an existing concrete context the significance will typically be manifested in the way the usage is applied either for *interpretation purposes,* viz. the agreement is interpreted in the light of the usage, or for *gap-filling* of the parties' (incomplete) contract, or both. This implies that the operation of international customs is limited to areas in which the legal position of the parties is fundamentally based on freedom of contract between the parties and not limited by mandatory statutory provisions. In the gap-filling situation the custom will replace or supplemt non-mandatory law rules. In an area of great practical importance such as the Convention on international sales (CISG) there are express rules on the importance of customs, cf. Art 9 of CISG for more details.

There is a wide variety of model contracts, standard terms, proposals for the drafting of certain types of contract terms etc. prepared by various international business and professional organisations for application in international sales of goods and supplies of services. Such materials may be valuable to the parties in individual contractual relationships when they are to decide the drafting of the contract between them. Often the materials are prepared with due regard to the balancing of both parties' interests and to existing international usages and the law otherwise applicable in the area. However, it is not a foregone conclusion that materials of this kind are in the nature of usages per se. Of course this does not exclude the possibility that the courts will take such materials into account, especially in support of – or to supplement – other existing source of law factors. Compared with usages proper, the weight of such materials will, however, be slighter.

6.4. Other international materials

6.4.1. Foreign Court decisions

With the rapid growth in international cooperation which has taken place since the end of World War II and the efforts undertaken in consequence of such cooperation of promoting international trade in various important areas by attempting to bring about an approximation of the various national legal orders, decisions from superior courts in foreign countries will also gain increased importance as a source of law factor (precedents) to Danish courts. One obvious example is the application and interpretation of CISG. As this Convention in central areas represents a uniform legal basis applying to a large number of countries there is no doubt that decisions from foreign courts regarding e.g. the interpretation of the Convention are of immediate relevance to Danish courts.

As was mentioned in Section 6.2.1 there are certain public international law conflict-solving bodies of a court-resembling character. Decisions from such bodies may also be a relevant source of law factor. Judgments under the European Human Rights Convention made by the European Human Rights Court e.g. have been highly significant in several cases decided at the Danish courts.

6.4.2. Nordic legislative cooperation

The tradition of cooperation between the Nordic countries goes back several generations and covers a large number of areas, including implementation of egislation of a uniform substance. On the organisational level the co-operation is now partly associated with the institutions, The Nordic Council and The Nordic Council of Ministers.

In the property and commercial law area, the co-operation has resulted in the implementation of important legislation in the individual countries with identical or almost identical contents in substantial areas. Where such legislation exists both travaux preparatoires from the other Nordic countries and decisions from their courts will be relevant source of law factors in Danish law.

6. 5. Reference places for international source of law factors

As already mentioned, treaties etc. to which Denmark has acceded will be published in "Lovtidende C". As regards international materials in general numerous possibilities of search – most of them quite excellent – are offered via the Internet, e.g. when starting out from the websites mentioned in

Chapter 1, Section 4, which provide links to a substantial number of international legal search facilities, or directly via one of these sites, e.g. "Lex Mercatoria" (www.lexmercatoria.org/). All international organisations of any significant importance also provide their own homepages often containing materials of a highly informative value, see e.g. on CISG where information on international case law practice decided under the CISG provisions in ordinary courts of law and arbitration tribunals can be found; or the homepage for the UN sub-organisation for international trade (UNCITRAL, http://www.un.org/), or the Danish site www.cisg.dk which provides i.a. Danish decisions made under CISG. On a trade organisational level various udeful material may be obtained via the homepage of the International Chamber of Trade (ICC) (http://www.icc.wbo/org/).

CHAPTER 4

Survey of the Danish court system

by Morten Wegener

1. Introduction

In this Chapter a brief account of a number of elementary matters regarding the Danish court system will be given, including the organisation of the courts, procedure in civil cases, and the possibility of appeals of court decisions, cf. Sections 2-5. When a judgment on a dispute has been pronounced such judgment may need to be enforced, cf. above Chapter 1, Section 2.1. The rules governing enforcement are described in Chapter 14. In Sections 6 and 7 some special types of conflict solution are described, viz. arbitration and hearings of certain consumer issues before special Consumers' Complaints Boards.

Danish courts hear both criminal and civil cases. With the general aim of this book only the last-mentioned will be treated here.

The most important legal regulation of the matters treated here is contained in the Administration of Justice Act, cf. Consolidated Act No. 815 of 30 September 2003.

2. Organisation of the courts

The *ordinary* courts are organised in a three-tier system reflecting the "instances" available: Town/city courts, high courts, and the Supreme Court. All permanent judges in the system have a fundamental legal education.

The local courts – *town/city courts* – currently numbering 82, cover a certain geographical area (a court constituency) typically corresponding to a minor amount of the smallest administrative units: municipalities. The largest constituencies will have several judges attached to the town/city court which will then operate in divisions but only one judge will preside in ordinary civil cases. The judge also undertakes the functions of a *bailiff* in enforcement proceedings, cf. below Chapter 14, as a *"probate administrator"* (where the town court is probate or bankruptcy court) e.g. in proceedings on estates of deceased persons and in bankrupt estates, cf. on the last-mentioned below Chapter 22, and the local *registration* transactions are also his province, cf. below Chapter 16.

The *high court* level comprises two courts. One for the Western region of the country with a permanent seat in Viborg, covering Jutland, and one for the Eastern region, with a permanent seat in Copenhagen, covering the rest of the country. Both high courts have a major number of judges attached presided over by a president. The courts operate in divisions. In ordinary civil proceedings three judges will participate.

The *Supreme Court*, situate in Copenhagen, is at the top of the hierarchy. It is composed of a President and 15 other judges. Prima facie, in supreme court proceedings, five judges will participate.

The three-tier system is organised so that appeals of judgments will normally lie to the court immediately above. Appeals of cases decided at the town courts as first instance will thus lie to the high courts and judgments in cases originating in high court may be appealed to the Supreme Court, cf. below Section 3 regarding first instance jurisdiction and Section 4 regarding appeals.

In certain areas a need for special expertise and/or involving special interests have led to the establishment of special courts with their own organisation. An important example is represented by the *Maritime and Commercial Court*, situate in Copenhagen, which mainly hears cases in which expert knowledge on maritime and commercial matters is deemed important. The Maritime and Commercial Court is presided over by a judge of legal training and at least two lay professional experts. Decisions may, prima facie, be appealed to the Supreme Court. Another practical example is represented by the rent tribunals. In the adjudication of most cases under the Rent Acts the town courts are supplemented by a representative of interest groups of houseowners and tenants and are then termed *"rent tribunals"*.

In principle judges are granted a constitutional right of *independence*, cf. especially s. 64. Thus the government in office from time to time is barred from giving directions to the courts as to the decisions to be made in a certain case or special types of cases. Judges are appointed upon recommendation from a special collegiate body – the *Judicial Appointing Council* – whose president is a Supreme Court judge, cf. s. 43a of the Administration of Justice Act. Matters concerning appropriations and administration are controlled by the Courts Board, cf. Act No. 401 of 26 June 1998. The Board is responsible to the Ministry of Justice but the Minister has no authority of instruction to the Board.

3. Procedure in civil cases

3.1. Parties and their claims

Usually only two parties will be involved in a case before a court, the party setting up a claim – *the plaintiff* – and the party against whom the claim is set up – *the defendant*. More parties may be involved, however, e.g. in cases where several people are entitled under a claim or where several people are co-debtors for the same debt. All natural persons may, irrespective of capacity, be parties in a case and the same applies to any socalled legal persons, e.g. limited liability companies, the state, and the local authorities. Having status as a party does not necessarily imply that such party may also dispose in the subject-matter of the case, e.g. in connection with agreeing a settlement with the other side. For minors such dispositions are normally made by the minor's guardian.

The parties will usually be assisted by lawyers, termed "advocates" in Denmark. Advocates are socalled "procedural agents" and not parties themselves. As a main rule the services of an advocate in civil cases are not obligatory, i.e. any plaintiff and defendant may normally conduct his own case. It is also possible to have certain close relations, e.g. a spouse, represent one in court.

The decision of the court is normally sought on a legal issue raised by the plaintiff in his *claim*. The issue may be contained in only one or several *allegations* made before the court by the plaintiff. As against the claim the defendant will set up his defence. Usually the defence will be to the effect that the claim be dismissed and the defendant be discharged. However, nothing prevents that the defendant may set up an independent claim which he asks the court to decide, e.g. where he has a counter-claim against the plaintiff. Incidentally, the same issue may be divided into several claims. Where the case involves e.g. a buyer's claim for damages for breach of contract on the seller's part the buyer may plead as his *principal claim* that he should be granted damages of a certain amount on various specific heads and – as a subsidiary claim – he *pleads "in the alternative"* that he should be granted a lower amount where the court is incapable of acknowledging all the damages items. Similarly the seller may plead several counter-allegations, e.g. principally dismissal of the plaintiff's claim, and in the alternative payment of a lesser amount than the amount claimed.

3.2. Procedural principles

The procedure in civil cases is as a main rule subject to a principle of *orality*, i.e. cases are tried orally and only where specially provided by statute will writing be used. Further, proceedings are subject to a principle of *directness*, i.e. the parties are to put forward their views and present their evidence directly before the judge who is to decide their case. It is also a principle that court sessions are public. Proceedings are normally conducted in open court unless the court, upon statutory sanction, decides otherwise.

A fourth important procedural principle is the socalled *adversarial principle*. This implies in particular that it is the parties – not the judge – who produce the procedural "substance" since this is made up of the allegations, representations and evidence which the parties rely on during the proceedings. In this connection the parties are placed equally, i.e. they have the same right to know and submit evidence used in the trial.

Though the adversarial principle is not applied unconditionally its main consequences may be outlined as follows: For one thing the parties will define the framework of the whole proceedings through their claims, representations, and material facts brought forward to support their claims. Thus a court cannot give a party more than he asked for in his claim and may only consider representations actually made and which have not been waived. Secondly, it is the parties who are in charge of the case through their production of evidence. Generally, the court has no independent initiative here and may not take information into account which has not been brought to light in connection with evidence production.

Thus the court is mainly referred to a passive role as regards the framework of proceedings and the elucidation of the case. The court may ask questions, however, and in the town/city courts the judge is under a duty to give guidance to anyone appearing without advocate representation.

3.3. The question of venue

The question of venue of proceedings is multi-dimensional. One dimension relates to the *substantive law jurisdiction* of a court. Apart from the Maritime and Commercial Court, cf. above Section 2, this refers to the determination of which court level is to hear the case at first instance. The main statutory rule is that civil cases are to be brought before the town courts. The most important exception from this main rule is that where the amount in dispute exceeds DKK 1,000,000 such case may be brought before the high court and if it has been brought at the town court it must be referred to a high court if one of the parties so requests. Basically the value of a case is decided by the claim made in the writ of summons, cf. the following Section.

The other dimension relates to the courts' *geographical jurisdiction* for courts at an equal level. The starting point is that proceedings must be brought at the defendant's home court, i.e. in the constituency of his residence or – where he has no residence – his place of sojourn. Companies etc. usually have venue in the constituency of their registered office. On a collective basis the jurisdiction rules imply that by far the majority of first instance civil cases are brought at the town courts in the constituency of the defendant's residence. The starting point may be derogated from in certain important cases. Thus, cases involving real estate may be brought before the court at the place where such real estate is situated. Similarly, cases involving damages in tort may be brought before the court at the place where the tortious act was committed.

3.4. Procedural steps in first instance cases

A civil case is commenced by the plaintiff's (in practice his lawyer's) taking out of a *writ of summons* against the defendant. The writ which is a procedural pleading in writing must normally contain the names and addresses of the parties, an indication of the court before which the case has been brought, the plaintiff's claim, a summary of the material facts supporting the claim, and a statement of the documents the plaintiff intends to rely upon. The writ is presented to the court which is to hear the case. Proceedings in the case are now *instituted*. The court will appoint a day of first hearing and clause the writ to such effect. The writ is then *served* on the defendant either by letter or writ server. The defendant will receive a copy of the writ at the service. He will also be instructed as to how he may safeguard his own interests.

At the appointed first court session the plaintiff (his advocate) must appear and submit the documents he intends to rely upon if they are in the plaintiff's possession. Failure to appear or failure to produce the documents will cause the case to be dismissed. When in the normal course of events the plaintiff does appear and performs the obligation mentioned the further proceedings will depend on the position adopted by the defendant.

Where the defendant *fails to appear* without lawful excuse the court will usually make a judgment in default whereby the claim of the plaintiff is *acknowledged* without further ado. The same applies if the defendant appears and admits to the claim. This is the way most civil cases – on the lines of pure debt recovery cases – are heard at the town and city courts.

Where the defendant appears (with this lawyer, if any) and *disputes* the plaintiff's claim he must account for his claim, counter-claims, if any, and the material facts supporting such claims (in first-instance high court proceedings such claims must be submitted in a written pleading, termed the defence). Hereupon the case will be adjourned and a new court session is appointed. This session may involve the *presentation of evidence* – e.g. examinations of the parties and witnesses – and a subsequent *trial*. At the trial the parties will expound their views on the factual and legal circumstances of the whole case in arguments by counsel. In major cases the presentation of evidence may involve several court sessions and the trial may be referred to a special session. Upon the closing of trial the court will set the case down for judgment. Judgements and interlocutory orders (decisions made during proceedings) in city court cases must normally be pronounced no later than six months after the date of setting down for judgemnt. For high court cases the similar timelimit is three months.

The court is obliged in all civil first-instance cases to attempt having a *settlement* agreed before the case is set down for judgment. Such settlement is entered in the court's records. Since a settlement is in the nature of an agreement there is no appeal against it.

Where a judgment is to be pronounced following presentation of evidence and trial the judge's decision is of the nature described in Chapter 1, Section 5. In that connection it is worth noting that the starting point in Danish law for *assessment of evidence* is that the judge is *free to consider it on its merits*. In other words the judge may decide the emphasis he will place on the evidence produced by the parties. Where lack of evidence on a certain issue acts to the detriment of a party in the decision the party in question is said to have failed to *"lift the burden of proof"* placed upon him.

Judgments are pronounced in open court. In their typical couching they will present the parties' claims, the material facts as stated and relevant, the representations made by the parties, the deliberations made by the court (the "ratio decidendi" of the judgment), and finally the decision proper. The party losing the case will usually be ordered to pay an amount towards the opponent's costs in the case (court fees, if any, expenses in connection with the production of evidence, lawyer's fee).

4. Appeals

As a main rule appeals against town court judgments lie to the high courts. Exceptions apply to judgments in cases where the amount in dispute is below DKK 10,000. For such cases leave to appeal may be granted by the Process Licence Board upon application if they contain a matter of general legal principle or special circumstances otherwise indicate that leave to appeal should be granted. The Board is a special body of professional jurists consisting of three judges, an advocate and a university jurist.

Judgments made by the high courts at first instance and by the Maritime and Commercial Court may normally be appealed to the Supreme Court.

As a main rule, there is no right of appeal of high court appeals to Supreme Court as a third instance court. However, leave to appeal may be granted by the Process Licence Board if the case involved contains issues of general legal principles.

The timelimit for appeals is 4 weeks for town court judgments and 8 weeks for high court judgments and decisions from the Maritime and Commercial Court to Supreme Court. The timelimits are computed from the pronouncement of judgment. The applications mentioned must also be lodged within 4 or 8 weeks, respectively. Since judgments may normally be enforced upon the expiry of 14 days from pronouncement (the socalled "enforcement timelimit" it will often be wise to appeal before the expiry of this shorter timilimit.

The appeal makes it possible to undertake a completely new trial of the case at the appellate instance. However, claims and representations which were not made in the lower court will – if the other side objects to their inclusion – only be considered with the leave of the appellate court.

A party who has received a judgment in default, cf. above the preceding Section, may apply for a resumption of the case where such application, in writing, is submitted within 4 weeks from the pronouncement of the judgment. By way of exception the court may grant resumption even if an application to such effect is not made within the timelimit but the application must be made within a year from pronouncement of judgment.

5. Legal Assistance and legal aid (court representation)

Whether a party acts as plaintiff or defendant litigation often involveees considerable costs. If the case is lost the loser will, as mentioned in Section 3.4, normally be ordered to pay the other party's costs. To this must be added his own costs for lawyer's assistance, etc. Thus the cost issue may well act as a barrier for a legal pursuit of justified claims or a reliance on just defences. In an attempt to counteract this disadvantage various private and public schemes have been created aiming for one thing at minimising the cost risk in certain cases, for another at ensuring that insufficient financial means do not act as a bar to obtaining legal advice.

Among the private schemes the socalled *legal expenses insurance schemes* stand out. Such insurance schemes will cover the costs of legal or other disputes which the insured may be involved in. The insurance is not taken out as an independent insurance but may be attached as an automatic supplement to some common insurance types, viz. family insurance covering house contents insurance, comprehensive building damage insurance, motor vehicle insurance with usual comprehensive cover and similar pleasure boat insurance. A number of issue types will be outside the area of coverage – in particular disputes in connection with the insured's business activity, disputes with authorities on tax or duties issues, and collection issues where justification and size of the claim is not in doubt. The coverage of costs refers both to own costs and to costs ordered on the party in question. A maximum amount of DKK 75,000 is set for each insured event and an own risk of 10 per cent of the total costs. These terms have been set aside by the

Competition Board and the coverage will now be set out in the individual principal insurance policies. Therefore it will vary in amount as some companies have maintained the former maximum while other companies have raised it considerably (up to DKK 125,000). It is a general requirement that the insured has applied for legal aid where the financial requirements for such application are present, cf. immediately below, and assistance must have been sought from the lawyer who has undertaken to represent the insured. Where the issue qualifies for a hearing before a complaints board, cf. below Section 7, that avenue must have been attempted. The costs involved here are not covered.

Outside the legal (advice and) assistance scheme any type of privately organised assistance is especially common from organisations within the same line of business or professional associations. These organisations sometimes extend legal assistance to their members and also regular litigation assistance where issues involving general principles are involved.

The *public* assistance schemes are mainly concentrated in the rules on *legal aid* (for litigation purposes). Leave to bring first-instance cases is granted, upon application, by the relevant county, for appeal cases by the Ministry of Justice, i.e. the Civil Law Directorate, which also acts as appeal instance for decisions made by the supreme administrative authorities. The grant will cover mainly the costs of the litigant's own lawyer, court fees, and costs ordered in favour of the other side, if any. It will cover all proceedings at the court in question, including enforcement of the decision made. When legal aid has been granted in first instance the grant will also cover appeals in second, and possibly third, instance where the decision is appealed by the other side and judgment has been given in favour of the legally aided party either in full or in part. Costs will only be covered to the extent that they are not covered by legal expenses insurance or other insurance, cf. above.

To qualify for legal aid the applicant is required to have a "reasonable case" to submit to a court (i.e. reasonable *grounds* for taking or defending proceedings – which does not mean that his prospects of winning are necessarily better than average). Certain case types are exempt, according to practice, e.g. disputes on commercial matters and clear-cut collection cases. An additional requirement is that the applicant is incapable of paying the costs in connection with the litigation without suffering considerable financial hardship. This *financial requirement* is regulated on the basis of certain tariff amounts, cf. currently Consolidated Act of the Ministry of Justice No. 948 of 25 November 2002. Where legal aid is granted the court will appoint an advocate to represent the party in question.

Another *public* scheme is a *legal advice and assistance scheme* which is available under Consolidated Act No. 1140 of 13 December 2002. Persons satisfying certain financial requirements may obtain legal advice by application to lawyers who are employed to conduct legal aid cases or to other lawyers who have undertaken such duty towards the town court judge. The assistance will be given in the form of advice and drafting of a number of applications and other writings, including an application for legal aid. Where a legal issue is already in progress extended legal advice may be provided. Depending on the character of the assistance two varying maximum fees are payable to the lawyer. For ordinary legal advice the state will disburse 75 per cent of the lawyer's fee and for extended legal advice 50 per cent of such fee while the rest will be payable by the applicant himself. Where legal assistance is granted with a view to obtaining legal aid for litigation the state will, however, pay the whole amount. Legal aid is not available i.a. for trader-litigants' cases of a predominantly commercial character.

6. Arbitration

A *voluntary* arbitration arises where the parties in a legal relationship have *agreed* that any legal disputes between them are not to be settled by the ordinary courts but are instead to be referred to a private court (arbitration court) consisting of one or more persons (arbitrators) who have been authorised by the parties to make a final, binding decision of their dispute. Such solutions may also, exceptionally, be prescribed as *mandatory*, e.g. in connection with certain labour disputes.

Agreements on arbitration (socalled arbitration clauses) are common in many contract relationships, especially in an international context. When arbitration is preferred to ordinary court hearing the argument is often that the process is speedier and more "professionally competent" and that the arbitration court – which is not subject to publicity requirements – makes for greater privacy where that need is present with the parties. On the other hand since the parties are to cover the costs of the arbitration court's activity such solution will often be more expensive than a lawsuit at the ordinary courts. Arbitration agreements may be combined with advance agreement on choice of law or whether the decision – unbound by law rules – shall be made on the basis of reasonableness criteria (i.e. what would be just and equitable).

The arbitration court may be established with a view to solving conflicts under a concrete, existing agreement (socalled ad hoc arbitration). The composition of the arbitration court is decided by agreement between the parties who also provide instructions as to the proceedings. A far more practical solution is agreements to refer disputes to permanent arbitration courts (socalled institutional arbitration) typically courts established or created in connection with national or international organisations within specified lines. An outstanding example is the permanent arbitration court in

Paris, established by the International Chamber of Commerce. The permanent tribunal in Denmark is the Danish Arbitration Institute situated in Copenhagen.

Where a valid agrement on arbitration has been made – as evaluated by ordinary validity criteria in contract law – the courts will refuse to hear cases on issues comprised by such agreement. As a main rule arbitration awards – also foreign – may be enforced in Denmark under the same rules as judgments. Provisions to this effect are contained in Act No. 181 of 24 May 1972 regarding arbitration, cf. below Chapter 22.

7. Complaints Boards' Hearings of Consumer Cases

Conflicts in the legal relationship between traders and their private customers are normally for moderate amounts. To facilitate customer's access to a speedy and inexpensive first opinion in certain types of conflict a number of special appeals or complaints boards have been established.

As from 1 January 2004 these issues are governed by Act No. 456 of 10 June 2003 on consumer complaints.The starting point is that complaints from consumers in respect of goods and services may be brought before an approved, private complaints or appeals board or before the Consumers Complaints Board and that such complaint may relate to all circumstances in the relationship between the parties. The distribution of work betwen the two boards means that only complaints which are not under the province of a private board are referred to the Consumers Complaints Board , i.e. this body will only have a "residual" competence. The Board is also barrred from hearing complaints for which a statutory complaint acces has been provided already.

A number of provisions in the Act (ss 2-4 and 16-17) are common to the approved private boards and to the Consumers Complaints Board. A consumer complaint may be directed towards anyone who may be sued under the provisions in the Administration of Justice Act before a Danish court in respect of the issues to which the complaint relates, which means that foriegn companies may also be sued under the circumstances. The consumer must pay a fee for the case to be heard but this fee will be reimbursed if he wins the case. In such instances the trader must pay an amount to cover the costs i connection with the proceedings at the Consumers Complaints Board and similar coverage of costs may also be provided before the private complaints boards. Arbitration agreements do not act as a bar to hearing before a complaints board. As regards the relationship between such hearing and a hearing before the ordinary courts it is stated that as long as a case is pending before a complaints board the parties are barred from bringing the same issue before the ordinary courts. On the other hand a case already brought before the courts may, prima facie – upon petition from the consumer – be adjourned indefinitely and transfered for hearing before the complaint board competent in the matter.

In principle decisions are not binding upon the parties and each party may subsequently bring the issue before the courts. Where the consumer's counterpart fails to observe a decision or settlement, the Consumers Complaints Board may, upon the consumer's petition bring the case before the courts on his behalf. If the consumer satisfies the financial requirements of free process, cf. above, such access is open to him both when he institutes proceedings himself with a view to performance of a decision made by an approved private board or by the Consumers Complaints Board and when his counterpart institutes proceedings on a plea of changing the board decision to the consumer's detriment.

The setting up of private boards within special trades or other delimitation and the rules governing their activities are subject to approval by the Minister of Trade and Industry. It is a condition that the board rules contain provisions on the composition of the board and hearing procedure – which must be reassuring to both parties- and on the payment of fees and costs. Under the Act governing the area up to 1 January 2004 (Consolidated Act No. 282 of 10 May 1988 on the Consumers Complaints Board) the number of approved private boards with trade delimitations has existed (e.g. the Real Property Provision Complaints Board, The Financial Services Complaints Board, and the Mortgage Credit Complaints Board.)

The Consumers Complaints Board consists of a president and represent-tatives of consumers and business life. The members are appointed by the Minister of Trade and Industry. The secratariat function is undertaken by the National Consumer Agency. The Minister may set up rules to govern the activities of the Board, e.g. delimiting its competence to exclude certain goods or services, and setting up minimum and maximum levels for the amounts in dispute. Although there are no such provisions at the time of writing it must be presumed that the former practice will be followed so that the proceedings are laid down (special forms to be used) that there will be a de minimis threshold (probably about DKK 800,-) and that a maximum threshold in respect of the payment made by the consumer will apply (so far DKK 24,000 and DKK 82,000 in respect of motor vehicles). It is also likely that a number of contractual relationships will be excluded from the access to complain(e.g. tenancy agreements) and that the access to bring complaints over goods and services deriving from public undertakings is governed.

CHAPTER 5

Compensation in Tort Law

by Bent Iversen

1. Introduction

Compensation may be relevant to an individual in many situations not only when suffering an unexpected loss and injury, as e.g. when a person is run over in a traffic accident but also when the loss is attributable to a contract partner's breach, manifested e.g. in delay in the delivery of a piece of production equipment or in delivery of defective goods. In the former cases in which the claim for compensation arises *outside* contract the claim is said to lie in *tort* and the compensation is described as *tort damages*. In the latter cases in which the claim for compensation derives from the obligations undertaken under a contract, the claim will lie *in contract*.

The account in this Chapter is limited to damages *in tort* – unless otherwise indicated. Damages in contract will be treated in the contexts of the specific types of contract, i.e. contracts of sale, financing, employment etc.

In contrast the account in the next Chapter, Chapter 6, on insurance deals with damages both *in* contract and *outside* contract (tort).

Where a person suffers an injury – or damage to his property – he will seek to recover financial compensation which in the modern world leads the victim to insurance rather than to compensation from a possible tortfeasor. Where the injured party does have a tortfeasor in mind it is also often really an insurance possibility he is contemplating, viz. the tortfeasor's liability insurance (if any).

The aim of insurance is to *restore the injured party's position* by compensating him for his loss – and since this consideration is also a substantial factor underlying the tort rules there is a close relationship between the law in the two areas. As regards *liability insurance*, i.e. insurance taken out against loss in incurring liability in damages towards others – the interplay is evident, but it is also manifest in relation to the very important rules in The Tort Liability Act Part 2, which is described below in Section

2.2.3. To this should be added that the very possibility of insuring against loss has played – and probably still plays – a significant role in the drafting of the compensation rules, cf. further in Section 2.1 below.

2. Tort damages

As was mentioned above in Section 1 most individuals who suffer injury or damage to their property will be concerned first of all with the possibility of recovering the loss by means of their own insurance. If the loss is covered through that channel, the injured party is satisfied and the tort law issue is left to be settled between the injured party's insurance company and the tortfeasor, cf. in this context the very important rules in the Tort Liability Act Part 2 *which to a considerable extent imply that tortfeasors who are not in business will not incur liability at all in respect of insurance-covered damage to property,* cf. further Section 2.2.3 below.

Where coverage cannot be obtained elsewhere the injured party will turn to the tortfeasor. However, it is not be deemed an ordinary rule that a person is necesarily liable in damages if his act or omission causes damage – as a main rule a further requirement for liability to arise is that the tortfeasor's conduct in the bringing about of the damage can be characterised as *negligent,* cf. below Section 2.1.1.

It is also a *necessary* requirement for tort liability to arise that there *is causation between the tortfeasor's act/omission and the resulting damage* but in most cases the satisfaction of this requirement is not adequate; a liability basis is also required – as *a main rule,* as already mentioned, a conduct on the part of the tortfeasor which could be described as *negligent,* cf. further in Section 2.1.1 below. As regards the *causation* problem it is possible that the courts will dismiss the injured party's claim in damages even if there actually is causation between the act/omission of the tortfeasor and the damage occurred (and indeed the necessary *liability basis* as well) if the damage is a *quite atypical consequence* of the tortfeasor's conduct – in such cases the damage may be said to be *"too remote"* or that there is a lack of *"proximity".* Where e.g. a passenger does not catch a plane – and thus loses the profit of a contract – the passenger cannot claim the loss of profit from the taxi-driver who took him to the airport – notwithstanding the certainty of the passenger's both catching plane and profit, if the driver had not bumped into a parked car on the way to the airport. There is causation but the loss which the passenger might seek to recover is too remote.

In the following it is presumed *that* the causation between the tortfeasor's act and resulting damage is capable of proof (for which the burden will prima facie lie with the injured party) and *that* there is no remoteness of damage issues. The first area to be treated is the most important problem of tort law: the basis of liability.

2.1. The basis of liability

2.1.1. Fault liability (Culpa liability)

The main rule regarding the basis of liability *in tort*, i.e. the cases in which the injured party's claim for damages is *not* based on a contractual relationship between the parties, is the so-called *fault* liability rule (*culpa* rule). Under this rule the tortfeasor will be liable in damages *where the tortious act or omission may be attributed to him as negligent or intentional.* Since establishing intention will only be possible in rare cases, the important element is to establish the criteria under which he may be said to have acted *negligently.*

Under the *traditional culpa definition* a tortfeasor commits the tort of negligence if he fails to show the degree which a reasonable, prudent man (a bonus pater familias) shows in similar circumstances.

This definition contains a valuable core in that it stresses that a condition for imposing liability under the culpa rule is that the damage could have been avoided if the tortfeasor acted differently.

In the assessment of the facts – whether culpa or no culpa has been shown by the individual tortfeasor – the traditional culpa definition is not very helpful. This ought not to be surprising considering the variety of circumstances to which the rule intended to be applicable. A rule which is meant to cover at one and the same time the circumstances under which a dentist will incur liability for a faulty treatment and the conditions under which a houseowner may be held liable for defective gravelling of his pavement must necessarily be couched in general terms.

When a judge is to assess whether in a concrete situation a tortfeasor has acted negligently he will therefore employ a different approach. First he will examine whether *it has been established by statute or statutory instrument what is deemed to be proper conduct in the area in question.* Various statutes, e.g. the Road Traffic Acts, the housing legislation, and the Workplace Environment Act contain several provisions setting out proper conduct in the areas concerned – the Road Traffic Acts contain rules of i.a. duties to give way, marking, and overtaking.

Proper conduct rules will primarily be described in statutes and statutory instruments issued by public authorities on sanctions derived from statute but they *may* also be established by *custom.* This is particularly true of professional areas in which experts may give opinions on the standard of care applied with a comparatively great amount of certainty.

Some situations are characterised by a lack of regulation by statute or custom as to proper conduct and unless the judge may find guidance in previous court decisions – case law is an important source of law in tort law – he must base his decision on general considerations of the conduct concept. Many different factors will be included in the deliberations, but among the most important are the *degree of danger* manifested in the act (the risk of damage inherent in it), the *capability of damage* (the likely amount of damage it will bring about) and the *measures which may be applied to avoid the occurrence of damage* (choice of alternative, less hazardous procedure, safety precautions, warnings etc.) which will decide whether the tortfeasor's conduct was negligent or not. *The higher* the degree of danger, capability of damage, and *the more* precautions the tortfeasor might have employed to prevent damage from occurring *the greater* is the likelihood of the court's holding culpa to be present. Since a professional conduct is typically more thoroughly regulated by guidelines than other stations of life and as they are also typically characterised by higher risks of harm it is no wonder that a culpa-liability assessment more often leads to liability in damages for professional conduct than for others.

In the context of the culpa-rule the distinction between "gross" negligence and "ordinary" negligence is not really of major importance since ordinary negligence is sufficient to find that a tortfeasor's conduct amounts to culpa – and therefore the statements made above relate more to the distinction between ordinary negligence and non-negligent conduct. In other contexts, e.g. in relation to several provisions in the Insurance Act (cf. Chapter 7, below) the difference between gross and ordinary negligence is, however, relevant. It may be said – somewhat crudely, perhaps – that gross negligence is present when the degree of negligence exceeds even the degree displayed by careless people (amounting to recklessness).

2.1.2. Vicarious liability

Under the provisions of the Danish Code of King Christian V of 1683, rule 3-19-2 (the figures refer to: Book, chapter, article) an *employer/master is liable in damages for the negligent acts committed by his employees/servants in the course of their employment.* Thus, where A is employed with B and negligently causes harm to C or C's property, C may sue the employer B in damages.

Vicarious liability undoubtedly represents an extension of the normal culpa liability in that although the employee must have acted negligently – the employer may be held liable under 3-19-2 even if he is at no fault himself.

Vicarious liability applies both *within and outside business contexts* and it comprises *all* employees from the company manager to the most junior office clerk. The *public sector* is also liable under the Danish Code 3-19-2 for torts of its employees.

Vicarious liability owes part of its existence to the employer's capability of instructing and controlling the employees and it is therefore well-justified that the tort must have been committed *within the course of the employment* for the employer to become liable under 3-19-2. In case law, however, the requirements of connection between "course of employment" and the harmful act have not been too rigorous; employers have i.a. been held liable for torts even when an employee was on a "frolic" of his own, e.g. when a messenger deviates from his regular route.

Employers are not liable under 3-19-2 for *abnormal* conduct or other tortious conduct which was *absolutely unforeseeable*.

> An employer who has had to pay damages as a result of his employee's negligent conduct can only claim recourse from the employee (i.e recover the amount from the employee) to the extent this is held reasonable with due regard to the fault displayed, the employee's position and the circumstances of the case, cf. the Tort Liability Act s. 23(1). Thus the main rule is evidently that the employer has no right of recourse against the employee but the higher the degree of negligence displayed by the employee the higher is the likelihood of an employer's successful recovery.

In the majority of cases the injured party will choose to sue the employer but occasionally he also has a claim against the employee – though this never applies to the case where the employee has merely acted with simple (ordinary) negligence and the damage/loss is covered by property insurance or consequential loss insurance taken out by the insured himself or a liability insurance taken out by the employer, cf. the rule in the Tort Liability Act s. 19(3). As regards the cases in which the injured party may have a claim against the employer in the first place, the Act provides in s. 23(2) that the employee's liability in damages towards the injured party may be reduced or lapse altogether where such reduction or lapse is deemed reasonable considering, *first*, the circumstances referred to in (1) (i.e. the s. 23(1) just mentioned), *secondly* the interests of the injured party. Where the rule in s. 23(2) leads to the exceptional result of the employee's having to pay damages to the injured party – the employee has recourse against the employer to the extent to which the employer would have been liable ultimately if the injured party had directed his claim against him.

An employee may inflict losses on his employer not only by harming *third parties*, he may also inflict more direct loss to his employer as e.g. when a shop assistant upsets a display of china figurines (possibly with an added infliction of personal injury to the employer at the same time). As regards losses of this type, the Tort Liability Act s. 23(3) provides that the reduction rule of (1) is correspondingly applied to the employer's claim against the employee.

2.1.3. Strict liability

In certain areas legislation provides that *the tortfeasor shall be strictly liable – on the objective basis of his act/omission having caused damage.* The requirements of causation and proximity (cf. above, Section 2) are upheld but the tortfeasor is liable *even if the act/omission cannot be attributed to his negligence or intention – he is "strictly" liable.*

Rules in the Danish Code of 1683 and provisions in Part 2 of the Field and Road Safety Act of 1953 imply that to a considerable extent there is strict liability for *damage caused by animals.* S. 8(1) of the Dog Act of 1969 sets forth in direct terms that liability in respect of *damage caused by dogs* is *strict* and in order to make such liability effective the owner of a dog is obliged to take out a liability insurance on his dog, cf. s. 8(1) – compulsory liability insurance).

Under the Act of 2003 on Railway Operation and the most recent Aircraft Act of 2002 there is a considerable extent of *strict liability in respect of damage caused by railway operation and airline traffic* and under the Nuclear Plant Act of 1974 the owner of the plant is *strictly liable for damage caused by nuclear accidents.*

Also other legislation – e.g. in relation to *oil damage, pollution of marine environment, natural gas supplies,* and *water supplies* contains single provisions of *strict* liability.

In 1994 an Act on strict liability in respect of environmental damage was passed. However, the strict liability – which applies to conduct after 30 June 1994 – is far from general. It only applies to damage "caused by business or public activity" and not even all such activity. An Appendix to the Act enumerates the enterprises which are strictly liable: primarily such enterprises as are required to seek special state environmental approval, e.g. iron foundries and cement works. Other enterprises are liable under ordinary negligence criteria (culpa).

Another important example of strict liability is represented by the rules of the Road Traffic Act, Part 16, regarding *compensation and insurance in respect of motor vehicles.*

Under the Road Traffic Act s. 101(1) a person responsible for a motor vehicle shall be liable for damage caused by such vehicle in road accidents (or by explosions) or fire stemming from the fuel tank in the vehicle notwithstanding that fault may not be attributable to the party responsible for the vehicle.

Under s. 101(2) 1st clause, the damages in respect of *personal injury* or *loss of breadwinner* may be reduced or lapse altogether if the injured party or the deceased *intentionally* contributed to the injury. The amount of damages may further be reduced and, in special cases, lapse if the injured party or the deceased displayed *gross* contributory negligence, cf. s. 102(2), 2nd clause.

The rules in s. 101(2) imply that contributory negligence by the injured party is judged with far more lenience than in an ordinary contributory negligence situation (c.f. below 2.3), the rules are in fact tantamount to allowing an injured party who has committed even gross contributory negligence in the injury inflicted upon him full compensation from the liability insurance company of the vehicle causing the injury – even if the driver was not at fault. Therefore it is important to note that s. 101(2) only applies to *personal injury and loss of breadwinner* (caused by a road accident involving a motor vehicle). As regards *property damage* the amount of compensation may be reduced or lapse if the injured party contributed to the damage intentionally or negligently (including to a "simple" extent) i.e. in such cases the ordinary rules of contributory negligence apply, cf. 2.3.

The Road Traffic Act, s. 103, contains provisions on liability for damage caused in collisions between motor vehicles.

Where a motor vehicle causes harm in a manner other than those referred to in s. 101(1) and s. 103, e.g. a car parked recklessly – the liability is not strict but follows culpa principles (cf. s. 102). Similarly there is "only" culpa liability where damage is caused outside the geographical area of the Road Traffic Act whose provisions are limited to "roads, used for ordinary traffic by one or several types of traffic".

To make the strict liability for motor vehicles effective the liability rules in ss. 101-104 are supplemented by a rule in s. 105(1) whereby liability insurance for motor vehicles is made *compulsory.* Under s. 105(2) the liability insurance shall be effected so that the current minimum coverage is up to DKK 84 million in respect of personal injury and property damage of up to 17 million in respect of the damage caused by a single event. Another special feature of the liability insurance is that it covers the injured party's loss even if the driver acted intentionally in connection with the road "accident", e.g. where he was drunk driving, was driving with worn tyres, had stolen the vehicle, was driving without a licence, etc. Thus from the injured party's point of view the liability insurance works as an accident insurance, cf. Road Traffic Act s. 108(1). In some of the cases mentioned – though by no means all – the insurance company will have recourse against the party responsible for the road accident, cf. inter alia the rule in the Road Traffic Act s. 108(2) (on recourse in gross negligence situations) but that is really no concern of the injured party – he will get his compensation in any event.

The liability under ss. 101-103, including the strict liability, is under s. 104(1) imposed on the owner or user of the vehicle actually using it or allowing it to be used. The driver of the vehicle incurs only ordinary fault liability – if he is a person different from the owner/user. The practical situations may be illustrated as follows: 1) If the owner drives his own car he is strictly liable, 2) If the owner is a passenger in his own car, driven by NN, the owner is strictly liable whereas NN is liable in fault liability, 3) If the owner has lent his car to NN for a longer-term use the strict liability will lie with NN (though he is insured via the car's liability insurance), and 4) If T has stolen the owner's car, strict liability will lie with T (who is not insured via the car's liability insurance in contrast to any third party upon whom T might inflict harm, cf. above).

Nothing prevents that a court may impose strict liability on a tortfeasor even if such approach is *not* warranted by statute. In the large number of areas in which legislation has not defined the basis of liability the courts have filled the gaps by holding that *fault* liability shall apply and this decision may be reversed by the courts themselves, thus introducing strict liability in one or several fields – or they may decide in a new area that strict liability shall apply.

Strict liability has been introduced sporadically through case law without legislative sanction, especially in respect of damage in connection with excavations with a certain amount of danger and damage caused by defective equipment, especially breaks in the public pipeline network (water pipes etc.). To this should be added a recent case, which has been much commented, in which the Danish Supreme Court imposed strict liability on an eternite factory for personal injury (asbestosis) which had been inflicted upon the employees of the enterprise in the course of eternite production. *But for the substantial part the courts have dealt with the need of liability extension which may easily arise in areas of a high amount of (large) danger potential by making the culpa rule stringent*, i.e. placing stricter requirements on the amount of care exercisable by a tortfeasor to allow him to escape a claim for negligence. It is evident that the courts hold the view that in politically controversial areas, as e.g. liability for pollution (environmental damage) it is for the legislators to decide whether (and how) the transfer from culpa to strict liability should be made.

Besides the courts have tightened the liability basis by establishing liability for *independent contractors* in several areas of conduct of a certain degree of danger, e.g. when imposing liability on a local authority for tortious acts committed by an independent contractor in the course of a piece of demolition work for the local authority, even if there was not an employer/employee relationship between the local authority and the independent contractor (cf. above, Section 2.1.2 on vicarious liability under 3-19-2 of the Danish Code).

2.1.4. Presumption liability

In an action for damages in tort the burden of proof lies prima facie with the *injured party* in respect of the tortfeasor's alleged negligence towards him. One of the methods which may be applied in the attempt to satisfy the need for liability tightening – without introducing strict liability – is to *reverse the burden of proof* so that the tortfeasor will only escape liability if *he* can prove that he did not act negligently – this method is described as culpa with reversed burden of proof or "presumption liability".

In case law such liability has mainly been imposed where defects in equipment have occurred and in situations of so-called "anonymous fault" in which the circumstances indicate that a negligent act must have been made within an organisation (e.g. a hospital) but where it is difficult to pinpoint exactly *who* committed the tortious act.

2.1.5. Children's liability and mentally disordered persons' liability

Under the Tort Liability Act s. 24a a child under the age of 15 is liable in damages under the same rules as persons above that age but the rule does not mean that the same standard of care is set up for the conduct of a child as compared to that of an adult. As regards children the culpa rule may be described as follows: *a child will incur liability if it has acted with less care than children of that age normally display in similar circumstances.* – In case law, children below the age of 4 are not liable under the culpa rule but especially as regards small children the parents *may* be liable (vicariously) *if* they have disregarded their duty of supervision of the child.

The fact that a child is liable (under the criteria indicated above) does not automatically imply that the same amount of damages is payable as an adult tortfeasor would have to pay, since a child's liability may – in the words of s. 24a – be diminished in consideration of "lack of development in the child, the nature of the act, and the circumstances of the case". The last general words allow the courts a wide scope for diminishing the liability of a child where appropriate. Main factors in the exercise of the court's discretion here are the insurance circumstances of the child and the injured party, cf. also the rules of the Tort Liability Act ss. 19, 20, and 24(1) referred to in Section 2.2 and 2.2.3.

Under the Tort Liability Act s. 24b there is a rule corresponding to the rule in s. 24a in respect of tortious acts and omissions made by persons who are incapable of sound and reasonable conduct *by reason of a mental disorder (insanity, permanent or temporary).* Under s. 24b the tortfeasor's liability will not be diminished if the incapacity is attributable to self-induced intoxication.

2.1.6. Objective defences

A tortious act which would principally attract liability in damages *may* be surrounded by circumstances which make it doubtful whether the tortfeasor incurs liability for it, i.e. an *objective defence* may be raised.

The most important defences comprise *self-defence, statutory authority or legal enforcement, necessity situations and "volenti" (consent) situations.* A situation of self-defence occurs where an act is deemed necessary to resist or prevent an unlawful attack, e.g. a jiu jitsu hold against an assailant. Legal enforcement is e.g. constituted by the exercise of police authority. A situation of necessity occurs where an act is deemed necessary to prevent an imminent danger of injury to persons or valuable property, e.g. when another person's rug is used to stifle a fire threatening a third party's valuable property (in this case it is presumed that the third party whose property is rescued, is obliged to indemnify the value of the rug).

2.2. The injured party's loss

The injured party may only recover compensation from the tortfeasor *if he has suffered a loss* and such loss may be attributed to the tortfeasor – cf. above Section 2.1. on liability basis. The measure of damages is based on a first principle of restitution – i.e. the injured party's loss is to be *compensated in full*, and secondly that the injured party should *obtain no enrichment* but these starting points are not always fully observed in either respect, cf. further below. The third fundamental principle of the measure of damages is that the injured party is under a *duty to mitigate his loss.*

Under s. 24(1) of the Tort Liability Act liability may – *under absolutely exceptional circumstances* – be reduced or lapse altogether where the imposition of liability is deemed an unreasonable burden on the person liable in damages or where quite special circumstances indicate that such an outcome is reasonable. The decision to allow reduction or lapse of liability will comprise deliberations on the amount of damage sustained, the nature of the liability incurred, the tortfeasor's circumstances, the injured party's interests, insurance cover, and the circumstances otherwise prevailing. In compliance with the travaux preparatoires of the Act the judges have shown great reserve in applying this possibility of diminishing liability.

2.2.1. Which losses will be recovered?

As regards property damage, *value losses* may be fully recovered and the measure of damages will follow the principles set out in the rules of the Insurance Contracts Act ss. 37-38, described in Chapter 7, Section 6.1.1.

The injured party may also claim full compensation for *consequential loss* from the tortfeasor. The principle regarding the injured party's duty to mitigate combined with the huge evidence problems encountered exactly with consequential losses imply that in practice the injured party will find it difficult to recover his actual consequential loss in full.

As regards *personal injuries,* the Tort Liability Act Part I contains a set of detailed rules as to the types of loss for which recovery may be sought and the amounts recoverable. *Loss of earnings* and *health recovery expenses* are indemnified in full. *Permanent injury, loss of capability to work, and loss of family breadwinner* are indemnified under standard rules which imply e.g. *that* an injured party who has lost his capability to work and had prior to the accident a yearly salary of DKK 350,000 will be entitled to a compensation of DKK 3,5 million for *loss of capability to work*, if he was under the age of 30 at the occurence of the injury, *that* the maximum compensation in respect of loss of capability to work is currently (2003) set at about DKK 6 miliion, and *that* the maximum amount recoverable for loss of breadwinner is currently about DKK 1,9 million. Pain and suffering will be recoverable at standard amounts – the current figures are DKK 140 per sickness day.

2.2.2. Limitation of plaintiff group

One tortious act or omission may lead to several losses. If a tortfeasor runs into a bridge e.g. it will not only be the owner of the bridge who suffers damage/loss – all the people who depend on the bridge for their business purposes will also suffer loss. Similarly, a personal injury may not only inflict loss on the directly injured party but also on his employer (where e.g. the injured party is an employee of an architect firm and is in the middle of a large project).

The main rule is that it is only the directly injured party who may seek recovery of his loss – the enterprises which are obliged to make a detour to deliver their goods owing to the damage to the bridge are barred from seeking recovery for their extra costs from the tortfeasor and the proprietor of the architect firm is likewise barred from claiming the loss he may suffer in having to put another employee on the project, perhaps starting all over again. The salary (less benefit paid out from the state – which the employer has to pay to the injured architect while he is incapable of working will, however, be recoverable from the tortfeasor as a *derived claim.*

In the event of the injured party's death as a result of the tortfeasor's act the persons who have lost a breadwinner may seek *compensation for loss of breadwinner,* cf. the Tort Liability Act ss. 12-14. Compensation for such loss is under standard measures, as mentioned above in 2.2.1.

2.2.3. May the injured party recover both from the insurance company and from the tortfeasor?

As was mentioned above in Section 1, it often occurs that the injured party's possibility of obtaining coverage is not absolutely dependent on his capability to hold the tortfeasor liable or upon the latter's *ability to pay* – the injured party has chosen to insure himself and may claim the insured sum from his own insurance company.

In such situations it is very important whether the injured party may *accumulate the two claims* (i.e. add the compensation from the tortfeasor to the sum insured) or *whether the sum insured shall be deducted in full or in part from the claim of compensation set up against the tortfeasor.* If the first option is chosen – the accumulation solution – the insurance company will have no recourse claim against the tortfeasor (who is in any event only obliged to cover the loss once) but if the other option is chosen – the socalled *compensation solution* – the next question arises: Should the loss lie with – and stay with the insurance company (in other words should the tortfeasor go free) or should the company be allowed recourse against the tortfeasor?

The decisive statutory provisions in this area are the rules in the Tort Liability Act ss. 19-22.

In life, accident or sickness insurance or other personal insurance – i.e. in practice fixed-sum insurance – the sum insured will normally *not* affect the injured party's claim against the tortfeasor: the injured party may accumulate the two amounts. It is therefore consistent that s. 22(2) provides that in personal insurance the insurance company has no claim against the party liable to pay damages. – The concept of fixed-sum insurance (and indemnity insurance) is explained in Chapter 6, Section 3.

In indemnity insurance, e.g. fire insurance – and in consequential loss insurance in which case the insurance will cover the injured party's loss fully, the injured party's situation is quite different and he is never capable of accumulating the two amounts. To the extent the injured party will have his loss covered by a property insurance company or a consequential loss insurance company – *he will have no claim whatsoever against the tortfeasor – and the insurance company which covers the loss will only have recourse against the party liable to pay damages if that party has brought the damage about intentionally or by acting with gross negligence, or where the damage has been brought about in the exercise of public or business activity,* cf. s. 19(1) and (2) of the Act. As mentioned above, the rules in the Tort Liability Act s. 19 (and s. 20) imply to a considerable extent that *tortfeasors who are not committing their tortious act in the exercise of their business will not incur liability at all when the damage is to insured property.*

Under s. 20 the state, a local authority or other public institution which is normally self-insurer, will in relation to the possibility of recourse claims be placed *as if* the public institution had effected an insurance themselves. Thus, where damage has been done to a state building the state's position towards the tortfeasor is as if the state had taken out insurance on the building – even if insurance is never taken out by the state.

The rules of the Tort Liability Act ss. 19 and 20 just referred to regarding the importance of the injured party's insurance or the injured party's status as a self-insurer do not apply to the liability in damages following from the rules in the Road Traffic Acts, the Airline Traffic Acts and the Maritime Act, cf. s. 21 of the Act.

The provisions in ss. 19-22 (and also ss. 23-25 which are also referred to in this Chapter) are applicable both to damages in contract and – of course – to damages *in tort*.

2.3. Contributory negligence from injured party

Where the injured party himself has contributed to the occurrence of the damage (contributory negligence) and his contribution is not of a trifling nature this factor will often lead to a reduction in his claim for damages (or perhaps a total lapse of claim). In such situations the courts will exercise a discretion by which the main emphasis is placed on a comparison between the degrees of negligence shown by the tortfeasor and by the injured party himself but regard may also be had to any difference in danger degree of the two acts.

The rules contained in the Traffic Acts on contributory negligence are mentioned above in Section 2.1.3.

Where a child below 15 years of age or a person comprised by the Tort Liability Act s. 24b is injured the rules in the Tort Liability Act s. 24a and s. 24b are applied analogously in the assessment of the injured party's contribution which may imply that the damages claim of the injured party will be subject to less reduction than would have been the case if the injured party had been an adult of normal mental function.

Under s. 24(2) of the Tort Liability Act the fact of contributory negligence *may* – exceptionally – be disregarded entirely or in part to the extent a reduction of the compensation would affect the injured party adversely to an unreasonable extent or where other very special circumstances justify such approach.

2.4. Joint tortfeasors

Where several tortfeasors are liable in respect of the same loss they are *liable jointly and severally* towards the injured party which is the equivalent of saying that the injured party if free to choose his defendant in the compensation claim.

When one of the tortfeasors has paid the claim the injured party leaves the arena but the issue of *distribution of the compensation burden among the tortfeasors remains to be solved – i.e. the issue of recourse*. Unless the problem has been solved already by a special rule as illustrated in e.g. the vicarious liability, cf. the rule in s. 23(1) referred to in Section 2.1.2, the mutual distribution will be based on the rule in s. 25(1) whereby the nature of the liability involved and the circumstances otherwise will decide what is a reasonable distribution. S. 25(2) contains rules allowing that regard may be had to any liability insurance of one or more of the tortfeasors.

3. Product Liability

Injury to persons or damage to property may occur as a result of dangerous propensities in a product. In such cases the issue of liability in damages will arise in respect of the loss the harmful/dangerous propensities have caused – the issue of *product liability*.

The product liability problems may be treated both in combination with the rules on sale of goods and supply of services and in combination with the rules on liability imposition – which latter context is chosen for the following account.

The product causing harm may be a hired product, or e.g. a product used in independent contractor relationships, but most often the product involved is a chattel transferred from seller to buyer in an ordinary sale and possessing dangerous propensities. The common reference to such product in daily parlance is a "defective" product but it is important to bear in mind that the legal rules applying to defects in individual contract relationships do not govern product liability. Thus, the Sale of Goods Act rules on defects in the goods (cf. Chapter 8) will *not* be applicable to a seller's product liability. It will be a *defect* in the Sale of Goods Act sense that a weed killer fails to kill off the weeds but it is a *defect in the product liability sense* if the weed killer causes the lawn to be ruined. Likewise, a sale-of-goods defect will lie if an engine has been filled with the wrong kind of oil whereas it is a product-liability defect if an oil causes the engine to break down. – Where an international sale is comprised by the UN Convention on International Sales of Goods (CISG) (cf. Chapter 9), the Convention rules (cf. CISG, Art. 5) will *also* comprise the seller's liability for *damage to the buyer's goods* but not the seller's liability for personal injury).

Product liability is not limited to contractual relationships. If a bicycle producer brings a bike on the market with defective handbrakes he may incur liability not only towards the buyer but also to third parties (non-contract parties) who may be injured as a result of the bike's incapability to brake.

Wrong use may bring practically any product to cause harm. But product liability is dependent on damage caused by properties in the product as a result of use which a party – typically the producer – must have contemplated. It is self-evident that to a large extent the marketing of a product decides the use which must have been contemplated and a producer may therefore diminish his own risk exposure by instructive and thorough marketing.

Before the Product Liability Act of 1989 which came into force on 10 June 1989 and which comprises damage caused by products (i.e. product items) brought into circulation on 10 June 1989 or later, the Danish rules on product liability were based on the product liability developed in case law. *Since* the 1989 Act (the Product Liability Act) implementing the rules on product liability which the EU member states were obliged to incorporate into their own law under a 1985-Directive – does not limit the injured party's access to compensation under the national rules on product liability – the Directive is a socalled minimum directive – *and since* the Product Liability Act has a restricted sphere of application the present legal position is, regrettably, rather complicated. *Within the sphere of application of the Act* two sets of rules are applicable: 1) the product liability based on the EU-Directive and 2) the product liability developed in case law. *Outside the sphere of application of the Act* only the product liability developed in case law will apply. The sphere of application is defined in particular in ss. 1 and 2 and in s. 3, referred to below in Section 3.

The EU rules on imposition of product liability in respect of damage occurring in products must be deemed per se to lead to the development of safer products but it should be mentioned that the EU is also actively concerned with this preceding link in the "product safety chain". A Directive from 1992 on *product safety* was incorporated in Danish law by Act no. 364 of 18 May 1994 on product safety. The directive/Act imposes general safety requirements to all products and establishes some general principles.

3.1. The product liability developed in case law

The product liability developed in case law attaches to a product concept comprising any product or service which may be subject to production, sale and use. The concept will – as mentioned above – especially relate to chattels but also services of any description (e.g. repairs) and real property, and as regards services, whether supplied in the course of business or not.

The imposition of liability is dependent on the product being defective/dangerous and *thereby* causing harm to person or property – i.e. a causal link must be present.

The defect/danger may consist in the *failure of an expected effect to show* in the product (e.g. a safety belt fails to work) but it may also consist in a wrong effect (a dyeing product producing a blue instead of the contemplated red colour) or a *side-effect* (a flavour additive producing cancer).

Liability is not imposed *merely* because a product is defective/dangerous and thereby causes damage. Prima facie, liability is only imposed if the defect/danger in the product is due to fault or neglect whether in construction, instruction, marketing, or manufacturing but in industrial production a deviating product – a "Monday product" – is also a manufacturing *defect.*

No liability is imposed for *development defects* – i.e. defects developing in the product which are due to a defect/risk unacknowledged at the time of production and hence beyond the sphere of knowledge which a producer ought to have. *System defects* – i.e. defects which are due to known, but unavoidable defect/risk in an otherwise "indispensable" product – will also escape liability imposition. The defence of "development risk" is dependent on observance of a duty to warn which arises as soon as a development risk ought to be known and it is obvious that the liability exemption for system damage presupposes, *for one thing* that – despite the inevitable danger – the launching of the product on the market was at all warrantable (e.g. for certain types of medicine), *for another,* that adequate warnings against the danger involved have been given.

In case law the damages claim may be set up not only against the link in the distribution chain who is genuinely at fault – subsequent (business) links, including retailers, are *liable* by virtue merely of their representing a link between producer and the injured party in respect of the liability imposed on one (or more) preceding links in the chain. This will often mean that the victim may claim either against the producer or against one or more intermediate traders.

3.2. The Product Liability Act

When reading the following account of the rules of the Product Liability Act it is important to bear in mind that the fact that a damage/injury is not comprised by the special rules of the Product Liability Act does not necessarily entail that coverage is unobtainable – the product liability based on case law referred to in Section 3.1 applies concurrently with the provisions of the Act, cf. also s. 13 of the Act in this respect.

The rules of the Product Liability Act are *mandatory* in the sense that they cannot be contracted out of to the detriment of the injured party or anyone taking the injured party's place in the compensation proceedings, cf. s. 12 of the Act.

3.2.1. The concept of "damage"

Under s. 2(1), 1st clause, the Act comprises "damages and indemnification for *personal injury* and compensation for loss of breadwinner" (emphasis added).

Property damage (including damage to real property and animals) are only comprised by the rules *of the Act* "if the object in question [the damaged property item] according to its nature was habitually designed for non-commercial use and was mainly used by the injured party in such manner" – i.e. the damage must be to "consumer" objects. When assessing damages *under the Act* for property damage an amount of DKK 4,000 is deducted by virtue of s. 8(1) of the Act though this amount may be changed by the Minister of Justice in accordance with subsequent EU-Directives to such effect. Where a defective product causes damage to several objects in the same event the DKK 4,000 reduction is only made once. – The emphasis on the words "*of the Act*" and "*the Act*" made here goes to remind that the product liability based on case law is not limited to damage to consumer objects nor does it provide for a deduction amount.

Under s. 2(2), 2nd clause, the Act does not comprise *damage to the defective product itself.* If the brakes of a car fail and the car is totally damaged the last-mentioned damage is, in relation to the car producer, a damage to the defective product itself. However, where the brakes were produced by a sub-supplier the damage in relation to such sub-supplier is to a product other than (and to more than) the defective product itself and the sub-supplier's liability is therefore a liability under the Product Liability Act.

3.2.2. The concept of product

For the purposes of the Product Liability Act a product is defined as "any goods whether manufactured or natural and whether incorporated as a component part of other goods or real property", cf. s. 3(1), 1st clause. Electricity e.g. will be a product in the sense of the Act.

3.2.3. The concepts of producer and intermediary

Under the Act a *producer* means "*any person* who makes a finished product, a component part of a product or raw material, *any person* who makes or collects a natural product, and *any person* who by putting his name, trade mark or other distinguishing mark on the product holds himself out to be the producer of such product" (emphasis added throughout), cf. s. 4(1).

Further, a *producer* is "*any person* who in the course of his business imports a product into an EU member state with a view to resale, renting, leasing or other kind of circulation", cf. s. 4(2).

An *intermediary* is "any person who brings a product into circulation without being considered a producer", cf. s. 4(3).

The rules in s. 4(1-3) are supplemented by provisions "transforming" intermediaries to producers (in the sense of the Act). The aim of these provisions is to ensure that the injured party may make his damages claim in an effective manner since he can both bring proceedings and enforce the claim within the EU.

3.2.4. The concept of "defect"

The determination of defect is a vital element for the assessment of the extent of liability imposed under the Product Liability Act. Under s. 5(1) "a product is defective if it fails to provide the safety which may properly be expected". In the assessment under s. 5(1) particular regard is attached to,

1) the marketing of the product,
2) the use of the product which may reasonably be expected,
3) the time when the product in question – i.e. the concrete product causing harm – was brought into circulation,

and it is added in s. 5(2) "that a product is not deemed to be defective just because a better product has been brought into circulation".

Where safety standards have been increased after the marketing of the harmful product specimen the safety standard prevailing at the time of the marketing of the product is the relevant standard – but safety requirements may of course be changed so dramatically that the producer is obliged to send out a warning/instruction in relation to the product specimens which were brought on the market earlier.

3.2.5. The liability

3.2.5.1. Producer's liability

The rules on producer's liability – and defences – are contained in the Product Liability Act ss. 6 and 7.

Under s. 6(1) a producer is "liable for damage caused by a defect in a product produced or supplied by him". Under s. 6(2) the injured party is to show 1) the damage, 2) the defect and 3) the causal link between the defect and the damage.

Prima facie, the rule in s. 6(1) would seem a genuine strict liability rule, cf. s. 2.1.3 – but a closer assessment of the liability basis reveals *that* the producer will only incur liability if the product is defective, *that* the defectiveness-assessment under s. 5 certainly leaves room for the *possibility* of holding the product non-defective where system defects are involved (cf. above s. 3.1), and *that* the defence rule of s. 7(1), no. 4, just referred to implies that no liability is incurred for development defects (cf. above 3.1).

Under s. 7(1) of the Act, in the listing of defences, a producer is not liable under the rules of the *Product Liability Act* if he can show

1) that he did not supply the product,
2) that he neither manufactured, collected, or brought the product into circulation in the course of a business,
3) that the defect is due to compliance with requirements imposed by a public authority, or

4) that the state of the scientific and technical knowledge at the time the product was brought into circulation was insufficient to discover the defect (at the time).

Further, under s. 7(2) a producer is not liable if the defect which caused the damage must be deemed not to have been present at the time when the product was brought into circulation by the producer in question.

Under s. 7(3) the producer of a component product is not liable if he can show that the defect in his component product is attributable to the design of the (subsequent) product into which his component product is comprised, or to compliance with instructions given by the producer of the finished/final product.

Under s. 9(1) the injured party's damages may be reduced or lapse if he contributes to the occurrence of the damage by an intentional or negligent act, i.e. the ordinary rule of contributory negligence, cf. on this concept above Section 2.3.

3.2.5.2. Intermediaries' liability

The EU-Directive underlying the Product Liability Act does not comprise the liability of intermediaries but at the drafting of the Product Liability Act it was found expedient to include a provision – in s. 10 – on intermediaries' liability. The travaux preparatoires of the Act reveal that the aim of s. 10 was to provide a rule which does not only comprise liability for intermediaries in the context of producer's liability following from the EU-Directive but to extend it to comprise the liability developed in case law in respect of fault committed in preceding production and distribution links (cf. above, Section 3.1).

The Product Liability Act s. 10 provides that an intermediary shall be liable in product liability *directly* towards an injured party and subsequent intermediaries (i.e. intermediaries closer to the injured party) in the chain of distribution (emphasis added) – thus, s. 10 clearly presupposes that a producer (further removed from the victim in the chain) will have a product liability.

3.2.6. Joint liability and recourse

Where two or more parties – e.g. a producer and an intermediary – are liable under the Product Liability Act for the same damage they are liable jointly and severally, cf. s. 11(1) of the Act. – This result is the same as obtains under the general Danish rules of joint tortfeasors, cf. above, Section 2.4.

Where producer's liability is incurred by two or more persons under s. 4(1), cf. Section 3.2.3. the distribution of liability among them is made – in the absence of contrary agreement – with regard to the cause of the defect, the single producer's occasion and opportunity of exercising control with the product, any available liability insurance, and the circumstances of the case", cf. s. 11(2).

An intermediary who has paid damages to the injured party or a subsequent intermediary, will – as is only reasonable – take the place of such injured party in his claim against preceding links in the production and distribution chain, cf. s. 11(3), 1st clause. The recourse claim under s. 11(3), 1st clause, may lapse or be reduced if the party seeking recourse has contributed, intentionally or negligently, to the occurrence of the damage or to increasing its extent, s. 11(3), 2nd clause.

3.2.7. Limitation

Provisions on limitation of claims under the Product Liability Act and claims under the rules on product liability developed in case law are contained in s. 14 of the Act.

These rules are very complex. In brief terms, *the main rule* is that a claim for damages in product liability is subject to a period of limitation of three years after the day when the injured party discovered or ought to have discovered 1) the damage, 2) the defect, *and* 3) the relevant producer's name and address, and that a *claim under the Product Liability Act* in all events will have lapsed 10 years after the day the producer brought the product in question into circulation.

The general rules on limitation in Danish law are treated below in Chapter 14.

3.2.8. The choice of law issue

Typically, Danish substantive law on product liability, i.e. the rules referred to throughout the present Section 3 – will be applicable when products are marketed in this country and cause damage here whereas Danish law will not be applicable when goods produced in Denmark are exported to a foreign country and cause damage in that country.

This legal position will subsist when the Minister of Justice, by virtue of s. 16 of the Product Liability Act, ratifies the Hague-Convention of 1973 on Choice of Law in Product Liability Cases.

CHAPTER 6

Insurance

by Lars Lindencrone Petersen

1. Introduction

The state is the largest insurer by virtue of the social insurance schemes – disablement pension, widows' pension, senior citizens' pension, labour market supplementary pension, National Health service, unemployment benefits, maintenance contributions, rehabilitation- and home help schemes are "heavyweight" types of personal insurance. This account is, however, limited to *private insurance*, i.e. the situation in which an individual or a group of persons (e.g. group life assurance) take out an insurance contract with an insurance company.

2. What is insurance?

It is impossible to know whether NN's real property will be burnt down or otherwise damaged – nor for that matter when it happens – but it is possible with an adequate number of properties to predict on a statistical basis the total amount of damage within a defined period of time and this creates the basis of insurance. When a large number of people – *the insured* – take out insurance against the same risk with the same *company* they will provide, through their aggregate premiums the basis for the company to offer financial compensation to the relatively few among them for whom the risk materialises. – The risk may be further levelled off by the process of *re-insurance* whereby the original insurance company "re-insures" with other companies or by pooling the risk accepted within a certain area by several separate companies, as eg. in employment risk insurance or environmental damage insurance.

3. Various Types of Insurance – Terminology of the Insurance Contracts Act

The main distinction in the Insurance Contracts Act is between *indemnity insurance* and *contingency insurance* (*fixed-sum insurance*). In indemnity insurance the measure of payment from the company is the measure of damage in money terms upon the happening of the insured event, e.g. fire insurance. In contingency insurance the sum payable by the company is stated in advance in the contract of insurance. Contingency insurance is common within personal injury insurance in which it is often difficult to measure the injury in money terms – basically, it is impossible to state the value of a loss of sound health in a human being in terms of money but it may be argued that in the event of e.g. a 50 per cent disablement a sum of DKK 2 million shall be payable.

As mentioned above in Section 2, the party taking out the contract of insurance is called *the insured*. Usually the insured will be the party to whom the insurance sum is payable upon the happening of the insurance event (in the terminology of the Insurance Contracts Act: *the party insured*) but this need not be the case – such party may be a person other than the insured. In personal insurance, especially life assurance and accident insurance, the insured party is usually termed *the beneficiary*.

4. The Contract of Insurance

The ordinary rules regarding formation of contract which will be examined in detail in Chapter 7 below also apply to contracts of insurance. A contract of insurance is normally made by the insured's submittal of an insurance proposal to the company – often with the assistance of an insurance agent of the company – and the company's returning an insurance policy. *In general contract terminology, which will be used in Theme 3, the insurance proposal is the offer and the insurance policy is the acceptance.*

The terms of the contract of insurance decide when the *company's liability*, i.e. their obligation to pay if the insured event happens, will become effective. In the absence of express agreement the company's liability will set in as soon as the company notifies its acceptance of the insured party's offer, cf. the Insurance Contracts Act s. 11. It is quite common to make individual agreements as to the operative date when liability commences.

The insurance policy is the document setting out the rights and obligations of the parties under the contract of insurance. Thus, when determining – upon the occurrence of damage – whether such damage is covered by the insurance the wording of the insurance policy is decisive. Where the company has exempted one type of risk from coverage, e.g. theft (in contrast to burglary) or certain items of property, e.g. jewellery (in contrast to other chattels) and the provision to this effect is of adequate clarity, the party insured must accept that the company is not obliged to meet his claim for compensation.

The provisions of the Insurance Contracts Act may always be contracted out of – against the interests of the company (with the exception of the rule in s. 39(1) mentioned in Section 6). Several provisions may also be contracted out of to the advantage of the company but for such deviations case law has developed special clarity requirements. Some of the provisions in the Insurance Contracts Act are described as mandatory in the statutory text itself in the sense that they cannot be contracted out of *to the advantage of the company*. At the drafting of the Insurance Contracts Act in 1930 the legislators were very conscious of the fact that insurance is an area in which one party, the company, is typically far more professional and deep-pocketed than the other, the party insured, and therefore certain limits had to be placed on the freedom of contract.

5. The Duties of the Parties

5.1. The Duties of the Company

The company is under a duty to pay the sum insured upon the happening of the insured event. The amount may be claimed 14 days after the company has been capable of obtaining the information necessary to evaluate the insured event and fix the amount of the insurance sum, cf. s. 24 of the Insurance Contracts Act. In return, as stated in s. 22 the insured party is under a duty to provide the company with all information in relation to the circumstances mentioned in s. 24 to the extent that such information is accessible to him.

As from the due date the party insured may claim *interest* on the amount at the official lending rate of the National Bank as at 1 January or 1 July, respectively, in the year in question, plus (currently) 7 per cent, cf. s. 24.

Under s. 29 of the Insurance Contracts Act the *time limit* for bringing actions on claims deriving from a contract of insurance is two years after the end of the calendar year in which the claimant became cognisant of the claim and that it was due for payment.

5.2. The duties of the insured and of the beneficiary

5.2.1. The duty to pay premiums

The main duty of the insured party is to pay the insurance premiums. If he fails to do so he may risk either that the liability of the company (their coverage duty) lapses, or in the event of serious delay in the payment of premiums that the whole contract will lapse or be cancelled by the company. The rules in this area which are quite complicated in their details – are stated in the Insurance Contracts Act ss. 12-17.

5.2.2. The duty of disclosure at the taking out of insurance

When an insurance is taken out the company tries to assess the risk they are taking over by asking the insured some questions – the extent and nature of the risk of course determine whether the company will effect insurance at all and in the affirmative the premium they will ask for it.

It is crucial for the company that the answers they receive from the insured are truthful and exhaustive and the Insurance Contracts Act contains a number of provisions in ss. 4-10 setting out the extent to which the company's liability (duty of coverage) will lapse or be reduced in the event of untrue statements by the insured at the formation of the contract, e.g. if he has failed to disclose a diabetes condition even if he was asked to that effect.

Where the insured was guilty of a *fraudulent misrepresentation* or non-disclosure of a circumstance which must be deemed of importance to the company, the company is not bound by the contract. The same applies where the circumstances of the insured have otherwise been of a character which would make it *contrary to common honesty standards* to let it stand, cf. the ICA s. 4. – The concepts of "fraud" and "standards contrary to common honesty" are also found (with the same implications) in the provisions of the Danish Contracts Act ss. 30-33 which are discussed in Chapter 7, Sections 4.7 and 4.10.1.

Where the insured made an *innocent misrepresentation* (i.e. he neither knew nor ought to have known that his statement was untrue) the company will be liable as if *no misrepresentation had been made*, cf. the Insurance Contracts Act s. 5 – in indemnity insurance the company may, however, terminate the contract upon a week's notice.

Where the insured misrepresented his circumstances *otherwise*, i.e. where the circumstances are not covered by s. 4 or s. 5, cf. immediately above, the company shall not be bound if it may be deemed that they would not have agreed to take the insurance if the true state of affairs had been disclosed, cf. s. 6(1)of the Insurance Contracts Act. Where the company would have accepted the insurance, but *subject to other terms* (typically a higher premium) the company will only be liable under s. 6(2) to the extent they would have committed themselves against the premium actually agreed upon (*the pro rata rule*). This rule may have unfortunate effects for the insured. Where e.g. a piece of real property has been insured against storm damage in an amount of DKK 600,000 on the basis of the insured's misrepresentations in respect of the construction of the property and the correct information would have brought about an increase of the premium by one half, it follows from s. 6(2) that the property is only regarded as being insured against storm damage in the amount of DKK 400,000 (2/3 x 600,000) which is normally the same as having *under-insurance* with the unpleasant consequences attached to this state of affairs, cf. below 6.3.

In *consumer insurance* and *personal insurance* it may be provided, despite s. 6(1-2), that the company shall be liable in full or partly where special circumstances so indicate. In evaluating the existence of such circumstances the determining factors are whether the misrepresentation must be deemed to have affected the occurrence of the insured event or the size of the loss/damage; the negligence shown by the insured, and the time which has passed from the statement of the misrepresenation until the occurrence of the insured event.

In *marine insurance* and other *transport insurance* (and *financial guarantee insurance)* the pro rate rule is exchanged for a rule under which the company shall be liable to the extent to which the insured may show that the fact misrepresented was of no influence to the occurrence of the insured event or the amount of the damage, cf. s. 6(4) (*the causation rule)* – it will e.g. be irrelevant if misrepresentations were made at the taking out of the insurance in respect of the packing of an article if the ship runs into a mine and is lost with all hands.

From the *wording of s. 6* it is evident that the rule *only applies to positive information.* With the reservation that the fact/circumstance *may* be subject to the rules of s. 4 or s. 5 at all, s. 7 provides that the insured's failure to disclose has no influence on the liability of the company unless he ought to have known that the non-disclosed fact was material to the company and his non-disclosure may be attributed to his *gross negligence* (thus *ordinary* negligence will not affect the liability of the company) – as regards the concepts of ordinary and gross negligence, cf. Chapter 5, Section 2.1.1.

5.2.3. Duty to disclose increased risks

It is not only relevant for the company to be told the risk they accept at the taking out of the insurance, it is also important if that risk is substantially increased – e.g. where an eternite roof is replaced by a thatched roof. The problem of increased risk is obviously largest in indemnity insurance. With life assurance it is self-evident that the risk of the company will increase day by day.

The rules governing the insured's duty to notify risk-increasing circumstances to the company – and the consequences of failure to observe such duty – are stated in the Insurance Contracts Act, ss. 45-50 (indemnity insurance) and in s. 121 (accident insurance and sickness insurance).

The rules on the duty to disclose increased risk resemble those applying at the taking out of the insurance though they are more *lenient towards the insured.* At the taking out of the insurance the insured is directly requested to inform of the asset insured – a similar request is not given to the insured regularly during the currency of the insurance.

5.2.4. The duty to observe safety regulations

An insurance policy will often contain provisions making the company's liability of coverage subject to the observance of certain safety regulations (the existence of safety regulations is also indicative of the company's attempts to reduce their risk).

Failure to observe a safety regulation – e.g. defects occurring in a compulsory alarm system – will not automatically cause a lapse of the insured's claim against the company. The insured must have *displayed negligence* and even if that requirement is satisfied the insured may still recover to the extent that he can show that the occurrence and extent of the insured event was not due to the failure to observe the safety regulation, cf. the Insurance Contracts Act, s. 51(1).

Under s. 124(1), the Insurance Contracts Act contains a special rule regarding the importance of safety regulations in sickness insurance and accident insurance.

5.2.5. The duty to refrain from causing the occurrence of the insured event

The purpose of insuring is also to be protected against one's own mistakes and it is therefore not possible to make a general rule to the effect that the insured will have no claim against the company if he has brought about the insured event himself. Anyone may forget to turn off a heater or mistake the reverse gear for the first gear. The degree of negligence displayed by the insured must determine the extent to which the company's duty of coverage lapses, cf. the rules in the Insurance Contracts Act ss. 18-20.

Where the insured causes the insured event to happen *intentionally* he will have no claim against the company, cf. s. 18(1). Where he acts with *gross negligence, the liability of the company is decided with due regard to the degree of guilt and the circumstances of the case*, cf. s. 18(2) – however, in *liability insurance* and *life assurance* where the need for security is felt to be especially high,, the company will be liable even if gross negligence was displayed (in the absence of express contrary agreement).

Where the insured has brought about the insured event by showing *ordinary negligence,* cf. Chapter 6, Section 2.1.1 on the negligence concepts, the company shall be liable in respect of all forms of insurance provided of course that the peril involved was covered by the terms of the policy. It *may* be provided in the policy that the company shall be exempt from liability if the insured has brought about the insured event in a state of self-induced intoxication and it may also be agreed that the company shall be capable of deducting up to 5 per cent even if only ordinary negligence has been displayed, cf. s. 20.

In the absence of express contrary agreement, the rules of s. 18 regarding lapse or reduction of the company's duty of coverage shall not apply if the insured party is *below the age of 14*, or where he was *incapable of acting reasonably* while in a state of mental disorder, such as insanity, temporary unsoundness of mind or similar mental condition, cf. s. 19(1).

The provisions governing the insured's duty to refrain from causing the insured event himself also applies in liability insurance – in which area it may bring very unpleasant consequences to the *injured party*. Where the tortfeasor has acted intentionally or under the influence of self-induced intoxication the liability insurance does not cover the act at all, cf. the Insurance Contracts Act ss. 18 and 20). This circumstance will primarily affect the injured party whose *sole realistic* possibility of coverage was perhaps exactly the liability insurance of the tortfeasor. – As referred to in Chapter 5, Section 2.1.3 above, the special drafting of the rules on compulsory liability insurance for motor vehicles was made to avoid that the unpleasant consequences may occur to the injured party in the case of a liability insurance for motor vehicles.

5.2.6. The duty to mitigate the loss/avert the damage

The insurance company may require that the insured seeks to avert or at least limit the damage/loss. The duty of the insured in this context is closely connected to his duty of observing any security regulations which explains why the two problems, as far as sickness and accident insurance are concerned, are treated collectively in s. 124 of the Insurance Contracts Act.

As far as indemnity insurance is concerned the rules regarding mitigation of loss are contained in s. 52 of the Insurance Contracts Act. Where the insured is in *deliberate (or grossly negligent)* breach of his duty under s. 52(1) to avert or limit the damage, s. 52(2) provides that the company is not bound to compensate damage which may be deemed to have been caused thereby.

The mitigation measures referred to in s. 52(1) will require regular financial sacrifice on the part of the insured and therefore s. 53 provides that the insurance coverage will also comprise loss and expenses inflicted on the insured through proper preventive or rescue action.

5.2.7. The duty to notify the insured event

Upon occurrence of the insured event the insured must notify the company forthwith if he intends to bring a claim against the company, cf. s. 21(1) of the Insurance Contracts Act.

A breach of the duty under s. 21(1) will not cause the claim against the company to lapse but the company will not, under s. 21(2) be liable to a greater extent than it would have been if the insured had given prompt notice of the damage.

The duty under s. 21 is, as indicated in the headline, a duty to notify *the occurrence of the insured event.* The company may supplement this duty – and the limitation rule in s. 29 of the Insurance Contracts Act – with a duty on the insured to *present his claim* within a certain timelimit, cf. the rules in s. 30 hereon. The limitation rule of s. 29 is described in 5.1.

6. The insurance compensation

As was mentioned in Section 3 it is a characteristic feature of indemnity insurance that the amount of the insurance sum is exclusively determined by the damage occurred in money terms whereas the insurance sum in a fixed-sum insurance is laid down in the insurance contract. Obviously this difference will manifest itself in relation to the detailed rules on the insurance compensation. The provisions mentioned below contained in ss. 35 -40 of the Insurance Contracts Act and the rules on under-insurance and double-insurance only apply to contingency insurance. The special problems regarding fixed-sum insurance are mentioned below in Section 7.

Under s. 35 of the Insurance Contracts Act any legal interest which may be stated in money terms is eligible for fixed-sum insurance. Under s. 39(1) of the Insurance Contracts Act the company is not obliged to give compensation which exceeds the loss suffered but the provision in s. 39 has not been deemed to prevent the introduction of *new-value insurance* by which the compensation is not reduced at the rate of any deterioration in value which the object's age and use may have brought about.

Under s. 36 of the Insurance Contracts Act a property insurance will prima facie only cover the interest attached to the fact that the *value* of the object is not reduced at the occurrence of the insured event – the socalled *capital interest.* Where the insured wants financial compensation for the *profit interest* of the object as well (e.g. the importance of a machine in the process of production) he will have to take out a consequential loss insurance too.

Often the owner of the object (the insured) will represent the full capital interest but this need not be the case. The object may e.g. have been sold in a credit sale under which the seller retains title (until the purchase sum has been paid) or it may have been placed as security (pledged or mortgaged) in which cases the capital interest will be on several hands. Under s. 54(1) of the Insurance Contracts Act a property insurance is deemed, in such cases, to have been taken out for the benefit of anybody representing a capital interest in the object. Thus a mortgagee or pledgee need not expressly agree with the mortgagor/pledgor that security comprises any insurance sum replacing the object secured in the event of its deterioration or destruction. This result follows from the rule in s. 54(1) of the Insurance Contracts Act.

Even if an insurance, under the rule in s. 54, has been taken out for the benefit of a third party too (e.g. a mortgagee) the third party in question may risk that the insured changes, cancels or terminates the contract with the company – or that he requires the total sum of compensation to be paid put to himself on the occurrence of the event, cf. the Insurance Contracts Act ss. 56 and 57. To avoid this, the third party must give the insurance company advance notification of his right.

In Chapter 9 on international sale of goods, insurance of goods in international sales is described. Such insurance represents an example of insurance cover comprising other interests in addition to those of the immediate owner.

6.1. The measure of insurance compensation

In the absence of agreement to the contrary in the insurance policy the provisions referred to in 6.1.1 and 6.1.2 below will apply.

6.1.1. Total loss

In the event of total loss the insured is entitled to receive a compensation from the company which, *upon deduction of deterioration in value as a result of especially age, use, and reduced applicability* – corresponds to the price he is to pay to *acquire another object of the same type and nature*, cf. s. 37(1) of the Insurance Contracts Act.

For *ready-made goods destined for sale* the *sales price* will determine the computation of the insurance compensation – when the insured himself has undertaken the processing, e.g. a basket-maker, cf. the Insurance Contracts Act s. 38 – and the same applies in those cases in which a re-acquisition as presumed in s. 37(1) is impossible, e.g. as would apply where a painting has been destroyed.

For *objects of household furniture, personal use objects* etc. the insurance is equal to the re-acquisition price *without deduction of deterioration of value caused by age or use*, cf. the Insurance Contracts Act s. 37(2). However, deduction for deterioration in value will be made for age and use if the *utility value* of the object was *considerably reduced* for the party insured at the time when the insured event occurred.

As mentioned above in Section 6 the principles governing the computation of the insurance compensation in s. 37(1) are deviated from at least in the case of socalled *new-value insurance* which is particularly common in insurance of real property but also – albeit with time limitations – in car insurance with comprehensive cover. Many new-value clauses in insurance policies are drafted so that it is a requirement for new-value compensation that re-acquisition is actually made.

It is also possible to deviate from the rule in s. 37(4) by agreement – which often happens. If this was not the case, e.g. thefts of bikes would be even more burdensome to the companies than they already are.

6.1.2. Partial loss

The Insurance Contracts Act has no rules on the computation of the insurance compensation on partial loss. Usually the insurance payment will be fixed at an amount equivalent to the *repair cost* of the damaged object – possibly with a deduction for any increase in value created thereby.

6.2. Over-insurance

Where the amount at which an object is insured (the *insurance sum*) is higher than the value of the insured interest – a painting e.g. worth DKK 70,000 is insured at DKK 250,000 – the situation is described as *over-insurance*. The rule mentioned above in Section 6 of s. 39 of the Insurance Contracts Act implies that it is not in the interests of the insured to be over-insured.

Over-insurance occurs partly because it may be difficult to assess the value of the objects insured and partly because the insured party/beneficiary wishes to take into account that the value of the objects insured increases during the insurance period, cf. below Section 6.3 on full value insurance.

6.3. Under-insurance

Under-insurance occurs when the insurance sum is lower than the value of interest insured – e.g. where furniture worth DKK 100,000 is insured at DKK 75,000. Under-insurance at the amount mentioned will not only mean that a total loss is only to be compensated by DKK 75,000 but that the company's compensation liability for any damage is reduced to 3/4 of the amount of the damage/loss in the absence of contrary agreement, cf. s. 40 of the Insurance Contracts Act. Thus a loss of DKK 16,000 is only compensated by DKK 12,000.

To avoid the unpleasant surprises of under-insurance a socalled *full value insurance* has been developed in recent years based on the principle that the insurance sum (and thus the premium) is regulated regularly to match the value of the interest insured – a problem which in inflation periods may be especially relevant in building insurance.

6.4. Double insurance

Double insurance arises when the same interest is insured against the same risks in several companies.

Double insurance will often result in over-insurance, cf. above in 6.2.

Externally, i.e. as towards the insured, each company is liable as if it was sole insurer, cf. s. 41 of the Insurance Contracts Act (though the insured will never recover more than his loss, cf. s. 39). *Internally,* i.e. in the relationship between the companies, the problems are solved by admitting recourse claims to be raised, cf. ss. 42-44 of the Insurance Contracts Act.

6.5. Own risk

An agreement between the company and the insured of *own risk* implies that the insured is liable for loss within the limits of the amount of own risk – and very often also that the amount of own risk is deducted from the compensation paid when a major loss has been sustained.

7. Special rules in respect of life assurance and accident insurance

A life assurance is often made for maintenance purposes – the assured desires that a sum of money is available to his dependants on his demise. Both at the taking out of the insurance and subsequently, the assured may *appoint a beneficiary* either by written notification to the company to such effect or by having the company include it in the policy, cf. ss. 102 and 103 of the Insurance Contracts Act. In most cases the beneficiary clause applied is for "persons of closest relation" and it is worth noting that the clause will normally imply that the spouse (or registered partner) of the assured is regarded as sole beneficiary, cf. s. 105(5). Only where there is no surviving spouse/registered partner will children (and thereafter other heirs) rank as beneficiaries.

On the death of the assured the insurance sum is – as an absolute main rule – paid direct to the beneficiary, i.e. out of the deceased's estate. In all circumstances the appointment of a beneficiary will imply that the insurance sum "escapes" creditors, if any, of the deceased's estate.

The rules in ss. 102-105 are correspondingly applied in accident insurance, cf. s. 122.

A life insurance may be mortgaged but is not *eligible to ordinary creditor enforcement procedures* (both from the creditors of the beneficiary and from those of the assured), cf. s. 116 of the Insurance Contracts Act. The principle of exemption from creditor enforcement procedures also applies to accident insurance, cf. s. 123.

In the event of the insured party's bankruptcy, his creditors have a modest chance of seeking invalidation of life assurance payments, cf. a rule to this effect in s. 117 of the Insurance Contracts Act.

8. Choice of law issues

Insurance may be trans-boundary and thereby, in principle, give rise to problems as to which country's law should govern any insurance disputes arising – i.e. the issue of choice of law or the problem of private international law ("conflict of laws"). In practice, the problem is limited, for one thing the position of the parties is regulated thoroughly in the policy, and secondly, the policy itself may appoint a certain country's law as governing law.

CHAPTER 7

Formation of contract etc.

by Morten Wegener

1. Introduction

When someone buys a house, hires a car, commissions a glazier to exchange a window pane, books a hotel room, feeds coins into a parking meter, etc. he or she enters into an agreement or a "contract" is said to have been formed. Contracts are the dynamic element of economic life, they are the prime instrument of transferring rights from one party to another. For the same reason contracts may reasonably be said to be the most important of all the commercial and property law disciplines. Any sale, any insurance, any tenancy arrangement will have a basis in an agreement and a judicial evaluation of the legal relationship between the parties will also focus on the agreement between them. Where the agreement is in writing it is often termed *a contract* and the law regulating agreements is often described as contract law. In the following agreement and contract are used interchangeably on the same fundamental matters.

For centuries it has been well-established in Danish contract law that agreements must be kept, cf. the rule in the Danish Code of 1683 5-1-2, but the detailed contents of this doctrine – the doctrine of freedom of contract – have alternated with the times. Sometimes the contractual freedom has been stretched so far that any contract which both parties had made voluntarily would automatically qualify as "reasonable" not only as between the parties but also from society's point of view. This supreme freedom of contract view was especially prevailing in the first part of the 19th century but developments brought the hollowness of the contract basis to light – the *voluntary* consent to the contract terms. Society could not watch passively while a development of social misery went on, manifested i.a. by the fact that many parents would enter into contracts obliging their under-age children to many hours of daily work in factories. The first instance of state authority intervention was within employment contracts – to be followed by legislative limitations of contractual freedom in other areas, *e.g.* in tenancy law, credit sale contracts law, insurance contracts law, competition law, marketing law, and interest law.

The principle of the binding effect of contracts has not only been cut by *setting up limits to what the parties may agree in a valid contract* but also by *allowing increased access for a party to withdraw from a continuous contract on the grounds of altered circumstances since the entering into it*, cf. especially below 4.10 and 4.11 on s. 36 of the Contracts Act.

It is implied in the freedom of contract principle not only that *the parties are free to decide the contents of their agreement* but also that they decide *which contracts they will make* and *who they choose as contract partners*. Intervention by state authority has proved necessary in these areas too, however, e.g. in competition law where concern i.a. to free trade has led to rules which may impose upon an enterprise to *sell* its goods to buyers in the market who wish to buy them. The rules governing competition are described in Chapter 12.

Apart from the limitations of contractual fredom mentioned, contract law developments throughout the last half of the 20th century have been characterised primarily by the growth in *standard contracts*. When establishing a building loan in a bank the contract is not written out on a piece of blank paper, instead the empty spaces provided for the purpose are filled out on a single specimen from the pile of "pre-made" building loan contracts of the bank, and the same goes for the buying of a car from a car dealer, the renting of a flat from a building company, the taking out of an insurance with an insurance company, etc. Standard contracts make it possible to take advantage of the accumulated experience in the companies within a line of business, and they also enable a better exploitation of modern technology, e.g. the application of EDP. Thus a good deal of positive comment may be made on standard contracts but they are not an unmixed blessing. The party drafting the standard terms (i.e. the manufacturer/seller, the line of business in question etc.) may be tempted to look to their own interests and thereby weaken the position of the other party (typically a consumer). This creates a need for making contract law rules which will weed out the undesirable specimens among standard terms. As will appear from the discussion below the requirements for *treating standard terms as agreed* are quite high in many areas. Further the trend is towards *interpreting standard terms against the draftsman* (or "contra proferentem"), (cf. in particular s. 38 b of the Contracts Act) and finally, some standard terms are directly *set aside* (i.e they are re-garded as non-binding). The authority for such setting aside will nearly always be sought in s. 36 of the Contracts Act.

Many examples of abuse of standard terms may be found, and in contract negotiations between two parties both using standard terms a regular "battle" may be fought as to whose terms are applicable – a sort of "battle of forms" – but the drafting of standard terms may also be a way to arrive at a solution which is tailor-made for this particular contract area and which delicately – and reasonably – sets off the conflicting interests against eachother. Where standard terms are drafted with an open mind, not just to safeguard the interests of the line in question but also their potential contract partners – such terms will be capable of achieving a status of gap-filling rules in the area and thus be cited as determinative in a conflict even if they were not agreed between the parties to the contract in point, cf. also Chapter 3, Section 6.3. above, on model contracts, standard terms etc. in international legal relationships.

In this connection it is important to keep in mind that some non-mandatory legal rules (i.e. rules which the parties may contract out of), e.g. the rules in the Sale of Goods Act, cover an area so wide that at least within certain fields of their coverage they will not tend to represent the best average best option but merely the best "reserve rule" – in those fields they function appropriately as "stop gap rules".

It is evident e.g. that the rules of the Sale of Goods Act which govern the purchase and sale of chattels (goods) are not equally suitable for regulating the legal position of a trader who has bought oranges or a machine made to specifications and now faces defective performance from the seller or delay in the delivery. The uncompromising and strict rules governing the buyer's remedies in the Sale of Goods Act – which may be deviated from – allowing the buyer to cancel his purchase are considerably better suited to the oranges' buying than to the machine buying, for which on the other hand, the buyer needs much more extensive rights to claim rectification of defects than the Act gives him. Therefore many organisations of trade – both on national and international level – have made agreed standard terms which the parties may incorporate into their otherwise individual agreements simply by referring to them.

As already mentioned, it is desirable that standard terms are drafted with equal regard to the two parties to the contract and obviously this is more likely to happen if both parties have a say in the drafting of the contract – as was the case when the equal-ranking building organisations drafted their "General conditions for works and supplies in building and construction enterprise" (*AB 92*) whose terms to a wide extent rank as gap filling rules in the building and construction field.

Generally, it is important to observe that the word "standard terms" is not unambiguous. Some standard terms are usual, others unusual, some are onerous, others are not, some have been unilaterally laid down by the draftsman/supplier (socalled *adhesion contracts*), some have been made through negotiation between equal organisations representing each party (socalled *agreed documents*) and in between there are all sorts of varieties. Statements concerning adoption, interpretation or setting aside of standard terms must therefore be read with due regard to the multiplicity of such terms.

Most of the contracts in contract law are synallagmatic contracts. One party's performance is given in exchange for that of the other party – as e.g. in a contract of sale. The opposite to such contracts is a gratuitous promise/contract (a *gift contract).* The following treatment will be limited to synallagmatic contracts and therefore a brief mention of the most significant points distinguishing gift contracts may be appropriate here. 1) With gratuitous promises the access to withdraw his promise is wider for the promisor 2) claims under gratuitous promises are especially weak in the event of the donor's bankruptcy – 3) the sale of goods rules relating to liability for defective quality and defective title, cf. below Ch. 9, are not immediately applicable to gifts (following the advice of not looking a "gift horse in the mouth", 4) several debtors will be liable jointly for the performance of a promise but normally not for a gratuitous one, 5) under the Bonds Act s. 9 the assignor of a claim warrants the existence of the claim but not when the assignment is a gift.

The rules governing contracts are principally to be found in the *Contracts Act* of 1917. (currently Consolidated Order No. 781 of 26 August 1996). The act comprises, under its title, "agreements and other legal acts in the area of contract and property law". the word legal act is an artificial term to denote private declarations of intention to create binding legal relations. In contract law such declarations are referred to as *promise, offer, command, acceptance* and *agreement.*

A *promise* is a unilateral declaration of commitment made by one person to another – a promise is said to "bind" the *promisor.* Sometimes the distinction is hard to draw between a promise declaration and a declaration of intention to be bound only in certain circumstances – a socalled *letter of intent* – cf. below Section 2.1.1.

An *offer* is a promise which loses its binding effect on the promisor if it is not accepted in due time.

An *acceptance* is the promisee's adoption of an offer and an *agreement* is established when an offer has been accepted within the time and manner prescribed.

Finally, a *command* is a unilateral declaration binding the addressee – as e.g. a buyer's notice to the seller regarding properties of the subject matter of sale, cf. below Chapter 8.

2. Further to the conclusion of the contract

As an absolute main rule the conclusion of a contract is not subject to form requirements. It is widely believed that a promise which has only been made orally is not binding but this is a misconception. For *evidence reasons it is advisable to have promises and agreements reduced to writing but for the validity of the contract writing is only exceptionally a requirement.* Part 1 of the Contracts Act (ss. 1-9) provides rules for the formation of contract. S. 1 provides that the rules in ss. 2-9 are non-mandatory and in practice the pattern of formation of contract often differs from the offer-acceptance model in the Contracts Act, cf. below s. 2.2. It is also important to keep in mind that foreign systems of law may have rules of formation of contract differing from the Danish ones, cf. below Section 2.3.

2.1. The model of the Contracts Act for formation of contract

The pattern of contract formation described in the Contracts Act is as follows: The offeror A sends an offer to the offeree B (e.g. an offer for 1,000,000 litres of oil at DKK 3,000 per 1,000 litres). B considers A's offer and sends an acceptance corresponding with A's offer which reaches A before the expiry of the timelimit set for acceptance. A contract is hereby concluded.

2.1.1. Offer

Most legal promises are *offers* which means that they cease to be binding if they are not accepted before the expiry of a certain timelimit – *the period for acceptance.* Gratuitous promises need not be accepted (except for *oral* gratuitous promises) – indeed the acceptance must normally be made forthwith, cf. s. 3(2) of the Contracts Act.

An offer is binding on the offeror *from the moment it has been communicated to the addressee* (offeree), cf. s. 7 of the Contracts Act. Therefore an offeror who regrets his offer is only capable of withdrawing it if he can manage to communicate his withdrawal so that it *precedes the moment of the offeree's cognisance of the offer itself* – or coincides with it, at the latest. It is self-evident what is implied in *"communicate"* here. A declaration has been communicated to the addressee when – in normal circumstances – he would have known of it (which is the case e.g. when dropped through his letter box or sent to him by telefax).

The rule in s. 7 means that there is a certain time interval in which the offeror is bound (by his offer) without a similar binding on the offeree, viz. from the time of communication to the offeree and until the expiry of the period for acceptance. The offeror decides the length of this interval for he is the party setting the period for acceptance.

The account so far has not questioned whether a declaration is an offer (promise) at all. The issue rarely causes doubt but in some cases it may be difficult to decide whether a declaration is an offer or merely an invitation to treat. When determining the status of two common situations – a window display and the mailing of price lists/catalogues – the former situation is an offer whereas the latter is generally held to be an invitation to treat. It has also been discussed whether advertising on the Internet qualifies as an offer or an invitation to treat but in a recent high court judgment this issue was solved. In the concrete case a car seller had advertised a comparatively expensive car for sale on his homepage at a wrong price and this ad was regarded as an invitation to treat. Thus an interested buyer was unable to accept the "offer".

Sometimes it may also be difficult to determine whether a declaration is so certain that a promise may be said to exist – a promise for something on which the party making the statement may be held bound or whether he merely declared that he intended to enter the contract. *Letters of intent* have become very common in business life. Both the party making and the party receiving such declarations should beware of regarding them as of no legal importance. It is extremely important to read the text closely to eliminate any doubt as to its status and as to whether the declaration is of such certainty that it is really a promise notwithstanding the description given to it in the headline.

2.1.2. Acceptance

2.1.2.1. What is an acceptance?

As already referred to, an acceptance is the addressee's adoption of the offer and the acceptance therefore contains both a *promise* and a *command.* A promise (to the offeror) that the acceptor will pay the consideration stated in the offer (DKK 3,000 per 1,000 litres of oil), and a command (also to the offeror)) that he is to be bound by his offer. When asking whether an acceptance is binding the answer must therefore be two-fold: the promise in the acceptance is binding (for the offeree) when it has been communicated to the offeror; the command in the acceptance is binding (for the offeror) when it has reached him. The special rules regarding the right to withdraw from certain contracts are mentioned below in 4.12.

2.1.2.2. The period for acceptance

Where the offeror has *stated the period for acceptance in his offer* s. 2(1) of the Contracts Act provides that *to qualify as acceptance in due time the acceptance must have reached the offeror before the expiry of the period fixed.* Where the offer is made by letter the period is computed from the day of dating of the letter. Where the offer has been made by telegram the timelimit is computed from the time of day at which the telegram was delivered at the telegraphic station, cf. s. 2(2). For telefax communication, the time stated on the fax is decisive.

The Contracts Act, s. 3, governs the situation *in which no period for acceptance has been stated by the offeror*. S. 3(1) determines the *legal period for acceptance* by providing as follows:

"Where an offer is made by letter or telegram and no timelimit has been set for its acceptance, the acceptance must have reached the offeror before the expiry of the period which he must have contemplated would pass at the making of his offer. At the computation of this period – where nothing else follows from the circumstances – it is presumed that the offer arrives in due time, and that the acceptance is sent promptly by the offeree after a reasonable deliberation time, and that it is not delayed on the way. Where the offer was made by telegram the acceptance is also to be made by telegram – unless it may arrive equally early by other means".

It is evident from the wording of s. 3(1) that the legal period of acceptance is composed of three elements: the time of sending, deliberation and return – *but so that the period of acceptance seen from the point of view of the offeree is a "unity"*. If he spends more time than is usual in deliberation, he may seek to gain what he has lost by making the return speedier than the sending, e.g. by replying by fax rather than letter. The decisive factor is exclusively whether the acceptance reaches the offeror before the expiry of the period for acceptance.

In the determination of the period for acceptance the variable is the *deliberation time* – what constitutes normal sending (and return time) is beyond doubt. A "reasonable" deliberation time is determined by what is customary in the line in question and as a general rule, the less complexity of the offer, the shorter the period for acceptance, also the more price fluctuation of the article contracted for, the less deliberation time, the more "commercial" the offer, the less deliberation.

Both the rule in s. 2(1) and the provision in s. 3(1) place the risk for the occurrence of a fortuitous event – i.e. an event beyond the control of the parties (or their employees, e.g. a postal strike) with the offeree. Whether the event affects the offer on its way to the offeree or the acceptance on its way to the offeror the risk lies with the offeree – *if the acceptance does not reach the offeror within the timelimit for acceptance*. The situation is one of *delayed acceptance* with the consequences attached to such situation – cf. below Section 2.1.2.3. In the cases treated in s. 2(1) where the offeror has set a period himself the risk is also on the offeree even if the offeror must have contemplated the occurrence of the fortuitous event (e.g. a labour conflict on which warning has been given); in the s. 3(1) cases (legal acceptance period), however, the risk is on the offeror if he ought to have known, *at the making of his offer*, that the event would arise – a subsequent knowledge which he ought to have had of the event does not, however, transfer the risk from the offeree.

2.1.3. Delayed acceptance

Where the acceptance does not reach the offeror before the expiry of the period for acceptance, the offer lapses from the moment of expiry. S. 4(1) of the Contracts Act provides that a delayed acceptance is regarded as a new offer, i.e an offer from the original offeree to the original offeror which the latter may treat as he likes (including throwing it away).

The principle of placing the risk with the offeree may imply *that* the offeree holds a reasonably justified belief that his acceptance was in fact made in time *and that* the offeror must realise that the offeree is mistaken in his belief (the dating or postal stamp may indicate this). As regards *these* – rather special – cases s. 4(2) provides that the offeror shall notify – upon receipt of the acceptance – the offeree without undue delay that his acceptance was delayed (and therefore not binding on the offeror). If the offeror fails to give such notification the acceptance is deemed to have arrived in time – and thus there is an agreement. Where the offeror sends the notification by letter, telegraph or other proper means of communication such as telefax or telex (and he can *show* that it has indeed been sent) the risk lies with the offeree if the notification is delayed or fails to arrive on account of fortuitous events, cf. s. 40 of the Contracts Act.

Communications of the *type* referred to in s. 4(2) are often termed *"notices"* (socalled obligatory notice) – the party in question must *give notice* in order to maintain his rights.

2.1.2.4. Rejection of offer

Where an offer is *rejected* by the offeree, it lapses definitively, cf. s. 5 of the Contracts Act. From the moment the rejection has been communicated to the offeror, he is free to dispose otherwise – in other words, the offeree is barred from withdrawing his rejection.

An offeree who would like to seek better terms than those contained in the offer and still hold the offeror to it must be cautious in his application to the offeror. As soon as the application has the character of a rejection of the offer – an assumption which is easily made – he cannot "change horses in mid-stream" and hold the offeror to the terms of his original offer against his will.

2.1.2.5. Non-conforming acceptance

An acceptance which adds to the offer or contains limitations and reservations which do not correspond with the offer is deemed a rejection (cf. s. 5 of the Contracts Act and immediately above) in connection with a new offer (counter-offer from the original offeree), cf. s. 6(1) of the Contracts Act. As regards the new offer the original offeror is not bound.

Sometimes it may be difficult to decide whether developments in a contract formation situation result in a non-conforming acceptance. An acceptance made by fax containing a supplementary "further particulars by letter" etc. would not qualify as an acceptance and therefore requires that a letter which does not correspond with the offer reaches the offeror before the expiry of the period for acceptance. Enquiries whose purpose are to bind the offeror to this offer but at the same time seek to elicit better terms than those contained in it will not always mean a non-conforming acceptance but especially in business matters such enquiries may imply that the offeror is no longer bound, cf. also Section 2.1.2.4.

The rule in s. 6(1) of the Contracts Act corresponds to the provision in s. 4(1) and just as for delayed acceptance there is a rule concerning non-conforming acceptance in s. 6(2) aimed at the situations in which the offeree reasonably believes his acceptance to be conforming to the offer and the offeror (exceptionally) ought to realise this. *In such cases* the offeror may not disregard the non-conforming acceptance – he must notify the offeree that the acceptance does not conform with the offer, failure to do so will mean that agreement is deemed to be made with the contents of *the acceptance*. As regards the offeree's communication the provision in s. 40 referred to in 2.1.2.3 applies.

2.1.2.6. Who is contract partner?

Even if the model of the Contracts Act for formation of contracts has been followed it may not always be evident who the contractual partners are. Many undertakings which have formerly been run or would formerly have been run as sole proprietorships are today organised as limited liability companies (A/S) or private companies (Aps) without the sole shareholder having realized *that* to the outside world it is not a matter of course that the person commonly known as GG, the electrician, runs his business as "GG, Aps" and *that* it may be relevant whether a contract is made with GG in person or with the company.

If the enterprise which a party, A, has established contact with, is in reality a company (and makes no attempt of concealing it) A must prima facie direct his claim against the company – *especially* if A took the initiative of forming the contract in the first place.

2.2. Formation of contract patterns other than that of the Contracts Act

The pattern described in the Contracts Act for contract formation with written exchange of offer and acceptance is quite old and may be said to reflect the conditions of trade prevailing at the time of the Act's origin, viz. about 100 years ago. As will have appeared, it is a comparatively simple model in its presumed concepts of oral or written (letter, telegram) exchanges of offer and conforming, punctual acceptance. It is still widely applied but by no means for all contract makings.

Presumably certain contract formations have always followed a pattern differing from the Contracts Act model, in particular contracts for the sale of land in that they are not the product of exchanges of single offer/acceptance declarations but rather a result of sometimes prolonged, difficult negotiations between a vendor and a purchaser. Many commercial co-operations are no longer established by correspondence in which single letters in a process of longer duration may be pinpointed as "the offer" and "the acceptance". Many of these relationships also involve complex objects of consideration from both parties and they will also often presume that the co-operation is to subsist for a very long period, 10 years or more. In such contracts it will often be impossible to determine the mutual obligations and the distribution of risk with absolute certainty and therefore the contract will necessarily become "open-ended" to some extent. Many types of "modern" contracts, e.g. management, franchise and ceratin licence agreements contain elements of this character. In contrast, in some contracts the formation procedure is so rudimentary that it may be difficult to trace the connection to the Contracts Act model – e.g. when a customer helps himself from an automatic vending machine or parks his car at a parking meter.

The possibilitites of making contracts electronically offers another set of problems in the application of the Contracts Act model. Under the wording of the Act the most advanced instrument of communication is the telegram and since Danish law is silent on the issue of electronic contract formation except for the socalled e-trade Act mentioned in Chapter 12 the provisions of the Contracts Act must be adapted to the new technology, in this case contract formation via the Internet.

In a contract law sense the term *"option"* is applied when a party has a right to enter a specified future agreement. Where A buys part of B's shareholding in a certain company C, A may also have been given the right to future acquisition of B's remaining holding of C-shares, i.e. A has an option for these remaining shares.

As has been indicated the situations which may occur under the head-line of "Other patterns for contract formation" are virtually without limit and in the following only a few typical instances will be treated.

2.2.1. Standard contracts – the adoption problem

As has been indicated above in the introductory section the "battle" against abuse of standard terms is fought on several fronts and one of the most effective weapons against a contract partner's exploitation of the powerful position inherent in the drafting of standard terms will naturally amount to considering the standard terms in question as "non-agreed" since that will bring them outside the scope of the contract entered into.

If the standard terms are printed in the contract which the parties sign, the terms are agreed whether or not their contents are given above the signatures of the parties or reference is merely made there to the terms printed "on the back" ("below" or "next page"). The position is considerably more doubtful if the standard terms are printed, e.g. on the back of the contract (and *no reference* is made to that fact above the parties' signatures) or if the contract does contain a reference to the standard terms and these are neither printed in the contract nor enclosed with it. Although in principle the problem of *adoption/non-adoption of standard terms* and the problem of *assessment of the contents* are separate issues it is indisputable that in the doubtful cases referred to above, the likelihood of regarding a standard term as adopted increases with the reasonableness of the term. Further, in relation to the assessment of the contents a presumption of reasonableness is made for standard terms applied by public authorities (railway companies, postal authorities etc.) which is also the case for terms which have been born as a compromise between equal organisations of rival interests (e.g. a national organisation of car dealers v. a national union of car owners).

Nor is it very doubtful that the likelihood of considering a standard term for adopted increases with the level of *expectation* that the area in question is characterised by standard terms. When driving on board a ferry the passengers will expect that the shipowners have sought to limit their liability in damages for injury to persons and (especially) damage to goods. The limitation clause is usually part of the ticket received.

For certain contracts, e.g. in a sale of durable household equipment, it is quite common for the seller at delivery (which will typically be *after* the making of the contract) to enclose a copy of his "Usual terms of sale", "of delivery" or whatever description his standard terms have found, which will often leave the buyer in a weaker position than he would enjoy under the *non-mandatory rules* in the Sale of Goods Act (the mandatory rules may, of course, not be deviated from). Naturally such standard terms will not become binding on the buyer merely because the seller has *enclosed* them at the delivery of the goods – there is no *"agreement"* of the terms involved. By the same token, a seller is also debarred from "sneaking in" standard terms deviating from non-mandatory rules for incorporation into the contract merely by stating them in the invoice accompanying the goods.

2.2.2. *Quasi contract*

A party will be bound not only by his *express promise* but also by any *implied* promise made (e.g. a creditor who accepts a late instalment but omits to terminate the whole loan arrangement).

For business (certainty and reliability) purposes it is sometimes necessary to hold a person to be bound *even if no express or implied promises can be ascribed to his conduct.* An example is provided where a person appropriates an article which is delivered to him by mistake – and such mistake is evident – in which case he must pay the price normally charged for such article.

2.2.3. *Will a party be bound by passivity?*

For some years the fierce competition on the consumer market led to the (mal) practice of sending "offers" to addressees by which the addressee was given to understand that a failure to react on his part would be regarded as "acceptance" – a method still used by some firms. A recipient of such unsolicited offers need not react, however. It is indisputable that the rules on the binding effect of passivity, cf. below, cannot be stretched to require such communication obligation. This is further enhanced by the wording of s. 4 of the Consumer Protection Act in respect of Certain Consumer Contracts referred to in 4.12 which reads: Where a trader sends or delivers unsolicited goods to a consumer and such sending or delivery is not due to a mistake [which the consumer may identify] the consumer may keep the goods free of charge."

A characteristic feature of the circumstances under which passivity may, conversely, result in a binding effect is that the non-reacting party by his own conduct *has* brought himself into a position under which the other party may reasonably infer that a contract relationship was sought and under which a reasonable safeguarding of his interests will imply that notice shall be given to him within a certain timelimit that a contract relationship is not desired on the terms stated in his application. A typical example is provided in the situation described in s. 9 of the Contracts Act: "Where a party in an application which would otherwise be deemed an offer has used the words "subject to contract" ... or the like the application will only be deemed an invitation to treat (i.e. to make an offer) in accordance with the terms stated therein. Where such offer is made within a reasonable time from the addressee(s) and the recipient must presume that his application provoked it he is bound to notify the offeror without unjustified delay if he intends to reject it. Where such notification is not given the offer is deemed to be accepted".

Thus there is no general rule obliging a party to react (give notice) if he finds that another party is under the impression that a promise has been given or an agreement entered. But the closer negotiations have been to agreement stage, the more relevant is the imposition of a presumption of a duty to react to an application of the character mentioned from the other party and the presumption of such duty will be further enhanced *if* a business arrangement is intended, *or* the parties have traded with eachother before, *if* the market price of the article contracted for is fluctuating, *or if* it is subject to inherent vice or is extremely fashionable.

2.2.4. EDI

EDI means *E*lectronic *D*ata *I*nterchange on a general level but in this context the concept is used in a narrower sense to describe electronic transfer of trade date to enable substantial data to be processed at the addressee's place immediately upon transfer. To achieve this immediate processing it is necessary that the trade data in question are structured on a model agreed by the parties in advance.

The advantage of a data structure model of such character increases with the amount of participants (in a common model). Thus it is not very appropriate that the banks make one model, the transport firms another, and the individual line of business a third etc.

The ECE (Economic Commission for Europe) has prepared a standard – a common language – for the EDI called EDIFACT (**E**lectronic **D**ata **I**nterchange **F**or **A**dministration, **C**ommerce **A**nd **T**ransport). EDIFACT has been recognized as a standard by the ISO – the international standardisation organisation. The ICC – International Chamber of Commerce – has also published a set of rules describing how EDI-parties should conduct themselves – the UNCID-rules (Uniform Rules of Conduct for Interchange of Trade Data). The aim of the standard is to establish a common reference in the way communication is effected in the mutual relationship between enterprises, in respect of public authorities and in the relationship between such enterpoises and the authorities. To the extent the standard is applicable, it will only be necessary to use one format.

Although EDIFACT has not been implemented by all lines, the application of EDI is already today an extremely important inter-trading factor. To illustrate, it may be mentioned that the use of EDI is well on its way to replace the old Bill of Lading system, cf. Chapter 8 for further details.

The application of EDI reduces the costs involved in paperwork – businesses may bring down the considerable expenses of writing order notes, confirmations, invoices etc. In addition they get more accurate information by the very fact of obtaining the relevant data sooner. It is quite relevant to a company (A) who must be able to deliver a certain article bought from another company B – if an order needs to reach B on April 20 to ensure that it is in stock with A at the time A's customers want to buy it – or whether it is possible to wait until 24 April – "stock ties up money" as is well-known – and also costs interest.

An example of EDI-application:
From the stock control system of company F, F's EDI system receives an electronic report on F's stock situation. In the EDI system criteria have been encoded concerning sales velocity, remaining stock, seasonal demand, market prices, etc. which enable the EDI system to "decide on its own" whether purchases should be made and what should be bought. If F's EDI system makes an order to company M, M's EDI system will be capable of executing the order on its own with the necessary automation – and possibly by the application to the EDI systems of other companies be capable of ordering raw materials and semi-produced goods, transport and storage-room. Man is involved in the production of systems and the EDI processing by random testings but to a considerable extent the computer really handles matters on its own.

2.3. Formation of contract on an international level

2.3.1. Introduction

The Danish rules on formation of contract are – of course – not the only way the problems may be solved. Thus, under German law an offer will bind the offeror already when it has reached the offeree. Under English law an offer will not bind the offeror unless he has been promised consideration and therefore an offer – unsupported by consideration – is freely revocable until it has been accepted. The consideration rule explains why it is sometimes seen in contract negotiations in England – and the USA – that the offeree will pay a certain sum of money to bind the offeror to the terms of his offer.

The rules of Part I of the Danish Contracts Act will apply when two Danish parties enter a contract in Denmark.

If a Dane – or more typically, a Danish enterprise – enters into a contract with a foreign business *(an international contract)* there is an immediate problem as to whether issues on the contract are to be settled on the basis of Part I or by applying the "corresponding" rules of the contract partner's legal system. The problem is termed *choice of law* and is dealt with in *private international law*, cf. also below Chapter 22.

The inverted commas with which "corresponding" was supplied above was quite deliberate – for the point of the choice of law issue is that the application of a foreign system of law may often lead to a different result than the Danish rules in the area. They may also imply the same – either by coincidence or because the national rules in the area have been subjected to *harmonisation* as a result of a very close cooperation between the countries (as was previously the case between the Nordic countries and today between the EU Member States in certain areas).

The choice of law issue may be illustrated by an example in the area of contract formation: Under *Danish* law an offer is binding on the promisor (offeror) from the moment the offeree is cognisant of it, cf. above 2.1.1. Under German law, as already mentioned, an offer is binding when it reaches the offeree. Under *English and American* law an offer will not bind in itself – the offeror A will not be bound until he has received "consideration" (in return for binding himself) *and also provided* that A finds such consideration "adequate" in terms of amount or nature. The rules also differ on the issue of acceptance in due time. Under *Danish* law an acceptance is in due time if it has reached the offeror before the expiry of the period for acceptance, cf. above 2.1.2.2. Under *German* law the acceptance need only have been sent before the expiry of the period for acceptance which also applies in *English* law.

The problem of choice of law is not identical with the problem of court jurisdiction – which is also true for international contracts. If a dispute between an Italian company from Milan and a Danish company from Copenhagen cannot be solved by negotiation and ends in court the *problem of choice of law* involves deciding on the application of either Danish and Italian rules of law whereas the *jurisdiction issue* relates to whether the case should be brought before the court in Copenhagen or in Milan. The two issues cannot always find a "synchronised" solution, even if the decision is to be made by applying Italian law, the court jurisdiction may still be in Copenhagen (rules on jurisdiction are set forth in *the EC Convention on Judgments* from 1968, cf. below Chapter 22).

2.3.2. Dispute solving through conventions

Naturally an issue such as the above mentioned involving a dispute between an Italian and a Danish company would find an appropriate basis for solution in an international set of common rules (a treaty or *a convention,* cf. above chapter 3, Section 6.2) where such exist to be applied. It will not prevent the parties from disagreeing – the preventive effect is no greater between such parties than between two Danish parties who are aware that disputes are to be solved under Danish law – but it will mean that the substance disagreement on a contract's formation (or interpretation of contents) is not further complicated by an issue as to which party's rules of law are to be applied. In other words: the choice of law problem disappears at the same rate at which international conventions are entered for individual contract types providing a set of common rules for the solving of contractual disputes between parties from different countries.

However, the legal systems of the various countries are so different that it is difficult to draft such international conventions and to have them ratified by the would-be participating countries. The most ambitious project so far – though by no means the only one – is the UN Convention on Contracts for the International Sale of Goods, cf. above Chapter 3, Section 6.2.. This Convention, which is usually referred to by its abbreviation, CISG, is described in more detail in Chapter 9.

As regards the issue of contract formation, Part II provides rules for *sales* contracts in relation to what may be deemed offers, when offers and acceptances are to be deemed binding, etc. These rules deviate considerably from the provisions in Part I of the Danish Contracts Act, and the Nordic countries – whose Contracts Acts are almost identical – declared at the signing of the CISG that they would not be bound by the rules in Part II, cf. below Ch. 10, Section 1. Therefore the rules in Part II are not applicable on international sales which will be governed by the law of one of the Nordic countries (including CISG, except from Part II) – but *since* many Danish companies are parties to international sales outside the scope of Danish law but subject to e.g. German, French, or Italian law (i.e. CISG *incl.* Part II) *and since* Part II represents the approach conceived internationally to be appropriate for solving legal issues on contract formation, a very brief an itemized account is given below of the most important rules of Part II:

1) An offer – cf. CISG Art. 14 – becomes effective when it reaches the offeree, cf. Art. 15(1) and Art. 24.
2) An offeror may revoke his offer until the offeree has dispatched his acceptance, cf. Art. 16(1).
3) The access to revoke just referred to until the offeree has dispatched his acceptance will not be applicable if it is indicated that the offer is irrevocable, cf. Art. 16(2)(a) – such indication having been made *e.g.* by stating a definite time for acceptance in the offer.

   An irrevocable offer will be binding when it has reached the offeree and a withdrawal will therefore only be effective if it reaches the offeree no later than at the same time as the offer, cf. Art. 15(2).
4) An offer which is rejected will lapse – when the rejection reaches the offeror, cf. Art. 17.
5) A contract is concluded at the moment when the acceptance becomes effective, cf. Art. 23 – which will occur when the acceptance reaches the offeror, cf. Art. 18(2), 1st clause, and Art. 24.
6) In order to be effective, a revocation of an acceptance must reach the offeree no later than at the same time as the acceptance, cf. Art. 22.
7) In order to be made in due time, an acceptance must reach the offeror before the expiry of the timelimit the offeror has stated, if any, or *where*

no limit is fixed, within a reasonable time, cf. Art. 18(2), 2nd and 3rd clauses, and Art. 20.

8) Art. 21 contains rules on the legal effect of late acceptance. In contrast to Danish law there is no general rule providing that late acceptance will be deemed a rejection combined with a new offer (cf. above Section 2.1.2.3).
9) Art. 19 contains rules on the legal effects of a non-conforming acceptance. Compared to the rules in s. 6 of the Contracts Act – cf. Section 2.1.2.5 – it is remarkable that immaterial modifications will not imply that the offer is rejected (combined with a new offer). With immaterial modifications – cf. the rule in Art. 19(3) – the contract is deemed to be concluded with the terms contained in the *acceptance* unless the offeror gives notice to the contrary without undue delay.

2.3.3. Solutions via choice of law

If the above problems which as a matter of principle will always occur in international contracts – are not solved by way of harmonised legislation (cf. Section 2.3.1) or through international conventions (Section 2.3.2) a solution may be found through choice of law – which country's law is to govern the dispute?

To a wide extent the parties may *agree* on the law applicable *(they may solve the choice of law problem by mutual agreement)* but otherwise the answer to that question is very much dependent on the character (type) of contract involved, money loan, employment contract, etc., cf. below Chapter 22 for more details.

2.4. The right to withdraw in valid contracts

When a contract is validly made the parties are bound by its terms. In a contract of sale the seller is bound to deliver the subject-matter sold at the time agreed and in proper condition for which the buyer is to pay the purchase price agreed in return. In a contract of employment the employee must perform the work agreed for which the employer is bound to pay him the wage agreed, etc. Where one of the parties fails to perform the starting point is that the contract has been *breached* for which – under the circumstances – the other party is offered various remedies, in particular an access to claim performance (*specific performance*), to withdraw from the contract *(rescisssion)*, and to claim financial compensation (*damages* and *proportionate price reduction*, see for further illustration the remedies on breach in sale of goods below, Chapters 8 and 9.

Danish law does not provide rules on a general access to withdraw from valid agreements to enable a party, in the absence of breach, to be released from his obligations under the contract unilaterally and at random. In a political/economic system based on market economy this is necessarily as it should be – as is also implied in the freedom of contract principle mentioned in Section 1 – since the system would otherwise collapse entirely. However this does not preclude a certain limited access to withdraw in ceratin groups of cases where the economic and social consequences of allowing such access must be deemed to be modest.

Currently the most important cases in practice where access to withdraw is exceptionally granted under certain conditions are comparatively new and relate to consumer contracts, cf. below Section 4.4. Another exception – quite limited and only ressembling a right to withdraw – has developed in case law on the basis of the provision in the Contracts Act s. 39, 2nd clause, which provides an access to withdraw promises after they have been communciated the promisee but before "they have induced him to act" as the wording goes. The time of withdrawal – in the requirement that it must reach the promisee as quickly or even immediately upon the promisee's cognisance of the promise proper – is thus generally of central importance and it is also to be presumed that considerations of reasonableness may be relevant. Presumably the exception margen is likely to wider in consumr contracts outside the stautory cases, cf. above, than in business contracts for which case law treats parties desiring to opt out of validly created obligations with rigour. This attitude was shown e.g. a high court judgment maintaining a business purchase of a trade van notwithstanding that the buyer had tried to withdraw already the day after the purchase and notwithstanding that her reasons – in her own circumstances – were justifiable.

3. Interpretation and Gap-filling in Contract

As mentioned above, most statutory rules in contract and property law are non-mandatory, which means that both in areas regulated by statute and areas regulated by case law – the parties are prima facie to determine the contents of their contract themselves. If the parties have gone into sufficiently minute detail they may unequivocally address any conceivable problem in the contract and any subsequent dispute may be decided from the wording of the contractual document.

In practice contracts are not made that way. The parties will only address material problems (price, quantity, delivery time etc.) in the contract, and often the document will use phrases and words which the parties interpret in different ways. Therefore real life will often present a situation in which the wording of the contract gives no clue as to how a dispute is to be solved and in that case the contract will need interpreting and its gaps must be filled.

As far as possible attempts are made to *interpret* the contract, i.e. it is sought via application of the contract's *individual* elements (cf. below Section

3.1.1) to determine the "reality" (contents) of *this particular contract*. Only when no more progress can be made by interpretation will *gap-filling* be resorted to – which means that the contract is supplemented by the rules of law, customs or principles applying to contracts of the particular *type*. Cf. Chapter 2, above especially Section 8, on the similar process in legislation.

Gapfilling is a kind of resignation in relation to interpretation – the attempt to hit "bull's eye" is given up for the satisfaction of at least hitting the target. Therefore interpretation precedes gap-filling but from an *evidence point of view* the contract party who claims that a decision was made at the entering into the contract which deviates from the result which will obtain on the basis of gap filling is faced with the burden of proof to that effect. *If* the parties agreed in the course of contract negotiations that a term which must be interpreted to the effect that an employee has been entitled to a notice of four months this term will take precedence over the rules of the law on employees giving him a notice of only three months but the burden of proving that the parties did agree to the term is on the employee if the employer disputes it.

3.1. Interpretation

3.1.1. Interpretation elements

The most important sources for interpretation are – naturally – *the words applied in the contract* but other factors are also relevant. Information (e.g. witness statements) in respect of the *negotiations preceding the making of the contract document* may clarify vague draftings in the contract and the same applies to any *previous contracts* between the same parties. The price agreed is typically a very important interpretation factor since it will indicate what sort of requirements may be imposed for the consideration.

Where the parties have a *common understanding* at the entering of the contract on a certain issue in the contract this consensus will be decisive – even if the conception of the parties deviates from normal ("proper") conception and even if one of the parties has *now* a different understanding of the contract term in question.

However, the typical situation (when a dispute arises) is where the parties had, originally, a different conception of one or more contractual terms – a difference which becomes apparent when the contract is to be performed. In these cases the test will be *"how an ordinary, reasonable person"* of the profession involved would interpret the words used in the contract. If this interpretation wholly or in the main part corresponds to the conception as alleged by one of the parties the interpretation problem is solved. But where the parties' divergent conceptions are equally valid the judge is in a more difficult situation especially if performance *has* already been made and no restoration to the parties' original position is possible for in that case the judge is incapable of finding that the parties are not to be bound, i.e. that the contract is deemed to have lapsed. The judge will not, however, be entirely left to his own devices in that the further interpretation data, as referred to above, i.e. those not expressly stated in the contract – will almost always provide at least a certain basis for the decision.

3.1.2. Principles of interpretation

As will have appeared from the above the borderline between interpretation and gapfilling is far from clear-cut and somewhere in the borderland – closest to interpretation – we find the socalled principles of interpretation:

Where it is doubtful what a promisor has intended to bind himself for a first principle is to interpret his promise to *the least onerous extent* – the socalled *minimum rule*. With synallagmatic contracts (cf. Section 1, above) in which both parties are promisors and their promises are given in mutual exchange the minimum rule is not very helpful. For gift promises on the other hand and other promises containing a certain amount of "generosity" or charity the rule is appropriate (examples include guarantee promises made by private individuals).

A principle of far more general application is the socalled *"ambiguity"* rule (in English law, the contra proferentem rule) upon which an ambiguity is interpreted against the party who drafted the contract.

The ambiguity rule is primarily important for the interpretation of standard terms the drafting of which will often be left to one party – the stronger – (the bank, the insurance company, the car dealer, etc.). Applying the rule is one of the methods by which undesirable elements among standard terms are weeded out, cf. above Section 2.2.1 on adoption problems in standard contracts and below in Section 4.11 on the setting aside of standard terms. By means of the ambiguity rule it is often possible to address a deliberate speculation in ambiguity whereby the party applying the standard terms has calculated on the other party's (the consumer's) conception of a standard term in one way whereas he (the draftsman) – in the event of dispute – will allege a different conception. – In 1994 following an EU Directive a new s. 38b was incorporated into the Danish Contracts Act which emphasizes the application of the ambiguity rule especially in *consumer* contracts. For the purposes of the Contracts Act a consumer contract is a contract made by a trader in the course of his business with another party (the consumer) principally acting outside the course of business, cf. the Contracts Act s. 38a(2).

It is important to keep in mind that the ambiguity rule should not be applied too rigorously. *Its application should be restricted to cases in which no result is obtainable by more individual interpretation factors* – and the ambiguity rule is not applicable merely because a term might have been drafted with greater *clarity* (indeed, this is probably always possible – in retrospect).

3.2. "Gap-filling"

The "gapfilling" rules of law in an area must be found in the same way as other rules of law.

Thus the first step is to examine whether *non-mandatory statutory rules* apply in the area in question- an example is provided by the Sale of Goods Act whose provisions are in the main a (detailed) set of non-mandatory rules, cf. the Sale of Goods Act s. 1(1).

Although non-mandatory statutory rules are not provided in the area concerned gapfilling rules may well exist. In almost all professional areas within trade life, *customs* have developed (trade customs and usages) on which information may be obtained – for Denmark with the Danish Chamber of Commerce. Where both a non-mandatory statutory rule and a custom exist in the same area the custom will usually have priority as the gapfilling rule of law, cf. the wording of s. 1(1) of the Sale of Goods Act.

For some of the more recent contract types, i.e types which have been born under the regime of standard terms (e.g. leasing of plant etc.) the *common standard terms of the line in question* will be capable of achieving status as gapfilling rules of law, sometimes in a judicially "censored" version, i.e. a version in which certain terms which the courts have considered too rigorous (i.e. too favourable for the line itself) in previous decisions, have been modified.

4. Invalidity of contract (promises)

4.1. Introduction

Part III of the Danish Contracts Act (ss. 28-38) contains a set of rules governing invalidity – or avoidance – of promises. The rules are not exhaustive nor do they represent the only factors which may avoid a promise. Under special statutes, e.g. the Rent Acts, the Employees Act, the Assistants Act, the Holiday Act, etc. a vast amount of rules address the *terms* which the parties may validly/lawfully agree in their contracts. Another example is provided by the terms in the Guardianship Act, mentioned in Section 4.4. below, governing the legal position of minors and mentally handicapped persons and the validity of contracts made by and with them. In addition invalidity rules developed in case law are applicable.

With the increasing use of standard terms the classical vitiating factors – duress, fraud and undue influence – have considerably declined in importance but on the other hand such terms have brought other problems as already mentioned. The most effective rule addressing these problems is undoubtedly the very important rule in s. 36 of the Contracts Act, mentioned below in 4.10 and 4.11.

A promise is void where – *on account of defects in the declaration of the promise* – the promise will not bind the promisor *neither on its immediate contents nor in respect to payment of compensation based on the interest of the promisee in its performance* – whether the defect in the declaration is attributable to the promisor's *person* (e.g. incapacity), the *manner of origination* of the promise (e.g. fraud on the part of the contract partner), or the *contents of the promise* (the promise may e.g. be contrary to a mandatory statutory provision).

Thus a promise will not be void *merely* because the promisor is not obliged to perform under its immediate contents (*specific performance*). Where A e.g. has sold his bike, whose market value is DKK 1200, to B for DKK 900 he will not be obliged to deliver specific performance if the bike is stolen from him before the delivery date agreed but his promise is still valid and he will have to compensate B for his loss of profit of DKK 300. On the other hand where A is a minor he will not be bound to deliver the bike nor to compensate B for his loss of profit. A's promise to B was *void* on account of his minority.

The fact that a promise is void does *not* mean that the promisor will never be liable in damages towards the promisee. The rules in e.g. the Guardianship Act s. 44(1) and (2) described below in Section 4.4. set forth that the minor A from the example above may well be liable in damages towards B – though the invalidity of the promise affects the measure of damages. A will not be liable to pay damages *placing B as if the contract had been performed (socalled "expectation interest" damages)* which would include B's loss but A may under certain circumstances be liable to pay damages to B *placing B as if the contract had never been entered into*, cf. s. 44(2) of the Minors Act (*"reliance interest" damages* covering B's – now futile – expenses in relation to the contract).

Where damages are referred to in the special area legislation e.g. in the Sale of Goods Act, which a party may claim upon a breach of contract by the other party – e.g. a buyer suffering a loss on the seller's late delivery of goods – the basis of computation is expectation interest. This implies that the statutory (and quite reasonable) point of departure is that agreements are valid. In this connection it should be mentioned that a *contract party who is entitled to claim damages on expectation basis will always be entitled to claim damages on reliance basis instead.* Sometimes it may be easier to show one's futile expenses than one's loss of profit (indeed it may be non-existent) nor is it always wise – from a commercial point of view – to show one's anticipated profit on a sale.

4.2. "Operative" and "non-operative" avoidance factors

The distinction in Danish contract law between "operative" ("strong") and "non-operative ("weak") avoidance factors relates to the fact that *some* factors – in this context called "*operative*" may be set up *against a bona fide promisee* whereas *others* (socalled *non-operative) may only be set up against a promisee in bad faith.* However, a rule which is so general as s. 36 is difficult to fit into this "system".

The operative avoidance factors, e.g. forgery and minority, are characterised by relating to situations beyond the promisor's precautionary control. Thus it is typically impossible to prevent that someone abuses one's name on an IOU or buys goods on credit in one's name – therefore forgery must be an operative avoidance factor and the protection of the innocent promisee must be subsidiary here.

With the *non-operative* factors (e.g. fraud) the situation is different – it would seem to be possible to avoid being deceived. No concern need be wasted on the promisee if *he* was the active deceiver or if he is in bad faith as regards deceit displayed by a third party) but if the promisee is innocent a choice must be made between protecting the promisor who might have avoided the situation or an innocent promisee – and in that situation the promisee's interests take priority.

Thus, as regards the non-operative avoidance factors it is absolutely vital whether the promisee was in good or bad faith. In this context (as elsewhere in Danish law) the *good faith concept denotes a state of mind whereby the promisee neither knew nor ought to have known the circumstances causing the promise to be liable to avoidance.* What he "ought to know" is decided (again as elsewhere in Danish law) on the basis of the knowledge which a wise and prudent man (or woman) would be deemed to have or become possessed of in a similar situation at the latest at the time when he *became cognisant* of the promise. What the promisor learns after that time is – as an absolute main rule – irrelevant for the presumption of good faith, cf. s. 39 of the Contracts Act.

As mentioned above in Section 1 the willingness to allow a promisor to withdraw his promise is greater with *gift promises* which is evidenced i.a. by the trend to regard weak avoidance factors as strong here – thus an innocent (gratuitous) promisee is not protected.

4.3. Forgery and fraud

When a promise is *forged* it is given in another person's name; when *fraud* occurs a promise someone else *has* given is changed so that its content deviates from that contemplated by the promisor (e.g. changing a figure from DKK 1,000 to 11,000).

Neither avoidance factor is mentioned in the Contracts Act but there is no doubt that they are both *"strong"* avoidance factors – on a line with registered minority, registered incapacity and mental illness etc. rendering a person unfit to act "reasonably".

Act No. 417 of 31 May 2000 on electronic signature introduced rules to protect the *authenticity* of digital declarations (i.e. that the declaration is truly originating from the sender alleged) and *the integrity* of such declarations (i.e. that unwarranted changes in the declarations have not been made).

4.4. Incapacity

A person under the age of 18 (*a minor*) or a person deprived of capacity to contract by court decision under the Guardianship Act s. 6, where such step has been deemed necessary, may be referred to, in Danish law, as persons under legal *incapacity*". Such persons have a special legal position in many areas, a position primarily laid down under the Guardianship Act (Act No. 388 of 14 June 1995).

The incapacity of a person implies that as a main rule such person is incapable of *disposing of his property on his own or entering into binding contracts. Minority* is a strong avoidance factor. A *court deprival of capacity* may only be set up against an innocent contract partner if the person deprived of capacity at the time of his incapacitation had been registered as such person at the place of his residence; where the person deprived of capacity owns real property a further requirement, as regards contracts on the property, is that the deprival of capacity has been registered on the page of the property in the Land Registry, cf. Registration of Property Act s. 48.

> Since the minor (or incapacitated person) cannot dispose of his property or otherwise enter into binding contracts it is necessary that others – a guardian – act for him when a valid contract is to be made.

The main rule providing invalidity on account of minority is not entirely without exceptions:

S. 42 of the Guardianship Act contains a very important exemption to the main rule providing that a *minor is free to dispose of property acquired by his own enterprise after attaining the age of 15 years, or where he has been deprived of capacity, after such deprival.* This special rule relating to own enterprise also applies to income of the assets obtained or benefits in lieu of such assets. But the rule does not affect the minor's access to undertake debt obligations. The minor will only be bound by his acts in relation to own enterprise if he has either paid cash or if the contract partner, in case the minority is later to be claimed in defence – decides to declare himself satisfied on the basis of instalments already paid.

The rules in s. 42 are also applied to property obtained by a minor/incapacitated person from a donor or testator for the minor's *free disposal.*

Where a minor is in possession – or obtains possession – of a business which may occur primarily by way of inheritance this business will normally be run by the guardian. It is, however, possible under s. 43 to allow the guardian – with the consent of the county governor office – to grant a person deprived of capacity leave to *engage in trade or other business on his own* in exceptional cases. Such leave will imply – under s. 43 – that the person deprived of capacity may validly enter contracts within the course of his business.

While the exemptions to the main rule just referred to have express statutory sanction this does not apply to the very important exemption of the socalled "*money rule*" under which a person who receives money in payment must be capable of relying on the payer's right to dispose of the money. This rule which is firmly established in case law has developed from considerations regarding the function of money as the common means of payment in society – and besides, "money is anonymous", which should also apply to payments by minors. Whether the contract partner in the situation is covered by the money rule – and will thus be allowed to retain the money even if the payer lacked the capacity to dispose of it – is decided upon an assessment of several circumstances of the case. What did the minor buy? How old did he appear to be? How big was the amount? The answers to these questions decide the legal position of the contract partner.

Where a contract is avoided for minority, i.e. none of the exemptions will apply, s. 45 of the Guardianship Act provides that *each party shall surrender what he has obtained or – to the extent that such surrender cannot be made – refund its value*. While the duty to surrender is unconditional for both parties, the compensation duty will only apply in full to the contract partner, the minor is only liable to refund to such extent as the benefit received has been put to use for his own "proper maintenance purposes" or "other purposes deemed to be of use to him", cf. s. 44(1). The intention of the rule is evident: it aims to protect minors against careless and ill-considered acts. The position may be illustrated thus: Where a minor has sold an object belonging to him and the sale is avoided for minority he may recover the object without incurring liability to compensate the buyer if he has spent the money on something "useless" for the purposes of the Act, e.g. theatre tickets. Conversely, if the minor has spent the money to defray expenses which were *necessarily* to be paid, e.g. payment of rent, he will be liable to compensate the other party for his payment since the money has been "put to his use".

The rule in s. 45(1) is very favourable to the minor and equally unfavourable to his contract partner. However, in situations in which the minor has misrepresented his minority status the need to give him legal protection is less felt and s. 45(2) therefore provides that the minor may be liable to compensate his contract partner not only to the extent of the "use" referred to in subsection 1 but on the level of reliance interest, where the minor *induced* the contract partner to enter the contract by his *misrepresentation*. Where the minor's misrepresentation amounts to a *criminal offence*, e.g. a forgery of his birth certificate, the contract partner has an unconditional claim for compensation on reliance interest measure, but *not* on expectation interest (cf. s. 45(3)).

4.5. Mental incapacity – unsoundness of mind

The Guardianship Act s. 46 contains rules on the effect of a mental disorder to the power to make contracts. The rules in s. 46 have been drafted on the "model" of those in s. 45, cf. the preceding Section.

4.6. Duress

4.6.1. Duress with physical, or threatened physical violence and mechanical duress

A promise which has been unlawfully provoked by personal violence or threatened immediate application of violence does not bind the party coerced *irrespective of the good or bad faith of the promisee*, cf. s. 28(1). This provision governing constraint on the will of the promisor (*duress with violence or threats*) may be applied analogously to *mechanical duress,* i.e. assumption of control of the organs of the party coerced, e.g. by leading his hand in writing.

The duress referred to in s. 28(1) need not be exercised by the promisee himself or with his knowledge and with a view to the cases in which the promisee is in good faith, s. 28(2) provides that the promisor – as soon as the constraint was stopped – is obliged to notify the promisee that the promise was given in a constraint situation. Where the promisor fails to give such notification, cf. the rule in s. 40 of the Contracts Act referred to above in 2.1.2.3, he will be bound by his promise.

4.6.2. Other constraint

Daily life provides many examples of promises made under threat where nobody would question their validity on account of the constraint imposed – debtors are signing voluntary settlements under threat of lawsuits against them if they don't, houseowners make their mortgage repayments under threat of compulsory sale of their property if they don't, etc.

Between the (rare) cases referred to in 4.6.1 of constraint with physical violence etc. and the – numerous – examples of lawful compulsion just mentioned there is a wide "band" in which the compulsion may well be *unlawful* but a promise made under it will only be avoided if the promisee was in bad faith as to the compulsion, cf. s. 29 of the Contracts act. To illustrate the wording of s. 29 a situation may be cited in which a promisor is threatened *with something illegal*, e.g. with disclosure of matters belonging to the sphere of privacy or to do something illegal (e.g. commit a crime) or *where the relationship between what the promisor is threatened with as against what he is threatened for is beyond reasonable proportion* (e.g. a president of a football club may threaten the thief caught in his strawberry field with information to the police if the thief does not agree to pay DKK 100 to his football club but not if the promise is to pay DKK 100,000 to avert information).

4.7. Fraud

Fraud will lie if a person *unlawfully and contrary to his own knowledge of the true state of affairs either makes misrepresentations as to such state or remains silent with the purpose of provoking a promise.* Fraud in contractual setting is governed by s. 30 of the Contracts Act and like the duress described in s. 29 only qualifies as a non-operative avoidance factor.

With the word "unlawful" the draftsmen indicate that the section is not applicable to any untrue statement or any failure to disclose even if it is done deliberately and the purpose is to provoke a promise. A seller is not obliged to reveal that the buyer may obtain the same article at a lower price from his competitor and likewise he may emphasize a car's excellent starting capabilities in the winter-time even if the newspapers' motor journalists have reached another conclusion in their test reports on the car – but a seller will be fraudulently misrepresenting if, contrary to the truth, he states that an article has been recommended by the National Consumer Agency, or the like.

4.8. Undue influence

Under s. 31(1) and (2) of the Contracts Act a promisee in *bad faith* has no claim on a promise provoked by *unduly exploiting* a promisor's considerable difficulties, lack of insight, recklessness or a relationship of dependence subsisting between them when the promise has been provoked or been conditional upon a benefit grossly disproportionate to the consideration.

To apply the avoidance rule in s. 31 several requirements must be satisfied: 1) the promisor must be placed in one (or more) of the inferior positions described in the section; 2) the promisee must be aware of this – he is required to *exploit* the inferior position of the promisor, 3) the promise is to leave the promisee with a benefit grossly disproportionate to the consideration, and 4) the promisee must be in bad faith.

The avoidance rule of s. 31 is often described as the "usury" provision of the Contracts Act and the term's aptness is illustrated by the fact that it is applied against unconscionable loan terms but s. 32 is not restricted to money loans. Where a court finds a promise invalid under s. 31 nothing prevents the judge from fixing another consideration, e.g. a lower interest on a money loan but otherwise letting the contract stand.

4.9. Disagreement between the will of promisor and the declaration given

The content of a promise may be different from what the promisor intended for several reasons. For one thing the promisor himself (or one of his employees) *may commit an error in connection with the drafting of the promise*, e.g. miswriting, cf. s. 32(1) of the Contracts Act; the promise may be subject to *distortion on its way from promisor to addressee*, e.g. on account of an error in the telegraphic office, cf. s. 32(2) of the Contracts Act, and it may occur that the promise externally is of the content envisaged by the promisor *but that he made it "pro forma"* (i.e. the agreement is only fictional), cf. s. 34 of the Contracts Act.

4.9.1. The rule in s. 32(1) of the Contracts Act

The provision in s. 32(1) is drafted as follows: "A party who has made a declaration of intention which on account of a misprint/clerical error or other mistake on his part has received a different content than envisaged will not be bound by the declaration if the addressee saw or ought to have seen that a mistake had occurred." The drafting leaves no doubt that s. 32(1) describes a *non-operative avoidance factor.*

As indicated in the text of the Act a clerical error will represent the most common source of error but the words "or other mistake" of s. 32(1) make no limitation in the factors to which it may be applied. There may e.g. be calculation errors or the promisor may have misunderstood the meaning of a word, e.g. mixed up gross and net concepts. However, the courts have taken this line further: At least with support in the principle in s. 32(1) it is generally deemed that a mistake which is *material* (for the promisor), and *evident* (to the promisee) will lead to the invalidity of the promise disregarding the type of mistake made by the promisor.

4.9.2. The rule in s. 32(2) of the Contracts Act

The rule in s. 32(2) 1st clause is drafted as follows: "Where a declaration of intention carried by telegraph or on oral presentation by messenger is misread on account of an error from the telegraphic office or by wrongful representation by the messenger, the promisor is not bound by the declaration in the form under which it was communicated even if the promisee was in good faith." According to the drafting, s. 32(2) 1st clause is clearly an *operative avoidance factor.*

The protection of an *innocent promisee,* if any, in s. 32(2) 2nd clause is safeguarded by imposing on the promisor a *duty to give notice* corresponding to the duty imposed on a promisor under s. 28(2) under the Contracts Act (cf. further in Section 4.6.1).

An error in a telefax is *not* covered by the rule in s. 32(2) on telegraphic errors – but by the rule in s. 32(1). However, it is presumed that the rule in s. 32(2) must be applied analagously in respect of errors occurring while a declaration is "in transit" by telex, fax or EDI (transmission error).

4.9.3. "Pro forma" promises – Contracts Act s. 34

Where the promisor and promisee agree that a contract was established pro forma (a contract whereby A "buys" B's valuable antique clock may have been entered to defraud B's creditors) the contract is not binding between the parties (nor is it binding on B's creditors who may take the clock in execution). However, pro forma promises should not be given lightly for if the promisee re-assigns the "right" he has been given under a (written) pro forma promise the promisor will be bound according to the contents of his promise as towards the assignee where such assignee is in good faith, cf. s. 34 of the Contracts Act.

4.10. Breach of basic assumptions – the general clause in s. 36 of the Contracts Act

When a person makes a promise he has certain preconceived ideas of the circumstances prevailing at the *making of the promise* and quite often he has certain (considered) expectations of the *future sequence of events*. In both situations the promisor may be wrong – in the first situation the basic assumptions are simply *false* – in the latter there is a *breach of assumptions* (as events did not turn out as presupposed). In both situations the promisor *must prima facie bear the consequences of his own misjudgment* but as mentioned below situations may arise in which the promisor will have access to withdraw his promise. For the following account a presumption may generally be described as an *assumption providing a basis for a promise*.

4.10.1. The Contracts Act s. 33

Where the promisor's basic assumptions have been false he *may* find support for a claim that his promise was void in the provision of s. 33 of the Contracts Act: "Even if a promise would otherwise be deemed valid the promisor is incapable of relying on it where circumstances, existing when the promise was communicated to him, and on which he must be deemed to have had knowledge allowing him to rely on it would be contrary to common honesty standards." Where A on his own initiative approaches B to buy a shareholding whose price, unknown to A (but known to B) has plummeted on the same day because the managing director of the company has turned himself in to the police with a confession of comprehensive fraud towards the company, B is barred from holding A to the offer made because this would be contrary to "common honesty standards".

The provision in s. 33 will not only be applicable in situations of mistake of the type referred to. The rule is also applicable to contract formation situations where none of the other more precisely defined vitiating factors can be shown but where the general picture of the situation would indicate that one of the parties should not be bound by the agreement entered. It is often difficult to show that a drunk person has been subject to undue influence (let alone show that he was in such a state as to be covered by s. 46 of the Guardianship Act, cf. above Section 4.5) but the information on his intoxication combined with the detrimental content of the promise he has made may be the factors which he can put to use – once he is sober – to withdraw from the promise in reliance of s. 33. There is no doubt, however, that with the introduction of s. 36 (in 1975) the more general rule of that section is more frequently relied on than the s. 33 provision.

4.10.2. S. 36 of the Contracts Act – the general clause of contract law

The introduction in 1975 of the socalled *general clause in contract law*, s. 36, was aimed i.a. at counteracting economic crime though that purpose was certainly not the only one.

Today the provision reads as follows:

"An agreement may be amended or set aside wholly or partly if it would be unreasonable or contrary to proper conduct to allow it to stand. The same applies to other legal acts.

In the decision under (1) regard will be had to the circumstances prevailing at the formation of the contract, contents of the contract and subsequent events."

The very general choice of words in s. 36 shows that the provision will sanction avoidance of a promise both on account of *circumstances at its making,* on account of its *contents*; on account of special *factors concerning the promisor's person*, and a *combination of two or more of the factors mentioned.* Thus a party who wishes to claim that a promise is not binding on him for *breach of basic assumptions* may also find support in s. 36 and the same applies – as already mentioned – to a party who claims that the *content* of his promise is of such character that he ought not to be bound by it. In the latter context s. 36 may *e.g.* apply to the socalled *agreed penalty claims,* i.e. agreements whereby a party (e.g. a master builder) agrees to pay a penalty in the event of his failure to perform an obligation imposed on him within a fixed time (e.g. completion of a building contract).

The introduction of s. 36 has also provided the courts with a *statutory provision* to set aside a promise wholly or partly with reference to a change in circumstances after its making – the situation traditionally called – and still sometimes referred to as – *breach of basic assumptions.* S. 36(2) gives express access to the possibility of taking subsequent events into account. This enables a judge who finds e.g. that a supplier shall no longer be bound by a long-term contract without notice access and whereby he is bound to deliver – at a fixed price – articles which have now been subject to a special levy or become more expensive on account of increasing raw material prices to refer to the provision in s. 36 of the Contracts Act – either to release him from his obligation or to increase his price wholly or partly by the amount of the special levy.

Among the avoidance rules in contract law, s. 36 is no doubt the one most frequently relied upon. In real terms, its wording is so wide that it is only rarely necessary to apply the rules governing duress, fraud, undue influence, etc. but the courts have chosen – quite wisely – to stick to the adopted course of applying ss. 29, 30 and 31 etc. when they are faced with a case involving one of these elements beyond a doubt.

After some hesitation in the first years following the introduction in 1975 the courts have gradually widened the scope of s. 36, e.g. by applying it to contracts between traders where there is an evident *discrepancy* between their bargaining positions. There is no doubt, however, that the courts' reluctance of applying s. 36 to contracts between traders still prevails. Its main area is contracts between on the one hand consumers and on the other hand traders, cf. below section 4.11 on (i.a.) the *setting aside* of standard terms. In 1994 a new s. 38c emphasizing the applicability of s. 36 on *consumer contracts* was incorporated into the Contracts Act following an EU-Directive. In real terms the introduction of s. 36(1), 2nd clause, changed very little in the legal position in Denmark although for educational purposes it is a good thing that the legal approach is expressed in the Contracts Act.

Apart from promises and contracts s. 36 may also be applied to change or set aside other legal acts, cf. s. 36(1), 2nd clause, e.g. commands (cf. above, Section 1) such as termination notices.

4.10.3. The presumption principle

As already mentioned, the invalidity-factors catalogue of the Contracts Act is not exhaustive. Apart from the invalidity rules in special legislation it has been deemed e.g. in case law that a mistake with the promisor *induced to him by the promisee* will, as a main rule, avoid the promise if the misrepresentation was a determining factor in the promisor's making of the promise (entering into the contract). This situation is not the same as where the promisee has deliberately or inadvertently (through negligence) provided wrongful information (since such misrepresentations are within the ambit of ss. 30 and 33 of the Contracts Act, or possibly s. 36) but relates to cases in which the promisee is in good faith as to the accuracy of the information, i.e. he had no reason not to believe in the accuracy of the information given.

In the situation just described the mistake of the promisor is that some of the presumptions he had at the giving of his promise and which were based on information provided by the promisee turn out to be wrong –but no blame attaches to the promisee. In case law wrongful assumptions or breach of assumptions have been relied on to uphold a promise to an even wider extent via the socalled *principle of assumptions*. Under this principle which may be conceived as a kind of *guiding line* (not a set of rules or doctrine) when determining which contract party should bear the risk – outside the other invalidity cases – of the breach of a certain basic assumption, three conditions must be satisfied in order that an assumption is *relevant*: 1) it must have *induced* the promisor to make his promise, 2) it must have been *evident* for the promisee, and finally, as a central point, 3) upon a comprehensive view of the circumstances it must be deemed that *the risk* of breach of the assumption should lie with the promisee. Where all conditions are satisfied, invalidity will lie and the promisor is accordingly released from his promise.

It has been debated whether the principle of basic assumptions has lost its relevance after the introduction of s. 36 of the Contracts Act. But in case law, despite the development in the courts' willingness to apply the provison, this has turned out not to be the case. However, the application area would seem to be limited to commercial contracts, in particular between equal partners, in which cases a starting point taken in one of the fundamental standard criteria ("unreasonable", "contrary to common honesty standards") in s. 36 would appear less appropriate.

4.11. Invalidity for contract contents – special note on the setting aside of standard terms

As has been mentioned several times in the preceding pages a promise may be avoided not only on account of circumstances prevailing at its making but also on account of its *contents*.

Special statutes contain a multitude of rules establishing that *contracts of a certain content cannot be validly made*. Where a contract is made contrary to such statutory provision the contract is prima facie invalid, i.e. not binding on the parties. An example of such rule is provided in the Assistants Act s. 4(1): "Contracts of employment [governed by the Act] cannot validly be made for a duration exceeding one year" and the provisions in the Interest Act s. 7(1) and (2) under which – for consumer contracts – a rate of interest exceeding the official discount rate plus – currently 7 per cent – cannot validly be agreed (the rules of the Interest Act are mentioned below in Chapter 14).

A promise may be invalid for its contents even if it is impossible to show a statutory rule *expressly* determining that a promise cannot validly have a certain content – the wording of s. 36 of the Contracts Act (cf. 4.10.2) certainly encourages the view that a court may hold a promise to be void *on the sole grounds* that it will find the result of binding the promisor to it "unreasonable".

With the rule in s. 36 of the Contracts Act the courts have been provided with an efficient weapon for the weeding out of the aberrations among standard terms. Even if a standard term has been agreed between the parties (cf. above 2.2.1) and even if the term is drafted with perfect *clarity and unambiguity* (cf. 3.1.2) it may be challenged – by way of setting it aside – where its enforcement would be deemed unreasonable or contrary to principles of fair conduct, cf. s. 36. The judges may use their discretion when evaluating the factors to stress in their decision but there is no doubt that a relevant point will be whether the term in general is usual or unusual within the line of business – and the extent to which the term places the contract partner in a less favourable position than a gap-filling rule in the area, will also be a vital factor, cf. Sections 3 and 3.2.

4.12. Competition clauses

As regards the socalled *competition clauses* (or *clauses in restraint of trade*) s. 36 of the Contracts Act is supplemented by a special set of invalidity rules in s. 38 (for salaried employees these rules are further extended by special provisions in ss. 18 and 18 a of the Salaried Employees Act, cf. below Chapter 20). Under s. 38 (1) of the Contracts Act a person who for reasons of competition has committed himself not to run a business or engage in other business activities of a certain nature or seek employment in such business may have such clause set aside if the commitment in regard to time, place, or other circumstance goes beyond what may be deemed requisite for competition protective purposes. The same applies if the clause is deemed to limit the employee's access to employment unduly. – Under s. 38(2) the employee shall not be bound by a competition clause if the employer dismisses him without reasonable cause, or where the employee resigns in a justified reaction to his employer's failure to observe his obligations.

4.13. Legal effects of the invalidity

When a promise is invalid the promisor is no longer bound to its terms towards the promisee. If he has already performed his part towards the promisee he is in principle entitled to recover what he has delivered against his own surrendering of the benefit he may have received from the promisee (cf. however Sections 4.4 and 4.5 on the provisions in ss. 45 and 46 of the Guardianship Act).

The promisee's *heirs* enjoy the same legal position towards the promisor as the promisee himself.

The promisee's *creditors* (including where relevant his bankrupt estate) will prima facie enjoy no better position towards the promisor than the promisee himself had. The absolute main rule in Danish law is that a person's creditors will have no better position at law than their debtor had.

Where the promisee has assigned his right under the void promise to an innocent assignee for value (normally a purchaser or mortgagee) the nature of the asset (real estate, goods, negotiable instruments, registered securities, or simple claims) will determine in the first place how the dispute between the promisor and the assignee is to be solved. These issues are treated elsewhere in the book, especially in Chapters 15 and 17.

4.14. The Consumer Contracts Act

Experience shows that consumers will sometimes enter into ill-considered contracts which they regret afterwards. On a general level there is of course no way to completely get rid of this phenomenon but some mandatory protection rules were introduced by Consolidated Act No. 886 of 1987 with subsequent amendments in respect of certain consumer contracts (the *Consumer Contracts Act).*

Under s. 1(1) of the Act its scope is limited to *consumer contracts* and such contract is defined in s. 1(2) whereby for the purposes of the Act a consumer contract is an agreement made between a trader acting in the course of his business and another party (the consumer) mainly acting outside the course of a business.

Under s. 2(1) of the Act a trader is barred from making an unsolicited approach in person or by telephone to a consumer at such consumer's address or workplace with a view to obtaining immediate or subsequent offers or acceptance of offers to enter into agreements. Under s. 3 a promise made by the consumer on the application of a trader contrary to these rules *will not be binding* (and under s. 18 the violation of the ban against unsolicited approach is punishable by a fine). – The ban contained in s. 2(1) against doorstep selling etc. does not apply to (i.a.) orderings of books, subscriptions for newspapers, weeklies and magazines, and insurance, cf. also s. 2 a on the information the trader is bound to supply.

Where a trader sends or delivers unsolicited goods to a consumer and such delivery is not due to a mistake which the consumer ought to realize – the consumer may retain the goods free of charge, cf. s. 4 of the Act. The same applies to unsolicited services supplied.

With the rules in Part 3 (ss. 5-9) of the Act the consumer has been granted a right to change his mind in some situations where invitations to conclude a contract are made in a way disposed to take advantage of the consumer's situation. S. 5(1) allows a cooling-off period for agreements for the sale of goods and services *made during a meeting with the trader outside his permanent place of business,* e.g. in a restaurant, during excursions, cinema shows, etc., and under s. 5(2) a consumer may also withdraw from subscription contracts for (i.a.) newspapers and magazines, cf. also s. 5(3-5) on exceptions from subsections (1) and (2).

Under Part 4 of the Act (ss. 10-13) a common cooling off period is also granted for *distance selling.* This concept includes under s. 10 a agreements for the sale of goods, services, or continuous delivey of goods or services concluded on the basis of distance communication and without meeting of the parties, where such agreemets are concluded as part of a system operated by the trader.The information duty on the trader is heavy both before and after the conclusion of such contracts, including the duty, cf. below, to inform the other party of the right to withdraw, cf. in more detail ss. 11 and 11 a. Agreements concluded via the Internet, e.g. by ordering from the trader's home page will generally be in the category of distance selling.

The right to withdraw under Part III must be exercised within a fortnight, cf. ss. 6 and 8 on the procedure. Where the trader has failed to notify the consumer *in clear writing* of the right to withdraw the agreement is *not binding* on the consumer. For distance selling the right to withdraw must also as a starting point be exercised within a fortnight but this timelimit may under the circumstances be extended to three months, cf. s. 12 a(1-2). It is no longer set forth that the agreement shall not be binding on the consumer if the duty to inform has been violated. Where such violation occurs the remedies as towards the trader may (apart from the timelimit extension mentioned) involve penal sanctions under the rules of the Marketing Practices Act.

Part 4 a of the Act (ss. 13 a-13) contains special rules on the right of withdrawal from insurance contracts and Chapter 5 (ss. 14-15) contains rules on the right to cancel *subscription contracts.* (e.g. concerning security and rescue services and on supervision or upkeep of real estate).

Special provisions on the consumer's right to withdraw are contained in other legislation: In practice the most important rules are found in ss. 6-13 in Act No. 391 of 14 June 1995 with subsequent amendments on consumer protection on *the purchase of real estate etc.* S. 9 of Act No. 472 of 30 june 1993 governing *package tours* allow the consumer a right to cancel a trip (against payment of a reasonable fee).

On an overall view provisions such as those mentioned represent an evident trend in the legislation of the most recent decades towards stregthening the consumer's position vis-a-vis the traders. The same trend can be traced e.g. in the rules governing consumer sale in the Sale of Goods Act, consumers' credit agreements in the Credit Contracts Act, and on default interest in consumer relationships. The same applies of course to the legislation on the Consumer Complaints Board and the approved private complaints boards, cf. above Chapter 4, Section 7, and on the consumer ombudsman institution, cf. below Chapter 12, Section 2.

5. Third party promises

In the majority of cases, agreements will purport to create a legal relationship between the immediate parties to the contract but it may be drafted in such manner that its principal aim is to *create a right for a third party* – as e.g. when a customer makes an agreement with a florist commissioning him to send flowers to a third party. In that case *a third party agreement/promise* is involved (the florist's promise to the customer is a third-party promise).

If the third-party promise entails that the third party in question may claim performance himself (at due date) the promise is a *"real"* third-party promise, cf. e.g. the rule referred to in Chapter 7, of s. 54(1) of the Insurance Contracts Act whereby a property insurance is deemed to have been taken out also in favour of a mortgagee. Where access to claim performance stays with the promisee of the third party promise (in the flower example – the customer) the promise is said to be an *"unreal"* third party promise (in the example, the florist's promise).

A third-party promise is *irrevocable* if it cannot be cancelled without the consent of the third party involved. By far most third party promises are *revocable* (as e.g. the florist's third-party promise to the customer would be).

6. Formation of contract via agents

6.1. Introduction

From what has been said in the preceding Section it is apparent that legal problems may fairly easily arise even if contract negotiations are carried on and agreement made between the two (or more) persons envisaged to be parties to the contract. Obviously the potential for mistake(s), void promises etc. will grow when one of the contract partners (or both) have others act for them in the course of contract formation but it stands to reason that for practical purposes society must be prepared to accept that contracts may be made through middlemen (agents) – the owners of a huge business are unable to serve all the clients themselves.

The simplest form of assistance during a contract formation is to employ a *messenger* to deliver declarations (offers, acceptances etc.) From the structuring of the Contracts Act – the placing of the rule on application of messengers in s. 32(2) of the Act – cf. above 4.9.2 – implies that the messenger's delivery is equivalent to an agreement made by the parties themselves. The messenger situation is, however, close to the area of agency law under which contact between the parties to a contract is established through an *agent* who has been authorized by one of the parties (the *principal*) to act independently with binding effect on the principal.

The most important statutory rules in agency law is *Part II of the Contracts Act on agency, the Contracts Act* and the *Act on Commercial Agents and Travellers*. The three sets of statutory rules are described below in section 6.2, 6.3 and 6.4-6.5, respectively.

The "agent" concept is not restricted to the above categories. The group also comprises *brokers* and other middlemen (estate agents, maritime brokers, commodity brokers, insurance brokers etc.) Section 6.6 below will include a brief mention of brokers and special agency relationships.

The formation of contracts through agents may cause several, diversified legal problems but the most important issue remains *whether the principal will be bound towards the third party under the agreement made by the agent with the third party.*

6.2. Agency – general

An agent (of general description) is a middleman who is authorized to make agreements with third parties in the principal's name and with immediate binding effect on the principal.

The parties to the contract are *the principal and the third party*. Immediately upon contract formation the third party has a claim against the principal (and conversely the third party will incur obligations towards the principal). If the contract is validly made, the third party incurs no liability or rights as towards the agent though his status is different from that of a messenger. Where the third party e.g. accepts towards a messenger the acceptance is not deemed to have been "communicated" – in a contract law sense (cf. s. 2.1.1 above) – until the messenger delivers the acceptance to his employer. Where acceptance is made towards an agent it has been duly communicated when it reaches the agent. The messenger merely operates to communicate the will of his principal whereas an agent – *in relation to the technicalities of contract formation* – and only in that respect, cf. above – is deemed to be the third party's contractual partner.

6.2.1. Agency without special identification

The simplest type of establishing an agency is where A informs B that he is authorized to act for C either in relation to a certain contract relationship, a group of agreements, or generally. Such agency will often be created by *oral* agreement but it retains its informal character even if issued/confirmed *in writing* (which may be desirable for evidence reasons) as long as the parties intend *that the written agreement is not to be shown to third parties.*

The characteristic feature of agency of this type is that the principal has not parted with anything as towards the third party. The principal has not furnished his agent with an outward appearance of authority – in other words, a third party contracting with the agent is referred to believing the latter's statement as to the existence of his authority.

Agency of this character is termed *"agency without special identification"* in Danish law. Sometimes the term *"assignment agency"* may be used, and the term "Section-18-agency" (reflecting the number of the relevant section in the Contracts Act) may also be met.

A third party who is approached by an agent of Section-18-authority will of course always have the possibility of conferring with the principal (e.g. make a phone-call to him) to verify that the person who approaches him has authority to act, but immediately the principal has confirmed the agent's status his authority becomes one of *"special identification"*. The confirmation provides the agency with the necessary appearance of authority and the third party is no longer referred to relying on the agent's representation as to his authority.

6.2.2. Agency of special identification

With the definition of agency without special identification made above in 6.2.1 it goes almost without saying that an agency of *special identification* is characterized by having an *external appearance towards third parties so that third parties are not referred to rely on the agent's representation of his authority.*

Agency of special identification may be created in various ways, *not limited to those mentioned in Part II of the Contracts Act.*

As mentioned in the preceding an agency of special identification may be created by *special communication to the third party in question*, cf. s. 13 of the Contracts Act.

Agency of special identification may also be created by *public announcement,* cf. s. 14 of the Contracts Act. When a company gives an employee power of procuration such power will be registered with the Commercial and Company Agency and thus be publicly announced (in the official Gazette, Statstidende).

Where the principal furnishes the agent with *written authority*, a *power of attorney*, and this document is designed to remain in the agent's possession for presentation to third parties, cf. above Section 6.2.1, an agency of special identification is also created, cf. s. 16 of the Contracts Act.

A very important form of agency of special identification is the socalled "*job agency*" – the authority usually inherent in a job description without special mention – cf. s. 10(2) of the Contracts Act. Almost any job will to a limited extent either by statute or by custom entail a certain access to bind the principal, the shop assistant may sell articles, the cashier accept payments, etc.

As mentioned above, agency of special identification may be created in a less traditional manner including passivity. If a business owner has for some time tacitly tolerated that a shop assistant has ordered goods with a supplier on his own he cannot suddenly refuse an order on the grounds that the employee previously acted as a buyer while his real status is only shop assistant. An *implied authority* has been established by the owner's passivity on the previous occasions.

6.2.3. The agent's scope of authority

The *actual authority* of an agent delimits the contracts he can enter with third parties on the directions of the principal. An agent who has been commissioned to sell his principal's car will typically have been instructed that the minimum price he is to ask is e.g. DKK 45,000 in cash payment – this minimum price is his *actual* authority.

The *scope of actual authority* is thus determined by the "signals" *the agent* has received from the principal. The *"apparent authority"* is determined by the signals the agent gives to *third parties*. Where A has informed NN that B is authorized to sell A's car (cf. s. 13 of the Contracts Act and above, 6.2.2) and A has directed B that the car is not to be sold below DKK 45,000 the *scope of B's authority* is defined by what he is to sell (the car, not e.g. A's motor bike) but the limits of his *actual authority* are narrower (the DKK 45,000 minimum price).

With *agency without special identification* the principal has not given signals at all to third parties and for such agency *the scope of actual and apparent authority is the same.*

With agency of *special identification* signals have been issued to third parties and in relation to the authority there will nearly always (as in the car example) be a narrower scope of actual authority, i.e. a minimum price when the agent is selling and a maximum price when he is buying.

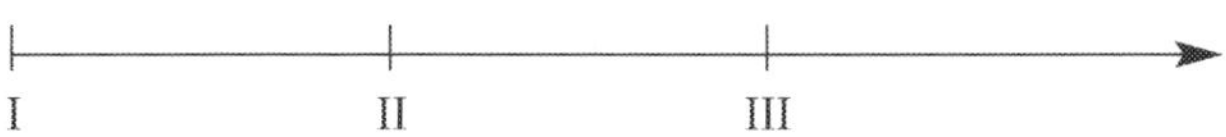

The line I-II illustrates actual authority, II-III the apparent authority.

6.2.3.1. Agency without special identification

For this type of agency there is only one problem, viz. that the agent *exceeds his actual authority* and thus also his apparent since they are identical here). Where this happens the principal is not bound towards the third party *notwithstanding good or bad faith with the third party,* cf. s. 11(2) of the Contracts Act. Since it is just as impossible to guard against an agent's exceeding his authority as it is to guard against forgery (cf. s. 42 and above, Section 4.3) it is only natural that such act will also constitute an operative avoidance factor.

Where the agent acts *within his actual authority* the principal will of course be bound since the agent is only doing what he was asked to do. But exemptions may occur. Where the agent in the car example mentioned above in 6.2.3. sells the principal's car for DKK 45,000 and at the same time receives DKK 1,000 from the buyer (in secret commission) the payment by the buyer is seen as an indication that the agent has failed to look after his principal's best interests and *under such circumstances* the principal will not be bound by the contract made.

6.2.3.2. Agency of special identification

With an agency of special identification the same effect as with agency without special identification will obtain if the agent *exceeds his authority* (e.g. by selling the principal's motor bike instead of the car in the example above) viz. that the *principal will not be bound by the agreement whether the third party was in good or bad faith at the transaction*, cf. s. 10 of the Contracts Act, conversely applied.

Where the agent at the entering of the contract keeps *within his actual authority* again the same effect will obtain – the principal will as an absolute main rule be bound by the agreement with the third party, cf. s. 10 of the Contracts Act.

A particular problem in agency with special identification relates to situations in which the agent *exceeds his actual authority but remains within the scope of his apparent authority* (i.e. he "operates" on the line II-III) e.g. by selling the principal's car for DKK 42,000 in the car example mentioned in 6.2.3). *Where the third party is in good faith,* i.e. he neither knew nor ought to have known that the agent exceeded his authority the principal will be bound towards the third party by the agreement made by the agent, cf. s. 11 of the Contracts Act. Where the third party is in bad faith the principal will not be bound (the concepts of good and bad faith in formation of contract situations are discussed in Section 4.2).

6.2.4. Revocation of authority

An agent's authority may normally be made irrevocable *but in practice most agencies will be revocable.*

The rules governing revocation of authority are set forth in the Contracts Act ss. 12-20. The general rule is that authority is revocable in the same manner as it was created (cf. above Section 6.2.1 and 6.2.2) and that it will normally suffice to revoke authority in such manner – thus, a job authority is revoked by removing the employee from his job. A notification to a third party that authority has been revoked will always be sufficient revocation as towards the third party in question, cf. s. 12(2) of the Contracts Act.

6.2.5. The legal relationship between agent and third party

As mentioned above in 6.2 no legal relationship will arise between agent and third party in the normal course of affairs. The legal relationship arises between *the principal* who acquires immediate rights and incurs obligations *towards the third party* by the agreement made between the agent and the third party.

Where the agent exceeds his authority, however, the principal will not be bound towards the third party (unless the principal accepts the agreement despite the agent's exceeding his authority) cf. above, Section 6.2.3.1 and 6.2.3.2, and such cases are addressed with the very important rule in the Contracts Act s. 25(1) *whereby an agent is to indemnify the third party for any damage/loss which he may suffer by the enforceability of the contract against the principal stated* – thus the agent is liable in damages on *expectation interest basis* (cf. above, Section 4.1). Naturally, the liability under s. 25(1) does not apply where the third party knew or ought to have known that the agent had no authority to conclude the contract he actually made, cf. s. 25(2).

6.2.6. The legal relationship between principal and agent

Part II of the Contracts Act provides no rules regarding the legal relationship between the principal and the agent but several of the provisions mentioned below in Section 6.3.2 in the Factors Act governing the relationship between principal and factor must be deemed to apply correspondingly to ordinary agency relationships.

6.3. Factors

In the same way as an agent acts for his principal's account a factor will act for his principal's account but in contrast to the agent – *in his own name.* Provisions on factors are contained in the Factors Act (Consolicated Act No. 636 of 15 September 1986. In its original drafting the Act was a contempoary of the Contracts Act. Even if factor relationships are now of far less practical importance than they used to be the Act is still important since it represents what may be termed a number of general agency principles in various ways.

The third party dealing with an agent knows that his real contract partner is the principal and if the contract is validly made the third party will only have a claim against *the principal* (cf. above, 6.2 and 6.2.5). Most often a third party dealing with a factor will have no idea that his contract partner is any other than the factor and whether the third party does know or does not know that the factor has a principal behind him the third party will only acquire a claim against the factor, *never against the principal.*

From this follows that it makes a vital difference to a third party whether he contracts with an agent or a factor. Where the third party sues the person he has contracted with on a claim of contract performance *the onus of proof lies with the person in question (the intermediary) in showing that he made it clear to the third party that he acted in another person's name* (i.e acted as agent) which excuses him from performance and means that the claim must be raised against the principal instead.

Several motives may dictate a principal's decision to avail himself of a factor's services rather than an agent's. The factor may e.g. enjoy wider credit access than the principal at the place where there is a market for the article, or the agent himself may claim appointment as a factor instead for competition reasons (he may wish to keep the principal in the dark as regards his business relations). The last consideration is of special importance in *trade* factor relationships i.e. with factors who are professional traders, and the acting as factors is within their course of business, cf. s. 4 of the Factors Act.

6.3.1. The legal position towards third parties

6.3.1.1. Who becomes liable towards third parties?

It follows from what was said in 6.3 that liability towards third parties is with the factor. The factor will be liable for the performance of the contract whereas the third party has no claim against the principal, cf. s. 56 of the Factors Act.

6.3.1.2. The property in goods in the factor's possession

Nothing prevents that a person may authorise another to sell and buy claims as a factor (e.g. a sale of securities via broker) but where reference is made in the following to "goods" (in 6.3.1.2 and below, 6.3.1.5) the reference is to goods in the sense of tangible *"chattels"*.

Goods in the factor's possession belong to the principal. This applies whether the goods involved are delivered to the factor with a view to re-sale, cf. s. 53(1) of the Factors Act, or whether the goods are purchased by the factor himself on the principal's account, s. 53(2).

Thus, a factor's creditors are *debarred from* seizing goods in the factor's possession in execution and in the event of the factor's bankruptcy the creditors must also respect the principal's property in the goods. Where the goods are unascertained (e.g. 500 kilos of King Edward potatoes as opposed to a painting) and the factor is in possession of more specimens of the genus concerned (King Edward potatoes) than the amount equivalent to what belongs to the principal the protection against creditor enforcement requires that an *unconditional appropriation* of the principal's goods has been made (which means that the factor must have appropriated ("earmarked") *the* goods he intends to apply in his performance towards the principal in such manner that he would be in breach as towards the principal if the appropriation was to be ignored.

6.3.1.3. The property in the claim against the third party

Where the factor's function was to sell the principal's goods for which the buyer has paid in cash a problem may arise as to the property in the money paid in, cf. 6.3.1.4.

Where the factor has sold on credit and the buyer has not yet paid the full purchase price a claim will lie against the buyer. *From a legal point of view the claim belongs to the principal – the factor's creditors are barred from levying execution on it.* But as a principal rule, rights against the claim (for its enforcement) lie with the factor, cf. s. 60(1) of the Factors Act which means that the buyer (prima facie) may be discharged by paying to the factor, cf. s. 62 following the view that a buyer often does not realize that his real contract partner could be a person other than the factor, cf. above 6.3.

6.3.1.4. The property in the money paid by the third party

Where the third party has *paid money* to the factor in accordance with an agreement to such effect, cf. above 6.3.1.3, *this payment belongs prima facie to the principal* but obviously the problem of "identification" (the appropriation issue mentioned in 6.3.1.2) is particularly felt with money and in practice this will often mean that the principal's right to the money is not protected against the factor's creditors. – Only where it has been agreed between the principal and the factor that the money is to be kept separate from the factor's other property (e.g. to be deposited in a separate bank account) and this agreement has been observed by the factor will the principal be entitled to claim priority rank as towards the factor's creditors.

6.3.1.5. The factor's unauthorized resale of the principal's goods

As mentioned above in 6.3.1.2 goods in the factor's possession belong to the principal. As regards goods purchased *for* the principal the intention is to deliver it to him, as regards goods *for resale* the principal has nearly always instructed the factor on a minimum price. For both kinds of goods *internal instructions* have been given *("actual authority")* but at the same time the factor is endowed with an *outward appearance* of authority *("apparent authority")* to sell the goods because he holds them in his possession (cf. above, Section 6.2.2 and especially 6.2.3.2 on the (almost) similar problem in agency of special identification.

An issue may arise as to the legal position *if the factor disposes of the goods in his possession in an unauthorized way*, i.e. by selling the goods purchased or going below a minimum price agreed.

For such situations s. 54(1) and (2) provides that it is vital whether the third party with whom the factor has contracted *acted bona fide*. Where the third party at the formation of the contract neither knew nor ought to have known that the factor disregarded the interests of the principal considerably or acted fraudulently towards him, the third party's legal position established by the transaction cannot be challenged.

The solution laid down in s. 54 of the Factors Act regarding the conflict between the principal and the third party also applies to situations in which the factor sells or engages in other unauthorised disposal of the principal's goods *after the termination of his authority* cf. s. 55 of the Factors Act.

6.3.2. The legal relationship between the principal and the factor

The provision mentioned in 6.3.1.5 above in s. 54 of the Factors Act sometimes implies that the principal – *as towards a third party* – will have to accept an agreement under which the factor has considerably disregarded the principal's best interests or even acted fraudulently towards the principal but in such situations the principal may, as towards the factor himself, disclaim the contract – which in practice will mean that the factor is liable to compensate the principal for any loss suffered, cf. ss. 15-16 of the Factors Act.

Otherwise the factor is under a general duty of *indemnity* towards the principal if he is breach of his duties towards him, cf. s. 17.

Prima facie, a factor will not be liable in respect of the third party's performance as towards the principal unless he has agreed to *act del credere* or such liability follows from trade usage or custom. The del credere liability implies that the factor will be personally liable to the principal for the third party's payment performance, cf. s. 14(1) of the Factors Act. Under s. 14(2) the principal may – even if the factor does not act del credere – require the factor to discharge the duties of the third party under the agreement if the factor has failed to notify the name of the third party with whom he has made the contract to the principal in his notification of the making of the contract.

A trade factor is entitled to *commission* on contracts made on behalf of the principal at least when the third party of the contract performs his duties under the contract, cf. s. 27 of the Factors Act. Outside trade factor relationships, the factor will only be entitled to commission where it has been agreed or such practice follows from statute or custom.

Under ss. 31-36 of the Factors Act the factor enjoys a certain right of lien on the goods received, *in security of his claim* against the principal (e.g. for commission, if any, or indemnification for expenses defrayed by him) and a trade factor even has a lien for claims deriving from previous factor arrangements for the principal. The more detailed implications of the lien security are discussed in Theme 5 below.

The Factors Act ss. 40-45 governs the extent and terms under which a factor may take the buyer's place in a sales factoring situation and the seller's place in a purchasing situation – the socalled *contracting for own account*. As it is quite difficult to deal honestly with oneself the access to adopt these functions is very limited.

6.4. Commercial agents

6.4.1. Introduction

With an Act on Commercial Agents and Travellers of 1990 Denmark implemented an EU Council Directive on co-ordination of the Member States' legislation on independent commercial agents. The purpose of the Directive was to create a considerably improved legal position for such agents.

A commercial agent is defined in the Act as an agent who undertakes for another (the principal) *against a consideration, independently and continously* to promote the sale or act in his interests in buying *on the principal's account* by procuring offers (orders) to the principal or making contracts to this effect in the principal's name, cf. s. 2 of the Commercial Agents Act. Thus, the rules on commercial agents in the Act ss. 2-30 will cover not only sales agents (who are largest in number and make up the most important group) and purchasing agents but also independent commercial travellers (separately discussed below Section 6.5). The difference between a commercial agent and a commercial traveller is that the traveller (representative) goes from place to place in his operation whereas a commercial agent has a permanent place of business.

The difference between a commercial agent and a factor is primarily in the factor's trading in his own name for the principal's account *whereas a commercial agent trades in the principal's name*. This applies whether or not the commercial agent has been authorised by the principal to enter into binding contracts with third parties and thus would be authorised as towards such third parties.

The difference between a commercial agent and an ordinary agent is primarily that the commercial agent's primary function is a *sales function* – he is to promote the sale of the principal's goods by establishing a link between production/importation and distribution – whereas the ordinary agent's prime function is to enter into contracts on the principal's behalf. *If* a commercial agent is authorised to enter agreements with third parties the difference between the functions of the two types of intermediaries will disappear in the specific contract formation situations but prima facie *a commercial agent will not be thus authorised*, cf. s. 16(1) of the Act and below, Section 6.4.2.

A *sole distributor* is characterized by having been granted the exclusive right to sell a certain article within a certain geographical area. While a commercial agent sells goods belonging to the principal the sole distributor sells in his own name and on his own account goods which he has bought from the supplier – manufacturer or importer – who granted him the sole distribution rights. The legal position of sole distributors is not governed by the agency law but partly by sale of goods law and partly by unwritten law principles developed in case law, possibly supplemented by agency law views. Incidentally, combinations of sole distributorship and commercial agency activity are quite common in practice so that a business may operate as an agent towards one or more principals while in regard to others it may have distributor status. Where issues arise between the parties the individual concrete relationship will of course determine the legal evaluation.

6.4.2. Will a commercial agent have authority?

As mentioned above in 6.4.1. the creation of an agency relationship *does not* suffice to endow the commercial agent with authority to make contracts which will be binding on the principal, cf. s. 16(1) of the Commercial Agents Act.

Even if an agent becomes authorised to conclude agreements – which he often will to a certain extent – he is not entitled to receive payments for goods sold, to give credit or to allow reductions in the purchase price without special agreement to such effect, cf. s. 20(1) of the Act. Similar rules apply to commercial agents acting as purchasers, cf. s. 20(3).

From s. 21(1) appears that an dissatisfied buyer may make complaints to the commercial agent where such agent has participated in the formation of the sales agreement but the agent cannot decide on such complaint without special authority to do so. Similar rules apply when the contract with the third party concerns purchases of goods for the principal, cf. s. 21(2).

A third party who has entered an agreement with the agent may often – and most often incorrectly – assume that the principal has authorised the agent to make the disposition in question, and therefore the principal is under a duty to give notice to a third party in good faith as to the agent's authority if he does not intend to be bound by the agent's dispositions. S. 16 and s. 20(2) contain separate rules to this effect.

6.4.3. The parties' duty of fidelity

Ss. 4-5 of the Commercial Agents Act provide that the agent is to safeguard the interests of the principal in the exercise of his duties, and that the parties to the agency agreement are under a mutual duty of fidelity and honesty.

Specific mention is made in s. 5(3) of the principal's duty to inform the agent withoin a reasonable time if he may foresee that the agency business will be of considerably less extent than the commercial agent could have contemplated in the normal course of events.

Failure on either side to observe these duties to the contract partner will attract liability in liability in damages to the injured party for the loss sustained thereby, cf. s. 6(1).

6.4.4. The commercial agent's right to commission

A detailed regulation of the agent's right to commission is contained in ss. 8-15 of the Commercial Agents Act.

Under ss. 9 and 10 the commercial agent is entitled to commission on agreements where such agreements are the result of the agent's effort – or if the agent has been entrusted with a certain geographical area or a certain group of customers – and the agreement in question (without resulting from the agent's effort) has been made with a third party belonging to this group/area.

Where a contract for which, in principle, the agent is entitled to receive commission is not performed the agent's claim for commission will lapse if the principal can show that the failure to perform is not due to circumstances within the control of the principal, cf. s. 14(1). Most instances of non-performance will *naturally* be due to the particular third party's incapability to perform his obligations under the contract and thus – under the wording quoted of s. 14(1) the risk of the third party's insolvency will be on the commercial agent.

6.4.5. Competition clauses

A competition clause will only bind the agent if it has been agreed in writing and is restricted to *that* geographical area and *those* products with which the agent has been engaged for the principal, cf. the Commercial Agents Act s. 30(1). The maximum period for such competition clause is two years from the termination of the agency contract, cf. s. 30(2).

For the sake of completeness s. 30(3) provides that a competition clause agreed with a commercial agent may be set aside under the conditions mentioned in s. 38 of the Contracts Act, cf. above 4.12.

6.4.6. *Termination of the agency contract*

The Commercial Agents and Travellers Act further protects commercial agents by providing rules on *termination notices* (ss. 22-23) and in addition to the provisions on termination notices rules of *compensation to the agent at the termination of the contract* (ss. 25-29). This last mentioned set of rules will imply that the agent is entitled to indemnification corresponding to a *maximum of one year's average commission pay* from the principal for his work – if he has procured new clients through his services (or has been instrumental in extending the trade with the existing group of clients considerably and considerable benefits will continue to flow from the connection with such clients. The Act does not contain provisions on compensation for lost investments. Such issues must be determined first and foremost on the basis of the contract between the parties and with due regard to the circumstances surrounding the termination of the contract relationship.

6.4.7. *How far may the rules of the Commercial Agents Act be deviated from?*

Under s. 1(1), 1st clause, of the Act, the rules of the Act may be deviated from by agreement unless otherwise stated in the Act. Apart from the rules in Part III governing employed commercial travellers the rules of the Act *cannot* be deviated from by custom or usage.

The Act is drafted so that for the individual provisions the extent to which they are mandatory is expressly stated. Many rules cannot be deviated from to the prejudice of the agent though a similar restriction presumably does not apply to deviations made to the prejudice of the principal.

The business of commercial agents is often of international character (and extending outside the EU) which means that rules of private international law on commercial agents are necessary – rules which as far as Danish interests are concerned are important both to commercial agents and to Danish undertakings with foreign agents. As regards private international law (or conflict of laws), i.e. the problem relating to which country's law will govern a certain legal issue (the choice of law problem) may be mentioned *that* the main rule of private international law is that the commercial agent's place of business determines which country's law rules must be applied, and that s. 1(2) and (3) of the Commercial Agents Act contain rules regulating the – *comparatively limited* – extent to which it is possible to deviate from the rules in ss. 22 and 25-27 regarding the termination of the agency contract via a choice of law agreement.

6.4.8. *The legal relationship between the commercial agent and the third party*

The Commercial Agents Act does not regulate the legal relationship between the commercial agent and the third party. In practice issues may arise in particular where the agent has claimed an authority (which does not exist) or where he has exceeded his (existing) authority. Such cases will be governed by the principles of s. 25 of the Contracts Act, cf. above Section 6.2.5.

6.5. Commercial Travellers

As mentioned above in 6.4.1 the rules of the Commercial Agents Act ss. 2-30 (and the EU directive which prompted the preparation of the Act) are directly applicable both to commercial agents and *independent* commercial travellers. As regards the concept of commercial travellers reference is made to Section 6.4.1 above.

As regards commercial travellers *under a contract of employment* the Commercial Agents Act contains in Part III (ss. 31-34) as an Appendix to the other rules in the Act – a number of special rules:

A commercial traveller (employed) may not during the course of his functions for the trading house promote the sale of other products or act in purchasing to others, cf. s. 32 of the Act.

As regards commission s. 33 extends a number of the provisions in s. 9-15 in the Act to commercial travellers as well.

In respect of the legal position of the principal (the trading house) towards third parties, s. 34 of the Act provides that the rules in ss. 16-21 regarding the legal position of the principal in agency relationships are correspondingly applied.

6.6. Other intermediaries

The making of contracts through e.g. estate agents and brokers is a good example of the flexibility of the law of agency. In the course of making one single contract such agent may act as both messenger, "ordinary" agent and factor. It is rare, however, that a real estate agent – or broker – will act as factor – despite the popular (legally imprecise) description of real estate agents as "agents having a house on commission" and where such agent – exceptionally – does so act he will normally not have access to the take the buyer's or the seller's place himself (contracting for own account).

The agent's chief function is to establish contact between the parties. If an agreement results he will as a main rule have earned his commission merely on the basis of having established contact. However, the parties will often find it difficult to reach agreement on their own and the agent may then – with an eye to his commission – act as mediator. For this task he will often be commissioned by one party to make an offer, sometimes with authority to draft it within defined limits. *Such* offer will be binding on the party in question as if he had made it himself but this does not imply an authority per se for the agent to actually make the contract himself. In most instances an estate agent will have messenger status so that he is to bring the reply to the offer to his client (principal) and only when the reply has come that far will it be considered communicated, cf. ss. 2 and 3 in the Contracts Act and above, 2.1.1.1. It is also possible that the agent has in fact been granted authority to make the agreement on a party's behalf. Such authority is prima facie an authority without special identification. Finally, the possibility of the agent's acting as factor cannot be *completely* excluded but as already mentioned this will be a rare occurrence.

Agents are found in many professions, sometimes under the description of brokers. In some cases their activities are regulated by special legislation, e.g. in regard to insurance agents in Consolidated Order No. 680 of 15 August 2002 on insurance provision and to real estate agents Consolidated Order No 691 of 2 July 2003 on conveyancing of real estate, cf. below Chapter 16, Section 3.3.

CHAPTER 8

Sale of Goods

by Bent Iversen

1. Introduction

A sales agreement is an agreement on the transfer of a property asset against a money consideration. The contract is an example of a synallagmatic agreement, i.e. an agreement which – in contrast to a gift disposition – imposes a duty on both parties to provide something in exchange for the other party's performance.

Both a transfer of full property in an asset and transfer of socalled limited rights and interests, e.g. of a security right, will be covered by the definition. Contracts on transfer of e.g. copyright, patent rights, goodwill etc. will also be comprised by the rules governing sales. On the other hand contracts of *conveyancing of real property* will be outside the scope of the Act, cf. s. 1a(1) of the Sale of Goods Act. Several provisions of the Act may, however, be analogously applied to such agreements.

In principle, a contract of *exchange* (barter) will be outside the definition of sales. The exchange contract differs from a sales contract in that the performance by both parties corresponds to that of a seller's in a sale. Nevertheless the rules governing sales will also be applicable to exchange contracts, cf. s. 2(3) of the Act.

Sales agreements are not conceptually attached to property assets of an economic value. Assets which are merely of sentimental value and which are therefore incapable of assesment in money terms under a general standard may be subject to sale. However, it is required that the property right may be transferred to a buyer and hence that is not inseparable from a certain person.

1.1. The rules on sale

In Danish law the fundamental legislation on sale has for a long time been the Sale of Goods Act of 1906.

In 1980 and 2002 this Act was supplemented by special rules on consumer sale (ss. 72-86). A consumer sale is, cf. s. 4a(1) of the Sale of Goods Act, a sale which is made to a buyer (consumer) from a trader acting in his course of business where the buyer in the main is acting outside his course of business.

The consumer sale rules – ss. 72-86 of the Sale of Goods Act – will be briefly discussed in the following account on sale of goods. The effect of some of the rules on consumer sale is to amend or supplement the ordinary provisions of the Act. This applies e.g. to the rules on the amount of the purchasing price, place of delivery, delay, and in particular to the rules on defects in the goods supplied. In addition, some of the rules of the sale of Goods Act are rendered ineffective as a direct result of the amending and supplementing provisions in the Act. Finally it should be noted that whereas the ordinary rules of the Act are non-mandatory, i.e. applicable only where the parties have not agreed otherwise or trade usage or other usage would dictate their application, cf. s. 1(1), several consumer rules are mandatory to the extent that they cannot be derogated from to the detriment of the consumer, cf. the enumeration in s. 1(2) and the more detailed account in the following.

The rules of the Sale of Goods Act are in many areas supplemented by other legislation. Apart from the Consumer Contracts Act, which is discussed above in Chapter 7, the Credit Contracts Act is of particular relevance to sale of goods. However, the Credit Contracts Act is not limited to sales on credit but comprises all types of credit arrangement, e.g. loan agreements.

Further, with effect from 1 March 1990 the UN Convention on Contracts for the International Sale of Goods (CISG) was introduced into Danish law and it now follows from s. 1a(4) of the Danish Sale of Goods Act that its rules will not apply to sales comprised by the international Sale of Goods Act. The Convention will be applicable to sales of goods contracts between parties having their place of business in different states, i.e. when the sale is of international character. The rules on international sale are discussed below in Chapter 9.

1.2. The Sale of Goods Act

1.2.1. Non-mandatory and mandatory rules

Apart from the rules on consumer sale, the rules of the Sale of Goods Act are non-mandatory (i.e. they may be derogated from) cf. s. 1(1) and will therefore only apply in the absence of contrary agreement or contrary implication in the contract, or where trade custom or usage does not imply otherwise.

In s. 1(1) the important view is stated that the common rules of the Act are not designed to settle all legal issues in connection with a sales agreement with binding effect. Apart from the fact that the Act only addresses the legal relationship between buyer and seller and only exceptionally includes the relationship of third parties its provisions will be subsidiary to any agreements between the parties (implied or express), including standard contracts, and also to customs and usages within individual lines of business or trade life in general.

In contrast, most of the rules on consumer sales in s. 72-86 are mandatory (not to be derogated from) and the mandatory character has been extended to a number of the ordinary rules when such rules regulate sales in a consumer setting, cf. s. 1(2).

1.2.2. Sale of specific goods and generic goods

An important distinction is the distinction between contracts for the sale of individually ascertained goods ("specific" goods) and contracts for the sale of unascertained goods ("generic" goods – where the subject matter is classified on the basis of "genus").

> In a sale of specific goods the seller can only perform the contract by delivering the object appointed in the contract. Similarly the buyer will be barred from claiming another object than that with which the seller is to perform. To illustrate: The seller S has agreed to sell his car of the make "Fiat" to the buyer B. S has no other car at his disposal which B is cognisant of.

A contract for the sale of unascertained goods implies that the seller is to deliver one or more objects appointed by the genus. In such contracts the seller is entitled to choose the subject-matter of the contract for his performance. To illustrate: S has undertaken to deliver 10 specimens of some standardised manufactured goods which are also available from other suppliers.

The examples illustrate that the distinction between "specific" and "generic" is not so much related to the properties of the subject matter of sale as to the way in which *the contract* has been concluded.

The distinction is important in several respects, cf. i.a. below on the passing of risk (s. 17 and s. 37) for the determination of the circumstances under which the seller will incur liability in damages on breach, cf. below ss. 23 and 24 and ss. 42-43, and for the determination of the seller's duty of specific performance and his right/duty to make redelivery, respectively.

The Sale of Goods Act provides some guidance for the interpretation of the distinction in the wording of s. 3, expressly applying the rules for unascertained goods not only to goods of a stated genus but also to sales of a certain quantity stated, i.e. socalled "semi-generic" sales. To illustrate: The seller is to deliver 1,000 bottles of wine from a certain wine region in France.

The relationship between the parties may be changed so that the seller's freedom of choice in a sale of generic goods is replaced by a duty to deliver specific goods. This situation may arise e.g. when certain objects have been appropriated to the buyer and sent to him.

1.2.3. Contracts for the supply of goods to be produced or manufactured upon specification

Sales contracts for the supply of goods to be manufactured or produced where goods are to be made according to given specifications are comprised by the Act, cf. s. 2(1) 1st clause, if most of the material etc. to be applied in the making of the product is to supplied by the party who undertook the preparation. Therefore the Act is applicable where e.g. a company has undertaken to supply a machine on specifications issued by a client (the buyer) if the company is to supply the materials for the construction of the machine. However, if the material to be applied in the process is in the main to be supplied by the party ordering the machine the arrangement will be outside the scope of the Sale of Goods Act. Nor is the Act applicable to contracts for the repair of goods even if the party who undertakes the repair is to supply spare parts etc. for the purpose. Finally, s. 2(1), 2nd clause, exempts contracts for the "erection of buildings or other establishment on real property". Such agreements will normally be categorized as construction contracts to which separate regulation applies.

In consumer sale, after the amendment of the Act in 2002, the application of the Sale of Goods Act under s. 2(1) has been changed so that sales contracts for the supply of goods to be produced/manufactured are now covered by the Act disregarding whether the seller or buyer (consumer) supplies the material necessary for the production of the subject–matter of sale involved.

1.2.4. Commercial Sale and other sale

A "commercial sale" relates to a sale between traders undertaken within or on behalf of their enterprise, cf. s. 4(1) and, as to the group of persons defined as traders, cf. s. 4(2). A sale which is not defined as a commercial sale, e.g. a sales agreement between two private individuals, has no special designation in the Sale of Goods Act but is usually described as a civil sale. When one of the parties (the seller) is a trader the rules on consumer sale apply.

The provisions governing commercial sales impose duties on the trader which are more onerous than those imposed on a non-trader. This applies e.g. to s. 6 (on notice towards invoices sent), s. 16 (on the buyer's duty to pay against delivery of documents), s. 21(3) and s. 28 (on delay), and ss. 27, 32, 51-52(1) (on notice requirements generally).

The background for imposing stricter rules e.g. on notice duties is that it will often occur in a commercial sale that a trader, A, who is to receive an article from another trader, B, has already re-sold the article before B has actually delivered it. Therefore it is important for A to know without delay whether he must make a covering purchase or take other measures to counteract the effect of B's possible breach.

2. Duties of the parties

2.1. Duties of the seller (delivery)

The seller's main duty in relation to the contract of sale is described in the Act as the duty to "deliver".

There is no express definition of the requirements under which a seller will be deemed to have performed his duty to deliver. The failure to define "delivery" is explained by the fact that for the purposes of the Act delivery is no unequivocal concept. It will depend on the agreement of the parties including whether the subject-matter of sale is to be collected by the buyer or sent from one place to another etc. Sometimes performance of the duty to deliver requires only a minimum of activity on the seller's part, e.g. if the subject-matter of sale is already in the custody of the buyer or if the seller is merely obliged to keep it ready for the buyer's own collection. In other circumstances – as dictated by the agreement – delivery will require a greater effort from the seller, e.g. if he has undertaken to bring the goods to the buyer's place of business or if he is to make arrangements with an independent carrier about the dispatch of the goods to the buyer.

A general description of the requirements of delivery must therefore be limited to saying that delivery is the total amount of acts on the seller's part required to put the buyer in possession of the subject-matter of sale in a proper manner. It is specifically emphasized that handing over and delivery will not always coincide.

2.1.1. Place of delivery

In the absence of contrary agreement, including the "special clause sales" below – the sale is one of collection. The buyer is to collect the goods sold at the place of residence of the seller at the time of sale or – if he had a business at that time and the sale is related to such business – at the seller's place of business, cf. s. 9(1). If the goods were at another place at the time of agreement than the seller's place of residence or business and the parties knew or ought to have known this, such other place is deemed to be place of delivery, cf. s. 9(2).

The rule in s. 9 corresponds to the rule in the Promissory Notes Act s. 3(1) whereby "money debts are debts to bring and *other debts* are to collect".

If the seller – in accordance with agreement with the buyer – is to see to the dispatch of the subject matter to the buyer to a destination within the limits of the "place", delivery is effected when the subject matter has been brought into the buyer's possession at the destination stated, cf. s. 11. The term "place" is defined as the area within which the goods are regularly brought out by the seller or his employees. Where the seller elects to employ the services of an independent agency of messengers the handing over to the buyer within the place will still constitute delivery.

In the same way as the main rule in s. 9, s. 11 will bring delivery and the physical handover to the buyer to coincide. In the absence of contrary agreement or custom the subject- matter of sale is to be transferred to the buyer's or his representative's possession and hence it will not normally suffice to place it at close quarters to the buyer's place, e.g. with a neighbour.

In a simple "dispatch sale", cf. s. 10, the goods are to be sent *beyond* the limts of the "place" according to the agreement of the parties or to custom.

S. 10 is applicable when the seller is to dispatch the goods to the buyer but no particulars have been agreed as to the place of delivery nor is there a custom to be traced on the subject. In such instances the dispatch will not be made on the seller's or his employees' arrangement and delivery is therefore deemed to have been effected when the *independent* carrier who has undertaken the forwarding from the place or, where dispatch is to be made by ship, when the goods have been brought on to the ship. The rule of delivery being effected when the goods are on the ship is to be applied whenever the first part of the carriage away from the place of delivery is to be made by ship and is unaffected by subsequent transportation by road. Where the seller instead of employing an independent carrier transports the goods himself to the buyer, delivery will not be effected until the goods are transferred to the buyer's custody either at his place of residence or at his place of business.

Where the seller leaves the carriage to an independent carrier the requirements under s. 10 are not satisfied until the carrier has received the goods and undertaken their transportation away from the place of dispatch (i.e the seller's place). Hence delivery is not deemed to be effected if the goods are handed over to a local carrier who has only undertaken the transportation within the place, e.g. to railway station or ship, in order to make the contract for further transportation there. On the other hand, the independent carrier need not have undertaken the transportation to the buyer's end completely but the seller may have agreed with the carrier that the goods may be brought to the buyer without further arrangement on the seller's part, e.g. if a carrier in Jutland has undertaken the transportation to Hamburg on the instructions of sending the goods from there by ship to e.g. Australia.

The costs of transporting the goods to the place of delivery are – unless otherwise agreed – to be paid by the seller whereas the buyer will pay the costs of transportation from the place of delivery. The seller will only be entitled – or obliged – to insure the goods for the buyer's account when agreed or such practice follows from custom.

In a consumer sale the provisions in ss. 10-11 are replaced by the provision in s. 73. If the seller has undertaken to send the goods to the buyer, delivery will – under s. 73 – be deemed to have been effected when the goods have been placed in the buyer's possession. When no agreement has been made on forwarding of the goods the rule in s. 9 will continue to apply also in consumer sale and delivery will be made on transfer of the goods to the buyer at the seller's place of business.

2.1.2. Transport terms

Trade life has developed a number of terms whereby the provisions of individual legislations as to delivery place, distribution of costs between buyer and seller, insurance issues etc. have been supplemented or amended.

A number of these transport terms have been collected and published by the International Chamber of Commerce (ICC) under the designation of *"Incoterms"*. The purpose of Incoterms is to offer contract parties in international trade a set of delivery terms which may be used by the parties to their own advantage hereby reducing the importance of any dissimilarities between the national delivery rules. When the parties have agreed to apply a term stated in "Incoterms" such dissimilarities may be disregarded since they have thereby adopted the interpretation of Incoterms which will govern any disputes concerning delivery etc. Incoterms are described in more detail in Chapter 9.

The Danish Sale of Goods Act also contains interpretation guidance in respect of some of the delivery clauses occurring in practice, cf. ss. 62-65. The transportation clauses of the Sale of Goods Act are not quite identical to those following from Incoterms and it is therefore necessary to specify in the sales contract whether a term is to be interpreted in accordance with the Sale of Goods Act or with Incoterms.

"FOB" – free on board, Sale of Goods Act, s. 62:

When goods are sold FOB from a stated place (the place of dispatch) the buyer is to charter ship or reserve shipping space for the carriage of the goods from that place, cf. s. 62(1).

> The seller's duty is to arrange and pay for the carriage of the goods to the place of dispatch and make such arrangement regarding their loading as is

incumbent on a carrier under the local law in force or according to custom, cf. s. 62(2).

In other words the place of delivery is the port of shipment and the seller is discharged (also in relation to further transportation costs) when the goods are on to the ship appointed by the buyer, cf. s. 62(3).

If the goods are to be sent to the port of shipment from another place, e.g. "Viborg FOB Hamburg" the FOB term will cause a derogation from the rule in s. 10 as the place of delivery has been moved from "handing over to independent carrier" in Viborg to the port of shipment in Hamburg.

"Cost & freight", "C & F", "cf" *– s. 63 of the Sale of Goods Act:*
When this term is used the *seller* is to see to chartering and payment of costs in this respect up to the place of destination and the seller will also bear the costs of transportation accommodation, cf. s. 63(1).

There is no express mention in s. 63 of the exact place of delivery which is relevant when the port of shipment is not the same as the place of dispatch. In that case place of delivery must be determined under the rule in s. 10 which implies that delivery has been effected upon handing over to an independent carrier at the place of dispatch. In contrast, in overseas trade it is considered customary for the port of shipment to constitute place of delivery even if the goods are – in the first place – to be sent from a place within the country.

"CIF" (cost, insurance, freight) – Sale of Goods Act s. 64:
The CIF term is interpreted in accordance with the C & F term except that the seller is to take out customary insurance for the part of the carriage which is after delivery.

The CIF term has been a popular term in overseas trade. From the buyer's point of view the term has the advantage that he is able to calculate in advance what the goods will actually cost him since all cost of their carriage to the place of destination are included in the price, and he may already before the goods have arrived calculate the price at which he may sell them.

"Franco" – Sale of Goods Act s. 65:
Under this term, the seller is to arrange and pay for the carriage of the goods to their place of destination which is also the place of delivery, cf. s. 65(1).

2.1.3. *Time of delivery*

Usually the time of delivery will be expressed in the contract of sale but it is also possible that circumstances will indicate prompt performance. This will often be the case when a buyer orders goods to be sent to him without indication of time. When the time for performance cannot be inferred from the agreement delivery shall be effected upon demand, cf. s. 12, i.e. the seller may postpone delivery until the buyer demands him to effect it.

Where there is a *time span* agreed for delivery to take place, e.g. "in November 2004", etc., the seller is free to fix time of delivery within this span of time unless circumstances indicate that the time span has been granted in the buyer's interest. This will e.g. be the case if the buyer is to arrange shipping space within the time span stated.

Expressions such as "in the beginning of", "mid-", or at the end of" a month are defined in s. 68(1) as: from 1-10, from 11-20 and 21 to the last day of the month respectively.

2.1.4. *The seller's performance*

The seller is to deliver the goods in their contractual state (i.e. "conforming to" the contract). What it takes to satisfy this requirement is primarily determined by the contract between the parties.

In a sale of specific goods the meaning of contractual performance is rarely in issue. In the absence of contrary agreement the goods are to be delivered in the state in which they were at the conclusion of the contract. Performance is not "contractual" if the goods lack properties expressly or implicitly warranted by the seller.

In a sale of generic goods the seller is – unless otherwise agreed – to deliver goods of a medium quality.

Usually there is no problem in deciding what the seller's main duty of performance consists of. It will normally be described in the agreement of sale with sufficient clarity or follow from the implied terms of the contract. A buyer of a car will normally be entitled to expect that its various components (engine, wheels, mudguards, etc.) are comprised by the agreement. The settlement of his secondary duties in respect of the sale may be more difficult and it may also be doubtful whether the agreed price covers the seller's assistance in the form of instructions in the use of the goods etc.

Generally, these questions are not solved in the Sale of Goods Act but in a few special areas the Act contains gap-filling rules as to the extent of the seller's performance.

As regards benefits/interests accruing from the goods, s. 18 contains a rule whereby benefits, such as a regular income from a renting of the goods, and a less regular income, e.g. bonus from a life insurance policy, etc. gained before delivery will devolve upon the seller. This does not apply, however, where the benefit could justly have been anticipated not to accrue until at a later time.

Benefits accruing after delivery devolve upon the buyer unless they could justly have been anticipated to accrue earlier. The term of delivery used in s. 18 denotes the term of delivery agreed where this term is a term other than the actual term of delivery which would be the normal thing to stress, cf. e.g. below on the passing of risk.

As regards dividends on shares or interest on written claims rules are provided in s. 19 and s. 20.

Where the extent of the performance required by the seller contains a certain latitude (about, approx., from/to ... etc.) s. 66 provides a gap-filling rule. S. 66 only applies to generic goods and will regulate latitude specifications for the quantity of the goods but not e.g. derogations from the time of delivery.

2.1.5. Passing of risk

The seller's duty is to deliver the goods in a contractual state, at the due time and at the proper place. When this has happened the seller's duties are discharged.

A buyer who does not receive his goods in due time or receives goods which are not conforming because of actual or legal defects will normally be entitled to *cancel* the agreement of sale, even if the delay in the delivery of the goods (or their destruction) or the non-conformity is attributable to circumstances beyond the control of the seller or his employees.

But since the remedy of the buyer of cancelling the agreement implies that he will thereby escape the duty to pay the price for the goods to the seller even if the defective performance is beyond the seller's control, it is necessary to set a timelimit within which the buyer may avail himself of such remedy. For the purposes of the Sale of Goods Act, s. 16(1) fixes *delivery* as the timelimit for the buyer's avoidance of the agreement when the lack of performance or defective performance is due to circumstances beyond the seller's control.

For it follows from s. 17(1) that the buyer shall bear the risk of the accidental destruction or depreciation of the goods when delivery has been made. S. 17(2) defines the implications of the buyer's bearing of the risk, viz. *that he will have to pay the purchase price even if the goods are accidentally lost or their value depreciated.* On the other hand, s. 17(2) does not mention the implication of the *seller's* bearing the risk (until delivery). However, it follows from other provisions in the Sale of Goods Act, including in particular s. 21 and ss. 42-43, that the buyer will normally still have the remedy of avoiding the agreement of sale, claim damages etc.

For the purposes of s. 17 accidental events means circumstances beyond both parties – and their employees' – control. Therefore the buyer will retain his remedy of avoidance if the goods are destroyed or deteriorated by fire before delivery even if a third party without the seller's knowledge started the fire. Conversely, the seller may claim the purchase price if the goods are destroyed or deteriorated in similar circumstances *after* delivery, e.g. after the goods – in a FOB sale – cf. s. 62 of the Sale of Goods Act, had been loaded on to the ship.

But where the destruction or deterioration of the goods is attributable to the seller or his employees the buyer will keep his remedy of avoidance and any other remedies for breach *notwithstanding that delivery has been made*. This will apply e.g. where the seller or his employees in pursuance of the agreement of sale – after delivery – undertook the supervision of the goods during their further transportation and in that process negligently caused them to be damaged.

The use of the term "delivery" in s. 17(1) is addressed at the actual implementation of the measures of delivery and not at the time of delivery agreed.

In situations covered by s. 17(2) and s. 37 the risk may pass from seller to buyer even if delivery has not yet been made, and under s. 58 the buyer may avoid a sale even if he himself – on the basis of the main rule in s. 17 – was to bear the risk of accidental destruction of the goods.

In s. 17(2) the sale relates to specific goods which are to be collected by the buyer. Where the time has arrived when the goods could be collected under the agreement of sale and they are kept ready for collection the buyer will bear the risk and will have to pay the purchase price even if they are accidentally lost or deteriorated. This may be illustrated by the following example:

The buyer B has made an agreement with S for the sale of a specific article which B is to collect himself at S' place of business "in the course of January 2005". In other words, the article may be collected on 1 January at the earliest and "must" be collected on 31 January at the latest. If S is ready to hand out the article in a contractual state e.g. on 1 January the risk will pass to the buyer from that date. Therefore, if the article during this period is subject to deterioration or destruction as a result of events outside the control of S, B will be obliged to pay the full purchase price even if he gets nothing in exchange or at best a less valuable article.

The direct application of s. 17(2) is for the sale of specific goods only and an analogous application of the rule to sale of generic goods will normally be excluded. The provision presupposes that the sale (as in the example) is a sale of collection (s. 9) and that a margin has been agreed within which the buyer may collect the goods.

S. 17(2) is not applicable to *consumer sales,* cf. s. 1a(3). The risk of accidental destruction or deterioration of the goods will not, in a consumer sale, pass to the buyer until actual delivery, i.e. in correspondence with s. 17(1). If the buyer fails, before the expiry of a period during which the seller is contractually bound to await the buyer's collection of the goods – to appear to collect the goods at all, there is a situation of *"claimant's non-performance"*, cf. s. 37 of the Sale of Goods Act. Also, in a consumer sale, the risk in such respect may pass to the buyer before delivery has been made.

Another exception from the main rule in s. 17(1) regarding passing of risk is the provision just described in s. 37.

S. 37 relates to situations of *claimant's non-performance*, i.e. instances in which the seller is *entitled* to discharge himself from his obligation to deliver. To illustrate: The goods are to be delivered at the buyer's place of business on a certain date. The seller takes measures to perform his duty to deliver but delivery fails because of factors within the buyer's control, e.g. lack of requisite storage space, or because he simply cannot be reached at the time of delivery when the seller tries to hand over the goods. The buyer's non-performance will attract a number of special legal effects to the benefit of the seller. One of these effects is that the risk in respect of the goods, as mentioned in s. 37, passes to the buyer.

S. 37 applies to sale of specific and generic goods alike. For the latter the passing of risk is, however, dependent on the seller's advance identification of the subject matter appropriated for contract performance, e.g. by a marking of the goods in such manner that no justified doubt may arise that the accidental event hit exactly those goods which were destined for the buyer in question.

A third and last exemption from the rule on passing of risk in s. 17(1) follows from s. 58.

S. 58 provides that the risk remains with the seller even after delivery if the buyer in accordance with the rules subsequently mentioned may avoid the sale. To illustrate: The seller has delivered non-conforming goods to the buyer who informs the seller that he wishes to avoid the sale on that ground. Before the seller has collected the goods – or before the buyer has made arrangements with a view to their re-delivery to the seller – the goods are stolen from the buyer's place of business without fault on the part of the buyer in relation to the theft. Under s. 58 the "destruction"/loss of the goods under such circumstances presents no bar to the buyer's remedy of avoidance even if he is incapable of surrendering the goods. For the buyer's (justified) avoidance of the contract will cause the risk to pass to the seller.

2.2. Duties of the buyer

The buyer's duty is normally to pay a money consideration to the seller at the due time at the right place.

Most often the parties will have agreed expressly the *amount* of the purchase price. Where this is not the case and no custom or usage can be traced in the area in question the buyer is to pay what the seller demands if such price is reasonable, cf. s. 5.

S. 5 does not apply to *consumer sales*. Instead s. 72 will apply whereby the customer in the same situation is to pay what must be deemed reasonable having regard to the nature and quality of the goods. The point in time relevant for the assessment of the reasonableness of the price is the conclusion of the contract. Any price increases which have occurred during the period between conclusion of the contract and delivery will not affect the price the consumer is to pay even if an exact price was not agreed in advance.

As regards *commercial sales*, s. 6 contains a special rule on the price. If the seller has sent the buyer an invoice the buyer is bound to give notice to the seller forthwith if he intends to challenge the amount on the grounds that a lower price was agreed than that appearing from the invoice. If he fails to give such notice he must pay the amount of the invoice unless he can show that a lower price was agreed or the price stated is obviously unreasonable. The buyer is under the same duty as regards other items, naturally listed in an invoice, such as e.g. place of payment, arrangements as to packing etc.

Where it has been agreed that the price is to computed on the basis of number, measures or weight, the quantity of the subject matter of sale at the time of passing of risk shall be relevant basis for the computation, cf. s. 7. This provision is an equivalent to that in s. 44 relating to the point in time which is relevant in the assessment of the conformity of the goods.

Where the purchase price is computed on the weight of the goods delivered, s. 8 contains a gapfilling rule whereby the weight of the packing ("tara weight") shall be deducted. This rule will often have been derogated from, so that the packing is to paid for "as the goods" (gross for net) or so that the weight of the packing is not be computed at its real amount (net tara) but on another basis (uso tara).

2.3. Temporal context between the duties of the parties

2.3.1. Cash sales

The synallagmatic character of the contract of sale implies that the parties are prima facie to perform at the same time, i.e. on a "performance against performance" basis. In pursuance of this principle the Sale of Goods Act provides that unless otherwise agreed or following from custom a sale is for cash.

Contracts whereby the seller allows the buyer to defer payment are credit sales, e.g. a sale with reservation of title, whereas a sale of advance payment means that the buyer is to pay the purchase price in full or in part before having the subject matter of sale placed at his disposal.

Ss. 14-16 govern cash sales and comprise all instances in which the performance of the parties is to be exchanged at the same time, i.e. also situations in which the simultaneous performance has been deferred till later.

The cash principle (performance against performance) follows from s. 14. Where no deferment has been granted from either party the seller is not bound to deliver the goods unless the price for them is paid at the same time and conversely, the buyer is not bound to pay unless he receives the goods at the same time.

The principle of s. 14 must be seen in conjunction with the rules of the Act relating to who is to take the initiative for the "discharge" of the sale, cf. s. 9, whereby the buyer is to collect the goods from the seller (collection sale), and s. 11 (delivery at buyer's address) i.e. a sale whereby the seller at the place of performance (the buyer's place of residence or business) is to offer to hand over the goods to the buyer. In both cases delivery of the goods will coincide with the actual handing over to the buyer and the buyer will therefore be capable of – and generally also entitled to – make an examination of the goods before paying the purchase price.

When the seller has undertaken to send the goods from the place of delivery (s. 10 and ss. 62-64) the simultaneous performance principle of s. 14 is not possible. The execution of the sale would be blocked if the seller was allowed to refuse to send the goods because he had not received the price. For such sales s. 15 will therefore apply, under which the seller, if the goods are to be sent from the place of delivery, is barred from omitting to send them but may prevent that they are handed over to the buyer. The difference from s. 14 is that the seller is to take the initiative for the discharge of a dispatch sale. In return he will have the right to make the surrender of the goods to the buyer dependent on payment of the purchase price. The only deviation in s. 15 from s. 14 is that the provision imposes upon the seller a duty to send the goods without the simultaneous exchange of the price but the provision is not contrary to the rule in s. 14 regarding the buyer's access not to pay before the goods are placed at his disposal. The buyer's access to examine the goods before payment will be the same, prima facie, as under s. 14. On the other hand, if the seller employs an independent carrier and sends the goods direct to the buyer, he can only completely ensure that payment is concurrent with handing over to the buyer if he stipulates cash on delivery (COD). Such dispatch method will often make it impossible for the buyer to examine the goods before payment and therefore the seller may only employ such dispatch – outside commercial sale, cf. immediately below – if it has been agreed with the buyer or follows from custom. Therefore if the seller wants to unite the buyer's interest in access to examination of the goods with his own interest in not handing them over except against cash payment he may send them to a forwarding agency instead who will see to the handing over of the goods on his behalf to the buyer after the buyer has had an opportunity to examine them.

In commercial sales there is a special "cash against documents" rule. Where, in a commercial sale a bill of lading (B/L) or consignment note is used in the dispatch of the goods from delivery place to destination place and the document is of such character that the seller can no longer dispose of the goods after delivery of the document to the buyer, the purchase price is, under s. 16 to be paid against delivery of the relevant document in accordance with the rules in s. 71. The same rule applies when the buyer is expressly bound to pay against documents, cf. s. 71, and when the dispatch is made under one of the transport clauses previously mentioned.

The dispatch documents capable of releasing the buyer's duty to pay must be of such nature that the seller is unable to dispose of the goods after their handing over to the buyer. Only in that case will the buyer pay the purchase price without risking that the seller gets a possibility of reclaiming the goods.

This effect is attached to Bills of Lading, i.e the receipts in respect of loaded cargo and cargo accepted for transportation issued by the carrier (shipowner) in pursuance of ss. 292-307 of the Maritime Act and to e.g. international CMR consignment notes. The dispatch documents must be accompanied by an invoice for the goods and insurance policy, if any, cf. s. 71(2).

From s. 71 follows that a clause involving cash against Bill of Lading will deteriorate the buyer's legal position in that the goods sold have not yet arrived – or he has no access of examining them before his payment against receiving the documents.

2.3.2. Special note on documentary credits

A seller granting credit may risk that the buyer fails to pay on the due date. When the purchase price is not paid the seller must contemplate suing the buyer with the inconvenience and risk involved of having to pay the costs of proceedings himself. Especially where the buyer lives in another country, legal proceedings may be both difficult and expensive. If the buyer refuses to pay on account of alleged defects in the goods, the seller will also need to contemplate whether a lawsuit is worth the expense. To this may be added that under s. 28(2) the main rule is that a seller is incapable of avoiding a sale and reclaiming the goods once they have been handed over to the buyer.

In a cash sale the seller may ensure that he receives his payment at the handing over of the goods. In a dispatch sale the seller may protect himself e.g. by having the goods addressed to a forwarding agent at the buyer's place. Further, he may have a bank act as "debt collector" by agreeing with the buyer on terms of cash against documents. Notwithstanding, the seller may risk that the buyer fails to pay and that the goods must therefore be sold elsewhere or stored with the risk of suffering a loss in consequence. If the seller wishes to protect himself against such risk he may arrange for the payment to be by way of *documentary credit* which is widely used in export trade.

The procedure in a documentary credit is that the buyer approaches his bank – the "opening bank" – with the sales contract asking the bank to open a letter of credit in the favour of the seller. The opening bank informs their connection at the seller's place – the "advising bank" – that a documentary credit has been opened and of the terms governing it. Subsequently the seller is notified by the advising bank. The seller now brings the goods to the ship (or other transportation means) and receives the carrier's acknowledgement of receipt of the goods by way of e.g. a Bill of lading. When the seller hands over the Bill of Lading and the other documents on the goods to the advising bank, the bank will, if a cash sale is involved, pay him the purchase price. The documents are sent by the advising bank to the opening bank and when the buyer pays the amount of the credit here, he will receive the documents and thus receive the goods. The Bill of Lading may be said to be "the key to the cargo".

Documentary credits and effects are discussed below in Chapter 9.

3. Seller's Breach

When the buyer fails to receive the agreed subject matter of sale at the right time or the goods fall short of the buyer's justified expectations a breach has normally occurred affording special remedies to the buyer. Where the defective performance is due to the buyer's circumstances. e.g. where, contrary to s. 9, he fails to collect the goods with the seller, or where he is not ready, as he should be under s. 11 in case the seller was to deliver the goods at buyer's address, such "claimant's default" will not entitle the buyer to regard the contract as breached on the seller's part. The rules on "claimant's default" are mentioned below. Nor will a failure to perform which is caused by a fortuitous event and setting in at a point in time in which the goods are at the buyer's risk entitle the buyer to claim that the seller is in breach.

Apart from these exceptional cases, the starting point in the Sale of Goods Act is, however, that the seller's failure to deliver the goods at the right time, at the right place and in the right manner, will release special remedies to the buyer's advantage. Thus, the contract issue is *which* remedies the buyer may rely upon.

The Sale of Goods Act distinguishes between three types of breach on the seller's part – delay, defects in the goods, and defective title. Therefore, it would seem that this structure of distinguishing is more convenient to follow than one based on the various remedies available.

3.1. Delay

The relationship of mutuality between buyer/seller means that the buyer (in a cash sale) is entitled to retain the purchase price upon the seller's non-delivery at the due time. Delay from the seller also entitles the buyer to the following remedies: he may still claim delivery (affirm the contract), he may cancel the sale (avoid the contract) and claim damages.

For the purposes of the Sale of Goods Act there is delay not only when the goods are not at the place of delivery until after the time of delivery agreed upon but also when the goods are never delivered, e.g. if they are destroyed/lost, hit by export bans etc.

3.1.1. Affirming the contract

The buyer's remedy of affirming the contract against payment of the purchase price follows from s. 21(1). The provision does not state the terms under which the buyer may claim this remedy. But it is evident that the buyer is incapable of affirming the contract if performance has become impossible, e.g. because the subject matter of sale (of which there was only one specimen) has been destroyed in a fire (sale of specific goods). In a sale of generic goods impossibility will only arise if there are no (longer) goods available equivalent to those agreed (impossibility of genus).

Apart from these extreme cases the buyer could, notwithstanding the delay, find it relevant to affirm the contract if the price of goods of the kind anticipated in the contract has risen after the conclusion of the contract since he would then either obtain the subject-matter of sale proper or be entitled to damages based upon the price conditions prevailing at the time at which he is seeking execution of the sale. If, on the other hand, the price has fallen the buyer might find it beneficial to avoid the contract of sale.

3.1.2. Avoiding the contract of sale

The buyer's (justified) avoidance of the contract of sale implies that both parties' right of performance lapses. Where performance has already been made each party must return what he has received. Thus if the buyer has received the goods – albeit too late – he must return them to the seller upon his avoidance of the contract (s. 57). Where the goods have perished the buyer is barred from avoidance unless their destruction was due to a fortuitous event (s. 58). The remedy of avoidance is not to be confused with the buyer's right to withdraw his order or the "cooling off" period granted to consumers by the Act on Certain Consumer Contracts (the "doorstep sales" Act) available to consumers for contracts made in doorstep sales, mail order sales etc.

Avoidance of the contract on account of delay normally requires that the delay was of *material* importance to the buyer, cf. s. 21(2). In a commercial sale any delay is deemed material, however, unless only a minor part of the quantity sold is affected by the delay, cf. s. 21(3). The "material character" requirement is also derogated from in socalled "fixed" sales i.e. sale in which the buyer has stipulated delivery exactly at a definite time.

In a *consumer sale* the rule granting the buyer the remedy of avoidance for material delay, cannot be derogated from by agreement, cf. s. 74 in conjunction with s. 1(2). Further, s. 74(2) and s. 75 provide that a consumer buyer – irrespective of the material character requirement and irrespective of any reservation made deferring the timelimit of delivery may avoid the contract if the seller fails to deliver the goods upon request before the expiry of a reasonable period of time fixed by the buyer – or where no such period has been fixed, within a reasonable time. There are no special requirements to the drafting of the buyer's notice requesting delivery. The notice, a parallel to which is found in i.a. Art. 47 of *CISG* on "Nachfrist" (below, Chapter 10) must be so specific that the seller may appreciate that the buyer is demanding delivery.

The remedy of avoiding the contract is not dependent on the seller's or his employees' fault in relation to the delay. Normally the buyer may avoid the sale even if the delay is attributable to non-delivery from the seller's supplier, or to other causes, e.g. strike, which the seller could not have foreseen at the conclusion of the contract. It is no requirement for avoidance that the buyer has given notice or warning to the seller in advance.

Sometimes, special circumstances allow the buyer to avoid the contract even before delay has actually occurred. Cases of anticipatory breach (delay) may occur when it is evident that the seller will not be able to perform in due time, e.g. because the subject-matter (in a sale of specific goods) has been destroyed, or where the seller's facilities of production have broken down, or if the seller has positively indicated to the buyer that he has no intention of performing (in due time).

A special effect from anticipatory breach follows from s. 22 governing sales on terms of *delivery by instalments*, i.e. a sale under which the seller is to deliver within stated intervals. The starting point of s. 22 is to consider each delivery as an independent contract in regard to the buyer's remedy of avoidance. However, from s. 22, 2nd clause it follows that the buyer may also avoid future deliveries if a repetition of delay may be expected, i.e. if the buyer may justly infer that similar breaches will take place with regard to the next deliveries. Further, the buyer may avoid the contract in its entirety if such avoidance is founded in the connection between the deliveries (e.g. when a machine is to be delivered in several parts for assembling at the buyer's place).

3.1.3. The remedy of damages

The buyer's interests will not always be absolutely safeguarded even if he is not to pay the agreed purchase price upon his avoidance – or when he recovers the price from the seller.

The seller's breach may well have caused him to suffer a loss and for such situations s. 23 and s. 24 of the Sale of Goods Act governing specific and generic goods respectively provide the terms under which the buyer may claim coverage of such loss from the seller.

The liability basis:

Under s. 23 the seller is liable in damages "unless he can show that the delay is not attributable to him". In tort terms s. 23 expresses a *fault* (or *"culpa")* rule. The seller is liable if he has been at fault but escapes liability if the delay is deemed to arise from accidental causes.

Under the wording of s. 23, the seller is prima facie liable in damages since he must show that he was not at fault to avoid liability. This means a tightening of the rules in relation to normal liability (outside contract) under which the injured party is (normally) to prove the tortfeasor's fault (breach of duty).

However, the seller will not always escape liability by lifting this "reversed burden of proof" and showing that the delay was not attributable to him. The seller will also be liable if the delay was due to the fault of his employees (vicarious liability in the Danish Law 3-19-2) and if the delay was caused by his own financial difficulties. Likewise, the seller is liable if delivery of the subject-matter was impossible already at the conclusion of the contract if he knew or ought to have known of the event making performance impossible.

Under s. 24 a seller of generic goods is liable "even if the delay is not attributable to him". Thus a generic seller's liability is stricter than that of a seller of specific goods. For it is evident already from the liability rule of s. 23 that the seller will be liable unless he has not – before committing himself – undertaken a reasonable inquiry into the possibility of any impediments to delivery in due time. Further it follows from s. 24 that the circumstances which may be relied upon in defence must be of *quite extraordinary character* and relate to factors which no reasonable seller would have contemplated.

Delivery impediments which are peculiar to the seller in question – but not to sellers generally – will not excuse the seller from performance. Therefore, a seller is not excused from performance if e.g. his supplier in a foreign country from whom he had contemplated buying the goods, is hit by export bans when suppliers in other countries are not subject to similar export restrictions. In other words, the impossibility must be outside a seller's contemplation and only quite extraordinary circumstances, such as war etc., will exempt him from liability. In short, the seller only escapes liability under s. 24 under "qualified extraordinary circumstances".

Where the impediment is only temporary the seller's duty to deliver – and hence his liability – will only be suspended. Where the buyer wishes to affirm the contract when the temporary impediment has ceased the seller may therefore be liable if he disregards the buyer's demand for delivery.

> In practice a seller will often have limited his liability for failure to deliver in concrete circumstances and s. 24 itself indicates that such limitation clauses may be applied with the wording "unless he has reserved exemption in such respect".

The measure of damages (the loss):
Upon the buyer's avoidance of the contract the measure of damages available under s. 25 of the Sale of Goods Act is, in the absence of other loss, the *difference in price,* i.e. the difference between the purchase price agreed and the price at the time of delivery for goods of the same sort and quality as the goods sold. The buyer may make a covering purchase on his own and unless contrary evidence is advanced the purchase price in such covering purchase is deemed to represent the market price. Other substantiated loss may also be claimed, e.g. consequential loss.

When the buyer *affirms* the contract he may claim the "time interest", i.e. loss suffered on account of the delay. This includes e.g. expenses incurred in hiring a similar object. Further, he will normally be entitled to claim loss of resale resulting from his own failure to perform a duty to deliver (in due time) as towards a buyer of the subject matter delayed.

3.1.4. The buyer's duty to give notice
The balancing of party interests implies that the buyer is not allowed to speculate in price developments indefinitely.

Therefore s. 26 of the Sale of Goods Act implies that – upon expiry of the timelimit of delivery and after non-performance is recorded – the buyer must, without undue delay following an inquiry from the seller, give notice regarding whether he wishes to affirm the contract as he will otherwise lose the right to claim delivery. The same applies, also failing an inquiry from the seller, if the buyer does not notify the seller within a reasonable time that he wishes the contract to stand.

Where delivery is delayed the buyer is to notify the seller if he intends to rely on the delay – in a business sale notification must be given forthwith and otherwise without unfounded delay, cf. s. 27. If the buyer fails to observe this notice requirement he is barred from relying on the delay at a later stage. The notice requirement is satisfied – initially – if the buyer states to the seller that the seller may expect a claim for damages at a later stage once the buyer has had a possibility of computing any loss the delay has caused him. A "neutral" notice such as this must, however, be followed by a notice within a reasonable time containing a specification of the items of loss the buyer will claim. Failure to make such itemised notice may prejudice the buyer's right to claim damages under the normal rules relating to passivity. If the buyer wishes to cancel the contract, in spite of delivery (delayed as it is) he must, however, without unfounded delay, notify the seller to such effect. Ss. 26 and 27 are built on the premise that notice is necessary to change a situation already existing.

3.2. Defects

For a sale which is not governed by the special rules on consumer sales in ss. 72-87, in this context particularly ss. 75a and 76, the Sale of Goods Act makes no attempt to define in detail when the subject-matter of a sale is "defective". The rules on defects are drafted with a view to defects in quality but it follows from s. 50 that the rules are also applicable to quantity defects, i.e. where the quantity delivered is less than agreed.

In the assessment of defect under s. 44 the emphasis is normally placed on the properties of the goods at the *time of delivery* (the time of passing of risk) to the buyer. S. 44 must be seen in conjunction with s. 17(1) under which the risk passes to the buyer *after* delivery in respect of accidental deterioration (or destruction) of the goods. Therefore defects occurring after delivery may not be relied upon unless such defects were caused by the seller's (culpable) circumstances. The rules on risk only govern *fortituous events* effecting the goods after delivery.

Under s. 44 the decisive element is when the defect arose and not when it became evident. Therefore, if the defect came in existence before delivery this circumstance could be relied upon by the buyer even if the defect does not manifest itself until after delivery was made.

The starting point in the assessment of the defectiveness of the goods is in the contract. If the contract allows the buyer to claim certain properties in the goods or stipulates that they should be free from certain (negative) properties the goods will be considered defective if the goods delivered have other properties than those agreed. This applies even if the value of the goods delivered is the same (or even higher) than that at which goods satisfying the terms of the contract may be assessed. If the contract allows the seller to deliver goods which would generally meet the description of "defective" the decisive point when assessing defectiveness remains the contract and not a more general evaluation of the quality. If the sale involves e.g. a car it will normally be considered a defect if the car lacks a bonnet and gearbox but the same is not necessarily the case if the car is sold "as she lies" for the breaker's yard.

The seller's *warranties* ("guarantee") as regards the existence of certain properties will also be relevant. A warranty will not exactly create a duty on the seller to eliminate defects in the goods, but s. 42(2) shows that the seller's warranting certain properties at the conclusion of the contract may attract liability in damages if it turns out, at delivery or later, that the goods do not possess the properties warranted.

The word "warranty" may sometimes be construed as a limitation of the buyer's right to claim remedies for defects. Thus a "warranty" may imply that the seller has undertaken within a certain period after delivery, to remedy certain defects in the goods (for which the buyer is presumed to "waiver" claims for defects, e.g. the right to avoid the contract). The expression "sold as examined/inspected" may, under certain circumstances (e.g. if the seller has acted fraudulently, or if the goods do not conform to the description under which they were sold) be held irrelevant.

In the absence of concrete indicating factors (including the purchase price agreed and the form under which the goods were offered for sale, e.g. "rejects") the buyer may claim goods of ordinary, satisfactory quality, suitability for use and value. Especially as regards goods sold as second-hand this rule will imply that the buyer is barred from relying on defects which in relation to the age of the goods, the price agreed etc. are natural consequences of (usual) wear and tear.

With a view to implementing some of the provisions of the EU Consumer Sale Directive of 1999 a new s. 75a has been included in the consumer sale provisions in the Sale of Goods Act which regulate the properties the subject-matter of sale is required to possess in order to conform to the contract. The provision relates to the genus, quantity, and other properties in the subject-matter and further lays down the requirement that the buyer is to receive the necessary information in connection with mounting, application, storage, and maintenance of the subject-matter of sale. The concept of defect in a consumer sale is further described in s. 75a (2) and in s. 76, in particular s. 76(1)no.4 under which the subject-matter of sale is deemed to be defective if it is of a different or poorer nature or usefullness than agreed or the circumstances of the sale otherwise would indicate. Under s. 77(1), where a seller has made a general reservation such as "sold as examined" or similar qualification such reservation shall be ineffective in a consumer sale unless the sale was made at a public auction, cf. for more details s. 77(2).

To a certain extent the buyer is required to observe for himself whether defects are present in the goods. Where the buyer has examined the goods prior to conclusion of the contract, or without reasonable cause refused to comply with a request from the seller to examine them, s. 47 of the Sale of Goods Act (the "caveat emptor" rule) provides that the buyer is barred from subsequently claiming defects which such examination ought to have revealed to him, i.e. visible defects which an examination would have uncovered. By the same token the buyer will of course be entitled to rely on a latent defect and the seller is barred from relying on the buyer's failure to examine if the seller has acted fraudulently, e.g. if he has tried deliberately to hide the defect from the buyer. For consumer sales a similar rule applies, cf. s. 77(b).

When goods have been bought at an auction, including at a compulsory auction sale, the buyer will often be barred from claiming subsequently that properties are lacking in the goods sold, cf. s. 48 and, as already mentioned *in consumer sales*, cf. s. 77(2).

Where the contract of sale involves a claim, e.g. a mortgage, there will be a defect if the claim turns out not to exist, cf. s. 9 of the Bonds Act. On the other hand, it is not normally considered a defect that the debtor is incapable to pay the debt, cf. s. 10 of the same Act.

The rules governing remedies in relation to defects are contained in ss. 42 and 43 governing specific goods and generic goods, respectively. In several respects, the rules are so uniform, however, that they may be treated together.

3.2.1. Proportionate price reduction

In sales both of specific goods and generic goods the buyer may claim a proportionate reduction of the purchase price if the goods are defective, cf. s. 42(1) and s. 43(1).

A proportionate price reduction implies that the agreed price is reduced so that the amount payable corresponds to the relationship between the value of the goods without defects and their value with defects.

Example: Where the value without defects is DKK 1,000 while the value with defects is reduced by 1/10 the buyer may claim the agreed purchase price reduced by 1/10. If the parties had agreed a price of DKK 800,- the buyer is to pay 9/10 of such amount, i.e. DKK 720. In other words, the proportionate reduction comprises DKK 80 (1/10 of DKK 800). If the agreed purchase price had been e.g. DKK 1,500 the proportionate reduction will comprise DKK 150 bringing the reduced purchase price down to DKK 1,350.

Neither s. 42 nor s. 43 requires special conditions to be met in order to allow the buyer the right to claim proportionate reduction. In particular there are no requirements that the defect must be material or that the seller is to blame for the defects in the goods. On the other hand the proportional computation, cf. the example, does require that the defect relied upon deteriorates the value of the goods so as to discourage claims for trivial defects.

In a consumer sale, the rules on proportionate price reduction are mandatory (s. 78(1), no. 1) whereas they may be derogated from in other sales.

3.2.2. The remedy of avoiding the sale

A material defect allows the buyer to avoid the sale both in a sale of specific goods and in a sale of generic goods under s. 42(1) and s. 43(2), respectively.

The assessment of whether the defect is material is generally to be made on a concrete basis as the decision is founded on whether the defect in relation to the particular contract and the other circumstances of the case may be considered important. In contrast to delay, cf. s. 21(3), there is no rule that any defect in a business sale is material. On the contrary, the right of claiming proportional reduction in the event of any value deterioration will often, presumably, imply that stricter requirements are imposed in order to regard the "material character" requirement, and hence the avoidance remedy, to be satisfied.

Like the reduction remedy the avoidance remedy is not dependent on fault with the seller or his employees.

Even if the defect is not material the buyer may avoid the contract of sale if the seller has acted fraudulently, e.g. in connection with the conclusion of the contract or by keeping silent about the defect at the delivery or seeking to hide it from the buyer, cf. s. 42(1) and s. 43(2). Likewise irrespective of the defect's being material or not a buyer of generic goods may avoid the contract if the seller knew the defect at a time at which he might have procured non-defective goods without unreasonable effort, i.e. made a *replacement delivery,* cf. s. 43(2).

Like the rules on proportional price reduction the rules on the buyer's right of avoidance may not be derogated from in a *consumer sale* (s. 78(1), no.4) whereas they may derogated from by agreement between the parties in other sales.

As regards sales by instalment deliveries s. 46 contains a rule corresponding to that on delay in s. 22.

3.2.3. The right to claim non-defective performance

A buyer of generic goods may, under s. 43(1) and (2) claim replacement delivery, i.e. non-defective performance under the same terms as apply to his right of avoidance. The classification with the avoidance conditions means that the buyer will normally only claim replacement delivery if the defect is material. However, a seller's fraudulent conduct (e.g. an attempt to hide the defect) will always entitle the buyer to claim replacement delivery. A claim for such replacement will not be dependent on the defect being material either, if the seller knew the defect at a time at which he could have provided non-defective goods without unreasonable effort. The remedy is not available, however, if it is impossible to procure non-defective goods.

When the seller has delivered less than agreed such breach is regarded as a defect if the buyer must assume that what has been delivered was contemplated to constitute full performance from the seller, cf. s. 50, 1st clause. In that case the buyer may under s. 50, 2nd clause, claim subsequent delivery of the rest of the goods whether that quantity is a material or immaterial part of the total amount.

The wording of s. 50 makes it most appropriate to generic goods but a buyer of specific goods has the same remedy of subsequent delivery.

The rules on the buyer's right to claim non-defective performance are mandatory in *consumer sales* and for such sales the buyer may also – under s. 78 (1) no. 1 – normally claim that the seller *"cure"* the defects, i.e. a change or repair of the goods. Outside consumer sales, on the other hand, cure of defects may only be claimed by the buyer if it has been agreed with the seller or follows form custom.

3.2.4. The right to claim damages

Both with regard to "original" defects, i.e. defects which were present in the goods at the conclusion of the contract and to "subsequent" defects, i.e. defects arisen after conclusion of the sale but before the risk passed to the buyer, the buyer may claim damages if the seller has acted fraudulently, cf. s. 42(2) e.g. by hiding the defect to the buyer.

In addition a buyer of specific goods may claim damages for original defects if the goods lack properties which will be deemed "warranted". This will include cases in which the seller has made an express promise to the buyer that the goods had certain properties. The expression "must be deemed warranted" indicates that the liability in damages will lie if the seller has merely made representations of some certainty as regards the existence of certain properties in the goods, e.g. that a wine is "of 1987 vintage". On the other hand, ordinary "puffing" or commendatory statements as to the excellence of a product ("best on the market") will not constitute a "warranty".

With subsequent defects, i.e. defects arisen after conclusion of the contract but before delivery, a buyer of specific goods will be entitled to damages under a fault liability rule, i.e. when the defect is due to the seller's or his employees' negligence, e.g. failure to secure proper storage or where the defect originates in the seller's poor financial situation.

Under s. 43(3) a seller of generic goods is liable even without fault on his part in respect of a defect. However, the seller may be exempt from liability under the same conditions as with delay (s. 24), i.e. where delivery of non-defective goods is impossible because of extraordinary circumstances which were outside any seller's contemplation at the conclusion of the contract.

If the buyer elects avoidance the computation of damages will be made on the same lines as apply with delay, cf. s. 45, which contains a reference to s. 25 (damages computation on delay from seller).

If the contract is affirmed the buyer may, if he chooses not to claim proportional price reduction, claim damages for the deterioration in value caused by the defect. Likewise he may claim damages in respect of other loss including in respect of expenses he may have had in the identification of the defect, etc.

For *consumer sales*, the seller's liability in damages is supplemented by a partly mandatory rule in s. 80. Liability is, however, also in such sales dependent on the buyer having suffered a loss. This condition is rather often – especially perhaps in consumer sales – not satisfied. Special problems in relation to tort law liability arise if the subject matter of sale causes injury to the buyer or his assignees due to dangerous properties of the goods (product liability).

When the subject matter of sale has dangerous properties (animal feed being poisonous, a herd of animals suffering from foot and mouth disease etc.) this will often cause the subject matter of sale to be considered defective to a degree offering the buyer the remedies described in the foregoing, including damages, but the liability rules in the Sale of Goods Act will not govern whether a claim lies in respect of the damage which those dangerous properties cause to *other* property assets etc. The liability of the seller in such respect, if any, is determined by the rules in the *Product Liability Act* or under general tort law principles.

3.2.5. The seller's right to cure a defect

Whereas, apart from consumer sales, the Sale of Goods Act does not entitle the buyer to claim that the seller cures defects by repair, the *seller* may – in all sales under the terms of s. 49 and s. 79 – make such repair with the effect that the buyer's remedies completely or partly will lapse. If the seller offers to remedy a defect by repair the buyer is under s. 49 bound to accept this if the repair can be made before the expiry of the time within which he is bound to await delivery (cf. s. 21) and it is evident that he will suffer no expense or inconvenience in the process. In a *consumer sale* it will suffice that repair is made "within a reasonable time".

On a line with the presumption of "materiality" of any defects in *commercial sales* (cf. s. 21) the seller's access to curing defects in such sales will be correspondingly limited. S. 49 will only have practical relevance if the seller under the agreement has been entitled to deliver within a certain period of time and chooses to perform before the expiry of that period. The parties may, however, have agreed that the seller's access to remedy defects by repair, shall be extended and the seller will normally also enjoy wider access to cure defects in a *sale on buyer's specifications.*

The effects of a successful repair within the lines posed by s. 49 (and s. 79) are that the buyer will be barred from cancelling the sale and claiming proportional reduction of the purchase price. If the buyer, before the execution of the repair, has suffered loss (e.g. on account of his deprival of a non-defective machine in the period of repair) his right to claim damages for such loss, e.g. damages in respect of reduced production capacity is unaffected, cf. s. 49(2).

3.2.6. Notice requirements

The buyer's right to rely on defects in the goods sold may lapse if he fails to give notice to the seller under s. 52(1) – in business sales forthwith and otherwise without unfounded delay. The duty to give notice under s. 52(1) is performed if the buyer merely makes a "neutral" communication to the seller without specifying the remedy in respect of the defect the buyer intends to rely upon. On the other hand, if the buyer intends to avoid the contract of sale or claim subsequent or substitute delivery he must notify the seller to such effect without unfounded delay. Where the buyer fails to give such notice he will lose the right to reject the goods or claim subsequent delivery. In *consumer sales,* s. 52 has been replaced by the less stringent rule of s. 81, 1st clause, requiring merely that the buyer is to give notice "within a reasonable time".

In addition it follows from s. 81, 3rd clause, that a notice given before two months after the buyer discovered the defect is always deemed to have been made in time. As opposed to s. 52(2) a consumer sale buyer may always make a neutral notice to the seller even if he intends to avoid the sale or claim substitute delivery.

In any event the timelimit under s. 52 for giving notice accrues when the buyer has discovered – or ought to have discovered – the defect. When he ought to have discovered it is decided on a concrete estimate. Among the factors to consider are whether the defect is of such nature as not to appear until some time after use of the goods or whether it is immediately ascertainable. In a commercial sale the buyer is to make a proper examination of the goods on delivery or when an agreed sample has reached him, cf. s. 51. If the goods are to be sent from one place to another the buyer is, however, not bound to examine them until they have been placed at his disposal at the place of destination. If the buyer has not performed his duty to examine, he will lose remedies in respect of defects which such examination would have revealed.

The buyer's duty to give notice is made less strict by the rule in s. 53 by which the provision of s. 52 regarding the buyer's loss of remedy will not be applicable if the seller has acted fraudulently or with gross negligence thereby inflicting substantial damage to the buyer. In *consumer sales*, the buyer's duty to give notice is further modified by the rule in s. 82. Under this rule the term of notice is suspended if the seller has acted contrary to principles of common honesty or with gross negligence.

Considerations for the seller's interests to avoid that the buyer may rely on his remedies for defects for a prolonged period of time after sale have dictated the provisions in s. 54(1) and s. 83(1) (consumer sale) by which the buyer will lose all remedies for breach if he has failed to notify the seller *within two years* after the handing-over of the goods that he intends to rely on the defect. In sales of building materials the timelimit is five years from completion and a maximum of six years from the handing over of the building materials, cf. s. 54 and s. 83(2). These timelimits are disregarded if the seller has undertaken to warrant the goods for a longer period, e.g. warranted the keeping qualities or durability of products for a period of several years. The timelimits will also be disregarded if the seller has acted fraudulently, e.g. by trying to hide the defect from the buyer or if the seller in a consumer sale has acted contrary to ordinary principles of honesty.

The limitation rules apply even if the buyer has had no possibility of discovering the defect. In real terms the rules are only of practical relevance for defects which the buyer has not identified nor ought to have identified. For in that case the remedies would have been lost long ago for his failure to give notice.

In consumer sales special rules apply as to where notice should be addressed. Under s. 84 notice may be given to a producer or other trader who has undertaken to remedy any defects in the goods in connection with the sale. S. 85, 1st clause requires a consumer buyer to give notice within a reasonable time after discovering the defect. Under s. 85, 3rd clause, a notice addressed to one of the third parties mentioned – corresponding to the provision on notice to the seller under s. 81 – given within two months after the consumer discovered the defect is always deemed to have been made in time. A notice serving to retain the consumer's right to claim repair of a defect from a business third party may also be addressed to the seller with binding effect against such third party, s. 85, 1st clause once again.

S. 61 contains a contract law rule to the effect that certain compulsory communications, including notices under s. 52 and s. 54 delivered for dispatch by mail, telegraph or other reliable means of communication, shall be deemed effective notwithstanding delays in their transportation or even loss so that they never reach the addressee. A similar rule applies in *consumer sales*, cf. s. 86.

3.3. Defective title

If the buyer, on account of a third party's title to the goods does not acquire the power of disposal contemplated in the contract or which he had justly anticipated the seller is in breach as regards the transfer of good title (i.e. his own title is "defective").

Completely defective title will lie where a third party owns the goods sold, e.g. in a case of theft, and partially defective title (limited ownership) will be present if the goods are e.g. subject to charge or other encumbrance.

The Sale of Goods Act only regulates title in s. 59 under which the buyer, even if the seller was innocently mistaken as to his right to sell the goods, may claim damages. This does not apply, however, if the buyer was in bad faith at the conclusion of the sale, i.e. he knew that the goods were not owned by the seller.

In relation to the other rules on damages, s. 9 is remarkable in that the seller is unconditionally liable even if he did not realize that he was incapable of transferring rights in respect of the goods to the buyer.

No reference other than in s. 59 is made to defective title in the Sale of Goods Act and the rule is limited to completely defective title. However, it is presumed that the provision also applies to partially defective title and likewise that the buyer may elect, instead of claiming damages, to avoid the contract of sale (when the defective title is substantial). In other words the rules on actual defects in the Sale of Goods Act may be correspondingly applied.

4. Buyer's breach

The main provision on buyer's breach is s. 28 which sets forth that actual (manifested) breach on the buyer's part is only possible in the form of delay. But a situation may arise in which it is evident even before the seller's performance that the buyer cannot or will not pay and for such "anticipatory breach" the Sale of Goods Act allows the seller certain remedies under certain conditions.

4.1. Delay

If the purchase price is not paid at the due time the seller may elect to affirm the contract or cancel it. Whether the sale is affirmed or cancelled the seller is also entitled to claim damages for the loss he may have suffered.

Under s. 28 the forms under which the buyer may be in breach are limited to situations in which the price is not paid at due date and where the buyer is to take certain measures as part of his payment performance. The measures upon which the payment of the purchase price depends referred to in s. 28(1) include e.g. that the buyer – when deferment of payment has been granted – is to accept a bill of exchange, that he is to open a documentary credit under the terms of the contract, or that he is to provide other security for the payment of the purchase price. The term will also cover cases which directly concern the seller's capability to deliver but which on account of the principle of performance against performance will also be relevant for the payment of the purchase price. Such situation will arise e.g. where the buyer fails to provide shipping accommodation where such duty is on him, e.g. in a FOB sale.

4.1.1. The remedy of affirming the sale

The remedy of affirming the sale means that the seller is entitled to claim the agreed purchase price and to claim that the buyer implements the measures necessary for payment to be effected. If the principle of performance against performance has not been derogated from, e.g. by agreeing that the buyer is to pay in advance, the seller's right to affirm is dependent on his concurrent delivery of the goods to the buyer.

4.1.2. The remedy of cancelling the contract of sale

In a *commercial sale* the seller may cancel the contract of sale upon the buyer's breach (delay) and the remedy is not dependent on the delay being material, cf. s. 28(1), 3rd clause, nor that the delay is attributable to the buyer. In other sales, a sale may be cancelled if the delay is material but it is no requirement in such sales either that the buyer is to blame for the delay.

If the subject-matter of sale has already been handed over to the buyer, the sale can only be avoided if the seller must be deemed to have made a reservation to such effect, cf. s. 28(2).

Most often a reservation for avoidance, in spite of the subject matter having been handed over, appears from a written agreement between the parties to such effect, e.g. a contract of sale with usual reservation of title. The expression "must be deemed to have made a reservation" shows, however, that the reservation allowing the seller to avoid the sale despite handing over need not be expressly agreed. Where e.g. the sale is for cash the seller may, if the subject-matter of sale has been handed over without payment, e.g. by a mistake on the part of the seller's employees, recover the subject-matter notwithstanding the handing over. The same applies if the buyer pays by a cheque which later turns out to be worthless (i.e. a "bouncing" cheque). In both cases the seller is required to rely on this cash reservation with reasonable speed as passivity may be construed as implied credit acquiescence.

Where the seller is to deliver in instalments and each instalment is to be paid for separately the seller may, when substantial delay occurs in the payment of a single instalment, avoid the contract of sale in respect of future deliveries unless there is no reason to believe that the delay will be repeated. This applies even if the seller – since the goods have already been handed over – is barred under s. 28(2) from avoiding the sale in respect of the instalment delivery for which payment was delayed.

Like s. 22, s. 29 also relates to sales by instalment deliveries. In contrast to s. 22, s. 29 contains a presumption that a buyer who has once breached the term of payment of one instalment will repeat his breach. The difference is attributable to the character of the performance since failure to observe payment terms is usually due to a buyer's inability or unwillingness to pay.

4.1.3. The right to claim damages

If the seller cancels the sale on account of the buyer's delay in payment he is entitled to damages for the loss he has suffered thereby. The reference in s. 30 to the liability rule in s. 24 shows that, unless the buyer disclaims liability in such respect in the contract, an exemption of the buyer's duty to pay will only arise in exceptional cases. In practice exemptions from such liability will only arise if statutory impediments prevent the buyer from paying or the monetary system collapses.

The most important head in the computation of damages is the *price difference*, i.e. the amount by which the agreed sales sum has exceeded the price of the goods of a similar nature and quality as those sold at the time of shipment, cf. s. 30(1). Where the seller manages within a reasonable time after avoidance to sell the goods elsewhere (self-help sale) the price obtained will be used as the basis for the measure of the price difference, cf. s. 30(2).

If the seller affirms the contract he will, apart from being able to claim the purchase price, have a claim for interest. Default interest is fixed under s. 5 of the Interest Act at a yearly rate corresponding to the official discount rate current form time to time plus (currently) five per cent. Apart from this the seller is entitled to damages for the loss which is not covered by the interest, e.g. a currency loss where the purchase price is payable in a foreign currency. On the other hand he may not claim other consequential loss, e.g. loss suffered because the delay has forced him to borrow money at a higher rate of interest than the rate he himself receives in his damages claim.

4.2. Buyer's inability to pay

When, in consequence of s. 28(2), the seller will be barred from avoiding the sale if the goods have been handed over to the buyer, a need may arise to protect him against the consequences of the buyer's inability to pay when manifested after conclusion of the contract but before the goods are handed over to the buyer.

Admittedly, s. 28(2) does provide some access to the seller for avoidance even after the handing over, viz. when he has made reservation for that event and the principle of "performance against performance" might entitle the buyer not to surrender the goods to the buyer without receiving payment at the same time. But considerations for the seller's interests may extend further as he may i.a. have a justified interest in being able to react to information on the buyer's poor financial situation if he has had no chance (or inducement) to stipulate reservation of title – and if, in reliance of the buyer's ability to pay he has agreed to waiver the principle of performance against performance.

On this background s. 41 provides the seller with a special possibility of avoiding the sale when the goods have been handed over to the buyer's estate in bankruptcy. The rules are primarily of practical importance in credit sales.

4.2.1. Right of stoppage

When the buyer, after conclusion of the sale, is declared bankrupt or negotiations for a compulsory composition are commenced against him, s. 39 allows the seller, even if the sale is for credit, to retain the goods, or where they have already been sent, to prevent their being handed over to the estate until adequate security has been placed for the payment of the purchase price at due date. Where the time of delivery has arrived and the estate fails to place such security on the seller's request he may cancel the sale. These remedies are also available to the seller if the buyer has suspended payment of his debts after conclusion of the sale or it turns out – e.g. in the course of an unsuccessful execution against the buyer's goods – that his property situation is such that he must be deemed incapable of paying the purchase price on the due date.

The factors governed by s. 39 are comprehensively termed "inability to pay". In contrast to manifested, existing breach the circumstances indicate anticipatory breach. The application of s. 39 requires that the buyer's inability to pay must have occurred "after conclusion of the sale" – but the provision is also applicable if the buyer, *without the seller's knowledge*, was insolvent already at the conclusion of the sale. The remedies in favour of the seller under s. 39 which collectively are termed "the seller's *right of stoppage"* (or *"lien* on the goods") are, as the provision shows, dependent on the buyer's inability to pay as it manifests itself after conclusion of the sale.

The right to retain the goods is of independent relevance alongside the principle of performance against performance when the seller, in granting credit terms, has waived cash payment.

The remedy of preventing the handing over to the buyer is not lost until the buyer is in possession of the goods and therefore the right is not barred by the fact that the goods have already been sent. Whether the buyer or seller has provided shipping accommodation is also irrelevant as long as the goods have not been physically handed over to the buyer. On the other hand, the handing over has occurred once the goods have been delivered to the buyer or his employees and the same will apply if the goods have reached a third party engaged by the buyer to process or store the goods. Concurrent with the exercise of the right of stoppage the buyer may require the buyer, or his estate, to place security for the payment of the purchase price on due date, If such security is not placed, the seller may avoid the sale when the time for delivery has arrived, i.e. at the point in time when the seller either may or is obliged to deliver under the terms of the contract.

4.2.2. Anticipatory lien

Even if the time of delivery has not arrived the seller may upon the buyer's adjudication in bankruptcy require that the estate decides without unfounded delay whether to take the buyer's place in the contract or not. Where the estate fails to adopt the contract, the purchase price is payable as a preferential claim in bankruptcy (Bankruptcy Act s. 93), cf. s. 40 of the Sale of Goods Act. The aim of s. 40 is to prevent that the estate will get an opportunity to speculate in the advantage/disadvantage of adopting the contract.

4.2.3. Retaining possession

Where, *after* the buyer's adjudication, the goods have been handed over to the bankrupt estate and the purchase price remains outstanding the seller may under s. 41 re-claim possession from the estate unless the estate adopts the contract and places security for the payment of the purchase price at the due date on the seller's request. If the estate has sold the goods or otherwise disposed of them so that they can no longer be recovered by the seller in a considerably unaltered state the seller may regard the estate as having adopted the contract. The aim of the rule is i.a. to prevent a race between the seller and the buyer's bankrupt estate in respect of goods sent by the seller before the adjudication and which have not reached the buyer at that stage.

4.2.4. Notice requirements

Under ss. 31 and 32 the seller is under a certain duty to give notice in respect of the payment default. The rules follow the same structure as ss. 26 and 27 governing delay on the seller's part and reflect the principle that the seller is normally only obliged to give notice on his own initiative if he intends to avoid the sale as a consequence of the delayed payment. The seller is not bound to give notice if he wishes to affirm the contract notwithstanding the delay in payment.

5. Claimant's non-performance

The foregoing discussion has mainly aimed at situations in which the discharge of a sale fails because of breach by one of the parties in the performance of the duties imposed on them under the contract. In relation to the breach of delay the temporal requirement in respect of occurrence of the breach is the point in time at which the parties are under a "duty" to perform their part of the contract, i.e. the "due date" (or maturity date).

In contrast to maturity date, the *time of payment* (or *discharge)* will refer to the point in time at which each party has a "right" to discharge himself of the duties imposed upon him under the contract. The time of discharge decides the temporal requirement for the onset of *"claimant's non-performance"*.

5.1. Claimant's non-performance by seller

Where the time has arrived at which the buyer has a right under the terms of the contract to discharge himself by payment, the seller will be in claimant's non-performance if he cannot accept the payment or refuses to take it. The situation may arise if the seller is not present when the buyer tenders performance or where he has failed to make the goods ready for surrendering to the buyer at the agreed time of delivery and the buyer shows up to collect them. The latter situation also involves a breach of the contract allowing the buyer the usual remedies in such respect.

In a "pure" claimant's non-performance situation (e.g. where the buyer has received the goods without being told who is to receive payment nor where it is to be made) the buyer may obtain discharge by depositing the purchase price with a financial institution under the rules of the Depositing Act.

5.2. Claimant's non-performance by buyer

From the provisions in ss. 33-37 it is evident that a claimant's non-performance is not generally seen as a "breach" in the Sale of Goods Act; the buyer has a right to the goods but is under a duty to accept them and only duties may be breached. – A contrary view is held in CISG, cf. below Chapter 9.

The situation will often result in certain changes of the circumstances surrounding the sale quite apart from the possibility that a buyer in claimant's default will also often be in breach of the contract. The aim is at one and the same time to protect the buyer's interests and prevent that his circumstances affect the seller's situation adversely by unduly increasing his burdens.

One of the relaxations which will set in, in case of buyer's claimant's default, follows from the rule mentioned in s. 37 under which the seller's loyal – but unsuccessful – attempt to perform *causes the risk of accidental destruction or deterioration of the goods to pass to the buyer.*

Further, it follows from s. 33 that in a situation of buyer's delay in taking delivery the seller is bound *to preserve* the goods until the delay ceases or the seller exercises the right to avoid the sale to which he might be entitled under s. 28. If the goods have been sent by the seller and have arrived at their destination the duty to preserve them will only apply if a person is available at that place to take possession of the goods on the seller's behalf and provided that the arrangement can be made without material expense or inconvenience.

The seller's duty under s. 33 to preserve the goods is not indefinite. If the seller is incapable, without material expense or inconvenience, of continuing to preserve the goods or the buyer fails to dispose of them within a reasonable time after being requested to do so the seller has a right to *sell* the goods for the buyer's account. The price obtained in such sale is final and the buyer is barred from disputing it provided that the sale has been made in a proper manner either by auction, published and properly held, or otherwise, cf. s. 34, cl. 1-3. Where sale is not possible or it is evident that the costs which are inherent in such sale cannot be covered by the sum obtainable the seller has a right of *abandonment* granted by virtue of s. 34, 4th clause, under which he may see to the "final removal" of the goods. Such abandonment will not affect the seller's claim for the purchase price.

As regards perishable goods or goods whose storage will imply disproportionate cost the seller is even *under a duty to sell*, cf. s. 35. On the other hand the seller is not deemed to have a duty to sell merely because the price of the goods is expected to go down.

The seller may claim the costs which he incurs in the preservation etc. of the goods from the buyer, cf. s. 36, and the seller has a lien on the goods in security for such costs. The remedy of avoidance, however, is normally not open to the seller unless the situation only involves breach on the buyer's part.

6. Special note on avoidance

Special problems may arise concerning passing of risk, duty of preservation etc. with regard to goods rejected by the buyer after they have come into his possession. A "rejection" may occur principally when the buyer avoids the sale (on account of the seller's breach) but similar problems will arise when the buyer demands substitute delivery, or where the seller has delivered prematurely and the buyer has no wish to receive the goods before the date agreed upon.

When the buyer refuses to take delivery of the goods he is bound to see to their preservation until they are placed at the seller's disposal, cf. s. 55 and s. 56.

The duty to preserve the goods sets in when the buyer has come into possession of the goods. While s. 55 covers situations in which the goods have come into the buyer's possession (e.g. because the seller delivered them at the buyer's business address) s. 56 implies that the buyer cannot always be obliged to take possession. S. 56 governs dispatch sales and will exempt the buyer from taking possession if the seller, or his representative, is present at the destination place, or if possession cannot be effected without concurrent payment of the purchase price by the buyer (e.g. if the goods have been delivered to a forwarding agent upon the seller's instructions only to hand them over on cash payment). The same applies if the buyer cannot take possession without material expense or inconvenience.

If the buyer neglects his duty to preserve the goods he will be liable in damages and he may also lose his right to avoid the sale under s. 57. For it follows from s. 57 that the buyer is not entitled to recover the purchase price unless he returns the goods received in substantially the same state and quantity as they were at the delivery. The buyer does retain his access to avoid, however, despite deterioration of the goods after delivery if such deterioration is due to accidental causes (e.g. a third party's arson activity in the buyer's warehouse), inherent vice in the goods, or measures taken before the defect which brings about the cancellation of the sale was discovered or ought to have been discovered (e.g. deterioration arising during testing of a machine), cf. s. 58. It follows from s. 57(1) that the buyer may cancel the sale even for an immaterial defect in which case, however, the buyer is to pay compensation for the deterioration, unless it originates in one of the circumstances mentioned in s. 58.

7. The passing of property

The discussion in the foregoing has mainly focused on the relationship between seller and buyer. But a treatment of the contract of sale cannot stop there. A sale of goods may create legal problems extending beyond the immediate contractual relationship – to the parties' creditors and assignees in contract. The relationship between seller and buyer is still – apart from the exemptions made in consumer sales – prima facie subject to a principle of freedom of contract, i.e. a principle which gives first priority to the agreement between the parties, and places statutory rules second. As regards creditors and assignees in contract, however, the rules are mandatory. These rules are commonly summarized with the label of "passing of property".

There is no rule in Danish law defining one certain phase in the process of sale as the moment of passing of property in the goods. In one relation property may pass already on conclusion of the contract whereas the passing in another relation may be attached to payment of the purchase price. Hence it makes little sense to speak of a passing of property to the buyer if the relation referred to is not specified at the same time.

Obviously the seller is the owner before the conclusion of the contract and equally obviously the buyer becomes owner when the goods have been handed over to him and he has paid the purchase price. Problems only arise in the period between these two phases in the discharge of the sale.

Where goods have been sold with a reservation of title (cf. the comments in Chapter 11, below) it makes sense to speak of the buyer having become owner – in the sense that he has actual possession of the goods. His power of disposal is limited, however, since he has no right to destroy or neglect the goods. The buyer may mortgage the goods but a mortgagee must respect the seller's right. Conversely, the right of the seller in the goods is also limited by the buyer's right. Whether the seller or buyer is designated owner is irrelevant and accidental.

In this Section only the relationship to the parties' creditors will be treated whereas the relationship to the parties' assignees in contract is included in the description of restitution in Section 9.

7.1. The relationship between the buyer and the seller's creditors

In a sale of *specific goods* (i.e. a sale of individually ascertained goods) the buyer obtains protection towards the seller's creditors already at the conclusion of the contract. That a risk exists that the seller may go bankrupt after the conclusion of the contract need not in itself deter the buyer from paying the purchase price in advance.

In a sale of *generic goods* the agreement creates no right to specified assets. The characteristic feature of such sale is that the seller, within the limits of the description of the goods made in the contract, may choose the items for his performance. In order that the buyer may acquire rights in respect of certain goods, such goods will need to be identified (appropriated to the contract). Since the seller's creditors are only bound to respect what the seller himself is bound by, the seller must in relation to the buyer have exercised his right to choose the goods for performance in a definitive manner. Thus the buyer does not obtain protection towards the seller's creditors until an unconditional appropriation of the goods has been made.

Such unconditional appropriation has been made if the identification has been made in the presence of the buyer or his representative, or if the buyer has been notified by the seller that the goods are appropriated to the contract. The same applies if the seller, in a sale upon buyer's specifications, has bound himself to appropriate the goods destined for the buyer gradually – as they are produced – and the seller has observed such duty.

The rules governing the buyer's protection towards the seller's creditors differ from those applying to charging of the goods by way of mortgage or pledge. A mortgagee/pledgee is not protected until the mortgagor/pledgor has been deprived of actual power of disposal over the assets charged (pledge) or upon registration of mortgage deed (mortgage), cf. further details in Chapter 18. This difference between sale and charging cannot be circumvented so that where a charge is really made the parties choose to make a contract of sale combined with the "buyer's" renting the goods to the seller so that ownership reverts to the seller when a rent corresponding to a repayment of the loan with accrued interest has been paid. The rules on charging are mandatory and are to be applied notwithstanding that the parties have termed their contract a sale "combined with hire".

It may be difficult to establish whether a sale is really a charge. Certainly a masked charge will not always lie just because the seller is to have the goods sold in his possession for a fairly long period. A person who has bought a horse but has no place to stable it may agree with the seller that the horse be stabled with him without risk of creditor challenge. One indicative factor in the determination of whether a legal act is a sale or charge is whether the legal act as seen from the assignee's point of view is solely relevant as security for indebtedness.

Where an asset is transferred on a pro forma level the creditors of the assignee are not bound to respect the contract. This applies no matter whether the contract appears as a sale or a charge.

7.2. The relationship between the seller and the buyer's creditors

As long as the goods have not been handed over to the buyer the seller's right of lien is protected and his rights in respect of the goods are therefore protected also as against the buyer's creditors.

Where the goods have already been handed over to the buyer the seller is, as a main rule, barred from cancelling the sale and therefore he has also lost his rights of the goods in relation to the buyer's creditors. This does not apply, however, if the goods, following the buyer's bankruptcy have been handed over to the estate (above Section 4.2.3).

Under s. 28(2) of the Sale of Goods Act the seller's access to cancel subsists also after handing over of the goods if he must be deemed to have reserved his right in such respect. This provision will comprise, apart from an outright reservation of title, situations in which a seller in a cash sale – without having received the purchase price concurrently – has handed the goods over to the buyer by mistake (above 4.1.2).

The last requirement of the seller's access to cancel the sale with binding effect towards the buyer's creditors is that the seller himself has a right to cancel the sale in relation to the buyer at all. On the other hand it is no foregone conclusion that a right to cancel in relation to the buyer per se will apply towards his creditors as well.

7.2.1. Cash sales

Where a seller in a cash sale has handed over the goods to the buyer without the purchase price being paid the sale will thus normally have been converted into a credit sale, cf. the remarks above in Section 7.2.. This does not apply, however, if the goods were handed over by mistake or payment was effected with a worthless cheque. In that case the seller is deemed to have made reservation and he may cancel the sale if he exercises the right with reasonable speed. On the strength of the provision in s. 58(3) of the Bankruptcy Act a presumption will also lie that a cash reservation extends to the buyer's creditors.

7.2.2. Sales with reservation of title

The Bankruptcy Act s. 58(3) implies that a reservation of title can be valid as against the buyer's creditors. A prerequisite is of course that such reservation of title is valid under the rules in the Credit Contracts Act, on these requirements cf. Chapter 11 below. Where the requirements of the Credit Contracts Act are satisfied the reservation of title will almost always extend to the buyer's creditors without more.

Quite apart from the requirements of the Credit Contracts Act a reservation of title is required to have been expressly agreed between the parties and it is also required that the agreement has been concluded before the goods were handed over to the buyer.

7.2.3. Consignment

The concept of consignment, under which a sale with reservation of title is included, and under which the buyer has a right of resale, is discussed below in Chapter 11 which also deals with the terms under which a consignor (seller) can be deemed to obtain protection as against the creditors of the consignee (buyer).

8. Restitution in sale of goods

When an innocent assignee acquires a right over goods by a contract with a person who is not entitled to dispose of them a conflict will arise between the true owner and the assignee. The conflict may be solved either by allowing the true owner's right to stand (restitution) or having it lapse to the benefit of the innocent assignee (extinction).

Danish law contains no general statutory rule on this issue. In the Danish Law of 1683 some rules regarding restitution do exist for special cases, whereas extinction is the rule in some provisions in contract and tort law.

As compared with the legal position in many other countries the right of restitution is quite wide.

In the debate on restitution versus extinction of rights a large number of legal political views have been advanced, considerations of legal security, considerations for "commercial interests" and risks, and concerns of a legally technical nature. But argumentations of this kind are hardly relevant when the legal position is to be described. The starting point must be taken in the way in which the asset has left the true owner's possession; whether it has been "traded" once or several times over is irrelevant.

8.1. Where possession is not based on contract

8.1.1. Theft

The true owner may recover the asset under the rule in the Danish Law 6-17-5.

8.1.2. Lost property

A person who has lost an asset may recover it by an analogous application of rule 6-17-5 of the Danish Law. This does not apply, however, if the asset has been sold at a lost property auction, cf. s. 4 and s. 7 in the Lost Property Act (Consolidated Act no. 591 of 1 September 1986).

8.2. Where possession is based on a void or voidable contract relationship

8.2.1. Operative invalidity factors

If the contract upon which possession is based is void as a consequence of one of the operative factors of invalidity – duress with violence or minority – the asset may be recovered.

8.2.2. Non-operative invalidity factors

Where the contract is void for one of the non-operative invalidity factors – ordinary duress, fraud or usury – the starting point is also that the owner may recover the asset.

8.2.3. Agency

Where an agent has exceeded his authority the principal is not bound and he may recover the asset which the agent may have assigned to a third party.

8.2.4. Invalidation in bankruptcy

Where a party has received an asset in a legal transaction which is invalidated under the rules in Part 8 of the Bankruptcy Act the right of the bankrupt estate is extinguished as against an innocent assignee, cf. s. 79 of the Bankruptcy Act.

8.3. Where possession is based on a valid contract with conditional or unconditional duty to return

8.3.1. Bailment

For bailment contracts of loan, hire or deposit the right to restitution follows from rule 5-8-12 of the Danish Law of 1683.

8.3.2. Pledge

A pledgor may on payment of the debt for which pledge was given under rule 5-7-4 of the Danish Law recover the object pledged from the third party to whom it has been sold by the pledgee.

8.3.3. Factoring

Under the Factors Act s. 53 the principal is the owner of the goods in the factor's possession. If the factor has the goods in his possession and sells them at a price which is lower than he ought to have obtained, or gives them in security by way of pledge or mortgage, or otherwise disposes of them after the expiry of his factoring functions, the rights of the principal are extinguished, cf. s. 54 and s. 55 of the Factors Act.

8.3.4. Reservation of title

For goods sold with a reservation of title the main rule is restitution. This area in particular has attracted criticism and the rule has been disregarded in some instances.

If the goods were delivered on consignment and the consignee acts contrary to instructions the rights of the principal are extinguished which follows either directly or analogously from the Factors Act s. 54 and s. 55.

8.3.5. Cash sales

In cash sales the problem does not arise at all. If the seller hands over the goods without payment there is normally, as already mentioned, a case of implied credit. Exceptionally, the seller may, as mentioned several times in the foregoing, avoid the sale after the handing over of the asset, e.g. if he has received payment with a worthless cheque. In that case the seller may recover the asset from the assignee on the same lines as in a sale with reservation of title.

9.4. Double transfer

Where an asset has been sold to two separate assignees the first buyer is the rightful owner. However, this right may probably be lost if the subsequent innocent assignee obtains possession of the asset – especially if he has paid for the asset and the first assignee has not.

CHAPTER 9

International Sales

by Bent Iversen

1. Introduction

The rules discussed in Chapter 8 above govern national sales of goods, e.g. a contract between a Danish buyer and a Danish seller who are both in business in Denmark.

Where the sale has an international element, e.g. a contract between a Danish seller and a foreign buyer, the sale may instead be governed by the Convention on Contracts for the International Sale of Goods, abbr. *"CISG"*. The Convention came into force in Denmark on 1 March 1990.

Where a sale is subject to CISG-rules and unless the parties have agreed otherwise, the rules in the Convention will override those of the Sale of Goods Act, cf. s. 1a(4) of the Sale of Goods Act.

The aim of the Convention was – as far as possible – to create uniform rules for the sale of goods all over the world. Thereby the uncertainty which might be involved in having sales contracts governed by various countries' legislation would seem to be reduced considerably. To avoid this uncertainty it has so far been the rule that the parties agreed in the contract which country's sales law would regulate their contract. Such *choice of law agreements* will still be necessary until the Convention has received general acceptance. On the other hand, if the countries to which e.g. a Danish seller exports his goods in the future decide to incorporate the Convention in their own legislation the need to make choice of law agreements will diminish – at least if the parties can agree that the Convention will meet their requirements.

The Convention has been adopted by a number of countries both within Europe and outside Europe.

At their adoption of the Convention, the Nordic countries made reservations to the effect that the CISG would not apply to sales which are concluded between parties having their places of business in Denmark, Finland, Sweden or Norway. Thus, for inter-Nordic sales the national sales legislation will apply, i.e. if Danish law is to apply, the Sale of Goods Act from 1906.

The CISG Convention is non-mandatory, cf. Art. 6. Thus the parties may agree that their contract is to be governed by other rules, e.g. the Sale of Goods Act.

The Convention consists of four Parts:

Part I contains general rules on the geographical and jurisdictional sphere of application etc. of the Convention. Part II concerns formation of contract and governs offer and acceptance. The rules deviate considerably from the inter-Nordic Contracts Act and Denmark (and Sweden, Norway and Finland) declared by their ratification of the Convention that they would opt out of these rules. Part III contains the sale of goods law provisions proper and will for most purposes cover the same aspects as the national rules. Part IV contains i.a. provisions on the reservations the states may make in relation to the application of the Convention.

2. Sphere of application etc. of the Convention

The Convention applies to contracts of sale of goods between parties whose places of business are in different states where:

a) the states are "Contracting States", i.e. states within which the Convention is in force
b) the rules of private international law would lead to the application of the law of a Contracting State, cf. Art. 1(1).

Thus, the Convention will be applicable e.g. between a Danish exporter and an American importer. Both Denmark and the US have adopted the Convention and it is therefore in principle irrelevant whether a dispute is to be governed by Danish or American law. On the other hand, the CISG-rules will not apply in a sales contract between a buyer and seller whose places of business are in the same country, nor by virtue of the Nordic "neighbouring country reservation" to contracts between a Danish buyer and e.g. a Swedish seller whose places of business are in Denmark and Sweden respectively.

Art. 1(1)(b) under which the Convention may be applicable even if only one of the countries has adopted it may be illustrated as follows:

A Danish seller receives an order from a buyer with his place of business in a state which has not adopted the Convention. If a dispute between the parties reaches a Danish court for decision it will follow from the rules of Danish private international law (mentioned below in Chapter 26) that if the seller has his business place in Denmark – governing law will normally be

Danish law and thereby the CISG-rules (as part of Danish law). If the case is brought before a foreign court the same result will obtain if the private international law rules of such country indicate that Danish law is applicable.

In determining whether the Convention is applicable no consideration is made to the nationality of the parties nor to the character of the sale as a commercial sale or civil sale, (cf. Art. 1(3)). On the other hand, the Convention does not apply to consumer sales, cf. Art. 2a and a number of sales enumerated in Art. 2(b-f). Sales for supply of goods to be produced or manufactured are, however, comprised, cf. Art. 3(1).

Where the CISG-rules do not apply to a sale, comprised by Art. 2, the sale is governed by the Sale of Goods Act (when Danish law is applicable) even if it contains an international element.

Under Art. 4 the Convention will only apply to the formation of contracts for an international sale of goods and to the rights and obligations of the seller and the buyer arising under the contract, i.e. the legal issues which in Danish law are governed primarily by the Contracts Act, Part 1, and by the Sale of Goods Act with the reservation following from Denmark's opting out of Part II of the Convention on formation of contract. Instead national Danish law on contract formation (Part I of the Contracts Act) will be applicable if the contract indicates Danish law as governing law.

Factors concerning validity and form of contract are not comprised by the CISG-rules, cf. Art. 4(a), and a contract for an international sale of goods is therefore valid even if it has been made orally, cf. Art. 11.

Legal issues relating to the importance of the contract of sale in regard to property in the goods sold are not comprised either, cf. Art. 4(b), which means that the Convention does not solve the special problems as to when the buyer obtains protection against the seller's creditors and assignees in contract nor as to when the seller may recover the goods upon the buyer's breach of contract.

Finally, it follows from Art. 5 that the Convention does not apply to the seller's liability for death or personal injury caused by the goods to any person, whereas damage to the buyer's goods are regulated. However, national rules on product liability will take precedence over the CISG-rules but this point is really irrelevant in Danish law since the Danish Product Liability Act only governs "damage to goods – in a consumer sale".

Among the other provisions in Part I may be noted that just as at the national level, by virtue of the Sale of Goods Act s. 1(1), the parties to an international contract are also bound by any usage agreed upon or by any practice which they have established between them in previous dealings (cf. Art. 9(1)).

3. Part III of the CISG Convention: Sale of Goods

Part III is the crucial Part of the Convention in that this Part (Arts. 25-88) governs the buyer's and the seller's rights and obligations and their remedies in the event of breach. The areas treated in the Convention are the same as in the Sale of Goods Act.

3.1. General provisions

Among the general provisions (Arts. 25-29), Art. 25 is of particular interest. This article provides the Convention's definition of "fundamental breach" (material breach of contract) which is relevant i.a. to the remedy of avoidance and the right to claim replacement delivery.

The determination of whether a breach may be regarded as fundamental is made on an objective basis. The decisive point is not how the *party in breach* conceives the expectations of the other party but on the effect of the breach to such other party.

The placing of Art. 25 among the general provisions indicates that the evaluation criteria of the concept of "fundamental" breach are the same with all types of breach – whether delay, defects, or defective title – and irrespective of whether the breach being evaluated was made by the seller or the buyer.

A party who wishes to avoid a sale must notify the party in breach to such effect, cf. Art. 26. Avoidance is effective once the declaration of avoidance has been made.

As regards the remedy of affirming the contract, e.g. the buyer's right to claim that the seller delivers the goods contemplated in the contract (i.e. a claim for specific performance), Art. 28 provides that a court of law applying the CISG-rules is not bound to allow such claim unless the court would be bound to do so under its own law in respect of similar contracts of sale not governed by the Convention.

The background of Art. 28 is the difference between i.a. Danish law and common law countries. Under Danish law it is generally possible to obtain a judgment for specific performance whereas under common law such claim would only be allowed to succeed when damages will not suffice to secure the claimant a reasonable satisfaction of his claim.

Art. 29(1) under which the parties may modify or terminate a contract is included to show that e.g. the rule in common law insisting on the presence of consideration does not apply within the Convention. In the course of the contract of sale a need may arise to change e.g. technical specifications for the goods ordered, delivery terms etc. and such modifications, which may cause one of the parties to incur additional costs, are therefore valid even if they appear as unilateral concessions from one party, i.e. even if no consideration is supplied in return from the other party.

3.2. The seller's obligations

The seller's main obligations follow from Arts. 30-52.

Summarized, the seller is obliged to deliver the goods, hand over the documents relating to them and transfer the property in the goods. The obligations of the seller will appear from the contract of sale and the gap-filling rules in the Convention which in the main correspond to the duties imposed upon a seller under the Danish Sale of Goods Act.

3.2.1. Delivery of the goods and handing over of documents

The Convention does not contain a definition of the concept of delivery. Arts. 30-34 only provide rules as to when, where and to a certain extent how delivery is to be made. Indirectly these rules indicate a number of acts which the seller is bound to perform with a view to putting the buyer into possession.

> Under Arts. 66-70 the risk will normally pass from seller to buyer when certain measures relating to delivery have been made. The time of passing of risk (and thus normally the time of delivery) will determine – in conformity with s. 44 of the Sale of Goods Act – when there is a delay or a defect in the goods.

Normally the parties will have *agreed* on the place of delivery. When the parties have not agreed a specified place, the place of delivery may be inferred by Art 31. The places of delivery designated in Art. 31(b) and (c) correspond to the main rule in the Danish Sale of Goods Act s. 9 (the seller's place of business or the place at which the goods were at the conclusion of the contract). Art. 31(a) correlates with s. 10 of the Sale of Goods Act.

The implication of the wording "placing the goods at the buyer's disposal" in Art. 31 (b) and (c) is that the buyer is to collect the goods. The seller's obligation is to see to it that they are *ready for collection* whereas the initiative for discharging the contract of sale and i.a. arranging transportation is on the buyer.

Where the seller fails to deliver the goods when he is obliged to do so under Art. 31 (a-c) there is a breach of contract and the buyer may claim the remedies under Art. 45, including the right of avoidance.

As to the time of the setting in of the duty to deliver and the seller's duties in connection with handing over of documents relating to the goods, cf. Art. 33 and Art. 34 respectively.

Art. 33 represents an equivalent to the statutory provisions in the Sale of Goods Act, viz. that the goods are to be delivered at the time *agreed* by the parties and Art. 33(b) correlates with s. 13 of the Sale of Goods Act. On the other hand, Art. 33(c) (which deals with cases in which delivery time has neither been agreed nor may be inferred from the circumstances of the sale) differs from s. 12 of the Sale of Goods Act. Under s. 12 delivery is to be made *upon demand* whereas under Art. 33 it is to be made "within a reasonable time after the conclusion of the contract".

If the seller's duty to deliver is coupled with a duty to hand over documents relating to the goods to the buyer such handing over is to be effected at the place and in the form required by the contract, cf. Art. 34, 1st clause.

3.2.2. Defects and third party claims

Arts. 35-44 of the Convention correspond to ss. 42-54 and s. 59 of the Sale of Goods Act governing actual defects and defective title, respectively.

The requirements of contractual conformity correspond to the concept of defect which has been developed in Danish law except that the Convention contains special rules in Arts. 41-43 on legal defects and intellectual property rights.

A first consideration in the evaluation of defects is the parties' *agreement* as regards quantity, quality, package etc., cf. Art. 35(1). Except where the parties have agreed otherwise the evaluation of the quality of the goods will be founded on the gapfilling individual rules of Art. 35(2) and (3).

The evaluation of the goods will, as already mentioned, be made at the time of passing of risk, cf. Art. 36(1). The passing of risk is specifically mentioned in Arts. 66-70 under which the risk will prima facie pass to the buyer on delivery, such time being – in a dispatch sale – the handing over of the goods to the first carrier.

The seller may *remedy* defects established in the goods when such remedying can be made without considerable inconvenience and expense for the buyer and the measures involved must be brought to an end before the expiry of the time of delivery fixed, cf. Art. 37. If the seller brings the goods into a non-defective state or makes a replacement delivery within the timelimit the buyer is barred from avoiding the sale but he retains his right to claim damages for the expenses which he may have incurred in the seller's remedy measures. If the goods, after remedy attempts have been made, are still defective the buyer retains all remedies available upon breach including right of avoidance, proportional reduction of purchase price, etc.

Under Art. 38 the buyer is to make an examination as quickly as possible of the goods with a view to ascertaining whether they conform with the contract.

When the buyer has discovered, or ought to have discovered, a defect he must in order to retain his right to rely upon the defect notify the seller of the defect within a reasonable time and at the same time specify its nature, cf. Art. 39(1).

> The construction of "reasonable time" is decided by the circumstances of the case. Usages and general practices in the area may be indicative but the buyer must normally give notice quite promptly. If the defect is not ascertainable until the buyer starts to use the goods the timelimit will not start to accrue until from that time. The requirement that the buyer is to specify the nature of the defect implies that a notice which merely states that the goods are defective will not suffice but it will probably suffice for an initial communication that the buyer describes the defect in general terms.

Under the equivalent rule in the Sale of Goods Act s. 52(1) notice is to be given forthwith in a commercial sale and in other sales without unfounded delay after the defect was discovered or ought to have been discovered. In contrast to Art. 39(1) there is no requirement in s. 52(1) that the nature of the defect is specified but only that the buyer relies on the defect.

Notice from the buyer must normally be given *within two years* from the date on which the goods were handed over to him, unless this timelimit is inconsistent with a contractual period of guarantee, cf. Art. 39(2) or the defect is due to factors which the seller knew or could not have been unaware of and which he did not disclose to the buyer, cf. Art. 40. Under s. 54(1) of the Sale of Goods Act the timelimit is also, following an amendment of the Act in 2002, *two years* computed from the handing over of the goods.

The seller is to deliver goods free from any rights or claims of third parties, i.e. free from any charge which the buyer has not agreed to take over, cf. Art. 41. A *legal defect* will lie if the buyer does not acquire title to the goods because they belong to someone else or e.g. are charged with a mortgage right.

If the goods delivered by the seller are charged with *intellectual property rights*, e.g. a patent, design, or trade mark right this may imply that the buyer is barred from using them in the way he contemplated. This may release remedies for breach, if the seller at the time of conclusion of the contract knew or could not have been unaware of the existence of such third party right or that a claim based on the right had been advanced, cf. Art. 42(1). However, the buyer cannot rely on the intellectual property right if he knew of the right himself or where the third party right or claim results from the seller's compliance with technical specifications furnished by the buyer, cf. Art. 42(2).

To retain his rights to claim in respect of legal defects and intellectual property rights, the buyer must notify the seller specifying the third party right or claim within a reasonable time after he has become aware of the right or claim, cf. Art. 43(1). On the other hand he is not required to seek verification of the right or claim of a third party through legal proceedings or otherwise.

4. The buyer's remedies in the event of the seller's breach of contract

Arts. 45-52 govern the remedies of the buyer in respect of the seller's delay in delivery and for defects in the goods.

The remedies relate to *failure of performance* on the seller's part and are not – like the Sale of Goods Act remedies – systematically divided into various remedies applicable for delay, and others referring to defects. The remedies may also be applied with other types of breach, e.g. if the seller fails to perform one or more of his *secondary duties*. However, certain remedies, e.g. the right to claim proportionate reduction, are only applicable for the seller's delivery of defective goods, and sometimes the application of one remedy may preclude application of others; naturally a buyer cannot at one and the same time rely on the remedy of proportionate reduction and the right to claim replacement delivery, cf. the express wording of Art. 46(1).

The rules governing *damages* upon the seller's breach of contract are contained in Part V of the Convention (Arts. 71-88) which comprises both the seller's and the buyer's liability in damages.

In his reliance on other remedies the buyer does not lose the right to claim damages, cf. Art. 45(2). Where the buyer has fixed a timelimit within which the seller is to perform his obligations he is barred from relying on other remedies except for delay in performance, cf. Art. 47(2). By remedying a defect the seller may prevent the buyer from avoiding the contract, cf. Art. 48.

The buyer may react towards the seller's breach either by affirming the contract (claiming specific performance, cf. Arts. 46-48) including a delivery of substitute goods, or subsequent delivery, remedying of defects, proportionate reduction combined with subsequent delivery, or by avoiding the contract (Art. 49).

4.1. The right to claim specific performance

Art. 46(1) does not set up special requirements in respect of the buyer's right to claim specific performance. However, the provision must be combined with Art. 28 under which a court of law will only be bound to enter a judgment for specific performance under special conditions.

With the modification following from Art. 28, the buyer may claim that the seller delivers an article which has not yet been delivered and that he delivers a part of the goods which may have failed to arrive. Further, he may claim that the seller make the arrangements necessary for the delivery of the goods. Art. 46(1) is applicable both to sales of specific goods and of generic goods since the Convention does not distinguish between the types of sale. In the nature of things, the right to claim replacement delivery is, however, limited to sale of generic goods.

The buyer may claim replacement delivery when the defect in the goods delivered is material, cf. Art 46(2). Where the defect consists in the buyer's having received only part of the goods, or in part of the goods being non-conforming, the buyer's right to claim specific performance will be limited to the missing part.

Further, the buyer may *claim* that the seller remedies a defect in the goods by repair unless such repair is deemed unreasonable under the circumstances, cf. Art. 46(3), e.g. if the places of business of buyer and seller are situated a long distance form eachother and it is possible for the buyer to have the defect repaired locally. On the other hand there is no requirement that the defect is material. Under the Danish Sale of Goods Act only a *consumer buyer* may require the seller to remedy a defect (The sale of Goods Act s. 78(1)) whereas a buyer in a commercial sale or civil sale has no corresponding right.

Where the goods are defective the buyer may claim a *proportionate price reduction*, cf. Art. 50. The right to claim reduction may be lost if the seller remedies the defect by repair without such repair affecting the value of the goods in a negative way.

If the buyer is in doubt as to whether a seller who has not performed his obligation to deliver or make replacement delivery or remedy defects, will be capable of performing within a period acceptable to the buyer he may by virtue of Art. 47(1) fix a "reasonable additional period" within which the seller is required to perform his obligations. In this way the buyer may eliminate doubts as to the material character of a delay.

For the seller's failure to observe the timelimit thus fixed will automatically imply that the delay is material and thereby attract the remedy of avoidance, cf. Art. 49(1)(b). The additional period must, however, be fixed at such realistic length that the seller has a practical possibility of observing it. If this is not the case the buyer is barred from avoiding until the delay is material on an objective view.

Art. 48 allows the seller to counter-act the effects of his defective performance even after the time of delivery in that the Article (48(1)allows him e.g.

to remedy a defect by repair and thus prevent the buyer from avoiding the contract. Such remedying is required to be made without unreasonable delay for the buyer and without causing the buyer unreasonable inconvenience or uncertainty of reimbursement by the seller of any expenses he may incur in that respect.

Under Art. 48(2) the seller may request the buyer to state whether – notwithstanding the breach occurred, e.g. delay – he will accept the seller's corrective performance. If the buyer fails to reply to such request within a reasonable time the seller may perform the contract within the timelimit he has stated in his own – unanswered – request.

4.2. The right to avoid the contract of sale

Under Art. 49 the buyer may avoid the contract

- where the seller's breach is "fundamental" (material), cf. Art. 49(1)(a)
- in case of non-delivery, where the seller fails to deliver within the additional period of time fixed, or where the seller himself declares that he will not deliver within the period so fixed, cf. Art. 49(1)(b).

4.3. The right to claim damages

Whether the buyer affirms the contract or avoids it he may claim damages from the seller for the loss he has incurred by the breach, cf. the common provisions in Arts. 74-77.

These Articles only contain rules on the *computation* of damages and the starting point is always that the seller is liable for *any* breach. Under Art. 79 the seller is exempt from liability if he shows that the failure to perform his obligations was due to an impediment "beyond his control", cf. Section 8 for more details.

5. Obligations of the buyer

The buyer's obligation to pay the purchase price and take delivery follows from the generally drafted provision in Art. 53 and the more detailed provisions in Arts. 54-60. Arts. 61-65 relate to the seller's remedies on the buyer's breach. Arts. 53-65 are supplemented by the common provisions in Arts. 71-88 on the buyer's and the seller's obligations.

5.1. Payment of the purchase price

The buyer's obligation to pay the purchase price also implies that he is to take such steps as the contract may require to enable payment to be made, e.g. open a documentary credit, apply for bank guarantee etc., cf. Art. 54. The buyer's failure to perform such obligations will amount to actual and not just anticipatory breach. However, the seller may under Art 63(1) set up a timelimit for the buyer's performance of such obligations.

Where the contract of sale does not fix the purchase price the parties are deemed to have agreed the price which at the conclusion of the contract is generally charged for similar goods where they are sold under comparable circumstances in the trade concerned, cf. Art. 55.

Where there is doubt as to the computation of the price of goods sold according to weight, the price is, according to Art. 56, to be determined by the net weight, i.e. the weight of the goods proper excluding package.

On a line with the main rule in the Bonds Act s. 3 (1) and the Sale of Goods Act s. 9(1) the purchase price is, in the absence of agreement to the contrary, to be paid at the seller's place of business or, where payment is to be made against handing over of the goods or of documents, at the place where the handing over takes place, cf. Art. 57(1). If the parties have agreed on documentary credit, payment is normally to be made at the financial institution at which the seller will present the documents agreed upon in the credit terms.

Unless the parties have agreed otherwise, the purchase price is payable when the seller places the goods or the documents controlling their disposition at the buyer's disposal in accordance with the contract, cf. Art. 58(1). The seller may make the handing over of the goods or documents contingent upon concurrent payment of the purchase price ("performance against performance"), cf. also Art. 58(2) whereby the seller, when the contract involves carriage of the goods, may dispatch the goods on the condition that they are not to be handed over except against payment in cash.

The buyer is not to pay the purchase price until he has had an opportunity of examining the goods. A prior examination may, however, be inconsistent with the procedure of delivery and payment agreed by the parties, e.g. if the parties have agreed "payment against documents", cf. Art. 58(3).

5.2. Taking delivery

Under Art. 60 the buyer is under an *obligation* to take delivery, e.g. make transportation contracts, apply for export or import licence, etc. where such arrangement lies with the buyer under the agreement made, and the obligation also includes a duty to take over the goods. The buyer's failure to take such measures is considered a *breach* in the CISG-rules and not – as would be the case under the Sale of Goods Act – as a claimant's non-performance. The Convention also contains rules on the duty of the other party to take care of the goods by way of preservation, sale or ultimate clearance, as prescribed in the Sale of Goods rules on claimant's non-performance, viz. in Arts. 85-88.

But these obligations are conceptually attached to a breach by the other party and not to his failure to take delivery.

6. The seller's remedies for breach of contract by the buyer

Art. 61(1) contains an overview of the seller's remedies for the buyer's breach of contact. The Article refers both to Arts. 62-65 and to the rules on damages etc. in Arts. 74-77. To the extent that they relate to an avoidance of the contract the provisions mentioned must be combined with Arts. 72 and 73 governing avoidance before the time for performance and avoidance in contracts of instalment deliveries, respectively, and with Arts. 81-84 on the effects of avoidance.

6.1. The right to affirm the contract

Art. 62 establishes the seller's right to claim payment of the purchase price. In addition the seller may claim that the buyer takes delivery of the goods and performs any other obligations he may have under the contract and at least this part of Art. 62 must be seen in the light of Art. 28 limiting the access of claiming specific performance. On the other hand it is doubtful whether Art. 28 of the Convention limits the seller's right to obtain judgment for the payment of the purchase price.

Under Art. 63(1) the seller may fix an additional period of reasonable length within which the buyer is to perform his obligations. Art. 63(2) debars the seller from exercising remedies for breach other than damages before the expiry of such additional period.

If the buyer – despite agreement to this effect – fails to communicate specifications on the goods (e.g. measurement, form, etc.) to the seller, Art. 65(1) allows the seller the right (though not a duty) to effect such determination of the properties himself after the expiry of a reasonable period following the seller's unavailing request to the buyer to provide the information. The seller is bound to notify the buyer of the making of the specifications and fix a reasonable time within which the buyer may make a different specification, cf. Art. 65(2).

6.2. The right to avoid the contract

The seller may avoid the contract on the buyer's fundamental breach. Further, the seller may avoid the contract within the timelimit which may have been fixed under Art. 63(1).

If the buyer has paid the purchase price the seller will normally – even if payment was delayed – lose his interest in avoiding the contract. However, Art. 64(2) allows the seller to avoid the contract if the avoidance can be made before the time at which the seller became aware that the buyer's delayed payment had been made. In similar circumstances the seller may avoid the contract if the buyer's breach consists in non-performance of obligations other than the obligation to pay the purchase price, cf. Art. 64(2)(b).

The contract has not been validly avoided unless the seller declares such avoidance by notice to the buyer in accordance with Art. 26.

In contrast to the rule following from the Sale of Goods Act s. 28(2) the seller's right to avoidance is not prejudiced by a handing over of the goods. However, in relation to i.a. the buyer's creditors the seller is only protected if he has made a reservation of title in the goods or similar safeguarding, compare Art. 4 under which the CISG-rules only govern the relationship between the seller and the buyer but are not concerned with the property in the goods.

7. Passing of risk

Arts. 66-70 on passing of risk govern the factors in connection with performance of a contract of sale which are solved by ss. 17 and 37 in the Sale of Goods Act. The legal effects of the passing of the risk from seller to buyer correspond to the effects under s. 17(1) of the Sale of Goods Act and both sets of rules are necessary supplements to the rules governing the buyer's obligation to pay the purchase price.

Art. 66 does not expressly address the legal effects of loss of the goods or damage to them *before* the risk passes to the buyer. However, it follows from Art. 36(1) that the seller is liable for defects which are present at the time at which the risk passed to the buyer. A destruction or deterioration of the goods before the risk passed to the buyer will imply that the seller will either be liable for delay because he cannot deliver the goods or alternatively for lack of conformity. The effect may be that the buyer may avoid the contract, and that the seller will not be paid and in addition may incur liability in damages.

The CISG-rules do not expressly tie up passing of risk with delivery in the strict manner provided in the Sale of Goods Act s. 17(1). But the rules are couched in such a way that the passing of risk will be attached to delivery all the same in a number of cases.

If the contract of sale involves dispatch of the goods and the seller is to send the goods without simultaneous agreement on handing over at a particular destination, the risk of the goods will pass to the buyer when the goods are handed over to the *first carrier* for transmission to the buyer, cf. Art. 67(1), 1st. clause. Where the goods are to be handed over to a carrier at a particular place, e.g. when the parties have agreed that the goods after transportation by road or rail to a specified port are to be handed over to a shipping company with a view to further dispatch by sea, the risk will pass to the buyer when the goods have been handed over to the shipping company in question, cf. Art. 67(1), 2nd clause. It is irrelevant for the passing of risk that the seller may keep the documents controlling the disposal of the goods.

The risk will only pass to the buyer if the goods have been clearly identified to the contract by marking, transport document, notice to the buyer or similar means, cf. Art. 67(2).

For cases which are not comprised by Art. 67 and Art. 68 the risk passes to the buyer when he takes delivery of the goods or – if he fails to take measures aiming at taking delivery at the due date and thereby is in breach of the contract – from the time at which the goods are placed at his disposal, cf. Art. 69(1). Article 69(1) therefore comprises cases in which the buyer is to take delivery of the goods at the seller's place of business and is to arrange transportation from that place himself. The rule will also apply when the goods are to be delivered by the seller at the buyer's place of business and when the goods are to delivered at a place on the way to the buyer without the seller being bound to transmit them from that place.

The implication of the wording "the goods are placed at the disposal of the buyer" means that the seller must e.g. have packed the goods if such duty is on him. Goods which are not *appropriated* to the contract from among the seller's other goods cannot be considered placed at the buyer's disposal until they have been clearly identified, cf. Art. 69(3). If the buyer is to take delivery of the goods at a place other than the seller's place of business, the risk will pass to the buyer when the time for delivery has arrived and the buyer is aware that the goods have been placed at his disposal at the place indicated, cf. Art. 69(2).

By *avoiding* the contract a buyer may "escape" the risk even if it had passed to him according to the foregoing, viz. when the seller has committed a fundamental breach, e.g. delivered defective goods entitling the buyer under the rules in Arts. 45-52 to take such step of avoidance, cf. Art. 70. A further requirement is that the buyer is capable of returning the goods, cf. below on Art. 81 of the Convention.

8. Common rules on the seller's and the buyer's obligations

8.1. Anticipatory breach and instalment contracts

Sometimes it is necessary to be able to regulate a situation in which one party needs to react towards the other party even if that other party has not yet actually breached any of his obligations but where it is likely that the other party cannot (or will not) perform his obligations at the due date. Cases of such anticipatory breach are governed by Arts. 71-73.

Under Art. 71(1) a party to a contract of sale may *suspend* the performance of his obligations if, after the conclusion of the contract, it becomes apparent that the other party will not (or cannot) perform a substantial part of his obligations as a result of serious inability to perform or for lack of credit worthiness, or on account of his conduct in the preparations to perform or in performing the contract. This does not imply that any new information incriminating the creditworthiness of the other party will entitle the other party to claim anticipatory breach. It is required that (new) circumstances materially changing the assumptions under which the contract was made, e.g. that the other party has also lacked financial capability or professional qualifications to perform contracts of sale with *other* contract partners. A premature avoidance as a result of a party's conduct "during the preparations of the contract" may be relevant if the buyer and seller are to cooperate in the processing of the goods and one party's performance in this respect falls short of the other party's justified expectations.

A seller who has dispatched the goods before the new information became available may prevent that the goods are handed over to the buyer, i.e. he may exercise *stoppage* of the goods. Stoppage may be effected even if the buyer has received a transportation document or other form of disposal controlling instrument giving him the right of possession of the goods, cf. Art. 71(2).

The party who suspends performance of the contract must under Art. 71(3) notify the other party to such effect forthwith and he must resume performance if the other party grants him adequate security, e.g. in the form of a bank guarantee that he will perform his obligations.

Where, before the expiry of the time for performance, it becomes *evident* that one of the parties will commit a fundamental breach of contract the other party may *avoid* the contract, cf. Art. 72(1). The phrase "becomes evident that a party will commit a fundamental breach" shows that to apply Art. 72(1) it must be much more certain than the requirement of one's own suspension of performance under s. 71(1) that the party will indeed be in breach and the anticipated breach is even required to be "fundamental". The more stringent requirements must be seen on the background that to a party in breach it is often far more onerous that his contract partner avoids the contract than a mere suspension would be. The party wishing to avoid must, if the time so permits, notify the other party accordingly to enable that party to provide adequate assurance of his performance, cf. Art 72(2).

No notification is to be given to the other party if the anticipated breach is founded on a declaration by the other party that he will not perform his obligations, cf. Art. 72(3).

If it turns out later that the basis for avoidance did not really exist the party who avoided will be placed as if he had cancelled the sale without just cause and this may release remedies for breach in favour of the other party.

Also cases in which a seller has concluded a contract with a buyer on instalment deliveries may proceed in such manner that one of the parties as a result of anticipatory breach will suspend performance or avoid the contract with the other party, cf. Art. 73.

8.2. The right to claim damages

Both Art. 45(1)(b) on the *buyer's* remedies for the seller's breach of contract and Art. 61(1)(b) on the *seller's* remedies for the buyer's breach set forth that the party in breach of the contract of sale may be liable in damages towards the other party. The duty to pay damages under the provisions mentioned will arise irrespective of whether the breach is attributable to the party concerned. In other words, it is the breach *per se* which releases a claim for damages, if any. However, the liability in damages is limited by the defence stated in Art. 79.

Under Art. 74(1), 1st clause, damages shall consist of a sum equal to the loss suffered by the innocent party as a consequence of the breach and may include lost profit. The amount of damages is to place the injured party as if the contract had been duly performed.

Both the principle of covering a party's expectation interest and the requirement in Art. 74, 2nd clause, that damages are only to cover loss which is not too remote (on a foreseeability test) are consistent with the rules of Danish (case) law regarding computation of damages both in contract and in tort.

Arts. 75 and 76 are supplementary to Art. 74 in that these provisions state that damages on avoidance of the sale may comprise the difference in price which is ascertainable i.a. in a self-help sale (the seller's substitute sale of the goods), by covering purchase (the buyer's obtaining similar goods from another seller) or otherwise, e.g. by showing a current price (market price) of the goods in question. A loss which is not covered by the rules in Arts. 75 or 76, e.g. in respect of use interruption and lost profit, may be recovered under Art. 74.

Where the contract is affirmed the buyer may by virtue of Art. 74 recover an *operational loss* which he has suffered because of the interruption in his production facilities registered within a period and of expenses he may have incurred in the repair of a defective article etc. A delay in the payment of the purchase price entitles the seller to claim interest as well, cf. Art. 78.

The party relying on a breach of contract is under an obligation to take reasonable measures of *mitigating* the loss brought about by the breach, cf. Art. 77, 1st clause. The duty to mitigate may imply that a buyer who fails to make a covering purchase – in order to avoid breaching a delivery obligation himself towards a third party – within a reasonable time after having learned that "his" seller will commit breach may not always rely on recovering his (full) loss from the seller. Similarly, by making a self-help sale a seller may mitigate the loss caused by the buyer's refusal to take delivery. Where a party fails to take such measures the party in breach may claim a reduction in the damages in the amount by which the loss should have been mitigated, cf. Art. 77, 2nd clause.

8.3. Interest

Under Art. 78 a party who fails to pay the purchase price or any other sum which is due is liable to pay interest on the amount. The rule relates primarily to interest on the purchase price but will also apply to e.g. interest on a sum which the seller is to return upon avoidance of a sale. The rule is applicable even if the debtor may rely on one of the defences in Art. 79.

The claim for interest on a money sum does not prejudice the right under Art. 74 to claim damages for loss, which is not covered by the interest.

8.4. Exemption from liability

The crucial CISG-rule in this context is Art. 79 which states the circumstances which may lead to an *exemption* from liability which a party would otherwise incur for breach of contract.

The exemption from liability must be seen in the light of the strict liability principle of Arts. 45 and 61 applying to a party in breach (buyer or seller) and imposing liability irrespective of fault in connection with the non-performance.

Art. 79 will exempt a party from liability in damages if he can show that the following conditions are satisfied:

– that an impediment of performance existed
– that such impediment was beyond his control
– that he could not reasonably be expected to have taken the impediment into account at the conclusion of the contract, and
– that he could not reasonably be expected to have avoided or overcome the impediment or its consequences.

There will be an "impediment" of performance if all goods contemplated for performance in the contract have been destroyed and where a party's performance or performance measures have failed as a result of force majeure situations hitting a seller's factory or raw material stocks, or government interference by way of export or import bans, sales prohibitions etc.

The requirement that the impediment must be outside the control of the party in breach means that only external events will qualify for the liability exemption in contrast to factors within a seller's own enterprise resulting in non-performance.

If the seller knew the impediment at the conclusion of the contract or had special grounds to expect that it would arise the requirement that he could "not reasonably be expected to take the impediment into account" is not satisfied.

The last requirement for exemption from liability "that he could not reasonably be expected to avoid or overcome the impediment" implies i.a. that the party exposed to impediments must inquire into alternative performance ways, e.g. whether goods which he had contemplated buying from a certain seller may be supplied by other dealers, or – where a contemplated transportation form is not applicable – whether alternative means may be used to bring the goods to their destination.

Where a party has engaged a *sub-contractor* to perform the whole or a part of the contract, and an impediment arises in respect of such sub-contractor, the party in question may only rely on exemption from liability if he can show that the impediment is of such nature that it will be comprised by Art. 79(1) both as regards the sub-contractor and the contract party himself. Thus a seller is barred from liability exemption if the impediment only exists for the third party engaged, e.g. an export ban in the country from which the third party contemplated exporting an article, if the seller himself or another sub-contractor was able to obtain the article from a country which was not affected by a similar export ban, cf. Art. 79(2).

Art. 79(2) only comprises impediments hitting a group of persons "engaged" by the party in breach to perform the contract in full or in part. If supplies from a third party are not connected with the sale in question, e.g. where interruption of energy supplies occurs at a seller's factory the issue of the seller's potential liability is exclusively to be evaluated on the basis of Art. 79(1).

The liability exemption has effect as long as the impediment exists, cf. Art. 79(3).

The party whose performance is impeded on account of the factors mentioned in Art. 79 must give notice to the other party of the impediment and its effect on the possibilities of performing the contract, cf. Art. 79(4). Where the other party does not receive such notification within a reasonable time after the party in breach became aware or ought to have become aware of the impediment the party in breach is liable for damages resulting from such non-receipt.

8.5. Effects of avoidance of the contract

Under Art. 81(1) a party's avoidance represents a termination of the rights and obligations of both parties to effect specific performance but the avoidance does not affect a party's obligation to pay damages to the other party. Nor will the avoidance affect provisions in the contract on the parties' rights and obligations attached to avoidance. A provision e.g. stipulating arbitration in the event of disputes will stand as will also e.g. a provision of an agreed penalty.

A party who has performed the contract wholly or in part may claim that the other party returns what the former party supplied or paid under the contract, cf. Art. 81(2) which corresponds to s. 57(1) of the Sale of Goods Act. Where both parties are obliged to make restitution they must do so concurrently.

A buyer's right to avoid the contract on account of the seller's breach will not lapse merely because he takes delivery. He may e.g. if he has received defective goods avail himself of all the remedies which are offered under Art. 45, including avoidance, cf. Art. 49(1) or substitute delivery, cf. Art. 46(2).

On the other hand it follows from Art. 82(1) that the buyer will prima facie lose the right to avoid the contract or claim substitute delivery if he is incapable of returning the goods in substantially the same condition as he received them.

Art. 82(1) which corresponds to s. 57(1) of the Sale of Goods Act, is modified by Art. 82(2) under which the buyer may avoid the contract or claim substitute delivery even if the goods cannot be returned in *substantially the same condition* as he received them, if the impossibility of making restitution is not due to an act or omission on the buyer's part but may be attributed to e.g. an accidental cause or inherent vice in the goods themselves, or is a result of the examination which the buyer is to undertake under Art. 38, or because the goods or part of the goods have been consumed or transformed by the buyer in the normal course of use before the buyer discovered or ought to have discovered the defect. The advantage to the buyer of avoiding the contract instead of claiming damages is that – if the market price of similar goods has fallen – he will be able to claim restitution of the (higher) sum of the purchase price. If on the other hand the market price has gone up a claim for substitute delivery or damages will be more attractive to the buyer.

The principles of Art. 82(2) correspond to s. 58 of the Sale of Goods Act.

A buyer who loses the right to avoid the contract or claim substitute delivery will retain all other remedies, e.g. the right to claim that the seller cures defects, the right to claim damages, and the right to claim proportionate reduction of the purchase price, cf. Art. 83.

On avoidance of a contract of sale the seller is bound, where he has received the purchase price, to pay interest on such price from the date on which payment was made, cf. Art. 84(1).

Similarly, a buyer is, under Art. 84(2), bound to pay an amount to the seller for the benefit he has had of the goods e.g. if prior to the return of a machine he has been able to put it to use in his enterprise or – where the goods have been sold and therefore cannot be returned – for the benefit of the price he obtained for them in the sale.

8.6. The preservation duty of the parties

Arts. 85-88 correlate with the rules of the Sale of Goods Act on claimant's non-performance, i.e. the rules in ss. 33-37.

The Convention does not use the terminology of claimant's non-performance because a buyer's failure to take delivery is treated as a breach of contract in the CISG-rules. Instead Art. 85 speaks of cases in which the buyer "is in delay in taking delivery" including cases in which the buyer fails to pay the purchase price where payment and delivery are to be concurrent acts.

If the buyer is to collect the goods with the seller at the seller's place of business but fails to do so, the risk of their accidental destruction or deterioration passes to the buyer, cf. Art. 69 and the seller's obligations are changed to a duty to preserve the goods, cf. Art. 85 under which the seller must "take such steps as are reasonable in the circumstances to preserve the goods".

The seller has a right to retain the goods until the buyer has indemnified him for the reasonable expenses he has incurred in such respect.

The substance of the seller's duty to preserve the goods varies according to the nature of the goods and their value.

The seller may have the right to deposit the goods at a third party's warehouse, cf. Art. 87, at the account of the buyer or he may have a right or duty to sell them, cf. Art. 88.

The buyer will be under a similar obligation to preserve the goods where he has taken delivery but intends either to avoid the contract or claim substitute delivery. If the buyer's non-acceptance of the goods is justified and the buyer has notified his intention to avoid the contract to the seller, cf. Art. 26, the storage of the goods is at the seller's risk and account and the buyer may retain the goods until the seller has indemnified him for reasonable expenses incurred thereby, cf. Art. 86(1).

The duty to preserve the goods also applies when goods have been sent to the buyer and have been placed at his disposal at the place of destination since the buyer may in that case take possession on behalf of the seller provided he can do so without payment of the price and without unreasonable inconvenience and expense, cf. Art. 86(2).

The party who is obliged on the other party's behalf to preserve the goods may if there has been an unreasonable delay by the other party in taking possession of the goods or in paying the price or expenses of the preservation sell the goods by appropriate means after notifying the other party that he intends to do so, cf. Art. 88(1).

If the goods are subject to rapid deterioration or their preservation would involve unreasonable cost a party who is bound to preserve them must take reasonable steps to sell the goods, cf. Art. 88(2). From the proceeds of sale he may retain an amount corresponding to the reasonable expenses of preserving the goods and selling them before paying the balance to the other party, cf. Art. 88(3).

9. Documentary credit

9.1. The concept

Briefly described a documentary credit arrangement is a device whereby a bank acting in accordance with instructions from a customer (the "applicant") or another bank commits itself to paying a sum of money to a third party (the "beneficiary") when such third party presents a number of documents as described in the contract of sale. The bank's commitment to pay may arise immediately upon presentation of the documents or at a later stage. In a documentary credit arrangement normally two banks will participate, cf. the procedure immediately below.

A documentary credit is a combination of a *method of payment* and a *bank guarantee* which is particularly useful when a seller wishes security for the payment of the goods he sends to a buyer in a foreign country and, conversely, where a buyer wishes security that by paying the credit amount he will have the documents concerning the sale handed out to him.

The International Chamber of Commerce (ICC) has prepared a set of rules governing documentary credits. These rules, "Uniform Customs and Practice for Documentary Credits" (ICC Publication No. 500, in the following referred to as "UCP") apply to the parties and the banks involved in the documentary credit arrangement when the parties have agreed to apply the rules.

A characteristic feature of a documentary credit is that the arrangement is an independent transaction *separate from* the contract of sale which the credit concerns, cf. UCP Art. 3. All parties in documentary credit transactions are concerned with *documents*, not with goods or services, cf. UCP Art. 4.

Comprehensively, Arts. 3 and 4 of the UCP express the essence of a documentary credit. The seller who may present the documents required under a documentary credit arrangement is *entitled* to have the purchase price honoured by one of the banks involved.

Even if a dispute may arise between the parties as to whether the seller has duly performed the contract (whether non-defective goods were delivered at the right time and at the right place) and even if the buyer may succeed in a claim before a court of law or tribunal alleging breach by the seller, such judgment or award will not affect the principle that the credit involves *independent* obligations for the parties which are released no matter how well it is substantiated that the seller has not performed his obligations under the contract.

Whether a documentary credit is to be opened depends, as mentioned, on whether the parties have agreed on this as a term in their contract, viz. the term concerning payment obligation.

Where the parties have so agreed the practical procedure is as follows:

1) the buyer instructs his bank (*the issuing bank*) to open a documentary credit in favour of the seller; 2) the issuing bank gives notice by a letter of credit to a bank in the seller's vicinity (the *advising bank*) stating a) that a documentary credit has been opened, b) the type of credit involved, c) the terms upon which the credit has been opened; 4) the seller, who is in this context referred to as *beneficiary,* is notified by letter (advice) from the advising bank that a documentary credit has been opened in his favour;

5) the seller now dispatches the goods and receives a receipt from the carrier, e.g. a Bill of Lading, or similar transport document; 6) the transport document and the *other* documents which the credit arrangement prescribes that the seller is to procure (e.g. insurance policy, customs documents, documents relating to origin or nature of the goods, etc.) are now presented by the seller at the advising bank and if the documents are in conformity with the requirements of the credit as regards number and contents the amount of the documentary credit is paid to the seller – or the bank makes a declaration that the amount will be paid out at a later date, cf. below on the socalled "long" documentary credit; 7) the documents are sent by the advising bank to the issuing bank which hands over the documents to the buyer against receiving the amount of the credit from him; 8) the buyer is thereupon entitled and authorized to have the goods handed over to him from the carrier at the arrival of the goods at their place of destination.

Each party has now obtained what they aimed at: The seller has received payment and the buyer the goods he is entitled to under the contract.

From the *buyer's* point of view the *security function* of the documentary credit arrangement is manifested in the knowledge that the seller is deprived of disposal once the transport documents have been handed to the advising bank, whether the transport document is a Bill of Lading, a CMR consignment note, a consignment note for sea transport or railway transport, or an air waybill. The buyer may rely on having the goods handed out at the destination place even if the transportation of the goods has been controlled by a Bill of Lading since the possession of this document authorizes the buyer to have the goods handed out from the carrier.

Where transport has been effected under a consignment note the goods will be handed out to the buyer if he is named as addressee in the consignment note. If the issuing bank will ensure that the goods are not handed out to the buyer until he has paid the credit amount to the bank, the bank must require as a condition for opening the credit that the bank or a specially appointed third party, e.g. a forwarding agent, is named as addressee in the consignment note.

From the *seller's* point of view the security of a documentary credit is that the procuration of the documents required in the credit arrangement suffices to ensure that the purchase price is paid irrespective of the buyer's ability (or willingness) to pay. This distinguishes this form of payment from the CAD device (cash against documents) whereby the seller may indeed arrange that the goods are not handed out to the buyer until he releases the documents but he cannot be certain that the buyer actually does show up at the place of document releasing to perform his obligations.

9.2. Various types of documentary credit

9.2.1. Revocable v. irrevocable credits

If a documentary credit has been opened as revocable the issuing bank may revoke the credit at any time. In practice the seller will invariably stipulate irrevocable credit terms to avoid that his dispositions are dependent merely on the bank's omission to revoke. If the parties have not addressed the issue expressly the documentary credit will be deemed irrevocable, cf. UCP Art. 6.

9.2.2. Confirmed v. unconfirmed credits

By *confirming* the credit the *advising bank* will make an unequivocal undertaking that the bank will also be liable for the credit amount provided that the terms of the credit are satisfied. By this confirmation the seller obtains security against "political risks" (e.g. a government embargo preventing the issuing bank from transferring currency to another country) and against other obstacles to the issuing bank's transfer of funds to the seller. A bank which has confirmed the credit cannot refuse to honour the claims of the beneficiary even if the bank may foresee that political instability in the issuing bank's country may jeopardize its own reimbursement of the amount paid to the seller. If the credit is *unconfirmed* the seller will only have a credit guaranteed by the issuing bank, i.e. a credit which is no better that the issuing bank and its country.

The honouring by the advising bank of the credit amount under a confirmed credit is *final*. The bank is barred from a subsequent *recourse* against the seller with a view to recovering the amount from him if the issuing bank fails to pay.

9.2.3. Payment documentary credit v. negotiation credit

A payment documentary credit is a credit which the issuing bank has made payable e.g. with the advising bank. This implies that once the advising bank has paid for the documents received from the seller the seller cannot be made liable to repay the money to the bank. Payment is *final* even if it turns out that the advising bank receives no coverage from the issuing bank. This applies whether the advising bank has confirmed the credit or not. Thus from a practical point of view there is no significant difference between a payment credit arrangement and a confirmed credit.

On the other hand the counterpart of payment credit, the *negotiation credit,* is made *payable with the issuing bank.* This means that the advising bank instead of final honouring of the seller's documents on behalf of the issuing bank will buy (negotiate) a *draft* as prescribed in the terms of the documentary credit drawn by the seller on the issuing bank or on the buyer, as the case may be, and which is accompanied by the documents required in the terms of the credit.

9.2.4. Sight v. long-term credits

A documentary credit is available both for cash and credit sales. Where a documentary credit has been opened for payment of the purchase price in a cash sale the credit is termed *"sight documentary credit"* and the bank will pay the beneficiary as soon as it has been established that the documents presented comply with the terms of the credit. A *long term credit* implies that the buyer has been granted deferment of payment and therefore the honouring of such credit will not be effected until at a later date, e.g. 60 days after shipment of the goods. In connection with a long-term credit drafts will normally have been issued which have been drawn by the beneficiary on the issuing bank or on the applicant (buyer).

9.3. The credit documents

As was mentioned initially, *documents* are vital in the context of this type of commercial credit arrangement.

The number and type of document which the seller is to present depends on the terms of the credit agreed by the parties already at the conclusion of the contract. Since the exact number and nature of the documents involved are therefore dictated by the contract no general indication can really be given.

However, the parties will almost always have agreed that one of the documents is to be a *transport document.* Requirements in respect of documents are set out in UCP Arts. 23-33. Where the parties have agreed e.g. on sea transportation which will call for a Bill of Lading to be presented such Bill of Lading must i.a. show that the goods have been loaded on board a named vessel or shipped by a named vessel. Thus, a Bill of Lading of receipt which merely acknowledges that the goods have been received for carriage will not satisfy this requirement. Where the agreement merely states presentation of "a transport document", a "dispatch document" etc., the normal practice is that any and all of the transport documents, including i.a. seaway bills and CMR consignment notes will satisfy the requirements of the credit in such respect.

Often a documentary credit will provide that the seller is to effect insurance in respect of the goods and that an *insurance policy* must therefore be provided substantiating that the seller has fulfilled this obligation, and the number of documents may comprise a *commercial invoice*, documents regarding the properties of the goods, e.g. *certificate of origin, certificate of quality* etc. and documents concerning customs handling, e.g. *customs invoice and/or consular invoice* etc.

The seller must realize that he needs to present all the required documents and that the contents of the documents must conform accurately to the terms of the credit to release a duty of payment with the banks concerned. Under UCP Art. 13 a bank must examine all documents with reasonable care prior to adopting the documents. Where the documents appear *on their face* to comply with the terms of the credit the bank may act in confidence to such appearance without liability i.e in paying, accepting or negotiating drafts etc.

UCP Art. 32 requires that the transport document is "clean" and a document which declares a defective condition and/or packaging in a clause by the carrier will be rejected by the bank. If the seller is to present a full set of "clean on board marine bill of lading" the transport document is also to comprise all original specimens of the document, it must be clean, i.e. without clauses indicating damage etc. and the bill of lading must be an on board bill of lading issued by a sea carrier.

Dependent on the contents and nature of the documents the buyer will obtain security that the goods delivered are conforming to the contract as regards number of units and weight. On the other hand the buyer will not obtain absolute security that the goods are non-defective. Even if the transport document will usually contain certain information on the quality of the goods the carrier will normally not be obliged to examine the properties of the goods on receipt. Only where it is evident that the goods received are of a character other than that described in the transport document will the carrier be obliged to make a clause to such effect on the document, cf. the comments in that respect in Chapter 12. However, often the carrier will have no possibility of ascertaining the quality of the goods with certainty. This would not be possible e.g. if the goods were transported in a closed container.

If the buyer requires greater security that the quality of the goods was satisfactory when they left the seller he may agree with the seller that a clause is inserted in the documentary credit terms to the effect that the seller is to deliver, among the necessary documents, a certificate issued by an organisation within the line in question or other body of control whereby the contractual conformity of the goods at shipment is certified. If a dispute between the parties on the conformity of the goods at dispatch arises such dispute will most often develop after the documents have been released for the buyer's account which will usually give the seller an advantage as towards the buyer. Any claims as to lack of conformity must then be settled after the seller has received the purchase price. The value of a claim against the seller (e.g. for damages in respect of defects in the goods) will depend on the seller's capability to pay and the disadvantage of having to enforce a claim against the seller in a lawsuit, often in the seller's own country.

10. Export Credit Schemes

To a Danish enterprise whose activities are completely or partly based on export it may sometimes be difficult to estimate a foreign customer's financial standing and whether such customer can be expected to pay outstanding amounts to the Danish enterprise as they fall due. And even if the foreign customer is able and willing to pay in his home country a situation may arise in which government interference in the country in question makes it impossible to transfer the amount to the Danish exporter.

To counter-act losses on export claims Denmark, on a line with most other Western countries, has provided special arrangements whereby a Danish enterprise may obtain security (*guarantee*) for the payment of an amount outstanding with a foreign customer irrespective of the customer's inability or unwillingness to perform his obligation. To strengthen the operational possibilities of export firms to finance exportation of goods and services a scheme of *state guarantee* has also been available for loans taken up by firms with Danish financial institutions.

The funds to finance the export credit schemes mentioned have until now, as far as Denmark is concerned, derived from the Danish Commercial Fund whose fund provisions and equity are now transferred to the Export Credit Fund (ECF).

Under s. 1 of the Act on the Danish Export Credit Fund etc. (Consolidated Act No. 199 of 12 September 1999 with subsequent amendments) the Fund's purpose is to secure to Danish export internationally competetive terms as regards coverage of extraordinary risks in connection with exports and to administer the provision of state assistance in the financing hereof.

Under s. 6(1) the ECF may apply coverage types corresponding to the insurance and guarantee products recognised in the market and in addition it may offer coverage forms necessary to perform the purpose of the Fund. The ECF may offer coverage towards business enterprises, financial institutions, insurance companies or other undertakings assuming a risk directly or indirectly in connection with the implementation of Danish exports, cf. s. 6(2) of the Act.

The ECF will only cover the risk of loss to the extent to which the private commercial insurance and capital market will not normally take the risk or insure against a risk in relation to Danish exports, cf. s. 6(3).

In practice, as seen from a Danish exporter's point of view, a guarantee will ensure that his enterprise is protected against the commercial and/or political risks which may be involved in dealing with a foreign client.

The commercial risk consists in the client's inability or failure to pay before the expiry of a certain number of months after the due date because of unsound financial circumstances. The political risk is the risk that payment is not made as a result of the political-economic conditions in the client's country of business, e.g. as a result of government interference involving restrictions in the access of transfer of currency out of the country.

A guarantee has the same function as an *insurance* in that the Danish exporter – against paymnt of a *premium* – protects his foreign claims in the same way as he would normally do in respect of other assets and interests. The "insured event" , i.e. the factor triggering off the payment of the insurance sum (the claim outstanding) from the instance placing the guarantee (the ECF) is that the client defaults in his obligation to pay the claim to the exporter. Upon indemnifying the Danish exporter the guarantor will subrogate to the claim outstanding. Usually only *part of a claim* against a foreign client may be guaranteed (normally 85-90 per cent). The rest of the claim is the exporter's "own risk".

The purpose of the guarantee is to further the posibilities of Danish export undertakings of financing exports of goods and services.

A guarantee is placed with primary liability towards (usually) a Danish financial institution. If the ECF's liability materialises the exporter will be liable in recourse for the amount paid.

Normally the guarantee access has been limited to *operational financing* to the exclusion of *capital financing*, such as investments in machinery and real property.

The main contents in the ECF Act are that short-term commercial risks in industrialised countries are to be covered in the private insurance market. But state export credit is designed for extraordinary risks, i.e. political and commercial risks on a medium-and long term as well as short-term commercial risks in e.g. developing countries.

11. Incoterms

11.1. Introduction

The main purpose of the *Incoterms* prepared by the International Chamber of Commerce (ICC) was to provide the parties to an international contract of sale of goods with a set of trade terms which in a succinct and unequivocal manner address the division of costs, risks and other obligations in connection with *delivery* between the parties. By agreeing that one of these terms is to apply the parties may, irrespective of nationality and legal conception, reduce the risk of encountering difficulties because they had diverging conceptions of the duties each of them had towards the other party in connection with delivery. An agreement that a certain Inco-term, e.g. FOB, is to govern the parties' obligations in connection with the carriage of the goods will make a choice of law decision in view of the international element of the contract unnecessary.

The most recent amendment of Incoterms was made in 1990. The amendment was made to accommodate a desire to adapt the terms to the increased use of electronic datacommunications. Therefore the clauses in Incoterms will be unaffected by a development in which paper documents issued in connection with a contract of sale including invoice, documents to be used at delivery or transport documents, may be replaced by electronic communications granting the parties the same legal position as they would have under a traditional paper document, e.g. a bill of lading.

Another main reason for the amendment of the Incoterms was the continued development of changes in transport forms, including consolidation of goods in containers, roll on/roll off traffic involving trucks and railway waggons and an increasing use of combined transportation types.

11.2. The structure of Incoterms

The structure of Incoterms enables the parties to ascertain their respective obligations step by step. For each of the 13 Incoterms the buyer's and the seller's obligations in respect of delivery are stated below 10 headlines, and each headline on the seller's page (the "A-page") will reflect the legal position of the buyer (the "B-page") in the same situation. Where it is stated e.g. below the headline A.3 (Contract of carriage and insurance) that the seller is to see to contract of carriage the corresponding heading for the B.3 will be "No obligation".

The 10 headlines are as follows:

1. Provision of the goods in conformity with the contract and payment of the purchase price
2. Licences, authorizations and formalities
3. Contract of carriage and insurance
4. Delivery and taking delivery
5. Transfer of risks
6. Division of costs
7. Notices to buyer and seller
8. Proof of delivery, transport document or equivalent electronic message
9. Checking, packaging and marking
10. Other obligations

The 13 terms are grouped into 4 categories so that each term within the individual category has the same initial letter, i.e. E-terms, F-terms, C-terms, and D-terms.

The parties will not have a free choice among all the terms in a given context. Thus, six of the terms are only applicable to sea transport, including transport via inland waterways (FAS, FOB, CFR, CIF, DES, and DEQ) whereas the remaining 7 terms are applicable to any transport mode, including multimodal transport. An appendix of the collective Incoterms is provided at the end of the book.

11.2.1. E-terms

This category has only one term, the EXW (ex works).

Where this term has been agreed the seller has performed his obligation to deliver when he has made the goods available to the buyer at his own premises, i.e. at the seller's place of business, factory, warehouse etc.)

The seller is not obliged to see to loading of the goods. This duty will lie with the buyer who is to provide means of transport (or engage a carrier). When the buyer has decided how the collection of the goods is to be made he must notify the seller accordingly.

When the goods have been placed at the buyer's disposal with a view to collection the risk passes to the buyer since the buyer is to pay the costs of transporting the goods to the place of destination. Unless otherwise agreed, the purchase price is to be paid with the seller at the same time as the goods are made available to the buyer, cf. the principle in s. 14 of the Sale of Goods Act and CISG Art. 57(1).

Where the goods are not collected by the buyer or by a carrier engaged by the buyer there will, under Danish law, be a situation of claimant's non-performance on the buyer's part and usually also a breach of contract.

Conversely, the seller will be in breach if he fails to make the goods available to the buyer at the time agreed.

11.2.2. F-terms

Under F-terms the seller is to deliver the goods to a carrier appointed by the buyer. The terms include *FCA* (Free Carrier), *FAS* (Free Alongside Ship) and *FOB* (Free On Board).

Under the *FCA* term the seller has performed his obligation to deliver when he has handed over the goods, in a customs-cleared state, to the carrier appointed by the buyer at the place named in the term. "Carrier" denotes any person who undertakes in accordance with a contract of carriage to perform or see to performance of carriage by rail, road or air, inland waterways or by a combination of such carriage modes. Where it has not been agreed that the buyer is to pay "cash against documents" (CAD) the purchase price is payable with the seller when the goods have arrived at the place of destination, cf. s. 15 of the Sale of Goods Act and CISG Art. 57(1). In the relationship between the seller and the buyer there is no obligation on the seller to effect contract of carriage since this duty is, as already mentioned, on the buyer who is to effect a contract of carriage of the goods from the place named. At this point s. 10 of the Sale of Goods Act is derogated from and the risk of accidental destruction or deterioration of the goods during the *preliminary transportation* to the carrier (e.g. a carriage terminal) is therefore with the seller who will not be released from such risk – and the costs involved in the carriage – until the goods are handed over to the carrier. However, the risk will pass to the buyer if he fails to effect contract of carriage and thereby debars the seller from handing the goods over to a carrier. In *multimodal carriage*, e.g. a road carriage from Odense to Hamburg which is subsequently combined with sea transport from Hamburg to Kuala Lumpur, the decisive point in a delivery context – and thereby the passing of risk and division of costs – is the identity of the first carrier since the handing over to "first carrier" constitutes delivery under the term. After that stage the buyer has the risk both in respect of the goods and of the costs involved herein.

The *FAS* term which is only applicable in sea transport and inland waterway transport implies that the seller has performed his obligation to deliver when the goods have been placed alongside the vessel in the port of shipment. Unless otherwise agreed, the purchase price is payable when the goods are handed over to the buyer at the vessel's side, cf. s. 14 of the Sale of Goods Act and CISG Art. 57(1). This difference as compared to the FCA term results from the fact that the FAS term does not involve the seller's contribution to the carriage of the goods. The contract of carriage is irrelevant to the seller since the duty to effect such contract is on the buyer who is also under a duty to notify the seller on the ship's name, loading place, and required delivery time. If the vessel named fails to arrive at the right time and the seller is thereby debarred form delivering the goods alongside it, the risk will pass to the buyer.

Where the parties have agreed that the *FOB* term is to govern delivery the seller has performed his obligation when the goods have passed over the ship's rail at the named *port of shipment.* After that stage the buyer will bear the risk of accidental destruction and deterioration. The term implies that the buyer is to choose carrier and make contract of carriage with such carrier and the buyer is therefore to notify the seller of the ship's name, loading place and required delivery time. Where the buyer fails to give such notification the risk of accidental destruction or deterioration will pass to the buyer, cf. s. 37 of the Sale of Goods Act and Art. 69(1) of the CISG. The purchase price is payable with the seller when the goods have been made available to the buyer at the place of destination, i.e. at the conclusion of the transport carried out by the ship to which the seller hands over the goods, cf. s. 15 of the Sale of Goods Act and Art. 57(1) of the CISG. However, the parties will often have agreed another arrangement, e.g. cash against documents (CAD) or such arrangement may follow from special rules and in that case the purchase price is payable against delivery of the documents involved.

11.2.3. C-terms

With all C-terms the *seller* is to make carriage contract and pay freight costs to the place of destination named in the individual term. The C-terms comprise *CFR* (Cost & Freight), *CIF* (Cost, Insurance and Freight), *CPT* (Carriage Paid To) and *CIP* (Carriage and Insurance Paid To).

The *CFR* term which is only applicable in sea transport or inland waterways transport, implies that the seller is to pay transport costs to the named *port of arrival.* However, the *risk* of loss or of damage to the goods will be transferred to the buyer once the goods have passed the ship's rail in the *port of shipment.* Unless cash against documents (CAD) or other payment arrangement has been agreed the purchase price is payable with the seller when the goods have arrived at the place of destination. When the goods have been loaded on board the vessel chartered the seller is to notify the buyer to such effect and make such other communication as is required in order to enable the buyer to take the measures necessary to take delivery, e.g. prepare unloading and customs clearance at the port of destination.

The *CIF* term has the same implication to the parties of the contract of sale as the CFR term except that the seller is also to effect – and pay premium in respect of – *marine insurance* to cover the buyer's risk of accidental loss or damage to the goods during their transportation to the place of destination (the port of arrival). The CIF term has a long tradition of being one of the most important terms of transport. However, after the introduction of container transport and the increased use of combined transport modes the term has lost some of its importance in favour of the terms Free Carrier (FCA) and Delivered Duty Paid (DDP) which are applicable in both sea and land transport.

The *CPT* term which in contrast to the CFR and CIF terms is applicable to all types of transport, including multimodal transport, implies that the seller is to pay the costs of the transportation of the goods to the named place of destination. The seller makes the carriage contract and the risk of the accidental loss or damage to the goods passes to the buyer when the goods are handed over to the carrier appointed. Where several carriers are involved in the transport delivery is made at the handing over to the *first carrier*. As mentioned in the description of the FCA term this term will also impose upon the seller a duty to hand over the goods to a carrier but in contrast to the FCA term, the CPT term will place the duty of appointing and making contract with the carrier on the *seller*. The seller is to give notice to the buyer on the carrier chosen so that the buyer may take the measures necessary to take delivery at the place of destination. Such place will be at the conclusion of the transport made by the carrier to whom the seller hands over the goods (where such carrier is the only carrier involved). Unless otherwise agreed, the purchase price is payable with the seller when the goods have been handed over to the buyer at the place of destination.

With the *CIP* term the buyer and the seller have the same obligations as with the CPT term except that under the CIP term the seller is to effect cargo insurance to cover the buyer's risk of loss or damage to the goods during the carriage.

The CIP and CIF terms are the only Incoterms which will impose a duty on the seller to effect insurance covering the buyer's risks during the carriage.

11.2.4. D-terms

The application of a D-term implies that the seller is to bear costs and the risk until the goods have reached their place of destination. D-terms comprise *DAF* (Delivered at Frontier), *DES* (Delivered Ex Ship), *DEQ* (Delivered Ex Quay (Duty Paid)), *DDU* (Delivered Duty Unpaid) and *DDP* (Delivered Duty Paid).

When transport is governed by the term *DAF* the seller has performed his obligation to deliver when he has made the goods available to the buyer, duty paid, at the place named in the term at the frontier but before the frontier line proper. The term is particularly practical for transport by road or by rail. Unless otherwise agreed the purchase price is payable with the seller when the goods are handed over to the buyer. The seller is to provide export licence for his own account and risk but the costs involved in the carriage of the goods after the time at which they are placed at the buyer's disposal are with the buyer.

With the *DES* term delivery is effected when the goods have been made available to the buyer *on board the ship* at the *port of arrival* named in the term. Since the seller and the buyer or their representatives are present at the same time payment of the purchase price shall be made with the seller, unless otherwise agreed, when the goods are handed over to the buyer at the port of arrival. The seller is at his own expense to arrange transportation of the goods to the port of arrival and is also to notify the buyer of the estimated time of arrival of the ship named. The buyer is to pay costs of *unloading* and customs costs etc. involved in the importation of the goods and the costs of the further transportation of the goods.

The *DEQ* term implies that the seller has performed his obligation to deliver when the goods have been placed at the buyer's disposal on the *quay* of the *port of arrival* named (delivery ex quay). The buyer is not required to be present on the quay or at the place of unloading but the seller must make sure that someone is there to take care of the goods. If he fails to do so he may be liable in damages for loss or damage to the goods.

As with the DES term the seller is to notify the buyer of the estimated time of arrival of the ship named. The *purchase price* is payable with the seller when the goods are handed over to the buyer. The costs in connection with delivery, including customs duties, taxes and public fees are payable by the seller. Where it has been agreed that the buyer is to be liable for import duties, the words "duty unpaid" will be used instead of the words "duty paid" and it may also be specified that only part of the duties shall be paid by the seller, e.g. "Delivered duty unpaid, VAT paid etc. ...".

The terms DES and DEQ may – in contrast to the two following terms (DDU and DDP) – only be applied for sea transport or inland waterways transport.

The place of delivery where the *DDU* term has been agreed is the place in the import country named in the term. Up to that place the seller will bear all costs and the risk of the goods. All customs duties, taxes and other public fees are payable by the buyer but as with the DEQ term the parties may specify that certain duties are payable by the seller. The purchase price is payable with the seller when the goods are handed over to the buyer, cf. s. 14 of the Sale of Goods Act and Art. 57(1) of the CISG.

The DDP term is identical with the DDU except that the DDP imposes upon the seller the obligation to obtain import licence and to see to customs clearance in connection with import as well.

As will have been apparent in the foregoing the carrier will often play an independent part in the delivery measures involved in long-distance contracts of sale. Therefore, where the goods are damaged during the transportation from the place of delivery to the place of destination agreed the issue of placing liability for the loss one of the parties incurs may arise.
The loss will typically affect the buyer since the risk of accidental damage to the goods has passed to him when they were handed to the care of the carrier (and thereby delivered).

The carriage of the goods from the place of delivery and to the buyer (the place of destination)- dependent on the contract and concrete circumstances-

will be effected via four different modes of transport, viz. carriage by sea, road, railway, and air.

During the most recent decades, with the increasing use i.a. of containers, it has become increasingly common that carriage of goods involves various means of transport each undertaking part of the total carriage from receipt of the goods up to their handing over to the buyer. Where the same means of transport is used for several stretches of such "successive transport" (e.g. by ship from Aarhus to Hamburg and then by another ship to a foreign continent) the term *"through transport"* is used. Where several means of transport are used (e.g. transport by road to Hamburg and then by ship) the transport is termed *"combined"* (or *multi-modal).*

All four modes of transport are regulated by statutes whereby the carrier is under a *stricter liability* than in ordinary tort law e.g. in respect of loading ("cargo") damage (physical damage to the goods or loss) and in respect of delay. In addition the carrier may be held liable for having handed out the goods to a person other than the proper addresee, and he may also be liable if, in connection with receipt of the goods he failed to examine whether the description of the goods in the transport document was correct.

In the following the conditions for the carrier's incurring liability will be examined with the starting point taken in the rules governing two of the major transport modes, carriage by sea and carriage by road.

Sea transport is regulated by the Maritime Act (consoldiated order No. 39 of 20 January 1998 with subsequnt amendments).

Within road transport the legal regulation of international and domestic transport differs:

Where the transport is international, which presupposes that the place of dispatch is in a country other than that of receipt of the goods, the contract will be governed by the CMR Act (Consolidated Act No. 602 of 9 September 1986). The term relates to the Convention (Convention relative au contrat de transport international de marchandises par route/ convention on the contract for the international carriage of goods by road) upon which the Act is based. Where both place of dispatch and place of recipt are in the same country the transport will be domestic, governed as far as Denmark is concerned – by no specific legislation except the rules following from the Traffic Acts.

The Maritime Act:

Under s. 275(1) and s. 278(1) of the Maritime Act the carrier is liable under *a fault rule with reversed burden of proof* for losses caused by damage to the goods, their loss, or delay, unless he can show that neither he nor his employees caused or contributed to the loss.

The carrier's liability for loss and damage will apply while the goods are in his care in the port of loading, during transport and in the port of discharge, cf. s. 274(1).

Where one of the *defences* mentioned in s. 276(1), no. 1 and 2, applies the carrier may escape liability if he can show that loss or damge was caused by default or neglect in the navigation or management *of the ship* on the part of the master, crew, navigator, or other persons employed in the service of the ship ("nautical" fault) or was brought about by fire, unless caused by the fault or neglect of the carrier himself.

Dealy in delivery will lie if the goods have not been delivered at the agreed time in the port of discharge named, cf. s. 278(2) and (3).

The CMR Act:

Under the CMR Act s. 24(1) a carrier is liable for damage to the goods, their loss or delay in connection with the performance of an international road carriage unless one of the defences mentioned in s. 24(1) applies. In a practical context the carrier is *strictly liable* since the exempting circumstances mentioned in s. 24(2) are really of *a force majeure* character. For loss and damage to the goods the carrier will escape liability if he can show that the loss/damage was attributable to one of the factors mentioend in s. 25 (use of open unsheeted vehicles, defective packing of the goods, inherent vice in the goods themselves, etc.).

Successive transport:

With a through document the liability attaching to the means of transport will normally extend to to all the carriers participating in the performance of the carriage. The carrier who entered into the contract with the customer will therefore normally be liable for the damage which may have occurred while the goods were with another carrier, cf. e.g. s. 285(1) of the Maritime Act.

With documents concerning *multi-modal transports* the documents themselves will usually specify the liability rules applicable if the goods are damaged in transit. On the other hand, where the liability rules are not evident from the documents, difficulties may often arise as to proving in whose care the goods were when they were damaged. This is because the damage will usually not be established until the goods are delivered to the addressee by the last carrier. Where liability is alleged towards the last carrier – in the absence of proof of the exact place for the occurrence of the damage- a presumption will lie that such carrier received the goods in an un-damaged condition from his predecessor. Normally, therefore, a claim for damages may be set up towards the last carrier under the liability rules applying for the last section of the carriage.

If the carrier has violated the liability rules applying to a particular transport area and is unable to rely on a defence the injured party (the cargo owner) is entitled to damages for the loss suffered.

However, transport legislation operates on a principle of *standardisation* and *maximization* of the items of loss an injured party may claim. In other words the measure of damages is not the same as the usual point of departure in Danish law, viz. *expectation interest basis*.
Where the goods have been damaged, or lost, the computation of damages will be based, as a starting point, on the value of the goods, and items of loss such as lost profit and consequential loss will not be compensated. Cf. s. 279(1) and the CMR Act s. 29(1) and (3), and s. 31. To this must be added that the damages amount is further maximized to certain "highest amounts", cf. e.g. s. 280 (1) of the Maritime Act, and s. 29(2), s. 31(2) and s. 32 of the CMR Act.

Special limitations to the compensation amount will apply when the carrier exceeds the delivery term *(liability for delay),* cf. s. 280 (2) of the Maritime Act (damages limited to an amount equivalent to two and a half the freight payable in respect of the delayed goods), and the CMR Act s. 32 (damages limited to the freight amount).

The carrier is barred from relying on defences or special limitations in the damages amount if the loss was caused by *his intentional misconduct* or *gross negligence*, cf. s. 283 of the Maritime Act, and s. 37 of the CMR Act.

Further, the carrier may incur liability for delivery to a person other than the person stated in the consignment note as consignee. The special rules of limitation of liability applying to *loss of the goods* are not applicable to such cases.

The transport documents are often – especially in international trade – important goods "tokens" (e.g. in connection with documentary credit, Cash Against Documents, etc.). Therefore the documents must contain information relevant from a sales law view on the nature, quantity, and extent etc. of the goods carried.

Throughout transport legislation this purpose is sought to be achieved by rules dictating the nature of information required in a consignment note amd by providing that the sender (normally the seller) is entitled to require introduction of special information into the document.

In the safeguarding of these considerations the carrier will also play an active role: *To the extent reasonably possible*, the carrier's function is to verify that the information in the transport document is accurate. He is also under a duty himself to inform in that he is obliged to provide the document with a reservation clause if the information on e.g. loaded units does not correspond with the number stated in the transport document, cf. e.g. the Maritime Act s. 298 and s. 11(cf. s. 10) of the CMR Act. Violation of this "duty of description" may cause the carrier to incur liability in damages.

13. Insurance of goods in international trade

A major part of the legal relationships will arise from contracts of sale between parties with a geographical distance between their places of business.

Therefore the parties must address the issue whether insurance should be taken out for damage which may hit the goods during their carruage – and in the affirmative – which party is to take such measure and who is to bear the costs involved.

The *CISG* convention contains no rules on the insurance issue which must therefore be settled in accordance with the contract the parties may have made.

Like any other insurance transport insurance is relevant if the goods reach the seller in a damaged state or never reach him at all because they are lost (or destroyed) on the way.

The insurance duty is closely connected to the issue regarding which party is to bear the risk of accidental loss of or damage to the goods but the contract may also provide that the seller is to effect insurance for the part of the transport for which the risk is on the buyer under the rules of sales law. This would be the case if the parties have agreed on using the CIF term. Apart from such cases it will be a matter for the risk-bearing party to decide whether transport insurance should be taken out.

13.1. Choice of insurance form

Insurance may be taken out as a *single insurance*, i.e. an insurance to be effected each time a shipment of the goods takes place, under a *general policy* whereby a mandatory insurance coverage within a certain period, e.g. a month, is obtained upon which premium settlement takes place or it may be taken out as a *floating policy* by which premiums are paid for a period, e.g. a year (advance premium) which is subsequently regulated by the end of the year on the basis of the actual sum of shipment for the individual areas covered.

13.2. Insurance terms

Where insurance is taken out on "Limited Danish Terms" the insurance coverage will comprise the socalled "serious accidents" (the "disaster risk"). In sea transport this will include i.a. damage sustained in total loss or as direct results of fire, explosion or of the sinking, capsizing, wreck, grounding, or collision of the ship, and in road and air transport i.a. damage caused by fire, explosion or by an accident which has affected the transport means, e.g. by collision, overturning or crashing of planes. These terms are in the main equivalent to the English terms often applied, the *Institute Cargo Clauses* (C) prepared by the Institute of London Underwriters.

To supplement "Limited Danish terms" the parties may agree on coverage of other damage, e.g. theft, damage caused by adverse weather conditions, or damage caused by other cargo ("Extended Danish Terms").

In international trade insurance is often taken out as a socalled *all-risks insurance* (Institute Cargo Clauses (A) (All risks)). This insurance covers all damage and loss to the goods during the carriage caused by external events with the exception of inherent vice or damage caused by delay in the arrival of the goods to the place of destination.

CHAPTER 10

Credit Agreements

by Bent Iversen

1. The Credit Agreements Act

The Credit Agreements Act (CAA), Act No. 398 of 13 June 1990 with subsequent amendments, which replaced the Credit Sale Act as from 1991 regulates the legal relationships arising in connection with granting of credit. In contrast to its predecessor, the Credit Sale Act, which was limited to sale on a credit basis, the Credit Agreements Act governs all types of credit contract in a *consumer setting*, including credit sale, agreements on money loans, account contracts etc., cf. s. 1(1) of the Act. In addition it follows from ss. 49-52 of the Act that some of the rules applying in consumer contexts including primarily a number of rules on sale with *reservation of title* are also applicable in a credit sale which is not a consumer sale. Under s. 7(1 and 2) such sale is subject to mandatory regulation, also outside consumer relationships, in that the rules are not to be derogated from to the detriment of the buyer. The following account relates to sales with reservation of title and not to the other forms of credit agreements in the CCA.

A sale with reservation of title implies as a characteristic under s. 6 in the CAA that the seller may recover the subject-matter sold if the buyer fails to observe his duties.

Under a valid reservation of title the seller obtains protection of his right as towards third parties, so-called "transfer protection", and he may recover the subject-matter sold from an assignee to whom the buyer has (illegitimately) sold it contrary to the title reservation. This applies even if the assignee was innocent, i.e. he had no knowledge of the reservation of title. Further the reservation of title enjoys protection against the buyer's creditors. This does not mean that the buyer's creditors are barred from seeking satisfaction in the goods sold. But if they do so they must *respect* the seller's better right (the reservation of title).

Part 10 of the Credit Agreements Act sets forth the requirements of a valid reservation of title. Further this part of the Act addresses i.a. the creditor's satisfaction, including the requirements for recovery of the goods sold, rules regarding computation of the claim and the value of the goods sold, procedure in a recovery, discharge and exemption rights, etc. The rules in Part 10 of the Act cannot be treated in isolation, however. For the Act is structured so that the rules of Parts 2-9 (ss. 8-33) are applicable to all consumer credit agreements including a sale with a retention of title. This combination implies that other parts of the Act, except Part 10 (e.g. the information duty under s. 9, the rule of payment in s. 25 etc.) must be included in a description of the reservation of title right.

Also the provisions in Part 6a of the Registration of Property Act governing i.a. the registration of reservation of title in certain motor vehicles (in the Car Register) must be observed. The rules of the Car Register in this respect are treated below in Chapter 17.

The comments in Section 1 relate to reservations of title in consumer relationships. The rules on reservation of title outside consumer contexts (in commercial sales) are mentioned in Section 2.

1.1. Validity of the reservation of title

The CAA is based on a one-string system which implies that a creditor in a consumer sale who wants to secure his claim is not allowed, in connection with the conclusion of the contract or upon delivery of the goods, to obtain a *mortgag*e in such goods to ensure that the consumer performs, cf. CAA s. 21(1). The option available to such creditor is therefore limited to a reservation of title. The mortgage ban affects not only a seller granting a respite in respect of payment of (part of) the purchase price but also a third party comprised by s. 5, no. 2. of the CAA who has granted a loan to the buyer under a preceding agreement to such effect with the seller (a so-called original tripartite relationship).

A mortage right granted in violation of s. 21(1) is void – both between the parties and towards a third party. However, the mortage ban does not prevent, under s. 21(2) that a creditor under the rules governing mortgage of real property obtains a mortgage right in the subject-matter sold as long as such goods constitute an appurtenant or constitutent part of real property cf. the provisions in ss. 37 and 38 mentioned below in Chapters 16 and 17.

Under s. 34(1) of the CAA an agreement of reservation of title shall be made at the latest at *the handing over* of the goods to the consumer which compared with agreements for sale of goods corresponds to the rule in the Sale of Goods Act s. 28(2) whereby a seller's right to cancel a sale will cease on the handing over of the goods to the buyer.

A reservation of title must be *agreed* between the parties and the seller is therefore barred from imposing such reservation unilaterally.

The agreement for reservation of title must comply with all the rules in the Act governing credit agreements. Therefore the agreement is to be made in writing (with a copy to the buyer) cf. s. 8, and it must contain the information mentioned in s. 9 and s. 14, as well as the other material terms of the contract Applied on a sale with reservation of title the seller must under s. 9 and s. 13 inform the buyer of the cash price, the down payment and the credit charges. In supplement to the statutory rules, case law adds the requirement that an agreement for reservation of title must be *unequivocal and express*. It must specify the subject matter upon which reservation of title has been made . Thus a reservation described in general terms such as "furnitue" or "machinery" will not be valid.

A special requirement for the validity of the reservation of title in a *consumer sale* is provided in s. 34(1) no. 4 whereby the seller at the handing over of the goods to the consumer must have received at least 20 per cent of the cash price, i. e. the price at which the goods might have been sold against cash at the conclusion of the contract. The seller is only considered "satisfied" for the down payment if he has neither directly nor indirectly a financial interest in the financial form by which the down payment is made. In more specific terms, this imlies that a seller is not satisfied if he has granted a loan to the consumer to cover the down payment or has placed a security by way of mortgage or guarantee for a loan taken up by the consumer to pay the down payment.

If the seller accepts (second-hand) goods in exchange the down payment requirement is satisfied if the goods substituting payment in money represent a value at least corresponding to the required minimum down payment.

Failure to effect down payment in a consumer sale invalidates the *retention of title* made. In that case the sale is treated as an ordinary credit sale which means that in the event of deafult by the buyer the creditor will be barred from recovering the goods sold. However, an application of s. 30(1) by the bailiff''s court may refer the creditor to seek satisfaction in a recovery of the goods sold, cf. also s. 30(2) which contains an express reference to the cases in which the requirements in s. 34 in respect of reservation of title are not satisfied.

Under s. 34(3) a contract of sale with reservation of title may not be "combined" with other transactions between the seller and the consumer, e.g. with debt obligations the buyer may have with the same seller, except from repair debts under the rule in s. 28(3). The reservation of title is only designed to protect sums which the seller may legitimately secure under s. 38 (the sum remaining outstanding, interest on payments due, and costs inherent in a recovery).

When the consumer has cleared off the debt under the contract the contract has served its purpose and it is not available for 2re-use" by the seller to secure new (other) claims.

1.2. Satisfaction of the creditor

When, on a consumer's breach, the creditor seeks satisfaction of his claim he *must* resort to the remedy of recovering the goods sold, cf. s. 35. When recovery has been made he is normally barred from setting up further claims against the consumer, cf. below, however, on the excemption cases following from ss. 41-42 of the CAA.

1.3. Requirements for recovery

Under s. 36(1) the creditor may recover the goods in an immediate execution without order of the court if

1) the contract of sale is duly signed by the consumer and he has been supplied with a copy, and
2) the contract contains a reservation of title.

Recovery may be made where the consumer is in material breach of his obligations under the contract. Whether a breach is material for the purposes of the Credit Agreements Act will follow from s. 29.

Under s. 36(1) the "necessity exemption" of the Administration of Justice Act will also apply to a sale with reservation of title. The necessity exemption, cf. s. 509(1) of the Administration of Justice Act restricts the assets a creditor may remove from a debtor's home and exempts assets "necessary to maintain a modest home for the consumer and his household". The exemption will attach to e.g. vacuum cleaners, refrigerators, ordinary TV-sets and radios etc. whereas assets of greater value, e.g. paintings, major stereo sets etc. may be recovered.

1.4. Computation of the claim

As already mentioned the reservation of title will only secure the special claims comprised by s. 38, i.e.

1) the sum remaining due, with deductions under s. 27(2-3)
2) interest on sums due, and
3) necessary costs incurred in the recovery of the goods sold, including collection costs unless s. 24 presents a bar hereto.

The starting point is that the creditor may claim the amount the consumer is still to pay. However, the claim of the creditor is to be reduced in accordance with the provision in s. 27, which must be seen in the light of s. 26 granting the consumer the right to early payment without limitation. The costs necessary in the recovery will include lawyer's fee, if any, transport costs and costs involved in an evaluation of the goods sold. The reservation in s. 38, no.

3, "unless s. 24 presents a bar hereto" refers to situations in which the creditor has failed to supply the information prescribed in s. 9. Where such information has not been supplied the creditor is normally barred from claiming indemnification for costs which would otherwise have been incurred as a result of the consumer's breach, cf. s. 24.

1.5. Evaluation of the goods sold

While s. 38 determines the items the *creditor* may include in his favour in connection with a recovery of the goods sold, s. 39 implies that the value of the goods recovered is to be credited to *the consumer*.

Under s. 39(2) the value assessment is dependent on the price the seller may obtain by selling the goods in a proper manner elsewhere.

The evaluation of the goods is made by the bailiff's court, possibly with the assistance of experts, cf. s. 47.

If the value of the goods sold exceeds the sum remaining owing to the creditor he will only be entitled to recover the goods if he pays the consumer the excess amount, cf. s. 40.

Where the remaining debt exceeds the value of the recovered goods the starting point is that the creditor is *barred from claiming such remaining amount* from the consumer. This rule is related to the rule referring a creditor to seek satisfaction by recovery of the goods sold (i.e. barring him from execution instead of recovery), cf. the remarks above in 1.1. on the "one-string" character of the CAA. Any claim remaining due to the creditor is, in accordance with this starting point, irrecoverable.

However, in some very special cases the creditor will maintain the access to claim an outstanding debt, cf. s. 41. This applies in particular where the consumer, as a result of negligence in the use or custody of the goods sold, has deteriorated their value and where the consumer has obstructed the seller's recovery of the goods sold.

The outstanding amount may not exceed the loss caused by the consumer's negligence etc.

Where the rule on necessity exemption in s. 36(2) bars a recovery of the goods sold the creditor may take the consumer's other assets in execution for an amount equivalent to the value assessment of the goods at the time of the execution, cf. s. 42(1). This places the creditor on the same financial level as if his application for recovery had been met. However, the creditor's access to claim a remaining sum by execution on the property of the consumer is also in that case subject to the restrictions laid down in s. 41. Hence the creditor may only seize goods in execution for the sum remaining due if the consumer has shown negligence in the use or custody of the goods sold or has obstructed the recovery.

If the goods are not in the consumer's possession the creditor may take the consumer's other assets in execution for the full amount at which his claim has been computed, cf. s. 42(2). In other words the risk of the goods' being irrecoverable is on the consumer.

1.6. The consumer's redemption and exemption rights

Where recovery has been effected the consumer may within a timelimit of 14 days redeem the goods sold against payment to the creditor of the amount at which his claim was computed in the recovery proceedings, cf. s. 43, 1st clause. Where the contract of sale comprises several items the consumer is entitled, in recovery proceedings, at his own discretion, to exempt one or more items of an entity against payment of an amount whereby the creditor's claim exceeds the value of the rest of the items, i.e. the items recovered by the creditor, cf. s. 44(1). The consumer may not single out items which are so incorporated with items recovered that the severance will cause material deterioration in value of the recovered goods, e.g. when the sale comprised a complete set of furniture composed on several, single components.

1.7. Recovery proceedings

S. 45(1) sets forth a number of procedural requirements which must be met by the creditor in order to execute recovery proceedings properly.

Petition for recovery must be presented to the bailiff's court within the district of the consumer's venue (his residence), cf. s. 45(2).

Where the creditor fails to appear at the recovery proceedings appointed the bailiff's court must dismiss the petition. If the consumer fails to appear at the court meeting he may be forced to appear with the assistance of the police and he is obliged, under oath, to supply the information required by the court to carry through the recovery proceedings.

Where the creditor has repossessed the goods without order of the court and without consent from the consumer (i.e. engaging in self-help, cf. s. 294 of the Criminal Code) the bailiff's court must under s. 48 dismiss execution proceedings which the creditor may later request on the sale or the recovery. Thus the creditor is barred from presenting a subsequent claim to the court for the levying of execution in respect of an amount remaining due, unless special circumstances warrant such step or the creditor has acquired a special legal basis after the recovery, e.g. a judgment against the consumer for a debt due.

2. Commercial Sale

Part 11 of the Credit Agreements Act modifies the starting point emphasised initially in this Chapter that the main aim of the Act is to regulate the legal relationship between a creditor and a *consumer*.

The term used in Part 11 is "non-consumer sale" which indicates that the provisions in Part 11 encompass both commercial sale and credit sale which are not consumer sale. The concepts of commercial sale and civil sale are mentioned above in Chapter 8.

The provisions are drafted so that s. 49 transfers certain provisions for credit agreements in a consumer setting to commercial *credit sale* as well while s. 50 delimits the extent to which the rules on *sale with reservation of title* are applicable to non-consumer sale. Finally, ss. 51-52 contain rules applying only to commercial sale with reservation of title.

The provision in s. 2, 2nd clause, of the Credit Agreements Act. limiting the sphere of application of Part 11 is discussed below in Section 2.3.

2.1. Common rules: The Credit Agreements Act s. 49

S. 49 provides that the following rules are common rules in consumer credit agreements and *credit sales* which are not consumer sales (commercial sales):

s. 22: the "general clause" of the Credit Agreements Act

s. 25: Re: the buyer's payment into a financial institution

s. 26 and s. 27. Re: the buyer's access of early payment of his debt and reduction of credit charges,

s. 28: Re: the buyer's access to appropriate payments to a claim out of several possible, and

s. 29. Re: determination of whether a consumer buyer's breach is material or not.

2.2. Special note on reservation of title

Under s. 50(1) all the rules in Part 10 of the Act relating to sale with reservation of title are prima facie also applicable to such sale outside a consumer setting.

Under s. 50(2) the following rules are non-applicable to commercial sales:

s. 34(1), no. 4:

- the effect of excluding the application of this provision to commercial sale is that e.g. in an agreement between a dealer and a trader for delivery of a machine to be used in the trader's enterprise there will be no requirement of a *minimum downpayment* for a valid retention of title clause in respect of the machine. The other requirements (mentioned in Part 10 of the Act) for the validity of a reservation of title must however, be met, including in particular the requirement that the reservation must have been agreed no later than at the handing over of the goods to the buyer, the ban against combining the sale with other transactions etc.

s. 35:

- in a commercial sale with reservation of title the creditor may decide at his own discretion whether to recover the goods on the buyer's breach *or* alternatively, whether he will seize other assets of the buyer in execution for the amount of his claim, cf. s. 51(1). In other words the creditor is not – as he was under s. 35 – subject to a "one-string" system to the effect that he is *required* to seek satisfaction by recovery of the goods sold. However, execution may not be effected against the goods themselves. Where execution would be deemed to bring about unreasonable loss or considerable inconvenience to the buyer the bailiff's court *may* refer the creditor to seek satisfaction as far as possible by a recovery of the goods sold, cf. s. 51(2).

ss. 41-42:

- commercial sale with reservation of title is governed by s. 51(3) instead of ss. 41-42. Where the creditor has still got a claim on the buyer after recovering the goods because the value of the goods recovered has been estimated at a lower amount than the creditor's claim the creditor may on the basis of the evaluation by the court seize other assets of the buyer in execution *for the remaining sum*. The same applies where the rule of necessity exemption debars recovery of the goods sold or where the goods are not to be found with the buyer in the course of recovery proceedings. The creditor's claim and his access to enforcement by way of execution is thus not dependent on a deterioration of the goods sold caused by the negligence of the buyer or his obstructing the recovery, such as was required in a consumer setting under ss. 41-42.

2.3. Special note on s. 2 of the Credit Agreements Act and credit consignment

Under the provision in s. 2, 2nd clause, Part 11 of the Act does not apply to traders purchasing for *re-sale* or to a sale of materials to be used in the production of the trader's enterprise. This limitation implies that the special rules on commercial sales will only apply to a sale of working plant whereas goods supplied for re-sale are not comprised.

A sale with a reservation of title with licence to re-sale is termed a *credit consignment*. In such arrangements, which only occur in commercial settings, the seller (the consignor) retains property in the goods until they have been resold by the buyer (the consignee) to a third party.

In several respects, credit consignment resembles factoring relationships and it is sometimes difficult to distinguish the two relationships. However, one distinct difference may be recorded: the factor sells in his own name for the account of the principal whereas a consignee sells in his own name and for his own account.

The reservation of title made by the consignor is, as already mentioned, not applicable as towards the consignee's assignees in contract but only as towards the creditors of the consignee in respect of goods which are in the consignee's possession as unsold. However, it would seem ill-advised to debar a person's creditors from satisfaction in respect of assets of which their debtor (the consignee in this case) has full power of disposal (in that he is entitled to sell the goods under the consignment agreement). Hence to obtain protection against the consignee's creditors further requirements must be met to ensure that the reservation of title is a reality between the parties and not only a security affecting the consignee's creditors. Under case law the main requirements are that the consignee shall settle with the consignor at fairly regular intervals at the rate of the re-sale of the goods and that the consignor shall ensure via adequate control that the settlement requirement is satisfied.

It is not possible to state in more detailed and specific terms the requirements which must be met in regard to settlement and control – they would no doubt differ according to type of goods involved anyway. In the determination, special emphasis will be placed on whether the consignee has made separate consignment accounts, whether a written consignment agreement has been made, and whether the consignee has a right to return unsold goods. Where these questions may be answered in the affirmative, the reservation of title is likely to be acknowledged. The opposite result will obtain if the consignee on the delivery of the goods paid by a bill of exchange, if he is to pay the purchase price partly in advance (on-account terms), and if the purchase price is to be paid at a certain point in time at the latest, or on expiry of a certain period. In these cases the purchase price is normally payable at a point in time other than the point of resale which defies a strict observance of the settlement requirement. Where the agreement purports that the consignee at the expiry of a timelimit which is fairly short, is required either to pay the purchase price or return the goods – which will usually be observed by the consignee – the reservation of title in respect of goods in the consignee's possession as unsold will usually be acknowledged. On the other hand, if the agreement allows that the purchase price is debited to the consignee's ordinary account on the expiry of the timelimit the goods are regarded sold on a fixed account whereupon creditor protection on the reservation of title will be denied – also as regards goods for which the timelimit has not yet expired.

CHAPTER 11

Intellectual Property Rights

by Morten Wegener

1. Introduction

Intellectual property law deals with the question of affording legal protection to a number of practically and financially very important assets, viz. to literary, artistic, technical, etc. works as well as to trade marks and other trade symbols. To a large extent, the protection is provided by specific Acts covering the individual types of performance and feature. The most important Acts are *the Copyright Act* (literary, artistic, etc. works), *the Patents Act* (inventions), and the *Trade Marks Act* (trade symbols in the form of trade marks). Disregarding the fact that the works mentioned all may be said to be of intellectual and intangible nature, the primary feature combining them in a special area of law is the fact that the legislation makes universal use of an *exclusive rights construction*: the person producing the work (the author, the inventor, etc.) is, in *certain* respects, granted the *exclusive access* to using the work. Such construction is indicative of one of the fundamental questions of intellectual property law: on the one hand, it is, in general, desirable that persons who make great independent efforts – e.g. an inventor – should be granted the possibility of reaping the financial fruits of such efforts. On the other hand, it may lead to socially detrimental effects, especially in terms of development and competition, if the protection is stretched too far. It is thus a matter of creating a reasonable balance between, first, the need for protection of the individual effort and the consequential "reward" of such effort and, second, the need for ensuring that said protection does not stifle social development and sales.

Since the exploitation of intellectual property to a large extent may be – and in reality is – of transboundary nature, there are clear indications of the need for comprehensive international cooperation in respect of the legal protection. Indeed, such cooperation has been progressing – and with Danish participation – since the end of the last century. Examples on a global scale thus include *the Paris Convention* (1883 with subsequent amendments) for the protection of so-called "industrial property" (particularly patents, designs and trade marks), and *the Berne Convention* (1886 with subsequent amendments) for the protection of copyright. The Conventions in particular lay down certain minimum requirements in respect of the protection to be provided by the various national statutes. In Europe, such cooperation mainly takes place between EU member states, resulting in certain common rules on patents, copyright and trade marks. Finally, a Nordic union has existed for many years, cooperating on protection in respect hereof, and intellectual property legislation in the Nordic countries is thus, to a large extent, uniform.

Intellectual property legislation is closely connected with competition rules and regulations as provided by the Marketing Practices Act, cf. Chapter 12, below. In practice, it will thus often be appropriate to consider the possibilities of applying various provisions in the aforesaid Act as a supplement or an alternative to the protection offered by the exclusive rights contained in the individual Acts governing intellectual property rights. The prohibition in s. 1 of the Marketing Practices Act of acts which are in conflict with sound marketing practice may be relevant, e.g. in situations where protection under intellectual property law is inadequate or questionable. Examples of such situations include cases in which an invention, on the one hand, does not fulfil the requirements to the "degree of originality" in order for the work to be protected under the Patents Act, but in which it is evident, on the other hand, that protection should be afforded against the attempt of a competitor to free-ride on the efforts of the inventor. The prohibition in s. 5 of the Marketing Practices Act, especially of the unauthorized use of the trade marks of others, may in a similar way work as a supplement to the protection offered to actual trade marks by the Trade Marks Act. A third important example of the interaction between the two areas of law is found in s. 10 of the Marketing Practices Act, affording protection to trade secrets. Such trade secrets will often be attached to the exercise of intellectual property rights, e.g. patents, but will – especially in the case of so-called "know-how" – not fall within the protection provided by intellectual property law.

In the following Sections, the individual Danish exclusive rights Acts will be treated separately. As the sanctions (penalties, damages, etc.) in respect of infringement of exclusive rights are of more or less uniform character, these will be treated together in the final section.

2. Copyright

2.1. What qualifies for protection?

Copyright protection is provided by the provisions in the Copyright Consolidation Act No. 706 of 12 March 2003.

Pursuant to s. 1(1) of the Act, literary and artistic works shall be protected, irrespective of whether the work in question takes the form of oral or written *fiction* or *non-fiction*, of a *musical* or *dramatic work*, of *films* or *photographs*, of *graphic works, works of architecture* or *works of decorative art,* or any other form. As the latter category indicates, the scope of protection is, in principle, directed towards any literary or artistic work, *irrespective of the manner of expression.* Maps, drawings and any other graphic or plastic art work of descriptive nature (s. 1(2)) are within the meaning of literary works as well as works in the form of *computer programs* (s. 1(3)).

> In some special cases, the copyright may be of "derivative" nature, i.e. the exercise of the basic rights in the work are subject to the consent of another author. Translation, transcription or adaptation of the work of others, or converting such work into another form of literary or artistic work may thus confer copyright (s. 4(1)) upon the translator, etc. in respect of the work in said derivative form, although such person should not, unless a new and independent work has been produced (s. 4(2)), exercise rights in the work in a manner infringing the copyright subsisting in the original work. Correspondingly, it is laid down (s. 5) that the arrangement of works or parts of works may form separate literary or artistic compilations – e.g. anthologies – in which the person who has arranged the work may claim (derivative) copyright. Acts, delegated legislation, judicial decisions and similar public instruments (s. 9(1)) fall outside the scope of protection, as does the manufacture of semiconductors ("chips", s. 10(2), cf. Section 6, below)).

On the basis of s. 1 of the Act, it is debatable whether requirements are made in respect of *originality, quality and quantity* for a work to acquire copyright protection.

S. 1(1) presumes that copyright is to be accorded to the person who *"brings into existence"* a work of the nature mentioned. Any work should thus be *original*, notwithstanding the nature of the work, i.e. be the product of the *independent skill and labour* of the author. In this connection, it is important to notice that copyright – unlike e.g. the patents right – is *not* a priority right ("first come, first served"). The requirement as to originality is thus not a requirement that the work should be "novel" in an objective sense. Accordingly, the copyright only offers protection against the unauthorized copying and use, cf. Sections 2.4 to 2.6 (below). It follows that – provided that the originality requirements are met – a legitimate situation with so-called "double products" could occur, i.e. works which in whole or in substantial part are identical and which are products of different authors.

The law is less clear in respect of whether requirements as to the *quality* of a product should be made. If it is "pure" art in the traditional sense of the word, e.g. in case of fictional literary works, there is no doubt that protection is not conditional upon qualitative restrictions, e.g. in respect of the lasting value of the work. In practice, however, such requirements are imposed to a certain (limited) extent on works with *a functional* purpose – for instance and in particular – applied art and industrial designs. To these ends, the said requirements are combined in a demand that the works in question must conform to a certain *degree of originality*. Consequently, the work must rise above the commonplace and – although taste is immaterial also in this connection – be the product of a documented and original artistic effort/intellectual activity. Since works of the aforesaid nature usually and to a large extent are subject to competition which should be safeguarded, case law indicates that only a narrow protective zone is normally meted out, i.e. the work is only afforded protection against plagiarism or close copying. *Computer programmes* present a special problem. The EU Directive of 14 May 1991 on the legal protection of computer programmes, which forms the basis of s. 1(3) of the Act, lays down that such programme shall enjoy protection provided it is original in the sense that it is the product of the intellectual labour of the author. The Directive expressly states that there are no other criteria as to whether a programme qualifies for protection. The travaux preparatoires of the Danish Act implementing the Directive are in perfect accordance with this aim. Notwithstanding that the issue has been debated in Danish legal literature it must now be deemed that requirements as to quality cannot be imposed. It would seem likely that this will have a mirror effect in relation to other works with a functional purpose so that the requirement regarding quality is also to be abandoned here.

Quantitative restrictions are only of practical importance in connection with linguistic works. In practice, the requirements are lenient. In a Danish Supreme Court judgment, it was thus held that a single sentence constituting the title of a book should enjoy independent copyright protection ("For Whom the Bell Tolls").

2.2. Subsistence of copyright

Copyright is acquired upon the *bringing into existence* ("the creation") of the work in question. Legal protection is thus not conditional upon the compliance with any specific form, upon registration with a public authority, or the like.

2.3. Who qualifies for protection?

Under s. 1 of the Act, copyright is afforded to the person who "brings into existence" the work in question, i.e. the *natural person* who "creates" the work ("the author"). In the event that there are more than one author and the individual efforts cannot be separated so as to constitute individual works, the copyright is afforded to all of the persons in joint authorship, cf. s. 6 of the Act.

The Copyright Act does not contain any general provisions on the rather common situation in which the work is produced in the course of *permanent employment*. Under case law, copyright is, prima facie, afforded to the employee, granting, however, to the undertaking the right to use the work within the limits defined to meet organisational needs. This provision is, however, subject to any agreement to the contrary by the parties, just as the custom of the trade may imply that the copyright is afforded to the undertaking to a larger extent. In the case of a computer programme which is produced by an employee during the course of his employment or in performance of the instructions of the employer, it is provided by a specific rule in s. 59 of the Act that the copyright shall be accorded to the undertaking, unless agreement to the contrary has been made, cf s. 53(4). Such transfer of copyright is final and complete.

Like the rest of the intellectual property rights, copyrights are property rights and may therefore be *assigned* in full or in part, so that the rights exercised in the work will be accorded completely or partially to the assignee, cf. s. 53 of the Act, but cf. Section 2.4.4 (below) for further reference on the so-called "moral rights". Naturally, assignment of copies of the work does not entail assignment of the actual copyright. Partial assignment in the form of publishing and licensing agreements is quite common, providing the assignee solely with publishing rights and the right of use in the work in question.

However, certain general limitations apply to the right of the assignee which may be said to be the result of the special nature of the right assigned. Pursuant to s. 53(3) of the Act, assignment of a right to use the work in a certain way or by certain means shall thus *not* confer upon the assignee the right to use the work in *any other way* or by *any other means*. Nor shall the assignee under s. 56(1), cf. s. 53(4), make *adaptations* to the work other than such adaptations which could be considered to be commonly authorized, expressly or by implication, unless agreement to the contrary has been made. Buildings and functional designs may, however, be subject to adaptation to a wider extent, cf s. 29.

It is also of importance to the author that s. 56(2) of the Act, cf. s. 53(4), lays down that the assignee shall *not*, without the consent of the assignor, *re-assign* the right, unless such re-assignment is authorized, expressly or by implication, e.g. where the customs of certain trades imply that various types of rights should be assigned in connection with transfers of undertakings. Under the previous state of law, there were no general stautory provisions in respect of the possible duty of the assignee to *use* the work, regardless of whether the author, for financial or moral reasons, could have a certain interest in such use. Now, however, s. 54 of the Act, cf. s. 53(4), lays down that the assignee undertakes a duty to use the work, unless agreement to the contrary has been made. If such use has not been made within a reasonable period of time or no later than five years after the proper performance of the contract by the author, the assignor can rescind the contract, i.e. he acquires a certain reversionary right in respect of the work. Such reversion is not subject to notice. According to the travaux preparatoires of the Act, the court has discretionary powers to decide what constitutes a "reasonable period of time", taking into consideration, however, the nature of the individual work and the form of use in question. In addition, the provisions contained in s. 55 of the Act, which are also non-mandatory, confer upon the author a certain possibility of terminating the agreement in the event that the assignment does not expressly state the individual forms of use comprised by the agreement. By giving reasonable notice, the author may terminate the agreement to assign the rights to the unspecified forms of use which have not been exercised by the assignee within three years upon the proper performance of the contract by the author. Finally, s. 57 of the Act contains general rules on settlement in respect of consideration relative to turnover, payable by the assignee to the author (royalties) and the subsequent supervision in respect hereof.

Copyright *devolves* upon the death of the author in the usual manner, cf. s. 61(1) of the Act. The rights exercised cannot, however, be subject to *creditor enforcement*, as long as the copyright rests with the original author, his spouse or his beneficiaries (unless such protection is waived), cf. s. 62(1), while a contrary starting point obtains in respect of existing *copies* of the work, cf. s. 62(2).

2.4. Copyright powers

2.4.1. General substance of the copyright

The general substance of copyright is set forth in s. 2 of the Copyright Act. Under subsection 1 of this provision, copyright shall, in general, afford the *exclusive right* in the work of *producing copies* of the work and of *making it available to the general public*, whether in the original or derived form, in translation, adapted into any other literary or artistic form, or any other technique. The concept of copy producing is defined in s. 2: Any direct or indirect, permanent or non-permanent and complete or partial production of copies in any manner and form whatsoever. Tranfers of the work to devices which may render it will be deemed to qualify as "prodcution". S. 3 lays down that the aforesaid making available has been carried out when *copies* of the work are offered for sale, on lease or as a loan, or are in any other way *distributed to the public* or *presented in public*, including when broadcast on television, or when the work is *performed in public*, including a broadcasting on radio or television. On the basis of s. 2 it may be said that the exclusive position accorded to the author in the Act contains a right of *reproduction*, of *distribution*, of *presentation*, and of *performance*, and no more.

2.4.2. Exhaustion of copyright

When the author has exercised his right of reproduction, and when copies later – e.g. by sale – are distributed to the general public, a practical question of paramount importance arises, viz. the question as to the relationship between the rights of the author and the owner of the copy in respect of the original work and the copy, respectively. To these ends, ss. 19 and 20 of the Copyright Act contain certain socalled "rules of exhaustion". The literal meaning of the word "exhaustion" is that something is "devoured" or "consumed". Indeed, the rules of exhaustion are concerned with the fact that any lawful assignment of copy, to a certain extent, causes the rights of the author to cease ("be devoured") in so far as the copies are concerned. The legal position, however, differs somewhat for the different types of work.

In respect of the *right of distribution*, the general starting points of the Act, cf. s. 19(1), is that a copy of a work – irrespective of its nature – may be distributed, provided that it is *sold* or in any other way *assigned* to others with the consent of the author. It follows from the above that it is of decisive importance whether *transfer of ownership* to the copy has taken place, i.e. licensing or lending does not provide grounds for free and unlimited right to further distribution.

The starting point is modified in several respects. Under s. 19(2), it shall apply to *all* works, except from buildings and works of decorative art, that although lawful assignment has taken place, no (further) distribution shall be undertaken by means of *licensing* without the consent of the author. In respect of copies of *films* and of *computer programmes* in digitised form, (further) distribution without the consent of the author shall also, as a principal rule, be prohibited, cf. s. 19(3). Using computer programmes for exemplification, it is seen that distribution is conditional upon the original assignment of copies with the consent of the author, and that lawful *further distribution* of such programs cannot be undertaken by means of lending or licensing, unless such consent has been given. In respect of copies of literary works, however, the initial lawful assignment causes the author to lose (exhaust) his right of distribution as regards further distribution by sale or similar assignment of ownership as well as by means of lending. Naturally, the distinction between lending and licensing is important in respect of those works which are not comprised by the prohibition in s. 19(3), e.g. in respect of books. The decisive element is whether a direct or indirect financial or comemrcial advantage is aimed at or whether mere coverage of expenses is sought. Where an advantage of the nature mentioned is aimed at, licencing will be deemed to lie.

The question of exhaustion of the *right of presentation* is treated in s. 20 of the Act. When a work is published or when a copy of an artistic work is assigned to others by the author, such publication and assigned copies shall be ready for public presentation under subsection 1 of the said provision. "Published" is defined in s. 8(2) as meaning the placing on the market of copies or its distribution to the general public in any other such way with the consent of the author. The presentation concept implies that a physical copy of the work is presented directly to a group of persons present. Thus film and TV recordings are not presentation in the sense of the Act, but performance in this respect.

As specified in the above, the rules of exhaustion *only apply to copies*, never to works, and they are solely directed towards the *right of distribution and presentation*. Any further exhaustion is fundamentally conditional upon the *lawful* placing on the market of the copies, i.e. with the consent of the author in the cases of first practical importance. Thus, *piracy copying* and other illegal measures can never make a basis for exhaustion.

The rules of exhaustion are national in the sense that in principle decision shall be made under Danish law as to the legality of the distribution in Denmark of copies which are lawfully placed on the market abroad. It is now expressly stated in s. 19(1) of the Act that exhaustion of the right of presentation applies *universally* for the whole EEA area (EU, Norway, Iceland, and Liechtenstein). Thus the exhaustion is what is normally termed *regional* (the whole area mentioned) in contrast to *national* (Denmark only) and *international* or *global* (universally for the whole world). This is of course of practical importance in particular to trade across borders, including socalled parallel importation. If e.g. a book is lawfully published in the UK, distribution of copies of such book to customers in the other EEA states can thus be undertaken without the consent of the author. Incidentally, the same result would obtain on the basis of the EC Treaty's provisions on the free movement of goods and services (Arts 28 and 30). In contrast it follows from s. 19(1) (and from the underlying EU-Directive 2001/29/EC of 22 May 2001) that lawful marketing outside the EEA area, e.g. in the US, does *not* imply exhaustion of copyright, and that e.g. parallel imports (though not private importation for own use) into Denmark will require the consent of the copyright owner.

2.4.3. Special note on the right of performance

Under the general provisions on the substance of copyright, the author, i.a., enjoys the exclusive right to perform the work *in public*, cf. Section 2.4.1 (above). However, s. 21 of the Act provides a few exceptions, e.g. in respect of performance of published works other than dramatic works or films during the course of education and church services.

As regards the principal rule referred to, it is of importance to determine the definition under the Act of the term "public performance". S. 2(4) goes some way to defining this by emphasising two examples of activities which could (also) be regarded as such performance. First, the section mentions wirebound or wireless transfer of works to the general public, including radio or TV broadcasting, and the placing of the work at the disposal of the general public in a manner so that access is given at an individually selected place and time (e.g. application of socalled "on demand" services via the Internet). Seecond, the provision lays down that the concept of public performance also comprises performance in a business undertaking to a comprehensive audience which would otherwise be considered to be non-public (the "music-while-you-work" situation). The fact that performance is "public" in the context present does not imply in itself that access must have been open to all and sundry. Indeed it is apparent from a number of judicial decisions that public performance may also occur in connection with types of performance other than those expressly stated in s. 2(4) when they are lacking a clearly private nature (e.g. certain club events, application of music in dancing studios, fitness centres, etc.).

It is further important to bear in mind that such public performance will not per se make distribution of the performed work legal without the consent of the author. This might imply what may be termed "re-newed public performance", possibly also copy production if the re- distribution does not coincide with the first performance. The issues arising here which are of particular relevance to music and film works have in some important practical areas been solved by the provision in s. 35 of the Act which endows the author with a claim for consideration in connection with the distribution via communal antenna systems and cable TV of simultaneously and unchanged broadcasts on radio and tv . However, the author's consent is not required, cf. s. 50 on socalled "agreed license" . Radio and TV companies' producers' rights (s. 69) are not comprised by s. 35 although they are governed by somewhat similar rules, cf. s. 48. Radio and TV brodcasts via satellite may be redistributed as long as distribution is also made via an earth based distribution network, cf. s. 30(5), and cf. s. 30(1).

2.4.4. Special note on moral rights

While the exclusive right referred to in the preceding Sections may be said to protect the immediate *financial* interests of the author in respect of the work, the provision in s. 3 of the Copyright Act concerns the socalled "moral" rights in the work in question. The Act contains two moral rights, viz. a right of paternity and a right of integrity.

The right of paternity is the right to be named as creator and acknowledged as such, both on copies of the work and when such work is made available to the public. The right is relative in the sense that the naming shall be carried out in accordance with "fair practice", cf. s. 3(1). Great variations may thus occur, depending in particular on the nature of the individual works. Infringement of the right of paternity upon expiry of the copyright (cf. Section 2.7 (below)) may be subject to public action if such infringement offends against cultural interests, cf. ss. 75 and 81(4) of the Act.

The right of integrity implies that a work may not be adapted or made available to the general public in any way or connection which could offend against the literary or artistic reputation or special character of the author, cf. s. 3(2). The right of integrity which does not afford any protection against actual destruction of the work, may be subject to public action on the same conditions as mentioned above.

Pursuant to s. 3(3), the author shall not waive his rights under s. 3(1-2), unless the nature and extent of the use of the work is limited. An assignment of copyright does not comprise the moral rights, cf. s. 53(1).

2.5. Other limitations of the exclusive right

The rules of exhaustion of ss. 19 and 20 of the Copyright Act mentioned above may be said to be in the nature of *general* limitations of the substance of the author's exclusive right. However, Part II of the Act contains a number of additional limitations which are more *specific* in character. The most important ones are the rules on the right to *private copying* and *reproduction.* Together these limitations are indicative of the balancing of social interests against the interests of the author, cf. Section 1 (above). Under s. 11(3) application of works under Part 2 requires that copy production on the basis of a reproduction of the works contrary to the powers of the author under s. 2 or on the basis of a circumvention of a technical measure contrary to s. 75(1) may not be effected, cf. on the latter in the following Section below. Thus the basis applied for the copy production under the provisions mentioned in the following must be a lawful one or represent a lawful rendering of the work and it is not to be contrary to s. 75c.

2.5.1. The copying right

The application of computer technology allows for a lot a copying of materials protected by copyright of a purely temporary and elusive character – e,g. automatic copying in the cache of the computer applied in connection with browsing on the Internet. Since temporary copying is is prinipcle comprised by the exclusive right of the author, cf. above, Section 2.4.1, it is necessary – to secure a reasonably unhindered application of the technical possibilities avialable, in cases where no genuine work exploitation is shown, to have an exception prooviosn in the Act on temporary copy production. This exception is found in s. 11 a. This provison allows the production of temporary specimens – to the exclusion of computer programmes and databases – under certain conditions, i.a. that the copies are random and do not represent an independent financial value. It is a requirement that the use of the work in question is lawful. The provision must be seen in connection with ss. 14-16 of the e-trade Act (Chapter 12 below) on distribution, caching and storing.

In respect of the private *right of copying*, s. 12(1) sets forth that any person shall be permitted to print or have printed a published work for private use, (thus to the exclusion of commercial purposes) provided that such copies are not put to use in any other way. Under s. 8(1), a work is published when it is lawfully made available to the general public. Copying, e.g. of published books, is thus lawful to the extent that it is for "private" use. It is not absolutely certain what this imprecise term denotes. As a guiding principle may, however, be said that copying for one's own use and for the use of persons to whom the producer is personally connected, e.g. and in particualr to his family, friends, and acquantainces and posisbly colleagues at his workplace – although the latter must not take the form of an application – directly or indirectly – for commercial purposes. Only "single" copies may be made, i.e. only the stricly personal need must be covered. The access to print lies only with natural persons, not to legal persons, e.g. companies. Prima facie, the assistance of another person at the printing is permitted but exceptions apply in this respect as regards musical works, films, decorative works of art and artistic works, cf. s. 12(3). Production of copies of musical works or films by means of facilities – such as coin-operated copiers – made available to the public, e.g. in libraries, is prohibited, cf. s. 12(4).

However important the right of copying may be to information and communication possibilities in today's society, it is evident that abuse may occur – indeed does occur to a considerable extent – particularly with the technological aids available to large parts of the public. Apart from the limitations referred to, a number of other restrictions therefore also apply, cf. s. 12(3) of the Act.

Presumably, the most important, in practice, of the situations mentioned here pertains to *computer programmes*. For such programmes, s. 12(2) no. 3, lays down, first, that the provision contained in s. 12(1), cf. above, will not give access to produce copies in a digitised form. Thus, the starting point is simply that private copying of such programmes is also prohibited. This prohibiton is, however, somewhat modified by s. 36(1), no. 1, , under which provision any person with the right to use a computer programme shall be permitted to produce such copies of the programme and to make such adaptations, including to correct any errors, *necessary* in order that he may use the programme *in the way it was intended*. This provision may be deviated from by agreement between the author and the assignee, e.g. to the effect that copying access is restricted. In pursuance of s. 36(1) no.2 any person exercising the right of use in a programme shall, however, always be permitted to produce a *soft copy*, irrespective of whether agreement to the contrary has been made, to the extent that such copy may prove *necessary* in respect of the use. A person authorised to use a computer programme will under s. 36(1) no. 3, cf. subsection 4, always be entitled to inspect, examine and test the programme to establish the ideas and principles underlying its individual components in so far as this is done in connection with such use of the programme as he is authorised to make (socalled "reverse engineering"). Further, under certain conditions a copy production of the programmes code and translation of the form of the code (from machine code to source code) is always possible as long as this is a requirement to procure the information *necessary* to suply inter–operativeness ability between an independently developed computer programme and other computer programmes, cf. s. 37 on socalled "decompilation".

On databases s. 36(2), no. 4, provides that the copying access under s. 12(1) does not give access to make copies in a digitalised form of such bases when the production is made on the basis of a reproduction of the database in a digital form. However, a person with a right to use a database is always authorised to perform such acts as *are necessary* to obtain access to the base contents and make normal use of such contents, cf. s. 36(2) cf. s. (39. No access to soft copy is provided.

One last limitation of practical importance in s. 12(2) provides that the access to copy relates to production of copies in digital form of works *other than* computer programmes and databases, cf. s. 12(2), no. 5. The limitation is less extensive than the foregoing in that such copying is permitted if the production relates only to single specimens and it is effected only for the personal use of the producer and his household. This may be of importance in particular in relation to copying ("burning") of music cds. The copies made must not be distributed outside the household.

Attempts to counteract abuse of the right of copying are made not only via legislative restriction but also through technical measures on the part of the authors and producers designed to prevent or impede illegal copying. This raises the question as to how the law relates to this issue.

Under s. 75 of the Copyright Act it is unlawful to *put in circulation* or to *possess* for commercial purposes – means whose sole purpose is to facilitate illegal removal or circumvention of technical devices applied to protect a *computer programme* (e.g. copy bars). The sanction for infringemnt is a penalty, cf. s. 78. Under s. 75 c it is unlawful without consent from the copyright holder to make a circumvention of effective techinal measures in products *other than computer programmes.* A vast number of preparatory acts are also prohibited (manufacture, importation, sale, possession for commercial purposes, cf. the enumeration in s. 75 c(2). "Effective technical measures" are construed under subsection 3 as any form of measure which, under its normal function aims at protecting works and other productions etc. protected under copy right law (including copy barrings and copy control, e.g. on cds and dvd films). From the travaux preparatoires of the Act it appears that s. 75 c cannot be deemed to comprise cases in which a circumvention of a code aiming at preventing or impeding the personal acquisition of a work (in contrast to codes aiming at preventing copying, e.g. circumvention of a region coding of dvd's). The sanction for infringement here is also a penalty, cf. s. 78.

In October 2003 the Danish government presented a bill which, if adopted, will imply rather considerable tightenings of the rules mentioned (Bill L 17 2003-04). The Bill proposes in particular to *prohibit* the production of copies in digitised form without the consent of the author on the basis of a specimen borrowed or hired (important in relation to the copy access under s. 12(2) no. 5). It will *also prohibit* external assistancee at the copying of literary works if the assisstant acts within the course of his business, *and* the copying of literary works where the technical equipment is made available in the course of business (copy stores, etc.).

2.5.2. The right to quote

From s. 22(1) of the Act appears that it is permitted to quote from a published work as long as such quoting is made in accrodance with proper practice and to an extent determined by the purpose. In principle the provision covers all types of work. Quotation is the same as a direct rendering – in fragmentary form – of the work in question. In contrast, the summary constitutes a freer and therefore usually adapted reference to a work or parts of such work. While the right of quotation is thus subject to a demand for due deference to "fair practice" and purpose-related relevancy, the right of summary is in principle, unlimited. When quoting from a work, reference to the source must, however, be made under s. 11(2).

2.5.3. Other limitations

From the other limitations in Part 2 of the Act may be mentioned that there are special rules first on copying etc. – in most cases against payment – in i.a. schools and universities and business undertakings (ss 13 and 14 in combination with s. 50), secondly on the use against payment made by radio and TV enterprises of published works, excluding dramatic works and film works (ss 30 and 35 in combination with s. 50). A certain compensation for the loss some authors suffer as a result of the copying access is aimed at by the imposition of fees in respect of blank sound and video tapes ("blank tape fees"), cf. ss. 39 et seq. It has been proposed to change the scheme in the Bill mentioned above (2.5.1) inter alia by imposing duties on digital sound media, image media and memory cards.

2.6. Infringement of the exclusive right by copying

As mentioned in Section 2.1, copyright protection is solely afforded against the unauthorised copying and use. The question of use will most often be connected with the rules of exhaustion and the additional limitations of the exclusive right. Assessment is made of whether the unauthorized copying by other persons of the protected work constitutes infringement of the exclusive right. The crux of the matter is, of course, whether sufficient similarity exists for the alleged infringing work to constitute a copy rather than "free adaptation", cf. s. 4(2) of the Act and Section 2.1 (above).

In practice, the answer to the question referred to will always depend upon a discretionary estimate, resulting, as regards the most important and frequent cases – i.e. in connection with works of decorative art and industrial designs, etc. – in a comparison between the works in question, providing an *overall assessment of the facts.* To this end, a few important general guidelines do, however, exist. First, copyright protection is only accorded to the work in *its present form*, i.e. any direct or underlying motives or fundamental ideas and principles will not enjoy protection. Such ideas and principles are, per se, subject to a kind of intellectual community property. A photographer e.g. is as incapable of claiming copyright in the depiction of a certain situation as an author of a book or a creator of a computer programme will be as regards an idea underlying their book or programme (the "algorithm" of such programme). Second, the nature of the protection is, perforce, conditional upon the alleged "imitator's" *knowledge of the other work* and *his use* of the work as the source of his own work, cf. Section 2.1 (above) for further reference on "double products".

2.7. Duration of copyright

Copyright normally expires 70 years after the death of the author, cf s. 63(1). In cases of joint authorship, duration is measured by the death of the last of the joint authors. A special rule applies in respect of films, cf. clause 2 of subsection 1. Copyright in works of unknown authorship normally subsists for 70 years from the end of the year in which the work was made public. For unpublished works and works of unknown authorship the period is 70 years from the end of the year in which the work was created. S. 64 of the Act covers a special situation, viz. where the copyright expires prior to publication of the work. Any person who, in this situation, publishes a work or makes it available to the public for the first time may exercise financial rights in the work similar to those of an author, cf. e.g. the – thus far unknown – symphony by Mozart which was found in Denmark a few years ago.

2.8. Related rights

Part V (ss. 65-72) of the Copyright Act lays down provisions on the protection of a number of rather different rights which are more or less connected to the actual copyright as provided by s. 1 of the Act, and where the circumstances may raise issues as to whether protection should be accorded under s. 1 or s. 5. Several provisons of this Part governing the socalled "related rights" are of great practical and financial importance, especially s. 65 (performers of literary and artistic works), ss. 66-67 (producers of sound and picture recordings), s. 69 (radio and television broadcasts), s. 70 (producers of photographs), and s. 71 (producers of catalogues, tables, data bases etc.). S. 65 affords protection, especially to the performing artist, against unauthorised reproduction on tape, film, etc. as well as against making the performance available to the public without the consent of the artist in question. By comparison, the remaining provisions are special in that they provide protection (against the unauthorized copying, making available, etc.) to producers of the works referred to, irrespective of any artistic effort. Several of the limitations of copyright apply correspondingly, e.g. s. 12(1) (the right of printing) to all the above provisions, and s. 22 (the right of reproduction) to all provisions except the last. In the above cases, the protective duration is fairly long, viz. 50 years from the end of the year of performance, recording, broadcasting, and producing, respectively (for catalogues etc. 15 years after the end of the year of production).

3. Patents

3.1. What qualifies for protection?

3.1.1. The invention concept

While the protection afforded by intellectual property law to works within literature and art (in the broadest sense) is spelt out in the Copyright Act, protection within the field of *technology* is mainly found in the *Patents Act*, cf. Consolidated Act No. 381 of 30 August 2001.

Essentially, ss. 1 and 2 of the Patents Act lay down the basic requirements for obtaining a patent. Under s. 1(1), there must be an "invention which is capable of industrial application". The starting point is that inventions qualify for patent in all technological areas. But the Act does not define the concept of invention in exact terms. As a principal rule, however, the phenomenon must be of a *technical* nature and have a *technical effect*, and it must be *reproducible,* i.e. repeatable, and *specifiable*. From s. 1(2-3) it is further evident that a number of matters of great practical importance are *not* deemed to be inventions. Examples include, first, discoveries, scientific theories and mathematical methods (no. 1 of subs. 2). In principle, the difference between a non-patentable discovery and an invention lies in whether the activity is *establishing* (discovery) or *constructive* (invention). In practice, it may be very difficult to draw the line between the two, e.g. in connection with chemical compounds and biological processes. Further, the Act excludes artistic works (no. 2 of subs. 2 – as mentioned above, these are protected under the Copyright Act) and schemes, rules or methods for performing a mental act, playing a game, doing business or a programme for a computer (no. 3 of subs. 2 – socalled "references to the human intellect"). The same applies in respect of presentation of information, e.g. by special means (no. 4 of subs. 2). Finally, *procedures* for surgical or therapeutical treatment or for diagnosing, used on humans or animals, are outside the scope of the definition (s. 1(3). Medical remedies – particularly in the form of medicine – and tools applied in the course of medical treatment are, however, patentable, cf. below.

It will be seen that under the wording of the Act computer programmes will not qualify for patenting (although they are comprised by the copyright law, cf. Section 2 above). However this does not exclude patenting in certain cases. Thus software may be protected under the Patents Act when it is incoporated into other (patentable) products as patent may also be given in respect of methods in the form of software solving a technical problem or providing a technical contribution (whereas the progamme in itself in non-patentable). Currently it is dicussed in the EU whether, on US inspiration, it might be appropriate to allow patents of software to a wider extent. The considerations in this respect have led to an EU directive on the patent capability of computer based inventions.

The requirement as to capability of "industrial application" is not to be taken too literally. Application within trades other than purely industrial ones – e.g. within agriculture – will suffice.

3.1.2. Exempt areas

Although a subject matter meets the above requirements for constituting an invention, it may still be a non-patentable invention. In recent years it has been debated whether to allow patent protection of inventions of a bio technological nature, including inventions which have implied application of modern gene technology in relation to plants, animals, and human beings, cf. EU Directive 98/44 on bio-technological inventions, implemented in the Patents Act as from 30 July 2000.

Under s. 1(4) of the Patents Act *plant varieties* and *animal races* do not qualify for patenting but patent may be obtained for an invention whose object is plants or animals if the exercise of the invention is not technically limited to *a certain* plant variety or animal race. Nor it is possible, as a starting point (s. 1(5), to obtain patent in respect of essentially biological processes for the production of plants or animals wheres patent may be granted in respect of *micro biological processes* or other procedures or a product made under such procedures. It is no bar to a patent ((s. 1(6))that the invention relates to a product consisting of or containing biological substance or that it relates to a procedure for the manufacture, processing or application of such substance. Where the biological substance has been isolated from its natural environment or where it has been produced by means of a technical procedure it may further be the object of an invention even if it already exists in natural form, cf. above on s. 1(2), no. 1. As regards human beings, s. 1 a (1) sets forth that the human body in all its stages of origin and development and the pure detection of part of it, including a sequence or part sequence of a gene, will not qualify for a patentable invention. Mostly on a line with the contents of s. 1(6) part of the human body isolated herefrom or produced in another way by a technical procedure – including a sequence or part sequence of a gene- may under s. 1 a (2) consitute a patentable invention even if such part of the human body is identical in its structure to the structure in a part naturally existing.

The patent law has for a long time contained provisons barring patents in respect of inventions whose commercial use would offend public decency or disturb the peace, cf. now s. 1 b(1). The practical importance of this bar has largely been non-existing but after the implementation of the EU directive mentioned above it has been revived in that s. 1 b(3) provides that a number of bio-technological matters concerning animals and human beings are comprised by s. 1 b (3, nos 1-3). This applies i.a. to procedures for the cloning of human beings and change of the genetic identity of human sex cells and application of human embryos for industrial or commercial purposes. (subsection 3, nos 1-3). As regards animals the exclusion is less extensive. Only procedures to change the genetic identity of an animal which may inflict suffering upon an animal which is not founded in a substantial medical useful value for human beings or animals, and animals produced in such procedures, are referred to s. 1(1) (3, no. 4).

In principle the exclusions mentioned might have unfortunate effects to the possibilities of protecting *plant breeding*. But although patent is unobtainable statutory protection against the commercial use by others is provided in special legislation, viz. in the Novel Plants Act (Consolidated Act No. 51 of 5 February 1996 as amended).

As regards the possibilities of obtaining patents for chemical compounds the position used to be uncertain. A certain area, viz. pharmaceuticals (medicine) was excluded from patenting in Denmark. The present legal position is, howver, that pharmaceuticals – and other chemical compunds – may be accorded patent protection in a manner similar to other inventions in such a way that the patent is directed towards either the compound as such (the substance) or towards the process in connection with the manufacturing of such substance, or towards its application, cf. s. 8(2) of the Patents Act.

3.1.3. The requirements of novelty and inventive step

The concept of invention implies per se that the invention should be considered to be new. S. 2 of the Patents Act lays down the requirements in respect hereof, providing that an invention should be novel relative to what was *known prior to the date of filing an application for a patent.* "Known" is defined in s. 2(2) as meaning all matter which has been made available to the public by written or oral description, by use or in any other way. In this connection, availability is not confined to Denmark. Novelty-infringing matter is thus in evidence when a large and indefinite number of people – anywhere in the world – has had the possibility of obtaining knowledge of such matter in such a way that any expert on that basis could have made the invention. It is likewise immaterial whether the inventor himself had prior knowledge of the matter. Conversely, the inventor may damage himself by the untimely publication of his own matter, i.e. prior to application for patenting. The novelty requirement is often boilt down to a requirement that the invention should constitute an *objective, global novelty*, cf. Section 2.1 (above) on the requirements in respect of copyright.

Where patent protection is sought in several countries the novelty requirement might be a hindrance since it will normally be impossible to hand in the application at the same time in all countries. This situation is provided for in s. 6(1) of the Patents Act with the socalled "convention priority" clause: Within a timelimit of 12 months, computed from the first application, the inventor may in subsequent applications (in other countries) request that such applications are deemed to be handed in at the same time as the first application. The same rule obtains within the European and international patent sytems, cf. below Section 3.8.

Under s. 2(1), the invention must be *materially different* from what has previously been known. This requirement is normally expressed as a requirement that the invention must represent the requisite *inventive step*. This is generally construed to imply that the invention may not appear as obvious to an expert in the field.

3.2. Acquisition of right

The acquisition of right is *formal*. In order to obtain Danish patent, application must be filed with the Danish Patent Office (www.dkpto.dk), cf. on procedure etc. Consolidation Act No. 6 of 6 January 2003 (The Patents Consolidation Act). The application must indicate the identity of the inventor, and further be accompanied by a specification consisting of a detailed description of the invention and a definition of the scope of the invention (the socalled patent claim). The application is subjected to a thorough and rather time-consuming scrutiny to establish whether the basic patentability requirements are met, cf. above. Currently, the case administration time is 2-3 years. If the application stands the test, patent is granted, whereupon any person may contest the patent for a period of nine months, cf. also Section 3.7 (below). A fee is payable for the proceedings involved and annual fees will be necessary to keep the patent in force, cf. on these fees Consolidation Act No. 119 of 12 February 2003. If the application is denied, appeal lies to the Danish Patents Appeals Board. Incidentally, purely Danish cases are of declining importance, cf. Section 3.8, below, for further reference on transboundary patents.

In contrast to copyright, the right of patent is a socalled *priority right*, i.e. the right is afforded to the first applicant, provided the application results in the grant of patent. The patent takes legal effect from the date of filing the application, cf. s. 2(1) of the Patents Act.

3.3. Who qualifies for protection?

The right to *take out* a patent (the right of invention) is afforded to the natural person who has made the invention, cf. s. 1 of the Patents Act. Where two or more persons have cooperated, the right of invention is granted to the persons in joint inventorship. Both the right of invention and the right in respect of the patent *taken out* (the right of patent) may be assigned to others in ownership, for use or as collateral, and both rights may be subject to creditor enforcement.

Special rules govern the area of employee inventions, cf. the Patents Consolidation Act No. 131 of 18 March 1986 as amended. Prima facie, all employee inventions belong to the employee. However, where an invention is made by an employee in the course of his employment, the employer may claim *the transfer* of the invention in respect of one or more countries, provided that the exploitation of such invention is within the business field of the undertaking. Where an invention is made by an employee during the carrying out of a defined task put before him by the undertaking, such invention also belongs to the employer, irrespective of whether the exploitation of the invention is outside the business field of the undertaking. The employee has a duty of disclosure towards the employer, and the employer must then, within a certain short period of time, notify the employee of whether he wishes to take ownership of the invention. If so, the employee generally has a right to fair compensation. The parties may contract out of the rules of the Act except for the rule on employee compensation. As regards inventions at public research institutions Act No. 347 of 2 June 1999 applies and in a number of points this Act contains provisions of the same substance as the 1986- Act.

3.4. Patent rights

The right of patent affords the exclusive right to the patentee of the *commercial use* of the patent. As a starting point, the protection only covers possible patent infringements undertaken in Denmark. However, s. 3(1)(1) of the Patents Act sets forth that any offering for sale, placing on the market or using of a product, which is manufactured by means of a process subject to patenting, or any importing or possessing of the product for such purpose shall be prohibited. This provision conferring socalled "indirect product protection" implies that to the extent that a certain process is protected by Danish patent, products which are lawfully manufactured abroad by means of such process (and which are not protected abroad) may not be imported to Denmark without the consent of the Danish patentee.

For the purposes of the relationship between the patentee and the purchaser of copies of the product protected by patent, s. 3 (3)(2) of the Act provides that the exclusive right shall not cover activities in relation to products which have been placed on the Danish market (or on any other market within the EU, cf. below) by the patentee or otherwise with his consent. Any copy which has been lawfully placed on the market may thus be further assigned without restriction, regardless of the method of assignment (sale, licensing, etc.). The patent is, in other words, *exhausted* completely upon the first lawful assignment of the specimen in question, cf. Section 2.4.2

on exhaustion of copyright. Within the EU (EEA) area, exhaustion applies universally, which means that a patent right cannot be used e.g. in order to prevent socalled "parallel imports" into Denmark from another EU country in which the specimens have been lawfully brought on the market.Thus, on a line with the exhaustion of copyright, the exhaustion is regional.

In the event that an issue arises in respect of whether the exclusive right conferred upon the patentee has been infringed, the patentee must bring an action against the undertaking which is presumed to have invaded the exclusive right. In practice, a comparison is normally made in such cases between the invention patented and the alleged infringing product. Assessment will always be made on the basis of a discretionary expert estimate, and the decision will almost always be the result of an overall evaluation of what sort of protection should be accorded the patentee. As a principal rule, the patentee carries the burden of proving that his patent was infringed. Exceptions are made, however, to the extent that the subject of the patent is a process for the manufacture of a new product. For this purpose, the Act (s. 64a) presupposes that the other product was produced by means of the patented process, unless evidence to the contrary is produced. In such cases, the burden of proof is thus reversed.

3.5. Special limitations of patents

The exclusive right acquired by patentees only provides protection against acts carried out for a *commercial purpose*, cf. s. 3(3), no. 1 of the Patents Act, i.e. private use by others is permitted. Where such acts are undertaken *for experimental purposes*, they are lawful even for commercial purposes, cf. no. 3 of the same provision. It is further provided by s. 5 that the exclusive right shall not afford protection against the use of the invention by others in connection with acts done on foreign vehicles, ships and aircraft temporarily or accidentally within the territorial grounds, waters or airspace of Denmark.

A certain relaxation of the priority effects of patents is provided by s. 4 of the Patents Act governing the socalled *right to continue use begun before the priority date*. Any person who, at the time of the filing of application for patent, was using the invention or had made substantial arrangements for such use may continue such use notwithstanding the patent. However, it is required that the use – which must not change in character – is not the result of an obvious abuse as against the patentee, e.g. in the event that the person in question has obtained knowledge of the invention in an unlawful manner. The right to continued use cannot be separately assigned, but only as an integral part of the activity out of which it has arisen.

Finally, the exclusive right is limited by the rules on *compulsory licence* contained in ss. 45-50 of the Act. The principal rule is found in s. 45, setting forth that if the invention is not exploited to a reasonable degree in Denmark and a period of three years from the granting of the patent and four years from the date of application has passed, any person wishing to put the invention in question to use in Denmark may, under this provision, be granted a licence to do so. In the first instance, licence and the terms in respect hereof, including the payment of compensation to the patentee, are pronounced by the Maritime and Commercial Court in Copenhagen. From s. 45(2) it appears that the Danish Minister of Business and Industry has powers to decide that putting an invention into effect in another country shall be comparable to putting it into effect in Denmark, and this may be subject to reciprocity. The provision in particular provides the possibility of the putting into effect or the exploitation of the patent in another EU Member State or country which is a member of the World Trade Organization (WTO), thus constituting exploitation in Denmark, cf. also s. 120 of the Patents (Consolidation) Act.

3.6. Duration of patents

Normal patent duration is *20 years* from the date of the filing of application for patent, cf. s. 40 of the Act, provided, however, that the yearly renewal fees are paid and that the patent is not revoked, cf. below. Upon expiration of the protective period, any person may, in principle, appropriate the invention.

Certain patented inventions are granted the possibility of renewal of the exclusive right for a period of up to five years through the issue, upon application, of a so-called "additional protection certificate", cf. s. 91 of the Act and Regulation no 1768/92/EEC. The possibility applies to medical remedies patents. The reason for this special arrangement is that such inventions typically are subject to substantive research and that they often cannot be exploited until a certain (additional) period of time has passed in respect of obtaining the necessary approvals from the Danish public health authorities.

A further extension of the time of protection has been proposed.

3.7. Revocation of patents

The grant of a patent does not provide any guarantee that the exclusive right is not contested at a later date in such a way that decision is made, on the basis of the challenge raised, in favour of the revocation of the patent or of the transfer of patent ownership. Actions for revocations on grounds of invalidity (especially claims contesting the satisfaction of the basic patentability requirements) may be brought by any person before the courts of law (s. 52 of the Act) or to the Patent authorities (ss. 53b-53c). The Patent authorities may, in addition, choose to keep the patent in force, but in a different form. If patents are deemed to be invalid, the revocation shall be effective from the date of the filing of application (s. 55a).

As regards the possibilities of contesting patents it is important that public notice of grant of such patents is required to be made and that the application documents must be made available to the public from the time of the grant of patent.

3.8. Transboundary patents

Inventions of substantive importance may, of course, be subject to simultaneous commercial use in several countries. It will thus often be in the interest of the inventor to seek patent protection extending beyond his own country.

The rather cumbersome starting point is that the inventor must file separate patent applications in each of the countries in which patent is sought. The international cooperation, e.g. on patent protection which has developed over the past century between the countries who belong to the Convention of Paris, cf. Section 1 (above), does not concern a common patenting procedure or a patent extending to all countries ("universal patent"). Such a patent is a figment of the imagination. The Convention merely lays down certain minimum requirements to the various national legal systems as well as an equal treatment demand for all Convention country citizens. The more recent international agreement – "The Patent Cooperation Treaty" – which is ratified by Denmark and a large number of other countries, does not provide the possibility of granting an actual international patent either. Transboundary patents may, however, be granted at a European scale. To this end, cooperation takes place between the 15 EU Member States and a limited number of other European countries under the auspices of the *European Patent Convention* (1973, signed by Denmark in 1989, cf. Part 10A of the Patents Act, ss. 75-90). Applications for socalled "European patent" are treated and patents are granted by the European Patent Office (EPO, main seat in Munich, www.european-patent-office.org). The basic patentability requirements are essentially similar to the ones contained in the Danish Patents Act. The applicant may choose in which of the Convention countries he wishes to obtain patent protection. Protection in e.g. Denmark is thus not automatically accorded, unless the applicant has explicitly selected Denmark. Protection is subject to payment of a fee, the amount of which is partly relative to the protection offered. In addition, an *EC Patent Convention* exists, concerning the legal effects of a patent granted (signed by Denmark in 1992, cf. Part 10 C of the Patents Act, ss. 92-97). This Convention, which is not yet in force, will empower the EPO to grant an EU patent which is universally valid in all EU Member States. For, in the event that the applicant selects one or more of these countries as protected area, such selection will prima facie be considered selection of all EU Member States. Since it has proved difficult to implement the convention a Regulation on European patent has been proposed.

4. Utility models

4.1. The Concept

Since 1992, inventions which do not meet the requirements contained in the Patents Act in respect of degree of originality, have been capable of obtaining intellectual property law protection under the Utility Models Act (Act No. 367 of 9 June 1998 on utility models etc.), which is inspired by German legislation. For the purposes of s. 1(1) of the Act a utility model is defined as "any invention which is capable of industrial application and which bears the solution to a technical problem". The last part of the definition ("technical problem") indicates that like in the case of patents, but unlike in the case of designs, the law is concerned with the strictly functional properties of the phenomena for which protection is sought. Protection for utility models may thus be seen as a small patent, providing protection under intellectual property law for small inventions. Inventors who do not wish to spend time and effort on obtaining actual patent protection shall, however, not be prevented from exploiting the more readily accessible, although more restricted possibilities provided by the Utility Models Act.

A number of inventions are outside the scope of protection by reason of their character. Some of these are repeated from the Patents Act, viz. discoveries, artistic works, and any variety of animal or plant. The Utility Models Act is, however, special in that protection thus far is not provided if the invention takes the form of a process (s. 2(1), no. 4)). The other basic requirements for protection also ressemble those provided by patent legislation, to which reference should be made in all respects to a large extent. The invention must thus be novel relative to what is commonplace at the material time, and it must depart in an appreciable way from such prior art (s. 3(1)). The threshold for the inventive step requirement is thus somewhat lower than for patents (depart in a "significant" way, cf. Section 4.1.3 (above). The requirement in respect of industrial application is to be widely interpreted as is the case with the Patents Act.

4.2. Acquisition of right

The utility models right is a priority right like patent and design rights. Acquisition is conditional upon the filing of an application with the Patent and Trade Mark Agency, specifying the invention in which the utility models right is sought, upon payment of a fee (Consolidation Act No. 119 of 12 february 2003) and upon subsequent registration, cf. on procedure etc.

Consolidation Act No 484 of 10 june 2003. Within a timelimit of 12 months from the application for utility model protection a patent application in respect of the same invention may be presented, cf. s. 49 of the Act, and it is also possible to convert a previously presented patent application into an application for utility models, cf. s. 6 of the Utility Models Act. Unless the applicant so requests, the Patent and Trade Mark Agency will not inquire into whether the statutory requirements of novelty and inventive step are satisfied (s. 12(2)). On the other hand, anyone may, upon registration, demand that such registration be revoked or invalidated, cf. Section 4.4, below. Appeals lie to the Patents and Trade Marks Appeals Board.

The right of registration is conferred upon the natural person who brought the utility model into existence. The right may be assigned, prior to or upon registration, in full or in part, to others, and it may be subject to debt enforcement. The Act governing employee inventions, cf. Section 3.3 (above), shall also apply to inventions which qualify for registration as utility models, cf. s. 51 of the Act. The same applies as regards the Act governing inventions in public reserach institutions mentioned above in Section 33.

The international co-operation on patents as formulated in "The Patent Cooperation Treaty", cf. Section 3.8, also applies to utility models.

5.3. Scope of the exclusive right

The utility models right grants the exclusive right to the commercial use of the utility model, cf. ss. 1(2) and 4 of the Act, and cf. also ss. 3-5 of the Patents Act. Consequently, any private arrangement or act for experimental purposes falls outside the scope of protection, and others may enjoy the right to continue use begun before the priority date, cf. Section 3.5. Further, there are certain possibilities of obtaining a compulsory licence, which is essentially similar in character to the one spelt out in the Patents Act, cf. ss. 30-31 of the Utility Models Act. Thus, exhaustion rules are – on a line with those applying in patent law – regional, cf. s. 4(2).

In the event of infringement of the utility models right, assessment will be based, as is the case in connection with patent and design rights infringement, on a concrete expert estimate, comparing the utility model with the alleged infringing product. In respect of the utility model, assessment will take its starting point in the utility models registration requirements as provided by the application and in the specification pertaining to such requirements, cf. s. 27 of the Act.

4.4. Duration of the exclusive right

Utility models registration lasts for three years from the date of application. The registration may – against payment of a renewal fee – be extended for two successive periods of three and four years, respectively, totalling a duration of 10 years, cf s. 28 of the Act. The maximum protective period is thus half of the protection provided by the Patents Act.

Under s. 32 of the Act, registration may be held invalid by judicial decree for various reasons, especially where the basic registration requirements – including the novelty and inventive step requirements – are deemed not to have been met. S. 34 lays down that any person may, in addition, request that the patent authorities, in full or in part, cancel the registration – for instance and in particular – to the extent that the basic requirements were not fulfilled at the time of registration. As in the case of patents, it is of importance to the surrounding world's possibilities of reacting that such registration be published and that the application documents be made available to the public, cf. ss. 14 and 16.

5. Design

5.1. What qualifies for protection?

5.1.1. The design concept

The legal protection of design rights is based on the Design Act, Act No 1250 of 20 December 2000 with subsequent amendments, which replaced the former Design Act as at 1 October 2001. The Act implements EC directive on legal protection of designs (98/71 EC) in Denmark. The rules of the old Design Act are still applicable to registered designs which are still upheld.

The design concept is defined in s. 2(1) of the Act as a product's or part of a product's appearance defined by the special features in the product itself or its ornamentation, in particular as regards lines, contours, colours, form, structure or material. Under s. 2(2) a "product" is an article made industrially or by handcraft including i.a. parts destined for assembling into a combined product, and packing, equipment, graphical symbols and typographical script types, with the exception of computer programmes. A "combined product" is a product consisting of several replaceable components so that the product can be taken apart and assembled again (s. 2(3).

It follows from the definitions that the object for protection is the *appearance* of a *product* or part of a product to a wider extent (including packing, equipment etc.), i.e. its exterior appearance which may be perceived visually, in contrast to the protection under patent and utility models of the technical function of a product. Even if the old design protection was also a protection of appearance it only applied to articles, not to the more extensive "products". Another difference in this context between the old and new Design Act consists in the capability of protection of parts of a product as the definitions imply, e.g. the design of the corner of a table, the set-up of screen images on a computer and the design of icons on a homepage.

Deisgn rights may be combined with protection under copyright law – i.e. double protection – cf. s. 10 of the Copyright Act and s. 50 of the Design Act.

5.1.2. Exempt areas

Under ss. 7-8 of the Design Act a number of circumstances excluding the obtaining of design right are enumerated. The most important of these are cases in which the design is contrary to an older design which has not become publicly accessible until after the date of the handing in of the application (s. 7(1),cl.2) or where the applicant either uses, in an unauthorised manner, another person's trade mark, firm or other business distinctive feature, or makes use of a work which is protected by copyright, or where the design contains an older design (s. 7(19, cl. 3 (b-d)). The aim of the design protection, cf. above, further requires that design right cannot be obtained in respect of those parts of a product which are exclusively determined by the product's technical function (s. 8(1), cl. 1). In other cases it will be posisble to combine design protection with patent or utiltity model protection so that the latter relate to the technical function of the product and the design protection relates to its appearance.

5.1.3. The fundamental requirements for design protection

The main requirements for obtaining design protection are contained in s. 3(1) of the Design Act: The design must be "novel" and possess an "individual character".

The *novelty requirement* is elaborated further in s. 3(2) and in ss. 5-6. S. 3(2) 1st cl. sets forth that a design is deemed to be novel if no *identical* design has become *publicly accessible* before the date of the filing of the application. The identity requirement does not contain a requirement of absolute similiarity since identity under the second clause of the provision is (also) deemed to lie if the special features of two designs only differ in immaterial areas. For the purposes of s. 5(1) a design has become "publicly accessible" if it was published in connection with a registration, or in other ways has become published, or where it has been displayed, used commerically or has become known in another way.

The determination in s. 5 of the meaning of "publicly accessible" indicates that the novelty requirement under the Design Act is to be construed in the same way as the requirement under the patent and utility model law (and under the old Design Act) i.e. an objectively global novelty is required. However, this indication is not altogether true: The rule in s. 5(1) is a main rule only and various exceptions are stated in s. 5 (2) and (6). Presumably the most important exception in practice is contained in subsection 6, cl.1 under which a design is not to be deemed publicly accessible if the publication has been effected within 12 months before the date of the handing in of the application by the designer or an assignee, if any, or by others on the basis of information conferred, or measures made, by the designer or a possible assignee. Under such circumstances the designer obtains what may be termed a "spare timelimit" in which publication of the design does not imply a detriment to the novelty of the design, cf. on the opposite solution in respect of patents and utility models, cf. above Sections 3.1.3. and 4.1. It is submitted that the spare timelimit is of particular impotance in cases in which there is a need to test the design and its position on the market. If such testing proves negative, the need for applying for design protection no longer exists.

The requirement of *"individual character"* implies that the overall impression the design affords to an informed user must be distinctive from the overall impression such user will have from other designs which are publicly accessible before the date of the filing of the application. The assessment will comprise a consideration of the degree of freedom which the designer had in the course of developing the design, cf. s. 3(3) of the Act, so that the requirement is less strict when the designer had limited access to develop a new design. The fictive "informed user" – which would appear a dubious element to a large extent – is to be perceived, under the travaux preparatoires of the Act, as a kind of hybrid between, on the one hand, an expert, and on the other, a non-expert user, who has no knowledge of the product nor of its application potential.

The requirements of novelty and individual character are of a special nature for combined products. Under s. 4 it is a condition, first, that the component, upon being incorporated into the combined product, is still visible in the course of normal use of the product. Second, it is a condition that it is the visble part of the component which must satisfy the requirements of novelty and individual character.

Lke the Patent Act and the Utility Model Act, the Design Act operates with rules of convention priority, see s. 16 and on the concept itself above in Section 3.1.3. Where priority has been claimed, the priority date – as an alternative to the filing date of the application, is important when deteriming the relevant points in time under ss. 3, 5 and 6.

5.2. Acquisition of right

Design rights are attributable to the "maker" of the design, cf. s. 1, which means that design must be created by man. Besides, the acquisition of right is formal, in that application must be filed with the Patent and Trade Mark Agency – by the designer or by an assignee. A fee is payable, cf. s. 13 et seq. (Consolidation Act No. 119 of 12 February 2003) and on the procedure, Consolidation Act No. 819 of 18 September 2001. The application must be accompanied by a reproduction of the design. The Agency will examine whether the application relates to a design, whether the requirements as to form are satisfied, and any obstacles of the kind mentioned in s. 7(1), no. 1 are applicable (public peace and decency) but no further testing will be made by the Agency on its own initiative, e.g. as to the existence of older, colliding designs. Where the requirements are satisfied, registration is made and published. The legal effects are computed from the date of reception of the application. Appeals of decisions of the Agency lie to the Board of Appeal for Patents and Trade Marks, cf. ss. 34-35 of the Act.

As will have appeared the right is assignable at any time and like other property rights it may devolve on the heirs upon death, and become subject to creditor enforcement. The Act does not contain provisons on designs made in the course of an employement relationship. It is submitted that, like the old Design Act, the new Act confers the right in such cases to the enterprise unless the design is also protected by copy right in which case the issue will need to be solved under copyright law, cf. above Section 2.3.1.

5.3. Scope of exclusive right

Under s. 9(1) of the Act, design right comprises a sole right to commercial use of the design, see the illustrative enumeration of acts of use at the conclusion of the provision. In a number of cases the right is incapable of being used, cf. ss. 10-11. The most important of these are acts for private purposes, testing purposes and reproduction for quoting or education purposes, in the latter cases provided that such acts are compatible with sound business ethics, that they state the source and do not harm the normal exploitation of the design unreasonably. Under s. 12 the exhaustion is regional. Parallel importation from one of the other EEA countries cannot be prevented on the basis of a design right if the product has been subject to a lawful marketing process in the country in question.

In collisons with other designs, the starting point is, under s. 9(2), taken in the consideration that the design right comprises any design which does not give the informed user (cf. above section 5.1.3) another overall impression and the degree of freedom which the designer had at the develoment of the design. The scope of protection in case of infringemnt will presumably be based on a concrete expert estimate. Where the overall imprission is the same the younger right must give way to the older. Thus design right is a priority right on a line with the patent and utility model rights.

5.4. Duration of protection

Desigh rights are protected for the period, or those periods, of five years for which the aplication was filed, computed from the date of application. Renewals may be made but the overall time of protection may not exceed 25 years, as a main rule, see s. 23(1-2) of the Act. Renewal requires payment of a fee.

The registration may further be terminated by decision of the Patent and Trade Mark Agency or by judgment, e.g. if one or more of the fundamental requirements for design right in s. 3 were not satisfied, cf. the provisions in Part 5 of the Act (ss. 25-33).

5.5. EU design and international design

The Euroepan Commission tried for a long time to make a legal basis for design protection, common to all the EU countries, via the drafting of a regulation in the area. The outcome was Council Regulation 6/2002 of 12 December 2001. The Regulation distinguishes registered and non-registered EU design. Protection under the first category, which is contingent upon registration with the EU Trade Mark Office in Alicante, cf. below Section 7.8, has been obtainable since January 2003 whereas the scheme for non-registered designs – which in principle only require publication within the Community – has been operative since March 2002. The national design acts continue to apply alongside the European regulation. The scheme is envisaged in the Danish Design Act, cf. ss. 42-43.

Further the Design Act contains provisions on international design registration, cf. Chapter 10 (ss. 53-59). The provisions refer to the socalled Geneva agreement from 1999 on international registration of design. Denmark has not ratified this agreement which prevents the Minister for Business and Industry from using the power in s. 60(1) of the Design Act to give efficacy to Chapter 10.

6. Semiconductors

Semiconductor is the technical term for the "chips" (integrated circuits) applied in computer technology. Intellectual property law protection in respect hereof is found in Act No. 778 of 9 December 1987 on Protection of Semiconductor Configuration (topography). For the purposes of s. 1(2) of this Act "topography" – which is the object of protection in the relevant products – is defined as "any number of connected images which, irrespective of the method of fixing or coding, constitute the three-dimensional design of the layers of which the semiconductor consists, and in which sequence every image forms, in part or in full, the design of a surface of the semiconductor in any stage of processing". The underlying ideas, concepts, processes, etc. do not qualify for protection, cf. s. 7 of the Act.

The acquisition of right is formal and subject to registration with the Patent and Trade Mark Agency. Under s. 2 of the Act requirements in respect of degree of originality are set up. Application for registration must be filed within two years from the date of first commercial use of the topography, cf.

s. 5, and cf. on the procedure Consolidation act No. 482of 10 june 2003. Registration is subject to payment of a fee (Consolidation Act No. 119 of 12 February 2003). The right is afforded to the producer or any assignee, cf. ss. 2 and 4 of the Act. In general, the protection implies the exclusive right in the topography of copying and commercial use as well as of importing the topography or any other semiconductor produced by means of such topography with a view to commercial use, cf. s. 6(1). Exhaustion in respect of commercial use and import applies universally within the EU, when the topography or any other semiconductor produced by means of the topography has been marketed by the proprietor in one of the Member States, cf. s. 6(2), no. 1.

Duration of the exclusive right is 10 years upon expiration of the year in which the right was established. The right takes effect on the day of the filing of application or – to the extent that prior use had taken place – on the day of the first commercial use of the topography, cf. s. 5(2-3).

7. Trade marks

7.1. What qualifies for protection?

7.1.1. The trade mark concept

In contrast to the items described in the preceding Sections, trade marks are in the nature of special *trade symbols* which are (may be) used when marketing goods and services, especially since they constitute one of the connecting links between a business and its customers by means of their symbolic value. Intellectual property law protection is first and foremost provided by the *Trade Marks Act*, cf. Consolidation Act No. 782 of 30 August 2001, as amended. A certain group of marks – so-called “collective marks” are afforded similar protection under Act no. 342 of 6 June 1991. The Acts referred to are, to some extent, results of the implementation in Denmark of an EU Directive on the harmonisation of Member State legislation on trade marks (89/104 EEC, the Trade Mark Directive). In addition, special EU legislation applies in the EU Member States and various provisions in respect of international trade mark registration are also applicable, cf. Section 7.8 (below).

S. 1 of the Trade Marks Act defines the general concept of trade marks as special marks for goods and services which are used, or the use of which is contemplated, by a business undertaking. In respect of the form of such marks, s. 2 lays down that a trade mark may consist of any type of sign capable of *distinguising* the goods or service of one business from those of other such businesses, and which is capable of being *represented graphically*. This implies that the mark must be suited for reproductive printing on paper.

Under s. 2, examples of the signs referred to include words, compounds, letters, numerals, figures and illustrations, and the shape of goods or of their attributes or packaging. Correspondingly, for practical purposes, distinction may be made in relation hereto between: *word marks* (e.g. the name "Danfoss"), *figure marks* (e.g. certain company logos), *slogan marks* (e.g. "Gillette – the Best A Man Can Get" etc.), *letter and numeral marks* (e.g. "BMW" and "4711") and *attribute marks* (e.g. a certain configuration of packaging for instance of bottles). However, not all features in relation to the attributes of the goods qualify for trade mark registration. Pursuant to s. 2(2), the right does not subsist in signs which consist exclusively of configuration pertaining to the nature of the article or which are necessary in order that a technical result be obtained, or in signs which significantly increase the value of the goods.

7.1.2. The distinctive mark requirement, etc.

One of the fundamental preconditions for obtaining trade mark protection is that the mark in question has the *necessary distinctiveness*, cf. s. 2 of the Act. It follows from this, first, that the mark must be special so as to distinguish it from other symbols used for commercial purposes. Second, the mark must not be of descriptive nature. This is specified in s. 13(2) of the Trade Marks Act, cf. s. 3(2), laying down that the mark shall not consist exclusively of signs or other indications which may, in the course of marketing, serve to describe the character, quality, quantity, application, value or geographical origin of the goods or service, or indicate the time of production of the goods or rendering of the service, or any other quality in respect hereof (e.g. words like "luxury", "extra", "first-class", etc.). Further, the mark shall not consist exclusively of signs or other indications which in the ordinary linguistic meaning or in accordance with general marketing practice may be considered an ordinary reference to the goods or services in question (e.g. "sun holidays", "gas concrete" and "station hotel").

S. 14 of the Act lays down a number of other general provisions. Under that section no protection may be granted to trade marks which are liable to mislead, e.g. in respect of the nature of the goods or services offered, or which, in an unauthorized use contains all or single components of the name of a person or business who holds lawful title to such name. Such infringement of the trade marks of others is treated below, cf. Section 7.6.

7.2. Acquisition of right

The trade mark right differs from the other intellectual property rights in that it may be obtained either by registration or by the use of the mark in question, cf. s. 3 of the Trade Marks Act.

Registration is conditional upon the filing of an application to the Patent and Trade Mark Agency, containing a reproduction of the mark, a depiction of the mark in so far as it does not consist exclusively of words, and an indication of the goods or services for which registration is sought. Registration is subject to payment of a fee (Consolidation Act No. 119 of 12 February 2003). The application will be subjected to an examination by the Agency, testing whether the statutory requirements of registrability are met. If so, the mark will be registered and the registration will be published. For reasons primarily of order, the marks are registered in different categories of goods or services. The registration may be challenged within two months from the date of publication, cf. s. 23 of the Act. The proprietor is not immediately under a duty to use the registered mark. If, within five years upon the conclusion of the registration, however, no use has been made in Denmark of the mark of the goods or services for which registration was sought, such registration may be subject to cancellation in full or in part. Correspondingly, if such use has been at a continuous halt for five years, the same shall apply, cf. s. 25. In the event that registration is denied, appeal lies to the Patents and Trade Marks Appeals Board.

Acquisition of right by the *use* of the mark is merely conditional upon the putting to use of such mark in Denmark. If the mark does not have the necessary distinctiveness when put to use, the right shall not subsist in the mark until, when, and if such distinctiveness is created upon the use of the mark, cf. s. 3(3) of the Act. Rights acquired by use are, in principle, just as valid as registered rights, although the latter carry various obvious advantages, e.g. and in particular as regards the possibilities of adducing evidence and as regards the material time of the institution of the right.

Regardless of the manner in which the trade mark right was acquired, it is, prima facie, a priority right, i.e. the right to a certain mark which was first instituted takes priority in case that two or more persons claim separate protection of such mark or of any similar symbol, cf. s. 7 of the Act.

7.3. Who qualifies for protection?

The right to trade mark protection is conferred upon the person or business (including companies) who has put the mark to use or undertaken registration, cf. s. 1 of the Trade Marks Act. The right may be assigned – in full or in part – like any other property rights and may be subject to debt enforcement proceedings. Licensing agreements in respect of trade mark rights are commonly included in substantive contractual relationships, e.g. franchising and distribution agreements. If ownership of a business is transferred, the right to the trade marks of such business is, under s. 38(2), assigned to the transferee as well, in the absence of contrary agreement. The transfer of the mark may be "loose" (socalled "trade mark merchandising") i.e. unrelated to the product(s) for which it was originally used, e.g. when the owner of a well-known mark with considerable sales power allows other producers by means of licensing agreements the use of the mark in the marketing of their products.

If a trade mark is created in the course of employment, the right of the mark belongs to the employer in the absence of agreement to the contrary.

7.4. Trade mark rights

The principal substance of trade mark rights is provided in s. 4(1) of the Trade Marks Act. The proprietor may prohibit any person who does not have his consent from making *commercial use of signs* which are *identical* with or *similar* to his trade mark. The use must, however, concern goods or services of the *same* or *similar* nature as those protected by trade mark, *and* there must be a possibility of *causing confusion*, including an alleged connection between the trade marks. Commercial use will especially occur when the sign in question is placed on the goods or on their packaging, or when such goods, by means of the sign, are offered for sale, imported/exported, or marketed or stocked for the purpose of sale, as well as when the sign is used on business stationery and for advertising purposes, cf s. 4(3).

When an article belonging to the trade mark owner is marketed within the EU by the trade mark owner or with his consent, the owner shall, as a principal rule, not be able to prohibit the use of such mark for the article in question, i.e. the further marketing of the article with the mark is lawful, cf. s. 6(1) of the Act. Within the EU, the trade mark right is thus exhausted universally: to the extent that the article has been marketed in a lawful manner in one Member State, the article can be imported freely to any other Member State. "Parallel imports" may thus not be stopped by reference to trade mark protection. A special issue, which has attracted some attention in recent years, relates to whether the parallel importer may re-pack the article and re-place the producer's trade mark on the re-packed articles/packaging. A number of decisions from the EC Court concerning first and foremost parallel imports of pharmaceuticals address the issue on the basis of whether a risk of splitting up of the common market would exist if re-packing was not allowed. If such risk was found to be present, re-packing was permitted (and re-placement of the trade mark) if a number of conditions were satisfied (no change of the product, a statement as to who had made the re-packing, notification to the trade mark proprietor, etc.). In recent years the Supreme Court in Denmark has decided quite a few cases in the matter of parrallel imports of pharmaceuticals with due consideration to the view mentioned and the conditions stated.

S. 6(2) provides an exception to the principal rule by laying down that the trade mark owner may prohibit the use of the mark, provided that he has reasonable grounds for resisting the continued marketing of the goods, especially if the condition of such goods has changed or deteriorated after the placing on the market. This exemption may be of particular importance in cases where such substantive repairs have been made to second-hand goods as to transform them into different products.

In (lawful) marketing *outside* the EEA areas similar questions may be raised as to whether the trade mark right is destroyed (exhausted) so that parallel imports – e.g. from discount countries – are made possible in disregard of the owner's rights. It would seem that the question is not absolutely clarified in all respects. An important European Court decision from 1998 (the socalled "Silhouette" decision) is presumably to be read to the effect that as regards the construction of Art. 7 of the Trade Marks Directive (corresponding to s. 6 of the Trade Marks Act) the Court applies the *"regional exhaustion"* view so that an owner of trade mark is not, prima facie, barred from exercising his trade marks rights in relation to parallel imports from countries outside the areas mentioned.

7.5. Special limitations of trade mark rights

As it appears from the above, the exclusive right is merely concerned with the *commercial* use of the trade mark. Any private use thus falls outside the scope of protection. Moreover, s. 5 of the Act provides a number of additional limitations of the exclusive right. Thus, the owner of the mark is in no position to prevent any other person from making, within the limits of sound marketing practice, commercial use of his own name and address, or of any other indication which pertains to the nature, quality, value, geographical origin, etc. of the goods or services. Further, the owner is debarred from prohibiting the commercial use of the trade mark to the extent that such use is considered necessary to illustrate the use of goods or services, especially in the form of accessories or spare parts. It is also in this connection a requirement that the use of the mark is in accordance with good marketing practice. The said limitation is of practical importance. A producer of unoriginal spare parts shall accordingly be permitted to market such parts on the grounds that they can be used with a certain main product, provided that the reference to the product (and the trade mark thereof) is necessary, and that it is clearly stated that the parts are unoriginal in such a way that possibility of confusion is ruled out.

Case law provides a certain further limitation in respect of socalled "comparative advertising", i.e. advertising which draws a comparison between the goods of the advertiser and those of any other person competing with such goods, presenting the competing products by means of their trade marks (e.g. advertisements showing a producer of a certain make of car comparing his own models with those of his competitors). For the purposes of trade mark law, such use of the marks of others is accepted, provided that it is fair and truthful, and in particular that it is not likely to cause confusion, cf. also Chapter 12, Section 2.5 below.

7.6. Infringement of trade mark rights

When the question of infringement of the trade mark right is raised in practice, the decisive factor will normally be whether the marks in question are *confusingly similar*. As mentioned above in Section 7.4, s. 4(1) of the Act lays down as a principal rule that confusion is only deemed to exist to the extent that the marks pertain to goods or services of the same or a similar nature. Thus the Act presupposes that both *similarity of mark* and *similarity of goods* are in evidence. In practice, the two requirements are not treated separately, and regard may also be had to other matters, e.g. the composition or nature of the customer portfolio. The result is rather an overall assessment as to whether a possibility of confusion is deemed to be present. The assessment will typically contain some flexibility, in particular so that the enforcement of the requirement of mark-similarity is less strict if the goods are identical and the requirements in respect of similarity of goods are correspondingly looked upon leniently where the similarity between the marks is evident.

Certain marks enjoy a particularly substantive protection against infringement. Pursuant to s. 4(2) of the Trade Marks Act, the requirement as to similarity of mark will not be upheld if the infringed trade mark is *well-known in Denmark*, and the use would constitute *undue exploitation* of the distinctive character or reputation of such mark or *be detrimental to* the such mark's distinctive character or reputation. The first purpose of the rule is to prevent an unfair advantage being taken of the goodwill which well-known marks normally enjoy. On the other hand, several owners of well-known marks squeeze the use of such marks by allowing – against payment – that the marks are used for a number of very different products, e.g. globally well-known motor cycle marks as spearheads of the marketing of fountain pens and other stationery.

7.7. Duration

There are no absolute time limits for the duration of trade marks. When the right is acquired by use, it will endure for as long as the mark is actually used, for which purpose, however, any suspension shall not be material. A registered trade mark takes effect from the day of application and lasts for 10 years from the day of registration. The right may be renewed – upon request and against payment of a fee – for successive periods of 10 years, cf s. 26 of the Act.

Registered trade marks are subject to a number of rules on revocation of trade marks, either for reasons already existing at the time of the registration, e.g. lack of distinctive character, or for reasons arisen after the registration. In addition to the requirement that the mark must be put to actual use within five years from the registration, cf. Section 7.2 (above), the provision contained in s. 28(2)(2) is of particular interest. Under that provision, the trade mark may be revoked, provided that the mark, by reason of the activity or passivity of the proprietor, has become the general term within the trade for the goods or services for which it was registered. In such cases, the mark is said to *degenerate*, i.e. the mark that used to be a special symbol of certain goods or services becomes a common name for all goods or services of the nature in question. This development is, of course, disadvantageous to the owner of the mark, which is why it is of importance that he seeks to keep the mark as his special symbol through his regular marketing and by his general "care" for the mark.

7.8. Details on EU trade marks, etc.

As mentioned above in Section 7.1.1, special EU legislation applies (from 1996), viz. Council Regulation No. 40/94 on the Community Trade Mark, in the Member States *concurrently with* the various national trade marks statutes. The Regulation establishes a Community Trade Mark System by laying down that registration (not use) can afford universal trade mark protection in all Member States. The registration requirements are more or less the same as the ones contained in the Trade Marks Act which also applies as regards the legal effects of registration and the duration of protection. In practice, the system is carried into effect by the "Office for the Harmonization of the Single Market", sitting in Alicante, Spain (www.oami.eu.int/en/deafult/htm). Application for registration may be filed either directly with the Office or with the registration authorities in the individual Member States. Appeals against decisions from the Office may be brought before a socalled "Appeals chamber" and further to the Court of First Instance, cf. above Chapter 3, Section 3.6.

International systems include the socalled "Madrid Arrangement" (1991) and the socalled "Protocol to the Madrid Agreement" (1989), both concerning the international registration of trade marks under the auspices of a subsidiary organisation of the UN (World Intellectual Property Organization, WIPO, www.wipo.int/). Denmark has ratified the Protocol, but not the Arrangement, cf. Part 8 (ss. 50 et seq.) of the Trade Marks Act for further reference on the Danish rules in relation to the international ones. Denmark has also acceded to the Trade Marks Treaty (the Geneva Treaty) from 1994 which is mainly concerned with various registration issues, cf. the Treaty publication of 7 January 1999.

7.9. Special note on domain names

Domain names are names of "addresses" on the Internet. The name will typically contain a designation for the owner or supplier (socalled second word domain"), e.g. "legal info" (in Danish "retsinfo" to indicate the law information service "retsinformation") , and a designation for the affiliation of the domain, either in the form of country code, e.g. "dk", "uk", or a generic code, e.g. "com", "gov", and "edu" (socalled top domains). The names act as very simple search systems which make it easier for internet users to find the pages on the internet they are looking for. The computers involved in the search do not use the names but use a special numeral system in which the names have been "translated" into figures.

The use of a domain name presupposes that it is registered. In most material respects this is effected on a basis which is not formulated in legislation but brought about in a private way, notably via various international and national organisations. As regards the national top domains registration responsibility lies with socalled "hostmasters", in Denmark "DK Hostmaster A/S" (www.dk-hostmaster.dk). The company is owned by "Dansk Internet Forum" (DIFO, www.difo.dk) an association whose menbers are various major interest organisations. In 2000 the association was granted the right to undertake the .dk-top domain by the Internet Corporation for Assigned Names and Numbers" (ICANN, www.icann.org). In this connection the association will define the overall aims and means for the Danish part of the Internet and hereby lay down the rules for the administration of, and issues, under the .dk. Domain. Such regulation lies i.a. and in particualr in the form of "Rules for registration, administration and conflict solution concernig domain names under the top level domain .dk" (the latest edition currently is the version of August 2003, which may be seen on DIFO's homepage).

Registration of a domain name in Denmark reqires an application to "DK Hostmaster A/S". Under the rules mentioned above such application may only be filed by a "domain registrator" acknowledged by the company to whom the customer (if he is not himself approved as a registrator) must apply. The rules contain only a few conditions for registration, including that the customer accepts the rules set up by DIFO from time to time, e.g. governing the determination of rights and obligations involved in the use of a domain name. Further the customer must warrant that the use or active application of the name applied for does not infringe third parties' name or trade mark rights and he must also declare that to his knowledge the use will not be contrary otherwise to Danish law. The hostmaster will examine that the registration conditions are satisfied and that the name is vacant, which is undertaken by the process described as "first come, first served" (waiting lists are provided against payment concerning already registered names). Where no impediment is raised the hostmaster accords the *right of use* of the name to the applicant. The periods of use are one year at a time. A modest fee is payable for each period for which the registration is to run. The right of use is transfereable. It is no bar to registration that the business applying for registration has its home base abroad.

Existing trade marks may of course be used as domain names and be registered as such. Conversely, domain names – except for the top level addition – will be capable of obtaining trade mark protection either via trade mark registration or on the basis of the rules of the trade mark law on use implementation, in both cases naturally under the condition that the fundamental trade mark conditions are satisfied, cf. above Sections 7.1.2 and 7.6.

The domain names have to a considerable extent become part of the external "image"of a business and often having the same function as a trade mark, viz. to act as a link between the business and its customers. It is therefore evident that the names contain a considerable potential for conflict, and that under the circumstances large economic interests may be at stake. Via DIFO's rules a special dispute-solving body has been established for the issues which a dispute over the use of a domain may raise, viz. the Appeals Board for Domain Names (in Danish: Klagenævnet for Domænenavne, www.domaeneklager.dk). Under the rules the Board shall have jurisdiction to hear cases on whether a domain name registration is contrary to Danish law or to the rules. The Board may decide to transfer, suspend or delete such domain names but it is not authorised to decide payment of compensation unless it is expressly stated in the rules. The complaint, in writing, shall be presented to the Board's secretariat and a minor fee is paid for the hearing (this fee will be reimbursed if the complainant wins the case). The hostmaster is obliged to enforce decisions made, e.g. on deletion. The reference to the Board of the case is no bar to a future institution of proceedings before a court of law and an injured party may naturally leap-frog the Board and go directly to the courts, e.g. to obtain an immediate view as to possible damages.

In its comparatively short life-time the Board has heard a large number of cases (currently about 400, as may be seen on the board's homepage) and its practice is therefore so comprehensive that it must be said to be illustrative. From the ordinary courts of law quite a few decions are also available now. The legal basis applied by both instances is first and foremost the Trade Mark Act, the Marketing Practices Act (ss 1 and 5), the Names Act and the provisions of the companies governing compnay names. From case law the following main guide lines may be outlined:

Socalled "domain name piracy" is counteracted by application of s. 1 of the Marketing Practices Act and general rules of law. Via a procedure as the one mentioned the "pirate" registers e.g. one or two well-known distinctive features, e.g. trade marks, as domain names with the aim of subsequent extortion of the owner of the distictive feature of an exorbitant amount for the transfer to him. If the domain name has been used commercially by the pirate, a decision of e.g. trade mark infringement will be made.

If the domain name is found to be liable to confusion with an existing trade mark, infringement of trade mark will be held under the ordinary rules in the Trade Mark Act, cf. above Section 7.6 if the domain name has been used commercially. If this is not the case, the matter is referred to ss. 1 and 5 of the Marketing Practices Act. Where two confusable domain names are in issue, which do not enjoy trade mark protection, the latter provisions are applied in favour of the first registered name provided that the use of the most recently registered name has been commercial and that the user has been cognisant of the other name at the registration.

The provision in s. 5 of the Trade Mark Act concerning spare parts, cf. above Section 7.5, does not confer upon un-authorised dealers of the product for which the trade mark is applied by the trade mark owner a right to use the mark as domain name. The matter is regarded as an infringement of trade mark and possibly to be contrary to ss. 1 and 5 of the Marketing Practices Act.

As mentioned in Section 7.1.2, the requirement of distinction prevents the obtaining of trade mark protection of socalled genus designations. Also in relation to domain nanes such designations are, in principle, free so that a domain name registration relating to a genus designation, e.g. the word "net bookshop" – will not give the user a special access to it. However, the use by others of the designation must be made with respect of ss. 1 and 5 of the Marketing Practices Act.

If a trade mark is used as a domain name for a socalled "hate page" where a consumer expresses his dissatisfaction with the product(s) marketed under the application of the trade mark, commercial use of the trade mark willl be held to lie and thereby infringement of such mark. Where the trade mark is incorporated as an ingredient of the domain name itself and the rest of the components signal the dissatisfaction (so that an Internet user is aware in advance that a hate page is involved) the situation may be different, notwithstanding the misrecommendation of the product aimed for. In a case involving the domain name "shit seat.dk" which had been registered by a (strongly dissatisfied) private buyer of a car of the make "Seat" the Board presumed that the registration was neither contrary to the Trade Mark Act nor to the Marketing Practices Act. The Board emphasised that what was involved was a hate page and that statements (in this case the domain name) which contain a subjective assessment of the value of a product cannot be deemed defamatory.

The responsibility for the generic topdomains lies with ICANN, cf. above, and the registrators approved by the organisation. As will have appeared, the Appeals Board for domain names is not competent in cases on names from these domains whereas Danish courts will have jurisdiction to decide both these and cases concerning other national top domains, if the ordinary conditions for instituting civil proceedings in Denmark are present. ICANN has prescribed a special – somewhat cumbersome – conflict-solving procedure in respect of generic topdomains ("Uniform Domain-Name-Dispute-Resolution Policy", UDRP), cf. the homepage of the organsiation.

By Regulation 733/2002 of 22 April 2002 the European Parliament and the Council have laid down guidelines for implementation of the topdomain "eu" with a view i.a. to facilitating the use of the Internet and extend the users' access to top domains. The aim is also to improve the visibility of the internal market and to strengthen the image of the EU in the global information networks. The Regulation envisages the appointment of a topdomain administrator to be in charge of the organisation and administration of the domain. The Commission will lay down more detailed rules for the implementation of the Regulation, including principles governing extra-judicial settlement of disputes. At the time of writing the scheme is not yet operative.

8. Special note on know-how

In a number of business enterprises, special knowledge – commonly referred to as *know-how* – is accumulated in respect of how different work processes, etc. are carried out in the most expedient way. Such knowledge, which may be of technical as well as of commercial nature, will, depending on the circumstances, be of substantial financial value to the individual enterprise in that it gives the enterprise – at least for a certain period of time – a competitive advantage.

Agreement on the definition of know-how has yet to be reached. It is, however, generally accepted that the knowledge in question, first and foremost, should be of practical nature, and that the knowledge package as a body or in the precise configuration and assembly of its components must be *secret* to the extent that it is not generally known or easily accessible, cf. in this respect Art 10, cl. 1, in the European Commission Regulation of 31 January 1996 on categories of technology transfer agreements (240/96) by which know-how is defined as a "technical knowlege which is secret, material and identified in appropriate form" (the Regulation is currently under revision). With this construction know-how will typically be related to a specific enterprise. The precise scope of the definition has, however, no immediate bearing on intellectual property legislation in that it does not imply an exclusive right, enjoying special protection like copyright, patents, etc. Protection in respect of the surrounding world must thus primarily be of factual nature: observation of strict discretion with the employees, business associates, etc., in order that no relevant information shall escape from the enterprise. In the event that the know-how may be considered a *trade secret*, it enjoys limited protection under the Marketing Practices Act, cf. Chapter 12, below, Section 2.9.

Know-how may be assigned which often happens in practice by means of licensing agreements. Asssignment of commercial know-how is often encountered in connection with the establishment of various long-standing working relationships, e.g. in respect of franchising.

9. Remedies for intellectual property infringement

All the above intellectual property Acts contain provisions in respect of *criminal liability* incurred by the person who infringes any of the exclusive rights referred to in the preceding Sections. In some cases, e.g. concerning patents and utility models, only intentional infringements will be punishable, while in other cases, e.g. concerning copyright, criminal liability will also lie for gross negligence. The sanction is normally modest, since the starting point is defined in terms of penalties. Where the offence was committed under aggravating circumstances, in particular where the infringement was intentional, and a considerable and evident unlawful enrichment was designed the punishment may be increased to simple detention or imprisonment of up to one year. In practice the remedy is invariably a (money) penalty.

Further, all the Acts contain provisions in respect of *civil liability* for infringements. Under the ordinary Danish rules of tort, damages are generally awarded for the loss suffered as a result of the infringement, e.g. for loss of sales and for market disturbances. In practice, the production of documentary evidence in respect of the size of the loss suffered normally presents great difficulties. To this end, rules have been made, laying down that any person who intentionally or negligently infringes the exclusive right shall always and as a minimum pay reasonable monetary consideration for the use of such right – normally an amount equalling an appropriate licence fee – and, in addition, provide compensatory relief for any further damage caused by the infringement. Moreover, some of the Acts contain provisions on payment in the event that the infringing person was acting bona fide, of a certain *reasonable pecuniary relief*, either fixed at an account of maximum profits gained by such person (as provided by the Copyright Act) or fixed at the loss of the owner of the right (as provided by the Patents Act). Finally, the Copyright Act contains rules on payment of compensation for *non-pecuniary damage* for the infringements of the rights of authors, photographers or performing artists.

In connection with infringement of intellectual property rights it is often of absolutely paramount importance that the proprietor acts quickly. Long legal proceedings for criminal and/or civil liability will therefore often be less practical, as compared to the possibilities of obtaining *restraining injunctions*, which may bring infringing activities to an immediate halt. In practice, such procedures are very common. The ordinary rules on injunctions contained in the Administration of Justice Act are followed, which mainly implies, first, that conclusive or presumptive evidence in respect of the alleged infringement must be produced, and, second, that security for costs must be provided if an injunction is to be issued, cf. the provisions in ss. 641 et seq. Often it will also be indicated that evidence of infringement and its extent should be sought as early as possible. The securing of evidence may be effected with the assistance of the bailiff's court in the form of a search with the party who is presumed to have violated the exclusive right, possibly with seizure, cf. the provisons in the Administration of Justice Act, ss. 653-653d.

If it is held by the court that the exclusive right was infringed, the court may, in pursuance of all the Acts, and upon a claim made by the rightful owner, order the *obliteration*, the handing over to the said owner, or the modification of any (illegal) products in the possession of the infringer.

CHAPTER 12

Marketing and competition law

by Morten Wegener

1. Introduction

The freedom of contract and the *freedom of competition* constitute the twin pillars of the type of occupational structure commonly referred to as "market economy". The freedom of competition provides any person engaged in commerce or industry with the possibility of participating in the battle with others for securing the largest possible share of total market turnover. The freedom especially manifests itself in the *competition* between market participants. From a business economic point of view this is generally taken to mean any measure aimed at *promoting the sale* of certain goods and services. Within legislation, the definition sometimes has an even wider construction, cf. section 2.1 (below).

It has long been recognised both that the freedom of competition cannot be completely unrestricted and that certain circumstances call for public measures, providing the competition with reasonable opportunity to unfold. As regards the former, it was established early that there could be cause for subjecting to a certain kind of censorship the *means* used by businesses *as against eachother* when marketing competing goods and services. To this end, rules were introduced laying down that competition should not be *disloyal* or *unfair*. The battle on and for the market was to be led with sharp-edged weapons in the form of competition on price, quality, and service rather than with blunted ones, e.g. like trade libel or denigration of competitors or their products, or any other type of free-riding on competitor performance. However, the marketing means applied have another side, viz. the one facing the *customers* which has been given increasing attention by politicians over the past 20 to 30 years, sometimes bordering on the extreme. The crux of the matter is the demand for *consumer protection* through a relatively high level of information when marketing, especially by banning marketing means which could prove *misleading*. Overall, the regulation of competition conditions in these two respects is termed *marketing* or *competition law*, and the principal statutory provisions governing this area are laid down in the Marketing Practices Act.

Different factors both in fact and in law may, however, impede the exercise of free competition. Traders may i.a. enter into mutual *agreements* with the purpose of restricting competition between the enterprises in order to create possibilities for imposing an unacceptably high level of prices for services offered. Another situation is where an undertaking or associations of undertakings attain market dominance in such a way that they more or less exercise a *monopoly* of supplying certain services and thereby make competition less effective or perhaps even illusory. The consideration for society as such as well as for other businessmen and for consumers may in both cases speak in favour of regulation, allowing for public measures aimed at keeping competition alive. Such legal matters of competition normally fall within the ambit of *anti-competitive practices law*. The most important governing law at national level is found in the Competition Act. In addition, the area also falls within EU regulation of great practical importance.

In the following, Danish marketing legislation will be treated in Section 2, the Danish Competition Act in Section 3, and the EU rules briefly in Section 4. As will have emerged from the above, the regulation is primarily focused on the possibilities of introducing certain public measures, i.e. it is "commercial regulation law", cf. Chapter 1, Section 1.1 (above). Given that the rules pertain to the marketing of goods and services, there is, however, a narrow connection both to law of contract and property law and sale of goods law, especially of course to the part governing the formation and validity of contracts on the one hand, and sale of goods and intellectual property law matters on the other.

2. The Marketing Practices Act

2.1. Scope of the Act

Under clause 1 of s. 1 of the prevailing version of the Marketing Practices Act (Consolidation Act No. 699 of 17 July 2000, as amended), the Act shall apply to any private business activity and to any public activity comparable with such activity. The term "private business activity" is broadly defined. Not only do ordinary private business activities, e.g. within trade, craft, industry, and agriculture come within the Act; it also covers activities within the field of services, e.g. banks, estate agents and the so-called "professions" (solicitors, accountants, etc.). Nor is it decisive whether a traditional entrepreneur's profit is the object of the said activity. Also co-operative societies, consumers' co-operatives and public utilities are within the scope.

As regards the public enterprise, the decisive factor is whether such enterprise is a market participant and, if so, whether it may – like private business activities – have competitive effects.

As a principal rule, the Marketing Practices Act has only territorial jurisdiction in cases where the business conduct pertains to the Danish market. In practice, however, the possibility of including activities pertaining to export markets in the scope has not been ruled out, provided that the prejudicial acts were committed in Denmark towards Danish competitors. As regards the access to sue for cross-border infringements of marketing practices, special rules apply, see below Section 2.13.2.

The concept of marketing in the Act as laid down e.g. in the title and in clause 2 of s. 1, cf. Section 2.3 (below) is extremely wide and not identical with traditional business conceptual perception, cf. Section 1 (above). According to the travaux preparatoirs of the Act, the term "marketing" aims at "any act carried out for the purpose of business", and thus not only at direct sales-promoting measures.

At present, the administration of the Marketing Practices Act falls within the authority of the Ministry of Business and Industry, cf. s. 24 of the Marketing Practices Act. The Minister may, however, delegate large parts of his authority to the National Consumer Agency, cf. below.

2.2. The Consumer Ombudsman

At the original passing of the Marketing Practices Act in 1974, a special (public) administrative body – the Institution of the Consumer Ombudsman – was appointed for the handling of certain tasks under the Act. Pursuant to s. 15(1) of the current Act, the Consumer Ombudsman shall be in charge of the *supervision* of the observance of the Act, especially for the purpose of protecting consumer interests, in that he may demand the disclosure of all information deemed necessary, including information for the purpose of deciding whether a matter falls within the provisions of the Act, cf. s. 15(2). The starting point is that through *negotiation* he shall seek to induce traders in commerce or industry to act in accordance with sound marketing practice and otherwise to observe the Act, cf. s. 16(1). Where any such person disregards a commitment made upon such negotiations, the Ombudsman may issue the *orders* necessary against the person in question for securing the observance of the commitment. Furthermore, s. 19(1) provides the Ombudsman with the possibility of *instituting legal proceedings* for the purpose of obtaining an injunction in addition to any derivative orders in respect of acts which are deemed to be in conflict with the Act, and, by virtue of s. 21(1) he is also endowed with certain powers to issue interlocutory injunctions.

In addition to these very concrete supervisory powers and pursuant to s. 17 of the Marketing Practices Act, the Consumer Ombudsman also performs a function of practical importance in that he prepares and publishes *guidelines* for marketing in certain fields which are considered to be material, especially in respect of protecting consumer interests. The guidelines, which in principle are of mere persuasive character, are drafted upon negotiations with the relevant trade and consumer associations. Where the guidelines have been approved by the organisations they may, upon agreement with such organisation, form the basis of a command but only in respect of those members who have acceded to the guidelines, cf. s. 17(2). Further, upon request, the Ombudsman files socalled *pre-publication vetting* under s. 18, stating his opinion on the legality of the marketing means to be applied. In general, such approvals are not, however, binding, but are mere restrictions on the possibilities of Ombudsman intervention at a later stage, cf. s. 18(2).

> In practice, the main efforts of the Ombudsman have been concentrated – entirely in accordance with the priorities established in s. 15(1) of the Act – within the fields where evident consumer interests prevailed, while mutual relationships between businessmen have largely been left to direct battles between the parties involved.

In pursuance of the Marketing Practices Act, the decisions of the Consumer Ombudsman cannot be appealed to any other administrative authority, cf. s. 15(4) of the Act.

2.3. The General Clause. General provisions

Clause 2 of s. 1 of the Marketing Practices Act sets forth that in any enterprise, comprised by the Act, acts which are *contrary to sound marketing ethics* may not be made.

The provision contains a socalled "general clause", cf. Chapter 1, Section 3.6 (above) on this concept. The concept of "sound marketing practice", which is the underlying principle of the Act, is so wide and imprecise that it only covers the more specific matters which are discussed in the following provisions of the Act (first and foremost ss. 2-5). These matters may thus be seen as examples of acts which will be contrary to sound marketing practices in all events. In consequence, the general clause is given independent importance, especially in that it gives possibility of intervention against undesirable conduct falling outside the scope of the more detailed regulation.

The concept of "sound marketing practice" cannot be defined in exhaustive and absolute terms. A survey of the procedures which may from time to time be considered unchallengeable can only be attained by analyzing case law, and even such analysis will never provide absolute certainty. Naturally, the problem is that the concept – and hence the general clause – is extremely elastic. The demands on marketing are changeable, not only from trade to trade, but also – and in particular – over time. What used to be acceptable 10 or 20 years ago is not necessarily acceptable today or tomorrow, if it is estimated, e.g. that there is a predominant need for tightening up the requirements.

As a general consultative basis for the assessment, the travaux preparatoirs of the Act provides that due consideration should be given to trade and industry interests, to consumer interests as well as to general social interests, so that in each case the invasion of these interests is balanced against the utility of the prejudicial conduct. It is thus established that good marketing practice is not merely the opposite of abuse, but that the demands on the persons engaged in commerce or industry may be extended beyond refraining from the unauthorized use of certain rights, etc. Somewhat more explicit guidelines are often provided by various codes of marketing ethics, etc., issued and designed by trade associations. "The International Chamber of Commerce" (ICC) (www.iccdanmark.dk) has drafted a number of socalled Marketing Codes which undergo continuous revision. Especially the existing Code of Advertising Practice is of great practical importance (although the principal provision governing advertising is s. 2 of the Act, cf. Section 2.5 (below)). In a number of court decisions, importance has been attached, upon application of the general clause, to whether the marketing means of the trader – e.g. his advertising – departed negatively from such codes of business practice. Examples of other such guidelines include the guidelines drawn up by the Ombudsman, cf. the preceding Section.

It is evident that a regulation technique which implies application of general clauses – as is the case with the Marketing Practices Act – fundamentally contains a possibility of a more flexible application of law than does a technique based on more accurately formulated rules. It does, however, also carry with it a considerable risk, especially by giving rise to uncertainty as to the law in trade and industry circles. Case law in respect of application of the general clause shows attempts to obviate the worst consequences of this kind by carrying out typological classification of the cases presented whenever possible. When taking this into consideration together with a similar practice exercised by the Ombudsman, it is to some extent possible to formulate reasonably tenable views on when an act is in contravention or in observance of the law, cf. the following Section.

The general clause in the law of contract (s. 36 of the Contracts Act, cf. Chapter 7 (above)) and clause 2 of s. 1 of the Marketing Practices Act partly overlap in connection with the use by businessmen of unacceptable contract terms, especially in standard agreements. For further reference, cf. the comments made in Sections 2.4.4 and 2.12.

2.4. The general clause. Application in practice

2.4.1. Disloyal market displacement

The field of application which is by far the most important in practice in respect of the general clause is cases of what is termed "disloyal market displacement". First and foremost, this occurs in situations where any person engaged in commerce or industry, in full or in part, tries to displace another such person from the market by certain forms of *imitation of* or any other form of *freeriding on* the efforts of the competitor. To this end, the general clause in particular functions as a supplement, both to the special provisions contained in ss. 5 and 10 of the Marketing Practices Act, cf. Sections 2.8 and 2.9 (below), and to the safeguard rules as provided by intellectual property legislation, cf. Chapter 11, Section 1.

It is, however, far from every kind of imitation that is considered unacceptable. In respect of goods, the law requires, first, that the product imitated has certain *external distinctive features*. Moreover, the infringement must be of such gravity – irrespective of the nature of the product imitated – that the imitation can be characterised as *proximate*. This normally implies market identity, i.e. that the goods or services in question are *likely to cause confusion*. Moreover, evidence that the imitator was acting *mala fide* must be present, i.e. that he intended the imitation with full knowledge of all relevant facts. The typical situation is where the imitator intentionally and systematically makes a close copy of the other party's product with the direct purpose of acquiring – without any effort of his own whatsoever – (part of) the market created by that other party. The infringement most often takes place during the preparation of the product, but other imitative/free-riding elements may be added or even override the original infringing act, e.g. in connection with features and advertisements. In respect of the latter, Art. 9(2) of the ICC Code of Advertising Practice, cf. above, lays down that advertisements must not take undue advantage of the goodwill attached to the name of a person, the trade name and symbol of another firm or product, or of the goodwill acquired by an advertising campaign. Imitation of other advertisements is prohibited, cf. Art. 11.

Disloyal market displacement may take a certain – and particularly malicious -form in cases where the imitation/free-riding is undertaken by former employees or other cooperative partners. In such cases, there seems to be a tendency towards tightening the demands to loyalty, at least for a brief period of time following the termination of the employment or cooperation. Former employees should thus be particularly cautious during the period of time following the termination, e.g. with getting in too close contact with the goods or services provided by the business they have recently left, cf. also Section 2.9 (below).

2.4.2. Indecent, etc. marketing means

In practice, the above-mentioned general clause forms the basis of a number of requirements to the *general* decency of the marketing means, i.e. to their conformity with prevailing general moral standards. Naturally, this is particularly important in respect of the marketing carried out in advertisements. Under the ICC Code of Advertising Practice, every advertisement must be prepared with due sense of social responsibility and may not contain statements or visual presentations which offend against prevailing standards of decency. Nor may advertisements, except for reasons, justifiable on educational or social grounds, contain any visual presentation or any description of dangerous practices or of situations which show a disregard for general safety. Special care must be taken in advertisements directed towards or depicting children or young people (Arts. 1-2 and 13-14). Such aspects will often be relevant, e.g. in connection with visual presentations in advertisements of violent crime and sexual situations. Further, it may be directly inferred from such aspects that advertising and other types of marketing a product the selling of which is illegal shall also be prohibited, and that steps may be taken in a similar way against the marketing of products which are dangerous or substandard.

Further, Art. 3(4) of the ICC Code of Advertising Practice lays down that advertisements may not endorse discrimination based upon race, national origin, religion, sex or age. Nor may they deprave human dignity in any way whatsoever. In conformity with this provision, the Ombudsman has found that it is in conflict with sound marketing practice to present foreigners in a "curious or stereotyped manner" in advertisements. The sometimes somewhat strained discussion on the use of persons of the weaker sex in various stages of undress as an advertising eye-catcher for various products is more than well-known. In a judicial decision, the court has issued an injunction under the general clause against a furniture shop, prohibiting the use of advertising of this nature. Under the above provision of the ICC Code of Advertising Practice (Art. 3(1-3)), it is further provided that advertisements are not without justifiable reason to play on fear and superstition, or contain anything which might lead to or lend support to acts of violence, or entice illegal or reprehensible conduct. The gap between direct indecency and general offence against public decency or plain nuisance is normally not that wide, and the provision referred to may be extended to comprising marketing means in general. Arriving at the address of a debtor in a car clearly marked with the words "debt collection" has thus been held to be in conflict with sound marketing practice in the debt collection business.

Other related areas include situations where pictures of certain persons are used for the purpose of marketing without the consent of the persons in question. Such actions have been considered to be in contravention of the general clause and are also included in Art. 9 of the ICC Code. The result may be the same in case of unauthorized use of the names of other persons. The Danish Supreme Court found that the use of the name of the late shipowner A.P. Møller in an advertising campaign without prior permission i.a. from the shipping company A.P. Møller A/S was contrary to sound marketing practice.

Advertising moving in the border areas may be especially controverisal if the medium is TV or radio. This area is subject to a detailed legislative regulation which in its main substance is on a line with the above, cf. Consolidated Act No. 194 of 20 March 2003 on TV and radio advertising.

2.4.3. Pyramid selling, etc.

One of the characteristics of the marketing technique termed "pyramid selling" is that an undertaking sells the right to practising certain activities, e.g. the sale of a certain product, within a given geographical area to a person who acquires the right to resell the right to other such persons operating under him. The procedure may be repeated in several levels in such a way that a pyramid of units and persons is formed. The financial motive force is the admission fee paid by anyone wishing to enter the system. By undertaking such multi-level operations, the basis of the pyramid can attain a size, allowing the founders to claim very large admission fees. The actual goods or services distributed play a totally insignificant role, if any at all. It has often proved to be the case that the system cannot support the pyramid in which event it tends to collapse. Those who have collected the admission fees will ultimately have enriched themselves at the expense of the other participants.

Schemes of this kind or of related nature, which in many ways resemble chain letter systems, are in flagrant conflict with sound marketing practice and will moreover often constitute actual criminal offences (fraud).

2.4.4. Unfair contract terms

According to the travaux preparatoirs of the Marketing Practices Act, the drafting of contract terms – whether for individual or standard contracts – is considered an integral part of trade and industry marketing. To this end, the Act – and hence the general clause – thus provides possibility of subjecting the content of such terms to a certain kind of censorship.

The principal precondition for holding certain contract terms to be in conflict with sound marketing practice is normally the identification of a *need for protection* with the person or persons on whom the term is imposed, i.e. typically that there is a presumption of imbalances in the relationship between the parties to the contract in such a way that one of the said parties is clearly at a competitive disadvantage. In this connection, the consumers constitute the immediate group of candidates. Further, the term in question is required to make the legal status of the parties depart in such a way from the ordinary rules of contract that there are grounds for saying that the trader, in an *unreasonable* manner, has made one-sided allowances for his own interests, thus making the term *unnecessarily onerous* on the other party to the contract. In practice, this situation will most often occur in connection with standard terms in agreements between undertakings, e.g. as provided in general terms of business, standard contract forms, and similar material.

It thus appears that assessment under s. 1 has a clear suggestion of the assessment of the importance of unfair contract terms in the *law of contract* laid down in the general clause contained in s. 36 of the Contracts Act, cf above Chapter 7, Section 4.10.2.. Assessment under s. 1, however, departs *in principle* from assessment under s. 36 in that it is *universal* and in that it relates to the term in question *as a type*, i.e. evaluating the *general* effect from the point of view of the consumers, cf. Section 2.12 (below) for further reference.

2.4.5. Hidden advertising

From cl. 12 in the ICC Code of Marketing Practice it appears that advertising must be capable of being clearly identified as advertising irrespective of the form it takes and the media applied. When an ad is published in a medium containing news or editorial matter it must be presented in a manner so that it will immediately be recognised as advertising.

Advertising which fails to satisfy the requirements mentioned is generally perceived as "hidden advertising". The marketing effort is disguised, so to speak, in that the message is incorporated in a neutral account, e.g. a text which may appear as official or of editiorial character. Such advertising which is quite common and which is may be take to even more refined finer tunes on the Internet ("interactive advertising") is on the one hand suited for affecting a consumers' decision basis but on the other hand it is indisputably contrary to s. 1 of the Marketing Practices Act (and may, under the circumstances come close to the rules on misleading, cf. the following Section. A comparatively recent decision from the Maritime and Commercial Court established e.g. that a local TV station could not, against payment, make a co-operation on a broadcast with a business making a certain product when the broadcast in issue appeared as edited journalistically but the main contents notwithstanding focused on the particular product.

The identity requirement is especially strict in connection with the sale of pharmaceuticals. This area is subject to special regulation, cf. Consolidated Act No. 793 of 10 September 2001 on the advertising of pharmaceuticals, as amended, which contains a detailed regulation of the requirements for advertising such products.

2.5. Misleading, etc.

Under s. 2(1) of the Marketing Practices Act, *false, misleading* or *unreasonably inadequate statements* which *may potentially influence the supply or demand* of goods, real property, and other assets as well as of facilities and services shall be prohibited.

The principal field of the provision is commercial *advertising*. It is, in essence, very similar to the provision in Art. 4 of the ICC Code of Advertising Practice laying down that advertisements may not contain any statement or visual presentation which directly or by implication, omission, ambiguity or exaggerated claim is likely to mislead the consumer, in particular with regard to characteristics, value, terms of payment, delivery, warranty terms, etc.

Advertising is considered misleading when a certain statement – irrespective of the medium used – may potentially impose on the market a false impression of the product marketed, and when such statement is relevant in respect of the reaction of the market, e.g. decisions to carry out a purchase. The statement must be deemed likely to have what is termed a "commercial effect". In principle, it is immaterial whether any person was in fact misled. The decisive factor is whether the statement, upon an *objective assessment*, could potentially influence supply or demand on the market to which the statement was directed.

Misleading information will normally be false, and conversely, false information will be deemed misleading. In case of the latter, there will, however, be certain modifications in respect of socalled *trade puff*, i.e. such – often exaggerated – commendations which cannot be verified and which should not, according to ordinary language usage, be taken literally (e.g. "The finest car in Denmark", etc.). Such statements are allowed. If, on the other hand, the statements are verifiable, the demands to truthfulness are strict. Most of the numerous cases tried have focused both on misleading indications of price, e.g. on false "before/now prices" or fabricated discounts, and on misleading statements of quality and quantity, e.g. the selling of second-hand goods without statement of quality grade.

A special kind of misleading advertising is the so-called *denigration*, which means misleading statements about *competitors*. Such denigrating advertising, which typically takes the form of false and discrediting statements about any other person within the same line of business, is prohibited under s. 2(1) of the Act and may, in addition, be subject to the provisions in s. 2(2-3), cf. below. In essence, these provisions correspond with Article 7 of the ICC Code of Advertising Practice, laying down that advertisements may not denigrate any firm, industrial or commercial activity/profession or any product, whether by bringing it into contempt or ridicule, or in any similar way.

Comparative advertising, i.e. advertising which draws a comparison between the goods of the advertiser and those of competing undertakings, carries with it a special danger of denigration, cf. also Chapter 11, Section 7.5.For the implementation of an EU harmonisation directive (97/55) express provisions were incorporated into the Marketing Practices Act s. 2 a governing this kind of advertising. Under subsection 1 of the provision comparative advertising comprises any advertising which directly or indirectly refers to a competitor or to goods and services offered by a competitor. Comparison is permissble under subsection 2 when a large number of requirements are satisfied which for the most part are consistent with the Danish practice applied so far. Apart from requiring that the comparison shall pertain to goods and services satisfying the same needs or serving the same purpose, it is required that such advertising must be *truthful, relevant* , *fair,* capable of *substantiation* as regards the factual subject-matter, and it must not be liable to cause *confusion.* If the ad in question contains a special offer it must be clearly stated i.a. when the offer will lapse, cf. s. 2 a(3). Comparative advertising is also touched upon in the ICC Code e.g. in Art 6 in which it is stated expressly that points of comparison must be based on facts which can be substantiated and that they are not to be unfairly selected.

S. 2(1) of the Marketing Practices Act is supplemented by the provision in subsection 2. Under this provision, the prohibition in subsection 1 shall include statements which, on grounds of their *form* or because they pertain to *irrelevant matters*, are *unfair* towards other persons engaged in commerce or industry or towards the consumers. Also in this connection, the statements are subject to the test of being potentially able to influence supply or demand, whereas it is immaterial whether such statements are truthful or unverifiable. The problem in relation to the form may arise, e.g. where the goods of the competitor are presented in a particularly adverse manner. Examples include information on the personal lives of the competitors or the race, nationality or religion of such competitors or of certain consumer groups. Assessment of whether a statement is deemed unfair is broadly connected to public social interest.

S. 2(3) of the Act is ancillary to both subsections 1 and 2, providing that misleading *practices* of importance to supply and demand similar to the influence provided in subsection 1 shall be prohibited, as shall practices with similar effect, provided that they are unfair towards other traders in commerce or industry or towards the consumers, on grounds of their special form or because they include irrelevant matters. The provision is, i.a. applicable to certain sales methods, where irrelevant matters are imposed on the customer contemplating a purchase, including to sales in connection with the socalled private "home-parties".

In respect of factual matters mentioned in connection with marketing, s. 2(4) of the Act lays down that, in general, substantiation of the truthfulness of the said matters must be available. Thus, the trader must be able to present evidence as to the truthfulness of the factual information used. The corresponding provision in the ICC Code is found in Art. 17, laying down that descriptions, claims or illustrations relating to verifiable facts must be capable of substantiation, and that advertisers should have such substantiation available so that they can produce evidence without delay.

2.6. Duty to provide directions for use etc.

Under s. 3 of the Marketing Practices Act, directions for use etc. must be given when an offer is made, a contract is concluded, or, depending on the circumstances, at the time of delivery, in a duly diligent manner, taking into consideration the nature of the property or the product, when such directions are material to the evaluation of the character and features of the property or the product, including, in particular, performance characteristics, durability, risks and possibilities of maintenance.

The provision is ancillary to ss. 1 and 2, imposing on traders in commerce or industry a *general* duty to provide directions for use and to disclose any information, prior to the more specific deliberations on the part of the customers concerning a possible contract. The duty covers all links in the chain of distribution, and hence not exclusively the final sale to the consumers. The basis of the provision is that directions for use are to be communicated upon conclusion of a contract. In relation to the expression "at the time of delivery", reference is only made to such information that may prove relevant and material in respect of *the use* of the product purchased, and thus not in respect of deliberations pertaining to the actual formation of the contract.

The specific nature of directions to be given and the form they should take depend on the object and nature of the contract. In this connection, trade customs may be used as advisory guidelines. As regards purchases of standard goods, the accompanying informative label and/or instructions will normally suffice. It is, however, usually not incumbent upon the trader to appraise the needs of the individual customer, unless circumstances – e.g. questions asked by such customer – call for such appraisal. Information on price is outside the scope of the provision. This does not, however, apply to information regarding other financial conditions – e.g. about any encumbrances on the product sold – which could be of relevance, especially in respect of contracts for comprehensive properties, e.g. when purchasing real property.

S. 3 of the Act is partly paralleled by the sales law rules on the vendor's "duty to disclose material facts" in connection with the sale of chattels and of real property, cf. Chapter 8, above.

2.7. Warranties

In connection with purchase of more durable goods, the seller will often grant a warranty on the features and/or durability of the product sold, i.e. assume a certain financial risk which in the contractual relationship would otherwise rest with the buyer. The warranty will normally be a relevant element in the buyer's decision to buy, and in general, warranties also perform a clearly sales promoting function. In this way, possibilities are opened for promises of warranties being used as well as abused. In practice, this will especially be carried out by making the contents of the warranty, in full or in part, fictitious: the legal position of the buyer towards the seller is not in reality improved (in fact it may even be aggravated) if compared to how the position would have been, had the ordinary rules of law been applied.

S. 4(1) of the Marketing Practices Act covers certain parts of this problem. Under this provision, a declaration that a warranty or the like be granted must only be used towards consumers in cases where the declaration provides the receiver with a significantly better legal position than the one he enjoyed under his statutory rights. It is immaterial whether the declaration of warranty is expressly stated in the actual contract or whether it is specified in a separate warranty certificate. The warranty or any other type of special guarantee, cf. the wording "or the like", must provide the receiver of such warranty with *actual, real improvements*, having regard to the terms of the contract *in its entirety*, i.e. that the receiver is not merely granted a number of rights vis-à-vis the supplier of the warranty which he would not have enjoyed otherwise, but that these rights are in fact of material importance.

Not only does s. 4 thus disqualify exemptions of liability disguised as warranties; it also lays down that declarations of such warranties are in fact no more than references to the ordinary rules of law, e.g. a buyer's remedies on the seller's default under the Sale of Goods Act. Examples of unacceptable practices thus include "warranty certificates" in consumer transactions, providing the buyer with the right to the free remedying of defects as found within one year after the date of purchase. The buyer already enjoys such a right under ss. 78(1) and 83 of the Sale of Goods Act, cf. also the Consumer Ombudsman's detailed guidance of 19 June 2003 on the application of warranty statements to consumers in advertising and contract terms. It is generally deemed in this guidance that a warranty is given if the trader without separate consideration – both in connection with the sale of the article or provision of service in question and also in connection with a reliance on the warranty – undertakes the risk for defective materials and functioning or other defects in the article sold for a certain period. The Consumer Ombudsman further presumes that the warranty period for new articles must, as a main rule, extend considerably beyond the timelimit of the Sale of Goods Act. For second- hand goods a warranty corresponding to or shorter than the statutory timelimit may be considered an improvement of the buyer's legal position if it is clearly stated in the warranty that defects under the Sale of Goods Act may in addition be claimed within the timelimit of the Sale of Goods Act.

If a warranty is given s. 4(2) sets up various requirements in respect of the contents and the accompanying circumstances. Thus the trader must inform of the warranty in a clear and unequivocal way and suply the information necesasary to rely on the warranty. Further, it must be stated in no uncertain terms that the consumer's statutory rights are not affected by the warranty. Upon request the warranty must be delivered in writing and in that case couched in Danish. It is submitted that neither these guidelines nor s. 4(1) are adhered to in practice to any noticeable extent.

S. 4 is also ancillary to ss. 1 and 2. Under s. 1, the terms of warranty may be subjected to actual censorship as regards contents, provided that the terms are deemed to be in conflict with sound marketing practice. Under s. 2, the misleading use of words such as "warranty" and the like as generally sales promoting arguments – for instance and in particular in advertisements – shall be subject to prohibition.

2.8. Business distinguishing features

Distinguishing features – names, trade names, trade marks, logos, etc. – are, as touched upon in Chapter 11, Sections 7.1 and 7.9 – one of the connecting links of prime importance for a business towards its customers. which is why such features often carry with them considerable commercial value. Accordingly, a need for rules exists, providing business undertakings with a certain kind of protection of their features. To this end, s. 5 of the Marketing Practices Act lays down that traders in commerce or industry may not make use of business features the like to which they do not have a rightful claim; nor may they use their own business features in such a way that they are confusingly similar to the features of others.

The concept of business distinguishing features is relatively broadly defined in that it covers all external factors which are connected with the business in question by the surrounding world (and in particular by the customers), e.g. – in addition to the above-mentioned factors – special decoration of shops and means of transportation, certain choices of form and colour used on signs and shop fronts, and certain staff uniforms. A certain distinctiveness (a certain degree of originality) is, however, required, but such distinctiveness may be attained through the regular use of the feature.

In practice, the principal problem under s. 5 of the Act is normally whether the feature applied is likely to cause confusion. Overall assessment of this matter is carried out on the basis of a large number of factors, especially the similarity as regards the sound and form of the trade marks applied by the parties involved, the geographical locations of the undertakings vis-à-vis each other, the trade positions enjoyed, and the customer bases. In the event that such confusion was actually intended (socalled "reputation free-riding"), the requirements to obtaining feature protection are normally relaxed, cf. also Section 2.4.1 above for further reference.

Certain features enjoy special statutory protection, to which s. 5 is thus a supplement. To this end, the rules on trade marks contain the principal provisions, cf. Chapter 11, Section 7.

2.9. Trade secrets

The term "trade secret" here means any such information on either *technical* (as regards production) or *commercial* matters in a business undertaking, which is *special* to a business and which the business in question tries to *guard from disclosure* to persons who are *strangers* to the business undertaking. The information will often be of first importance or in any case material to the competitive position of the business as is the case, e.g. if the business is the only one in the market with knowledge of and experience with a certain (advantageous) production process or who has developed particularly efficient business methods. As these examples illustrate, special *know-how* developed in an enterprise will normally be considered a trade secret, cf. Chapter 11, Section 8.

The protection of trade secrets under Danish law is provided, partly by the rules in the Penal Code governing industrial espionage, and partly by the provisions in the Marketing Practices Act, in particular by s. 10 of this Act. While the provisions in the Penal Code are directed towards the penetration by *strangers* of the undertaking, the Marketing Practices Act rules cover the undertaking's relationship with *employees* and *cooperative partners*. This Chapter only deals with the latter rules.

Pursuant to s. 10(1) of the Marketing Practices Act, any person engaged in employment or working relations with an enterprise, or who otherwise performs a duty for such enterprise shall be prohibited from acquiring or attempting to acquire, in an improper manner, knowledge or possession of the trade secrets of the enterprise. For this purpose, the concept of trade secrets has the same definition as mentioned above. The first requirement is thus that the information protected is not *common knowledge*, e.g. information obtained in the course of general vocational training. In addition, it is a requirement that the enterprise has shown due diligence in guarding the information from disclosure to anyone but *relevant persons* (those whom it "concerns"), including to persons within the enterprise itself. In the event that all employees e.g. have enjoyed free and unlimited access to the information, irrespective of whether for reasons justifiable on workrelated grounds, the information will not enjoy protection. "Employment or working relations" is widely interpreted as meaning any form of cooperative relationship, whether of casual or permanent nature. However, persons who are merely visiting the enterprise are outside the ambit of the definition.

S. 10(2) concerns persons who have *lawfully* acquired knowledge or possession of the trade secrets of a business enterprise. If so, the information in question may not be *communicated* or *utilised* without authorization for a period of three years upon termination of the employment, working relations or of other duties. Under this provision, it is thus illegal for trusted members of staff to terminate their employment and immediately start competing with the former employer, using the trade secrets acquired from such employer.

Under s. 10(3), any person who, during the discharge of occupational duties or otherwise for purposes of business, has been given access to technical blueprints, descriptions, recipes, models, etc. in confidence, shall not make unauthorized use of such material or enable other persons to make such use. In cases of this nature, the material does not need to fall within the definition of trade secrets. The provision is i.a. of practical relevance in respect of sub-suppliers or persons who have received material of the nature mentioned for the purpose of reproduction or making an offer.

S. 10(4) deals with the "handling of stolen goods" in respect of trade secrets. Under this provision, traders in commerce or industry may not utilise a trade secret, if knowledge or possession of the secret has been obtained in a manner contrary to s. 10(1-3). In such cases, the person "handling" the secret is presumed to be acting *mala fide*. Examples of such situations include cases where an undertaking – e.g. against payment – acquires information on a competitor's trade secrets from persons in the employ of the competitor.

Also s. 10 is supplemented by the general clause contained in s. 1. This provision may e.g. form the basis of temporal protection being extended beyond the period laid down in s. 10(2).

2.10. Marketing prohibition

Ss. 6-9 of the Marketing Practices Act contain a number of prohibitions of the more specific marketing means which are generally – albeit sometimes ill-advisedly so – considered to be particularly adverse and also suited for more detailed regulation.

2.10.1. Premiums

A premium in this context means the reception of a subsidiary product without separate consideration upon the purchase of a main product or service. Such techniques may serve to obscure prices, which is the principal rationale underlying the prohibition in s. 6(1). This provision lays down that traders may not, by selling goods or real property to consumers, or by rendering facilities or services to consumers, grant any premiums or other consideration comparable to such premiums, unless the premium is but of token value. Advertising such illegal premiums is also prohibited. In pursuance of s. 6(2), a supplementary product which is of the exact same nature as the main product or service shall not be considered a premium. Quantity discounts ("two for the price of one", etc.) are thus not deemed to be premiums.

Giving away products without obligation to buy – e.g. free samples as promotional gifts – and providing customary installation or service in connection with a purchase, e.g. adjustment of clothes purchased, are thus outside the scope of the premium definition. The same goes for the so-called "tie-up purchases" where two or more products or services are bought together, having either a natural connection (e.g. developing a film and supplying the customer with a new film) or being separately purchasable.

Delimitation as regards the concept of premiums of "token value" has given rise to a number of cases, and court practice is strict: the value of the supplementary product, estimated as an independent purchase object, must not exceed a total value of a few Danish kroner, notwithstanding the price of the main product or service. In addition to this absolute limit, there is, however, also a relative one. The value of the supplementary product may also be balanced against the value of the main product or service, and in the event that the value of the latter is comparatively low, the premium value must only be microscopic. Outside the context of the s. 2 situation the nature of the premium is irrelevant.

The provisions of s. 6 only apply to sales to end users. Hence, premiums are allowed in the intermediate stages of the chain of distribution, always provided, however, that the activities are kept in observance of sound marketing practice, cf. the general clause.

S. 6(3-6) lays down special provisions in respect of the socalled "flight bonus programmes". Under such programmes, which must be offered on an international scale, premiums are granted when a flight is booked, e.g. in the form of free flights, hotel accommodation, and rental cars. According to the conditions laid down in the above-mentioned provisions, premiums of this nature are not prohibited. Under s. 6(7), similar schemes are permissible for undertakings other than airlines, etc., provided that such undertakings are subjected to similar international competition.

2.10.2. Quantity and customer restrictions

Under s. 7(1) of the Act, retail businesses may not impose caps on the number of units of a certain type of goods, purchasable by the individual customer. In addition, such businesses may not refuse to sell to certain buyers. Under subsection 2, these rules do not apply to actual clearance sale goods.

The provision aims at protecting small retailers against the use by large retail businesses of so-called "bargain merchandise" or "loss leaders" which are sold to the customers at a price far below the wholesale price. Whether the said provision will prove efficient, and whether it is in fact desirable considering the competition, is somewhat doubtful. For one thing, the rules exclude the possibility of imposing restrictions in respect of marketing – including advertising – on the number of items or the quantity purchasable by the individual customer, provided the goods are in stock, e.g. "max. 3 pcs per customer". For another, it is impossible to exclude certain customers – in practice primarily small retailers – and they thus have the possibility of purchasing from the business in question the entire stocks of the goods on offer. However, the uncertainty of the provision is illustrated in a case in which the Maritime and Commercial Court exonerated a discount store from alleged infringement of the prohibition in a suit brought by the Consumer Ombudsman. The store had advertised the sale of Christmas beer at a very favorable price but with the proviso that the offer was only applicable at the purchase of a maximum of two cases. If a customer wanted more cases the price would be considerably higher. The store had made the restriction on the grounds of preventing that other traders bought up whole quantities of the spot article for re-sale. The Court held that the marketing was not comprised by s. 7(1).

It is, however, not prohibited to give notice by means of advertisements, etc. that the goods are only in limited stock. Incidentally, s. 7(1) comprises only goods, not services, e.g. – as has been decided in case law – mobile subscriptions.

The escape clause covering "actual clearance sale goods" is not particularly effectual. It is very difficult to delimit the scope of this criterion with certainty. There are (no longer) limitations in respect of the right to have clearance sales, and in practice, the goods offered as clearance sale goods are far from always unmarketable or of a quality inferior to ordinary goods. However, in general, groceries will probably not be deemed "actual clearance sale" goods.

2.10.3. Trade stamps, etc.

The granting of discounts, bonuses, etc. may also give rise to pricing being obscured. S. 8 of the Marketing Practices Act contains a few rules aimed at counteracting such practices.

Under s. 8(1), discounts or other consideration may not be granted in the form of stamps, coupons or the like, by traders *prior to* the purchase of goods or upon rendering facilities or services. The provision is directed towards the use of coupons or the like in daily and weekly papers, periodicals, flyers, advertising material, etc. The provision does not, however, prevent that organised discounts are granted, for instance and in particular to members of certain societies, provided that the discount arrangement is not based on the use of stamps and coupons in the manner referred to.

S. 8(2) of the Act deals with discount arrangements as regards the use of stamps, coupons or the like, used *in connection with* the sale of goods or rendering facilities or services, and with a view to the later cashing of the stamp or the coupon. Such arrangements are permitted, provided that every stamp is clearly and explicitly marked with the issuer's name or undertaking, indicating also the declared value in Danish currency. The issuer must cash the stamp in Denmark at face value, when stamps at an amount further specified by the Minister of Trade and Industry are presented for cashing. It follows from the above that the stamp issuer cannot demand that goods be taken instead of cash. At present, the above-mentioned cap is DKK 20, cf. Consolidation Act No. 197 of 20 March 2003.

Ordinary cash and quantity discounts are outside the scope of s. 8. The same applies to dividend which – e.g. in consumers' co-operatives – is distributed in relation to operating result. This was illustrated in a Supreme Court decision in which the judges held that the member bonus system of the Danish co-operative FDB (Coop Denmark) was not comprised by s. 8, nor was it contrary to s. 1. Finally, the provision does not apply to the flight bonus programmes treated in s. 6 (3-5), cf. Section 2.10.1 (above).

The actual use of discount systems, including the issue of stamps under s. 8 may in some cases be practised in such a way that it could prove misleading or be in conflict with sound marketing practice, i.e. on the facts of the case, the conduct may be within ss. 1 and 2 of the Act.

2.10.4. Lotteries and prize competitions

Prize competitions etc. used to be one of the most popular marketing means. For these purposes, s. 9(1) of the Marketing Practices Act provides that promoting the sale of properties or services to consumers by means of offering to consumers the chance of winning a prize by participating in a lottery, a prize competition, or in any other form of arrangement whose outcome depends, in part or in full, on chance, shall be prohibited, provided that such participation is conditional upon purchase. Under subsection 2 of the same provision, the Minister of Business and Industry may impose de minimis limits. Under Consolidation Act No. 1152 of 16 december 1994 s. 9 does not apply if the value of the individual prize does not exceed DKK 100 and the total prize value of the entire marketing effort is below DKK 1,000. For measures directed towards children under the age of 15 in particular the lower limits are DKK 5 and DKK 50.

The prohibition contained in s. 9(1) is thus directed towards so-called "lottery participation conditional upon purchase". Accordingly, the provision does not apply to cases which do not stand the test of being matters of chance. Performance-related competitions, i.e. competitions in which the best performance is rewarded, and which provide reasonable security that this will indeed be done, are thus not affected by the prohibition. The same goes for competitions which are open to everybody, and in which all correct solutions are rewarded.

Under s. 9(3), the prohibition does not apply to periodicals – i.e. especially daily and weekly papers and the like – as such periodicals may initiate lotteries, awarding prizes in connection with solutions to prize competitions. Practical examples include crossword and picture puzzles. The competition must be initiated solely by the periodical and thus not be undertaken in cooperation with trade and industry persons who are in any case excluded under s. 9(1). Plain advertising folders – i.e. publications without socalled editorial articles – are outside the scope of s. 9(2).

2.10.5.Direct marketing

S. 6 of the Act is directed against certain forms of "direct marketing", where a trader approaches one or more specific persons (i.e. not unadressed mail) without considering whether such unsolicited approach is made on the basis of their names, postal addresses, telephone numbers or the like. The provision was incoporated into the Marketing Practices Act 2000 to implement the provisions in the EU Directives 97/7 and 97/66.

Under s. 6a(1) a trader is prohibited from addressing anyone by means of electronic mail, an authomatic call system or telefax with a view to selling goods, real property and other property assets as well as work and services unless the addresee had asked for it beforehand. The term "anyone" indicates that the ban is not limited to consumers but to all and sundry irrespective of whether the addressee is a consumer or a trader, and irrespective of whether the adressee is a natural or legal person. In this light there is no doubt that the sending of e-mails or telefax of socalled "spam" for advertising purposes is prohibited. Under the not very lucid travaux preparatoires of the provision an assessment as to whether the approach is for sale purposes must place considerable emphasis on whether "the trader has an interest himself in the dispositions on the part of the customer which the trader's applications concern". Evidently, direct invitations to buy will be within the scope of the ban. But a certain limitation of its scope with a view to some important situations in practice will now follow from the new rule, incorporated in 2003 into s. 6a(3). This allows a trader who has received the electronic address from a customer in connection with a sale of an article or provision of a seervice to market other similar products/services of his own via electronic mail. It is a condition that the customer may decline to receive such material both in connection with the giving of his address to the trader and in connection with later approaches. Applications by means other than distance communication and optings out of applications are regulated by s. 6a(3-6).

There is a certain similarity between s. 6a and the provisions in the Act on certain Consumer Agreements (the "doorstep sales" Act) ss. 2 et seq. regarding unsolicited applications to consumers, cf. above Chapter 7, Section 4. This is borne out at the conclusion of s. 6a(3) which says that these provisions apply along side s. 6a(3) to approaches to consumers by telephone.

2.11. Labelling and packaging regulations

Ss. 11 and 12 of the Marketing Practices Act vest various powers – partly inspired by the EU – in the Minister of Trade and Industry to lay down more specified rules in respect of the labelling and packaging of goods, including indications in the various intermediate retail stages in the chain of distribution of the country of origin of the goods (s. 11(1)). Under the powers vested, a number of ministerial regulations have been drafted – which are not treated here – including detailed rules of the nature referred to in respect of certain categories of goods.

As to the statement of prices s. 1(1) of Consolidation Act No. 209 of 28 March 2000 on labelling and displaying of prices etc. sets forth that a person who offers his goods for commercial purposes in a retail sale by labelling, displaying by signs or in other ways must *clearly* inform of the price including VAT and other taxes in respect of the article or article unit advertised. Where organised discount is granted all the entrance doors of the shop or in connection with distance sales must state the various information details hereon (ss. 1(2) and 5(2)). If credit sales are engaged in the seller is under s. 2 of the Act under the same obligation to inform about the cash price, credit costs and the annual costs, cf. also ss. 9 and 14 of the Credit Sale Agreements Act (Chapter 10, Section 1.1, above). Finally it appears from s. 5(1) that when informing of prices towards consumers in advertising of any manner the information must satisfy the requirements in s. 1(2) and (3). In administrative practice the Price Labelling Act is deemed to comprise trade in and advertising of goods and servcies on the Internet and by means of similar electronic communication forms, compare Section 2.12.2 below on s. 8 of the e-trade Act and above, Chapter 7, Section 4.9.1 on s. 32(1) of the Contracts Act.

2.12. Special note on e-trade

As mentioned in Chapter 7, Section 2.2 the Contracts Act model for contract formation is in principle also applicable to agreements made electronically although an adaptation is made on account of the tools applied at the formation which are of course materially different from those known at the beginning of the last century. In relation to the Marketing Practices Act a similar starting point may be made in that the rules are applicable to e-trade contracts as well, in particular the rules which are relevant before and at contract conclusion.

However, there are also various important rules which are especially directed towards e-trade and which are designed to *supplement* general marketing law. The most important law in this respect is *Act No. 227 of 22 April 2002 on services in the information society, including certain aspects of e-trade* (the e-trade Act) which is the Danish implementation of the EU Directive 2000/31/EC of 8 June 2000. The aim for the Directive (minimum directive) is to secure the free movement in the internal market for the implementation and exercise of socalled "information society services" , e.g. advertising and invitations to buy goods and other servcies on the Internet, cf. on the concept in the immediately following. Such services may automatically and simultaneously be accessible in all countries within the EEA area and are thereby of trans-boundary character to a particular degree and therefore also in particular need of harmonisation via Member State legislation.

2.12.1.Application area

Under s. 1(1) of the e-trade Act, the rules are applicable to services in the information society. S. 2, no. 1 prescribes that the aim is to secure *any service* with a *commercial* purpose which is delivered *on-line* (electronically over a certain distance) upon the *individual request* of a service recipient. Services which do not satisfy *all* requirements are outside the scope and the same applies (under s. 1(2) of the Act) to certain subject-matter areas and types of activities (e.g. tax matters and personal data protection). The party supplying the information servcie is termed the *service supplier* whereas the recipient (and user) is of course called the *service recipient*. The subject-matter delivered between the parties is *commercial communication*. This implies any form of communciation which is directly or indirectly aimed at furthering the sale of goods and services or at establishing an image for an enterprise, an organisation, or a person engaging in trade, industry or craftsmanship trade or another trade regulated by law (s. 2, nos. 2, 4, and 6).

Based on the *nature* of the services supplied, the application of the Act is thus, first and foremost internet access servcies, e-mail, advertising and on-line sale of goods and services, including by application of socalled "banner (standard) advertising" – WAP and SMS servcies, search machines (also freely accesible ones) – and general on-line information about an enterprise no matter if they represent advertising proper or not. If the ordering of an article is made electronially, e.g. via the homepage of a business, while the delivery of the article is made off-line in traditional manner, the Act applies to the ordering whereas the off-line part is subject to the ordinary rules of the Marketing Practices Act, the Contracts act, and the Sale of Goods Act. Speech telephony, telefax, and telex services and services provided over the phone, fax, and telex, are however outside the scope and the same applies to services which do not have the required commercial purpose, e.g. private individuals' hompages. Since it is a requirement that an individual request can be traced from the service recipient (e.g. where such person has visited the homepage on the Internet) it follows that text TV and radio and TV broadcasts sent via cable or satellite are not comprised by the Act. The supplier may be both a natural and a legal person and under the circumstances also a public authority if the offer of services from that quarter is made on a commercial basis.

As regards the *geographical* scope of application, s. 3 of the Act sets forth that an information service supplied by a supplier *established* in Denmark must, within the socalled "co-oordinated area" as it is called, be exercised in accordance with Danish law irrespective of whether the service is solely directed towards another country within the EU/EEA. A supplier is established in Denmark under s. 2, no. 3, when he engages in commercial trade in this country by means of a permanent arrangement within a non-specified period of time. The co-ordinated area is defined under s. 2, no. 8. as "rules which are set forth in the EU Member States and enforced by the authorities of the Member States, and which pertain to requirements in respect of information society services or requirements to suppliers of such services when activities as a supplier are started or exercised". When these obscure designations are translated into Danish it means that the business offering the service must have a physical and permanent presence in Danish territory of such quality that the relevant economic activities can in fact be – and are in fact – exercised, e.g. when a company established and registered in Denmark has its business seat in Denmark. The decisive element in the assessment of application within the co-ordinated area. i.e. the entire EEA – is thus not where the *techonology* applied was situated or where a given page on the Internet is accessible but where the supplier of the service *engages in his commercial trade*. A Danish enterprise with a home base in Denmark which has directed its marketing efforts against e.g. the German market via the Internet, must oberve Danish law whereas a German enterprise in the opposite situation must observe the requirements under German law. In this respect the Act and the Directive underlying it contain important rules of mutual recognition betwen the Member States, cf. s. 4 of the Act.

Under the travaux preparatoires and under the Directive the regulation made focuses on *public law* rules, i.e. rules which are enforeceable by authorities within the public administration. This statement is of a somewhat problematic natuere, cf. as regards s. 12(2) of the Act in the following Section. However, it is evident that it is irrelevant fore the choice of law and venue issues in regard to private disputes, cf. below Chapter 22, and it is also apparent from the Directive that it is not to apply to contractual obligations in connection with consumer agreements. A number of other circumstances are unaffected by ss. 3 and 4 of the Act, cf. s. 5.

2.12.2.The marketing practices requirements posed to the supplier

Ss. 7-13 of the e-trade Act contain a number of provisions, which may be said collectively to represent a number of ordinary marketing law rules with a view to application in relation to electronic marketing and trade. Some of the provisions are non-mandatory, where the agreement is a non-consumer one, see s. 13(2), cf. s. 10, 11(1) and s. 12.

S. 9(1) sets forth that all commercial communication which is part of or constitutes an information society service must be drafted and presented so that it appears with certainty on whose behalf it is sent out. Further it is required under subsection 2 that when discounts, premiums, and gifts are allowed the conditions for participation must be readily accessible and be presented in clear terms. The same applies with regard to permitted sales promotion competitions and games. As will be seen, s. 9 is aimed first and foremost at hidden or obscured advertising, e.g. via the Internet, cf. above Section 2.4.5.

Under s. 7(1-2) the supplier is under a general information duty concerning various basic information for the identification of the enterprise, its placement, affiliation to schemes of approval (name, address, e-mail address etc). Under s. 3 easy and permanent access for the recipient and the authorities to the information in question is required. From the travaux preparatoires of the Act it appears that the requirement implies that the information is to be given collectively and in the most adequate way under the form of technique applied in that the widest requirements will probably be posed via marketing via the Internet where the technical potential of detailed information is currently best.

S. 8 deals with price information. The price is to be stated clearly and it must be apparent if it is inclusive of taxes and delivery costs. The provision applies not only towards consumers but also towards service recipients who are traders and thereby it becomes a supplement to the provisions on price information in the Price Labelling Act and the Consumer Contracts Act, cf. above Section 2.12 and Chapter 7, Section 4.14.

S. 10 contains rules on certain information which the supplier must give *in advance* to the recipient before agreement is concluded. Thus, information on the technical parts in connection with the contract formation must be given, whether the contract made shall be stored by the supplier and whether it is to be accessible, the technical tools required to find and correct typing errors, and the languages in which the contract is concluded (subsection 1). The Directive prescribes that the information which the recipient may e.g obtain by clicking on to an icon in the screen image must be clear, understandable and unequivocal. This is adhered to in the travaux preparatoires of the Act where it is presupposed that the information must be emphasised so that it is readily recognisable, and that it must be couched in a way so that it is not unduly difficult to learn. Further the supplier must state (subsection 2) the relevant conduct codes to which he is affiliated and the electronic access to them, cf. on such codes below. Moreover s. 10 is to be seen in conjunction with s. 11. Under subsection 1 of this provision the supplier must, before an order is made, provide the recipient with adequate, effective and accessible tools to enable him to find and correct typing errors (e.g. so that the recipient before the giving of an order, on a screen image, is presented with a survey of information stated with an access to correct such information or leave the ordering process altogether). Further, the supplier must (s. 11(2)) present contract terms and general sales conditions in a manner so that the recipient is able to store or reproduce them (e.g. of relevance to the recipient if the supplier does not store the contract himself, cf. s. 10(1) no. 2.

It will be seen that ss. 10-11 concern various technical matters concerning the formation of the contract. However, the information duty for the supplier under these two provisions is not isolated. Since sales via the Internet is generally to be regarded as long distance sale the sale is, apart from the information duty, subject to the rule of cooling-off period under the Consumer Contracts Act, cf. above Chapter 7, Section 4.14.

S. 12 of the e-trade Act governs order confirmation and reception. In s. 12(1) the supplier is obliged, without undue delay, to confirm the receipt of an electronic order. Thus it will not suffice to send the confirmation by letter. The confirmation period must be deemed to be quite short. Under s. 12(2) the electronic order and confirmation are deemed to be received when the addressee has access to them. From the travaux preparatoires of the Act it appears that an e-mail with attached file which for technical reasons or because of technical breakdown cannot be opened by the recipient is probably not to be deemed received since the receipient has had no chance of knowing the material. The same applies under the travaux preparatoires if the

Internet supplier has closed the access to the electronic mailbox. The travaux preparatoires finally state that the electronic order confirmation does not determine when an agreement is deemed to be concluded and that the main area of ss. 10-12 of the Act is to secure the service recipient against making an order which does not match what he wanted. The confirmation is not however, designed to determine when agreement has been concluded. However, it must be remarked in this context that s. 12(2) corresponds to the ordinary rules of Danish law as to when contract law "commands" , e.g. an acceptance, become binding for the addressee, cf. Chapter 7, Section 2.1. above (the "communication" criteria). In situations in which Internet marketing must be deemed to be an offer for the purposes of contract law – which they will probably be in most cases, also when standard goods are involved – the provision thus supports the view that a supplier is bound when he has received the electronic order.

Under s. 13(1) the provisions in ss. 10, (1) and 12(1) do not apply to contracts which the parties make *exclusively* by electronic mail exchange or similar individual communication (since it will often be the service receipient who chooses the communication form). Exceptions comprise both consumer agreements and agreements between traders. If the communication is started via the service supplier's homepage the exception does not apply, cf. the word "exclusively". The term "similar" is first and foremost aimed at SMS messages.

The code of conduct under s. 10(2) cf. above, is primarily represented by a labelling scheme termed " Danish Electronic Labelling Arrangement" which contains a number of guidelines especially for trade and marketing on the Internet and for the application of electronic mail. The guidelines have been made by a large number of interest organisations with the assistance of the ministry of business and industry and the ministry of research. Traders may apply for affiliation. If the application is met an agreement is made between the administrator of the labelling scheme and the trader, under which the latter commits himself to observe the guidelines. Subsequently he will be accorded an electronic label. Control and appeal access is available, cf. for further details on the scheme: www.e-fokus.dk. Excellent surveys of the legal position of consumes and traders in respect of e-trade are available on the Consumer Ombudsman's homepage for net trade www.net-tjek.dk.

2.12.3.Other rules

The e-trade Act also contains a number of special rules governing the conditions of liability exemption for a supplier who is merely undertaking "pure transmission", e.g. access to network, or who undertakes, via transmission, an automatic, intermediate and temporary storing of information (s. 15, socalled "caching") or who administers various host services, e.g. in the form of socalled web-hotels (s. 16, "hosting"). The rules are not elaborated here. As mentioned in Chapter 11, Section 2... there is a certain correspondence to the provisons in copyright law on temporary copy production.

2.13. Enforcement

2.13.1. Sanctions

The majority of the prohibitory rules contained in the Marketing Practices Act are enforceable by sanctions, cf. s. 22 of the Act. S. 1 (the general clause), s. 3 (the rule on directions for use), and s. 4 (the warranty rule) constitute exceptions. The principal remedy is penalties which may also be imposed upon companies as such. Violation of s. 10 (trade secrets) may, however, attract custodial sentences in the form of simple (short-term) detention or imprisonment of a maximum of two years. In practice, the sanctions imposed by the courts are generally lenient.

The question of instituting criminal proceedings is normally raised by the Consumer Ombudsman towards the Prosecution Service who then passes the right of prosecution to the Ombudsman under s. 19, if he so desires. In respect of infringement of trade secrets (s. 10), legal proceedings are conditional upon the request of the injured party. In cases of denigration as treated in s. 2(2-3) of the Act, the injured party must institute criminal proceedings himself.

The e-trade Act does not contain provisions on the sanctions for infringements of the various rules of the Act, including the penalty they may attract. Hence, the legal enforcement must be effected by adapting the marketing practices law to the matter.

In the event that knowledge of marketing conditions is of material importance to the decision, the criminal case will be tried in the Maritime and Commercial Court in Copenhagen. All other cases are heard in the ordinary courts of law, cf. s. 14(2).

2.12.2. Injunctions and orders

Acts which are in contravention of the rules contained in the Marketing Practices Act may be *prohibited* by court decree, cf. s. 13. Proceedings may be instituted by anyone with a legal interest in such proceedings, i.e. especially by the aggrieved parties and further by the Ombudsman. It must be deemed that the issue raised must have an appropriately concrete character. This view was taken by the Danish Supreme Court in a case in which the Court rejected a request from the Consumer Ombudsman to order a bank to change its socalled "validation" rules. The Court held that such interference would have repercussions throughout the banking world and affect its income structure. Thus, on its real merits the case concerned a general set of problems which the judges found unsuited for regulation via a prohibition under the

Marketing Practices Act. Proceedings are normally commenced at the Maritime and Commercial Court, to the extent that the application of the rules of law is of material importance, but the parties to the case may, however, agree on another forum. Proceedings are governed by the general rules for civil cases, cf. Chapter 5, above. Both in connection with decisions in cases for injunctive relief and with later independent cases, the court may issue certain *orders*, e.g. such as may be necessary to ensure that the prohibition is duly observed, including decisions that contracts concluded in a manner contrary to a prohibition shall be void, cf. s. 13(1), no. 1, and no. 2 of the same provision in respect of orders for redress. As mentioned above in Section 2.2, orders may further be issued by the Consumer Ombudsman upon negotiation with a trader for the purpose of performance of a commitment expressed by such trader. Non-compliance with such orders or injunctions is separately punishable by sanctions, cf. s. 22(1).

In the event that there is an apparent danger that the objective of an injunction issued by the court will not be met if performance is conditional upon the decision of the court, the Ombudsman may issue an *interlocutory order*. In such cases, proceedings for affirmation of the injunction must be instituted at the court no later than the following weekday, cf s. 21(1). Violation of an interlocutory order carries sanctions under the provisions of the Danish Administration of Justice Act.

> As regards consumers' possibilities of recovering money payments made to traders and comprised by an order made by the court or by the Ombudsman it is important that such consumer case qualifies for legal aid (cf. above, Chapter 5, Section 5) provided that the financial requirements for such aid are met, cf. s. 23 of the Act.

In former practice, decisions on cross-border marketing practices infringements were quite difficult to enforce , e.g. where a business with a home base abroad had grossly and systematically violated provisions of Danish marketing practices law. By Act No. 1257 of 20 December 2000 on prohibitions for the protection of consumer interests (implementing Directive 98/27 EC of 19 May 1998) this state of affairs is comparatively improved, as far as the EEA area is concerned. The Act is applicable to cases in which a trader in a Member State violates EU consumer protection rules such as represented in a vast number of directives and *which carry effect to other Member States*. Proceedings against violations infringing consumers' collective interests may in such cases be instituted by the authorities of the state in which the effect has been noted. Proceedings are instituted on a claim for injunction in the Member State if which the business has its home base, cf. for more details ss. 2-3 of the Act and on recognition of enforcing authorities s. 4. In Denmark authorities recognised to institute proceedings before the courts of other Member States include i.a. the Consumer Ombudsman and the Pharmaceutical Agency.

2.13.3. Damages. Invalidity. Remedies for breach of contract

The Marketing Practices Act contains a few provisions on the possible *civil law* consequences of violation of the Act. First, s. 13(2) lays down – as a matter of course – that in accordance with the ordinary rules of Danish law, any act contrary to the Act shall inflict liability for damages upon the person in violation, cf. Chapter 5, above for further reference on these rules. In practice, such actions for damages will first and foremost occur between traders, e.g. in case of disloyal market displacement, denigration or any other unlawful acquisition or abuse of trade secrets. The attitude of the courts to the question of liability is clear: if conduct contrary to the rules of the Act is in evidence, civil liability is incurred, provided that the conduct in question is injurious in such a way that a loss has been suffered as a consequence of such injurious conduct. Whether the necessary subjective conditions (intent, negligence) are fulfilled, does not normally present a practical problem. The vast majority of wrongful acts within the scope of the Marketing Practices Act are committed deliberately, and often with malicious intent. It is, however, often difficult, as is the case with infringements of intellectual property rights, cf. Chapter 11, Section 9, above, to establish the extent of the pecuniary injury. Therefore, if compensatory damages are awarded, they are often computed on a discretionary basis.

The losses inflicted upon consumers by violation of the Act will often be of such modest size that they do not provide ample inducement to bring an action for damages before the courts in view of the inconvenience involved with such a case, and the risk of incurring costs, in particular in cases where the defendant undertaking is domiciled outside Denmark. Upon the amendment of the Marketing Practices Act in 1994, the possibility of instituting class actions was introduced. If a number of consumers have identical claims for damages in respect of violation of the Act, the Consumer Ombudsman may upon request (from the consumers) bring a collective action for damages under s. 20 ("cumulate the individual actions" as it is normally put). If the case is decided in favour of the consumers, the claims will also be considered an entity in connection with enforcement – including enforcement abroad.

Another civil law question in respect of violations of the Marketing Practices Act rules is raised in connection with the effect of such violations on concluded contracts, including in particular whether such violations may operate to *vitiate*, in full or in part, the contracts made or give reason to rescission on grounds of *breach of contract*. The question is especially important in connection with contract terms which are found to be in contravention of the general clause contained in clause 2 of s. 1 of the Act, in that it is debatable whether such terms may be set aside under s. 36 of the Contracts Act. Although it must be maintained that the Marketing Practices Act is not concerned with the consequences in contract and property law of certain marketing means, and although, in principle, assessment under clause 2 of s. 1 is not entirely similar to assessment under s. 36, cf. Section 2.4.4 (above), such assessments will, in practice, be identical. A contract term which is deemed to be in conflict with sound marketing practice will thus in general also be set aside on grounds of being unfair under s. 36. Correspondingly. Failure to perform or defective performance of the obligations under the e-trade Act s. 10(1) (duty to inform about various technical amtters) may imply that a consumer inadvertently submits an order he would not otherwise have made. On an isolated view the defective information basis per se would be contrary to sound marketing practices for e-trade. However, it is quite likley that in the assessment of whether the consumer should be bound by the order made a rubbing-off effect may set in. On the same lines, the fact that misleading is deemed to have taken place (s. 2 of the Marketing Practices Act) may be relevant in the law of sale of goods when establishing whether the goods sold were in fact defective, cf. s. 76(1), nos. 1-3 of the Sale of Goods Act. The act of misleading may accordingly afford provide grounds for provdiding the buyer with remedies for breach of contract as against the seller, e.g. the right to cancel the sale and/or the right to claim damages, cf. ss. 78 and 80 of the Sale of Goods Act.

3. The Competition Act

3.1. Introduction. Purpose of the Act

Government intervention against undesirable anti-competitive practices is ordinarily based upon a *control principle* or a *prohibition principle*. If a control principle is applied at the drafting of a given piece of anti-competitive legislation, one or more of the public authorities empowered thereto will try to supervise any specific anti-competitive practices in order to be able to intervene against the alleged adverse effects of such practices, e.g. by issuing orders against the enterprises involved that they bring the unwanted situation to a halt. No act is prohibited in advance. If, on the other hand, a principle of prohibition is applied, legislation will prohibit *per se* a number of specific anti-competitive practices in such a way that any undertaking infringing the prohibition will summarily risk legal sanctions, especially in the form of criminal sanctions. It follows directly from the above that prohibitory legislation in general will provide more speedy and expedient legal protection against detrimental anti-competitive practices than will controlling legislation.

Until 1998, Danish competition legislation was largely based upon a control principle, while existing EU competition rules (cf Section 4 (below)) as well as national legislation in by far the larger part of other European countries are framed as prohibitory legislation. With the adoption of a new Competition Act in the 1996/97 session of the Danish Parliament, Folketinget – Act No 384 of 10 June 1997, taking effect for the major part on 1 January 1998 – Danish legislation was brought in compliance with the typical European pattern. The Act is a prohibitory act, the substance of which has largely been adapted to EU legislation, cf. Section 3.2.3 (below) for further reference on the relationship between national rules and EU rules. S. 27 of the Competition Act lays down certain interim provisions, cf. especially s. 27(4) on old anti-competitive agreements. Various subsequent amendments have been made to the Act which in its consolidated form is available as Competion (Consolidation) Act No. 539 of 28 June 2002.

The rationale of the new Act is based upon a common competition policy objective in that s. 1 provides that the purpose is to *promote efficient social allocation of resources through effective competition.* For these purposes, efficiency shall be in evidence when goods and services are produced and distributed at the lowest possible costs and when the supply of said goods takes place in such quantity and combination so as to reflect user and consumer preferences. Such efficiency must be present, both in the short and in the long term (so-called "static" and "dynamic" efficiency). In respect of short-term efficiency an instant picture or at least rather narrow time limits are employed, while long-term prognosis implies an evaluation of the undertakings' abilities to adapt to changes in the sense that they are able, due to the constantly changing nature of the markets, to develop adaptations or innovations in the form of new manufacturing processes, products or services. The desired efficiency is presumed to be best attained by the exercise of "effective competition".

According to the travaux preparatiores of the Act, this concept aims at matters in respect of the *structure* of the market in question as well as at the *behaviour* of the undertakings on such market. For the purposes of *structure*, a market with "effective competition" is thus i.a. characterised, on the one hand, by the number of market players being sufficiently large in consideration of economies of scale, and on the other, by the possibilities of operating on the market in question not being impeded or restricted by the presence of so-called "admission barriers" of factual and/or legal description(e.g. where access to the market requires very considerable invetsments which will be wasted is the business desires at a later point to abandon its efforts, socalled "sunk costs"). In respect of the *behaviour* of undertakings, the law is i.a. based on the assumption – hardly very realistic in practice – of independent decisions taken by undertakings who are active market players. Competition is thus presumed to be expedient and effective only to the extent that business enterprises enjoy the fundamental freedom of contract and of making transactions in financial relationships, including of adapting to competitor market behaviour. Accordingly, the Act is directed towards anti-competitive practices, irrespective of whether such practices are results of agreements (commonly referred to overall as "cartels"), cf. Part 2, or of the abuse of undertakings of a dominant position on the market ("monopolies"), cf. Part 3.

Other legislation provides provisions supplementing the Competition Act and such legsilaiton may also provide the competition authorities with a variety of powers, e.g. to state an opinion or undertake a certain supervision. These areas will not be touched upon in the following.

3.2. Scope of the Act

3.2.1. Principal rule on activities covered

Under s. 2(1) of the Competition Act, any form of business activity and subsidies under public means for business purposes is within the ambit of the Act.

The concept of "business activity" is widely interpreted as meaning *any economic activity taking place in a market for goods and services*, irrespective of whether a financial gain was intentionally sought and regardless of how the activities were organised (sole trader, limited company, cooperative society, etc.).

It was a very problematic feature of previous competition legislation that there was no real possibility of intervention against anti-competitive practices resulting from business activities carried out by government or local authorities. Pursuant to s. 2(1) of the prevailing Act, however, public and private business activities are, in principle, of equal rank. In general, the competition authorities thus also have powers to intervene against activities carried out under the auspices of central or local government, provided that such activities are of business nature in the above-mentioned meaning of the word, i.e. that they concern the supply or demand of goods or services on a market. Examples include public activities in connection with energy supply, etc., public transportation and refuse collection, and so-called public activities covered by external funds. In the event, however, that a public authority, e.g. a district council starts production for the authority's – the district's own consumption ("in-house production"), the Act shall not apply. The same applies to the administration authorities' unilateral, authoritative, general or concrete decisions in relation to the citizens under applicable law which have a character of so-called "authority order".

Business under public subsidies is treated below in Section 3.7.

3.2.2. Exemption in respect of certain effects of public regulation
Pursuant to clause 1 of s. 2(2) of the Competition Act, Parts 2 (prohibition of anti-competitive agreements) and 3 (prohibition of abuse of dominant position) will not apply, if anti-competitive practices are *a direct or necessary cause of public regulation.*. According to the travaux preparatiores of the Act, the exemption from s. 2(1) is based on a wish to secure that political regulation of importance to competitive matters of business undertakings are not to be set aside by the competition authorities in that such regulation would possibly be drafted for the protection of public interest rather than of competition. Thus, general health and environmental matters may dictate that the protection of competition is disregarded. It follows that the provision does not distinguish between private and public activities. If the requirement in respect of the causal connection between the anti-competitive practice and public regulation is satisfied, the exemption will apply accordingly, irrespective of whether the business activity is withnin the private or public regime. However, it must be deemed that the requirement of "direct or necessary" cause will impy that the sanction basis for the competition restriction is evident and that the public regulation in question cannot be implemented without it.

Incidentally, the concept of regulation applied is rather widely construed in that "public regulation" does not only include legislation and general delegated legislation (consolidating acts), but also general budgetary rules, documents pertaining to the Danish Finance Act, obligations under EU regulations and under ratified international law agreements (treaties), as well as the rules on the non-statutory duties of local government (the socalled "municipal power of attorney"). There are no certain requirements as to the substance of the wording of legislation, but it rests with the public authority in question – and not with the undertakings – to spell out the purpose of the legislation. Non-used authority provisions in the legislation may e.g. not be relied upon by the undertakings in support of anti-competitive practices.

The exemption, which in character and by means of the parallel in existing EU legislation, undoubtedly should be interpreted quite narrowly, could cause practical problems, especially at local government level. To this end, clause 2 of s. 2(2) of the Competition Act lays down in respect of anti-competitive practices undertaken by a district council that such practices shall only be considered a direct or necessary cause of public regulation when the practice is deemed necessary in order for the district council to be able to perform the statutory duties incumbent upon it. The last part implies that it must follow from legislation that the council is responsible for or must carry out a certain task. All anti-competitive practices undertaken by local government fall within the scope, and it is further required that the specific substance of the said practices may be directly inferred from the governing law of the district in question (district council decisions, district council regulations, etc.). If the task can be performed in various different ways, the district council has an obligation to choose the one likely to cause the least distortion of competition, cf. the requirement that the anti-competitive practices must be "necessary". Decisions made by boards in so-called public utilities – e.g. the joint operation by two or more districts of a power plant – are treated like decisions made by district councils, cf. s. 2(3) of the Act.

Whether or not an anti-competitive practice is within the ambit of the exemption contained in s. 2(2) is decided under s. 2(4) of the Act by the authority who drafted the regulation or made the decision in question, or, to the extent that such regulation was stipulated by statute or by any EU Regulation, by the relevant minister in charge. The question of whether s. 2(2) provides the necessary authorization may be tried before the courts of law. The competition authorities, on the other hand, are not granted such right of action. They do, however, if a competition limitation is comprised by subsection 2 – or otherwise impedes an effective ressource application from a society point of view – under s. 2(5), have the possibility of giving a reasoned opinion to the minister in charge and to the Minister of Business and Industry pointing out any detrimental effects imposed upon competition by the regulation, etc., and propose competition promoting measures within the field. Replies to opinions must be made within three months, including motivated decisions in respect of any proposals put forward by the competition authorities. The opinion and the reply may be subject to publication, cf. s. 13(2) of the Act.

3.2.3. Exemption in respect of pay and working conditions

Under s. 3, the Act shall not apply to pay and working conditions. For these purposes, reference is only made to actual pay and working conditions as those existing in the relationship between employer and employees, irrespective of whether such relationships are regulated by collective agreements. The main reason for excluding such relationships from competition law is that the regulation of these areas is primarily based on policies of social consideration. However, the provision mentioned does not, debar the competition authorities from demanding information from organisations and undertakings in respect of pay and working conditions, cf. s. 3, 2nd cl.

3.2.4. Delimitation as towards EU law

As mentioned in Section 3.1, the substance of the Competition Act stems, to a large extent, from the EU competition rules. Additional and very important similarities exist in terms of structure. The decisions made under the fundamental European competition rules by the EU competition authorities and by the European Court of Justice must thus be presumed to be important advisory guidelines at the construction and application of the principal provisions contained in the Competition Act to the extent that questions of fact in Denmark resemble such European questions. The far-reaching identity between the two bodies of rules – and on the whole between the EU rules and most national competition law regimes in Europe – is naturally not only of material importance to the undertakings in respect of the planning of production and marketing; such identity also plays an important part from a society point in enhancing the possibilities of securing, on a broad front, effective competition within the EU.

For the purposes of the mutual relationship between the Danish and the European rules, the Competition Act only concerns the detrimental effects of anti-competitive practices undertaken within Danish territory other than the Faroe Islands and Greenland, cf. s. 29 of the Act. In respect hereof, the EU competition rules cover cases in which anti-competitive practices may affect trade between Member States, cf. Section 4 (below). Such affecting of trade does not, however, necessarily require that the undertaking or undertakings involved have a connection with the various Member States. Even in cases where several participant undertakings are all domiciled in the same Member State – e.g. in Denmark – and direct their activities towards the Danish market, trade may be affected within the meaning referred to, especially in cases where the practice creates barriers, preventing enterprises from other Member States from penetrating or staying on the Danish market. It follows from this that the fields of application of the Competition Act and EU competition law partly overlap, creating a possibility of problems with concurrent jurisdiction.

The possible conflicts in the relationship between national law and EU law which are formally inherent in this state of law, are normally forestalled by applying the principle of EU law supremacy, cf. Chapter 3, Section 4.6.4, above. Further, the acceptance of a socalled "one-stop-shop principle" may be discussed. This principle should rule out any possibility of parallel case management of the same subject-matter by the EU authorities and the national competition authorities under several different bodies of rules. Anti-competitive practices must *either* be tried under EU law *or* under national competition rules. As regards approval of mergers, cf. below, Section 3.8, in accordance with this view, such mattter shall be dealt with either by the European Commission (prima facie under the threshold values in the merger control regulation applicable) or by national competition authorities. The Competition Act s. 4 touches upon another aspect of the principle in determining that the provisions in Part 2 of the Act shall not comprise anti-competitive agreements, decisions, and concerted practices which have obtained exemption under the EC Treaty, or which otherwise satisfy the conditions under a regulation on the exemption or exclusion of certain categories of agreements, etc. Individual approval of certain contract terms under Art 81(3) of the TEC or the fact that the terms satisfy the requirements of a socalled "group exemption scheme" under the same provision will thus imply per se that the agreement obtains the same legal validity and benefits in law as if it had exemption granted by the Danish competition authorititeis under s. 8(1) of the Competition Act, cf. on this provision in Section 3.5.3, below.

The new scheme of administration which takes effect as at 1 May 2004, see below Section 4, will, however, imply that the issue of parallel procedure before various authorities will generally be less important, and that e.g. Danish authorities in the overlapping area mentioned will be able to apply both national competition law and community law.

3.2.5. Special note on corporate groups

In pursuance of s. 5(1) of the Act, the provisions on the prohibition of anti-competitive agreements (Part 2) are not applicable to agreements, decisions, and concerted practices within the same enterprise or within a corporate group. Detailed rules in this respect are fixed by the Minister of Business and Industry, cf. s. 5(2) and on the use of this power Consolidation Act No. 1029 of 17 December 1997.

It appears from the travaux preparatoires of the Act that the administration of s. 5(1) is presumed to be undertaken in accordance with decided cases under EU competition law in so far as corporate groups are concerned. As a starting point, it is thus necessary to distinguish between *vertical* and *horizontal* groups. In respect of the former, a parent company exercises, by means of economic ownership or voting rights, a controlling influence on one or more subsidiaries, cf. s. 2 of the Companies Act, and s. 3 of the Private Companies Act. Thus, where the subsidiaries constitute a group economic unit within which they have no real freedom of action in respect of the independent economic policy making, any anti-competitive agreement, etc. between the subsidiaries within the group will not be governed by the competition rules. Conversely, horizontal groups are not characterised by one of the companies in the group being superior to the rest and hence exercising a controlling influence on the others as above. Rather, the undertakings have – usually on the basis of an agreement – placed themselves under joint leadership, just as they often have mutual share holdings, socalled "cross holdings". If a discretionary assessment establishes that effectively exercised joint leadership is in evidence to which all cooperation participants are subordinate, and if an arrangement exists between the undertakings, equalising all business and economic risks, the cooperation will be deemed to be an association of undertakings. Accordingly, the participant undertakings will be considered a group economic unit, carrying the same consequences in competition law as is the case with vertical groups, cf. above. Under s. 2, cf. s. 5, in the 1997 Consolidation Act, cf. above, internal agreements in co-operative undertakings are viewed in the same way, if they are limited to what is necessary to secure a satisfactory operation of the co-operative and maintain a contracting strength.

3.3. Administration of the Act

3.3.1. The Competition Council and the Competition Agency

The administration of the Competition Act and of the regulations issued thereto shall be undertaken by the *Competition Council* which is a collegiate body under the Ministry of Business and Industry, consisting of a chairman and 18 other members, cf. s. 14(1) of the Act and in respect of the composition and rules of procedure of the Council, s. 15(1) and Consolidation Act No. 862 of 5 September 2000, respectively. At the administration of the Act, the Council acts independently of the Minister of Business and Industry and is thus not subject to any instructions from the Minister in respect of case management, nor may decisions made be reversed or set aside by the Minister, cf. also s. 20(1). The *Competition Agency* functions as a secretariat for the Council, taking care of the day-to-day administration of the Act on behalf of the Council, cf. s. 14(2) and Consolidation Act No. 951 of 2 December 1997. Information on decisions made by the Competition Council, the Competition Appeals Board (cf. below) and the Agency itself may be found via the Agency's homepage (www.ks.dk) and links are also provided to the EU competition authorities and to competition authorities in other countries.

Proceedings may be instituted under s. 14(1) by the Competition Council itself, upon notification, on the basis of a complaint, or as a result of a reference made by the European Commission. The Council must decide whether the complaint provides adequate inducement to instigate investigations. Since no ordinary obligation thus exists to handle the complaints received, the Council may prioritise its own and the Board's efforts, e.g. by refusing case treatment in respect of complaints deemed to be of minor importance. In addition, the Council may decide not to handle cases, if the European Commission is considering the same case under the EU competition rules, cf Section 3.2.4 (above) on the one-stop-shop principle. The Council (the Agency) undertakes the collection of information in respect of the case and may to this end under s. 17 demand all information deemed necessary for the activities of the Council or for establishing whether a practice falls within the scope of the statutory provisions. If there seems to be evidence of a criminal offence, an information must be preferred in order that any further investigation of the case be undertaken by the police. S. 18 further authorizes the Competition Agency to make control inquiries, authorised by warrant, at the premises, i.e. with the enterprises, and sometimes with police assistance. Further s. 18 allows a fairly liberal access for the Board upon judicial order to make on-site control examination, i.e. at the undertakings porper and possibly with the assistance of the police (socalled "dawn-raids"). Finally, the Agency is to some extent entitled to pass on information to the competition authorities of other countries, cf. s. 18a.

As a principal rule, the right of public access to documents under the Open Administration Act shall not apply to cases under the Competition Act, cf. s. 13 and the listed exemptions therein. The parties' right of access to documents as provided by the provisions contained in the Administrative Act will, however, remain unchallenged. Where a consultation of the parties is to be made under the Administration Act (s. 19) the access to such consultation comprises the entire decision draft, cf. s. 15a.

By the provision in s. 23 a which was incorporated into the Competition act in 2000 the Competition Agency has also become entitled to check the observance of the provisions in Arts 81-82 of the EC Treaty as nationally competent authority under regulations and directives issued under Art 83 and in accordance with Art 84. Arts. 81 and 82 are directly applicable. So far the provision has been of minor practical importance but this will change after 1 May 2004 when a recently implemented reform of the procedures surrounding the application of Arts. 81 and 82 becomes effective, cf. Section 4, below.

3.3.2. Appeals rules and judicial review

The *Competition Appeals Board* is the appeals body for the vast majority of Competition Council decisions, cf s. 19(1) in respect of decisions which may be appealed against, s. 21 in respect of the composition of the Board, and on the Board's activities Consolidation Act No. 1032 of 17 December 1997. The most important exclusion from appeal access is, in practice, found in cases where the Competition Council refuses to entertain a complaint, cf s. 19(3). Such decisions cannot be appealed against. Appeal access, which is governed by the general principles of administrative law, is granted by s. 19(2), affording such access, first, to the person to whom the decision of the Competition Council is directed, and second, to any person with an individual, material interest in the case in question. The Appeals Board shall decide whether such interest is in evidence, e.g. if trade or consumer associations have, under the circumstances, documented such interest in a specific case that they qualify for appeal access. Appeals must be filed within four weeks from the day the decision was communicated to the person in question, cf. s. 20(2). Under s. 19(4), the appeal may act as or grant a stay of proceedings.

In cases where there is a possibility of appeal to the Competition Appeals Board, judicial review is not to take place until the decision of the Board is available, cf. s. 20(1). Under s. 20(3), the case must be brought before a court of law no later than eight weeks from the day the decision was communicated; otherwise the decision by the Board shall be final and conclusive.

3.4. General meaning and character of the delimitation of markets

When assessing whether anti-competitive practices are in evidence – irrespective of whether such practices are the result of an agreement, cf. Part 2 of the Competition Act, or of abuse of dominant position, cf. Part 3 – a more *specific definition* of the markets with which the practice was concerned is generally needed. The same applies to the assesment of whether a merger is to be approved, cf. Part 4 of the Act. Although both the EU competition authorities and the national competition authorities in their practice have long ago determined the criteria which must be deemed relevant in this context, a provision to this effect was incorporated in the Competition Act in 2000, viz. s. 5a. In principle an utterly superfluous and not very lucid provision, it delimits the relevant market on the basis of surveys of demand and supply substitution and potential competition (subsection 1, cl. 1) The latter shall be examined when the position of the undertakings involved on the relevant market has been sustantiated and this position makes it doubtful whether the Act has been observed (subsection 2). Notwithstanding that there will be nuances in the factors to which attention will be paid in connection with decisions under Parts 2, 3 and 4, it is possible to establish a few important overall features in relation to s. 5 a and the practice so far in the market delimitation, cf. also the guidance isusued by the European Commission in 1997 on market delimitation under Arts 81-82 of the EC Treaty. .

First, markets have a product dimension. The relevant *product market* as it is commonly termed, comprises all goods or services which may *substitute* for each other, i.e. one product can substitute without difficulty for any other product *(demand substitution*). Whether specific products/services accordingly can be said to belong to the same product market shall first and foremost be assessed – although the undertakings' own perceptions of the nature of the market may be taken into consideration – primarily on the basis of *consumer interests*. In general, an overall estimate will be made, attaching particular importance to whether the products/services in respect of their intended end use, properties – including quality – and level of price can satisfy the same consumer needs. Depending on the circumstances, more subjective consumer traits may be included in the assessment, especially in cases where there are grounds for assuming that factors like taste, fashion, brand preferences, etc. play an important part in the selection of products which in technical terms are completely identical and thus completely interchangeable. Calculations of the socalled "cross-elasticity" may provide further theoretical guidance, providing a measure of the relative effect of a change in price in respect of a certain type of goods on the consumption of an alternative product. The more similar the products are in respect of qualities and intended use, the sooner an increase in the price of one of the products will result in the increased demand for and sales of the other. High cross-elasticity, which i.a. is found with numerous common and practically identical consumer goods, marketed by different producers under separate brands – e.g. oil and petrol products, ordinary detergents and cleaning liquids, dairy products, etc., etc. – naturally points towards the goods in question belonging to the same product market. In addition to demand substitution, a number of cases, e.g. in connection with the delimitation of the market concept under s. 11 of the Competition Act, may call for an examination of *the possibilities of supply-side substitution*, i.e. of whether other suppliers of similar goods can switch production without substantial capital expenditure and at short notice from one type of goods to another within the present market definition.

In addition, markets carry a *spatial* dimension. The relevant *geographical market* is, in general, considered to be the area 1) in which the undertakings market their goods or services, 2) which has sufficiently homogeneous competitive conditions, and 3) which may be distinguished from adjacent geographical areas on the basis of material differences in the competitive conditions. It follows from the above that establishing the geographical market also will imply the catering for consumer possibilities of substitution, but in this connection between suppliers marketing the relevant goods or services within different territories. Important factors for the purposes of assessment in respect of the above include the nature and properties of the product/service, existing possibilities of distribution, the product's dependency on transport in a physical and economic sense (e.g. perishable goods), divergences between consumption habits and local prices, and the existence of possible barriers to entry to the (local) market in question. Also in this connection, the cross-elasticity provides a certain kind of theoretical guidance, illustrating the relative effect of a change in prices in one geographical area – e.g. Copenhagen – on demand met by suppliers marketing the relevant product in another area, e.g. North Jutland. The relevant geographical market may thus be the entire Denmark or, depending on the circumstances, a smaller territory – a certain part of the country, a certain region or district, etc.

The substance of the concept of "potential competition" is not very clear. Most often it will indicate that the area of focus is whether there are undertakings which are not currently operating in the particular market but which on a medium-term view might establish themselves there (cf. on the time horizon above on supply substitution). An assesment at this level will necessarily imply that the possibilities of such undertakings of entering the market will be evaluated and thereby also the possible strength they may obtain. Thus, under the circumstances the assessment may have the character of an extremely uncertain prognosis.

Mention of potential competition is made in both the 1st and 2nd clause of s. 5a. Its inclusion at the market delimitation itself is contray to the practice of the European competition authorities and the Competition Agency so far, since such practcie has focused on establishing a momentary view and an impression of the immediately predictable which is of course what is geenrally relevant from a competition point of view. This makes it a good question what the idea of s. 5(1) is in this connection: whether to change former practice or whether the mention of potential competition in the first clause of the provision is superfluous so that it will only need to be addressed under the condition mentioned in the second clause, i.e. following a traditional market delimitation (the momentary view). The latter option is to be preferred.

3.5. Prohibition of anti-competitive agreements, etc.

Part 2(ss. 6-10) of the Competition Act deals with the prohibition of certain anti-competitive agreements. In s. 6(1 and 3) the fundamental prohibition standard is formulated (Section 3.5.1). In pursuance of s. 7, there are, however, certain lower thresholds (Section 3.5.2), and as ss. 8 and 10 provide individual or group exemptions from the prohibition (Section 3.5.3). S. 9 prescribes a specific procedure for obtaining a declaration from the Competition Council that a given agreement is not covered by the prohibition (Section 3.5.4). Agreements in group economic units are outside the scope, cf. Section 3.2.5 (above). The provision in s. 4 of the Act (exemption under the EU rules) as mentioned above in Section 3.2.4 also belongs to the rather complicated system with prohibition, lower thresholds, and possible exemptions.

3.5.1. The principal rule contained in s. 6

Under s. 6(1), enterprises, etc. shall be prohibited from making *agreements* which have as their *direct* or *indirect object* or *effect* the restriction of competition. The same applies under subsection 3 of the same provision in respect of decisions by *associations of undertakings and concerted practices.*

3.5.1.1. Definition of agreement, etc.

The agreement concept contained in s. 6(1) is very broad. Thus, it will suffice that the enterprises involved (albeit not group economic units, cf. Section 3.2.5 (above)) have attained sufficient consensus between them as to the bargain to which they have mutually committed themselves, and no requirements exist in respect hereof that the agreement must be in writing or legally binding. It is likewise immaterial how the agreement was termed or formed and whether the anti-competitive practices were the sole subject of the agreement or whether they merely formed part of a greater whole as certain terms and conditions, including whether expressed as (parts of) standard terms. It is further of no importance whether the agreement is *horizontal*, i.e. exists between undertakings at the same level of production or marketing, or whether it is *vertical,* i.e. concerns undertakings at different such levels, e.g. producers and wholesale/retail traders. In addition, the agreement need only be binding on one of the parties. It goes without saying that unilateral acts fall outside the definition of agreements, but to this end, it is important to notice that such unilateralism must be strictly clean, i.e. without any form of express or implied contractual connection. If an agreement exists, any unilateral act for the purposes of securing the performance of such agreement will thus be considered to be part of the overall agreement. Since "concerted practices" have been placed on an equal footing with agreements, cf. below, it is normally not of material importance to prove that such agreement was in fact concluded.

The wording "decisions by associations of undertakings" covers decisions or resolutions made by the authorized bodies of an association of undertakings, irrespective of whether such decisions are legally binding on the members of the association – for instance and in particular – decisions made by the authorized bodies in trade associations. "Concerted practices" means that two or more undertakings co-ordinate their market behaviour without having concluded an agreement properly socalled between them, thus knowingly substituting for the risks of competition practical co-operation between them. Prima facie, the coordination thus intended must be capable of being deemed to be the result of a direct or indirect contact between the parties, e.g. in the form of meetings held or information exchanged, but according to the decisions taken by the EU competition authorities and also in pursuance of the travaux preparatoires of the Competiton Act, no further proof that the co-ordination was actually reflected in the *de facto* behaviour of the undertakings on the market need be produced. The mere participation in such meetings for the purposes of exchanging information on production, price, business terms and other conditions relevant to competition thus carries with it considerable risks for the participant undertakings. If no intentional coordination has taken place, but the undertakings in question merely act in a consistent manner on the market (socalled "parallel behaviour"), the prohibition will in principle be inapplicable but – seen from the undertakings' point of view – they would be wise to note that the existence of parallel behaviour may, under the circumstances, constitute an implication of concerted practice.

3.5.1.2. The restriction-of-competition requirement

The definition of restriction of competition contained in s. 6 is also extremely wide, containing both internal and external elements. Restriction of competition is said to be in evidence where an agreement, etc. *both* has caused a restriction of the commercial freedom of action for at least one of the parties, *and* a restriction of the possibilities of choice of any third party, e.g. in respect of possibility of entering into contracts with the parties to the agreement. In principle, s. 6 comprises any form of anti-competitive practice within the aforesaid meaning. It is thus of no material importance whether the restriction in fact takes the form of prevention of competition, or whether said competition is merely reduced or distorted and both present and future matters are included. Further, horizontal as well as vertical relations fall within the meaning of s. 6, cf. Section 3.5.1.1 (above). It is likewise immaterial whether the restriction concerns competition between several similar goods of different brands, e.g. between beer or mineral water producers (so-called "inter-brand" competition) or whether it concerns several retail traders, all marketing "Carlsberg" beer, but at different prices and/or on different terms (so-called "intra-brand" competition). Finally and in pursuance of the wording of s. 6(1), it is of no importance whether the agreement, etc. has as its object or effect the restriction of competition. The prohibition is applicable both to agreements which *have as their object* the restriction of competition irrespective of whether any effect is in evidence, and to agreements which *have as their effect* the restriction of competition irrespective of whether it was the object. The provision thus poses no requirements that the competition was *de facto* affected.

3.5.1.3. Examples of prohibited agreements/terms

S. 6(2)(nos. 1-5) of the Competition Act enumerates a number of *examples* of agreements which are prohibited under subsection 1. The list, which is thus *non-exhaustive*, covers a variety of classic anti-competitive situations.

S. 6(2), no. 1, concerns agreements involving the fixing of purchase or selling prices or other business terms. Pricing agreements have almost always been considered particularly invidious for the purposes of competition law in that they remove one of the central competition parameters or at least reduce materially its importance. Since the prohibition contained in s. 6(1), as earlier mentioned, applies both to horizontal and vertical agreements, s. 6(2), no. 1, is i.a. of importance both to pricing agreements between several producers of the same article, and to decisions between a producer and his distributors in respect of the prices to be applied by the latter in the subsequent levels of distribution. Pricing co-operation agreements of directional nature will also come within the Act, including horizontal list prices, issued by trade associations to the members of the association. The term "other business terms" especially covers mutual anti-competitive selling terms, including uniform guidelines in respect of payment for services rendered, defects liability, warranties, and discounts.

S. 6(2), no. 2 of the Competition Act deals with agreements which restrict or control production, marketing, technical development or investment. Such agreements will sometimes be in the nature of self-restrictive agreements with the object for the participant undertakings of maintaining a high level of prices in respect of certain goods through the restricted supply of such goods. Other examples include agreements between two or more present or future competitors that they confine their production to certain areas (specialisation agreements) for the purposes of optimum allocation and application of resources, as well as agreements for the arrangement of special sales systems, implying limitations in the possibilities for the parties or one of the parties of selling to any third party, which is the case, e.g. with distribution and franchising systems. The provision further applies to collective boycott measures towards an individual undertaking, and competition clauses in connection with transfers of undertakings exceeding the limits of what is necessary in respect of duration, product scope and geographical application.

The sharing of markets and sources of supply are mentioned in s. 6(2), no. 3. Horizontally, such systems may be in evidence in the form of agreements between competing producers or traders on market sharing according to geographical areas, sales quotas or categories of customers. Vertical market sharing under the same guidelines most often takes the form of agreements between producers and distributors or solely within the trade links, e.g. between wholesale and retail traders.

S. 6(2), no. 4, concerns the application of dissimilar conditions to equivalent transactions with other trading parties, thereby placing them at a competitive disadvantage. As the wording implies, especially in respect of "dissimilar conditions", reference is made to discriminating agreements. Such agreements will typically take the form of vertical anti-competitive practices, resulting in discriminatory pricing, or discount and bonus arrangements discriminating buyers or categories of buyers. In respect of the latter, the Act is normally not concerned with discounts founded on cost, but rather with forms of discounts, etc. founded on demand or sales, in particular such discounts which have as their object the protection of a customer relationship (so-called "loyalty discounts"). Horizontal agreements on discounts are within s. 6(2), no. 1, cf. above. It follows from the general provisions contained in s. 6(1), cf. Section 3.5.1.1 (above), that the unilateral behaviour of any individual undertaking, resulting in discrimination, shall not come within no. 4 of subs. 2. Depending on the circumstances, such behaviour may, however, constitute abuse of dominant position and thus be prohibited under s. 11 of the Act.

Finally, s. 6(2), no. 5 concerns agreements whose conclusion is subject to acceptance by the other party of supplementary obligations which, by their nature or according to commercial usage, have no connection with the subject of such agreements. Such situations normally occur when an undertaking deals in an attractive product, the sale of which is subject to the obligation on the buyer – by means of a so-called "tying clause" in the agreement – to buy *other* goods or services from the undertaking, notwithstanding that these have no connection with the principal subject of the agreement and that the goods or services could have been obtained in a quality superior and at a price inferior elsewhere. As was the case in connection with s. 6(2), no. 4, it is important to note that no. 5 of the same provision only applies to agreements in respect of the aforementioned conditions, typically of the terms and conditions for future supplies. Requirements of immediate purchase of supplementary products, imposed by the seller as a precondition for the individual conclusion of a contract are outside the scope of s. 6(1), but may be affected by s. 11. For further reference in respect of the opposite situation in which the buyer is attracted by means of other products, cf. Section 2.10.1 (above) on s. 6 of the Marketing Practices Act.

As the last example s. 6(2), no. 6, mentions agreements etc. under which two or more undertakings co-ordinate their competitive behaviour via the establishment of a joint venture. The provision which was incorporated into the Act in 2002 specifies that joint-venture agreements which are not comprised by the merger control rules, cf. below, Section 3.8, will be within the ambit of s. 6 in so far as regards their competitive effects, cf. also s. 12c (2) of the Act on asseessments both under the merger control rules and under ss. 6 and 8.

3.5.1.4. Orders

In the event that the Competition Council finds that s. 6(1) has been infringed, a need will often exist that the continuous unlawful state be remedied as soon as possible. For these purposes and in pursuance of s. 6(4), the Council may thus issue the necessary orders. To this end, it is immaterial whether the proceedings were instituted on the initiative of the competition authorities, upon the filing of a complaint or whether the case was assigned by the EU competition authorities, cf. Section 3.8 (below) for further reference on orders under ss. 6 and 11.

3.5.1.5. Vitiating factors

Under s. 6(5) of the Competition Act, *agreements* and *decisions* prohibited under s. 6(1-3) shall be automatically void, unless subject to exclusion under s. 7, exemption under ss. 8 or 10, or otherwise covered by a declaration under s. 9 (or exempted under the EU rules, cf. Section 3.2.4 (above) on s. 4 of the Act).

The invalidity, which is effective both towards the parties to the agreement and thirs parties, is not conditional *per se* on the subsequent manifestation by the Competition Council or a court of law, but will take effect without more from the conclusion of the agreement. To the extent that the anti-competitive terms merely constitute part of the agreement, that part alone will be invalidated, unless such anti-competitive stipulations cannot be distinguished from the remaining part of the agreement. What other legal consequences the invalidity may cause, for instance and in particular in respect of return of consideration already exchanged and/or in respect of payment of damages, is decided under the ordinary rules of Danish law, cf. Section 7, Section 4.13, above.

3.5.2. The lower thresholds contained in s. 7

3.5.2.1. The exclusions in s. 7(1)

It follows from the account in the above Sections that the prohibition contained in s. 6 has an extremely wide coverage. Disregarding one-off transactions, numerous types of agreement, etc. between business undertakings will – especially, of course, such agreements which result in or are conditional upon a long-standing and more comprehensive co-operative relationship – almost perforce lead to anti-competitive practices within the meaning of the Act. It is, however, far from always that solely odious competitive intentions underlie established cooperative arrangements involving restrictions on the freedom of commercial action of the parties, and/or any damaging effects thereof. Although a given agreement imposes material restraints on the autonomy of the parties to do business, the purpose and the effect may, nevertheless, directly or indirectly intensify competition, which is often the case, e.g. when an undertaking organises, for the purpose of penetrating new markets in the most efficient way, its distribution system on such markets with the exclusiveness inherent in sole distribution agreements. The picture is thus not always all black and white: negative effects on competition of restrictions on the parties may – and indeed in practice often will – be more than offset by the positive effects of the co-operation. Just as s. 6 does not provide any possibility of shadings which take into consideration such qualitative problems, the said provision does not contain any quantitative criteria either. Provided that anti-competitive practices pursuant to the Act are in evidence, not only agreements between large undertakings with substantial market shares shall be affected, but also totally insignificant arrangements in respect of competition between small or medium undertakings which have no real power on the market. The difficulties for the trade and industry as well as for the competition authorities which would have been caused, had s. 6 stood alone, by the fundamental non-distinguishing between large and small, are met by s. 7 of the Act, trying to exclude by means of lower thresholds non-appreciable anti-competitive practices from the scope of the prohibition.

Under s. 7(1)(1), the prohibition contained in s. 6(1) is not applicable to agreements between undertakings, decisions by associations of undertakings, and concerted practices between undertakings, provided that the participant undertakings have a total annual turnover of no more than DKK 1bn *and* a total market share as regards the goods or services in question of no more than 10 per cent. S. 7(1)(2) provides that an additional lower threshold exists, in respect of which the size of the market share is immaterial, implying that the prohibition will not apply either if the amount of annual turnover of the participant undertakings is less than DKK 150m.

Under s. 7(1), computation of *turnover* may give rise to questions of doubt in a number of instances of practical importance. To the extent that one of the participant undertakings forms part of a group, the computation must be made on the basis of group turnover, i.e. the total group turnover less intra-group turnover between subsidiaries. In the event that an undertaking has made a number of similar agreements with other undertakings on the market, it is the aggregate amount of the participant undertakings' total turnover which should form the basis of computation. Turnover in trade associations ("decisions by associations of undertakings") is total turnover for all members of the association in addition to the turnover of the actual association. Incidentally, detailed rules in respect of calculation of turnover are deemed to be drawn up by the Minister of Business and Industry, including rules that the turnover thresholds should be calculated on the basis of other figures (than plain turnover) in financial undertakings, cf. s. 7(3). Since turnover may fluctuate from year to year, it is of importance that the exclusion under s. 7(1) applies even though the undertakings overstep the thresholds in two successive years, cf s. 7(4), cf. Section 7(4), and Consolidated Act No. 895 of 21 September 2000 made on the basis of the authority contained in s. 7. According to the travaux preparatoires of the Act, s. 7(4) may not be relied upon for the purposes of circumventing the turnover and market share thresholds, for instance and in particular by large undertakings taking over small undertakings who have made anti-competitive agreements. Calculation of *market share* under s. 7(1)(1) necessitates a delimitation of the relevant market, i.e. the product market and the geographical market. In essence, such delimitation is carried out on the basis of the views presented in Section 3.4 (above). Since it is never an uncomplicated matter neither in respect of turnover criteria, nor as regards the size of the market share, to determine whether a case falls within or outside the scope of exclusion, it is further of importance to the undertakings that specific cases of doubt may be referred to the Competition Council in order that an informal statement on the issue be made.

3.5.2.2. The modification in s. 7(2)

Some contract terms are generally perceived as so harmful for competiton that they are outside the scope of lower thresholds under s. 7(1). Pursuant to s. 7(1)(2) this applies, first, when undertakings or associations make agreements, co-ordinate or decide prices, level of profit etc. in respect of the sale or re-sale of goods or services. The nature of the price agreement (minimum/maximum) etc.) is irrelevant. Under no. 2 of the provisions agrements, etc. on advance regulation of bids etc. are outside the scope of s. 7(1). This latter modification extennds the ban against "bid cartels" within the building and construction industry to comprise all lines of trade.

Nor will the thresholds under s. 7(1) apply to agreements etc. between undertakings where such agreements in concert with similar agreements act to delimit competition, cf. s. 7(3). The presence of a network of similar agreements within a certain line of trade, typically various forms of distribution agreemenst may under the circumstances create large or even invincible barriers to market access so that in real terms potential competitiors are barred from entering the market (socalled "network effect"). Where such situation is in evidence it goes in principle without saying that the lower thresholds cannot be upheld for the individual agreement, etc.

3.5.3. Possible exemptions under ss. 8 and 10

3.5.3.1. Individual exemption under s. 8

As mentioned in Section 3.5.2.1, agreements, etc. involving anti-competitive practices may often carry not only negative effects, but also positive effects on competition. Under ss. 8 and 10 of the Competition Act, possibilities exist of exempting under specific guidelines agreements from the prohibition in s. 6(1), provided that the positive effects outweigh the negative ones. Exemption may apply either individually by the specific decision by the Competition Council (s. 8) or en bloc for entire groups of agreements in pursuance of general rules in respect hereof (s. 10). Irrespective of whether any such exemption is based on one or the other of the aforesaid arrangements, exemptions distinguish themselves, in principle, from the exclusions provided by s. 7(1) (the lower thresholds) in that agreements which may be subject to exemption are prima facie prohibited. As stated in the above section, agreements which fulfil the requirements in s. 7 are, however, permitted per se.

Under s. 8(1) of the Act, the Competition Council may upon notification exempt agreements between undertakings, decisions by associations of undertakings and concerted practices between undertakings from the prohibition contained in s. 6(1), if the Council finds that two positive and two negative conditions *all* have been met (nos. 1 and 2 of s. 8(1), and nos. 3 and 4 of s. 8(1), respectively).

The agreement, etc. in question must first contribute to improving the production efficiency *or* distribution of goods or services, etc. *or* to promoting technical and economic progress (s. 8(1)(1), the so-called "positive alternative conditions"). "Efficiency" is not only to be taken to mean efficiency in a business or marketing economic sense, but also – and in particular – societal efficiency, cf. Section 3.1 (above). Numerous common types of agreement between business undertakings, involving certain kinds of anti-competitive practices, may be likely to satisfy such conditions. Specialisation agreements (Section 3.5.1.3 above) may i.a. by taking advantage of economies of scale, lead to improvements of both production and distribution; sales agreements (Section 3.5.2.1 above) to improvements of distribution in that the distributor (vendor) can concentrate his sales efforts within certain sales areas; licensing agreements in respect of patents and/or technical know-how may contribute considerably to the dissemination of new technology and thus boost the technological development, etc.

Further, the agreement must allow consumers a fair share of the benefit resulting from the activities contained in no. 1 (s. 8(1), no. 2), the so-called "obligatory positive condition"). The definition of consumer should be widely interpreted as meaning not only actual consumers, but also any intermediate links in the chain of distribution (users). The benefit should not necessarily be of cost-related nature, but may e.g. also manifest itself in improved distribution possibilities, environmental improvements or in a higher level of quality and/or service. Nor is it necessary that the exact consumer share is established. Since present and future competition intensity will normally decide whether, and to what extent the undertakings are allowing such benefits to the consumers, assessment under s. 8(1), no. 2 will generally be closely connected with assessment under s. 8(1), no. 4, cf. below.

Pursuant to the first of the negative conditions, the agreement, etc. should not impose on the undertakings involved restrictions which are not indispensable to the attainment of these objectives (the benefits) under no. 1 (s. 8(1) no. 3). The provision, which is an example of application of the well-known EU law principle of *proportionality,* cf. Chapter 3, Section 2 (above), requires that the parties to the agreement are not able to attain the objectives by less intervening arrangements than the restrictions applied. Thus it will not suffice that such restrictions carry with them benefits under no. 1; the restrictions must, in addition, be deemed necessary for the agreement to attain those particular benefits.

The other negative condition contains a requirement that a minimum of competition be maintained in that the agreement, etc. must not afford the undertakings the possibility of eliminating competition in respect of a substantial part of the goods or services, etc. in question (s. 8(1), no. 4). Assessment in this respect must both consider the extent of the remaining competition between the parties to the agreement, and the possibilities of competition from other undertakings on the market in question. If the agreement causes the competition between the parties to be more or less suspended, such agreement can only be exempted to the extent that other undertakings are expected to exert a material competitive pressure. If the agreement only restricts competition between the parties within narrowly defined limits, a large market share held by the participant undertakings will not *per se* prevent exemption. In general, it may, however, be said in this respect that the larger a share of the market an anti-competitive agreement, etc. covers, the more difficult will it be for the parties to the agreement to satisfy the condition in s. 8(1), no. 4.

Exemption is conditional upon the filing of a notification of the agreement, etc. to the Competition Agency, for which purpose the Competition Council may lay down specific procedural rules, including on the use of special notification forms, cf. s. 8(2) of the Competition Act and Consolidation Act No. 211 of 26 March 2003. Agreements of which no notification has been made can thus not be exempted. The burden is on the participant undertakings to prove that the individual conditions contained in s. 8(1) are satisfied. If this is deemed to be the case, exemption is granted for a certain period of time, but takes effect no sooner than from the time of notification, cf s. 8(3), and no possibilities thus exist for the agreement, etc. to be granted retrospective validity – cf s. 6(5) – exceeding beyond the said time of notification. Duration of the exemption will depend upon the certainty of the examination of the conditions underlying the exemption, including, of course, also in respect of future developments. Certain additional conditions may pertain to the exemption, for instance and in particular in respect of a duty to report to the Competition Agency. Exemption may be extended upon renewed notification, cf. s. 8(4), just as certain conditions may conversely give rise to the alteration or revocation, e.g. if factual matters have changed in a manner decisive or if the parties have given false or misleading information, cf. s. 8(5).

3.5.3.2. Group exemption under s. 10

Under s. 10 of the Competition Act the Minister of Trade and Industry shall, having submitted the matter to the Competition Council, lay down rules in respect of exemption from the prohibition contained in s. 6(1) of the Act for groups of agreements, decisions and concerted practices, satisfying the conditions in s. 8(1). Also this field of the Act is rooted in EU competition law, which for these purposes contains a number of regulations, exempting entire categories of agreements – e.g. on vertical agreements, transfer, of technology agreements, specialisation agreements as well as research and development agreements – from the prohibition of anti-competitive agreements contained in Art. 81(1) of the EC Treaty (which is essentially similar to s. 6(1-3) of the Competition Act), taking into consideration the predominantly positive effects of the agreements, cf. Art. 81(3) (which is essentially similar to s. 8(1) of the Competition Act), cf. also Section 4 (below) and Section 3.2.4 (above) for further reference on the effects of EU exemption in Denmark. Taking into consideration the nature of the type of agreement in question, the said regulations enumerate a number of – normally very detailed – conditions for exemption, i.e. in respect of acceptable and unacceptable terms and conditions. In the event that a specific agreement satisfies the conditions, the agreement will be *automatically* exempted from the prohibition, without prior notification and without prior administrative decision. Regulations are adopted for a certain currency – normally 10 years – and contain a safety valve in that the competition authorities have the right to withdraw the benefit of group exemption from individual agreements if it is estimated that such agreement has effects which are incompatible after all with the general conditions for exemption contained in Art. 81(3) of the Treaty. In a competition law system which is based on prohibition, arrangements of the aforesaid nature are, of course, not only resource economical for the competition authorities, but also contain, through the automatic exemption on the basis of a number of pre-specified conditions, in principle, obvious benefits to the undertakings in respect of time and due process.

The Danish group exemptions can be found in quite a substantial number of consolidation acts, see e.g. Consolidation Act No. 353 of 15 May 2000 on vertical agreements. The majority are similar to the EU rules as regards their nature, structure, and contents.

3.5.4. Negative clearance under s. 9

Since it may be of material importance to the undertakings to be able to establish whether agreements contemplated or already concluded are within the scope of the prohibition contained in s. 6(1), s. 9 of the Competition Act provides a possibility that the Competition Council may, upon approach by the undertakings, make a declaration in respect hereof.

Pursuant to this provision, the Council may, upon notification from an undertaking or association of undertakings, declare that an agreement, decision or concerted practice does not, to the knowledge of the Council, fall within the prohibition in s. 6(1), and that no grounds for issuing an order under s. 6(4) thus exist. As in the case of notification under s. 8, notification is presumed to be subject to the use of notification forms, cf clause 2 of s. 9.

If a notification has been filed, the Competition Council is – notwithstanding the wording of s. 9 – under an obligation to make a decision. If a declaration is made (a "negative clearance" in EU terminology), which as mentioned in s. 9 shall be binding on the Competition Council, provided that the basis of the decision does not change, and that no influential factors existed at the treatment of the notification case of which the Council was not informed. Nor will any penalties be imposed in pursuance of s. 23 of the Act, cf. Section 3.8.2 (below). If, conversely, the Council finds that no clearance can be given under s. 9, the agreement, etc. shall accordingly be subject to prohibition under s. 6. In the event that such agreement is sought upheld, it is strongly advised that the undertakings apply for exemption under s. 8 as an alternative way of obtaining negative clearance, if such exemption was not sought already in connection with notification under s. 9. If notification is filed for the sole purpose of obtaining negative clearance, the Competition Council does not have the investigative powers to determine whether the conditions for exemption under s. 8 are satisfied.

3.5.5. The practical route through the system

As generally noted in Section 3.5 and as stated in detail in the following Sections, the existing body of rules concerning the treatment of anti-competitive agreements is rather complex. It may thus be useful to outline in conclusion how the participant undertakings to an agreement in general should act in practice insofar as doubts remain as to whether the agreement falls outside the scope of prohibition under s. 6(1) of the Competition Act. Initially, it should be examined whether the agreement is covered by the lower thresholds contained in s. 7. If this is not the case, or if no settlement of the question is possible, the next issue is whether a group exemption regulation applies (under national or Community law) to the area and if so, whether the terms and conditions of the agreement are in conflict with such regulation, cf. ss. 10 and 4 of the Act. If uncertainty remains in respect of whether the agreement may be realised without infringing s. 6(1), the possibilities of applying to the Competition Council for negative clearance under s. 9, alternatively for individual exemption under s. 8 must be relied upon.

3.6. Prohibition of abuse of dominant position

Under s. 11(1) of the Competition Act, the abuse by one or more undertakings, etc. of a dominant position within the Danish market or part of such market shall be prohibited. If the abuse is the result of an agreement or concerted practice between two or more independent undertakings, it is subject to prohibition under s. 6, cf. above. S. 11 thus deals with the unilateral use of considerable market strength which in the specific case may be characterised as abuse. As was the case with s. 6, public undertakings fall within the scope of the provision, cf s. 2 of the Act and also Section 3.2 (above).

3.6.1. What is "dominant position"?

According to the travaux preparatoires of the Competition Act, "dominant position" is defined in conformity with the judicial decisions made by the EU competition authorities in pursuance of the provision contained in Article 82 of the EC Treaty, the corollorary to s. 11. The practice of the Competition Council follows this construction. In general the concept will be taken to mean any position of *economic strength* enjoyed by an undertaking which enables it to prevent effective competition from being maintained in the relevant market by giving it the power to *behave to an appreciable extent independently* of its competitors, customers and ultimately of its consumers.

The existence of a dominant position may derive from several different factors which taken separately are not necessarily determinative, but among these factors a highly important one in EU case law is the existence of very *large market shares*. Very large and stable market shares are per se deemed sufficient evidence of market dominance, unless special circumstances exist. The limit is presumably to be fixed at 50 per cent. If the share is below this level, but above 40 per cent, there is, to the extent that the share has proved stable over a certain length of time, a presumption of dominant position. Shares between 25 and 40 per cent will not constitute dominance or presumption of such dominance without more. In such cases, a thorough concrete assessment will be made, taking into consideration not only the market share, but also various other matters, including the number and market share of competing undertakings, the future competitive situation, the general economic strength and technical resources of the alleged dominant undertaking, any lead-time created by the undertaking towards its competitors as a result of the possession of intellectual property rights, and its behaviour on the market. Finally, if the share is below 25 per cent, there will normally be no grounds for presuming dominance. Calculation of market share is necessarily conditional upon a precise definition of the relevant market, both in terms of product and geography, cf. Section 3.4 (above). As indicated by the wording of s. 11(1) and as presumed in practice, a position such as the one mentioned may be taken by two or more enterprises in concert ("collective dominance").

Upon enquiry, the Competition Council shall give an opinion as to whether one or more enterprises take up a dominant position, cf. s. 11(2).

3.6.2. When is a dominant position "abused"?

3.6.2.1. The general substance of the concept of abuse

The holding or attainment of dominant position by an undertaking will not in itself constitute infringement of the prohibition contained in s. 11(1). The position must in addition have been abused. The underlying rationale appears to a certain extent from the examples in s. 11(2), cf. below, but the EU competition authorities have incidentally on several occasions given rulings in respect of the general substance of the concept of abuse. These rulings indicate that the concept is of *objective* nature, comprising any action taken by a dominant undertaking which by its nature may influence the structure of a market on which competition is already, as a result of the presence of the undertaking in question, weakened, and which causes barriers to the maintenance of the continuing existence of competition on the market or of the development of such competition, resulting from the use of other means than those used in the course of normal competition for the marketing of goods and services, taking place on the basis of the products of the undertakings.

Substantiation of abuse which lies in principle with the competition authorities, is thus not conditional upon the assessment of the subjective conditions of the undertaking (good/bad faith, etc.) Further, the EU competition authorities have, on several occasions, indicated that dominant undertakings hold a special responsibility that effective and undistorted competition should not be compromised by their actions. But it does not suffice that an enterprise is a dwarf among giants – which is the impression which seems to be presumed in the political discussion of recent years on a couple of large Danish food undertakings – a discussion which to a large extent on a factual level leaves much to be desired.

3.6.2.2. Examples of abuse

S. 11(2) contains four *examples* of abuse under subsection 1 of the provision. As in the case of s. 6(2), s. 11(2) is thus non-exhaustive.

Under s. 11(2), no. 1, abuse will lie, first, by the direct or indirect imposing of unfair purchase or selling prices or other unfair trading conditions. The basis of assessment in respect of price is the prices which are created on a market with active competition. The provision is initially directed towards the application of unreasonably *high* prices, but may also be used in the opposite situation, e.g. where a dominant undertaking has made use of unreasonably *low* prices for a length of time, i.e. prices which are not conditional upon economies of scale efficiency, for the purposes of eliminating a market competitor (so-called "lethal price war"). Cases in which a dominant undertaking imposes requirements that minimum prices or profits be observed in connection with resale in subsequent levels of distribution shall also fall within the scope of abuse.

S. 11(3), no. 2, concerns the limitation of production, markets or technical development to the prejudice of consumers. Examples of practical importance include refusal to supply, in which cases the dominant undertaking refuses to supply to certain buyers, e.g. such buyers which do not satisfy certain demands set by the undertaking. The basis of assessment of acts of this nature is that the undertakings enjoy the fundamental freedom of choosing its potential trading partners. Under case law, refusal to supply may, however, constitute abuse under s. 11 in certain circumstances, viz. if 1) the access to supplies is of material importance to the person seeking the supply, 2) the supplier has a dominant position on the market, and 3) the supplier has not provided an objective, factual and reasonable statement as a defence for the refusal to supply, which is the consistent policy of the undertaking.

Abuse will further lie when dissimilar conditions are applied to equivalent transactions with other trading parties, thereby placing them at a competitive disadvantage, cf. s. 11(3), no. 3, and Section 3.5.1.3 (above) for the corresponding provision contained in s. 6(2), no. 4. Abuse in this respect is in particular constituted by the application of discounts and bonuses which are not granted to other buyers of similar quantities, i.e. discount or bonus arrangements founded on supply or sales ("loyalty discounts", etc.).

In conclusion, s. 11(3), no. 4 provides that it is abuse if the conclusion of contracts is made subject to acceptance by the other parties of supplementary obligations which, by their nature or according to commercial usage, have no connection with the subject of such contracts, i.e. tying clauses, etc., cf. also in this connection Section 3.5.1.3 (above) for further reference on the corresponding provision contained in s. 6(2), no. 5.

3.6.3. Orders. Negative clearance

It may often be important, also in connection with abuse of dominant position, to bring the unlawful practice to an immediate halt. As was the case with s. 6, the Competition Council thus has powers to issue orders for the cessation of the infringement of s. 11(1), cf. subsection 3 of this provision and also Section 3.9.1 (below). Similarly, negative clearance may be granted upon notification from the undertaking, cf. s. 11(5). In the nature of things, the prohibition may not be subject to exemption, and no system equivalent to the exemption possibilities under s. 8 thus exists in respect hereof.

3.7. Anti-competitive subsidies

The EC Treaty contains some important provisions on state subsidies. Under Art. 87(1) state subsidies or subsidies granted by means of public funds under any form whatsoever, which act or threaten to act in an anti-competitive way by favouring certain enterprises or certain productions are prohibited as a main rule to the extent that such subsidies affect trade between the Member States. It is mandatory to notify the European Commission on the existence of subsidies and the Commission may order the state in question to abandon or change the subsidising measures, cf. Art. 88 (2) and (3).

The Competition Act contains rules on what is termed "competion distortive" subsidies in s. 11 a (incorporated in 2000). Under this provison the Competition Council may issue an order to the effect that subsidies granted by means of public funds in favour of certain forms of business activity must be terminated or repaid. The conditions underlying such order appear from subsection 2. The subsidy must directly or indirectly aim at or result in competition distortion and it must not be legal under public regulation. Under the travaux preparatoires of the Act and in accordance with the EU authorities' practice under Art 87, cf. above, the subsidy concept is to be construed widely comprising any form of subsidy and indirect suppoort facilitating the various burdens which normally lie on a business budget and which thereby, without being a subsidy in the proper sense of the word, are of the same nature and have a similar effect. The aim of the subsidy is irrelevant. The concept of "public funds" is also to be construed widely as comprising both subsidies from the state and other public authoritites , in practice, presumably, notably from local municipalities.

The most difficult of the conditions in respect of issuing of orders is the condition governing the legality of the subsidy under public regulation. The regulation concept corresponds to the simliar concept in s. 2(2) of the Competition Act s. 2(2) and shall be construed in the same way, cf. Section 3.2.2 above, i.e. to the inclusion of a wide range of different legal bases. On a line with the assessment under s. 2(4) the legality is not as a starting point to be decided by the Competition Council but by the minister in charge or – as regards municipalities – by the competent supervisory authority, cf. s. 11a(3). Where an order of repayment is made such order may, under s. 11a(4), be directed towards a large group of addressees, including of course private business undertakings. Further, rules are provided on limitation of repayment and on notification of negative clearance, cf. subsections 5 and 6 of the provisions as well as on notification of public subsidisation and on repayment, cf. Consolidation Act N0. 880 of 21 September 2000 and Consolidation Act No. 949 of 18 October 2000, respectively.

S. 11 does not apply to cases in which the public subsidies granted are comprised by Art. 87 of the TEC.

3.8. Special note on mergers

One of the fundamental elements, on a principle level, of the EU competition rules is the control over mergers (fusion of two or more previously independent enterprises) and over certain other company acquisitions, where one or more persons already controlling at least one enterprise, or one or more enterprises acquire direct or indirect control of the whole or parts of one or more other enterprises, cf. the provisions contained in Council Regulation 4064/89 of 21 December 1989 and 1310/97 of 30 June 1997. If a merger or an acquisition of the nature referred to has a Community dimension (implying i.a. the fulfilment of considerable turnover requirements), it must be notified to the European Commission and may not be implemented before approval has been obtained by the Commission. The decisive factor underlying the Commission's assessment is whether the merger, etc. creates or strengthens a dominant position in the Common Market or a substantial part thereof. If so, approval is denied. Almost all Member States within the EU have fundamentally similar national control systems, the general basis of course being a fear that concentrations of undertakings, irrespective of whether such concentrations might generate positive effects, per se will restrict competition decisively to the detriment of consumers.

The Competition Act did not originally contain any provisions on merger control but such provisons were incorporated in 2000, cf. ss. 12-12g. The basis for the provisions is to a large extent the EU Regulation mentioned above. Prima facie,, the Act is not applicable if a merger is comprised by the EU rules, cf. s. 12(5). The following account is limited to certain main principles in the control procedure.

The merger concept is defined in s. 12a. It comprises, on the one hand amalgamations of two or more previously independent undertakings into one enterprise, and on the other hand, cases where one or more people, who already control at least one undertaking, or one or two undertakings by buying up shares or assets via agreement, or otherwise, acquire the direct or indirect control of the whole or part of one or more other enterprises (subsection 1, cf. in part subsection 3). The establishment of a joint venture which on a permanent basis undertakes the collective functions of an independent enterprise (socalled concentrative joint ventures) are perceived as a merger of the latter nature (subsection 2). Outside the scope are a number of cases which would otherwise have been comprised where the capital possession is temporary and the voting right released by such possession is not exercised, e.g. the temporary possession by financial institutions of parts of an enterprise with a view to resale (subsection 4).

In order to be comprised by the Competition Act the merger must satisfy some threshold values set up in s. 12. The main rule is expressed in two alternative categories in s. 12(1). Either, the collective turnover of the participating undertakings in Denmark must amount to at least DKK 3.8 bn and at least two of the participating undertakings must each have a collective turnover in Denmark of no less than DKK 300 million. *Or* at least one of the participating undertakings must have a total turnover in Denmark of no less than DKK 3.8 bn and at least one of the other participating undertakings must have an annual turnover worldwide of at least DKK 3.8 bn. The computation of the turnover is subject to Consolidation Act No. 895 of 21 September 2000, cf. Section 3.5.2.1, above. Special rules on stage-wise mergers are provided in s. 12(3) cf. subsection 2.

A merger satisfying the conditions in ss. 12-12a must be notified to the Competition Agency no later than one week after the conclusion of the contract, acquisition of control etc., cf. s. 12b(1) and on the Agency's publication of the notification, the same provision subsection 2, and further Consolidation Act No. 235 of 27 March 2003. The competence to decide whether a merger is to be approved or prohibited lies with the Competition Council, cf. s. 12c(1) and the merger is not to be carried through before the Council has approved it. The procedure in such case may be two-phased. First, the Council will consider whether the merger is immediately approvable or whether a separate inquiry is to be made into it. To reach this decision the Council has four weeks computed from the receipt of full notification, cf. s. 12d(1). Where a separate inquiry is initiated, decision of approval/prohibition must be made no later than three months after receipt, as mentioned, cf. s. 12d(2) and on the effects of exceeding the timelimit, subsection 3 of the same provision.

The decisive conditions for approval/ prohibition are provided in s. 12c(2). A merger whereby one or more undertakings do not create or strengthen a dominant position causing effective competition to be impeded must be approved. In principle, the assessment may take a two-phase direction. First the dominance question is to be considered. If this is answered in the affirmative, the next problem to address is the effect of the dominance to competition. In many cases, this issue will probably involve an overall assessment. Apart from the fact that the evaluation will comprise a number of the elements known from assessment under ss. 6 and 11, it may be of relevance to point out the merger's predictable implication for the future structure of competiton. The central point is the merger's future effects towards the future competition structure. It goes without saying that a prognostication in that respect will often be fraught with difficulties in particular when markets of considerable movement are involved, e.g. on account of rapidly developing technical innovations.

Where approval is granted, certain conditions may be attached, e.g. on the selling of certain enterprises or assets, cf. for further details s. 12e, and the approval may in certain circumstances be revoked, cf. s. 12f.

3.9. Enforcement

3.9.1. Orders

As mentioned in Sections 3.5.1.4 and 3.6.3 above, the Competition Council has powers to issue orders that infringements of ss. 6(1) and 11(1) be terminated. To this end, s. 16 of the Act contains specific provisions in respect of such orders, especially as regards their possible substance, cf. the non-exhaustive enumeration in s. 16(1), nos. 1-4. Orders may i.a. imply the rescission, in full or in part, of agreements made, that specified prices and profits are not to be exceeded, that a duty to supply exists, and – of practical importance, especially within transport, communications, and energy supply – that a duty to grant (to any third party) access to the infrastructure facilities necessary in order to be able to offer goods or services must be observed. Orders may be granted for a duration of up to one year at a time, cf .s. 16(2).

3.9.2. Default fines

Under s. 22 of the Act, failure to observe the duty to report to the Competition Council, cf. Section 3.3.1 (above), and disregard of orders issued, cf. above, may be punishable by the Council's imposing daily or weekly default fines on the offending party which, if necessary, may be recovered by statutory debt collection.

3.9.3. Criminal sanctions

Intentional or grossly negligent violation of a number of the provisions in the Act is punishable by penalties, cf. the list contained in s. 23(1). Criminal liability may be imposed on legal persons. Where a negative clearance has been issued under ss. 9 or 11(5) no penal sanctions are, as mentioned, applicable.

The measure of penalty for violations of ss. 6(1) and 11(1) is presumed, under the travaux préparatoires of the Act, to be effected with due consideration to the financial benefit obtained or aimed at by the violation, although it will presumably often be quite dificult to show this with certainty. A large number of other factors may also be relevant to illustrate the relative

detrimental potential of the violation, including the number and value of the goods and services comprised by the violation, the number and size of the undertakings comprised, the duration of the violation, and any attempts to withhold information about the violation from the competition authorities. Each individual undertaking must be assessed separately. The level of penalties is not intended to be in any way comparable to the level applied under the EU rules, cf. Section 4 (below).

3.9.4. Damages

The Competition Act does not contain any provisions in respect of damages.

However, under the general Danish law of tort, any anti-competitive practices which are in conflict with the Act and which have inflicted financial damage upon a natural or legal person, will normally attract civil liability, providing the injured party with the possibility of bringing an action for damages before the ordinary courts of law. If e.g. a loss is substantiated as a result of a refusal to supply, cf. Section 3.6.2.2 (above), the aggrieved enterprise may recover such loss. In practice, however, the number of compensation cases is very low.

4. The EU competition rules in brief

The overall governing EU law in respect of competition rules related to undertakings is found in Arts. 81-86 of the EC Treaty. If follows from the above account of the far-reaching identity between EU rules and Danish rules, and the interpretative effect that the former together with case law thereof have on the latter, that a presentation of the EU provisions may be given in brief. The principal rules in the TEC are formulated in Arts. 81, 82, and 86, concerning unacceptable anti-competitive practices within EU territory, cf. Section 3.2.4 (above) for further reference on delimitation in relation to Danish competition legislation. As mentioned in Section 3.1, the law is founded on a principle of prohibition. The rules are based, partly on the need for protection of competition, including aspects of effectiveness, cf. Section 3.1 also in this connection, partly – and in particular – on the need to secure that the integration process within the EU is not compromised by artificial barriers. In addition to the provisions of the Treaty, important secondary regulation is made, e.g. in the group exemption regulations mentioned in Section 3.5.3.2 (above). To this must be added the comprehensive case law and practice from the European Court, the Court of First Instance and the European Commission.

Art. 81 concerns anti-competitive agreements and is, as mentioned, essentially similar to s. 6 of the Competition Act. Art. 81(1) lays down the fundamental prohibition and ancillary exemplification, cf. s. 6(2) of the Competition Act. The anti-competitive practice must be liable to affect trade between Member States. In practice, the concepts of agreement and anti-competitive practice are normally very widely interpreted and of partly technical nature, which is why the prohibition has a considerable field of application. Any prohibited agreements/conditions will by virtue of Art. 81(2) automatically be void, cf. s. 6(5) of the Competition Act. Under Art. 81(3), the prohibition may be declared inapplicable if the anti-competitive practices mainly carry positive effects of a specified nature similar to s. 8(1) of the

Competition Act. Exemption may be granted individually or en bloc, cf. ss. 8 and 10 of the Competition Act.

It is presumed in practice that the anti-competitive practices are noticeable. By way of guidance – i.e. to decide whether a restrictive practice will not be caught by Art. 81(1) the Commission has issued a socalled "de minimis notice whose most recent version derives from 9 December 1997, which compares with s. 7 of the Competition Act. The notice distinguishes beteween horisontal and vertical agreements. For horisontal agreements the market share limit is 5 per cent and for vertical agreements 1o per cent so that, prima facie, agreements under which the total market share of the participating undertakings is below these levels will not attract competition law sanction. This starting point is, however, modified in practice for agreements of a particularly suspect character, e.g. horizontal price or quota agreements which have been included in a special "black list" in the Notice (socalled "hard-core terms"). Such agreements are always perceived as contrary to Art. 81(1) irrespective of market share. Further, a number of special (less stringent) rules apply to agreements between small and medium size undertakings.

Art. 82 deals with the abuse by undertakings of a dominant position within the common market or in a substantial part of it. The provision is similar, also in respect of the exemplification of prohibited acts, to s. 11 of the Competition Act. Negative clearance may be given, cf. s. 11(4), but no exemptions are granted.

Public undertakings and undertakings to which certain rights have been granted by the public authorities, are also in pursuance of Art. 86 in conjunction with Arts. 81 and 82, covered by the competition rules, cf. s. 2 of the Competition Act. Under Art. 86(1), the Member States shall in respect of such undertakings be under an obligation to refrain from creating or maintaining arrangements which are in conflict i.a. with the competition rules.

Infringement of the prohibitions contained in Arts. 81 and 82 may carry penalties, cf. s. 23 of the Competition Act. Assessment of the amount of such penalty will be made on the basis of the turnover of the undertakings at issue and the economic importance of the (prohibited) practice in question. The penalty level is, in general, high, and in practice amounts well into eight or nine figures are quite common.

The main actor in competition law for both minor and major parts has so far been the 4th Directorate General of the European Commission (DG IV). However, as from 1 May 2004 substantial changes will take effect in the procedure and – especially – in the distribution of casts between the Commission and the national competition authorities and courts, such as defined in Council Regulation 1/2003 (EC) of 16 december 2002. The Regulation prescribes, first (Art 1) that agreements etc., which are comprised by the prohibition in TEC Art. 81(1) and which do not satisfy the conditions of Art 81(3) are prohibited per se (i.e. without the necessity of a prior decision to this effect). Conversely, agreements comprised by the prohibiton but which do satisfy the requirements under Art 81(3) are not prohibited per se which means that for such agreements there is (no longer) a requirement of access to advance notification to the competition authorities. Abuse of a dominant position as mentioned in Art. 82 TEC is banned in a similar way per se.

Further, Art. 3(1) of the Regulation prescribes that when national competition authorities or courts apply national competition law on agreements etc. which may affect the trade between Member States they must likewise apply Art. 81 in the evaluation of the matter (including a consideration of whether the exemption criteria of subsection 3 have been satisfied). In the same way, in the application of national law on abuse of a dominant position, they must also apply Art. 82. In the overlapping area between national law and Community law (the mutual trade criteria, cf. above Section 3,2.4) the national competition authorities and courts will be accorded a considerably larger competence than they used to have. Since, as mentioned, the former access to notify the Commission of agreements with possible prohibited terms with a view to exemption is no longer available the undertaking will need to carry a considerably larger risk itself for its agreements to be beyond reproach from a competition law point of view. In the borderline between national and Community law it is important in principle that the the Regulation (Art. 3(2) 2nd cl.) sets forth that the Member States are not disbarred by the Regulation from adopting a more restrictive national legislation prohibiting or sanctioning unilateral conduct on the part of undertakings and to apply this legislation in their area.

The Commisssion continues to play a major part but as regards the continuous hearing of concrete cases its place has become more withdrawn. The Commission will not be barred from instituting concrete cases or from entering a concrete case with Community aspects pending before national authorities (which would then need to resign). In addition the Commission enjoys considerable co-ordinating functions. As regards cases before national court – which may be expected grow in number – Art. 234 of the TEC secures that the need for co-ordination is observed (cf. Chapter 3, Section 3.6 on preliminary rulings).

CHAPTER 13

Basic elements of financing law

by Lars Lindencrone Petersen

1. Sources of finance

All business enterprise is dependent on capital though the capital needs obviously differ e.g. for a newspaper kiosk and a publishing house. Since the number of businesses in which the owner is capable of providing the total financing himself is extremely small the provision of loan capital is a social necessity. This function is undertaken by enterprises in the financial sector including in particular financial institutions and mortgage credit institutions. Also the state – albeit in a more indirect and selective manner – is a provider of finance with its range of commerce and export assistance schemes.

In the main, a mortgage credit institution can only grant a loan against security in real property. The loan is provided by the issuing of bonds by the mortgage credit institution which are subsequently sold (at the Copenhagen Stock Exchange). Mortgage credit loans will typically be long-term, up to 30 years. Out of consideration i.a. to stability in the bond market certain value limits are imposed by statute which the mortgage credit institutions are not allowed to exceed. Nevertheless, losses at the credit institutions (in particular during periods of depression in the property market) are unavoidable.

While the mortgage credit institutions are exclusively concerned with capital financing, the loan business of financial institutions, which is in principle built on deposits (private and commercial) is concentrated on operational financing. Nothing prevents, however, that financial institutions may also grant loans for capital assets which indeed they do to a fairly large extent.

One ingredient of the banking engagement of a business is nearly always a cash credit account. This account which consists of a certain range of credit is designed to offset liquidity variations of the business and is used as a convergence point of the daily money flow. However, the financial institutions have a wide range of other offers to their business clients. Thus, loans in terms of foreign currency may be provided e.g. to buy working plant and a financial institution may offer to guarantee a client's performance of obligations under a contract. A business engaged in imports or exports may cover its rate of exchange risks on obligations or rights fixed in a foreign currency etc.

Alongside financial institutions – often established as subsidiaries of one or more financial institutions – specialized enterprises such as factoring or leasing companies are operating. A factoring company extends loans against security in respect of the outstanding claims of a business and a leasing company finances the acquisitions of machinery and other working plant on the basis of hire contracts.

Professional loan granting will always involve an assessment of the borrower's capability to pay the interest and repayments on the loan but a lender may of course adopt a more or less risk oriented loan profile. In the credit assessment, a large number of elements will be included – apart from evaluating the security offered, emphasis will be placed on the applicant's financial situation and future prospects, such as they appear in his accounts and budgets, and forecasts within the line of business involved will also be relevant. Naturally, an important factor is also any previous experience gained from a cooperation with the customer in question.

In financing law literature a large number of concepts and terms are used. A central place is occupied by the concept of "claim" or the law of claims.

2. The law on claims

A claim in this context is a legally protected claim for (i.e. "right of") a performance. The holder's right may consist in a claim for the payment of a money debt by the debtor, for a supply of goods, the placing of a real property at the disposal of the creditor, the performance of a carriage, a piece of work etc. Thus, the legal sense of a claim differs somewhat from the use of the word in ordinary language which will usually denote a claim for money only.

The concept of claim in this sense may perhaps seem abstract. However, it should be noted that claims usually appear in synallagmatic contract relationships. In other words a claim is usually one side of an agreement. In a contract of sale of goods the seller has a claim for the payment of the purchase price and the buyer has a claim for the subject-matter of sale, and in an employment contract the employee has a claim for a money consideration while the employer has a claim for a work performance. Claims may, however, by unilateral in that the "debtor's" commitment is not dependent on a consideration form the creditor. This would apply to a claim based on a gratuitous promise, and usually to a claim deriving from a guarantee, and a claim for damages in tort.

"Proper" performance signifies the performance contemplated on the part of the debtor in order to terminate a claim by performance. A claim for a debt will terminate when the debtor pays, a claim for a piece of work when such work is performed, etc.

A statement that the debtor is obliged to provide proper performance is not absolutely adequate. The legal protection of a claim does imply that the creditor may enforce his claim with the assistance of the legal system in the event of the debtor's failing to perform voluntarily but this protection does not always imply that a claim is enforceable under its immediate terms (i.e. specific performance). Often the creditor will have to tolerate that non-money claims are converted into money claims. Thus a claim for a piece of work is not subject to specific performance. A claim for an individually ascertained object, e.g. a specific bike or some specific bikes may be enforced in specific performance whereas it is doubtful whether the same applies to a claim for unascertained goods, identified by genus only, e.g. 20 Italian bike frames.

A common feature of all claims is that the debtor is liable personally, i.e. to the whole extent of his property. The realisation of the personal liability requires that non-money loans are converted into money loans to undertake a qualified estimate of the extent of the debtor's property which will go into the satisfaction of the claim (which would otherwise be impossible to make).

As has appeared, the money claims are the most important of all claims. More than half of the claims arising from synallagmatic contracts are money claims and claims for compensation in tort are always computed in money terms. To this should be added, as already mentioned, that non-money claims must usually be converted into money claims to be enforced and that it is always necessary to convert a claim to money terms in order to realise the personal liability. Considering that money is the means of payment and economic-value yardstick authorised by the state authority this is not surprising. In all circumstances the money claim is absolutely vital in a description of the part of the legal system governing financing of business enterprise.

3. Individual enforcement and collective enforcement

Where the debtor fails to perform voluntarily the creditor is, as already mentioned, entitled to assistance from the legal system in the enforcement of his claim. In the law of enforcement the distinction is between individual and collective enforcement.

The most important type of individual enforcement is execution which is the tool commonly applicable for enforcement of money claims. In an execution the debtor is seized of assets to the extent presumed adequate (if possible) to cover the creditor's claim (after sale at a compulsory auction).

Bankruptcy is the central instrument for collective enforcement. A bankruptcy involves total settlement between a debtor and his creditors in that the total property of the debtor is realised with a view to equal satisfaction of the creditors. Bankruptcy is only relevant if the debtor is (has become) insolvent. As long as the debtor is capable of paying his debts the creditors are adequately protected (against unwillingness to pay) in the rules on execution.

4. Liability of several debtors

Several debtors may be liable in respect of the same debt. This applies e.g. in guarantee and partnership relationships.

Prima facie, where several debtors are liable their liability is joint and several ("one for all, all for one") (the Bonds Act s. 2(1). This is the main rule.

This rule, which may be contracted out of, imposes equal liability on all debtors which implies that the creditor has a free choice, at the due date, as to who is to pay his claim. On the other hand, there may be an agreement – or an arrangement may be built into the legal relationship – implying that one debtor is to be liable in preference to the other(s). Thus a guarantee commitment will never materialise for the surety unless the debtor himself is in default.

A debtor in a joint and several debt relationship may have limited his liability. A guarantee e.g. may be limited to a maximum amount, less than the total sum of the claim against the principal debtor. The liability is then termed "partly joint and several". For "joint" liability will lie if only the total liability amounts exceed the debt.

In the internal relationship between debtors who are jointly liable the starting point is an equal distribution of liability. However, another distribution may have been agreed or may be inferred from the debt relationship itself. Thus, a surety who has performed his obligation towards the creditor will have full recourse against the debtor whereas the debtor upon payment will – naturally – have no recourse against the surety.

The parties may have agreed that the liability of several debtors shall be proportional or in rateable shares. In that case the claim is really composed of several individual claims. Each debtor is liable for his part of the debt and the creditor has no possibility of a choice of debtor. In a proportionate liability relationship there will of course be no recourse problems in the debtors' inter-relationship.

5. Sole proprietorships and companies

A business may be run in several organisational forms. The historical starting point is the one-man business (sole proprietorship) in which the owner runs the business as his own master. On the other hand the corporate organisation form has a century-long tradition. Danish company law is built on the basic doctrine of contractual freedom but, nonetheless, especially limited liability companies and private companies are subject to a comprehensive and detailed legal regulation in the Companies Act and Private Companies Act, respectively. From a financing law point of view the issue of liability for an undertaking's debts is of course vital in the evaluation of the possible organisation forms.

In a sole proprietorship the owner is liable personally and there is no distinction between business debt and private debt. On the other hand, the owner has put his entire financial existence at risk.

The same applies to the partners in a partnership (cf. Chapter 21, Section 2). The partners are liable personally, on a joint and several basis, and directly, for the debts of the partnership. Thus a creditor may address his claim against one of the partners without first setting it up against the partnership. Conversely, where property is available in a partnership – which there may not always be – the partners will have priority rights in respect of such property as towards creditors (separate creditors) whose claims are held against each individual partner.

In principle, the position of a sole proprietor (or partner) is unaffected by the fact that he/she is married. Though s. 15 of the Act on legal effects of marriage (the Legal Effects of Marriage Act) provides that all property owned by a spouse at the contraction of marriage or acquired later shall be part of their community of property (unless it has been made separate property) the community of property is practically of no effect in respect of liability as long as the marriage subsists.

Under the Legal Effects Act s. 16(1) each spouse has the full disposal of all property introduced by such spouse into the marriage. This rule will comprise not only property owned by the spouse at the contraction of marriage but also any later acquisitions. This distribution into property contributed by each spouse is also reflected in s. 25 of the Legal Effects of Marriage Act under which each spouse is liable in respect of the part of the common estate at his/her disposal and in respect of his/her separate property for obligations incurred by that spouse before or during marriage. Exceptions to this rule may be found. In particular, liability for tax claims is joint and several (Tax at Source Act, s. 72(2)). But the basic principle remains that a spouse is liable only to the extent of his/her contributed property (and separate property, if any). At one extreme this means that one spouse may be subject to bankruptcy proceedings whereas the other spouse is financially sound. Whatever the position, it may be ill-advised to include the property situation of a spouse in an evaluation of a potential debtor's creditworthiness.

The community of property will not really show until it ceases to exist, upon death, on divorce or judicial separation. Under the Legal Effects of Marriage Act s. 16(2) each spouse – or heirs – will take out half of the joint property held. This rule means that each contributed property is computed separately followed by a settlement of net halves. Where one contributed property is solvent and the other insolvent, the solvent spouse – without otherwise incurring liability for the debt of the other spouse's contributed property – is only to relinquish one half of his/her net contributed property.

Under the Legal Effects of Marriage Act various separate property arrangements are allowed. As a main rule, the arrangement will require a marriage settlement (s. 28 of the Legal Effects of Marriage Act). During the marriage there are no liability differences between separate property and community of property but a difference will show on judicial separation or divorce in that the equal sharing standard (s. 16(2)) is avoided as a result of the separate property arrangement.

As regards corporate debt in a limited liability company or a private company the company is solely liable. The members (shareholders) have limited their risk to the capital they have contributed. Sometimes, however, the liability is illusory only. Where the capital in a company – in relation to the business operated (or contemplated to be operated) – is inadequate it may be regarded as highly likely that a professional evaluation on a loan application of the business will result in a requirement of a guarantee (and perhaps mortgage as well) placed by the owner(s) of the company.

In a limited partnership (cf. Chapter 21, Section 3) the partners' liability is not the same. The general partner will be liable personally and directly whereas the limited partners' liability only extends to the amount they have contributed, or a definite amount (in addition). But within the range of such amount each limited partner is of course personally liable. The general partner may be a limited liability company or a private company. Thus, from a liability point of view – except that limited partners (in contrast to the requirements of members in limited liability companies and private companies) need not have contributed the amounts subscribed – the same result will obtain in a limited partnership as with the limited liability companies of either description. In practice limited partnerships operating with a limited liability company as general partner are almost exclusively applied as a framework for tax arrangements.

6. Security of credit

In the concept of claim the personal liability of the debtor is an important element. Where a debtor's property is adequate to cover his debts the personal liability appears, from the creditor's point of view, satisfactory. On the other hand, where the debtor's indebtedness exceeds the value of his property a creditor cannot be certain of (full) satisfaction and where the debtor has no assets the claim is (currently) worthless.

The personal liability is not fixed to the debtor's property at a certain point in time but to his property as it stands from time to time. Thus, it is possible that a borrower who was completely solvent when the loan was granted may prove incapable of performing his payment obligation when it falls due. Thus, there is a need of securing a claim in advance against a debtor's insolvency.

Insolvency security may consist in a mortgage, placed by the debtor himself or a third party. The effect of the mortgage is to give the mortgagee a priority right of satisfaction under the asset mortgaged, e.g. a real property. A similar security may be obtained in a credit sale of goods by a retention of title clause. Leasing is also in reality applied as a tool of insolvency security.

In addition claims may secured by holding several debtors liable in a joint and several liability. A guarantee is the most important example of such security. But the value of the security will naturally be absolutely dependent on payment capability of the surety (when his liability materialises).

7. Constitutive acts

A mortgage right may be provided with transfer protection, i.e. protection against the mortgagor's other creditors and subsequent assignees in contract. While the mortgagor is bound as towards the mortgagee at the conclusion of the contract, transfer protection is dependent on a formal constitutive act which may consist in registration, deprival of power of disposal, or notice to a third party.

It is often said that a constitutive act is required for the protection of a mortgage right against third parties. But this statement lacks precision. It is only to obtain protection against legal proceedings from the mortgagor's other creditors (by way of execution or bankruptcy) and against the mortgagor's subsequent dispositions in favour of a bona fide assignee that a constitutive act is required. As towards others – e.g. on the mortgagor's death, his heirs – the mortgage right is protected from the conclusion of the contract creating it.

The constitutive act required will depend on the type of asset involved. For mortgage of real property the constitutive act is registration (Registration of Property Act s. 1). Mortgage of chattels may be secured either by registration (s. 47(1) of the Registration of Property Act) or by deprival of power of disposal. Mortgage of claims is incapable of registration (s. 47(5)) and since claims are intangible, deprival of power is also impossible. This does not apply, however, to claims in connection with a negotiable instrument since such claim is deemed attached to the document proper. The constitutive act required by mortgage of a negotiable bond is therefore deprival of power of disposal (the Bonds Act s. 14 and s. 22). As regards ordinary claims the constitutive act – since deprival of power is impossible – is to give notice to the debtor under the claim mortgaged (s. 31(1 and 2) of the Bonds Act)). The constitutive act required with mortgage on listed assets will be registration (Securities Tradings Act s. 66(1)).

Incidentally, the issue of transfer protection will not only arise in a mortgage situation but also in a sale. While constitutive acts are always required in a mortgage the conclusion of a contract will, in certain cases, suffice to protect the buyer against the seller's creditors but not immediately as towards his bona fide assignees in contract as well. This applies in particular for sales of specific goods.

8. Total indebtedness clause

In a business engagement with a financial institution several accounts and securities will usually be involved. Therefore mortgage contracts with financial institutions usually contain a clause of "total indebtedness", i.e. a clause to the effect that the mortgage is to serve as security for any claim which the financial institution may have, or acquire, against the mortgagor.

Such clause which may combine several loan relationships and several securities progressively, and fulfil the purpose of adding flexibility to comprehensive credit arrangements is valid but must be seen with the limitation that the claim involved must be a claim connected to the mortgaging from a credit point of view.

In a guarantee the application of a total indebtedness clause would not seem reasonable and is not practised by the financial institutions either – except for guarantees in respect of a company's commitments provided by the sole – or main – owner.

CHAPTER 14

Money claims – contents, termination, and enforcement

by Lars Lindencrone Petersen

1. Introduction

No single Act regulates money claims collectively. A number of basic principles on e.g. place of payment and time of payment are set out in the Bonds Act. Also the Interest Act and the Payment Cards Act contain more general rules on money commitments. Further, rules on money claims may be found in the Acts regulating the individual contractual relationships, e.g. the Credit Agreements Act, the Sale of Goods Act, the Rent Acts and the Insurance Contracts Act. Some of this legislation is irrelevant in a business context either because it is in the main limited to consumer agreements (the Credit Agreements act) or governs problems which in practice will only arise in relation to consumer settings (the Act on Means of Payment).

Usually, a money claim will terminate by the debtor's payment of his debt. But other legal termination grounds may operate to terminate a claim, e.g. waiver, set off, limitation or other statutory barring founded on passivity.

Like any other claim a money claim is protected in law. This means that the creditor is provided with legal means of enforcement if the debtor fails to pay voluntarily. The most important enforcement instrument of money claims is execution (distress).

The statute law on money claims is only to a limited extent rooted in international law. Exceptions are provided by the Bonds Act which is largely a result of Nordic legislative co-operation and the Credit Agreements Act which is partly a product of EU law. On the other hand the general principles on money claims are mostly common on an international level but this has not led to completely uniform single rules.

2. Contents

2.1. The debtor's obligations

The debtor's obligations are primarily based on the agreement between the parties. Where the agreement is silent the non-mandatory rules applying to the contractual relationship in question will be applied. The most important legislative rules which dominate in consumer relationships are only of limited importance in business financing.

The amount of the debt is usually fixed in the agreement. This applies unconditionally for money loans. Otherwise the gap-filling rules for the individual contract relationships are applied. Where no agreement has been made, e.g. as to the amount of a purchase price, the buyer is, under s. 5 of the Sale of Goods Act to pay what the seller demands unless such price may be deemed "unconscionable" and a similar rule is deemed to apply to a piece of work performed according to account rendered by a workman.

2.1.1. Means of payment: Legal tender

The debtor's main obligation is to pay a certain sum of money. In a purely Danish contract the obligation will (almost always) be in Danish kroner. However, a Danish financial institution may well extend a loan to a Danish client which is fixed in terms of a foreign currency. In that case, under the Bonds Act s. 7 payment may be made in Danish currency according to the rate of exchange current at the date of payment.

Generally, a cheque is not considered legal tender in the sense that a creditor cannot refuse to accept payment by cheque. However, the fact that a creditor may refuse to accept a cheque is not really important at the clearing off of a payment obligation but the importance shows where the provision of consideration is to be concurrent with payment.

2.1.2. Time of payment

The time of payment may be looked at as the point in time at which the creditor may demand payment or as the point in time at which the debtor may demand discharge by paying off his debt. In ordinary parlance the word "due date" will often be used to cover both sides of the payment time. In legal parlance the distinction will be between maturity date and discharge date.

The maturity date is the point in time at which the creditor may demand payment. Normally the date is fixed in the agreement between the parties which applies in particular to money loans. Otherwise the maturity date may be construed from the contract or be fixed by statute or custom within the individual contractual relationships. Where no basis can be found for an extension of the maturity date to a future date, the creditor may under the Bonds Act, s. 5, demand payment at any time. If the date of maturity is on a national holiday, a Saturday or the Danish Constitution Celebration Day (5 June), the date of maturity is normally postponed to the following workingday (s. 5(2) of the Bonds Act).

Sometimes the debtor is allowed a period of grace after maturity which means that payment within a certain timelimit is still deemed to be made at the right time. A provision of grace does not imply deferment of maturity which is evident in that the debtor is to pay default interest, not from the expiry of the period of grace, but from the date of (first) maturity. The debtor is not entitled to a period of grace unless it has been agreed or must be deemed to be implied in the contract or follows from special rules of law on the individual contractual relationships. If a bond is for payment on (11) June term or (11) December term seven days of grace are deemed to have been agreed (the Bonds Act s. 5(3). Where the timelimit expires on a holiday or a Saturday it will be extended to the following workingday. Another example of days of grace is provided in s. 33(3) of the Rent Acts under which a payment is considered made in right time if made no later than on the third weekday after maturity, or where such weekday is a Saturday, the following workingday.

The time of discharge is the point in time at which the debtor is entitled to clear off his obligations by payment. The word entitled does not mean that the creditor is obliged on his part to accept payment but only that acceptance obstacles with the creditor will amount to claimant's non-performance.

The time of discharge may be stated in the contract, e.g. in a clause providing that the debtor is entitled to discharge at any time or upon a certain notice. Where the contract states the time of maturity without mention of discharge the usual rule is that the debtor is not entitled to early discharge. Where neither maturity date nor discharge date are mentioned in the contract and such dates are not to be inferred from it the debtor is entitled to pay at any time, cf. s. 5(2) of the Bonds Act.

2.1.3. Place of payment

The main rule is that the place of payment is at the creditor's residence or at his place of business, if any (cf. s. 3(1) of the Bonds Act)). The creditor may require payment at another place within the boundaries of the country unless such arrangement causes considerable inconvenience or expense to the debtor.

Payment may be made through the post and will have been effected when it reaches the creditor. Payment may be made by postal order even if this means that the creditor is to collect the money at the Post Office. Payment has been made when the note regarding the payment has reached the creditor even if he has no possibility of collecting it on the same day.

The debtor's obligation consists in payment at the right time and place. Therefore, where the place of payment is with the creditor, payment must in order to have been made at the right time have reached the creditor before the expiry of the payment term. Thus payments made by post are not made at the right time even if the debtor sends the money before the expiry of the payment term if it fails to reach the creditor until after the timelimit. Exceptions to this rule are made under s. 42a(1) of the Registration of Property Act which provides that payments under a mortgage deed in real property to (the post or) a financial institution for transmission to the place of payment is made at the right time when made within the term of payment under the mortgage deed. Under s. 42a(3) this rule is mandatory in favour of a debtor. This does not mean, however, that payment has been made at the paying of the amount to the (post or) financial institution. Payment has not been made until the amount has reached the creditor. Thus, the risk of the sending is on the debtor who will have to repay if the money is lost on the way.

2.1.4. Interest

Under the Interest Act, s. 2, interest is not payable for a period of time prior to maturity (credit interest). Thus, in a credit sale, the buyer is, prima facie, not bound to pay interest on the purchase price within the credit period. The rule in s. 2 of the Interest Act may be contracted out of, however, and a contrary intention may also follow from trade usage or custom. For money loans the starting point is that the parties are deemed to have agreed that the borrower is to pay interest during the currency of the loan.

2.2. Breach

If the debtor fails to perform his obligations he will be in breach of contract unless performance is prevented by the creditor's circumstances. In all events the debtor will bear the risk of performance until payment is effected and only in extreme situations will the debtor's obligation terminate as a result of changed conditions.

2.2.1. The creditor's right to claim premature payment

On a default by the debtor in the payment of instalments or interest, the creditor may demand payment of the whole debt if the delay is material. This effect is not dependent on the delay being attributable to the debtor. Whether the delay is material will depend on the contract and its construction, and where the contract is silent the non-mandatory rules governing the specific contractual relationships will provide the answer.

One mandatory rule in favour of the debtor, is, however, found in the Registration of Property Act s. 42a(2). Under this rule, where interest or repayments under a mortgage deed in real property are not paid at the right time, the creditor may only demand payment of the entire debt if the debtor has failed to pay interest or repayments no later than 7 days after a demand in writing has been sent or made. The creditor's demand must have been made after the last day on which payment was to have been made and must state in express terms that the capital will fall due if the repayments and interest are not paid before the expiry of the timelimit now stated.

2.2.2. Damages

A debtor who defaults on a contractual obligation is, where the requirements for liability are otherwise satisfied, obliged to pay damages to the creditor on expectation interest. This also applies to money obligations but in the same way as insufficient funds will not excuse a debtor from his duty to pay, the loss arising from the creditor's financial situation is normally excluded from the damages rule on default in money obligations. Therefore the creditor is usually only entitled to default interest.

The rules on default interest are set out in the Interest Act. The rules of the Act governing interest on money claims in the sphere of contract and property law are non-mandatory, cf. s. 1(3). Exceptions are made in s. 7 which contains mandatory rules in favour of a consumer for contracts between a trader and a consumer.

Under s. 3(1) of the Interest Act interest is payable from the date of maturity if such date is fixed beforehand. Where this is not the case, s. 3(2) provides that interest is not payable until a month after the day on which the creditor sent or made a demand for payment. Where the existence or size of the claim is doubtful – and notwithstanding whether the maturity date has been fixed in advance or not – interest is not payable until a month after the date on which the debtor was able to collect the information deemed necessary to assess the justification of the claim and its size (s. 3(3). If the creditor initiates legal proceedings for the payment of the debt interest is payable, notwithstanding that the maturity date was not fixed in advance and even if doubt subsists as to its justification and size, from the date on which legal proceedings were initiated s. 3(4).

Under the Interest Act, s. 5, default interest is fixed at an annual rate corresponding to the lending rate of the National Bank as per 1 January or 1 July, respectively, in the year in question, plus (currently) seven per cent. Where the creditor could demand a higher rate on another basis he will retain the right to do so under s. 6. Such "other basis" will lie, not only when a higher rate of default has been agreed but also where the interest on the claim is higher in the normal course of events, i.e. where a credit interest rate exceeding the rate of default interest is payable.

Under ss. 9a and 9b of the Interest Act the creditor may claim compensation from the debtor of his reasonable and relevant costs in connection with a frustrated execution of an unpaid claim. Compensation of execution costs may be claimed under the rules of Order No. 601 of 12 July 2002 whereas in regard to reminders the compensation is subject to a ceiling of DKK 100,- incl. VAT, cf. s. 9(3) of the Interest Act.

2.3. Claimant's non-performance

When payment is obstructed by the creditor's circumstances there is a situation of "claimant's non-performance". The situation presupposes that the time of discharge has arrived and that the debtor is capable of paying. Claimant's non-performance will set in if the creditor refuses to accept payment or if he has moved or has transferred the claim without informing the debtor where payment is to be made. Other situations of claimant's non-performance will comprise a creditor's refusal to take measures legitimately required by the debtor as a condition for paying or if there is justified doubt as to who is the rightful creditor.

The creditor is not obliged to accept payment but where his circumstances prevent the debtor from performing his obligation certain legal effects in favour of the debtor will set in. Thus, where the debtor is said to be entitled to discharge by payment at the commencement of the period of discharge, this does not imply that the creditor is obliged to accept payment but merely indicates that the debtor's duties are modified if the creditor obstructs performance.

The debtor's obligation to pay does not lapse but will be suspended as long as the situation of claimant's non-performance subsists. If the debtor is to pay interest on the debt his obligation to do so will cease from the point in time at which claimant's non-performance sets in (The Interest Act s. 4(1)). Exceptions are made where a reasonable safeguarding of creditors' interests in view of the particular character of the obstacle involved would require that the debtor deposits the amount with a financial institution as the debtor in that case is to pay the creditor the amount which would have accrued by such disposition (s. 4(3)). The application of this rule depends primarily on the character of the obstacle, i.e. whether the creditor's circumstances are fairly excusable or whether he has prevented the debtor from paying without cause. Secondly, it is considered whether the obstacle may be presumed to be of longer duration and whether the amount in question is of such size that it justifies the imposition of inconvenience on the debtor to make special measures at all.

The most important effect of claimant's non-performance is that the debtor may be discharged from his obligation by depositing the amount in accordance with the provisions in the Depositing Act. A deposit may be made if the performance consists of money or securities and a situation of claimant's non-performance has set in.

The Act lays down a number of requirements in order for the deposit to result in discharge. Under s. 6 the depositing is to be made at the Central Bank or another financial institution or a public institution authorised for such purpose by the Minister of Justice. S. 2 makes it a condition that the debtor has not reserved the right to reclaim the amount, and under s. 3 the debtor must, at the depositing of the amount, state in whose favour the depositing is made and the debt relationship the deposit relates to.

The legal effect of such deposit is that the debtor is deemed discharged of his obligation (s. 1(1)). On the other hand the deposit creates a right for the creditor to demand payment of the amount deposited. His claim for the performance will lapse after the expiry of 20 years. For one year after such expiry the debtor may reclaim the deposit. Where such claim is not made the deposit will fall to the ultimate beneficiary, the Treasury (s. 5).

3. Termination by means other than payment

3.1. Waiver

A claim may cease by the creditor's waiving his right under it. A waiver may be part of a synallagmatic agreement or it may be unilateral in the sense that the creditor demands no consideration in return for it. The waiver may be complete or limited to part of the claim.

An important example of a unilateral waiver of part of a creditor's claim is a voluntary composition. Compulsory composition will also in part imply a waiver since a (qualified) majority must accept the debtor's proposal for a compulsory composition in order for it to be capable of ratification by the bankruptcy court.

In a synallagmatic contract waiver may arise by means of the creditor's waiving his right against other consideration than the original one agreed, e.g. goods instead of payment.

Where the parties have mutual claims they may agree that their claims are to terminate by mutual waiver. Such voluntary set-off is not subject to the requirements applying to compulsory set-offs, cf. immediately below.

3.2. Set-off

A claim may cease to exist by set-off which means that the claim is settled to the extent it is covered by a counter-claim. A decisive feature of the rules of set-off is that where certain conditions are met, the settlement may be enforced against the creditor's opposition which has led to the frequent application of the term "compulsory set-off". A set-off is not an automatic device but requires that the party desiring to set off approaches the other party to such effect.

When a set-off is considered as a termination device it will be most appropriate, as far as possible, to use the same terms as have been used so far in the present Chapter. The claim terminated is called the principal claim, its holder the creditor, the party requesting the set-off is called the debtor and the claim whereby he terminates the claim against him is called the counter-claim.

In the main, the requirements of set-off are not statutory but derive from generally accepted legal principles (with the notable exception of the rules on netting in the Securities Trading Act, ss. 57-58). The main requirement is mutuality which means that the claims must subsist between the same persons.

The justification of the set-off rules is the convenience it offers to the parties in that they avoid engaging in measures for performance. However, this justification is not tenable for a compulsory set-off. The most important justification for a compulsory set-off is the security of performance inherent in a set-off right. A party who has a right to set-off is certain of satisfaction in an effective and simple manner. The rules in compulsory set-off delimit the possibilities afforded by the legal system in respect of such security.

3.2.1. Equalization capability

The performance to which the counter-claim entitles its holder must be capable, according to its nature, of being applied in the performance of the principal claim. This means that set-offs are in practice virtually limited to money claims.

3.2.2. Maturity

In a set-off declaration the debtor demands the counter-claim to be performed and that he wishes to apply such performance to perform the principal claim. As regards time requirements for set-off, this means that maturity date must have set in for the counter-claim and time of discharge for the principal claim.

3.2.3. Mutuality

As already mentioned, a main requirement for set-off is mutuality. However, if the requirement of mutuality was without exception, the set-off rules would not be satisfactory from a security point of view since any transfer of the principal claim would deprive the debtor of the right of set-off. To safeguard security interests it is necessary to allow a right of set-off also against an assignee of the principal claim. This right need not be unlimited since for set-off purposes it will suffice that 1) the requirements have been met or 2) the debtor justly believed that they were met, or 3) the debtor justly believed they would be met in the future.

On a transfer of ordinary claims the security consideration is safeguarded by the rule in the Bonds Act s. 28. Under s. 28, 1st clause, a debtor may apply a claim on the assignee in a set-off unless he acquired the claim after the point in time when he was notified of the transfer or presumed transfer had been made. This rule protects the debtor where the condition of mutuality has been satisfied and when he justly believed that the condition was satisfied. Since set-off is also dependent on maturity, s. 28, 2nd clause, provides that the claim, if it was not due for payment when the debtor was notified of the transfer or presumed such transfer had taken place, is only applicable in a set-off if its maturity date coincides with that of the principal claim at the latest. This limits the right to set-off to situations in which the requirements governing the maturity have been satisfied or where the debtor may have relied on their becoming so in future.

On a transfer of a negotiable promissory note, set-off considerations are defeated in favour of assignee considerations. Where the principal claim is attached to a negotiable note the debtor is therefore barred, under s. 18(1) of the Bonds Act, the access of set-off as against assignees of the note. To prevent transfers whole sole purpose is to debar set-off, access to set-off is allowed, however, if the assignee knew that the debtor held a claim applicable for set-off and that he would suffer a loss in the transfer if such transfer would debar set-off.

3.2.4. Exclusion of set-off

A claim is incapable of set-off if the creditor from social protection considerations is entitled to effective payment. This applies e.g. to claims for maintenance payments and claims for holiday pay, and presumably to claims for pay for work performed. Further, set-off may be excluded by agreement or under the non-mandatory rules of specific contractual relationships. A party who has promised to grant a loan is thus barred from discharging his obligation by set-off. An agreement for sale stipulating cash payment will not exclude set-off unless the contract in question provides a basis for inferring such exclusion.

3.3. Limitation

After the expiry of a certain period of time a claim may terminate on account of age. This termination form is called limitation (or statute-barring). The provision of rules of limitation of claims in the legal system is primarily to be viewed as manifesting the consideration for security and clarity in legal relationships. It will often be difficult after a long period of time to substantiate the true facts of a legal relationship whether the issue is in respect of a claim's valid creation or its proper performance. Another factor in favour of time limitation rules is the avoidance of inconvenience of keeping old receipts indefinitely.

Limitation causes the claim to terminate by operation of time without more. When a claim is barred on account of time limitation claims for interest will cease too, even if the claim for interest was not barred independently. A retention of title clause will also lapse once the seller's claim for the purchase price is barred by limitation. On the termination of a claim by limitation any surety's obligations will also lapse even if the guarantee obligation was not barred on an independent assessment. This does not immediately go for claims secured by mortgage. Under s. 42 of the Registration of Property Act the mortgage right for the capital under a registered mortgage deed for a stated sum will not be barred. A similar rule applies to security rights in respect of pledge of chattels, and security rights in claims. Other rights of security will lapse on the time limitation of the claim.

The main rule on limitation of claims is contained in the Danish Code 5-14-4 under which the period of limitation is 20 years. However, a number of claims, important in practice, will be barred after five years which is the limitation period under the Limitation Act. Further, limitation rules in respect of special claims are provided in various statutes.

3.3.1. Danish Code 5-14-4

Under its wording, the rule in the Danish Code 5-14-4 will only comprise promissory notes but it is commonly held that the rule applies to claims in general. The rule is mandatory to the extent that the parties cannot agree to postpone limitation to a later date.

Time begins to run from the creation of the claim. As regards claims created by agreement this means that the timelimit is computed from the making of the promise upon which the claim was created.

The limitation is interrupted upon the debtor's acknowledgement of his obligation. An acknowledgement will lie if the debtor signifies his willingness or obligation to perform. Acknowledgement may be implied from the debtor's conduct where such conduct may be equalled to direct acknowledgement. Payment of interest is an implied acknowledgement since the interest claim derives from the entire debt. On the other hand, payment of instalments will not in itself constitute acknowledgement of the outstanding debt.

The limitation period is also interrupted if the creditor gives notice reminding the debtor of the claim's continued existence. The reminder is not subject to formal rules and an oral demand will suffice. If the creditor wants irrefutable evidence that the debtor has in fact received a reminder he may have it served by a writ server.

Upon interruption, a new limitation period of 20 years will begin to run.

3.3.2. The Limitation Act

The Limitation Act provides a limitation period of five years for certain claims. Even if the Limitation Act is the most important regulation in practice it represents, from a legal point of view, an exception to the main rule in the Danish Code 5-14-4. Consequently, it is only applicable to the claims enumerated in s. 1(1) and its sphere of application may not be extended by analogy.

Under s. 1(1), no. 1, the Act comprises claims based on agreements of sale or other transfer of goods or other chattels which are sold as appurtenant to a piece of real property, use of real property or chattels, provision of accommodation, food and boarding, carriage of persons or goods and performance of work or provision of a personal service of any nature. The Act comprises any claim based on the agreement including claims for damages for breach. Examples of important claims outside the scope of the Act include claims based on agreements for money loans and conveyancing of real property.

Only a few of the remaining claims comprised by the Act under s. 1(1), nos. 2-6 will be mentioned here. Claims for interest due will be statute-barred after 5 years even if the debt is not comprised by the Act. A claim under a guarantee made in respect of a claim comprised by the Act is barred after 5 years which means that the surety's obligation is subject to independent limitation. The Act further comprises claims for damages in tort unless the damage was caused by a criminal offence.

Under s. 1(2) the limitation period of 5 years is not applicable where a promissory note has been issued or upon provision of other "special legal basis whereby the creation and amount of the claim have been acknowledged by the debtor or have been established by other written means".

The exclusion of limitation after 5 years upon acknowledgement by the debtor is not unqualified. Under the wording of s. 1(2) the acknowledgement must be in writing but it does not suffice that there is an agreement in writing between the parties. Further, the acknowledgement must be unilateral so that the debtor's obligation is separate from the legal relationship underlying it. Apart from promissory notes, which are expressly mentioned in the Act, a voluntary settlement will meet these requirements. The same applies to a voluntary composition which has been adopted by the debtor in writing. The fact that a bill of exchange has been issued does not suffice to exclude the five-year limitation. From the wording in s. 1(2) may be inferred that the five-year limitation is also excluded where a claim is established by judgment, settlement made before a court of law, compulsory composition, or debt rescheduling process. A claim which under s. 1(2) has been brought outside the application of the Act will be subject to the general rule in the Danish Code 5-14-4.

Under s. 2, 1st clause, the five-year limitation period begins to run "from the time at which the creditor may claim payment", i.e. from the day of maturity. Where the creditor, on account of unforeseeable ignorance of his claim or of the debtor's whereabouts, has been incapable of setting up his claim the time does not start to run, however, until the time at which the creditor was, or – under usual diligence criteria, would have been – capable of demanding payment of his claim (s. 3). A similar suspension of limitation is not applicable under the Danish Code 5-14-4.

The five-year limitation is interrupted in the same way as the twenty-year limitation by an acknowledgement by the debtor of the debt (s. 2, 2nd clause). Where the creditor intends to suspend the limitation s. 2, 2nd clause, requires him to take "legal steps" against the debtor and that he pursues these without undue delay with a view to obtaining settlement, judgment or other decision in law, whereas a reminder will not suffice to suspend limitation under the twenty-year-rule. Legal steps may include bringing an action, presenting a petition for attachment proceedings, presenting a bankruptcy petition or notifying the claim in the debtor's bankrupt estate (the Bankruptcy Act s. 241).

The effect of an interruption is a fresh accrual of a five-year period or that the claim will be subject to limitation only under the Danish Code 5-14-4 provided that the requirements under s. 1(2) are satisfied.

Under s. 4, time under the general rule of limitation after 20 years will run alongside the five-year limitation. That a claim comprised by the five-year limitation is also subject to the main rule in the Danish Code 5-14-4 is of practical relevance where the claim falls due more than 15 years after its creation, and in cases in which the five-year limitation has been suspended for more than 15 years (s. 3).

3.3.3. Other limitation rules

Apart from the Danish Code 5-14-4 and the Limitation Act various statutes will provide limitation rules whose application is restricted to claims deriving from special legal relationships. Examples include s. 54 and s. 83 of the Sale of Goods Act and s. 29 and s. 30 of the Insurance Contracts Act.

3.4. Barring of claims upon preclusive notice

In certain cases a public notice to a person's creditors or to the creditors in an estate will cause a claim to lapse in respect of creditors who fail to report their claims within a certain timelimit. The claim is said to terminate upon preclusive notice.

The need to establish a final list of creditors is especially marked on an administration of an estate (on death or bankruptcy). However, a notice with exclusive effect is not applicable in any administration. A notice in a deceased person's estate always operates with preclusive effect whereas a notice in a bankrupt estate has no such effect. Further, in special cases, e.g. in an emigration situation, a person may be granted licence to convene his creditors on preclusive notice (s. 25 of the Constitution Act).

The barring sets in even if the creditor is not to blame for the failure to report his claim. The fact that the issuer of the notice knew of the claim's existence will usually not exclude barring.

4. Enforcement

Where a claim is not performed voluntarily the creditor may demand enforcement either by performance or realisation of assets belonging to the debtor. In respect of money claims execution is the central element of the enforcement process. Execution jurisdiction lies with the first-instance local courts (town and city courts) which are termed "bailiff's courts" for this function. Thus, the local judge (or deputy judge or, most typically, a clerk) acts as bailiff.

4.1. Execution basis

A claim does not immediately provide a basis for execution. It is required that the claim has been established in a special, authoritative manner – in short, an "execution basis" needs to be provided. The documents which qualify as execution bases are (in principle) exhaustively enumerated in the Administration of Justice Act.

A money-judgement is applicable as execution basis upon the expiry of 14 days (without appeal) from the date of pronouncement of judgment. An arbitration award also qualifies as an execution basis. The same applies to court settlements between the parties. Out-of-court settlements between the parties satisfying certain formal requirements and bonds may also qualify – provided that they are claused to such effect – and the same applies to mortgage deeds, cheques, and bills of exchange.

A number of claims sharing the feature that the creditor is a public authority instance are provided with execution remedy by statute. This applies in particular to claims for taxes and duties. Such claims are immediately applicable in execution proceedings.

4.2. The procedure

An execution is commenced by the creditor's presentation of a petition for execution, accompanied by substantiation for the execution basis, to the bailiff's court in the circuit of the debtor's residence. Subsequently the bailiff appoints a day for the hearing, either at his office or at the residence of the debtor. If the debtor fails to appear after being summoned to the bailiff's office the creditor may usually ask for police assistance to secure the debtor's presence. During the course of proceedings the debtor is obliged to give details on his property.

Money in the debtor's possession, if any, will be applied immediately for payment of the creditor's claim. Otherwise the bailiff will seize (other) assets in execution. Where a choice between several possible assets may be made such choice is usually made by the debtor. Where the debtor owns no assets which may be seized the proceedings must be closed as abortive – the debtor presents an "insolvency declaration". Hereupon, another six months must pass, as a starting point, until a new execution process may be initiated against the debtor.

4.3. The subject-matter of execution

Prima facie, a debtor is liable to the full extent of his property. Therefore, likewise prima facie, execution may be levied on all assets owned by the debtor. However, a number of exemptions are made to this first rule. The debtor is not to be totally deprived. In particular he is allowed to retain assets necessary for keeping up a financial subsistence level and necessary tools of work to a modest extent. Access to levy execution is also limited as regards wages which have not yet been paid out, claims under synallagmatic contracts, and – by virtue of other legislation – pension payments and other special deposits.

In business relationships the importance of execution to private creditors is only modest whereas execution for public claims on the basis of a distraint order is quite common. Where a business enterprise faces an unsurmountable financial crisis the end result will almost invariably be bankruptcy upon a decree made on the petition of a private creditor (or the debtor himself). As the subject-matter for creditor enforcement is more or less the same, whether one or the other remedy is applied, the detailed account of this subject is included in Chapter 19 on business collapse.

4.4. Legal effects of the execution

As between the execution creditor and the debtor the execution will imply, in principle, that the creditor is entitled to sell the goods seized at a compulsory auction if the debtor fails to pay the claim. However, removal of assets of a considerable use value to the debtor or his family may under the circumstances be deemed unfair in view of the modest amount the goods will normally fetch at a forced sale. Hence the debtor is not normally deprived of possession of the goods and he may continue to use them. In execution of chattels the bailiff's court may direct that the goods are to remain in the debtor's possession as long as he keeps an instalment arrangement fixed by the court and of a duration which is normally not to exceed 10 months. On similar lines the court may decide that execution levied on real property serving as dwelling house for the debtor or his household will not entail a power of sale as long as the debtor keeps an instalment arrangement fixed by the court and approved by the debtor. However, these limitations do not apply to a mortgagee seeking satisfaction on his mortgage. To secure the possibility of collecting the goods seized in execution with a view to sale the debtor is deprived of the (legal) access to dispose of the goods in a manner which may be detrimental to the execution creditor's right.

The execution creditor's right is often termed a right of "charge by order of the court". This implies that he has a right somewhat similar to a charge created by party disposition (on the parties' own will and therefore binding). Accordingly, conflicts arising between several execution creditors in respect of the same asset are solved by a priority principle of "first come, first served". Thus, the best ranking priority is to receive satisfaction before secondary rights may be covered. The criteria for deciding the priority are determined first and foremost by the nature of the asset seized in execution. For execution upon i.a. real property, registered ships and aircraft, registered securities and patent rights it is provided that the execution shall obtain protection as towards other creditors' instituting legal proceedings only upon the terms applying to securing the mortgage right arranged by party disposition – this means that a constitutive act is required (registration etc.) The priority position is then determined by the point in time at which the necessary constitutive act was made. For execution levied on chattels and unsecured claims the execution creditor is protected without constitutive acts. The priority position of executions in such assets is determined by the date at which the creditor presented an execution petition to the bailiff's court (i.e. not the date of its actual performance). However, where the execution was made on the basis of a distraint order the priority position of such distraint is the date of its actual performance.

Naturally the rights of the execution creditor will lapse if the claim for which execution was levied is paid. In addition special rules on independent time limitation of the rights under an execution are applicable notwithstanding that the claim secured is still valid.

4.5. Compulsory sale

The execution creditor's right entails that he may claim the goods seized in execution to be sold at a compulsory sale. However, for the reasons outlined above only a few executions will lead to such sale.

Where execution is levied on an asset, otherwise unencumbered, belonging to the debtor the execution creditor will be paid out of the proceeds to the extent of his claim and any surplus is paid to the debtor. Where an asset is charged with several execution orders or other mortgage rights, which is typically the case for real property, the claims are settled on their respective priority basis and claims which are not covered will lapse as unsatisfied.

CHAPTER 15

Transfer of claims

by Lars Lindencrone Petersen

1. Introduction

Like other property rights, the right under a claim may be transferred to a new creditor. If the claim is transferred by agreement the arrangement is known as an assignment. In accordance with the terminology of the Bonds Act assignment will be used to denote transfer of a claim by agreement and the parties in the relationship will be referred to as debtor, assignor and assignee.

Claims are often unsuitable for transfer to third parties on account of the uncertainty of the debtor's capability to pay and the risk that a person other than the assignor is entitled to it. To this must be added that the legal protection is primarily designed for the debtor to ensure that his obligation is not increased by reason of a transfer. Exclusions from this apply to claims attached to negotiable instruments for which the rules are designed with the very purpose of facilitating transfer.

The most important Act on assignment of claims is the Bonds Act which in Part 2 contains rules on negotiable bonds and in Part 3 on ordinary bonds. The Act is only directly applicable if a bond has been issued but the rules in Part 3 may be applied analogously for claims in general. Part 3 is also analogously applied to assignment of non-money claims. Claims whose assignment is governed by the rules of Part 3 directly or by analogy are termed ordinary claims corresponding to "ordinary bonds". Alongside the Bonds Act the rules on electronic securities in the Securities Trading Act also play an important part.

2. The relationship between assignor and assignee

In the main the same rules apply to the relationship between assignor or assignee whether the claim is attached to a negotiable bond or not.

As regards conclusion and validity of the contract the ordinary contract law rules in the Contracts Act and the Guardianship Act apply. Where the assignment is invalid, e.g. on account of fraud, the assignor still holds the claim. As regards negotiable bonds an exception is made to this rule in case the assignor is a minor. Further, under s. 14 of the Bonds Act a bona fide assignee who has acquired possession of a negotiable bond will get a good title even if the assignor was a minor. An almost similar rule applies for money. Also in an assignment of registered securities the minority defence may be defeated towards a bona fide assignee (Securities Trading Act, s. 69).

The rights of assignees are determined – subject to defences, if any, on the debtor's part – primarily by the agreement and its construction. Unless otherwise agreed, an assignment of a claim comprises the security rights attached to the claim whether in the form of a retention of title, mortgage, or guarantee.

Under s. 9 of the Bonds Act the assignor warrants the existence of the claim. This does not apply for gifts or where the assignee knew or had reason to suspect the claim's non-existence. On the other hand, where a debtor is unwilling or unable to pay, the assignor is not liable unless he had warranted such payment (s. 10 of the Bonds Act). Such warranty will lie if the assignor has transferred the claim under an "indemnity clause" in favour of the assignee. In that case the assignor will be liable as an ordinary surety for the debtor's performance.

3. Ordinary claims

The main view underlying Part 3 of the Bonds Act is that the debtor's obligation should not be increased on an assignment of the claim. The rules protecting the debtor's interests may be divided into rules on the debtor's defences and rules on "apparent (payee) authority".

3.1. The debtor's defences

In accordance with the principle that the debtor's obligation should not be increased by an assignment of a claim the main rule provides that an assignee will not obtain a better right than the assignor had (the Bonds Act, s. 27). In other words the debtor retains towards an assignee any defence (i.e. objection to the claim) he had as towards the assignor even if such assignee was in good faith as regards the existence of any such defence.

From s. 27 it follows that the debtor may rely on the defence that the claim was not validly created whether the vitiating factor ranks as an operative or non-operative factor (i.e. whether it may set up against innocent third parties or not). The fact that the vitiating factors mentioned in ss. 29-39 of the

Contracts Act are defeated as towards a bona fide promisee does not imply that they are also defeated as towards a subsequent assignee.

Where the debtor paid the claim prior to the assignment he may rely on such defence towards the assignee as well (s. 27). The same applies to other changes in the debt relationship, e.g. part waiver in connection with a voluntary composition.

Where the claim derives from a synallagmatic agreement, e.g. a sale, the debtor (buyer) may, by virtue of s. 27, refuse to pay to the assignee (e.g. a financial institution) if he was entitled to cancel the sale on account of breach from the assignor (seller) and similarly the assignee (the financial institution) must tolerate a reduction in the claim if the debtor (buyer) may demand a proportionate reduction. In consumer sale, the corresponding rule (s. 33 of the Credit Agreements Act) is mandatory in favour of the buyer.

The fact that the assignee will not obtain a better right than the assignor will apply under s. 27 unless a contrary inference follows from special rules of law. Such a rule is provided in s. 34 of the Contracts Act under which the defence that a written declaration of indebtedness was issued as a sham will be defeated as towards a bona fide third party acquiring rights under the document.

3.2. Apparent payee authority

The debtor is not necessarily told of a transfer of a claim and it is also possible that he has been told of an assignment which turns out later to be invalid. To protect the debtor against the risk of paying twice the Bonds Act provides rules in s. 29 and s. 30 whereby the debtor may be discharged on a bona fide payment to the assignor or assignee, respectively as "apparent payee".

A debtor who does not know that the claim has been assigned is protected by the rule in s. 29 of the Bonds Act where the debtor may pay to the assignor with discharging effect unless he knew that the assignor was no longer entitled to the payment or he has failed to show the care required in the circumstances.

A debtor who has been notified of an assignment which later turns out to be invalid is protected, to a certain extent, by the rule in s. 30 of the Bonds Act which provides in its 1st clause that when the debtor pays to a party to whom an original promissory note has been assigned his discharge will not be barred by the invalidity of such assignment. For claims which are not attached to a promissory note the condition of applying s. 30 is that an assignment declaration in writing has been made. The rule is also applicable if the assignor informed the debtor that assignment had been made.

The debtor will not obtain discharge if he knew or had cause to suspect that the assignment was invalid (s. 30, 2nd clause). Under this provision the debtor is not discharged either – if the assignment was invalid for one of the reasons stated in s. 17, i.e. if the assignment was a forgery, signed on behalf of the assignor without his authority, or invalid on account of duress with violence, or because of minority.

The Bonds Act contains no rule as regards the requirements the debtor may impose as a condition for paying to the assignee. However, this issue is closely related to s. 30 as the debtor must, it is submitted, be entitled to claim that the assignee substantiates his right in such a way that there will be no risk of the debtor's paying to an assignor whose right later turns out to be invalid. This will require that the assignee can show a written assignment declaration, or that the debtor has received notification from the assignor of the assignment (s. 30, 1st clause).

3.3. Transfer protection

In an assignment of ordinary claims the same issue arises as with transfers of other assets as to the requirements for protecting an assignee's right against the assignor's creditors and subsequent bona fide assignees.

A transfer of an ordinary claim to hold or to mortgage is under s. 31(1) of the Bonds Act invalid as against the assignor's creditors "unless the debtor had received notification from the assignor or the assignee about the assignment". The validity of the assignment as against the assignor's creditors is in other words dependent on the performance of the constitutive act of notification of the debtor. The notification, which may be given by either assignor or assignee, is not subject to special formal requirements and therefore an oral communication will, in principle, suffice. As regards the contents of the notification it follows from the words in s. 31(1) that it must be apparent that an assignment has taken place. This means that a notice stating that "all payments are to be made to ..." will not meet the requirement in s. 31(1) as it is not apparent whether the claim has been assigned or whether a mere collection authority has been issued.

As against subsequent assignees in contract, the assignee will obtain protection in the same way as against the assignor's creditors, i.e. by notice to the debtor. This follows from s. 31(2) of the Bonds Act whereby a subsequent assignee will take precedence over an earlier assignee if the debtor received notice of assignment from the former first, and provided that the assignor was in good faith at the notification.

3.4. Invoice and contracts discounting

Ordinary promissory notes are to a large extent only used as a basis for the loan business of financial institutions and mortgage credit institutions, and as such documents are (almost never) subject to transfer the rules of the Bonds Act, Part 3, would be of no practical relevance if they were to be applied to ordinary promissory notes only. As already mentioned, however, these rules also comprise transfer of (other) ordinary claims which adds considerably to their practical sphere of application.

An importer or producer selling on credit to distributors will often finance his credit business by raising loans on his claims with the distributors in a factoring company or a financial institution. In this financing model, termed invoice discounting or factoring, the credit security element is that the factoring company or the financial institution, with the rules of Part 3 of the Bonds Act as the legal basis, will obtain a charge on the importer's or the producer's credit sale claims. Incidentally, it is also common for a building contractor to create credit for himself by mortgaging his contractual rights to a financial institution.

Expensive chattels, such as cars in a consumer sale, were formerly often sold on credit basis with reservation of title and it was common for the dealer to finance his credit extension in such sale by means of "contract discounting", i.e. by placing his contractual rights as a security basis. However, as a result of the heavy protectionary rules in favour of the buyer in the Credit Contracts Act this finance model is no longer very popular. Instead, financing is often effected by the buyer's contracting a loan, enabling him to pay cash, from a finance company or a financial institution against a registered mortgage right of the subject-matter.

4. Negotiable instruments

4.1. The concept

The rules on negotiable instruments are designed to facilitate transfer of such instruments which aim is achieved by securing the assignee's rights via special (apparent) authority rules, lapse of former holders' rights and lapse of some of the debtor's defences. The fact that debtor considerations are second to assignee considerations within the framework of these rules must be seen in the light of the presumption that by issuing a negotiable instrument the debtor is deemed to have accepted the risk inherent in such step.

While the rules on ordinary promissory notes of Part 3 of the Bonds Act may be analogously applied to a money claim which is not attached to a promissory note, it is a condition for applying the rules in Part 2 on negotiable instruments that a bond is involved. Therefore in relation to Part 2 it is vital to establish the requirements which must be met in order to identify a document as a bond.

The Act does not contain a definition of a bond. Such instrument is commonly perceived, from the angle of rights conferred, as a declaration in writing conferring a unilateral, unconditional claim for a certain sum of money, and from the angle of obligation, as a unilateral, unconditional declaration in writing whereby the debtor either undertakes to pay or acknowledges that he owes a certain sum of money. The "unilateral" requirement means that a document containing a synallagmatic agreement is not within the definition of a bond. That the creditor's right and the corresponding debtor-obligation is to be unconditional means that a document containing a synallagmatic agreement is incapable of becoming a bond even if it has obtained a unilateral character by one party's performance of his side of the agreement. Therefore, e.g. a contract of sale under whose terms the seller has supplied on credit is not a bond.

For a document to be within the scope of negotiable instruments the document must be comprised by the Bonds Act s. 11(2). Under this provision the following are defined as negotiable instruments: 1. Bonds of payment to bearer or not stating the payee (bearer bonds). 2. Bonds of payment to a specified person or to order (bonds to order). 3. Bonds conferring mortgage rights in real property, registered ship or aircraft unless the words "not to order" or similar reservation has been made. 4. Bonds of payment to a specified person (registered bonds) where they expressly state that they are to be regarded as negotiable.

4.2. The document as representing the claim

In contrast to chattels and real property a claim is an intangible asset. In order to make a claim into an asset suitable for transfer it is necessary artificially to convert it to a tangible asset. This explains the creation of the legal fiction that the document itself represents the claim which is provided in s. 13 of the Bonds Act. With bearer bonds the presumption is under the first clause of the rule that the person holding possession of the bond ("the bearer") is entitled to set up the claim. This makes the document proper into the asset represented by the claim. Note that the rule is to the effect that the bearer is deemed to have the right to the claim but not that he necessarily has such right in real terms. A thief of e.g.a premium bond is of course not owner of such bond but the outside world may, by virtue of s. 13, rely on the presumption that a premium bond is owned by the bearer. The same artifice is behind the concept of money. Money represents claims on the Treasury and a person holding money in his possession is deemed to be owner of such money though this is not necessarily the case.

With other negotiable instruments, e.g. ordinary mortgage deeds in real property, the right under s. 13, 2nd clause, is deemed to lie with "the party holding the deed in his possession whether made out to him, or assigned to him or to bearer by written assignments appearing as a coherent string of assignments". Thus the requirement is not that the assignments are linked in real terms, only that they appear to be so. It is irrelevant that an assignment may be a forgery. The decisive element is that the holder of the instrument has an apparent, lawful title to it.

The rules on lapse of rights, lapse of defences and on apparent authority in negotiable instruments are based on the legal fiction set up in s. 13.

4.3. Lapse of rights

Under s. 14 of the Bonds Act a former owner's rights in respect of a negotiable instrument may be defeated as against an assignee of the document. This rule is applicable no matter how the document has left the owner's possession whether on an invalid agreement, by theft or robbery.

The requirements for lapse of the former owner's rights are *that* the assignee's right was created by an assignment, i.e. by an agreement, *that* the assignment is valid in itself, that the assignee holds the document in his possession and *that* he was in good faith as regards the assignor's (e.g. a thief's) right to dispose of the document. Where bearer documents are involved no further requirements are set up for the lapse of a former owner's rights (s. 14(1). For other types of negotiable instruments, e.g. mortgage deeds in real property, a further requirement is that the assignor held the document on an apparently lawful title (s. 14(2)).

4.4. Lapse of defences

In itself the fact that a debtor has signed a negotiable instrument will not imply that he loses defences ("objections") he may have had in respect of the legal relationship underlying the issue of the instrument, e.g. the purchase causing the issuying of the instrument (cf. s. 1 of the Bonds Act). But when the document has been transferred some of the debtor's defences may be defeated as against the assignee. The rules governing the defences which are defeated (non-operative or "weak" defences) and defences which are not defeated (operative or "strong" defences) are contained in the Bonds Act ss. 15-17. The main principle underlying the rules is that a defence may be lost if a diligent debtor could have prevented the occurrence of the factor relied on as a defence whereas a defence will not be defeated if a diligent debtor could not have avoided its occurrence.

For a defence to be lost, s. 15 requires *that* the right of the assignee was created in an assignment, *that* the assignment itself was valid, *that* the assignee holds the instrument in his possession, and *that* he was in good faith in regard to the defence of the debtor. The defences a debtor may lose comprise under s. 15(1): 1. that the instrument was invalid under the rules of ss. 29-33 of the Contracts Act, or that – upon being signed by him – it has been issued contrary to his will, 2. that he has not received the consideration agreed or holds other defence from the legal relationship which underlies the issue of the instrument, and 3. that payment had been made prior to the assignment, or that the debt relationship had otherwise terminated or been modified by agreement, set-off, renunciation, or judgment.

To protect the debtor a defence under s. 15(3) is retained if the instrument is claused in a way which is not easily removable regarding payment or other factors capable of supporting the defence, even if the clause was actually removed prior to the assignment. A pencil-written clause or a clause placed so close to the edge of the paper that it may be cut off will count as "easily removable".

An important exception to the rule that a defence may be lost is contained in s. 16 under which defences in respect of interest falling due before the day of assignment, and time-bound (ordinary) repayments falling due before this point in time will be retained as against an innocent assignee. Thus, as regards payments which under their terms should have been made before the date of assignment the assignee will obtain no better right than the assignor had.

Under s. 17 of the Bonds Act the debtor may even towards an innocent assignee allege in defence 1) that the instrument was a forgery signed on his behalf without authority to do so or that it is invalid for duress with violence (Contracts Act s. 28), incapacity by reason of minority and registered guardianship with deprival of legal capacity or incapability because of a mental condition, and 2) that the instrument had been declared null and void, or that the claim had terminated or been modified under statutory rules of deposit, time limitation, statute-barring upon preclusive notice, compulsory composition, or debt re-scheduling. A common feature of all the defences in 1) is that even a careful, diligent debtor could not prevent their occurrence and a common feature of the defences under 2) is that they are all statutory termination grounds whose purpose would be defeated if the defence were to be lost as against an innocent assignee.

4.5. Rules of apparent authority

The rules on apparent authority may be divided into two groups. 1) the rules relating to the payee to whom the debtor may pay with discharging effect, and 2) rules relating to the issue of the conditions on which the debtor is to pay. Naturally, the rules are interrelated to secure the overall objective that a debtor may be certain of his discharge when the conditions for his payment are properly met.

Under s. 19(1) of the Bonds Act a debtor paying in good faith to a holder of a bearer bond will obtain discharge even if the payee was a minor or lacked the right to take the payment. Under s. 19(2) it is a requirement with other negotiable instruments, e.g. a mortgage deed in real property that the holder had apparent lawful authority. The rule in s. 19 under which the debtor may obtain discharge upon payment to e.g. a thief of a negotiable instrument will comprise any payment under the instrument.

A special rule on interest due and timebound repayments due, is contained in s. 20(1). Under this rule, upon an assignment of a negotiable instrument, a bona fide debtor may make such payments to the assignor. Thus, the assignee has a strong incentive to give notice to the debtor of the assignment before the first payment term sets in.

S. 21(1) and (2) sets out what the debtor may require as a condition for paying. Failure to observe these conditions will entitle the debtor to refuse to pay without incurring liability for breach and he is also free to discharge himself by depositing. As a condition for redeeming a negotiable instrument (paying off the remaining debt) the debtor may under s. 21(1) claim delivery of the instrument to him. For instruments other than bearer bonds he may also claim a receipt to be given on the instrument. With payments of timebound repayments due, s. 21(2), 1st clause, only provides the debtor with a right to a separate receipt whereas with other repayments, e.g. a payment on ownership change in respect of a mortgage deed in real property, he may also claim that the deed is claused to such effect (s. 21(2), 2nd clause).

4.6. Transfer protection

As with transfers of other assets an assignment of a negotiable instrument will also raise the question of what is required in order that the assignee's rights are protected against the assignor's creditors and bona fide assignees in contract.

With transfers to hold, the assignee is protected as towards the assignor's creditors from the time of assignment. Where a sale of an individually ascertained negotiable bond – or several bonds – is involved the buyer will thus be protected already from the conclusion of the contract, whereas in an unascertained sale the requirement is that the seller has made an unconditional appropriation of the bond(s) by which he intends to perform his obligation under the agreement.

On a mortgage or other charge in security s. 22 of the Bonds Act will require that the assignee has obtained possession of the instrument.

From s. 14 of the Bonds Act it follows that an assignee of a negotiable instrument will not be protected against subsequent bona fide assignees until he has obtained possession of the instrument.

5. Registered (electronic) securities

Under the Securities Trading Act s. 59(2) which is linked with subsection 1 of the same provision under which securities may be issued and transferred electronically ("dematerialised") registered securities (i.e. electronic securities) are defined as negotiable dematerialised securities, registered with a central securities depository (a Securities Centre). These rules are unintelligible to the un-initiated but that is the way the legislators apparently have seen fit to express themselves. Included in the concept of registered securities are in particular listed shares and bonds, and so far only one securities depository has been established.

5.1. The registration system

The registration system entails that securities registered with the securities depository are entered in accounts belonging to the individual owners. Registration comprises not only title but also limited rights such as mortgage rights, and any limitations of power of disposal, e.g. minority.

The registration of rights is made at the securities centre but will be governed by the account-keeping institutions. Thus, applications for registration must always be made to an account-keeping institution. The scrutiny in connection with registration is made both at the account-keeping institution and at the securities centre.

The account-keeping institutions are listed in s. 62(1) of the Securities Trading Act. Under this rule the right to make registration at the Securities Centre is in particular with the Danish National Bank, with financial institutions, mortgage credit institutions and other bond-issuing institutions as far as electronic securities issued by the institution in question are concerned.

5.2. Legal effects of registration

In a contract and property law context the principle is that registration is to replace the fiction of the document as representing the claim. Thus the registration is the main axis in relation to transfer protection, (s. 66), extinction of rights (s. 69), lapse of defences (s. 70), and apparent authority (s. 71). Otherwise the rules on legal effect are inspired – with the modifications required by the electronic registration system – by the corresponding rules in the Registration of Property Act and the Bonds Act governing real estate and bearer bonds, respectively.

5.2.1. Transfer protection

Under s. 66(1) rights in respect of electronic securities must be registered in the securities centre to obtain protection against legal proceedings and assignees in contract. Thus, the constitutive act for transfers of electronic securities is registration.

In accordance with the usual principles of extinction of rights s. 66(2) provides that an agreement or legal proceeding calculated to defeat a non-registered right must be registered itself and that an assignee in contract is (further) required to be in good faith at the notification to the account-keeping institution.

The legal effects of a registration are, under s. 66(3) computed from the time of final scrutiny at the securities centre.

5.2.2. Lapse of rights

When an agreement on rights in respect of electronic securities has been finally executed at the securities centre a bona fide assignee under an agreement registered under s. 69, 1st clause, is protected against challenges on the validity of such agreement. S. 69, 1st clause, will however still allow the challenge that the agreement is invalid by reason of forgery or duress with violence or threatened violence.

A bona fide assignee who fails to obtain rights on the securities or loses rights obtained is entitled to compensation by the securities centre to the extent of his loss. Thus the credibility of the registration system is guaranteed.

5.2.3. Lapse of defences

S. 70 brings the rules of the Bonds Act ss. 15-18 governing defences and set-offs to apply analogously to a debtor under electronic securities so that final registration with the securities centre replaces possession of the debt instrument.

5.2.4. Authority

Where the securities centre, on behalf of the issuer, makes a payment in good faith to a person registered as payee the securities centre is discharged under s. 71(2), 1st clause, even if the payee was not entitled to receive the payment or was a minor. Under s. 71(2), 2nd clause, this will not apply if the person entitled under the register has based his right on an agreement which is void by reason of forgery or duress with violence or threatened violence.

5.2.5. Liability in damages

Under s. 80(1), 1st clause, the securities centre is liable in damages for loss on account of errors in connection with registration, alteration or cancellation of rights or payments even if the error was accidental. However, where the error is attributable to an account-keeping institution the liability will lie with such institution. Where the injured party has contributed to the error either intentionally or negligently damages may, however, under s. 80(3) be reduced or lapse altogether. Under s. 80(2) the securities centre is further, as already mentioned, liable towards an innocent assignee who has suffered a loss on account of the rule on forgery and duress with violence or threatened violence in s. 69, 2nd clause.

6. Cheques and bills of exchange

6.1. Concepts, terminology and application

A creditor whose claim is for money may require payment by the debtor at the right time and place. On the acceptance of the creditor, however, nothing prevents that another mode of performance may be effected e.g. by a third party's payment under an order issued by the debtor to the creditor.

Performance through order involves the debtor's issuing of a request to a third party to pay a sum of money to the creditor. If the creditor is willing to accept the order and the third party subsequently pays under it the claim has been duly performed. If the third party refuses the debtor's request the claim is of course still existing. The most important examples of orders are cheques and bills of exchange, governed by the cheques and bills Acts.

The aim of these Acts, both rooted in a comprehensive international cooperation is to make cheques and bills of exchange into suitable instruments for payment. This purpose is manifest not only in the special negotiability of cheques and bills of exchange which they share with other negotiable instruments but also the immediate obligation of a party signing a cheque or a bill as transferor. This means that a cheque or bill of exchange is easily transferable as long as the document contains a reliable name.

Cheques and bills of exchange are required to be made in a particular form. In order that a document may be regarded as a cheque or a bill of exchange the formal requirements set up in ss. 1 and 2 of the Acts are satisfied. The requirements which are largely identical for the two types of document include e.g. that the designation cheque/bill of exchange is introduced in the body of the document proper, not just as a headline. The satisfaction of the formal requirements poses no problems in practice. The financial institutions supply their customers with cheque forms and bills of exchange forms are available from any stationery. It must be emphasized, however, that both a valid cheque and a valid bill may be issued without using the forms supplied as long as the instructions governing form of the document are (otherwise) met. As regards cheques, however, the banks would no doubt resent that an account-holder writes out cheques without using the forms provided for the purpose by the bank itself.

In the terminology of cheques and bills of exchange the issuer of the document (debtor) is termed a drawer. The party to whom the document is issued (creditor) is called the payee and the party ordered to pay or on whom the cheque/bill is drawn is called the drawee. To a certain extent the parties may be one and the same person but in that respect the rules are not quite identical for the two types of document on account of their separate areas of application.

In contrast to bills of exchange which may be drawn on everybody cheques may only be drawn on commercial banks and savings banks (s. 3 of the Cheques Act). A cheque is said to be a means of payment but this expression is not absolutely precise. Admittedly, a cheque is always to be paid on presentation in accordance with s. 28 of the Cheques Act, and antedatings, if any, are considered unwritten. Nevertheless, the expression means of payment is not absolutely correct since payment is not truly effected until the payee has had the cheque honoured (paid) at the drawee bank. Still a cheque's true character of means of payment is evident in e.g. a cash sale in which the seller agrees to take a cheque instead of ready money without such sale being converted to a credit sale on that account and with the important result that the seller, in contrast to his position under a credit sale governed by s. 28(2) of the Sale of Goods Act, may recover the goods if the cheque "bounces".

Cheques may be issued to "self" though it would seem to make little sense, at first sight, that an account-holder draws a cheque to himself unless he uses such device to draw from his account to obtain cash. However, the true function of a cheque is not evident until it is transferred.

A bill of exchange is termed a means of credit which is more appropriate than the expression means of payment is of a cheque. The maturity of a bill may be stated as a definite point in time (in the future) or the bill may be a "sight" bill, i.e. payable on presentation to the drawee, or at a certain time after sight (s. 5 of the Bills of Exchange Act). The basic model used for the provisions of the Bills of Exchange Act involves the three persons already mentioned: drawer, payee and drawee. Such bill which is called a draft may be applied to the payment of the purchase price in a credit sale in that the buyer (drawer) draws a bill to the seller (payee) for one of his debtors (drawee).

In contrast to a cheque a bill may be drawn on the drawer himself. Such bill which is termed a "promissory note" is not really an order, but a debt instrument issued as a bill of exchange. A promissory note may be applied in the financing of a credit sale in that the buyer issues a bill to the seller drawn on himself whereupon the seller may transfer the bill (discount it) to a financial institution which will pay out the amount of the bill after deduction of a financial consideration (for the discounting of the bill).

Party coincidence on a bill may also appear when the drawer issues the bill to himself. In that case the bill is a draft to own order. In a credit sale a draft to own order may be used in the financing of the sale in that the seller draws the bill on the buyer to himself after which he may discount it at a bank in the same way as a promissory note issued by the buyer.

6.2. The relationship between drawer and payee

The issuing of a cheque in a debt relationship will not immediately imply that the drawer is discharged of his commitments towards the payee. The debt relationship does not terminate until the payee has had the cheque honoured at the drawee bank. If the cheque turns out to be worthless (for lack of funds) the payee may demand the amount from the drawer (s. 12 of the Cheques Act). The payee is, however, provided with a special, easy access to enforcement of his claim since a cheque may serve as execution basis with the drawer.

On the other hand, the party issuing a cheque will not lose access to challenge the legal relationship underlying the issue of the cheque. A party who e.g. has bought a quantity of goods against payment of a cheque may cancel the sale if the goods suffer from material defects notwithstanding the issue of the cheque. If the seller (payee) has already cashed the cheque with the drawee bank the buyer is of course referred to demanding the money from the seller, but when the cheque has not yet been cashed the buyer may revoke it as towards the drawee bank which will imply, under s. 32(1) of the Cheques Act, that the bank is not entitled to honour it unless it has been certified.

For bills of exchange the rules are almost identical to those governing cheques. A bill is regarded as a means of credit and it is therefore self-evident that a debt relationship is not terminated by the issue of a bill. The debt relationship does not terminate until the drawee has paid on the due date. If the drawee on a draft refuses to pay (or to accept) the bill, the payee's position is the same as with a cheque and he is left to demand the sum from the drawer (s. 9(1) of the Bills of Exchange Act). The issue will of course not arise with a promissory note since this document is a debt instrument made out in bill of exchange form. Like cheques bills of exchange may also serve as execution basis with the drawer.

6.3. The relationship between drawer and drawee

Whether an issuing of a cheque is justified in the relationship between drawer and drawee will depend on the existence of an agreement to such effect. Under s. 4 of the Cheques Act the drawer is required to have funds available at the drawee bank for his disposal by cheque, either under an express or under an implied agreement. Whether such agreement exists is rarely in issue in practice. As already mentioned cheques are usually issued in sets of forms delivered to the cheque issuer at his bank and the fact that a bank delivers such forms will of course indicate an acceptance that disposal of the account may be made by means of cheques. Where the funds available in the account are no longer sufficient it is equally evident that the bank will not be bound to honour the cheques the drawer may issue.

It should be noted that the rule of s. 4 of the Cheques Act is not relevant to the question whether a valid cheque has been issued but only states the obvious limitation that the drawing of cheques is only allowed if the issuer holds an account in the bank in question over which he may dispose by means of cheques.

The Bills of Exchange Act does not contain a provision similar to s. 4 of the Cheques Act. In other words, the Bills of Exchange Act imposes no requirement that the drawer has funds available with the drawee over which he may dispose by means of a bill of exchange upon agreement. Where the drawer has no debt outstanding from the drawee or where no other factors lead him to expect that the drawee will pay for him it makes little sense to issue a bill of exchange. To this must be added that generally the drawee need not meet the bill's order to pay just because he owes money to the drawer. On the other hand, where the drawer has a claim with the drawee there is no reason to believe that the drawee would reject to honour the bill to discharge his debt. The issues in the relationship of drawer/drawee will of course not arise with a promissory note.

6.4. The relationship between payee and drawee

The issuing of a cheque will not imply that the drawee bank becomes liable as towards the payee. This applies even if there is a cheque agreement between the drawer and the drawee bank and even if the drawer's account holds sufficient funds to cover the cheque amount. Thus, the drawee bank may refuse to honour a cheque as towards the payee but it would normally be hard to see the bank's interest in doing so if funds are available in the drawer's account to cover the amount.

Exceptions from the rule just mentioned apply where the drawee bank has provided the cheque with a signed clause which may be interpreted to the effect that the cheque will be paid (e.g. by adding words such as "certified" or marked") or where the bank's signature is placed on the front of the cheque. Under s. 25 of the Cheques Act a bank is bound to honour a cheque thus marked if it is presented for payment before the expiry of the term of presentation of 20 days fixed in s. 29, computed from the date of issue of the cheque.

In order to reduce the indisputable risk inherent in taking a cheque instead of ready money the Danish financial institutions have established a scheme of warranty under which they undertake, under certain conditions, to pay cheques not exceeding DKK 1,000 even if the funds in the drawer's account will not cover the amount. It is to be noted, however, that this cheque warranty scheme has nothing to do with the cheque access proper.

On a line with the rules applying to cheques the issuing of a bill of exchange will not imply that the drawee will be committed as against the payee. The drawee will only incur an obligation if he accepts the bill of exchange (s. 28(1) of the Bills of Exchange Act). When the drawee has accepted the bill he is called "acceptor". The acceptance is written on the bill and is expressed by the word "accepted" or similar designation, and will be signed by the acceptor.

In an attempt to remove the uncertainty as to whether a drawee at maturity will be willing to pay the bill, s. 21 of the Bills of Exchange Act provides that any holder of a bill of exchange (i.e the payee or a subsequent assignee) up to the date of maturity of the bill, may present the bill for acceptance by the drawee at the place of residence of such drawee.

6.5. The obligation in cheques and bills of exchange

As will have emerged, only the drawer is the debtor in relation to cheques or bills. Where a cheque is certified the drawee bank is also committed and where a bill is accepted the drawee (acceptor) is also bound.

A cheque or bill may be transferred by indorsement. The indorsement, entailing a transfer of all rights under the cheque or bill, must be made on the document or on a slip of paper applied to such document (allonge) and must be signed by the indorser (transferor). It is not remarkable that transfer can be made. But it is remarkable indeed that the indorser warrants the payment of the cheque or bill unless he has made reservation to such effect (s. 18 of the Cheques Act and s. 15 of the Bills of Exchange Act). Thus, by his indorsement of a cheque or a bill the payee will become debtor under the document. This rule creating as it were a new debtor every time a cheque or bill is transferred is one of the pillar elements in the negotiability of these documents.

6.6. Transfer of cheques and bills of exchange

6.6.1. The negotiability basis

Cheques and bills of exchange are negotiable documents. The fiction of the document itself representing the claim is set up in s. 19 of the Cheques Act and s. 16(1) of the Bills of Exchange Act, respectively. In these rules it is provided that a holder of a cheque or bill of exchange is deemed rightful holder if his title is evidenced by an unbroken line of indorsements even if the last indorsement is "blank", i.e. an indorsement not containing the name of the transferee. In slightly briefer terms a holder of a cheque or bill of exchange with a formally (i.e. apparent) lawful title is deemed holder of the right under the document.

6.6.2. Apparent authority

From the principles of the document representing the claim it follows that the drawee bank may pay, for the account of the drawer – i.e. with the effect that the amount is debited from the drawer's account – to the presenter of a cheque provided that he holds the document on a formally lawful title. The drawee bank is required to be in good faith, however, which implies under s. 35 of the Cheques Act that the bank is to verify that the line of indorsement is duly unbroken but verification is not made of the signatures' authenticity. Thus a cheque may be paid to a person who is not rightful holder, e.g. a thief. The loss incurred hereby lies with the party from whom the cheque was stolen (the payee or a subsequent assignee) whereas the drawer is discharged.

To provide some protection against the risk of payment being made to an unlawful holder of a cheque s. 37 and s. 38 provide rules for crossing of cheques. The crossing which consists in drawing two parallel lines across the front of the cheque may be made by the drawer or by the holder of the cheque. Crossings may be general or special. Where general, the crossing will consist of two lines only, or words may be added between the lines such as "to banker" or a similar expression; a special crossing is one adding the name of a specified bank between the two lines. The effect of a general crossing is that the drawee bank may only pay to another bank or to one of its own customers and the effect of a special crossing is that the drawee bank may only pay to the bank named, or where such bank is the drawee bank itself, to one of its customers. A crossing offers some security, though far from absolute, against the risk that a cheque is paid to an unlawful holder. However, by providing the cheque with a false blank indorsement a thief may create the formal (i.e. apparent) lawful title needed and if he is a customer with a bank he may have the cheque cashed despite the crossing.

For bills of exchange s. 40(3) provides that a bill of exchange debtor paying when the bill is due will be discharged of his obligation unless he has shown fraud or gross negligence. This implies that he will obtain discharge if he has verified that the payee is holder of the bill with a formally lawful title. However, this will not apply if he knows or has just cause to suspect that the bill has gone astray.

6.6.3. Lapse of rights

The rules applying under s. 21 of the Cheques Act and s. 16 of the Bills of Exchange Act, respectively, regarding lapse of rights are fairly similar to the rules on negotiable bonds in s. 14 of the Bonds Act. A thief of a cheque or a bill of exchange will of course not become owner of the document. But if he creates the necessary "formally lawful" title for himself by indorsing the document with a false blank indorsement and subsequently re-indorses it to an assignee, the former owner's rights are defeated as against the assignee unless such assignee acted mala fide at the acquisition. Where the assignee did not know that the document had gone astray nor had just cause to suspect it, the good faith requirement is satisfied merely by his having verified the transferor's formal title.

As regards cheques it is commonly held that a crossed cheque is exempt from the rule on lapse of rights. This is, however, a misconception. A crossing has the effects mentioned above but a crossing will not entail that a stolen cheque, however duly crossed, may be reclaimed from a subsequent bona fide assignee. The statement which is often made of the special security of payments by crossed cheques sent to a creditor by registered letter is therefore somewhat misleading. Admittedly, if the cheque reaches the creditor (payee) the debtor (drawer) is discharged even if it is subsequently stolen and the creditor's right is defeated as against an innocent subsequent assignee. But if the cheque is stolen in transit the debtor will bear the risk which means that he may be liable as against a subsequent assignee of the cheque, without being discharged as against the creditor. Only by adding the words "not to order" or similar limitation may a cheque be brought outside the rule on lapse of rights in s. 21 of the Cheques Act.

6.6.4. Lapse of defences

As regards lapse of defences in relation to a cheque or bill of exchange the rules are contained in s. 22 of the Cheques Act and s. 17 of the Bills of Exchange Act. The construction of these rules, which are expressed somewhat summarily, is more or less on a line with the equivalent rules in s. 15 and s. 17 of the Bonds Act on negotiable bonds. This means that the rights of an innocent assignee of a cheque or bill of exchange may only be challenged upon "strong" (operative) grounds, not upon "weak" (non-operative) grounds.

6.6.5. The difference between lapse of rights and lapse of defences

While it is comparatively easy with negotiable instruments to distinguish between lapse of rights and lapse of defences it may be difficult with cheques and bills of exchange to see this dividing line as a result of the rule whereby any signer of a cheque or a bill of exchange is committed under the document. Where a cheque or bill of exchange, lawfully indorsed to an indorsee A, is stolen and the thief, after providing the requisite formal "title" by indorsing the document with a blank indorsement whereby he has become A +1, transfers the document to an innocent assignee A +2, the issue of both title to the document and (lapse of) defences will arise in the relationship between A and A +2. Under the rule of either s. 21 of the Cheques Act or s. 16 of the Bills of Exchange Act A +2 will have lawful title to the document. A's name is on the document and may therefore qualify as one of the indorsees against whom A +2 may set up the claim under the cheque or bill. But the signature is a forgery and A will therefore not be obliged to pay since forgery is within the defences which may relied on as against an innocent assignee under s. 22 of the Cheques Act and s. 17 of the Bills of Exchange Act. In other words the end result will be to endow A +2 with the same legal position held by the former indorsee A; i.e. he will have access to set up the claim against the debtors above him but not against A. A +2 may of course also set up the claim against A +1.

6.7. Recourse and protest

As already mentioned, the position with cheques and bills of exchange is that any signer to such document becomes liable on it. Thus with each indorsement yet another cheque- or bill-debtor is added. The debtors are liable on an equal footing which means that the holder of the document may claim payment from any of them. An indorsee who is left with the payment obligation may claim the amount (in recourse) from any of the indorsees ahead of him on the document.

In order that the holder may implement such recourse the cheque or bill must be protested. The rules on protest, contained in Part VII of the Cheques and Bills of Exchange Acts will only be briefly mentioned here.

Where the drawee bank refuses to honour a cheque, protest may be effected by the bank's dated declaration of dishonour on the cheque indicating also date of presentation for payment. Protest in respect of a bill of exchange may be for non-acceptance or for non-payment. Protest, which is subject to very short timelimits, must be made by a notary – i.e. the local judge (town and city courts judge). Upon un-availing request to the drawee to accept or pay the bill the notary may draw up the protest.

CHAPTER 16

Real estate – sale and mortgage

by Lars Lindencrone Petersen

1. Introduction

Real property consists primarily of a plot of land. Buildings and other fixtures built on the land by the property owner will automatically become integrated in the real property. If a building is constructed on leased land the landowner will of course not become owner of the building. Nevertheless, though it may seem somewhat artificial in ordinary linguistic parlance a building on a leased site is regarded as a "real property". An owner-occupied flat is also an independent real property.

The division of the land of the country into individual property holdings is based on a century-old system of title numbering. Each property consists of one or several "title numbers". The main axis of the title numbering is the Development Act. The title numbering system provides the basis for land registration including registration of rights over real property.

When a purchase of real property is contemplated a number of complicated issues may arise which are generally non-existing when a purchase of other assets is involved. The purchaser of real estate will e.g. almost always need to seek external financing in the form of loans from a mortgage credit institution.

Mortgage rights in real property are vital for the security provision in money loans. This will apply not only in connection with construction or conveyancing of real estate but also as regards operational financing of a business enterprise.

2. The registration system

2.1. Sources of law

The rules on registration are contained in the Registration of Property Act. Title I of the Act (ss. 1-42b) governs land registration and Title II (ss. 42c-49a) governs registration of chattels and property generally. The account in this Section will be limited to the rules on registration of rights in respect of real property whereas the rules on registration of chattels are treated in the next Chapter.

The Registration of Property Act, dating in its origin from 1926, has been amended several times over the years but the fundamental rules of the original Act have survived almost unchanged. In 1992 the technical rules of title I were adjusted in preparation for computerised registration. The process of computerisation which has been going on for several years is now largely completed.

2.2. The formal rules on registration

2.2.1. Registration authority

Land registration is within the scope of jurisdiction of the town and city courts. Each court has a registration department attached, comprising the properties situate in the district in question. Registration is made by the judge. The placing of registration authority with the courts implies that appeals against a registration decision lie to one of the High Courts – and only there.

2.2.2. Registration basis

Registration requires a document (under s. 9(1)) of the Registration of Property Act). A copy is to accompany the original document when lodged for registration.

The original document is not required to be made on a particular form, except for mortgage deeds which in accordance with s. 50f of the Registration of Property Act must be made out on the forms approved by the Minister of Justice. While no form is obligatory for the original document – other than mortgage deeds – the copy of a registered document must be made on the copy paper approved by the Ministry of Justice.

Both document and the copy must state, at the top of the first page, the title number of the property or its page in the Registry and the applicant's name and place of residence. The lodger of a registration application is commonly a lawyer but others, e.g. a financial institution, are also entitled to act as applicants.

A mortgage deed must be accompanied by the latest registered deed of conveyance ("title deed") of the property. This rule aims at reducing the risk of false mortgage deeds.

As regards title deeds and mortgage deeds the signature of the issuer must be confirmed by a lawyer or two other attesting witnesses. The witnesses' occupation and residence must be stated and they must attest the authenticity of the signature, the accuracy of the date and the capacity of the issuer.

To qualify for registration under its terms a private document must under s. 10(1) of the Registration of Property Act purport to "determine, create or cancel a right over real property". In summary form s. 10(1) goes to establish that only rights over real property are eligible for registration. Thus a deed containing only a personal obligation for the owner does not qualify. The most important examples of documents establishing rights over real property are deeds of conveyance and mortgage deeds.

To qualify for registration a document must (likewise in accordance with s. 10(1)) be lodged as issued by the person authorised under the Land Register to dispose of the property in question or as issued with his consent. A document concerning a property belonging to a company must be accompanied by evidence of the signer's power to sign for the company, e.g. in the form of an extract from the Companies Register.

2.2.3. The register and the files

The Land Register reserves a page for each property in the district – termed the property page. The property contains only summary information on the rights registered.

Fuller information is to be gained from *the files*, kept for each property and containing copies of the various documents registered on the property. This system is an appropriate way of combining the interests of quick reference and complete registration.

2.2.4. Registration process

A document for which registration is sought must be sent or delivered to the Court Registry of the district in which the property is situate. When the document has been received at the Court Registry it is said to be lodged for registration.

The first phase of the registration process consists in entering the document in the application book. The application book is kept for all business days of the Registry Office.

At the entering of the document into the application book a certain inquiry is made on the eligibility for registration of the document. Where evident defects appear in the document it will be rejected from entry in the application book. This would apply e.g. where a document lacks the issuer's signature, where a deed of conveyance or mortgage deed lacks signatures of attesting witnesses, or if a registration copy has not been attached.

Upon entering in the application book the judge's scrutiny of the document's eligibility will follow. This scrutiny is to be made as soon as possible and no later than 10 days after the lodging of the document.

Where a document satisfies the formal requirements and is fully conforming to the Register, it will be entered on the Register. Where the requirements are not met the result may be rejection of the document, or registration may be made with a timelimit for setting the defect right, or registration may be made with a cautionary clause.

Rejection will occur if the document suffers from a defect which is typically irreparable. Where a person in possession of a conditional deed of conveyance has issued a mortgage deed which fails to specify the conditional character of the issuer's title the mortgage deed will be rejected for registration. If the issuer finds the rejection unjustified the decision of the judge may be appealed to a high court.

Registration with a timelimit is applicable where the issuer of the document has failed to attach evidence of his power to dispose of the property, e.g. a power of attorney or an extract of the Companies Register. Since such defects are normally remediable the document will be entered in the Register with a statement of a timelimit. Failure to procure evidence before the expiry of the timelimit will cause the document to be deleted from the Register unless the judge agrees to extend the timelimit.

If a document does not state older encumbrances (primarily mortgage rights) which the document is to respect in accordance with the Register, registration will be made with a clause of caution to such effect. The clause will warn the recipient of the document, e.g. a purchaser or a mortgagee, of the existence of a mortgage right which does not appear from the document. Often the new right under the document is not really contrary to the older right on which caution has been given. An older mortgage deed may have been paid or reduced without such act being apparent from the register.

Some, though not all, registered documents are published in the Registration Gazette which is published as a section of the Official Gazette, Statstidende. Documents comprised by the rules of publication in the Registration Gazette are especially deeds of conveyance and mortgage deeds.

Under s. 25, 1st clause, of the Registration of Property Act a document is deemed to be registered when entered on the Register. However, partly in view of the timelag which may lie between the lodging of the document for registration and its ultimate registration, s. 25, 2nd clause, provides that the legal effects of registration, unless otherwise expressly provided, is to be computed from the day at which the document was lodged for registration. Provided that the document is not rejected from registration the registration will thus generally have retrospective effect as from the date of entering into the application book. Documents lodged for registration on the same day rank equally, cf. s. 25, 3rd clause. This will of course be different if one document expressly respects another.

The application book, the Register, and files are open to public inspection. The staff of the Registry Office are to assist the public in searching and at the same time to verify that no documents are removed nor amendments made to the registrations. Anyone may obtain extracts (photocopies) of the application book entries, the Register, and files against a fee.

When purchasing real property or advancing loans for real property a request for a Register certificate, i.e. an extract of the page of the property on the Register, is usually made. Where a loan against mortgage rights in real property is to be paid out before the mortgage deed has been finally registered the appropriate measure will be to ask for an extract from the application book as well. This may contain execution orders which have not yet been registered on the Register.

2.3. The legal effects of registration

A number of legal effects are attached to registration of real property. The most vital effects are stated in s. 1 and s. 27 of the Registration of Property Act. The rules in s. 1 and s. 27 relate to priority conflicts (the priority effect) and chain conflicts (validity effect).

A priority conflict is a conflict between two rights deriving from the owner of the property. Priority conflicts may be illustrated thus:

A is the owner of the property. B's right, which was created first, may be e.g. a mortgage right and C's right, which has been added later, may e.g. be an execution right. Such conflicts will be decided under s. 1 of the Registration of Property Act.

A chain conflict may be illustrated as follows:

A – B – C

A is the original owner of the property. B has acquired rights over the property but his rights are not validly created. The agreement between A and B may e.g. be void for fraud. C has acquired right over the property in reliance of B's formal title. The chain conflict between the original owner (A) and the bona fide assignee (C) is to be decided under the rule in s. 27 of the Registration of Property Act.

2.3.1. The Registration of Property Act s. 1

S. 1(1) of the Registration of Property Act which may be said to be the "platform" rule of the registration system provides: "Rights over real property must be registered in order to confer validity onto agreements in respect of real property and to provide against legal proceedings regarding the same."

This rule establishes that the constitutive act for rights over real property is registration.

The rule in s. 1(1) does not imply that a right over real property in all respects will need registration to be valid. The requirement – like other requirements of constitutive acts – is only directed against "agreements in respect of the real property and against legal proceedings".

As long as a right has not been registered the holder is at risk of having his right defeated by a subsequent agreement or legal proceeding. However, an un-registered right will not be immediately defeated if legal proceedings are taken against the property or where a subsequent agreement – irreconcilable with the un-registered right – is concluded. The requirements, as stated in s. 1(2) of the Registration of Property Act, for a document or legal proceeding to be capable of defeating a un-registered right are that the agreement or legal proceeding itself is registered and that the assignee under the agreement was in good faith as regards the un-registered right.

Where legal proceedings are involved (execution or bankruptcy) registration will be the only requirement of defeating an earlier un-registered right, whereas for an assignee in contract (purchaser or mortgagee) the additional requirement of good faith as regards the un-registered right is imposed.

Normally bad faith comprises intention (knowledge) and any negligence, both gross and ordinary. For the purposes of s. 5, 1st clause, of the Registration of Property Act, good faith means that "the assignee had neither knowledge of the unregistered right nor was to blame for his ignorance by reason of gross negligence". That ordinary negligence is thus within the good-faith scope means that an assignee who had knowledge of the existence of the un-registered right will only be bound to make more detailed inquiry if he harbours reasonably justified suspicions of the existence of such right. Under s. 5, 2nd clause, good faith must be present at the time at which the agreement is lodged for registration. Thus the decisive element is that the assignee was in good faith when his right was entered in the application book. The fact that his good faith is perhaps converted into bad faith before entering in the Register is irrelevant.

The rule in s. 1 of the Registration of Property Act providing that registration of rights over real property must be registered to obtain transfer protection is subject to a number of exceptions stated in ss. 2-4.

Under s. 2 registration is not required for an assignment or other transfer of a registered mortgage deed. The issue of transfer protection on assignments of registered mortgage deeds is to be decided under the rules of the Bonds Act.

Rights of use established on time terms exceeding those usually made are valid against all the world without registration under s. 3 of the Registration of Property Act. This rule is primarily aimed at tenancy agreements. It is to be noted, however, that the protection granted to a tenant in statute law is also to be respected by all the world without registration.

Under s. 4 any taxes and duties payable for real property and fire insurance premiums will have priority against all the world (including older rights) without registration. A similar priority applies to contributions for the maintenance of roads and continued supply of water, light, heat, etc. of the property as well as arrangements for diversion of water or other substance. Under special statutory provisions payments for water consumption from public works and construction contributions for roads and sewers are usually secured against all the world without registration.

2.3.2. The Registration of Property Act s. 27

The drafting of the Registration of Property Act is as far as possible designed to protect bona fide assignees acting in reliance of the Register from suffering a financial loss thereby. The rules to this effect are mainly concentrated in the provisions of s. 27. The conflicts regulated by s. 27 may as mentioned above be illustrated thus:

A – B – C

S. 27, 1st clause, provides: "When a document has been registered and delivered or sent from the Registry Office the validity of such document cannot be challenged as against a bona fide assignee of rights over the property under registered agreement – or under assignment of a mortgage deed."

Even if the agreement between A and B is void for e.g. fraud, C's right over the property may still prevail (i.e. A's right will be defeated) provided that the requirements of s. 27, 1st clause have been satisfied.

B's (invalid) document must have been registered, delivered, or sent from the Registry Office. C's document is to be registered, i.e. entered in the application book or – where a mortgage deed – assigned to C. C must be an assignee in contract (purchaser/mortgagee) and he is required to have been in good faith. Where these conditions are all met A's right will be defeated as against C's.

The rule in s. 27 may only be relied on by an assignee in contract. A's right will not be defeated as against B's creditors. In the event of B's bankruptcy the bankrupt estate must therefore respect A's right even if the adjudication order is registered on the property.

The rule of A's right being defeated in favour of C is not always a foregone conclusion even if the requirements of s. 27, 1st clause are met. Where the validity of the document (i.e. B's document) is challenged for falsification, forgery, duress with violence or threatened application of violence, or the issuer's (A's) minority, s. 27, 2nd clause, will not allow the innocent assignee's (C's) right to prevail. Thus the defences ("objections") which may be lost under s. 27 are in the category of non-operative objections whereas operative objections will stand.

The rule in s. 27, 2nd clause, will prima facie imply that where an operative objection applies there is a gap in the principle of protecting the innocent party acting in reliance on the Register against loss. But the gap is filled with the provision in s. 31 whereby the innocent assignee who, in consequence of the rule in s. 27, 3rd clause, does not acquire right over the property is entitled to compensation from the Treasury. Under s. 34 the Treasury compensation is also available to a party who loses a right or does not obtain the right contemplated upon the information in the Register because of errors in the registration process. The aim of these compensation rules, which are not of an extent to threaten the Treasury unduly, is to strengthen the principle of the Register's reliability.

3. Conveyancing of real property

3.1. Sources of law

The conflicts which may arise on a conveyance (sale) of real property in relation to third parties – e.g. in the relationship between the purchaser and the vendor's creditors – are subject to the rules in the Registration of Property Act including in particular the rules i s. 1 and s. 27. As regards the inter partes relationship in a conveyance, no single statute exists but some individual elements are regulated in the Consumer Protection Act on real property conveyance.

The Sale of Goods Act, which governs all other sale, expressly excludes real property in its s. 1a(1). However, since the Sale of Goods Act rules to a wide extent reflect ordinary contract law principles, in the absence of special statutory regulation these principles are also to be applied to a conveyance of real property. Thus, the end result is that despite its express exclusion in s. 1a(1) the Sales of Goods Act will often be applied all the same when deciding conflicts concerning conveyances of real property.

The Consumer Protection Act on real property conveyance entitles, under Part 2 (ss. 6-13), the purchaser of a real property which is in the main contemplated as residence for the purchaser the right to withdraw from the contract within six (business) days from the purchase. This right of withdrawal is dependent on the purchaser's payment of 1 per cent of the purchase price to the vendor. The purchaser is not bound to pay such compensation if the agreement was made with a vendor who built the property with a view to selling it or whose main business trade is conveyancing. The Act also contains rules – in Part 3 (ss. 14-18) on withdrawal rights in agreements for purchasing or construction of entire buildings. Further, the Act on consumer agreements providing rights of use of real property on a timeshare basis contains consumer protective rules including a withdrawal right of 10 days.

3.2. Conclusion of the contract

Contracts for the sale of real property are subject to the ordinary rules governing conclusion and validity of contracts. On a line with the rules in other areas no form requirements are set up which implies that an oral contract of sale of real property, in principle at least, is binding.

However, such contracts will usually imply such complexity and mass of detail that the terms per force must be reduced to writing in the form of a contract note. To this may be added that the negotiations are also often prolonged and involve several phases. The contact between vendor and purchaser is almost always established via a real estate agent. On the basis of the estate agent's sales prospect and calculations a draft contract note is prepared. If the ensuing negotiations lead to an agreement on the terms of the sale a final contract note is drawn up which is signed by the parties. This process – with some variations – is so established in practice that it would seem virtually impossible to substantiate that a contract of sale had been made unless a contract note signed by the parties can be produced.

3.3. Real estate intermediary business

Professional intermediary business in real property for private use is regulated by the Act on Trade in Real Property. The Act which is one of many elements in the consumer protection legislation applies to commercial supply and sale of real property, intermediary business involving purchase and sale of real property and other commercial advice and assistance in relation to sale of real property. Authority to act as real estate intermediary is restricted to real estate agents, registered with the Commerce and Companies Agency, lawyers, financial institutions, mortgage credit institutions, and insurance companies. Among the conditions of registration as a real estate agent are certain requirements in relation to practical and theoretical training.

3.4. Deed of conveyance – conditional or unconditional (conclusive)

A contract for sale of real property may well be made from the outset in the form of a deed of conveyance. Most often, however, a contract note will be prepared which will subsequently form the basis of the deed of conveyance.

The deed is usually written by a lawyer (representing one of the parties). The fact that the documents are written in separate stages – first contract note, then deed of conveyance – may lead to the assumption that the contract note is only regarded as a "draft" for the deed but this is a misconception. The contract note contains the agreement between the parties and must therefore be closely adhered to when the deed is drafted. A term deviating from the contract note may only be introduced into the deed if the parties so agree. A party wishing to consult his lawyer will thus need to do so during the negotiations preceding the preparation of the contract note or make his obligation under the contract note dependent on lawyer's approval.

A deed of conveyance is defined under s. 6 of the Registration of Property Act as a document transferring the property in a specified real property. Deeds may be unconditional (conclusive) or conditional. The condition may relate to the purchaser's payment of the purchase price but could also relate to other things, e.g. the obtaining of a development licence.

A deed made conditional on payment of purchase price is in reality a sale with a reservation of title. The vendor holds security in the property and may claim repossession if the purchaser fails to pay the purchase price in accordance with the agreement. On the other hand, the purchaser may claim a conclusive deed of conveyance upon payment of the purchase price.

3.5. The obligations of the parties

Pursuant to the principle of contractual freedom the obligations and rights of the parties in a conveyance of real property are prima facie to be determined from the terms of the agreement between them (the contract note). Where the agreement is silent the non-mandatory rules of law applying to sale of real property will be applied.

These rules are not statutory but have been built up gradually in case law. Despite the express exemption of real property (in s. 1a(1)) of the Sale of Goods Act the rules of this Act may provide guidance to a ceratin extent.

3.5.1. The vendor's obligations

The vendor's obligation is primarily to procure title to the purchaser to the property and place it to the purchaser's actual disposal.

The property must correspond to the description in the agreement. Where this is not the case there will in principle be a defect. However, it may be extremely difficult in practice to decide whether a piece of real property suffers from a defect. Apart from serially-produced (new) single-family houses a piece of real property is a distinctly unique asset. The issue of defect must therefore be determined with reference to the age of the property, the price paid, and other concrete factors.

With a sale of real property the same rule applies as with sale of goods that the purchaser cannot set up defects which he has found or ought to have found by usual inspection, if he has either made such inspection or failed to make it despite a request from the vendor to do so. In support of this standard the contract note will often specify that "the property is sold as it is and as inspected by the purchaser".

In the case of a latent defect – i.e. a defect which is difficult or even impossible to detect – the purchaser may set up the defect. This applies, prima facie, even if the property is sold "as it is".

The purchaser must give notice within a reasonable time after he discovered or ought to have discovered the defect. However, a long period of time will often pass before a defect becomes so manifest that a purchaser ought to detect it.

The remedy for defects most often applied in real property sale is proportionate reduction of the price. If the vendor has failed to observe his duty to inform on the condition of the property, or if he has provided a special warranty (which fails to hold) the purchaser may be entitled to damages. Rescission of a contract of sale of real property is only rarely possible. For such remedy the defect must be very serious indeed, the vendor must have provided a massive warranty, or the purchaser must have stated to the vendor at the conclusion of the contract that he was buying the property for a certain purpose (which the defect makes it impossible to fulfil).

The Act on Consumer Protection in Conveyance of Real Property provides in Part 1 (ss. 1-5) – with its provisions on present condition report and information re change of ownership insurance – a possibility of eliminating the consequences of construction defects in the relationship between vendor and purchaser. These rules apply to agreements for sale of real property where the property is primarily used for residence for the purchaser. The rules state that a purchaser who has received a report on the physical state of the building (a report on current condition) and information on change of ownership insurance shall be barred from setting up construction defects as against the vendor. The condition report is to be signed by a construction expert, assigned by the Ministry of Economic Affairs, Business and Industry, and to be covered by a liability insurance, and the information on change of ownership insurance must contain an unequivocal offer to the purchaser of an insurance which for a period of at least 5 years, with a possibility of extension to at least 10 years, will cover defects in the physical condition of the building which were present at the date of takeover and of which there is no mention in the condition report on the property.

3.5.2. The purchaser's obligations

The purchaser is bound to pay the purchase price. This will usually involve several elements since the purchaser will only rarely be capable (or willing) to pay the entire purchase price in cash.

One element will almost always involve a fresh establishment of loans with a mortgage credit institution. Where there is a balance between on the one hand the loan granted and the deposit payable, and on the other hand the purchase price, such discrepancy will either be financed with a loan taken by the purchaser against mortgage security in the property, or become settled by the vendor's issuing of a mortgage deed equivalent to the balance.

4. Mortgage rights over real property

4.1. Function

Real property plays a vital part in practice as an object for security by way of mortgage in loan establishments. Un-mortgaged privately owned property is extremely rare to come by.

Most of the loans established against mortgage in real property are granted via mortgage credit institutions. The borrower issues a mortgage deed to the mortgage credit institution in question, which then issues bonds which the borrower may proceed to sell. Sometimes the mortgage credit institution may grant index-linked loans with bonds attached. The trade in bonds is governed by the price whose rate is fixed in the daily trading of securities at the Copenhagen Stock exchange.

Apart from the loans granted through mortgage credit institutions a considerable amount of banks' loans is also secured by mortgage in real property. The financing of a building project is often a co-operation between a bank and a mortgage credit institution whereby it is agreed, at the initial stage of the construction work, to make a building credit available against mortgage rights in the property which on completion of the work may be replaced by a fixed loan granted by a mortgage credit institution.

4.2. The relationship between mortgagor and mortgagee

The agreement between mortgagor and mortgagee is subject to the general rules on contract formation and validity. An oral agreement will thus be valid but since mortgage rights are to be registered with a view to validity towards the mortgagor's creditors and assignees in contract a mortgage deed will need to be made.

In accordance with the basic rule of contractual freedom the relationship between mortgagor and mortgagee is to be determined under the terms of the mortgage agreement. Where the agreement is silent the non-mandatory rules governing mortgage relationships are applicable. As regards mortgage deeds in real property the principle of contractual freedom is broken by the mandatory rules of s. 42a and s. 42b of the Registration of Property Act.

Mortgage documents comprise three types: Ordinary bonds, indemnity bonds and owner's mortgage deeds.

The most important examples of ordinary bonds secured by mortgage are mortgage deeds issued to mortgage credit institutions and vendor's mortgage deeds. Such mortgage deeds contain terms on payment of interest and instalments and redemption of the debt. The mortgage security comprises the claim including interest, default interest and costs in collection etc. Under the Bonds Act, s. 11(2), no. 3, a bond providing mortgage right in real property is a negotiable bond unless the words "not to order" or similar restriction has been added. Such a *restrictive clause* is contained in the mortgage deeds of mortgage credit institutions which – in contrast to the private mortgage deeds – are not traded.

An indemnity bond is a document whereby the mortgagor grants mortgage security of his current or future debt to the mortgagee. The security may cover all indebtedness but may also be limited to a specified claim, e.g. a recourse claim i relation to warranties or personal guarantees. To be eligible for registration an indemnity bond must contain a maximum amount for the debt. An indemnity bond may be applied in security for a debt arising progressively, e.g. a building credit, or a debt of varying amount, e.g. a cash credit. As regards arrangements with financial institutions an indemnity bond is thus immediately suitable as a mortgage document but in practice this type of deed has for several years lost ground to owner's mortgage deeds.

An owner's mortgage deed provides security for a definite amount and is comparable to an ordinary mortgage deed in several respects except that the mortgagor issues the mortgage deed to himself. Since it is impossible really to owe oneself something, the mortgage is a fiction as long as the mortgagor himself holds the deed. However, an owner's mortgage deed may be applied in a pledge and may thereby serve the same function as an indemnity bond to secure a debt of varying size.

Under s. 50(1) of the Registration of Property Act mortgage deeds lodged for registration must be made on forms approved by the Minister of Justice. This rule brings the terms of the mortgage deed forms to operate in the same way as non-mandatory statutory rules. Where no special clauses apply in the individual text of a mortgage deed the standard terms of the form will apply.

For mortgage deeds in real property several forms are available. The starting point is that all mortgage deeds must be made on Form A. For mortgage credit institutions there is an alternative Form B which they will use instead. Among the multitude of terms contained in Form A specific mention may be made of the provisions in clause 8 and clause 10.

Under clause 8 it is provided that the principal debt does not fall due on a change of ownership unless the mortgage deed provides otherwise. This rule is to the advantage of the mortgagor, especially considering that private mortgage deeds (owner's mortgage deeds) are usually issued at a discount. The property may be sold without such act creating access for the mortgagee to demand redemption of the mortgage debt. The individual text of the mortgage deed will, however, usually include a term to the effect that on a change of ownership an extraordinary instalment (change of ownership instalment) of e.g. 10 per cent of the remaining debt is payable.

Clause 10 contains a term to the effect that in the absence of contrary agreement, the mortgage deed will remain in the property in the event of a compulsory sale. This means that a compulsory sale of the property is not in itself a redemption- releasing factor and that a purchaser at the compulsory sale against payment of the amounts due may take over the mortgage debts even if such debts had become due for redemption before the compulsory sale on account of breach. The purpose of the compulsory-sale term in clause 10 is to encourage the obtaining of bids approaching the value of the property when sold on the ordinary property market.

Though owner's mortgage deeds are to made on Form A the terms in clauses 8 and 10 are of no practical importance where an owner's mortgage deed has been pledged. An owner's mortgage deed will always include an individual term allowing the mortgage deed to be called in at short notice (e.g. 14 days) or without notice.

The mortgagor is bound to pay the interest and instalments under the mortgage deed at the right time and place.

Under Form A, clause 1, mortgage deed payments, completely in accordance with the ordinary rule in s. 3 of the Bonds Act of the place of payment of money obligations, are to be made at the creditor's residence or at another place appointed by the creditor. Payments made through the post are thus, prima facie, not made at the right time even if the debtor sends the money before the expiry of the term of payment, if it does not reach the creditor until later. Exceptions are made in s. 42a(1) of the Registration of Property Act under which payments under a mortgage deed in real property are deemed to be made at the right time when such payment was handed in to (the Post office or) a financial institution for transmission to the place of payment within the time limit for payment applying under the deed. This rule, which is mandatory under s. 42a(3) to the benefit of the debtor, is repeated in Form A, clause 2. This does not imply, however, that payment has been made at the paying in of the amount to the Post Office. Payment has not been made until the amount has reached the creditor. Thus the risk of transmission is on the debtor who will have to re-pay if the money is lost on the way.

Under Form A, clause 2, which is largely corresponding to the rule on days of grace in s. 5(3) of the Bonds Act, all payments – with additional modification in respect of non-business days i.e. holidays, Saturdays and the constitutional celebration day – are made at the right time when made no later than 7 days after maturity, for settlement-date payments the date is no later than 7 days after first settlement date. However, a breach will not automatically imply that the creditor may demand redemption of the entire remaining debt. Under s. 42a(2), where interest or instalments under a mortgage deed in real property have not been paid at the right time, the creditor may only demand payment of the principal if the debtor fails to pay interest and instalments no later than 7 days after a demand in writing has been sent or made. The creditor's demand must be made after the last payment date and must state in express terms that demand for redemption of the principal may be made if interest and instalments are not paid within the timelimit stated. This term, which is mandatory under s. 42a(3) to the benefit of a debtor, is repeated in clause 9a of Form A.

Under s. 42b of the Registration of Property Act a creditor is barred, despite a contrary provision in the mortgage deed from demanding redemption as a result of 1) non-payment of taxes and duties or other payments due to other mortgagees, 2) execution being levied on the property, 3) possession being taken of the property, 4) a meeting being held following an application for compulsory sale, 5) the debtor's estate being administered in bankruptcy, or 6) the debtor's estate becoming administered by a trustee. In real terms this rule implies that default in payments under the mortgage deed and material deterioration of the mortgage are the only types of breach counting as lawful redemption factors for mortgage debt in real property.

4.3. The relationship between successively created mortgage rights

S. 1 of the Registration of Property Act provides that the constitutive act for mortgage rights in real property consists in registration. Priority conflicts between two mortgage rights created successively will therefore, prima facie, be settled according to the date of registration.

A mortgage deed may provide that the right of the mortgagee is to be postponed in favour of subsequently created mortgage rights. Such postponement clause may cause a mortgagee's right to become illusory in that priorities are created to such an extent that the value of the property no longer covers the mortgagee's claim. From the mortgagee's point of view a postponement should therefore be limited to such effect that he will not risk holding a less favourable priority position in the end than he had originally. From a security point of view no reserve need be held against a clause whereby the mortgage deed is to be postponed in favour of a subsequently created mortgage deed against a proviso that the net proceeds on the additional loan shall be applied towards reducing the mortgagee's claim. Nor is there a vital security bar to a clause purporting that the mortgage deed is to be postponed in favour of a mortgage-secured loan applied in the improvement of the property mortgaged.

4.4. Advancement right

Where priorities in an established order are changed by the redemption of a mortgage or its reduction by instalment payments the question will arise whether subsequent mortgage rights will advance correspondingly in priority or whether a gap will arise which the owner may use for further mortgaging. This question is treated in s. 40(1) of the Registration of Property Act which provides that the owner, despite contrary agreement with a subsequent mortgagee or others, is entitled to fill the vacant place – either forthwith or later – with a new mortgage right unless he has renounced such right at the termination or later. This provision which is mandatory to the extent that it is not possible to agree in advance that a mortgage right is to advance, establishes as a main principle that a mortgage right in real property will retain the priority at which it was placed at the outset.

The rule governing fixed priority rank is built on the premise that the terms upon which a loan secured by mortgage in real property may be taken depends on the priority position the borrower may offer the lender. The better priority, the better terms of currency and rate of interest. Thus the justification of the rule is that a mortgagee should not be allowed to obtain a better priority position than contemplated by him at the creation of the mortgage right without the mortgagor gaining the more favourable terms for his loan which this priority rank would allow him.

However, this consideration will not justify an absolute rule of fixed priority. To the extent that advancement may be predicted on the creation of a mortgage right, a right to such advancement may be a factor to be emphasized by the mortgagor to negotiate better terms for his loan. Consequently s. 40(3), 1st clause, of the Registration of Property Act provides that the parties may validly agree in a mortgage deed of lower ranking that the right under it is to advance to the extent a deed ranking above is reduced by payment of instalments or upon redemption of such higher-ranking deed at a date stated in advance. "Instalments" in s. 40(3) will only cover instalments whose date of maturity will appear from the mortgage deeds whereas extraordinary instalments, such as instalments on change of ownership, will be outside the agreement of advancement right.

With the important exceptions in s. 40(3) the main rule on fixed priority rank in s. 40(1) is limited to extraordinary redemption of a mortgage debt and payments of extraordinary instalments. A place becoming vacant in the priority rank in this way is termed an owner's mortgage.

To avoid too much uncertainty about the priorities s. 40(1) provides that advancement will be effected if the mortgagor who has redeemed a mortgage debt cancels the mortgage right without availing himself of the right to fill the vacant place with a new mortgage right, unless he demands a clause to such effect entered in the Register.

An owner's mortgage may be applied in further mortgaging. But an owner's mortgage cannot be made subject to creditor enforcement. Even if an owner's mortgage is available in the priority rank on a property an execution will take the most extreme place, i.e. after the very last mortgage deed registered. If the property is put up for compulsory sale, however, an owner's mortgage will accrue to the subsequent mortgagees.

4.5. The extent of the mortgage right

A mortgage right in real property comprises the plot of land which the property constitutes as a unity for title purposes. The mortgage right will also comprise anything integrated (or becoming integrated) into the property. At this point the limit of the scope of mortgage is fixed in the rule in s. 38 of the Registration of Property Act. When a building has been constructed, in full or in part, and when instalments of wiring, heating, household machines and similar equipment have been made at the owner's expense for use of the property, separate rights of the building's materials and the fixtures and fittings mentioned cannot be reserved, whether as property rights or otherwise.

The legal effects of objects being comprised by the rule in s. 38 is that separate rights cannot be reserved "whether as property rights or otherwise". Separate rights in respect of a s. 38-object will thus lapse whether the right is defined as a retention of title, a chattel mortgage, or property right in leasing relationships. S. 38 is applicable not only for the benefit of mortgagees in the property but may also be relied upon by execution creditors in the property and the owner's bankrupt estate.

A building constructed by the owner is always comprised by s. 38. The building concept of the section comprises residential houses and commercial buildings of any description. It is irrelevant that a building is more or less valuable or whether it is placed on the site on a loose construction but caravans, on-site (workplace) huts, and similar mobile constructions are not caught by s. 38.

Apart from the building proper, s. 38 will comprise "wiring, heating plant, household machines, etc. ... installed in the property ... for the use of the property". This signifies that objects integrated with the property are comprised. A random selection of objects for mentioning may include oil burners and other types of heating plant, fixed electrical installations and fittings, lifts and sinks, toilet bowls, and bath tubs. The word "household machines", aimed particularly at residential housing might have a wide construction. However, since the items must be "installed in the property" the rule is limited to "machines", brought into physical connection with the property or which at least are "stationary". S. 38 will comprise cooking stoves, exhaust hoods, refrigerators, dishwashers, washing machines, tumble driers, and freezers.

Trade equipment including stationary machines will not be caught by the rule in s. 38. This applies even if the equipment is constructionally integrated in the property. However, such equipment will be comprised by the rule in s. 37 of the Registration of Property Act. This rule which, in contrast to s. 38, does not cause a lapse of separate rights is discussed in the next Chapter.

CHAPTER 17

Security rights over chattels

by Lars Lindencrone Petersen

1. Introduction

Mortgage rights are the central credit security tool in contract and property law. A retention of title also functions as a security right but this tool is only applicable in connection with a change of ownership (purchase/sale). A further example is provided by leasing which creates, from a security point if view, the same effect as a retention of title.

Security rights over chattels may be created either by pledge or mortgage. The difference between the two is in the requirements for constitutive act. In a pledge the constitutive act will consist in deprival of power of disposal whereas the constitutive act for a mortgage right is registration.

As a starting point a pledge or mortgage right may only attach to a certain asset (or certain assets). Where a business is operated from premises owned by the business proprietor, however, it is possible to mortgage the working equipment and working plant. A similar rule for mortgage rights applies to a business run from hired premises. The equipment mortgage right is, however, to respect separate rights created in connection with the acquisition of business equipment.

2. Pledge

2.1. Concept

In a security by way of pledge the constitutive act is deprival of power of disposal. This reduces the application effectively to tangible (physical) objects.

A pledge is immediately available for chattels. And even if the idea may seem artificial a real property could theoretically be pledged as well. However, s. 1 of the Registration of Property Act provides that rights over real property are to be registered in order to obtain validity against agreements in respect of the property and against legal proceedings which in reality will imply that real property can only be subject to mortgage.

A claim, e.g. a seller's claim for the purchase price in a credit sale, is not a tangible asset and is therefore not eligible for pledging. The constitutive act for a mortgage right of claims is under s. 31 of the Bonds Act a notice of the mortgage to the debtor of the claim secured by mortgage, i.e. for a mortgage right of a seller's claim in a credit sale a notice of the mortgage to the buyer.

Some claims are made tangible by fiction. This applies to claims attached to negotiable instruments including in particular negotiable bonds. The fiction consists in rules to the effect that the right of a claim is attached to a document (proper) thus creating the possibility of pledge.

2.2. The relationship between pledgor and pledgee

A pledge is created by agreement between the pledgor and the pledgee. The agreement is subject to the general rules on contract formation and validity.

In accordance with the fundamental principle of contractual freedom the agreement determines the relationship between the parties. Where the agreement is silent, reference must be made to the gap-filling or non-mandatory rules regarding security. Unless otherwise agreed, the parties are e.g. deemed to have agreed that the pledgee may appropriate any fruits and benefits from the pledge held.

2.3. Constitutive act

The constitutive act in a pledge consists in deprival of power of disposal. On a line with other cases requiring a constitutive act to be performed such act is necessary to confer transfer protection, i.e. protection against the pledgor's creditors and subsequent bona fide assignees in contract. In the inter partes relationship, on the other hand, the pledgor will be bound from the conclusion of the contract.

The constitutive act may be executed by transferring possession of the object pledged to the pledgee. To obtain legal effect the deprival of power of disposal must be effective which means that the pledgor must be barred in actual fact and not just formally from using the object pledged. Where a car e.g. has been pledged the right of pledge is not protected against the pledgor's creditors if he is allowed to drive it occasionally even if he parks the car with the pledgee again immediately after use. Such deprival will not be "effective".

The decisive factor in the protection is not that a pledgee has possession of the object but the effective deprival of the pledgor's power of disposal. Thus a valid pledge may be created by keeping the object pledged under lock and key in a room to which only the pledgee will have access (and the key – hence such pledge is pledge is termed: pledge secured by key transfer).

The constitutive act with pledge of chattels may – on a line with the key-transfer consideration – be effected by transferring possession to a third party. The third party in question must be a person independent of the pledgor who has undertaken in agreement with the pledgee not to deliver the object pledged to the pledgor. To illustrate the "independence" point an employee (e.g. a department manager) of the pledgor's business will not qualify as a person capable of keeping the object on behalf of the pledgee.

2.4. Application

From a historical perspective pledge of chattels was the security basis used primarily when obtaining loans from pawnbrokers. Apart from the State Pawnbroking Agency (an authorised government lending institute) in Copenhagen, professional pawnbrokers used to be active in extending loans against pledges of chattels, e.g. jewellery and clothing. The need for loans of this category has for several years been extremely modest. Hence the State Pawnbroking Agency has been abolished and the pawnbroking business – in the traditional sense – has ceased to be among the living professions.

It goes without saying that the requirement of an effective deprival of power of disposal reduces the application of pledge in a commercial financing context. Thus, pledge of working plant is not even to be considered. However, pledge may be suited for security in goods or raw materials.

3. Mortgage

3.1. Sources of law

The rules regarding mortgage of chattels are contained in Title II of the Registration of Property Act under the headline "Registration in respect of chattels and property generally". This Title consists of Parts 6a (ss. 42a-b) and 7 (ss. 43-49a) under the headings of "Registration in the Car Registry" and "Registration in the Personal Registry", respectively. Both these Parts contain independent and separate rules on chattel mortgage, which will not exactly earn them a prize for clarity of lay-out. However, in legislation explanations can usually be traced for anything.

In Danish law on security rights in chattels it is a basic rule that only mortgage rights are required to be registered (and indeed capable of registration) following the rules to this effect in Part 7. The Car Registry Part introduced into the Act in 1992 and aimed at protecting car buyers against disappointments as a result of hidden debts represents an exception from this rule. Thus, this Part will require registration not only of mortgage but also of reservations of title and, prima facie, also of legal proceedings (s. 42d(1)). The Car Registry assets are defined as "motor vehicles, trailers and semi-trailers for cars, and caravans" (s. 42c). On the other hand, assets which are not comprised by this definition are expressly excluded from the rules on chattels in Part 4 (s. 43 and s. 47(1)).

Mortgage deeds conferring mortgage rights on chattels are, as will have emerged, always required to be registered. Whether a mortgage deed is comprised by the rules of Part 6 or Part 7 depends on whether the asset mortgaged fits the definition of the Car Registry entries or not. However, the rules on mortgage in the two Parts are so uniform that they may be described together (though with the burden of parallel statutory reference throughout).

3.2. The relationship between mortgagor and mortgagee

A mortgage right over chattels is created by agreement between the mortgagor and mortgagee. The agreement is subject to the general rules on contract formation and validity.

In accordance with the fundamental principle of contractual freedom the agreement will prima facie determine the relationship between the parties. Where the agreement is silent, reference must be made to the non-mandatory rules regarding security. As regards mortgage rights the principle of contractual freedom is on a few points broken by mandatory statutory rules (not to mention the rules of the Credit Contracts Act governing consumer credit relationships).

Under s. 42/47(2) of the Registration of Property Act the mandatory rule in s. 42a regarding maturity effect on default of payments under a mortgage deed in real property shall be applied to mortgage deeds on chattels as well. A mandatory rule of a somewhat different structure is contained in s. 21(1) of the Credit Contracts Act under which the creditor in a consumer sale is barred from obtaining mortgage of the goods sold in security of the buyer's performance of his obligations. This rule carries the drastic effect of invalidating the mortgage agreement.

Under s. 50f(1) of the Registration of Property Act mortgage deeds lodged for registration must be made on forms approved by the Minister of Justice. For mortgage deeds on chattels the form prescribed for such chattel – or car – shall be applied. By virtue of the application of forms contained in s. 50(1) the terms of these forms which are largely identical will operate in the same way as non-mandatory statutory rules. Unless otherwise stated in the individual text of a mortgage deed the standard terms of the forms shall apply.

The Chattel/Car Form differs in several respects from Form A, the general form for mortgage deeds in real property. As an example may be mentioned that clause 7e of the Form in contrast to clause 8 and clause 10 of Form A provides that a change of ownership both on a voluntary sale and on a forced sale will act as redemption-releasing factor in respect of the mortgage debt.

3.3. The registration process

The main emphasis in the Registration of Property Act is on the rules on real property. Compared to these rules the provisions on chattel mortgage are more or less of an appendix character.

Under s. 42e(1)/s. 43a(1) registration of chattels is made in the Car/Personal Registry which is kept for the whole country at the Court of Aarhus. The registration is computerized.

The mortgage deed is lodged with the Court Registry and entered in the application book on the same day. When the judge has established that the formal requirements for registration have been satisfied the document is entered in the Car Register/Personal register. This registration must under s. 42f(3), cf. s. 16(4)/s. 44(2) be made no later than 10 days after the lodging of the document for registration. A mortgage right on chattels is under s. 42g(1)/s. 46 deemed to be made when the mortgage deed has been entered in the Car/Personal Register and delivered or sent from the Court Registry but the legal effects of registration are computed from the date of lodging for registration, i.e. the date of entering in the application book.

With very few exceptions all land in Denmark is comprised by the registration system. This makes the rule in s. 1 of the Registration of Property Act whereby rights in respect of real property are to be registered practicable. In the nature of things a similar requirement is not possible for chattels and hence a general rule requiring registration of rights over chattels is unthinkable. From this follows that registration of mortgage rights over chattels does not afford – indeed cannot afford – any guarantee to the mortgagee that the mortgagor is entitled to grant a mortgage right over the object at all. Even the existence of the object or its imminent coming into existence is no certainty. However, as a consequence of the extension of the registration requirement to reservations of title and legal proceedings in addition to mortgage rights and the fact that chattels comprised by this system are registered in the Central Registry for Motor Vehicles, the Car Registry will at least for these two vital areas afford better security to a mortgagee than the Personal Register.

Attempts have been made to introduce a certain security against fictional mortgage deeds by the provisions governing the basis for registration of mortgage deeds. However, it must be emphasized that the registration judge does not inquire into the existence of the object described in the mortgage deed. If the object does not exist the mortgagee's right is a fiction and this is his own risk.

Registration of a chattel mortgage requires that the mortgagor's personal register number/VAT No, name and address are stated in the deed and the mortgagor's signature is to be certified in an attestation clause verifying the authenticity of the signature, the accuracy of the date and the capacity of the issuer. Where the mortgagor is a company a power to sign emerging from an extract of the Companies Register of reasonably current date must be attached.

The mortgage deed must contain an accurate enumeration and description of the object(s) mortgaged. The further requirements are to some extent dependent on the character of the mortgage. A car must be described with indication of frame number, make and registration number, if any, whereas for a mortgage right over a horse it will suffice to state the age, colour and sex of the horse. A mortgage deed over cattle must contain information on the number, breed and age. A fairly similar requirement applies to mortgage deeds granting rights over pigs, chickens, minks etc.

To avoid an accumulation in the Car/Personal Register of rights which no longer exist, s. 42g(2)/s. 47(3) contain a "clearance" rule whereby mortgage deeds over chattels are deleted after 10 years from the registration of the mortgage deed if an application of renewed registration has not been lodged within this period. The effect of deletion is that the mortgage right, where – exceptionally – it continues to exist will no longer enjoy protection against the mortgagor's creditors and bona fide assignees.

3.4. Identification

The fact that the registration requirements for describing the mortgage are satisfied does not imply that the object mortgaged will be identifiable on the basis of the text in the mortgage deed in due course. If it turns out that the object mortgaged can no longer be identified as a result of its mixture with similar objects or for other reasons the mortgage right will lapse. Thus, the decisive point is that the enforcing authority (i.e. the bailiff) may trace the object on the basis of the mortgage deed.

The requirement of identification is not only set up for mortgage rights over chattels. A seller's right of recovery in a sale with a retention of title clause is dependent on the identifiability of the subject-matter of sale. This requirement applies without exception as a condition for obtaining rights over a certain (or some certain) object(s).

3.5. Legal effects of registration

Under s. 42d(1)/s. 47(1) of the Registration of Property Act mortgage deeds over chattels must be registered to obtain validity against agreements made bona fide with the owner of the chattel mortgaged and against legal proceedings. Thus the constitutive act for mortgage of chattels is described as registration.

The effect of registration is – in the same way as other requirements for constitutive acts, e.g. the requirement for notice to the debtor on security rights in respect of ordinary claims (the Bonds Act s. 31) that the right hereby obtains protection against subsequent creditors and subsequent bona fide assignees. On the other hand, as already mentioned, the registration provides no guarantee of the existence of the object mortgaged, or for its capability of identification in due course.

Nor does the registration afford a security of the mortgagor's actual power to dispose of the object mortgaged. Thus a mortgagee will need to respect execution orders made before the lodging of the mortgage deed for registration and a retention of title in respect of the object is also overriding the mortgagee's interest. Thus, on registration, the mortgagee only obtains protection against creditor enforcement and subsequent assignees in contract whereas the registration will not cause rights created earlier to be defeated. Where a mortgage right in a Car Registry asset is involved, the right will, however, by virtue of the rule in s. 42d(1), be capable of extending the currency of an unregistered reservation of title or an unregistered execution.

3.6. The subject-matter of a registered mortgage right

A mortgage right over chattels can only be created in respect of a certain object (or some certain objects). Thus under s. 47b(1) of the Registration of Property Act chattel mortgage rights cannot be created over "collections of uniform objects or objects defined for a common use, which are described in general terms unless a contrary intention follows from other statutory provisions". This rule which is really a ban on mortgage rights on objects defined by description only ("concepts") means that no valid mortgage right can be created in a "stock" of commodities or generally in chattels described solely on their connection to a collection or similar grouping with a possibility of exhaustion/addition. An exception to the ban on "conceptual" mortgage is contained in the Registration of Property Act, s. 37 and s. 47b(2), governing equipment mortgage rights.

4. Equipment mortgage rights

4.1. Characteristics

Where a real property is designed, on a more permanent basis, with a view to a special business activity a registered mortgage deed on the property will comprise, under the Registration of Property Act s. 37, in the absence of contrary agreement, the appurtenant working equipment and working plant –

including machinery and technical plant of any description, and, for agricultural holdings, the appurtenant livestock, manure, crops and other produce insofar as they are not appropriated in the regular running of the holding in question. Thus the parties cannot validly agree that a mortgage deed in real property is to comprise objects which are not caught by s. 37, e.g. the stock of an industrial enterprise whereas it may be agreed in a mortgage deed that the mortgage right is not to comprise a certain (or some certain) machine(s), and that the mortgage is not to comprise the s. 37 equipment at all.

Where a business enterprise operates from hired premises the proprietor may, under s. 47b(2), 1st clause, mortgage the working equipment and working plant, including machines and technical plant of any description, and where agricultural holdings are concerned, the livestock, manure, crops and other produce of the property. However, under s. 47b(2), 2nd clause, the mortgage will present no bar to an appropriation of the objects mentioned in the course of the regular running of the holding.

In the description of the subject-matter of the mortgage right, s. 47b(2) corresponds completely to s. 37. At this point there is no doubt that the two provisions are to be construed in the same way. The difference is that s. 37 is concerned with enterprise operated from a property owned by the mortgagor whereas s. 47b(2) governs enterprise operated from premises hired by the mortgagor. Another – technical – difference is that the right under s. 37 will automatically be attached to a mortgagor's right over the property ("in the absence of contrary agreement") whereas a right under s. 47b(2) must be registered in the same way as a mortgage right over chattels.

4.2. Requirements of localisation

The equipment mortgage right under s. 37 can only be attached to a (mortgage) right over real property which on a more permanent basis has been designed for a special business activity. The requirement under s. 47b(2) is merely that the business is run from hired premises.

S. 37 will comprise not only real property in the usual sense. A building on a hired site (Registration of Property Act, s. 19) will be capable of entertaining the s. 37 mortgage right. The same applies to an owner-occupied flat. S. 47b(2) requires that the enterprise is to be run from hired premises but the tenancy is not required to comprise the entire property. Thus it will suffice that the business is run from a flat. To an enterprise without local connection to a hired property s. 47b(2) is not applicable.

In spite of its presence on the statute book since 1928, s. 37 has not been fully construed as to its meaning of "more permanent design for a special business activity" but a first requirement must be that the property is dominated or at least considerably marked by the business run by the owner.

Industrial and production properties of the usual description will satisfy this requirement without more. It is no requirement that the property is used exclusively for commercial purposes. S. 37 is e.g. applicable even if one or more residential tenancies are included in the property in addition to the business carried on by the owner. A contractor's or haulier's property, with an office, garage etc. will be within the scope of s. 37 even if the property includes a building designed for the owner's private residence. On the other hand, where the property is completely without commercial distinction, typically a single-family house or other dwelling-house, from which the owner runs his business such property will not qualify as a s. 37 property. The rule in s. 47b(2) does not set up similar requirements and must therefore be applicable to commercial enterprise, run from residential premises. However, the business is required to have its operational focus in the premises hired.

4.3. The extent and substance of the mortgage right in equipment

The mortgage right in equipment under s. 37 or s. 47b(2) comprises the working plant, or with a slightly different term the means of production of a business. The mortgage right does not comprise (nor can it be brought by agreement to comprise) raw materials, semi-manufactured goods, or products (commodity stock) and supplies of oil or other fuel. The same applies to objects used for demonstration purposes.

The mortgage right in equipment is not limited to chattels physically connected to the property (the premises). Mobile working plant will also be included. However, s. 37(3)/s. 47b(2), 3rd clause, provides that the rules on mortgage of equipment is not applicable to vehicles comprised by the Car Register system (s. 42c).

The mortgage right in equipment comprises the working fixtures and fittings and working plant. A machine which is sold will thereby be outside the scope of the mortgage and a new machine bought for the business will be included in the mortgage. Compared to mortgage on chattels the mortgage right in equipment has the benefit of being capable of replacements without changing the underlying contractual relationship and without registration measures but on the other hand it suffers the disadvantage that it may gradually be reduced.

4.4. The agricultural holding rule

For agricultural holdings the mortgage right in equipment comprises the appurtenant "livestock, manure, crops and other produce insofar as they are not appropriated in the regular running of the holding in question". For agricultural holdings the mortgage right will thus catch not only the means of production but also the produce of the holding. The justification of the special rule on agricultural holdings must be related to the traditional form of running farms characterized by the impossibility of making a clear-cut distinction between means of production and produce. However, buyers of produce from the holding will be outside the agricultural holding mortgage.

A necessary consequence of the produce mortgage right in agricultural holdings is that the mortgage right will have to cease when the production is appropriated under "the regular running of the holding." The more detailed contents of such description must depend on an individual assessment. However, there is no doubt that a product of sale, e.g. grain, will not be excluded from the mortgage just because it is ripe for selling. It is also required to have been sold.

4.5. Mortgage rights over equipment v. separate rights

The rules in s. 37 and s. 47b(2) are no bar to a separate financing on the basis of chattel security right. This is due to the fact that equipment security, whether in the form of a reservation of title, a leasing right, or mortgage will be bound to respect the separate security rights.

The separate right must exist at the moment the asset is included in the category of equipment in the business. Where the asset has been brought into the equipment mortgage as unencumbered a subsequent separate financing is not possible, unless the equipment mortgagee is willing to waive his mortgage right. Where a s. 37 mortgage right is involved in a property, even if encumbered only to a moderately massive extent, the creation of a separate right is usually not possible.

The fact that the mortgage right in equipment is to respect a separate right in an equipment asset does not imply that the asset in question is not comprised by this mortgage right. For the equipment right will catch the free value which the asset may still represent (apart from the separate encumbrance).

An asset acquired subject to retention of title will be included in the equipment mortgage from the outset at the value matching the deposit which may have been paid. Apart from deterioration of value as a result of wear and tear and obsolescence the equipment mortgage is improved at the rate of instalment payments and when the last contractual payment has been made, the asset will be included in the mortgage right in full. Assets charged with a chattel mortgage, with a free value, will also be included in the equipment on the same pattern.

5. Retention of title

Denmark has traditionally recognized a retention of title clause in relation to a buyer's creditors. Naturally such recognition is dependent on the validity, under the rules of the Credit Contracts Act, of the retention between the immediate parties, seller and buyer.

The retention of title system may be viewed as an exception to the ordinary principle that third party validity of an agreed security right is dependent on a constitutive act. The main premise is that the seller (in a credit sale) instead of completely renouncing his right to the asset may choose to make the buyer's final acquisition dependent on payment of the purchase price. Where absolute title to the object of sale has already been transferred to the credit buyer a valid agreement on retention of title cannot be made since security rights over the object in question for the benefit of the seller (or another creditor) in that case will require constitutive act (deprival of power of disposal/registration).

A retention of title must be expressly agreed between the parties. A unilateral reservation on the seller's part, e.g. on an invoice or bill accompanying the subject matter of sale, is not valid even if the buyer does not object to its inclusion. Nor will a custom or usage (in the parties' own relationship) suffice whereas a valid retention of title may well find support with reference to a framework agreement.

In accordance with the basic consideration of the reservation of title system, the fundamental validity requirement is that an agreement on retention of title was made before the seller's power to cancel the sale was definitively lost in relation to the buyer, i.e. before the delivery to the buyer of the subject matter on a credit basis (The Sale of Goods Act, s. 28(2). A subsequent agreement on security rights in the subject matter of sale for the purchase price (or other claims on the buyer) is subject to the rules on mortgage right and thereby to the requirement of constitutive act.

Likewise in accordance with the reservation of title right conceived as an exception to the general principle of security rights in chattels, a retention of title clause is only capable of securing the seller's claim under the contract of sale to the exclusion of claims deriving from other legal transactions. Thus, a contract of sale with a retention of title clause may not contain a total-indebtedness-clause.

A retention of title clause is only allowed to comprise the subject matter of sale and is not capable of extension to other objects owned by the buyer. This limitation is also in harmony whit the main view of reservations of title representing exceptions to the mortgage right rules: The seller's title never extended to objects other than the subject-matter of sale in the first place.

The attraction of a retention of title is, as will have emerged, that a constitutive act is not required. As regards motor vehicles this attraction has been removed, however. Apart from the usual validity conditions and limitations on power of disposal a retention of title clause in a Car Register asset is required to be registered under s. 42d(1) of the Registration of Property Act. Thus the retention of title will not represent a competitive alternative to mortgage in this area. However, for constructions comprised by the mortgage ban in s. 21(1) of the Credit Contracts Act a retention of title is the only security tool applicable.

6. Leasing

The leasing concept which has gained international recognition is not altogether unequivocal. The concept usually refers to an agreement for long-term hire of commercial chattels. In the international leasing terminology the leasing company/owner and the user/hirer are termed lessor and lessee, respectively.

Leasing differs from traditional hire in that the leasing company's property title to the asset leased is used in reality as security for a loan. The leasing company will buy the asset (e.g. a machine) required by an enterprise and subsequently rent it to the enterprise. The leasing charge (rental) is calculated so that the total (monthly) rentals upon deduction of the (expected) residual value of the machine at the end of the rental period corresponds to the purchase price plus interest. Consequently, a standard provision of the leasing contract will be to the effect that where the lessee gives notice to terminate the contract before the end of the leasing period he is to pay the difference between the total sum of the remaining rentals discounted on a retrospective basis up to termination and the value of the asset.

Thus leasing is in reality an alternative to purchasing subject to a seller's retention of title (or a purchase financed by loan and secured by granting a mortgage on the goods). In a choice between outright purchase and leasing, elements of both business economics, credit, and tax will need to be considered.

CHAPTER 18

Guarantee

by Lars Lindencrone Petersen

1. The concept of guarantee

A guarantee is a means of securing claims. The security consists in the guarantor's (surety's) undertaking that the debtor (the principal debtor) will perform his obligation towards the creditor. The obligation may be of any description but the dominating practical application of such security is for a money loan.

A common feature with all guarantee is that the guarantor's obligation will not materialize until the principal defaults on his obligation. A guarantee establishes, in other words, a joint debt relationship characterized by one debtor's (the principal debtor's) liability occurring in advance of the other debtor's (the guarantor's).

In the same way as in other joint debt relationships the creditor's security is that several debtors are liable for the debt but where it turns out, in due course, that the surety is (now) unable to pay the security has of course been illusory. Nothing prevents, however, that a guarantee is further strengthened by the surety's own placing of security for his guarantee commitment, and it is not an exceptional occurrence that a third party without undertaking a personal debt liability, i.e. without becoming a surety himself, agrees to place mortgage for the debtor's debt.

In the loan business of the banks, guarantees are applied to secure purely private loans or loans for the establishment of or take-over of minor business enterprises. For such purposes the guarantee will most often be provided by a family member. However, unless an enterprise is thoroughly consolidated a bank loan for a private company will almost invariably be dependent on a guarantee from the company owner(s). On the other hand, a guarantee is also applicable in a professional version, e.g. placed by a (guarantee) insurance company and a security- placing resembling guarantee – and given that name

– is also part of the commercial banks' and savings banks' range of products for their commercial clients.

A private guarantee is normally unilateral in the sense that the surety does not stipulate a consideration for his commitment (from the creditor or from the principal debtor). Where a guarantee insurance is involved a premium will of course be payable and payment will also be demanded by a bank in return for the placing of a guarantee.

In contrast to traditional guarantee by surety, a guarantee placed by banks or insurance companies is a vital element in international financing. Consequently the law on personal security by surety is principally of a national character whereas the law on professional guarantees is built on standards of international background.

2. Establishment

A guarantee relationship is established by a promise made by the guarantor to the creditor. A declaration to the debtor implying a promise to act as guarantor will not establish an obligation of guarantee in itself but may create an obligation to make a guarantee promise to the creditor. The creditor may also seek out a guarantor himself and the debtor may not even know that the payment of his debt is secured by guarantee.

A guarantee promise is subject to the general rules on promises and contracts in the Act on Guardianship and in the Contracts Act. Thus a minor is incapable of committing himself by a guarantee promise (The Guardianship Act, s. 1(2) or s. 6. Nor will a promise made by the minor's guardian bind the minor (The Guardianship Act, s. 27).

Like other promises a guarantee promise is binding on the promisor when it has been communicated to the promisee (s. 7 of the Contracts Act). Acceptance is only required for promises requiring consideration and a guarantee promise (for which no consideration is required) is therefore binding without acceptance.

Whether the guarantor may withdraw his promise on account of defects in its making must be evaluated under the general rules of vitiating factors in Part 3 of the Contracts Act. Where the principal debtor has e.g. induced the guarantor to make his promise by misrepresenting his financial status in his accounts the guarantor will not be bound if the creditor was in bad faith as regards the misrepresentation, whereas he will be bound if the creditor was acting bona fide (s. 30 of the Contracts Act).

3. Reality of the guarantee promise

Guarantee commitments are subject to the general rule of contractual freedom in Danish law. The starting point for an evaluation of a guarantor's commitment is therefore the guarantee promise and its construction. Where the promise is silent the reality of the guarantor's obligation must, on a line with other contractual relationships unregulated by mandatory statutory rules, be determined by reference to non-mandatory rules of law. The Danish statutory law on guarantee is sparse and therefore the rules are primarily to be sought in case law and legal tradition.

3.1. Validity of the principal obligation

The guarantee promise implies a warranty of the payment capability of the principal debtor but the guarantor does not warrant that the principal debtor is in fact obliged to pay. Therefore, a guarantor's liability will lapse towards a creditor where it turns out that the principal debtor's obligation does not exist. Exceptions to this rule will occur if the guarantor undertook the guarantee in the knowledge that the principal debtor was not bound which may occur e.g. on a guarantee for a bank loan to a minor.

3.2. The subject-matter of commitment

As a main rule, the claim for which the guarantee is provided will have been agreed. At least it must be considered reckless (and probably not fully valid in a consumer setting) if a guarantor provides a guarantee "for any claim which the creditor may have or acquire against the principal debtor". The guarantor sometimes limits his liability to an amount less than the debt, e.g. DKK 50,000 of a loan for DKK 100,000 or to a fraction of the claim, e.g. one half of a loan.

It is doubtful whether a guarantor will be liable for ordinary interest on the claim secured without agreement to such effect. As regards default interest and costs in abortive enforcement attempts with the principal debtor there is no doubt that the guarantor is not liable if his guarantee is of primary liability character whereas it is doubtful whether he will be liable for such claims in an ordinary guarantee.

3.3. Various types of guarantee

A common feature of all types of guarantee is that the obligation of the guarantor will not materialize until the debtor has defaulted in his obligations.

Where the guarantee involves the guarantor's liability as a principal debtor himself (i.e. where he has assumed primary liability) default on the part of the debtor will suffice for the creditor's access to claim the sum from the guarantor instead. In an ordinary guarantee a further requirement is that the debtor's inability to pay has been substantiated. Such inability may be shown e.g. if the creditor or another creditor has attempted enforcement of the claim by execution. Where the guarantee declaration does not state otherwise or a contrary intention cannot be inferred by construction, e.g. if the undertaking is for "prompt payment of the debt", the guarantee granted is "ordinary".

It may have been agreed that a guarantor is to be liable as a "surety in respect of loss" which means that he will be liable for the loss a creditor may suffer in his dealings with the principal debtor. In most respects a loss guarantee corresponds to an ordinary guarantee.

4. Termination

4.1. Termination in connection with the principal obligation

Where the principal obligation terminates by payment by the principal debtor the guarantee obligation terminates as well. The same applies if the principal obligation lapses by set-off, renunciation (waiver), or deposit. The guarantee obligation will also terminate if the principal debt lapses by time limitation, or statute barring on preclusive notice, even if the guarantee obligation was not barred on an independent view.

Where the creditor agrees on a partial waiver of his claim, e.g. in connection with a voluntary composition, the guarantor's obligation will terminate to the same extent. On the other hand, if the creditor's claim against the principal debtor lapses in part on a compulsory composition the guarantor's obligation will still stand in full – even if the creditor voted in favour of the compulsory composition (s. 191 of the Bankruptcy Act). The same applies if the principal debtor's obligation is reduced or lapses on a debt rescheduling (s. 226 of the Bankruptcy Act).

4.2. Independent termination of the guarantee obligation

A guarantor will of course be discharged from his obligation once he has paid the debt secured. But like other claims discharge may also be obtained on a set-off by the guarantor or if he deposits the amount due under the rules of the Deposit Act. A guarantor's obligation may cease by limitation, even if the principal debt is not time-barred itself which, for claims comprised by the Limitation Act, follows from s. 1(1), no. 3. A guarantor's obligation may also cease by statutory barring on preclusive notice.

Where the creditor without consent from the guarantor agrees to give time to the debtor the guarantor's obligation will cease unless it is substantiated that the guarantor's risk has not been increased thereby. On the other hand, the guarantor is not released if the creditor merely chooses not to attempt enforcement of the claim. Where the guarantee is for a bank loan and the debtor defaults on the payment, the guarantor is required to be given notice by registered letter of such default within 6 months after the date of maturity. Failure to observe this requirement will cause the bank to lose the claim as against the guarantor to the extent that his recourse claim against the debtor has been deteriorated by the failure (s. 41 of the Act on Commercial Banks and Savings Banks). This rule is not to be applied analogously to other guarantee relationships. In non-business guarantee relationships notification shall be made within three months after the time of maturity of the payment and failure to observe the timelimit will imply that the surety will only be liable for the amount which the secured claim would have represented if the debtor had made all payments in time up to three months before notification was given.

5. Right of recourse

A guarantor who has paid the claim secured may claim indemnity from the principal debtor. The claim is automatically transferred to the guarantor. Any security attached to the claim, e.g. mortgage or retention of title, will also be transferred to the guarantor. Exceptions to the rule on guarantor recourse will apply if the guarantor has promised to guarantee a claim which was not validly created or if the claim on the principal debtor has been reduced by a compulsory composition or a debt rescheduling.

6. Joint guarantors

Where several guarantors are liable the question as to their separate liability cannot be answered unequivocably. One guarantor may be liable with secondary liability, another may have assumed primary liability, one may be liable in respect of the whole debt while another has limited his liability to a definite amount or a fraction of the debt. The liability may joint and several, or on pro rata basis, and the guarantors may have committed themselves collectively or separately from eachother. To describe two of the many variations imaginable the terms "co-guarantee" and "secondary guarantee" may be used.

6.1. Co-guarantee

A co-guarantee will lie where several guarantors have been able to count on the liability of eachother. In the absence of contrary agreement, co-guarantors are liable on a joint and several basis (The Bonds Act, s. 61, cf. s. 2).

The guarantor who has paid off the debt will of course have a right of recourse against the principal debtor. If this claim is wholly or partly worthless, which will often be the case, the question remains how the loss is to be distributed among the guarantors. In the absence of express agreement on such distribution the loss is to be shared by the guarantors in equal proportion. If the guarantors have separately limited their obligation to a certain amount the starting point is that they are liable among themselves for the loss in proportion to the amounts to which they have limited their obligation separately.

6.2. Secondary guarantee

Secondary guarantee will lie where one guarantor (the secondary guarantor) warrants to the creditor that another guarantor (the principal guarantor) will perform his obligation.

The principal guarantor may be liable either on a primary liability basis or on ordinary (secondary) liability basis for the principal debtor's obligation and similarly the secondary guarantor may assume liability either on primary basis or secondary basis. Unless otherwise agreed, the secondary guarantor is liable as an ordinary guarantor for the principal guarantor's obligation.

In the same way as a guarantor who has paid the debt will have recourse against the principal debtor a secondary guarantor who has paid off the debt may claim indemnity from the principal guarantor.

CHAPTER 19

Business Collapse – liquidation or reconstruction

by Lars Lindencrone Petersen

1. Introduction

A business forgetting the importance of a continuous adjustment of its basic ideology and the targets aimed at may easily find itself on the road to becoming an "ailing" business. Management and organisational problems left unsolved may also sap the dynamics necessary in any enterprise and external factors such as suppliers' failure to deliver and losses on debtors may also cause a business to face a crisis.

In most cases where a business is no longer viable the activities may be closed down voluntarily and without loss to the creditors. Thus, where a company is involved, the Companies Act and the Private Companies Act regulate liquidation of solvent companies. But where the financial crisis of a business has reached a stage at which the debts can no longer be paid in full, the situation calls for a more drastic remedy. The most drastic remedy available is that of bankruptcy (winding up).

A bankruptcy may sometimes be averted by a compulsory composition, i.e. an arrangement whereby the debtor's debts are reduced. In contrast to bankruptcy such an arrangement will imply a re-organisation of the debtor's finances and may even provide for a mechanism of survival for his business.

Bankruptcy proceedings are brought at the local (town and city) court, for that purpose termed the "bankruptcy court". The compulsory composition scheme is also within such court's jurisdiction.

The rules on bankruptcy and compulsory composition are contained in the Bankruptcy Act. Apart from these rules the Act also governs suspension of payments and debt rescheduling.

To a fairly wide extent the Bankruptcy Act is a result of inter-Nordic cooperation. Within EU-context (excluding Denmark) a Regulation on

Bankruptcy became effective on 1 July 2002 containing in the main a number of rules of international private and procedural law character. A harmonisation of the substantive part of bankruptcy legislation is probably still quite low on the agenda. But the fundamental principle of equal (or "pari passu") satisfaction of the debtor's creditors is recognized internationally.

Bankruptcy is an expensive and econimically inappropriate way to close a business. It is only rarely possible to sell a bankrupt business in "one piece" or to arrange for survival of some of its divisions. Usually the assets need to be realised at very low prices, workplaces are lost, and the bankruptcy proceedings usually turn out only a modest dividend to the ordinary creditors. After the bankruptcy the debtor is still liable for the part of his debt that remained outstanding, cf. s. 156 of the Bankruptcy Act. Therefore bankruptcy is seen as a legal remedy which should only be applied when the possibilities of providing an arrangement of the debtors financial affairs have been attempted in vain.

A debt arrangement will almost always be dependent on composition, i.e. debt reduction. Where all creditors agree to waive part of their claims the scheme will be implemented as a voluntary composition. Where (only) a minority object to the scheme it may under certain conditions be possible to establish an arrangement as a compulsory composition.

The rules on suspension of payments in Part 2 of the Bankruptcy act – which are not reviewed in this account – are designed to support attempts to stave off bankruptcy in favour of a debt arrangement. The underlying idea is that the debtor, by notifying suspension of payments to the bankruptcy court may to some extent neutralize his creditors and thereby obtain the necessary peace to try out the possibilities of averting bankruptcy. The suspension of payments system is aimed primarily at voluntary debt arrangements but its structure is such that it allows it to be used as a preparation for compulsory composition negotiations immediately.

2. Date of notice

A prime function of the date of notice is to mark the basis for computation of invalidation notices but the date of notice is also a vital time factor in relation to other issues in bankruptcy, compulsory composition and debt rescheduling.

For the purposes of s. 1(1) of the Bankruptcy Act the date of notice is defined as 1) the date at which the bankruptcy court received notice of suspension of payments or a petition for composition negotiations or an application for debt rescheduling or bankruptcy, 2) the date of the debtor's death where the estate is administered under the rules on insolvent estates in the Administration of Estates Act, 3) the date upon which a resolution is taken to wind up a public limited liability company or a private (limited liability) company, provided that the bankruptcy court receive, within three months after such decision, a notice of the suspension of the company's payments or a petition for composition negotiations or a bankruptcy petition, or the earliest of the dates mentioned.

In practice a notice of suspension of payments and a petition for bankruptcy are by far the most important bases for the date of notice. A petition for bankruptcy may be presented by the debtor himself or by a creditor (s. 17(1)). A petition for debt rescheduling will only rarely be applied with the other date of notice bases since the debt rescheduling system is limited to (hopelessly indebted) debtors who are not in independent business.

The rule in s. 1(1), no. 2, will determine the date of notice in a deceased person's estate for which the probate court has ordered insolvency proceedings. The date of notice rule in s. 1, no. 3, is aimed at situations in which liquidation of a public limited liability company or private company has been started under the rules of liquidation of solvent companies and it turns out during the proceedings that the company is in fact insolvent.

If the basis for the date of notice lapses the immediate effect is that the date of notice lapses too. However, s. 1(2-5) contains rules whereby the original date of notice may be maintained. The technique of these rules is that the date may be maintained if a new date of notice basis is presented to the bankruptcy court within three weeks after its lapse.

3. Bankruptcy

3.1. Purpose and main principles

In a bankruptcy the debt relationships between a debtor and his creditors are settled collectively. The starting point is that the debtor's property is realized whereupon the proceeds are applied in satisfaction of the claims owed by the debtor at the moment of bankruptcy. Thus bankruptcy is an extremely draconian remedy and will only be applicable towards an insolvent debtor. As long as a debtor is solvent his creditors will have adequate security in the rules on execution. However, these rules are not always satisfactory if the debtor is incapable of paying his debts since they may sometimes bring about the effect that some claims are covered in full whereas others will remain unsatisfied in full or in part. The bankruptcy rules, in contrast, are built on a main principle of equal satisfaction of the debtor's creditors, the pari-passu principle. Thus the aim of bankruptcy is to apply the debtor's property in an equal satisfaction of the creditors who had claims on the debtor at the commencement of the bankruptcy (the bankruptcy creditors). To ensure proper execution of the pari-passu satisfaction it is necessary that the debtor is deprived of the power of disposal of his property at the commencement of the bankruptcy and that the creditors from such point in time are barred from execution upon the assets of the bankrupt estate.

To counteract the uncertainty of timing when an adjudication of an insolvent debtor may be expected and the risk that a debtor facing imminent bankruptcy may try to prefer some creditors over others or attempt to withhold assets from the bankruptcy proceedings, the Bankruptcy Act contains rules on avoidance of acts which provides the rules with a certain retrospective effect.

3.2. The bankruptcy requirements

3.2.1. Insolvency

The main condition for bankruptcy is that the debtor is insolvent. Under s. 17(2) a debtor is insolvent "when he is incapable of paying his debts as they fall due unless such inability may be deemed to be of temporary character only".

When judging whether the debtor's inability to pay may be deemed to be temporary only, it is submitted that emphasis must be placed not only on income which he may rely on for paying his debts but also on the state of his balance sheet. This will apply in particular where the debtor has assets which may easily be realized and which may be evaluated with a fairly high degree of certainty.

The couching of s. 17(2) indicates that a creditor who has petitioned bankruptcy must be able to show that the debtor is insolvent. Where proof of insolvency has been submitted, however, the burden is on the debtor to show upon a balance of probabilities that the inability to pay must be deemed to be temporary only.

Where the debtor admits insolvency the bankruptcy court will normally presume that his estimate is correct. Other circumstances which will bring a prima facie presumption of insolvency to operate include, under s. 18, that the debtor has suspended payment of his debts, or that no coverage has been obtainable from a debtor upon execution levied within the three months immediately preceding the bankruptcy petition. Incidentally, it will almost always be evident that a debtor against whom a bankruptcy petition has been presented is insolvent.

3.2.2. Bankruptcy on a creditor's petition

Only a third party who is a creditor may petition the debtor's bankruptcy. Thus a party who has contributed in a business as a shareholder or limited partner will be barred from provoking bankruptcy on that account.

It is no requirement that the creditor's claim has been established by judgment or other (execution) basis, cf. s. 478 of the Administration of Justice

Act, but sufficient proof of its existence must be put forward within the framework of the comparatively modest advancing of evidence allowed in the bankruptcy court. Where some presumptive evidence is advanced and the creditor has a particularly strong interest in provoking bankruptcy, a bankruptcy decree will, under the circumstances, be available subject to security placing on the lines of s. 28 of the Bankruptcy Act.

The claim is not required to have fallen due. Admittedly, it is normally impossible to set up a claim against a debtor before maturity but in a situation in which a provocation of bankruptcy is aimed at the requirement of maturity will not be well-founded. A creditor with a claim which has not yet fallen due will certainly share the interest of a creditor with a claim which has fallen due in having the debtor declared bankrupt while he still owns unencumbered assets .

Under s. 20(1), no. 1, a creditor cannot claim adjudication of the debtor if his claim is adequately secured on a mortgage on the debtor's property. The justification of this rule is that bankruptcy represents a remedy of such violent character towards the debtor that it must be a requirement that the creditor initiating the process has a genuine financial interest in applying the remedy. Under s. 20(2), other similar types of security rank equal with mortgage. This includes e.g. a retention of title. On the other hand, the fact that a claim is secured by ordinary guarantee or mortgage placed by a third party will be no bar to a creditor's petition for bankruptcy (s. 20(1), no. 2 and 3, and s. 20(2)).

3.2.3. Bankruptcy on debtor's petition

In order to petition bankruptcy a debtor must be of age and of sound mind. As regards insolvency and proof of such insolvency the same requirements apply in principle whether the petition is presented to the bankruptcy court by the debtor himself or by a creditor. However, in the nature of things, a debtor who presents a petition himself will admit to being insolvent.

3.3. Legal effects of bankruptcy

Upon pronouncement of the adjudication order the debtor will, under s. 29, lose the right to assign or abandon his property, to accept payments and other services rendered, to accept terminations, complaints, and similar declarations, to incur debts, or to dispose in any other way of his property. This firmly establishes the principle of the debtor's deprival of power of disposal.

The fact that the debtor upon pronouncement of the adjudication order is barred from disposing as regards the estate does not mean that this applies towards third parties as well. Only after the expiry of the day and night on which publication of the bankruptcy has been made in the official gazette, the Statstidende, will the debtor's deprival of power be effective as towards the whole world (s. 30(1), 1st clause)). Until this point in time, the deprival of his power to dispose is effective only against a party who knew or ought to have known of the bankruptcy (s. 30(1), 2nd clause)). This means that a third party who has made a contract with the debtor in the interval between the pronouncement of the order and its publication will prevail in his right as towards the estate if he acted bona fide as regards the pronouncement of the adjudication order. Thus the contract is treated as if made before the bankruptcy. The rule in s. 30 comprises not only dispositions whereby claims are created against the estate but also payments to the debtor. A party who has made a bona fide payment of his debt to the debtor before the publication of the order will thus be discharged as against the bankrupt estate.

Under s. 30(2) the provision in s. 30(1) will only apply where a contrary intention does not follow from the rules on securities and on registration at the Land Registry or other registration. A party who has paid bona fide as regards the publicized bankruptcy under a negotiable bond, cheque, or bill of exchange will be discharged if the debtor has the instrument in question in his possession. As regards real property the Registration of Property Act, s. 1, provides that the bankruptcy order must be registered in order to remove the debtor's access to dispose in benefit of a third party who was bona fide as regards the bankruptcy.

After the pronouncement of the bankruptcy order execution may not be levied on the property comprised by the bankruptcy (s. 31(1) of the Bankruptcy Act), cf. Section 3.1.

3.4. The assets in the bankrupt estate

3.4.1. The debtor's property at the moment of bankruptcy

At the outset, the assets of the bankrupt estate will comprise "any property owned by the debtor at the time of pronouncement of adjudication order"(s. 32). Conversely a provision in s. 82 sets forth that "property items belonging to third parties or property ineligible for inclusion in the estate for other reasons shall be delivered to the rightful owners".

An asset borrowed or hired by the debtor is thus to be delivered to its owner and the same applies to items the debtor may hold as a bailee for a third party. Where the debtor has bought an asset in a sale with retention of title the bankrupt estate must respect the seller's better right. Where the estate wishes to keep the asset in question it will thus have to pay the (remaining) purchase price.

3.4.2. Debtor's acquisitions during the bankruptcy

S. 32 provides that not only the property owned by the debtor at the moment of adjudication is to be included in the estate but also any property which may accrue to him during the bankruptcy proceedings. Thus, inheritance devolving upon the debtor during the bankruptcy proceedings may be demanded by the estate under s. 34.

An important exception to the rule of the debtor's (after)acquired property is stated in s. 33 whereby income from the debtor's own enterprise during the bankruptcy proceedings and any benefits in lieu thereof will not be comprised by the estate. The provision is mainly aimed at salaries/wages income.

3.4.3. Assets exempt from bankruptcy

It follows from s. 36 that some assets may be exempt from bankruptcy. Admittedly, the fact that a debtor is personally liable means that he is liable to the full extent of his personal property, but the legal system has acknowledged that exemptions may be made if the justification to do so is properly shown.

Settled assets – in particular inherited assets and gifts – cannot be made subject to creditor enforcement. The same applies under s. 116 of the Insurance Contracts Act to the debtor's rights under a life assurance policy. However, the bankrupt estate may demand, under s. 117 that disproportionately large premium payments shall be re-paid into the estate. When the company has paid the insurance sum to the insured the sum will be included in his property and thus in his bankrupt estate. On the death of the insured the insurance sum is paid directly to the party named as beneficiary in the policy (s. 102) and only where there is no beneficiary will the amount be paid into the deceased person's estate.

The Pensions Savings Act contains rules corresponding to the creditor rules on life insurance. This Act comprises capital and instalment pension at a financial institution.

Certain assets are exempt from creditor enforcement as a result of their personal character. This applies e.g. to the copyright of literary work and art work (The Copyright Act, s. 62). Where the copyright holder has disposed of his work by sale or conclusion of a publishing contract, however, the consideration may be made subject to creditor enforcement.

To ensure that the debtor retains the essential financial means of a subsistence level, the Administration of Justice Act provides in s. 509 that execution may not be levied in assets necessary to keep up a modest home and a modest living for the debtor and his household. The exemption right which is granted in s. 509 is a "necessity" exemption.

3.5. Invalidation

3.5.1. Application and function

When an act made before the bankruptcy is "invalidated" (avoided) the estate may disregard it when the satisfaction of the creditors makes such invalidation necessary. The rules on invalidation are set forth in the Bankruptcy Act, Part 8 (ss. 64-81).

The invalidation rules may be applied in bankruptcy, compulsory composition (s. 184) and debt rescheduling (s. 221). Under the Administration of Estates Act, s. 70(1), these rules are also applicable in connection with administration of insolvent estates. On the other hand they are not applicable on a voluntary debt arrangement whether the debtor has notified suspension of payments or not.

The rules governing invalidation comprise three groups of acts: Creditor preference, execution and impairing dispositions. However, it will not suffice that an act is impeachable by its very nature. A number of other requirements varying from rule to rule must also be satisfied. Most invalidation rules contain certain timelimits. These limits are computed on the basis of the date of notice.

In relation to persons connected to the debtor the invalidation timelits are particularly long. For the purposes of s. 2, no. 1, of the Bankruptcy Act connected persons are defined as spouses, relatives in ascending or descending lines, siblings, spouses of such persons, and other persons who have had a specially close relationship to another. A person and a company or two companies may also be so closely connected that their alliance will be caught by the definition in s. 2, nos. 2-4.

Where invalidation is dependent on an act's or execution's being made before the expiry of a certain time the condition under s. 73 of the Bankruptcy Act is deemed to be met when registration or another constitutive act has been made within such time. Where a mortgage right e.g. is claimed to be avoided it will be decisive whether the mortgage deed had been lodged for registration within the avoidance timelimit.

Traditionally, avoidance is contingent upon the debtor's being insolvent when the act was made and that the beneficiary was in good faith as regards the insolvency of the debtor (the subjective conditions of avoidance). However, most avoidance rules in the Danish Bankruptcy Act are objective, i.e. it will be no requirement that the debtor was insolvent. Avoidance in relation to connected persons is, however, where the extended timelimits apply, dependent on the debtor's being insolvent. These rules are drafted so that in order to escape invalidation the connected person is to prove that the debtor was solvent.

3.5.2. Invalidation of creditor preferences

A creditor preference is an act whereby the debtor has sought to procure to a single creditor, whose claim was to have been covered on an equal footing with the ordinary bankruptcy claims either full or partial satisfaction of, or security for, his claim. Thus a redemption of a loan which was not secured by a mortgage right on assets belonging to the debtor will be a creditor preference. Invalidation is particularly possible against creditor preferences falling under ss. 67, 70, or 74 provided that the preference satisfies the other requirements for invalidation named in the individual provisions as well.

S. 74 of the Bankruptcy Act comprises "dispositions which unduly prefer a creditor at the cost of the other creditors". The requirement of "undue" preference signals that the debtor may safely make the payments required in the average interests of the creditors. This includes i.a. payments of wages/salaries, rent, telephone bills, and similar claims necessary to keep the debtor's business running. Similarly, payments on a cash credit, secured in full or in part, will usually be excluded if the movements recorded have the character of ordinary business routine..

Even if an act is comprised by s. 74 it may be difficult to carry the invalidation through since the estate is required to be capable of showing that the debtor was insolvent when making the act and that the creditor preferred was in bad faith as regards the insolvency of the debtor.

As regards the delimitation of the impeachable dispositions s. 67 and s. 70 of the Bankruptcy Act are narrower than the rule on creditor preference in s. 74.

From a temporal point of view s. 67(1) and s. 70(1) are limited to dispositions made later than three months before the date of notice. These rules are objective which means that invalidation may be made even if the debtor was solvent. In relation to connected persons the timelimit of invalidation under s. 67(2) and s. 70(2) is extended to two years before the date of notice, cf. above Section 3.5.1.

For one thing, the rule in s. 67 may be applied where payments have been made with "unusual means of payment ... provided that such payment did not appear as ordinary under the circumstances". This includes in particular a payment in goods rather than in money. From the wording of the rule it follows, however, that it will not be any supply of goods instead of money payment which will attract invalidation. An important factor will be whether the creditor agreed to receive goods instead of money because he genuinely wanted the goods or whether he accepted this for lack of alternative. Further, s. 67 will catch payments "before the due date ... provided that such payments did not appear as ordinary under the circumstances". Before the "due date" must imply before maturity date which means that s. 67 is applicable to a payment made before the maturity date, unless such payment appears ordinary. Outside the scope of s. 67 are e.g. payments on a cash credit which is still used in the normal way. Finally, the provision in s. 67 is applicable to "payments in amounts which have substantially impaired the debtor's ability to pay his debts provided that such payment did not appear as ordinary under the circumstances".

S. 70 of the Bankruptcy Act comprise "mortgage and other security types which were not granted to the creditor at the establishment of the debt or had not been protected against legal process without undue delay after such establishment". Conversely a mortgage right in security for contemporaneously created debt cannot be invalidated. However, a mortgage right whose establishment coincides with the establishment of the debt may be invalidated under s. 70 if the right has not been secured against legal process "without undue delay after the establishment of the debt."

Under the rule in s. 72(1) "payment of debts made after the date of notice may be invalidated unless such debts were covered by the rules relating to priority of debts in bankruptcy or payment was necessary to avert losses". Invalidation under s. 72(1) which is temporally limited to dispositions made after the date of notice is dependent on the creditor's bad faith as regards the date of notice. However, the provision is drafted so that to avoid invalidation the creditor must show that he neither knew nor ought to have known that the date of notice had set in. Where a supervisor, appointed to the debtor during the period of suspension of payments, had approved the payment, invalidation is only possible if it is evident that the supervisor has exceeded his authority.

Both on a formal and practical level it represents an important limitation in the invalidation access that the provisions of s. 67, s. 70, and s. 72 are inapplicable towards acts comprised by the rules in Part 18a of the Securities Trading Act governing agreements on financial security placing and final settlement etc.

3.5.3. Invalidation of execution

The rule governing invalidation of execution is contained in s. 71 whose structure is completely parallel to ss. 67 and 70.

3.5.4. Invalidation of impairing dispositions

A debtor faced with an imminent bankruptcy may feel tempted to make sham transfers to keep part of his property from creditor enforcement. In such cases avoidance rules are not really necessary since a transfer which does not bind the debtor will not bind his creditors either. But where the debtor has reduced his property by a valid disposition such act can only be challenged by invalidation.

Gifts which have been effected later than six months before the date of notice may be invalidated under s. 64(1). This rule is objective. A similar rule applies to a disclaimer of inheritance which has devolved upon the debtor, cf. s. 65(1).

Gifts effected earlier but later than one year before the date of notice, and disclaimers of inheritance made earlier but later than two years before the date of notice may be avoided unless it is established that the debtor was solvent (cf. s. 64(2), 1st clause, and s. 65(2). These rules are not limited to connected persons. The corresponding rule in s. 64(2), 2nd clause, governing gifts effected later than two years before the date of notice is, however, limited to connected persons.

Where the debtor has paid remuneration in favour of a connected person later than six months before the date of notice in the form of wages or other remuneration for work which evidently exceeds what would be considered reasonable considering the work performed, the income of the business in question and the circumstances of the case, such payment may under s. 66(1) be invalidated to the extent of the excess amount. This rule is objective. Where the excessive wages have been paid earlier, but later than two years before the date of notice, invalidation may be effected unless the connected person can show that the payment was made while the debtor was still solvent.

Under s. 72(2) of the Bankruptcy Act, which temporally is limited to dispositions made after the date of notice, other dispositions – i.e dispositions not comprised by s. 72(1) – may be invalidated "unless such disposition was necessary to maintain the debtor's business, represents a reasonable safeguarding of the creditors' common interests or of meeting the necessities of daily life". This rule will comprise any disposition by the debtor which, as seen from the point of view of the bankrupt estate, it would have been better that he had not made. Whether a disposition subsequently, as viewed from the bankrupt estate, was necessary to maintain the debtor's business or a reasonable safeguarding of the creditors common interests is difficult to evaluate at the time when the disposition is made. To protect a third party, invalidation is therefore excluded towards a "party who justly believed that the disposition was necessary as stated". Where a supervisor has approved a disposition such disposition can only be avoided if the supervisor has "evidently exceeded his authority".

Apart from undue creditor preferences, s. 74 of the Bankruptcy Act comprises unduly impairing dispositions. That s. 74 is only applicable to "unduly" impairing dispositions must mean that a transaction in the normal course of business is not voidable even if the debtor suffers a loss in it. Only in cases of aggravated circumstances, e.g. where the contract partner has exploited the debtor's financial situation will s. 74 be applicable. Invalidation under s. 74 is contingent upon the bankrupt estate's capability to show that the debtor was insolvent when the disposition was made and that the contract partner was in bad faith as regards the insolvency of the debtor.

3.6. Priority of debts – the liabilities of the estate

As already mentioned, the aim of bankruptcy is to apply the debtor's assets in an equal satisfaction of the bankruptcy creditors. The equality principle is not completely realized, however, as some bankruptcy creditors are satisfied in priority to others. To this must be added that the claims which arise in connection with the bankruptcy and the proceedings in the bankrupt estate must necessarily be satisfied in priority of the bankruptcy creditors' claims. These claims are called preferential claims. The rules governing priority of debts, i.e. the order in which the claims against a bankrupt estate are satisfied are contained in Part 10 (ss. 93-99) of the Bankruptcy Act.

3.6.1. Preferential claims

The individual groups of preferential claims are enumerated in s. 93, nos. 1-3.

Under s. 93, no. 1, costs and expenses at the commencement of the bankruptcy shall be paid as preferential claims. This provision will include a creditor's costs in having the debtor declared bankrupt. Under s. 93, nos. 2 and 3, costs and expenses in the adminstration of the estate and debts incurred by the estate during proceedings will be included. S. 93, no. 3, will in particular comprise claims under agreements made by the trustee on the part of the estate.

3.6.2. Suspension of payments claims

S. 94, nos 1-3, of the Bankruptcy Act comprises claims arisen in an attempt to avert bankruptcy. This will include e.g. a fee to the lawyer or composition association who has assisted the debtor in the attempt to avert bankruptcy in favour of a voluntary debt arrangement or a compulsory composition.

Debts contracted at the time of the suspension of paymemnts are satisfied as ordinary claims in bankruptcy – usually simple claims (s. 97) although debt contracted after the date of notice with the consent of a supervisor appointed by the bankruptcy court will have a status as a preferential claim under s. 94.

3.6.3. Wage and salary privilege

The wage and salary privilege under s. 95(1), no. 1, comprises persons who have performed work in the debtor's service. The privilege will extend to anyone who has undertaken fully or partly to place his labour at the debtor's disposal by agreement. This includes salaried employees, assistants and other staff as well as employees employed temporarily. A person who has undertaken management functions only, which would apply in particular to a managing director in a limited liability company/private company will have no privilege as he is not employed in the debtor's service. Further exception from the privilege may be made by court order towards connected persons under certain conditions (s. 95(2).

> The privilege comprises, as a starting point with a certain amount of temporal limitations, cf. however s. 95(1), no. 5, claims for wages/salaries and other consideration for work performed (no. 1), claims for compensation as a result of discontinuation of the employment relationship (no. 2) and other compensation (no. 3). Cliams for holiday pay rank as preferential claims (no. 4) for which the only time barring is contained in the limitation rules of the Holiday Act.

Apart from their inclusion in the bankruptcy privilege wage and salary claims comprised by s. 95 are also secured by the Wage-Earners' Guarantee Fund.

3.6.4. Suppliers' privilege

Under s. 96 privilege status is conferred on a supplier who, within a timelimit of 12 months before the commencement of the bankruptcy, had supplied dutiable goods for resale for the duty part of the purchase price. The privilege comprises all so-called excise duties/taxes (i.e. to the exclsuion of VAT for which a special reimbursement system applies).

3.6.5. The ordinary creditors

All claims which are not comprised by the rules mentioned above are satisfied as ordinary claims (s. 97). The ordinary claims usually comprise by far the largest amount of the bankruptcy claims. When a bankrupt estate has provided e.g. 10 per cent dividend this means that the ordinary creditors have received 10 per cent of their claims whereas the privileged claims have been satisfied in full.

3.6.6. The deferred claims

Under s. 98 three types of claim shall be satisfied after the ordinary creditors have been paid. The deferred claims will be satisfied in the following order: 1) Claims for interest, accrued after adjudication on the claims stated in ss. 95-97, 2) claims for fines, penalties and payments of additional tax in consequence of wrongful or non-submission of tax return and similar claims of a penal nature against the debtor, and 3) claims under gratuitous promises. The order of priority given in s. 98 is of very little practical relevance since the deferred claims will only rarely be covered at all.

3.7. The legal position of mortgagees

A mortgagee whose claim is fully covered by the value of the mortgage will of course have no claim for dividend. If a mortgagee obtains part cover for his claim he will only be entitled under s. 46 of the Bankruptcy Act to dividend on the balance of such claim. Thus, where a claim for DKK 100,000 is secured by mortgage bringing in DKK 60,000 the creditor will have a claim for dividend of DKK 40,000.

The traditional distinction of mortgage rights is between mortgage rights which may be enforced independently of the bankruptcy (secured creditors' rights) and mortgage rights which must be satisfied upon realization by the bankrupt estate of the asset mortgaged. The rules of ss. 85-91 of the Bankruptcy Act limits the first-mentioned group of secured creditors to creditors who hold a "pledge or similar security right" (s. 91(1)) i.e a mortgage right in claims – both ordinary claims and negotiable bonds – and mortgage right in listed securities registered in the Danish Securities Centre.

Under the main rule in s. 85(1) a compulsory auction sale of the debtor's assets during the bankruptcy proceedings may only be made upon request by the estate or with its consent. Thus a mortgagee of real property and a mortgagee of chattels must resign themselves to awaiting the decision of the estate to realize the secured asset(s). The rationale behind these rules is that the bankrupt estate should have the best possibilities of maintaining the debtor's business with a view to a sale in its entirety or at least a more appropriate realization than a compulsory sale of the individual assets in the business.

3.8. The administration and conclusion of the bankrupt estate

Immediately upon pronouncement of the adjudication order the bankruptcy court will appoint one or more trustees. This appointment is, prima facie, definitive. Where it is deemed appropriate the bankruptcy court may appoint a creditors' committee and a separate meeting may also be called to elect such committee.

The trustee will be in charge of the realization of the assets of the estate and prepares a statement of the financial position of the estate. A creditors' committee's function is advisory and supervisory only and is therefore not to be compared with that of a company board of directors.

The bankruptcy court supervises the proceedings in the estate and may intervene, if necessary. The court may also settle any disputes which may arise in the estate.

When the debtor's property has been realized, dividend will be paid out under the rules of priority in bankruptcy and when dividends have been paid the proceedings are closed. Creditors whose claims were not covered in full will, under s. 156 of the Bankruptcy Act, retain their claims against the debtor for the remaining amount and therefore the debtor's financial position is not really cured in the bankruptcy process.

4. Compulsory composition

4.1. Voluntary composition or compulsory composition

A voluntary debt arrangement is an agreement between the debtor and his creditors whereby the debtor's finances are re-organised by a reduction of the debt (composition), a deferment of payment (moratorium), or liquidation. There are no special statutory rules on voluntary debt arrangements. The statutory basis for establishment of a voluntary debt arrangement must thus be sought in the general rules on contract formation.

A voluntary debt arrangement will only bind the creditors who have expressly or implicitly agreed to the scheme. A voluntary arrangement may well be made without the concurrence of all creditors. A creditor's acceptance of a proposed debt arrangement will, however, generally be contingent upon the acceptance of all the other ordinary creditors.

The most important characteristic of a compulsory composition is that the composition effect may be forced upon a minority of the debtor's creditors. Further compulsory composition allows the rules of invalidation to be applied. However, the most important advantage of a compulsory composition is that it is binding on creditors who have failed to react whereas a voluntary composition will only bind those creditors who approved the arrangement.

The compulsory composition rules also act to a ceratin extent as a model or incentive for voluntary debt arrangements.

4.2. The compulsory composition process

The first formal step in the compulsory composition process is the debtor's presentation to the bankruptcy court of a petition for composition negotiations to be opened. Prior to that, however, the substantial part of the composition basis must be provided in order that negotiations can be commenced. This result obtains from s. 166 which provides that the petition shall be accompanied by the composition proposal, declarations of approval from 40 per cent of the creditors in terms of number and in value, and the documentation which is to be produced by the fiduciary appointees. Thus a formal characteristic of the compulsory composition process is that its wheels will not be set in motion until the scheme contemplated is fully prepared. In other words, the crucial element of the composition proceedings is really in the preparation of the composition negotiations which is conducted during the period of notified suspension of payments.

The debtor attempts to set up a composition proposal and at the same time he must approach two persons to assist him as composition "fiduciary appointees" one of whom must be skilled in accounting s, and the other a professional expert of the debtor's line of business (s. 164). The fiduciary appointees are in particular to prepare a balance sheet and an account of the principal reasons for the debtor's petition for a compulsory composition and make a declaration as to whether in their opinion the proposal put forward is reasonable and recommendable/adequate (s. 165). Thereupon the proposal is – together with the documentation prepared by the fiduciary appointees – to be sent to the creditors with a request for their approval.

When the requisite basis is established a petition for commencement of composition negotiations may be submitted to the bankruptcy court. The commencement of negotiations is not automatic. The bankruptcy court will examine whether the requisite materials have been brought forward and may refuse to commence negotiations if there is no reasonable prospect that the composition will be approved, ratified and performed (s. 167 and s. 168). The bankruptcy court will publish the commencement of the composition negotiations in the official gazette, Statstidende (s. 169) .

For the approval of the compulsory composition s. 176 sets up a requirement of acceptance by a certain qualified majority of the creditors both according to number and in value. Under s. 176(1) approval is contingent upon acceptance by 60 per cent of the creditors participating in the vote. Apart from this majority requirement, which refers to the number of creditors participating in the vote, s. 176(2) sets up a further requirement that the creditors approving the composition shall represent a certain majority of the total amount conferring voting rights. The requirement is approval by the same percentage rate as the proposal is below 100. However, approval from 60 per cent of the total amounts entitled to vote will always be a requirement.

The last step in the compulsory composition negotiations is the bankruptcy court's ratification of the composition (s. 178). Ratification is not a foregone conclusion upon approval of the composition. The court must refuse ratification if the composition is fundamentally defective (s. 179) and may refuse ratification where defects of more or less serious nature occur in the composition (s. 180).

4.3. Types of compulsory composition

Under s. 157 compulsory composition may imply 1) a percentage reduction of the ordinary debts (ordinary compulsory composition), 2) a distribution of the debtor's property or part of it among his creditors against discharging the debtor for the part which remains uncovered (liquidation), and 3) postponement of payment (moratorium). The rule in s. 157 is exhaustive in that no other forms of compulsory composition than the three stated may be made but combinations are possible. In practice the main rule is that ordinary composition is combined with a moratorium. A proposal for an ordinary composition providing for 40 per cent may e.g. contain a provision to the effect that 10 per cent will be payable at the ratification of the composition and the rest to payable in instalments falling due at certain specified times or at certain intervals.

4.4. The claims in compulsory composition

The priority of debts in bankruptcy is quite complex with several classes of debts involved. The system is more simplified in compulsory composition under which the claims against the debtor are only divided into three groups: 1) the claims which are not comprised or affected by the composition (the non-affected claims), 2) the composition claims, and 3) the claims which lapse upon the composition (the eliminated claims). The justification for this simplification is that a dividend of at least 25 per cent must be available for the composition claims and therefore the need to distinguish between various degrees of priority does not exist.

4.4.1. The non-affected claims

The claims which are not affected by the composition cannot be grouped into one single category. Some are not affected because they were not created until after the commencement of composition negotiations whereas others are outside the composition e.g. by virtue of priority rights in bankruptcy.

The Bankruptcy Act s. 158(1) sets forth that composition comprises claims created before the commencement of the composition negotiations. This implies that debts incurred after this point in time are not affected by the composition.

Outside the scope of the composition, according to s. 158(2), no. 2, are claims which have priority to ordinary claims in the event of bankruptcy. This exception from the main rule that the composition comprises debts created before the commencement of composition negotiations is almost self-evident. It would hardly make sense if a debt which was to be fully met in bankruptcy were to be caught by the composition effect by force. The elements of the priority ranking in bankruptcy which s. 158(2), no. 2, incorporates into compulsory composition are the rules in ss. 94-96.

Under s. 158 (2), no. 3, debts contracted before the commencement of the composition negotiations with the consent of the two fiduciary appointees with a view to continuing the debtor's business shall be outside the scope of the composition. This rule aims at enabling the debtor to obtain the necessary credit in the preliminary stages of a compulsory composition but will have no efefct if the composition attaempt is abortive and results in bankruptcy. However, the Bankruptcy Act affords another possibility. If the debtor notifies suspension of payments he may contract debts with the consent of the supervisor which will be comprised by s. 94, no. 2. A debt comprised by this rule is not only exempted from the composition effect but will also be equipped with priority rights in the event that the composition attempt fails and ends in bankruptcy.

The Bankruptcy Act s. 158 (2), no. 4, allows that the composition may exclude claims below a certain minimum amount from the composition.

4.4.2. The composition claims

Under s. 158(1), the composition comprises debts contracted before the commencement of composition negotiations. As has already appeared, debts equipped with priority rights in bankruptcy will be outside the scope of the composition. This leaves the debts which in bankruptcy would rank among the ordinary claims (s. 97) to carry the composition effect. However, it is not absolutely correct to say that a debt which in bankruptcy would rank as an ordinary claim will always be affected by the composition. Debts contracted with the consent of the fiduciary appointees will escape the composition effect and there may also be a provision in the composition scheme granting full cover of small claims.

4.4.3. The eliminated claims

S. 159(1) describes the claims which will lapse in a compulsory composition context. The claims involved are all among the deferred claims in bankruptcy. The most important eliminated claims are claims for interest accrued on the claims comprised by the composition during the period after the commencement of composition negotiations. The interest lapse rule implies that interest may no longer be claimed in respect of the composition claims even after the ratification of the composition.

4.4.4. The pari passu principle

Like other types of insolvency proceeding the compulsory composition scheme is built on a fundamental principle of equal ("pari passu") satisfaction of the debtor's creditors. This principle is manifested in s. 160 under which the creditors "otherwise" i.e. with the modifications following from s. 158 and s. 159 – are to be treated equally unless they consent to a less favourable treatment. S. 160 contains the obvious reservation that a creditor may consent to a less favourable treatment. Such a clause for negative special treatment may be to the effect that the creditor consents to receiving a lower amount of dividend or that the dividend shall not be payable to him until after the ordinary composition period.

4.4.5. Minimum dividend

Under s. 161 the claims in compulsory composition cannot be reduced to less than 25 per cent of their amounts unless very special reasons warrant it or the creditors consent to further reduction.

4.4.6. The legal position of mortgagees

The rule on the legal position of mortgagees in compulsory composition is contained in s. 158(2), no. 1. Under the 1st clause of this rule it is provided that claims secured by mortgage shall be outside the scope of the composition to the extent of the mortgage. However, under the second clause mortgagees are bound by the composition in respect of the part of their personal claims against the debtor which may not be covered by such security in due course. It is almost self-evident that a debt which is fully secured by mortgage will be outside the scope of the composition. In respect of debts where the security is inadequate to cover the whole amount, s. 158(2), no. 1, provides what is in reality two rules – a dividend rule and a time rule. The dividend rule says in all simplicity that the part of a secured creditor's personal claim which is not covered by the security will be caught by the composition and the time rule implies that the mortgagee may put off seeking satisfaction on the mortgage.

4.5. Legal effects of the compulsory composition

The main legal effects of compulsory composition are set forth in s. 190. The rule in s. 191 regarding sureties and other co-debtors' position is closely linked to this rule.

Under s. 192, 1st clause, the composition will also bind creditors who have failed to react. Thus the composition will bind potentially unknown creditors. Under s. 190, 2nd clause, the composition attaches to any claim whether set up by the creditor or existing in the form of a recourse claim from a co-debtor, e.g. a surety. On the other hand, the composition does not affect a creditor's claim against sureties or other co-debtors who are liable jointly with the debtor.

5. Debt rescheduling

The rules on debt rescheduling contained in Title IV (ss. 197-237) in the Bankruptcy Act are aimed at hopelessly indebted debtors. For this category of debtors who have generally very little to offer their creditors the compulsory composition scheme (or a voluntary composition) usually holds little attraction.

While the rest of the Bankruptcy Act rules are focused on business enterprises the debt rescheduling scheme is drafted with a view to debtors who are not in independent business (any more). Another contrast to the insolvency forms regulated in the Bankruptcy Act (bankruptcy and compulsory composition) which presume a certain amount of unencumbered assets a debt rescheduling presupposes that the debtor does not possess unencumbered assets (any more).

The main condition for the bankruptcy court's access to make a debt rescheduling order (on the debtor's application) is that the debtor is incapable of meeting his debts and within the next few years will have no prospects of meeting such debts. A further requirement is that the debtor's income circumstances and other factors indicate that such order should be made. In that evaluation special regard is had to the debtor's interest in a debt rescheduling, the age of the debt, circumstances surrounding its creation, payments made so far, and the debtor's income during the rescheduling process.

An order for debt rescheduling may call for a total lapse or reduction of the debt. The access to an order for total lapse of the debt is especially aimed at debtors of senior citizen status. In connection with the reduction alternative the main rule in practice is that an agreement for instalment payments of the rescheduling dividend will be made.

Apart from senior citizens and debtors of similar income bracket an order for debt rescheduling will purport that the debtor's debt is reduced to a percentage payable over five years. The dividend percentage is to be determined on the basis of an estimate of the amount the debtor is capable of paying out of his expected income during the period of rescheduling while allowing him to keep up a modest living. The estimate will take account of the debtor's family commitments but also, where this is relevant, to the financial situation of a spouse. The higher the income of a spouse, the larger the share the debtor will have to pay out of his own income.

The procedural rules, with modifications for practical purposes, are similar to those governing compulsory composition and the effects of a debt rescheduling order are the same as the effect of such composition.

CHAPTER 20

The legal relationship between employers and employees

by Morten Wegener

1. The employment law and its sources

Employment law as a legal discipline contains the rules on socalled contracts of service, i.e. agreements on the performance of personal work by which one party – the employee (or "servant") places his labour at the disposal of another – the employer (or "master") in such a way that the latter has a regular power of instruction and control as towards the employee. The substance of the legal discipline may thus be characterised as the study of the rules governing the legal relationship between employers and employees. Although no exact definition of employees exists, they are often referred to – including sometimes in legislation – as "wage-earners".

The starting point for establishing the legal relationship between the parties is – as within other areas of the law of contract – the agreement made by the parties to the individual contract of service. Employment law is, however, characterised i.a. by the fact that to a large extent this starting point has only formal importance. For one thing, extensive legislation exists both in respect of the individual classes of contract of service (e.g. as regards salaried employees), and in respect of various important elements inherent in most contracts of service (e.g. as regards holiday, equal pay, and equal treatment). The legislation usually offers *mandatory protection* in that it cannot be contracted out of to the detriment of the employee. Secondly, principal parts of the legal relationship between the parties within the framework of this legislation are very often not based upon individual contracts between these parties, but rather upon socalled *collective agreements*, i.e. upon contracts between employers' and employees' associations for pay and working conditions of their members within certain fields – for instance and in particular – within certain trades. Although in principle nothing prevents the parties from making agreements which differ from the collective agreement governing the area, in practice, such individual agreements are almost never formed. In respect of the aforementioned central questions, the legal relationship is instead based on the provisions contained in the collective agreement to the effect that such agreement replaces any terms and conditions agreed to individually by the parties. The socalled *industrial relations law* generally deals with the legal relationship between the associations and the legal questions arising from the formation, the substance, and the enforcement of collective agreements.

The industrial relations law is touched upon briefly below in Section 2. Section 3 treats some typical principal issues in the legal relationship between the parties to the individual contract of service based on existing legislation and prevailing collective agreements. Section 4 gives a brief account of the different formalised cooperative relations within the individual places of work.

2. Industrial relations law

2.1. The legal basis

The principal constituents of industrial relations law *as provided by collective agreements* are *general trade agreements, principal agreements,* and *workplace agreements.*

General trade agreements are made between the individual employees' trade associations and the corresponding employers' associations. The collective agreements typically lay down rules on pay and working conditions within the different trades, on the settlement periods and on how disputes about the application and interpretation of the collective agreements are to be resolved. In respect of the latter, the basis is normally the "Code of practice for resolving industrial disputes" agreed between the central associations, cf. Section 2.2 (below) for further reference on this Code. If no adequate arrangement has been made between the parties to the agreement for the resolution of disputes, the rules of the Code will automatically apply, cf s. 22 of the Act on the Industrial Court (cf. immediately below).

The provisions contained in a given general trade agreement are only applicable, on employers' level, to employers organised in employers associations. If a non-organised employer and the union at issue so specifically agree, the agreement may, however, apply also to the relevant employer's enterprise (a so-called "adhesion agreement").

The *principal agreements* are made between the central labour market associations within the various occupational areas, e.g. the agreement made between the Danish Employers' Confederation and the Danish Federation of

Trade Unions in 1973 concerning the greater part of the private sector labour market (most recently amended in 1993). Such agreements lay down different principal and longer-term conditions in respect of the legal relationship between the labour market parties, e.g. as regards notice of termination, renewal of general trade agreements, the right to unionise, strikes, shop steward arrangements, and the fundamental right enjoyed by the employer to manage and distribute work.

Workplace agreements are ancillary to general trade agreements and principal agreements in respect of special pay and working conditions within the individual undertakings. Such agreements are normally formed between undertakings and the local trade union branch office.

> In the agreements, the employers in question promise to offer pay and working conditions to both unionised and non-unionised employees which at least meet the minimum requirements laid down in a given collective agreement. Although conditions inferior to such requirements may be validly agreed with the individual employee, cf. Section 1 (above), such agreement will, in principle, contravene the collective agreement with the union. Conversely, the union undertakes a duty on behalf of itself and its members, especially to refrain from instigating any disputes in respect of the area covered by the agreement during the settlement period ("no-strike agreement").

In addition to the above agreements, there is some *legislation* which must be considered to fall within the ambit of industrial relations law, including, first and foremost, rules to create an institutional framework for the resolution of various types of disputes between the labour market parties. The principal Act is Act No. 183 of 12 March 1997 on the *Industrial Court* and Consolidated Order No. 709 of 20 August 2002 on conciliation of labour disputes (the *"Official Conciliator Act").*

2.2. Resolution of disputes

2.2.1. The lawful means in industrial conflicts

In Denmark, there is a fundamental freedom to instigate industrial conflicts. This freedom is, however, subject to a number of important limitations, especially to the effect that no collective disputes may be instigated in the settlement period of a collective agreement, cf. the following Section. In addition, there are some restrictions as to the means of action which may be applied. Lawful means of action on the part of the employee include omission to perform the work (*strike*), resistance against taking up employment (*blockade*). The latter should not be confused with socalled "picketing" where access is e.g. denied to the workplace of the employer. Such action is not considered lawful means in industrial disputes. On the part of the employer, the lawful means of action include exclusion from work (*lockout*) and resistance against employing (*boycott*). It is thus seen that means of action which are liable to punishment and which e.g. consist of violent acts may not be applied. In practice, it is further assumed that a certain reasonable balance must exist between the means of action and the goal pursued, which is why it is generally considered to be unacceptable to take industrial action with the sole overall purpose of destroying the other party.

A single group of employees – public-sector employees who are governed by public servants legislation – do not enjoy the right to strike.

2.2.2. Legal disputes and conflicts of interest

Within industrial relations law, there is a fundamental – albeit not quite clear – distinction between legal disputes and conflicts of interest.

A *legal dispute* concerns issues in respect of contravention of prevailing collective agreements and disagreements in respect of construction of provisions contained in such agreements. A *conflict of interest*, on the other hand, concerns cases where an employees' association and an employer and/or an employers' association disagree on whether or on what conditions a collective agreement between the parties should be concluded or renewed. Disagreement between the parties as to the nature of the conflict will constitute a legal dispute.

The distinction is of importance to the resolution of the dispute/conflict, cf. the three sections below.

2.2.3. Resolution of conflicts under prevailing collective agreements

As mentioned above, a no-strike agreement exists in principle between the parties during the settlement period, i.e. they have a duty not to disturb the industrial peace by taking industrial action. It follows from this that the no-strike agreement does not prevent either party – the individual employee or the individual enterprise – from exercising his/its rights under the *individual* contract of employment. The employee may e.g. give notice to terminate his contract of employment or, where such termination is founded in the employer's breach of contract terminate it summarily. Similarly, the employer may, where operational needs justify such step, dismiss employees while observing existing terms of notice, or dismiss employees summarily where such dismissal is founded in the employee's breach of contract. Under general practice, exemptions also apply in respect of unionised employees from the no-strike agreement in connection with *strike work* (work affected by a lawful industrial dispute in a similar undertaking), as well as socalled *loyalty conflicts* (support of a lawful industrial dispute comprising employees with whom a certain close connection exists, which is deemed to justify trade solidarity).

Apart from the above exceptions, the principle underlying no-strike agreements implies a duty conferred upon the parties by virtue of the "Code of practice for resolving industrial disputes" mentioned in Section 2.1, to seek, in the first instance, the differences resolved – irrespective of the nature of such differences – through *negotiation*, first internally in the enterprise, and secondly, if such negotiations end in a deadlock, through *conciliation* with the participation of the associations involved. Where such conciliation does not resolve the matter either, the further procedure depends upon the nature of the disagreement. Where the dispute relates to the construction of an agreement which is not a principal agreement the dispute must be resolved by industrial arbitration upon the request of one of the parties. The arbitration tribunal is composed of an even number of representatives of both parties and of an umpire. If, on the other hand, the dispute concerns a violation of the collective agreement or the construction of a principal agreement, the dispute is referred to the *Industrial Court*, consisting of an even number of employers' representatives and employees' representatives, and chaired, normally, by a Supreme Court judge or High Court judge. Cases containing elements of both violation and construction of an agreement, which occur frequently in practice, are brought before the Industrial Court which then either makes a decision or refers the case to settlement by industrial arbitration.

It is thus seen that the disputes referred to which are settled by industrial arbitration or heard by the Industrial Court are in the nature of legal disputes. The Industrial Court is, however, further empowered to deal with certain types of conflicts of interest, e.g. in respect of the legality of official collective industrial action or any notice given in that connection, cf. s. 9 in the Industrial Court Act. Conflicts of interest may also be settled by industrial arbitration – for instance and in particular if the conflict falls outside the scope of an collective agreement – if the parties so agree.

Cases within the jurisdiction of the Industrial Court usually cannot be brought before the ordinary courts of law, cf. s. 11 of the Industrial Court Act. Incidentally, this Act lays down a number of provisions in respect of proceedings. The starting point is application of the rules contained in the Danish Administration of Justice Act on civil proceedings, cf. Chapter 4 above. An action is brought by and against the employers' or employees' association at issue; cases involving sole traders which are non-members of an employers' association are, however, brought by or against the undertaking. Where the issue relates to the question as to whether a strike launched is in contravention of a collective agreement, the respondent association will in practice in most cases admit to the wrongfulness already during a preliminary hearing so that the remaining issue before the court is the position it will adopt on liability for penalties, if any, cf. the following Section. Where no such admission is made, the Court may, however, make an interlocutory order on the contravention or non-contravention character of the action launched, referring the question of penalties for later settlement. The decisions of the Court are enforceable under the ordinary Danish rules contained in the Danish Administration of Justice Act on enforcement of judgments, and any settlements made are enforceable under the provisions contained in the same Act on court settlements. The same applies to awards by industrial arbitration tribunals and decisions made during conciliation and association meetings.

2.2.4. Sanctions against violation of collective agreements

In connection with violations of collective agreements, e.g. by strikes in contravention of the agreement, or by remuneration below agreed minimum rates, the Industrial Court has powers to impose upon the infringing party – i.e. the person or persons who have taken active part in the violation of the agreement – the payment of a socalled *penalty*. This is a financial sanction, fixed in consideration of all relevant facts pertaining to the case in question, including both the possible need to "punish" the infringing party and – conversely – any mitigating circumstances surrounding the violation, cf. s. 12 of the Industrial Court Act. The penalty is thus not necessarily connected to the loss inflicted by the violation. In respect of strikes in contravention of a collective agreement, the penalty is in general and as a starting point determined in respect of the individual participants on the basis of fixed rates per strike hour. The penalty is liable to increase if the strike continues after the employees' association has admitted to its wrongfulness during a preliminary hearing, cf. above. As regards lockout in contravention of an agreement, the penalty imposed is normally fixed at an amount at least equal to the loss of earnings incurred during the period, often, however, with the addition of a certain "punitive charge". The same applies to remuneration below an agreed rate. If an association bound by a collective agreement has taken part in the violation, such association may incur separate liability for penalties.

The penalty is awarded to the aggrieved party to the collective agreement. This party will decide whether transmission of payment shall be made to injured members. Persons who are not parties to the collective agreement – e.g. non-unionised employees – cannot incur separate liability for penalties.

2.2.5. Resolution of conflicts in the absence of a collective agreement

The absence of a collective agreement may be caused by the expiration of an existing agreement without negotiations for renewal having been successful. Another reason may be that a collective agreement for the area in question or for the undertaking in question has never been made before so that there is no precedent for solving a topical disagreement as to whether such agreement should be made and the terms it should include. While the former instances normally involve associations on both sides and hence a large number of undertakings and employees, the latter typically concerns individual non-unionised undertakings and (groups of) employees within such undertakings. Notwithstanding the reason for a conflict of interest, the last resort in respect of means of resolving such conflicts is the instigating of industrial action, first and foremost strike or lockout.

Before this stage is reached, however, various rules must be observed. Thus, strikes are subject to *notice*, and copies of such notice must be forwarded to the *State Conciliation Board*, cf. s. 2(4) of the Official Conciliator Act. The Conciliation Board ("the official conciliator") may summon the contending parties for negotiations, recommend that concessions be granted, and finally require substance negotiations to be initiated. Under s. 3(3) of the Official Conciliator Act, notified industrial conflicts may be required to be deferred for a period of no more than two weeks for the purposes of continued conciliation. Where the strike is likely to affect vital social institutions or functions, or if it is otherwise deemed to have far-reaching social consequences, it may be subject to deferment for another two weeks, cf. s. 4(5) of the Act. If the official conciliator estimates that there is a possible solution to the problem which could be accepted by both parties, he is authorised to propose such solution (socalled "proposed settlement"). Such proposed settlement must then be put to the vote within the associations at issue. If the vote takes the form of a ballot, rejection on the part of the employees requires that a majority of the voters have voted against the proprosal. If less than 40 per cent of the employees entitled to vote participated in the voting a rejection will further require that at least 25 per cent of the number entitled to vote voted against the proposal. Especially in recent years interference from the legislative power has occurred if a negative result or a proposed settlement has been rejected and a labour dispute has materialised as a result.

The work of the Conciliation Board is naturally first and foremost of mere practical importance to the renewal instances referred to. In connection with conflicts concerning individual non-unionised undertakings, e.g. refusing to enter into agreement with one or more employees' associations, the conflict is, in practice, more likely to reach the stage of actual industrial action.

3. The legal position in the individual contract of employment

3.1. Introduction

As mentioned in Section 1, the legal relationship between the employer and the individual employee is determined by the concrete contract of employment. The contract must be seen in the light of any mandatory legislation governing the area in question, and will further, to the extent that the legal position remains unclear, normally be subject to gap-filling partly by relevant rules in any non-mandatory legislation partly by terms of any collective agreements. In addition, customs of the trade in question, if any, may be considered. Since a contractual relationship is at issue, the courts may as a last gap-filling resort consider ordinary fundamental principles of the law of contract, particularly in connection with an assessment of whether breach is in evidence and as to the remedies to which such breach may entitle the injured party.

The statute law available is often of a general character which means that it will in principle comprise all or most types of employment relationships. This category comprises e.g. the law on access to part-time employment, cf. Act No. 815 of 26 September 2002, on fixed-term employment, cf. Act No. 370 of 28 May 2003 on holidays, cf. below Section 3.4.2 and on equal treatment and equal pay, cf. below Section 3.2. and 3.4.1.

The class of contract of employment which is by far the most important of those governed by special legislation of importance, e.g. to private undertakings, is the *salaried employment contract*, cf. the rules contained in Consolidation Act No. 691 of 20 August 2002 with subsequent amendments on the legal relationship between employers and salaried employees (the Salaried Employees Act). For the purposes of s. 1(1), salaried employees are defined as 1) persons who in full or in substantive part are engaged in *commercial or clerical work* or in *inventory control* similar thereto, 2) persons who in full or in substantive part are engaged in *technical* or *clinical aid work* not pertaining to trade and industry, and other assistants performing like work, and 3) persons whose work consist in full or in substantive part of *managing or supervising* on behalf of the employer the execution of the work of others. It is immaterial in respect of all three categories whether the enterprise is a private or public sector enterprise.

The Act also comprises fixed-term employment contracts – within the categories mentioned, cf. s. 1(4) and Act No. 370 of 28 May 2003 on fixed-term employement. For the purposes of the latter Act and under s. 1(4) such employment is defined as employment for which the time of termination of the labour relationship has been fixed upon objective criteria such as a definite date, performance of a certain task, or the occurrence of a certain event. Since successive re-engagements of the same employee may suggest mis-use on the part of the employer, s. 1(4) provides that renewals of the employment relatioship are only to be effected if the conditions in s. 5 of the Act on fixed –term employment are satisfied, i.e. the renewal must, as a starting point, be justified in objective circumstances, e.g. unforeseeable factors such as sickness, pregnancy and child birth.

Under s. 1(2), the Act shall only apply to cases where the employee in question is employed by the employer for an average of *more than 8 hours* per week, and where he is under a *contract of service*, making him *subject to the instruction of the employer*. It has been deemed in case law that this latter part shall not apply e.g. to employees in temping agencies (which are also outside the ambit of the Act on fixed-term employment) and this inapplicability also extends towards the agency itself.

3.2. Formation of the contract of employment

In general, an employer is free to employ any person whom he finds suitable for any vacancies. Thus, he will be capable of engaging both unionised and non-unionised employees. This freedom may, however, be curtailed by the so-called *closed shop clauses* in collective agreements, i.e. provisions laying down that the employer may only or mainly employ members of certain employees' associations, cf. Section 3.5.2 for further reference in this respect. In addition, Consolidating Act No. 711 of 20 August 2002 on equal treatment of men and women in respect of employment and maternity leave, etc. (the Equal Treatment Act) lays down various fundamental limitations of the freedom. The general equal treatment concept is laid down in s. 1(1) of the Act. No discrimination on the grounds of sex must be made and this applies both to direct discrimination and to indirect discrimination in particualr with reference to pregnancy or marital or family status. Thus men and women are to be treated alike by the employer in connection with appointment, transfer, and promotion, and working conditions in undertakings employing persons of both sexes must be uniform. Nor is it lawful to specifically state when advertising for labour that persons of a specific sex are required or preferred, cf. ss. 2, 4, and 6 of the Act in this respect.

The Prohibition of Labour Market Discrimination Act No. 459 of 12 June 1996 (the Non-Discrimination Act) provides other – quite far-reaching – limitations. Under s. 1 of this Act, discrimination shall be taken to mean any direct or indirect discrimination on grounds of race, colour of skin, religion, political persuasion, sexual orientation or national, social, or ethnic origin. Prima facie, employers are prohibited from discriminating employees or applicants for vacancies in connection with appointment, dismissal, promotion, or in respect of pay or working conditions, and any indication in advertising that a person of a certain race, etc. is required or preferred for a certain position or vocational training programme is also prohibited, cf. ss. 2 and 5 of the Act. S. 4 of the Act further provides that employers shall not, in connection with the appointment of an employee or during the course of his/her employment request, collect or receive and make use of information in respect of the factors enumerated in s. 1.

At the appointment, the employee is under a duty, on his own initiative, to disclose any information on matters which he knows or ought to know will be of material importance to the employer, e.g. about serious illness. Any questions asked must, of course, be answered truthfully. Failure to observe these duties may provide justification for dismissal of the employee and for imposition of liability in damages towards the employer.

At the commencement of the employment, the employee must be on time and place his labour at the disposal of the employer. Conversely, the employer has a duty to receive the employee. If these obligations are not met, the other party may, depending on the circumstances, have a right to terminate the contract, and the party in breach may incur liability in damages, cf. Section 3.6 (below).

As a starting point, contracts of employment are not subject to *formal* requirements. Thus, an oral contract will be valid. However, from Consolidating Act No. 692 of 20 August 2002 on the duty of the employer to inform the wage-earner of the terms and conditions in the contract of employment, it follows that the employer undertakes a duty in all contracts of employment, except those concluded under the Seamen's Act, which have a duration of more than one month and an average working week of more than eight hours, to provide written particulars of the material terms of employment (the nature of the work, the working hours, pay, holidays, notice of termination, etc., cf. s. 2(2) of the Act. The particulars which may be of different description (letter or contract of employment, separate documents) must be communicated no later than one month after the commencement of the employment. In the event that the employer fails to perform this obligation, the employee may bring an action before the courts for compensation, whereas the validity of the contract remains unchallenged. Following a Supreme Court judgment of 1997 the starting point in respect of the amount of compensation is DKK 5,000 unless disagreement on the legal relationship has occurred or a concrete risk of such disagreement exists in which case the starting point is DKK 10,000. If a collective agreement imposes a duty upon the employer to provide information to an extent at least equal to the statutory requirement, the Act will not apply.

3.3. The duties of the employee

3.3.1. The principal duty

The principal duty of the employee is to *perform the agreed work* in accordance with the instructions of the employer. The employee must perform the work, exercising *reasonable care and skill*, setting an *ordinary pace*, and carrying out the task in the *agreed place*.

The instruction powers enjoyed by the employer are fundamentally connected with the right to manage and distribute work. In addition to the actual performance of the work, these powers comprise the right to instigate control measures, to lay down provisions in respect of workplace conditions, and to schedule the daily working hours and possible breaks, provided, of course, that no agreement to the contrary follows from the contract of employment. The powers vested are, however, subject to various general limitations. First, the employer is not empowered to order the employee to perform a task which involves a risk to his "life, honour or welfare". Further, he may not make unilateral variations of the contract of employment to such an extent that the basic assumptions of the establishment of such contract are thereby breached. Existing collective agreements often impose certain restrictions, especially in connection with working hours, on standard hours and on the time of day or night the work is to be performed. Finally, under the Working Environment Act (Consolidation Act No. 784 of 11 October 1999, as amended) a continuous daily period of rest of no less than 11 hours within each 24-hour period and one weekly day of rest shall be provided.

Non-compliance with the principal duty may, depending on the circumstances, justify summary dismissal and give rise to liability in damages, cf. Section 3.6.

3.3.2. Ancillary duties

In addition to the principal duty, a number of ancillary duties apply, among which, in general, the most important is the employee's duty of *fidelity* to the employer. One particularly important example of such duty applies under s. 10 of the Marketing Practices Act and relates to the duty of secrecy in respect of trade secrets, cf. above Chapter 12, Section 2.9 Non-compliance with this duty will almost always provide justification for summary dismissal and liability in damages.

In addition, socalled restraint of trade clauses may be established under the contract, prohibiting the employee from performing similar duties for a certain period of time upon the termination of the employment, see generally Chapter 7, Section 4.12 on s. 38 of the Contracts Act for further general reference in this respect. S. 18(1) of the Salaried Employees Act lays down that such clauses shall only be binding on salaried employees in positions of *trust* or who have entered an agreement with the employer on exploitation of an invention made by the employee. The validity of the commitment is dependent on compensation to the employee for the period of the duration of the commitment and it is also a requirement that the claim for compensation and its amount appear from a written contract. The compensation is to constitute at least 50 per cent of the salary at the time of leaving. The Act also limits the access to use socalled *client clauses* in relation to former employees, e.g. by inserting a ban against having business relations with the former employer's clients to a certain extent and during a specified period after the employee's leaving, see for more details s. 18a of the Salaried Employees Act.

3.4. The rights of the employee

3.4.1. Pay and other remuneration

The remuneration to which the employee is entitled as payment for work performed is normally fixed in the contract of employment. If no such (specific) agreement has been made, and if the employer is a party to a collective agreement, terms from such agreement will usually be implied to the effect that the contract of employment is deemed to be subject to the terms of such agreement. Incidentally, the employer will, in such cases, undertake a duty under the collective agreement to observe the rates of wages, etc. provided therein.

The part of the remuneration constituted by wages/salary may be fixed on various calculation bases. *Time wages* are calculated relative to the time spent, e.g. per hour, week or month. They may take the form of *standard wages* or *minimum wages*. The former is the rate of wages prevalent within the trade in question. As regards minimum wages, however, only a lower threshold exists which may then be supplemented, e.g. in consideration of the qualifications, seniority, etc. of the employee. Especially *performance related wages* contrast sharply with the latter in that such remuneration is proportional to certain performance results. Common examples include so-called *piecework wages*, granting to the employee e.g. a certain amount per unit produced. Furthermore, wages may take the form of *commission* where the remuneration is a certain percentage of the sales effected by the employee. In supplement of these forms of wages, certain kinds of allowances, e.g. *bonus* or *commission on profits*, granting a share of the undertaking's operating result to the employee may be provided. *Overtime work*, etc. is normally subject to separate (fixed) remuneration.

Cash payment of wages may be combined with *payment in kind*, e.g. in the form of certain comprehensive "perks" (free residence, free car, etc.). Consideration of this nature will, of course, constitute remuneration to which the employee has a lawful claim.

Remuneration is paid at a point in time agreed or specified in the collective agreement; time wages are generally payable in arrears for certain periods of time. The employer will normally be debarred from making *set-offs* against the pay claim, cf. Chapter 14 above. On the employer's *bankruptcy* pay claims shall enjoy a certain preferential status in the order of priority, cf. Chapter 19 above, and additional protection by the Wage-Earners' Guarantee Fund.

Special questions in respect of wages arise in the event that the employer wishes to make a differentiation of wages based upon the sex of the employee. Under s. 1 of the Consolidation Act No. 756 of 21 August 2003 on Equal Pay, (the Equal Pay Act) such differentiation is, in principle, prohibited whether it is direct or indirect. The latter will lie under s. 1(2) when a term, criterion, or practice which is apparently neutral has the effect of placing a considerably larger number of persons of one sex in a weaker position unless the term etc. is appropriate and necessary and may be justified in obejctive, non-sex related factors. Any employer engaging both men and women shall provide equal pay, including equal pay conditions for like work or for work rated as equal. In the latter context an overall evaluation is made in which relevant factors such as qualifications are considered, cf. s. 1(3) and (4).

Where the employer is in breach of his duty to remunerate, such breach will normally afford grounds for rescission of the contract of employment, cf. Section 3.6 (below).

3.4.2. Holiday

The principal provisions on holiday and holiday pay are found in Consolidation Act No. 396 on Holidays of 31 May 2000 with subsequent amendments. Prima facie the Act comprises all employees, defined as persons who receive consideration for personal work in an employment relationship, cf. s. 1 and on exceptions, s. 2. The employee may not renounce upon his right to holiday, holiday pay, holiday bonus, and holiday allowance under the Act and the provisions of the Act are not to be derogated from to the detriment of the employee, cf. s. 4(1). However, nothing prevents that an employee is given more extensive rights, e.g. and in particular by collective agreement, cf. subsection 2 of the provision.

Under s. 7(1) the employee earns a right of 2,08 days paid holiday for every month of employment in a calendar year (the socalled *accumulation year*) cf. on non-accumulation periods in subsections 2-4. However, under s. 8(1) the employee is entitled to 25 days' holiday a year notwithstanding whether a right to paid holidays has been accumulated under s. 7. Basically junior cleerks and students under a training contract are entitled, under the Vocational Training Act (Consolidation Act No 724 of 25 july 2000) to 25 days' paid holidays during the first and second full holiday year after the commencement of the employment relationship, cf. s. 9 of the Act.

Holiday must be taken in the year following the accumulation year, running from 1 May to 30 April (the socalled *holiday year*), cf. s. 12(1) of the Act, and so that the holiday is taken by five days a week, cf. subsection 2-3- of the provision. Under s. 15 the scheduling of the holiday lies with the employer, upon negotiation with the employee, with due consideration to the operation of the enterprise but also so that the employee's wishes are adhered to as far as possible. Notice of holiday scheduling must be given as soon as possible, and no later than three months or one month prior to the holiday, depending on whether it is the principal or residual holiday, respectively. The *principal holiday* has a duration normally of at least 15 consecutive days in the period between 1 May and 30 September (the socalled *holiday period*). The *residual holiday* may be taken outside this period, e.g. as individual rest days, if prompted by organisational needs. The principal holiday may not, however, be split up. Special limitations exist in respect of the employer's right to schedule the principal holiday for the period between notice of termination given by the employer and the actual termination of the employment, cf. further on scheduling of principal and residual holiday ss. 14-18 of the Act. Under s. 13(1) the holiday begins at the commencement of working hours on the first holiday and ends at the end of working hours on the last day. If the employee is sick when his holiday begins he is not under a duty to begin his holiday – nor will he be capable of starting it if, at the commencement of holiday, he is a participant in a strike or lockout, cf. s. 13(2-3).

In respect of employees engaged on a monthly basis or longer term basis and who are entitled to full non-Sunday holiday- and sickness pay, payment of the holiday generally takes the form of *paid holiday* and with a *holiday bonus* of 1 per cent of the wages earned in the accumulation year, cf. s. 23(1-4) Alternatively such employees may demand a *holiday allowance* of 12 per cent of wages earned in the accumulation year, cf. s. 23 (5), and on resigning employees subsection 6 of the same provision Employees who are not comprised by s. 23 will under s. 24 receive a holiday allowance of 12.5 per cent of the wages earned in the accumulation year. The employer is obliged to make continuous payments into a special scheme (the "Holiday Account") from which the remuneration will be paid to the employee when the holiday is taken, cf. ss. 24(1) and 28-29.

3.4.3. Lawful absence, etc.

The employee may, in certain circumstances, as a result of personal matters be permitted to omit to perform his duty, without such omission carrying – at least summarily – consequences for the existence of the contract of employment. In some cases, he may even preserve, in full or in part, his right of remuneration from the employer.

The most important example of such instances is the *sickness* of the employee. Under s. 5(1) of the Salaried Employees Act, sickness which causes incapacity for work, and which is not intentionally or by gross negligence contracted during the performance of the contract of service, or otherwise fraudulently withheld at the assumption of the position is considered "lawful absence". The salaried employee shall thus be entitled to claim his usual wages from the employer during his period of sickness. The employer may, however, demand medical documentation, and agreement may be made in connection with permanent illnesses to the effect that termination may be subject to shorter notice, cf. s. 5(2).

Several collective agreements contain provisions outside the scope of the Salaried Employees Act, laying down that lawfully noticed termination may not take place in cases of unprovoked sickness. Summary dismissal is, obviously, also prohibited. The question of payment during sickness will normally be settled under the rules contained in Consolidated Act No. 761 of 11 September 2002 as amended governing benefits in connection with sickness and confinement (the Benefits Act). Under this Act, the starting point is that the employee shall receive sickness benefits. In respect of private contracts of employment, benefits are to be paid by the employer for two weeks from the first full day of absence and otherwise by the local government authorities. In the event that the employer pays wages during sickness for a period extending beyond the statutory minimum, he shall be able to claim reimbursement from the local authorities of an amount equal to sickness benefits. Certain employment requirements shall apply, cf. ss. 3 and 4 of the Act. The sickness benefits paid are (considerably) lower than normal wages, cf. s. 9 of the Act in respect of calculation.

In connection with absence from work on grounds of *pregnancy and maternity leave*, the employee shall under ss. 11 et seq. of the Benefits Act be entitled to benefits from the local authorities. The main rule is that the mother is entitled to benefits for the first 14 weeks after giving birth and the father enjoys a similar right for two consecutive weeks in the same period. Subsequently the parents together have a right to benefits for 32 weeks until the child is 46 weeks old, cf. s. 13 (1-2). Special rules apply under the same provision (3-6) in cases where the parents choose to have their leave until the child is 54 weeks old, or postpone the benefit periods, or partial resumption of work is effected. S. 7 of the Salaried Employees Act accords to the mother a right to 50 per cent of the wages from the commencement of the maternity leave and up to 14 weeks after giving birth. If wages are paid by the employer in such period the employer may receive the benefits in full or partial reimbursement from the local authorities as was the case with the sickness benefits. The actual *right of absence* (not the extent of payments from the employer or out of public funds) is incidentally treated in ss. 7-10 of the Equal Treatment Act, cf. above Section 3.2. S. 7(1) specifically provides that any female wage-earner has a right of absence on grounds of pregnancy and maternity leave from the point in time where four weeks remain until the estimated date of birth. After the birth she is obliged to take two weeks' absence and thereupon she is entitled to a further 14 weeks of absence. The father is entitled to two weeks' absence after the birth or after reception of the child in the home or upon agreement with the employer within the first 14 weeks after the birth. Upon expiry of the 14th week each parent has a right to an absence from work for 32 weeks with a possibility of extension, if leave is taken and with a possibility of postponement of part of the right of absence, cf. s. 7(2-4). S. 9 prohibits dismissal of an employee on the grounds that the employee has demanded exploitation of the right of leave, that he/she was absent under the terms of s. 7, or on other grounds based on pregnancy and maternity. However both male and female employees are obliged to notify the employer under s. 10 (on time of birth and period of absence).

The possibilities of longer-term absence in connection with child care are contained in Act No. 402 of 31 May 2000, as amended, on child care leave. The scheme, which is administered by the Job Service, relates to the care of own children at the age of 0-8 years and it is a condition that the leave is taken with the child. It is also a condition that leave granted on such grounds debars, or limits, the possibilities of exploiting public day-care options, see ss. 2 and 3 of the Act, which also contain certain employment requirements. For employees in employment s. 4(1) allows a right of leave – i.e. a claim proper for freedom from work – during a consecutive period of a minimum of 8 and a maximum of 13 weeks or – if the child had not had its one-year birthday at the time of the commencement of the leave, a minimum of 8 and a maximum of 26 weeks. The Act contains rules on notification of the employer who may – to a certain extent – demand that the leave be postponed, s. 4(2-4) and s. 5. It is possible to place the leave in immediate extension of the maternity leave, cf. above. The access of leave may be applied once for every child within the first 9 years of the child, cf. s. 4(5).

In addition to the right of leave under s. 4, s. 7 allows an access to agree leave with the employer in consecutive periods of at least 8 weeks, but leave under the two provisions – which comprise both parents – may not exceed a total of 52 weeks, cf. s. 7(2) and s. 10. Normally the amount of leave benefit is 60 per cent of the maximum amount of unemployment benefit, cf. s. 12.

In the same way as s. 9 of the Equal Treatment Act, cf. above – s. 4(7) prohibits the dismissal of an employee on grounds of requests made by the employee for childcare leave, on grounds of the employee exercising his/her right to such leave, or on grounds that he/she has been absent as a result of such leave, cf. on the requirements as regards the leave benefits Consolidation Act No. 577 of 21 June 2001.

Finally, special rules apply under Consolidation Act No. 981 of 14 December 1993 on military service leave and leave for UN service, etc. in respect of right of absence from work caused by the performance of *military service* and *contractual UN service*, as well as in respect of the right, under certain circumstances, to return to work. S. 6 of the Salaried Employees Act lays down somewhat similar rules in respect of the conscription for military service of salaried employees. Finally, s. 16 of the same Act provides a freedom to *seek employment elsewhere* without loss of wages, after the salaried employee has received or given notice of termination of the contract of salaried employment.

3.5. Normal termination of the contract of employment

3.5.1. Introduction

By far the majority of contracts of employment are of indefinite period, i.e. the termination date is not to be fixed in advance on the basis of the contract. Contracts of employment may thus normally be terminated by either party without giving rise to liability, upon giving a certain – short or long – period of *notice*. Other contracts are agreed for a *fixed term* and thus terminate, e.g. after a certain specified period of time (a season, etc.) or for the performance of a specific task. Such contracts terminate per se upon expiration of the period of time or when the task has been performed. Whether such fixed-term contracts may be terminated by notice is a matter of construction, but often this is not the case.

"Normal" termination is, in this connection, taken to mean the termination of the contract of employment by lawful notice, or termination per se of fixed-term contracts. The opposite case arises, particularly where the contract is terminated (summarily), typically because either of the parties is in breach of the contract, cf. Section 3.6 (below).

3.5.2. The reason for termination

The starting point in respect of contracts subject to termination by notice is that either party may terminate the contract *freely* by giving notice within the period specified for the contract in question. In other words, no *reason* for the termination need be given. On the part of the employer, this starting point is, however, to a considerable extent of mere theoretical nature in that legislation or collective agreements either exclude certain reasons from being lawful, or in other ways seek to provide a certain kind of protection against the unfair or (otherwise) wrongful dismissal of the employee.

The first group includes the prohibitions contained in the Equal Treatment Act and in the leave of absence legislation, governing dismissal in conncection with pregnancy, maternity leave, childcare leave and conscription leave. In addition, s. 4 of the Equal Treatment Act prohibits any sexual discrimination in respect of dismissal, just as any such dismissal may not be founded on racial, etc. grounds, cf. the Prohibition of Labour Market Discrimination Act mentioned in Section 3.2 (above). In addition, ss. 1 and 2 of Consolidation Act No. 443 of 13 June 1990 on protection against dismissal on grounds of association matters debar, as a principal rule, any employer from making dismissals because an employee is a member of an association or a specific association, or because he is not a member of an association or a specific association. Further, health and safety representatives and employee board members enjoy a certain kind of protection against dismissal under provisions contained in the Working Environment Act and company legislation, cf. below. Apart from the statutory rules, various terms in collective agreements apply, e.g. in respect of prohibition of dismissal in connection with sickness and leave and as regards special protection of shop stewards.

Unfair or wrongful dismissal is further discouraged by imposing, in certain circumstances, requirements that written substantiation be submitted, cf. e.g. s. 4(3)(a) of the Principal Agreement in respect of written particulars of the reason for dismissal to employees who have been in the continuous employment of the undertaking in question for a period of at least nine months. In addition, certain negotiation rules may apply, or rules ordering the employer to provide compensatory relief to the person dismissed, cf. Section 3.5.4 below in respect of the latter.

3.5.3. The period of notice

The duration of the period of notice is specified in a few cases by legislation. The most important is s. 2 of the Salaried Employees Act, laying down that the notice period in respect of termination by the employer shall depend on the duration of the employment, to the effect, however, that statutory maximum notice shall be fixed at six months with discharge at the end of a month and statutory minimum at one month with discharge as above (for the first six months of employment). As for the salaried employee, the notice period is one month, regardless, normally, of the duration of employment. The parties may agree on a trial period of up to three months during which the employer has two weeks' notice and the salaried employee may summarily leave his position.

In cases beyond the scope of the statutory provisions in the Salaried Employees Act or other legislation, the period of notice must, in so far as no agreement on notice has been made under the contract, be "reasonable", taking into consideration the nature of the contract of employment and the duration of such employment. To the extent that a collective agreement applies to the area, rules in respect of notice will often exist therein. However, the variations between the individual collective agreements are considerable in this area.

3.5.4. Other forms of protection against dismissal

Only few statutory provisions are applicable as to the procedure for terminating employment. Examples include the rules on *collective dismissals*, cf. Act No. 414 of 1 June 1994 (as amended) on notice, etc. in connection with large-scale dismissals. The Act applies prima facie to contemplated dismissals for reasons which cannot be imputed to the employees, to the extent that the number of dismissals within a period of 30 days exceeds certain shares of the labour force, e.g. 10 per cent in undertakings which normally employ at least 100 and no more than 300 employeess. Any contemplated dismissals must first be negotiated with the employees, especially for the purposes of limiting or avoiding such dismissals. If they are still to be carried out, the employer must notify the labour market authorities and the employees. The dismissals can then take effect no sooner than 30 days upon such notification. The duration of the notice period shall rise to eight weeks in respect of dismissal of over half of the employees within workplaces normally employing at least 100 employees.

In respect of employment governed by collective agreements, s. 4(3) of the Principal Agreement lays down that dismissal shall not be carried out arbitrarily, cf. also Section 3.5.2 above. Complaints of unfair dismissal may be the subject of negotiations, and may in addition, to the extent that such negotiation ends in a deadlock, be considered in a special dismissal board appointed by one of the central labour market associations. The board may order the re-instatement of the person dismissed, or in the alternative award compensation of a maximum amount equal to 52 weeks' wages. In the event that dismissals are effected in connection with transfer of undertakings, such dismissals are deemed not to be founded on reasonable grounds, cf. s. 3 of Consoludated Act No. 710 of 20 August 2002 on the legal rights of employees in connection with transfers of undertakings.

If the rules of notice have not been observed at the termination of employment, damages may be claimed in respect of loss suffered, cf. Section 3.6.2 (below). In addition, a number of dismissal cases may give rise to awarding pecuniary relief to the employee as a way of "softening the blow". This applies i.a. under the rules in the Principal Agreement, but also in pursuance of s. 2b of the Salaried Employees Act. If, in the case of dismissal of a salaried employee who has reached the age of 18 and who has at least one year of continuous employment with the undertaking in question prior to the dismissal, no reasonable cause for the dismissal is provided by the personal matters of the salaried employee or by organisational needs, the employer shall by virtue of the aforementioned provision pay compensation to the salaried employee. The amount is fixed in consideration of the duration of employment as well as of the other facts of the case, but may not exceed the salary of the employee for a period equal to half of the notice to which he is entitled. In connection with long-term employment, the stated maximum may be raised to the effect that such compensation may, after 15 years of continuous employment, amount to six months' pay at the most. It is thus seen that the possibilities of pecuniary compensation are inferior to those provided by the Principal Agreement, cf. above.

Additional compensation rules are provided by ss. 14-16 of the Equal Treatment Act. In pursuance of s. 15, any employee may, if he is dismissed on grounds of demands of equal treatment, be awarded a compensation of up to 39 weeks wages. The amount of the award in the individual case is settled on the basis of seniority and the circumstances of the case. If the dismissal is effected in connection with maternity leave, etc., the upper limit is – on the same considerations as above – 78 weeks' wages, cf. s. 16. The awards granted in practice are generally considerable – corresponding to 6-9 months' pay. The burden of proving that the dismissal was not founded on the circumstances in question is on the employer. Under the somewhat problematic provision in s. 16a of the Act, a reversed burden of proof may also apply in other possible discrimination situations. Where it is shown on the facts of the case that it is indicated that a direct or indirect discriminatory treatment has occurred the other party, typically the employer, will need to prove that the equal treatment prinicple has not been violated.

Compensation rules prinicpally on a line with those of the Equal Treatment Act are now to be found in various acts e.g. in the Equal Pay Act s. 3(2-3) (above Section 3.4.1). The same applies for dismissals in contravention of the provisions of the Act on Child-care Leave, cf. s. 4(10) of this Act which limits, however, the compensation award to 26 weeks' pay. Dismissal in contravention of the Act of Collective Dismissals, cf. above, will release a duty on the part of the employer to pay a compensation corresponding to 30 days' pay (8 weeks if the dismissals affect nore than half of the employees in undertakings with a workforce exceeding 100 employees). Further, any infringement on the part of the employer of the Prohibition of Labour Market Discrimination Act, cf. Section 3.2 (above), will make him liable in damages, including in cases of dismissal, cf. on awards also Section 3.2 of the Act on substantiation of employment.

Finally, a marked social measure is introduced by s. 2 a of the Salaried Employees Act, providing for payment of lump sums by way of redundancy compensation to salaried employees dismissed after having been in the continuous employment of the same undertaking for 12, 15 or 18 years. The compensation, amounting to one, two or three months' pay, respectively, is not payable if the salaried employee starts receiving state pension. The same applies if the salaried employee upon termination of employment qualifies for retirement benefit from the employer and if he has been a paying member of the pension scheme in question before reaching the age of 50. However, early retirement benefit or voluntary early pension will not debar compensation under s. 2 a.

3.6. Summary termination. Damages

3.6.1. Summary termination

As in connection with other types of contract, the contract of employment may be subject to summary termination, if either party has committed a *serious breach* of the obligations under it. In practice, more far-reaching requirements are imposed in respect of the employer's access to rescind the contract (summary dismissal) than in respect of the employee's right to do so. Often rescission is dependent on a prior warning having been given which remains unheeded by the other party.

3.6.2. Damages

If the contract of employment is prematurely terminated (including in connection with too short notice of termination), the injured party may bring an action for damages in respect of any loss suffered. In some instances, the law contains certain statutory minima, cf. e.g. ss. 3 and 4 of the Salaried Employees Act, i.a. laying down that the employer's claim for damages, in cases of unlawful absence or quitting of service by the salaried employee, shall be equal to no less than half a month's pay. To this end, various collective agreements contain similar rules.

Claims for damages on the part of the employee may be set up in addition to the compensatory claims mentioned in the above Sections.

4. Different kinds of cooperative relations within the workplace

4.1. The shop steward arrangement

The shop steward arrangement is established, partly under the existing principal agreements, partly in the general trade agreements. For this purpose the employees in an undertaking or within departments of such undertaking elect a shop steward from their own group. In large undertakings with several shop stewards, these stewards may sometimes elect a senior shop steward. The elected person is normally subject to approval by the relevant trade union, and the employers' association must be notified of the election.

The task of the shop steward is to protect the interests of his colleagues towards the employer, e.g. in connection with local negotiations on any dispute or local negotiations of pay and working conditions. Further, the shop steward is to encourage good working relations within the workplace. In general, he must perform his ordinary duties in addition to the shop steward task.

The dismissal of a shop steward must normally be founded on compelling grounds and shop stewards thus enjoy a better protection against dismissal than their colleagues at the workplace. A "comppelling ground" will usually lie if the shop steward commits a serious breach of his contract of employment, e.g. by calling strikes in contravention of the collective agreement, or disregarding his duty of secrecy in a material way, cf. above Section 3.3.2. Usually dismissal is prohibited until the competent industrial authority has had access either to negotiate the dismissal with the employer or to subject the dismissal to review before an industrial tribunal.

4.2. Works councils

The works council arrangement is established under an agreement between the central associations. The councils consist of management and employee representatives, and may be involved in discussions of an extensive catalogue of questions concerning organisational conditions, ranging from essentially social issues (e.g. welfare issues and retraining of personnel) to essentially production-related issues (e.g. the introduction of new technology and incentive pay schemes). The councils must further be notified of the financial situation of the undertaking, the prospects, etc.

4.3. Health and safety representatives

Under the Working Environment Act (Section 3.3.1 (above)), the employees in an undertaking shall elect health and safety representatives for the performance of local health and safety tasks. In undertakings with a workforce of more than 20 employees, a socalled safety committee must, in addition, be appointed, consisting of employer and management representatives as well as of the health and safety representatives. The committee is to undertake the coordination of the performance of the tasks referred to. The health and safety representatives enjoy the same protection against dismissal as shop stewards, cf. s. 10 of the Working Environment Act.

4.4. Employee board members

In public limited liability companies and private companies, which have engaged an average of at least 35 employees within the past three years, the employees are entitled by virtue of s. 49 of the Companies Act and of s. 22 of the Private Companies Act to appoint members for the Board of Directors, cf. also the detailed provisions contained in Consolidating Acts nos. 942 and 943 of 9 December 1993 (as amended). In principle, the employee board members shall thus take part in the day-to-day work of the board on equal terms with any other member of the board. They enjoy the same statutory protection against dismissal as shop stewards, cf. s. 32 and s. 33, respectively in the consolidating Acts mentioned.

CHAPTER 21

Business Organisation Company Law

by Lars Lindencrone Petersen

1. Introduction

A business can be run in many types of business organisation. The starting point is the sole trader, a business run by the owner as his own master. Such business will not imply a legal distinction between the person and the business. A "private" party to whom the owner owes money may seek satisfaction in those business assets which are not reserved by priority rights for the "business creditors" – and conversely a party who has sold a machine for use in the business may seek satisfaction in the owner's "private" property as well.

Where several persons have joined together to run a business they will do so in a company. This does not apply the other way round – with the inference that a single individual is barred from running a business on company basis – for under the statutes governing companies of either main category, public limited liability companies ("A/S") and private (limited liability) companies ("Aps"), both categories may be owned by a single person in that the person in question holds all shares and such "sole traders" are quite common in practice.

The most important types of company comprise *public limited liability companies, private (limited liability) companies, partnerships, limited partnerships, cooperative societies, joint-ownership shipping companies,* and *independent institutions/foundations or funds*. These types of company will be discussed below.

Danish law recognizes the principle of contractual freedom in company law in that the participants of a joint business enterprise are free to decide the organisation form they find best suited for their needs. *If* the participants decide to set up a limited liability company, a joint ownership shipping company, or a foundation, their company will be regulated by the rules governing the specific organisation, in the Companies Act, the Private Companies Act, Part 5 of the Maritime Act, and the legislation on funds, respectively.

Otherwise the choice of organisation is generally free and the legal position of the individual types of company must be determined through application of court decisions in previous cases (case law) and general legal principles – with the modification that the recent Act on Business Enterprises (1994) contains a number of mandatory rules regarding registration, notification, accounts, auditing and publication.

The participants' choice of company type will be determined by several different considerations. The liability issue is an important factor but tax considerations and the desire of facilitating a business transfer to the younger generation may also be included. Some types of business – commercial banks, savings banks, insurance companies, and mortgage credit institutions are *required by law* to be organised in a specified company type or the choice is limited to certain specified types.

2. Partnerships

2.1. Introduction

Apart from the rules in the Act on Business Enterprises there is no legislative regulation of partnerships. Thus the legal position must be inferred to a considerable extent from general legal principles, case law and the circumstances of the individual case. Therefore it is appropriate that the participants – the partners – set down their inter-partner relationship in an agreement – the *partnership agreement.*

A partnership will often have only a few owners which makes a close cooperation between the partners both possible and necessary.

2.2. The relationship between the partners

2.2.1. Capital investment – surplus and deficits

An initial capital may be unnecessary or financing may be made on the basis of loan capital. The normal thing, however, is that partners contribute an investment capital and working capital and they will generally have agreed how much each partner is to contribute.

If the contributed capital proves inadequate the individual partner will not be bound as towards his partners to contribute more unless otherwise agreed.

A partner need not accept, without more, that one or more partners contribute with more capital.

In the book-keeping, capital investments are entered to the credit of *capital accounts* in the partners' accounts.

The partnership agreement will often determine the proportion in which the operating profits are to be distributed among the partners. Where the agreement is silent and no special circumstances would indicate a contrary intention the partners must be deemed to have agreed to share equally in the profits. As regards individual contribution towards losses the same presumption of equal contribution is made as a starting point.

Profits (and interest or consideration, if any) are credited to the capital accounts of the partners, and losses will be debited. Thus the accounts will show the partners (current) investments in the firm from time to time.

2.2.2. *The property relationship in the partnership*

The net value of a partner's share is often difficult to calculate while the firm subsists. Instead a partner's property right as towards the other partners is described as his gross share of the firm's assets (socalled constructive share). The amount of the individual partner's constructive share may be stated in the partnership agreement. In the absence of such clause the non-mandatory rule is that the property relationship is determined on the basis of the partners' current balance on their capital accounts.

2.2.3. *Obligations of the partners*

Unless otherwise agreed, the partners all have a duty of participating in the running of the firm. The partnership agreement may and will often contain more specific terms regarding the area of work of the individual partner, and such division may simply follow from the training and professional expertise of the individual partners.

Apart from the obligation to contribute capital and the duty to work for the firm the partners are under a general duty to look after the interests of the partnership.

2.2.4. *Management of the partnership*

The participation in the management of the partnership is not only an obligation for the partners, it is also a right – unless otherwise agreed.

On account of the close cooperation and the joint liability the non-mandatory rule must be that the partners must concur in all decisions, apart from trivial or absolutely necessary decisions. The agreement may spell out which decisions can be made by an individual partner and often an internal practice will become established in the business in that regard.

2.2.5. New partners

In view of the typical character of close cooperation between the partners an admission of a new partner – including a spouse or heir of a deceased partner – requires the consent of all partners, unless otherwise agreed in the partnership agreement. Similarly, a transfer of a partner's gross share in the firm will require the consent of all the other partners.

2.3. The relationship to third parties

2.3.1. Who may bind the partnership towards third parties?

All commercial partnerships are to be notified for registration at the Commerce and Companies Agency: At the notification must be stated who has power to sign for the partnership, i.e. who will bind the firm as towards the outside world.

Apart from the rules governing power to sign the general rules on authority and power of procuration in s. 7 of the Act on Business Enterprises will be applicable.

2.3.2. The liability towards the creditors

2.3.2.1. To the partnership creditors

The partners are liable personally, jointly and severally, and directly towards the partnership creditors. An incoming partner will, prima facie, not be liable for the existing debt in the partnership. An outgoing partner will, again prima facie, not be liable for the part of the partnership debt created after his retirement.

As a result of the direct liability the creditors need not first seek satisfaction in the common property.

2.3.2.2. To the individual partner's creditors (separate creditors)

As regards a partner's private debts only he himself is of course liable.

Such "private creditors are barred from levying execution on the firm's individual assets. On the other hand they may levy execution on the debtor's (the partner's) rights in the partnership, e.g. a claim he may have for pay and dividend or net share in the partnership. On the basis of such execution a creditor may demand payment of the capital share via termination of the agreement unless the agreement is interminable (for a certain period). If the agreement is interminable the execution made will be of a temporary nature, i.e. it will not be capable of forming a basis for a compulsory sale.

On a partner's bankruptcy his "private" creditors (his bankrupt estate) may, in a similar way, rely on his rights in the partnership, including his net share.

2.4. Dissolution of a partnership

Any partner may require the dissolution of the partnership if its activities were meant to be limited to a certain period of time or until the achievement of a specific purpose. Unless agreement to the contrary must be deemed to have been made any partner must also be deemed to be capable of giving notice to dissolve the partnership at an appropriate time and on appropriate notice.

Further, any partner may demand dissolution where there is a material change of circumstances vital for the continued running of the business.

3. Limited partnerships

In a limited partnership there are two kinds of partners. The *general partner(s)*, liable personally for the debts of the firm and the *limited partners* who are not liable beyond the capital they have contributed under the limited partnership contract.

As a result of the contractual freedom the rules in force will present no bar to placing an additional liability on the limited partners in the contract, e.g. a personal and joint liability for a loan to the firm, which is a common occurrence in practice.

Otherwise the rules mentioned in Section 2 regarding partnerships will be correspondingly applied to limited partnerships. For anyone dealing with a limited partnership it is always important – as it is with a partnership – to examine the real contents of the partnership contract.

4. Joint ownership shipping companies

Where a ship is owned by a joint ownership shipping company – whose ownership access is incidentally limited to one ship – each of the joint owners will only be liable for the ship's commitments to the extent of his share of the ship, cf. the Maritime Act s. 102. Thus a joint owner will be liable personally, on a pro rata basis and directly towards the company's creditors, unless otherwise agreed.

Where a ship share is transferred from A to B, A will remain liable as towards the creditors for the liabilities of the company at the transfer. B will not be liable to the creditors for these "old" commitments but on the other hand he will be liable for the commitments which are created after the transfer. If the transfer has not been notified to the Shipping Register, A will also be liable for the last-mentioned commitments towards a third party who was in good faith as regards the transfer, cf. s. 115(2) of the Maritime Act.

Joint ownership shipping companies are – as will have appeared from the foregoing – registered in the Shipping Register.

5. Cooperative societies

In Denmark a number of organisations on cooperative basis (companies and societies), especially in relation to farmers' professions and trade unions, exist in which the members' rights as towards the company/society – including first and foremost the right to share in the profits – are typically dependent on their amount of dealings with the company.

The relationship between members of the society is usually regulated in the articles. For cooperative societies the traditional rule is that a member has only vote – but a contrary intention may be expressed in the articles.

To the outside world the cooperative society is not represented by the members but normally by a board with power to sign for the society – under the rules prescribed in the articles.

The liability of members for the debts of the society is primarily dictated by the provisions in the articles to such effect – and it is therefore very important that a party who contemplates contracting with such societies examines their articles. Presumably the members must be deemed to be liable personally (and jointly) if the articles fail to indicate a limitation of the liability for a society's debts.

6. Funds – independent institutions

A certain amount of property – including one or more enterprises – may be placed with a view to furthering a specific purpose without designating specific persons as owners, partners or participants. In that case the joint forces will have the character of an independent institution – or the more modern terms, foundation or fund. If a foundation's purpose is solely to manage capital it will often be termed a trust fund but whether one or the other term is used the institution is comprised by the Consolidated Act No. 698 of 11 August 1992 on funds (and certain associations) or Consolidated Act no. 547 of 20 June 1996 on commercial funds.

A fund is usually created by a unilateral disposition whereby the founder in a deed of gift or by will appropriates the property of the institution from his property. The valid establishment of a fund requires that a definitive appropriation of the property of the institution from the founder's property is made, that the purpose of the fund is indicated, and that the Board who is to manage the institution (independently) is stated. The terms under which funds are to be managed are called the trust deed.

Funds are often set up exclusively or partly with a non-profit/charitable purpose but this is not a requirement.

The management are appointed under the guidelines stated in the trust deed and the scope of action of the members of such management is solely limited by the terms of such deed and – naturally – by the legislation governing the areas of the fund's activities.

The creditors of the fund are referred solely to the institution's property for satisfaction of debts. But the managers may – like the managers of other companies – incur liability in damages for negligent conduct towards third parties.

7. Limited Liability Companies

7.1. Introduction

A *public limited liability company* (A/S) is a (commercial) company in which none of the members (the shareholders) are liable personally for the debts of the company but only to the extent of the capital contributed by the shareholders (the share capital) and the rest of the company property.

A *private (limited liability) company* (Aps) is a commercial company in which none of the members – the shareholders – are liable personally in respect of the company debts but only to the extent of the capital contributed by the shareholders – the contributed capital – and the rest of the company property.

With very few exceptions the promoters of a company with limited liability are free to decide between the two types of company and the choice will often be dictated by an evaluation of which set of governing rules holds the greater attraction to the company members. For large companies with considerable capital, many members and many employees the public limited liability type will often be most appropriate (a private company is e.g. ineligible for listing on the Stock Exchange); for the large group of minor companies the private company form will typically hold greatest attraction, cf. also the EU effect described immediately above. – In the absence of express contrary provision the rules on non-company matters (e.g. tax law provisions) are the same for the two types of company.

The formation of a company must be notified to the Commerce and Companies Agency and be made public in the official gazette, Statstidende. The same applies to subsequent alterations in company matters or circumstances.

7.2. Formation

The initiative to form a company is taken by the promoters. The subscription is made on the memorandum of association. The minimum capital of a public limited liability company is DKK 500,000; the minimum capital of a private company is DKK 125,000.

The promoters are obliged to prepare and sign a memorandum of association which is also i.a. to contain draft articles for the company.

Where shares (in both categories of company) may be subscribed against non-money payment (socalled *payment in kind*) – e.g. against securities or real property – or where such assets are to be taken over by other means than against consideration in shares, the evaluation basis must be accounted for on the grounds of shareholder and creditor protection, and both the Companies Act and the Private Companies Act contain rules to ensure that payments in kind are of a value corresponding to that stated by the promoters.

The company articles which represent the set of rules which – subject to the rules of both Companies Acts – are to govern the specific company's relations, must contain i.a. clauses on the purpose of the company, the amount of capital and shareholders' voting rights.

7.3. Registration

Both categories of company must be notified for registration at the Commerce and Companies Agency. Registration is contingent on the contributed capital being subscribed with binding effect and paid in. The registration must be published forthwith in the official gazette, Statstidende.

A company of either category will not become a legal person until it has been registered (not just notified for registration). Until registration it is incapable of acquiring rights or incurring liabilities. Often several dispositions need to be made in the interval between formation and registration. For such dispositions a joint and several liability is incurred by the persons who made the dispositions or participated as co-responsible parties. On registration the company will take over the commitments following from the memorandum of association or which have been incurred by the company subsequently which releases the contracting persons' liability – *provided that* the contract partner was informed at the conclusion of the contract that it was concluded *on behalf of the company*.

7.4. Increase of capital

Decisions on increase of capital by issue of new shares or transfers of company reserves to share capital (issue of *bonus shares*) are made by the company in general meeting. A similar principle applies for private companies.

Where the share capital is increased by new issue whereby payment is made for the new shares (both categories of company) the former company members will prima facie be entitled to a proportional subscription of the new shares. A detailed set of rules seeks to prevent that a majority may exploit their majority position to keep a minority from subscription of new shares. For to the extent a new subscription is not made proportionally there will be a shift of influence in the company and if the new shares are subscribed at a price below their real value the imbalance will be even more felt in the distribution of the company funds. However, special rules take account of a situation where the employees of the company (or its subsidiaries) are granted a right to subscribe (at favourable prices) since such subscription is encouraged by the legislators.

Where the capital is increased by the issue of bonus shares no interference may be made with the priority rights of the company members. For bonus shares no consideration is paid to the company in respect of the new shares – an issue of bonus shares merely represents a distribution of the same equity values in the company on a share holding which after the issue of the bonus shares will have a larger total face value than before.

7.5. Reduction of capital – Own shares – Shareholders' loans

As has been mentioned several times, the vital element of a company of either category is that the members are not personally liable – i.e. that the creditors are referred exclusively to the company property for satisfaction. Therefore it is important not only to ensure that the required capital is actually paid in on the formation of the company and a subsequent increase of capital, if any, but also to draft the rules of the Companies legislation so that they afford protection against an uncontrolled reversion of the company funds to the shareholders.

7.5.1. Reduction of capital

The statutory rules to this effect are generally the same for both categories of company.

As a predominant main rule, reduction of capital may only be decided at a general meeting. The resolution is to state the reduced amount and it must be notified to the Commerce and Companies Agency in the usual way.

7.5.2. Own shares

Prima facie, a company is barred from acquiring own shares against consideration because the capital basis of the company is thereby diluted. On the other hand a purchase of "loose" shareholdings may contribute to preventing an undesired intrusion into the company and it is also a way to exercise a reasonable price management so that fortituous variations may be avoided. These contrasting considerations – whose importance varies in a limited liability company and a private company – have led to the following rules:

A *private company* is barred from acquiring own shares. This rule is, howver, subject to a few exceptions.

A *public limited liability company* may not acquire more than 10 per cent of its own shares in share capital. This rule is also subject to certain exceptions.

7.5.3. Shareholders' loans

A company (of either category) is barred from extending loans or placing security for shareholders, directors or managers in the company or its parent company. Nor may loans be granted or security placed for "connected persons" to this group of persons whether the connection is by marriage or family relationship in ascending or descending line.

A security placed by the company will be binding, however, if the lender had no knowledge of the security's having been placed contrary to these rule-s.

Provisions regarding limitation/bans of the access to grant shareholders' loans etc. do not prevent that companies within a group may borrow from eachother and place security for eachothers' debts.

7.6. Company management

7.6.1. Internal management

In both Companies Acts management of the company is with the board of directors and the management. Day-to-day management is with a managing director.

> A public limited liability company is reqired to have a board of at least three members. Basically, a private company is also required to have a board of three members but in companies where the employees are not entitled to representation on the board the articles may provide that the board shall consist of less than three members or indeed that the company shall have no board at all. In all events the majority of the board *must* be elected by the general meeting.

The company employees are entitled to elect a number of board members corresponding to half the number of the other board members if the company employed at least 35 employees during the past three years.

In the absence of contrary indication in the articles the board elects its own chairman. The necessary quorum is formed when more than half of the members are present and decisions are made by simple majority of votes – unless stricter requirements are made in the articles.

In a public limited liability company the board must appoint a management of one or more members. Private companies are also required to have a management.

The managers undertake the day-to-day management of the company whereby they are to act on the guidelines and instructions made by the board. For dispositions of an extraordinary nature or major importance the consent of the board is required.

7.6.2. Who may bind the company towards third parties?

The rules which are the same in both Companies Acts are of the following main contents:

Members of the board and management represent the company externally.

The company will be liable for legal transactions made on the company's behalf by the whole board and also, prima facie, by transactions made by one director or one manager. The articles may provide that the individual management and board members' *rights to sign for the company* – in contrast to the board collectively – is limited so that the right to sign may only be exercised by one or more specified members together or more members together. This – socalled collective signature – is the only limitation to the power to sign for the company which is capable of registration.

It is not altogether unlikely that a person who has no power to sign may bind the company anyway since the ordinary rules on authority (including the authority usually inherent in a job function without special mention, "job authority") will of course also apply to companies acting as principals.

7.6.3. The General Meeting

The general meeting is the forum where company owners, i.e. the shareholders, meet to decide on company matters. *The general meeting is the highest authority of the company* and the board and management are, with a very few exceptions, bound to implement the decisions ("resolutions") made at general meetings.

Within five months after each accounting year an ordinary (annual) general meeting ("AGM") is to be held. At the AGM decisions regarding approval of the accounts must be made and regarding the application of any profits or coverage of loss.

Any company member has the right to attend the meeting and speak at the meeting. He has the right to demand discussion of a certain item at the AGM if a written requisition to such effect is made with proper notice before the meeting. Any share issued after 1 January 1974 is to carry voting rights but the articles may provide for increases of the voting rights of some shares – though such increase may not exceed the voting right of other shares of the same amount by more than 10 times. Similar powers are not applicable to private companies which means that shares may be without voting rights.

General meetings are presided over by a chairman.

At the general meetings all matters are decided by simple majority of votes unless the articles provide otherwise, cf. below in 7.8. In the event of a tie a proposal for decision will lapse whereas on matters of elections of persons, a drawing of lots must be effected unless otherwise provided in the articles.

7.8. Protection of minority interests

A resolution on *alterations to articles* will require, outside some special cases, a qualified majority, i.e. for *public limited liability companies* at least 2/3 of the votes cast and of the vote-carrying share capital represented at the meeting.The double majority requirement of this rule will provide a special protection of minority interests in companies where the shares do not carry the same voting rights. For *private companies* the rule is the same, but non-mandatory, since the articles may set lower requirements for the size of the majority.

Some alterations to the articles are only valid if at least 9/10 both of votes cast at the general meeting and of the amount of voting share capital represented at the meeting concur in the resolution, and some alterations in both categories of company even require the concurrence of *all company members*. Such requirements of very qualified majority apply in particular to proposals whereby the company members' right to dividend or distribution of the company funds are decreased in favour of parties other than company members (always providing for the special rules in the situation mentioned above regarding employees' pre-emption right for new shares at favourable prices).

Both Companies Acts set forth that a decision made in general meeting is invalid when it is evident that it may be used in the procuration of undue advantage to some shareholders or others at the cost of other shareholders or companies. This provision is a sort of *general clause for protection of minority interests*.

With certain cases of intentional majority abuse the courts may decide that the company be dissolved.

7.8. Annual accounts – dividend – auditors

7.8.1. The annual accounts

For the creditors and the company members the capital notified for registration is one thing whereas the current general financial state of the business is yet another. The interest in this context is shared by the outside world and public authorities. Thus the preparation and publication of correct and informative annual accounts will be relevant in several respects. The rules governing this area are contained in the Company Accounts Act.

The annual accounts, which the board and management must cause to be prepared, consist of a *balance sheet*, a *profit and loss account*, and *notes* to the accounts, and for each accounting year and a *management report* must also be prepared and for the parent company, *consolidated accounts*. The common denomination of these accounts, reports and notes is an *annual report*.

The annual accounts, the management report and consolidated accounts, if any, must be signed by the board and management. The annual report must be sent to the Commerce and Companies Agency immediately upon approval and no less than five months after the end of the accounting year, whereupon it will be accessible to the general public.

7.8.2. Dividends

A company may distribute for shareholders' dividends the profits of the year in accordance with the approved accounts for the past accounting year, any profits transferred from previous years and other reserves which are not tied under statute or company articles.

The authority to determine the amount of dividend is with the general meeting. The Companies Act does, however, contain a provision under which the general meeting may not decide on distribution of amounts in excess of the amounts proposed or approved by the board. A similar provision does not apply to private companies.

7.8.3. Auditing

The general meeting will elect one or more auditors. At least one auditor is required to be a state-authorised public accountant or a registered public accountant. For companies listed on the Stock Exchange two auditors must be elected one of whom must be state-authorised. An auditor is barred from being a member of the company management or board or an employee of the company, nor may he have close family relation to any of the members of the company management. An auditor may not have loans in the company or in companies within the same group.

The auditor is under a duty to review the annual accounts (including the information in figures appearing in the annual report) in accordance with proper accounting principles. Where the company is a parent company he is also to review the consolidated accounts and the accounting relations between the group enterprises mutually.

The auditor must confirm, in a clause on the accounts, that he has reviewed the said accounts (and consolidated accounts, if any). Where the auditor finds that the accounts should not be approved he must state so in his clause.

For the use of the board the auditor will prepare auditor's minutes stating in particular the nature and extent of auditing work performed and any defects he may have found in the book-keeping and accounting of the company. These minutes are submitted to any board meeting and any addition to them must be signed by all board members.

7.9 Dissolution of companies

7.9.1. Liquidation

Unless otherwise provided by statute, the decision to dissolve a solvent company of either category is made by the members in general meeting and will be performed by liquidation. To undertake the liquidation the general meeting will appoint one or more liquidators.

The liquidators are to prepare a profit and loss account for the period from the end of the past accounting year to commencement of liquidation and a balance sheet as per the latter date. As soon as possible the accounts, duly reviewed, must be presented for inspection by company members and creditors at the company's office apart from being sent to the Commerce and Companies Agency. Further, as soon as possible the liquidators are to request the creditors by notice in Statstidende of at least three months to notify their claims. The notice referred to is *not* preclusive. At the same time as the publication notice, separate notice is also given to all the company creditors.

Upon expiry of the notice period and payment of the debts to the creditors, a distribution of the surplus of the liquidation estate may be made.

Where, during the proceedings in the estate, the liquidators may find that the liquidation will not give full coverage to the creditors the liquidator must convene a general meeting for deciding a presentation of a bankruptcy petition.

7.9.2. Merger

A merger may arise where one company (the take-over company or continuing company) integrates another (the company taken over or discontinuing company) or where both companies combine to make one new company.

Mergers require approval by a majority as required for article alterations in the company ceasing to operate. In the continuing company the decision on merger *may*, prima facie, be made by the board.

Payments to shareholders in the discontinuing company can and will often for tax purposes be made in shares but *may* of course also be made in money or in kind.

A merger will also affect the creditors of the companies concerned. The creditors cannot oppose the merger and on a merger the liabilities of the discontinuing company will be transferred to the continuing company. Where the creditors' possibilities of satisfaction will suffer (in real terms) by the merger a creditor may demand redemption of his claim (or that security be placed if the debt is not yet due).

7.9.3. Splitting up

Under the Companies Act the general meeting of a public limited liability company may decide – with the majority required for article alterations – to split up the company. On such splitting up the assets and debts collectively are transferred to several existing or newly-established public limited liability companies or private companies against consideration for the shareholders of the split-up company.

The Private Companies Act contain no rules on splitting up.

7.10.4. Converting a public limited liability company into a private company – or vice versa

A conversion of a public limited liability company into a private company – or the other way round – may be decided by the company in general meeting with a majority as required for alterations of articles.

8. Groups

Where the shareholding of a public limited liability company or private company in another company is to such an extent that it controls the majority of the voting rights in that company the former company is termed a *parent company* and the latter a *subsidiary company*. The parent company and the subsidiary company/ies together compose a group. If a subsidiary or parent company together with one or more subsidiaries collectively hold so many shares in another company that they control the majority of votes in that company, a group relation will also lie.

The existence of a group relation will – as already mentioned – typically consist in the parent company's holding of the majority of the voting rights in the subsidiary but a controlling influence may also find other forms creating a group relationship, cf. the rules in s. 2 of the Companies Act and s. 2 in the Private Companies Act.

In principle any company within a group is a single legal person concluding its own contracts, acquiring its own rights, being liable to its own creditors (but not to the creditors of the other companies), etc. However, the controlling influence of the parent company in the subsidiary will imply that it may be unwise to treat each company as a separate unit in all respects and the Companies Act, the Private Companies Act, and the Company Accounts Act therefore contain certain rules seeking to counteract the possibilities of abuse of the group relationship.

CHAPTER 22

International choice of law and international procedural law

by Lars Lindencrone Petersen

1. Introduction

If a Danish employee who has been employed with a Spanish enterprise is sued for breach in Denmark it may seem an obvious inference that the Danish rules on employment contracts are applicable. But this is not the case. Admittedly, a Danish court is to apply Danish law but for the situation referred to here Danish law will in fact prescribe that the law of the workplace, i.e. Spanish law is, prima facie, applicable.

The rules determining whether foreign law is applicable instead of Danish law are termed choice of law rules. These rules delimit the scope of application of Danish law in relation to foreign law. If a choice of law rule refers to foreign law the Danish rules comprised by the choice of law provision must be replaced by the corresponding parts of the foreign law system in question. Thus, the choice of law rule does not give a solution of the dispute itself but merely determines whether the decision is to be made under Danish or foreign law.

The choice of law rules are categorized in this country and in other countries under the area of *private international law*. The word *international* may be misleading since international law is not involved here. Danish private international law is a component of Danish law and the same applies in other legal systems. It is the conflicts that are international, not the rules. The wording "*private law*" indicates that the choice of law mechanism will only attach to matters of Danish private law, including contract law.

When a conflict relates to several states the parties must also address the issue as to which forum a case may or must be brought before. Where the contract beteen the parties is silent or if they cannot subsequently agree the issue relates to the proper venue – or put in another way – the international competence lying with the court/s before which the case may be brought. However, often the parties have provided guidelines as to how conflicts between them may be decided, either at the making of the contract or at a later time. Such guidelines may be in the form of an arbitration clause, cf. above Chapter 4, Section 6. Alternatively they may have agreed on a particular venue, i.e. apppointed a certain national court to decide any conflicts beteen them.

The solution of the forum issue does not imply per se that the court or arbitration court deemed competent is required to apply the law in the country in which such court is situated when the mutual rights and obligations of the parties in the matter in disputeare to be evaluated.

Anotther important issue raised by interntational legal relationships of the character mentioned relates to the recognition and enforcement of foreign court and arbitration court decisions. A venue agreement appointing e.g. the Maritime and Commercial C ourt as a forum in a case between a Danish and an American contract party is of no immediate use to the Danish party if the judgemnt of such court is nor recognised in the USA and therefore cannot be enforced in that country.

Uncertainty about forum and enforcement possibilities may – just like differences between the individual legal systems, cf. above in Chapter 3, Section 1 – acts a bar to international exchange of goods and services. In the light of this an international cooperation with a view to minimizing this uncertainty and facilitating international trade has been in progess.

2. Background and relevance

It is a fundamental legal principle that a case should be evaluated in the same way no matter where it is brought. For purely national matters this principle is observed by means of general legal standards (especially statutory rules) whereas in international constellations it may be infringed upon as a result of differences between the legal systems involved.

The choice of law issue arises because of differences between the national systems of law but the choice of law rules do not contribute to meeting the need of uniform evaluation. In the same way as other legal requirements the choice of law rules are inherent to the individual country's legal system and may therefore differ from state to state. On an extreme view, a conflict related to Denmark and Sweden (in an area where Danish and Swedish standards differ) brought before a Danish court as a result of a Danish choice of law rule will be evaluated under the Swedish rules whereas, had it been brought before a Swedish court under the Swedish choice of law rules it would have been determined under Danish rules on the area in question.

The aim of a uniform evaluation may be achieved (on community basis) by prescribing uniform standards of private law. But even within the EU this approach is only possible to a limited extent and at a moderate speed. However, in one area – in particular company law – the EU harmonisation has come a long way. On the Nordic level legal uniformity has been achieved within major areas of private law.

Another possibility is to provide convention-based legislation on international matters. The International Sale of Goods Act (CISG) referred to in Chapter 9 is the best example of such legislative measure.

Common choice of law rules (again convention-based) are a third alternative for solving the uniform evaluation issue. The most important example of this solution model is the Sale of Goods Act and the EU Convention on International Contracts referred to in Section 6 and 7, respectively.

It must be emphasized that uniform rules will not per se imply uniform evaluation since the same rule may be subject to different construction from one court to another. Thus effective uniform evaluation is ultimately dependent – as evidenced by the European Court of Justice – on a common court of international competence.

3. Sources of law

The Danish choice of law rules are integrated in Danish law. Therefore the question of sources in private international law are no different from the source of law questions in other areas of law. In summarized form the sources of law may be described as legislation, legal custom, case law, and the circumstances of the case. The relationship to foreign law, however, of the particular substantive law area, has to some extent provided its source of law bases with an international character.

The international choice of law system is only to a limited extent characterized by legislation. However, this does not apply in the area of contract law. The most important legislation in that area is Consolidated Act No. 722 of 24 October 1986 regarding which country's law rules shall be applied on international sales of goods (The International Sales of Goods Act) and Act No. 188 of 9 May 1984 regarding implementation of the Convention on which law should govern contractual obligations etc. (the Choice of Law Convention).

The International Sales of Goods Act based on a Hague Convention of 1955 contains a fairly precise set of choice of law rules. The Choice of Law Convention which is an EU product and which was incorporated into Danish law by the implementation Act (Act No. 188 of 8 May 1984) will prima facie comprise all contract matters but on the other hand it will be superceded, under its own terms (Art. 21), by other convention-based statutory rules including e.g. the Sale of Goods Act. Reflecting the wide aim of the Convention the choice of law rules are generally rather flexible. This makes for some uncertainty as to the legal position in many areas but this is really an inevitable price to pay for flexibility.

The Danish choice of law system does not contain many rules based on custom. As an example may be cited the rule that a person's capacity is to be determined under the law of the country in which he resides.

The available case law on intenational choice of law issues is so sparse and limited that it affords slender grounds for setting up differentiated choice of law rules.

Where neither legislation, custom or case law provides clues to the solution of a conflict the judge must base his decision on the circumstances of the case which really means that he is referred to finding a solution which may be regarded as best suited as a future guideline. However, this model is not particularly appropriate for predictions of the law in an area in which positive law is already limited such as it is in private international law.

In Nordic private international law a basic standard has been coined in the sentence "a legal relationship is primarily to be determined under the law of the country to which it is most closely connected or has its principal origin". The approach thus indicated is called the *individualising method.*

The individualising method which also exists in other legal systems in various forms is incorporated in the Choice of Law Convention which provides in Art. 4(1) that an agreement – in the absence of choice in a valid clause – shall be subject to the law of the state "to which it is most closely connected". This assessment is governed by a presumption that the closest connection is to be found where the party who is to effect the performance which is "characteristic of the contract" has his habitual residence (Art. 4(2)).

It may occur that a rule of a foreign legal system is heavily at variance with Danish legal conception. In that case it will not be applied. This disregard is possible under the basic principle of viewing any choice of law clause on public policy considerations ("*ordre public*") whereby (foreign) rules which are contrary to fundamental Danish legal principles are not applicable. For such effect, it will – naturally – not suffice that the foreign rule is not in harmony with a Danish rule. Nor may a foreign rule which leads to a result which is unrealistic or unfair under Danish conception be disregarded on that ground. The result must be really unacceptable.

4. Formation of contract

4.1. Capacity

The Danish main rule on capacity is that a person's capacity is determined under the law of the country of his domicil. There is no general statutory rule prescribing the domicil principle and the Choice of Law Convention will not apply – save for the special rule in Art. 11 – to issues of natural persons' capacity (Art. 1(2), par. a)). However, the domicil principle as a vital determinant of capacity must be deemed to have been established by legal custom. The alternative to the domicil principle is the nationality principle which is observed in most European countries. Only England and Norway share the Danish conception of domicil as a vital determinator for connection in capacity issues.

However, a result in favour of the law of the forum is contained in Art. 11 of the Convention. When an agreement has been concluded between persons present in the same country, a natural person who would have capacity under the law of that country may only rely on lack of capacity under another legal basis – under Danish private international law the domicil law of the person in question – if the contract partner knew or ought to have known of the lack of capacity at the conclusion of the contract. A foreigner who is a minor but would be of age under Danish law is thus bound if he makes a contract in this country with a bona fide contract partner. Conversely, a Danish minor (sued as defendant at a Danish court of law) is correspondingly bound by a contract he has concluded abroad if he would have been of age under the law of the country in question. Thus, within the framework of Art. 11 of the Convention the status of minority changes into a non-operative vitiating factor.

4.2. Formation of contract and validity

The rules regarding conclusion of contracts and invalidity contained in the Contracts Act, Part I and Part 3 respectively are among the key provisions of contract and property law. Thus there is no probably no doubt that – in the absence of express sanction – Danish courts will be extremely reluctant to set aside the rules of the Contracts Act on formation of contract and invalidity of contract in favour of foreign legislation of materially different substantive content. However, such sanction is provided with Art. 8 of the Choice of Law Convention.

Under Art. 8(1) of the Convention issues on the existence and validity of an agreement or a term in an agreement are determined under the law applicable under the choice of law rules in the Convention provided that the agreement or term is itself valid. Where a contract between a Danish importer and a German exporter (under s. 4(1) of the Sale of Goods Act) is subject to German law, an issue regarding e.g. whether the exporter's standard terms of sale may be deemed (by a Danish court) to have been adopted or not, must be determined under German law.

Art. 8(2) contains a modification to the principle of application of the law of the Convention. Under this rule a party may rely on the law of the country of his residence to show that he has not consented to the agreement or the term and the circumstances show that it would not be reasonable to determine the effects of his conduct under the law appointed by Art. 8(1) – i.e. the law of the contract. This reservation in favour of a party's domicil law is especially aimed at persons who are inexperienced in international trade relations. It may be used e.g. to protect an unprofessional party against contract rules prescribing obligations by passivity which are more extensive than the corresponding rules contained in his own domicil law.

4.3. Agency

The Choice of Law Convention is not applicable to issues on an agents' power to bind his principal (Art. 1(2) par. f). This goes for all the various agency relationships and also for the power of members of company organs to bind the company as towards third parties.

The explanatory statements on the Sales Act reveal that this Act is not directed to issues on authority in agency relationships either. Thus, Danish law contains no statutory rules on choice of law in the issue regarding an agent's power to bind his principal towards third parties.

The rules on agency in the Contracts Act, Part 2, are, like the rules in Part I and Part 3 in the same Act, on formation of contract and invalidity of contract, respectively, among the vital parts of contract law. This will no doubt imply, on a prima facie view, that a Danish court will be reluctant to set aside the fundamental principles manifested in these rules.

However, this does not imply per se that foreign agency rules are never applicable. An engagement of an agent may under the rules of Part 2 of the Contracts Act lead to the principal being bound within certain limits even if the agent has exceeded his authority. Therefore it may well be compatible with the principles underlying Part 2 of the Contracts Act to leave the issue of the scope of authority to a foreign system.

If an agent is permanently based in a foreign country the rules on scope of authority which apply in such country are applicable. The same applies if the agent has been sent out to a specified country. Only where the agent acts outside the express or implied geographical scope of his authority will the application of Danish law be indicated as a starting point.

5. Tort damages

In the law of tort the main rule is that the law applicable is the law of the place at which the tort was committed. The rule comprises – at least prima facie – all tort conditions including liability towards others, the extent of liability and the computation of loss.

The law of the place of the tortious act is not applicable if upon an individualising evaluation of the relationship it is found to have closest connection to another legal system. To reach this result it will not suffice that the tortfeasor and the injured party share law of domicil – especially if the tortious act was made in this country. But even in cases where the act was committed in another country where both parties reside the rule will not be superceded by Danish law immediately.

6. Sale of Goods

6.1. The (Uniform Laws on) International Sales of Goods Act

International sales of goods are regulated by the (Uniform Laws on) *International) Sales of Goods Act* based on a Hague-Convention of 1955. The Act is a result of the international efforts of achieving uniform evaluation. Apart from Denmark, a number of countries have ratified the Convention but the Act is also applicable in relation to other countries. However, the practical importance of the Act has been radically reduced by The International Sale of Goods Act (referred to in Chapter 9).

6.2. The scope of application of the Act

The scope of application of the Act is set out in s. 1 and 2. The rule in s. 1 indicates the contracts comprised by the Act and the rule in s. 2 contains a delimitation – albeit in negative terms – of the legal issues which will be within the scope of the Act.

6.2.1. Which contracts?

S. 1(1) provides – in conformity with the full title of the Act – that the Act is applicable to sales of goods of an international character. The text does not specify what is meant by "international character" whereas s. 1(2) and (3) contain rules defining and delimiting "sales of goods".

A sale is international if a direct geographical connection to more than one law system is involved but a more indirect connection to another law may also make a sale international. Thus, a contract concluded between two Danish parties may be international if it is contingent on an international sale which is not yet discharged – e.g. if a Danish importer re-sells a consignment of goods to a Danish buyer before the goods have arrived in the country. On the other hand a sale will not become international just because the parties have agreed that disputes are to be settled by foreign arbitration, or that payment is determined on the basis of a foreign currency.

Under s. 1(2) the Act is not applicable to sales of registered ships or aircraft, sales of securities, forced sales in enforcement procedures or otherwise by court measure, and to consumer sales. The exclusion of consumer sales was made in connection with the implementation of the Choice of Law Convention which provides special rules on certain consumer agreements in Art. 5 including certain consumer sales agreements. These rules are treated in Section 7.3.3.

Under s. 1(3) agreements for supplies of goods which are to be manufactured are within the definition of a sale if the materials necessary for such manufacture are to be supplied by the manufacturing party. Thus the same delimitation is made on this point as the Danish Sale of Goods Act provides in s. 2(1).

6.2.2. Which legal issues?

The Act does not contain a positive delimitation of the legal area comprised by the contract choice of law. There is no doubt, however, that the Act covers the legal issues which in Danish law are regulated by the Sale of Goods Act and the Credit Contracts Act. Thus if the Sales of Goods Act appoints a foreign system of law these Acts will be superseded by the corresponding legislation on the subject in the foreign legal system.

S. 2 of the Act contains a negative delimitation of the legal issues comprised by the Act. Under this rule the Act is not applicable to issues governing the parties' capacity to enter into contracts, form of contract, or the legal effects of the sale to third parties.

The Act does not contain rules on formation of contract and validity or on agency issues. However, issues on formation and validity are, under Art. 8 in the Choice of Law Convention, comprised by the rules in the legal system appointed by the Sales Act whereas the position as regards agency is more doubtful.

6.3. Choice of law rules in the International Sales Act

6.3.1. Parties' autonomy

Under s. 3, 1st clause, the buyer and seller may agree that the sale shall be subject to the legal rules of a certain country. The contractual freedom under this rule is very extensive. The parties may choose any country's rules of law and the choice is not limited to the legal systems to which the contract is connected.

Under s. 3, 2nd clause, the contract choice of law must be made in an express term or to be inferred unequivocally from the contract. This means that an implied assent cannot be based on circumstances outside the contract. It is a requirement that the parties have considered the problem and have agreed to apply the legal rules of a specified country. An agreement on jurisdiction will not suffice per se. Only where other circumstances indicate such construction will a jurisdiction agrement be interpreted as a contract choice of law.

6.3.2. The non-mandatory choice of law rules

Where the parties have not agreed to apply the legal rules of a certain country, s. 4(1), 1st clause, provides that the rules of the seller's residence at the time when he received the order shall be applicable. "Order" is defined as the buyer's offer to buy or his acceptance of the seller's offer. Where the order is received at a business place of the seller's s. 4(1), 2nd clause, provides that the rules of the country in which such business place is situate will apply and therefore the seller's residence is rarely of importance in commercial sales. The seller's business place is the place from which he operates his business on a permanent basis, not a place where he stays only temporarily for business purposes e.g. in connection with a fair or an exhibition. If a contract is concluded at such temporary place of staying the law of the seller's place of business is applicable unless otherwise provided in s. 4(2).

The rules of the country where the buyer is resident or where the business place from which the order was given is situate will be applicable under s. 4(2) if the seller or his agent received the order in that country. For the application of the rule it is irrelevant whether the agent has power to conclude contracts on the seller's behalf or whether he may only take orders which are to be confirmed by the seller subsequently. The rule is quite unambiguous where an order made towards the seller's agent is later extended by the buyer with an order direct to the seller.

For commodity exchange sales or auction sales the rules of the country of the exchange or auction place shall be applicable under s. 4(3).

6.3.3. Procedure in examination of the goods

As regards the procedure in the buyer's examination of the goods, timelimits and notices for such examination, and measures to be made if the subject-matter is rejected, s. 5 provides that the rules of the country in which the examination is to be made shall apply, unless otherwise expressly agreed. This rule is limited to questions of a more formal character. Whether examination is necessary at all and, in the affirmative, where it is to be made, issues of notice duty, and whether the goods may be rejected are determined under the law governing the sale generally.

7. Other contract relationships

7.1. The Choice of Law Convention

The Choice of Law Convention is a result of the efforts within the EU of harmonising private international law. The Convention was transformed into Danish law by Act no. 188 of 9 May 1984. In the same way as the Sales Act the Convention is not limited to relationships with a connection to the Convention states.

7.2. Scope of application of the Convention

The scope of application of the Convention is in particular defined in the rules of Art. 1 and Art. 10. But some of the other provisions in the Convention will also be of importance in this respect.

7.2.1. Which contract relationships?

Under Art. 1(1) the Convention terms are applicable to contractual obligations in all situations in which a choice between the laws of several countries is to be made. Thus, the Convention will prima facie comprise all contractual relationships.

There is no express requirement that the contract relationship is international. However, under Art. 3(3) the parties' agreement to apply the law of a foreign country – where all other circumstances of importance at the time of conclusion of the contract are connected to only one country – will not imply that non-mandatory rules of that country are set aside. This really limits the principle of party autonomy, which is a main principle in the Convention, to (genuine) international contract relationships, i.e. contract relationships with a real geographical connection to more than one legal system.

Art. 1(2) sets forth a number of issues to which the Convention is not applicable. Examples include contract-based issues relating to matters of succession and family law and issues of obligations under negotiable instruments, including obligations under bills of exchange and cheques.

7.2.2. Which legal issues?

The choice of law rules of the Convention cover the legal issues normally perceived as contract-law related. Art. 10 contains a listing of (some of) the issues under the heading of "scope of the applicable law". Under s. 10(1) the law appointed by the choice of law rules in the Convention is, in particular, to be applied in issues of interpretation, performance, consequences of breach, including the assessment of damages, the various methods of "extinguishing" (discharge) of obligations, including limitation and other lapse of rights as a result of exceeding timelimits, and the effects of nullity of the contract. However, s. 10(2) provides that as regards the manner of performance and steps to be taken in relation to defective performance regard shall be had of the law of the country of performance.

While Art. 1(2), par. a is not – save for the special rule in Art. 11 – applicable to issues of capacity, nor, under Art. 1(2), par. f, to agency issues, the choice of law rules in the Convention will under Art. 8, prima facie comprise all issues on contract formation and validity. These issues are all referred to in more detail in Section 4.

7.3. The choice of law rules in the Convention

7.3.1. Party autonomy

Under Art. 3(1), 1st clause, an agreement shall be governed by the law chosen by the parties. Under Art. 3(1) 3rd clause, a choice of law may comprise the entire agreement or only part thereof and under Art. 3(2) agreement on choice of law (or on amendment of a previous choice) may be made at any time i.e. also in the course of discharge of the contractual relationship.

On a line with the corresponding rule in the Sales Act s. 3 the freedom of contract under Art. 3 of the Convention is extremely wide. Thus the parties' choice of applicable law is not limited to the legal systems to which the contract is connected. Generally the contractual freedom under Art 3. (3) is limited to international contract relationships and with the rules in Arts. 5 and 6 certain consumer contracts and individual employment contracts are brought outside the sphere of contractual freedom.

Under Art. 3(1), 2nd clause, a choice of law must be made in express terms or appear with reasonable certainty from the contract or the circumstances of the case. This rule is not as strict in its couching as the corresponding rule in the International Sales Act s. 3, 2nd clause, under which a choice of law must be made by express term or appear unambiguously from the contract. However, it is submitted that a jurisdiction agreement will not suffice on its own. Presumably, other objective circumstances may also be taken to indicate – without an express choice of law clause – that the parties have made such choice.

The substantive content of the international party autonomy is that the parties may contract out of mandatory rules in the legislation which would otherwise – i.e. in the absence of choice of law – govern their contract. However, Art. 7 of the Convention contains a reservation in respect of rules in the legislation superseded in the choice of law made (Art. 7(1) or in the legislation of the forum (Art. 7(2)) which will be mandatory in the sense that they are to be applied irrespective of the law otherwise applicable to the contract. Such internationally mandatory rules may especially, though not exclusively, occur in (a convention-based) legislation on international contract relationships. The Commercial Agents' Act s. 1(2) contains an express internationally mandatory rule.

7.3.2. The non-mandatory choice of law rules

To the extent that no valid choice of law has been made the contract is under Art. 4(1) governed by the law of the country with which it is "most closely connected". This general description which corresponds to the contents of the individualising method is not in itself very instructive as a guideline since an objective balancing of various connection factors is not possible without more. Where e.g. an agreement has been made between a Dutch party and a Danish party in Holland to be performed in Denmark it is not possible without some sort of measure of the relevance of the connection data available to decide whether the contract is most closely connected to Holland or to Denmark. This uncertainty has been overcome with a number of presumption rules in the Convention.

Under Art. 4(2), 1st clause, there is a basic presumption that the closest connection is to be found in the country where the party who is to effect the performance which is "characteristic of the contract" has his habitual residence or, in the case of a company or other legal person, its central administration. However, if the contract is concluded in the party's course of business the presumption under Art. 4(2), 2nd clause, is transferred to the principal place of business, or if performance is to be effected from another place of business, e.g. a branch, to the country in which such other business place is situate.

The performance characteristic of the contract is deemed to be the performance representing the main purpose of the formation of the contract or which distinguishes it from other contracts. Thus, the presumption in Art. 4(2) appoints e.g. for contracts for work and materials the contractor's law, in tenancy matters the landlord's law, in financial institution relationships the bank's law, and for sales of goods, of which some are not comprised by the Sales Act (s. 2(2)) the seller's law. If the presumption rules are of no avail, e.g. because the contract is one of pure exchange, the closest-connection issue must be solved without presumptive guidance (Art.4(5)).

The presumption rule of Art. 4(2) is not applicable under paragraphs (3) and (4) to contracts concerning rights in immovable property and contracts for the carriage of goods. As regards rights in immovable property, including a right of use, there is a presumption, which can hardly surprise, of closest connection in favour of the country where the property is situate, and as regards carriage of goods there is a presumption that the carrier's country has closest connection but only if that country is also the country of loading and discharge or is the place where the consignor's principal place of business is situate.

The presumption rules in Art. 4(2-4) will be superseded – as indeed the very system of closest connection would indicate – if it appears from the circumstances as a whole that the contract is more closely connected with another country. For this result to obtain it will not suffice, of course, that a connection to another is shown to lie. The requirement must be that the connection factors on a collective assessment will take precedence over a reference indicated by the presumption rule.

7.3.3. Certain consumer contracts

Art. 5 of the Convention contains special rules on certain consumer contracts. These rules act as limitations both on the principle of party autonomy in Art. 3 and on the sphere of application of the presumption rules in Art. 4.

For the purposes of the Convention, Art. 5(1) defines consumer contracts as contracts for supplies of goods or services to a person ("the consumer") with a view to an application which must be deemed to be outside his business, or a contract for the provision of credit for such application. This definition is on a line with – and will in all events be construed as – the corresponding definition in other statutory law, e.g. the Credit Contracts Act s. 1.

Under Art. 5(2) the choice of law of the parties in a consumer contract – irrespective of the rule of free choice of law in Art. 3 – will not imply that the consumer is deprived of the protection afforded to him under the mandatory rules of the law of the country of his habitual residence, and in a more or less similar way Art. 5(3) provides that a consumer contract without choice of law – irrespective of the presumption rules in Art. 4 – is governed by the law of the country in which the consumer has his habitual residence. However, these limitations only apply to contracts concluded under specific circumstances -as enumerated in Art. 5(2) – and sharing the feature that the conclusion of the contract was preceded by some international canvassing for business. Other international contracts will be subject to the general Convention choice of law rules, including the rule in Art. 3(1) regarding the parties' free choice of law.

7.3.4. Individual employment contracts

Art. 6 of the Convention contains specific rules on individual employment contracts. In the same way as the rules on certain consumer contracts in Art. 5 aim to protect the consumer the aim of the rules in Art. 6 is to protect the employee to a certain extent although the methods differ.

Under Art. 6(1) the choice of law of the parties in an employment contract, notwithstanding the rule of party autonomy in Art. 3, will not imply that the employee is deprived of the protection to which he is entitled by virtue of mandatory rules in the law which would have been applicable in the absence of a choice of law. Thus, the employee protection is to the effect that mandatory rules in the law otherwise governing the contract of employment, i.e. without a choice of law, are applicable even if the parties have agreed a choice of law. This legislation is determined by the special choice of law rule in Art. 6(2).

In the absence of a choice of law, an employment contract is, notwithstanding the presumption rules of Art. 4, subject under Art. 6(2) to the law of the country in which the employee habitually carries out his work in performance of the contract, even if he is temporarily employed in another country, or, if the employee does not habitually carry out his work in any one country, to the law of the country in which the place of business through which he was engaged, is situate. This standard will be superseded, however, under its own terms if it appears from the circumstances as a whole that the contract is more closely connected to another country whose law will then be applicable.

Both on a linguistic level and on substance level the choice of law system governing individual employment contracts in Art. 6 of the Convention is rather complex. Expressed in summary terms (with the inherent risk of imprecision) the system is merely to the effect that the law of the workplace is applicable as a starting point, and that mandatory rules aiming at protecting the employee cannot be derogated from by means of a choice of law.

8. International procedural law

8.1. The EU-Convention on Judgments

8.1.1. The area of application etc. of the Convention

As at 1 November 1986 Denmark acceded to the Convention on the competence of the courts and enforcement of civil court decisions, including decisions in commercial cases, (the Judgments Convention) with protocol attached and protocol of 3 June 1971 regarding referral of interpretation issues to the European Court of justice, cf. Act No. 325 of 4 June 1986 (the Accession Act) and Consolidated Act no. 724 of 22 October 1986. Later amendments and an agreement made in 1988 ("the Lugano-Convention") with the then EFTA countries (i.a. Finland, Norway, Sweden, and Austria) of more or less the same contents as the Judgments Convention were adopted by accession in Denmark in 1996, cf. Consolidation Act No. 152 of 18 March 1999.

As between the rest of the 14 EU states the Judgments Convention was replaced from 1 March 2002 by Council Regulation 44/2001 on the courts' competence and on recognition and enforcement of court decisions in the civil and commercial law area (the Judgments Regulation).

The Judgments Convention is a socalled double Convention which means that it regulates the Member States' rules both on the international competence of their courts and on recognition and enforcement of judgments made in other Member States. The contrast is single conventions which only address the latter issue, cf. for an example the Nordic Convention referred to below in Section 3.3. In relation to the national legal systems the Convention will prima facie provide that the courts apply the rules of venue stated in the Convention in preference to the national rules, cf. section 2 of the Accession Act and s. 247 of the Administration of Justice Act.

Under Art. 1(1) 1st clause, of the Judgments Convention the Convention shall be applied to civil and commercial matters whatever the nature of court or tribunal. "Civil matters" are cases of private law character as opposed to a case of public law. The distinction is not too precise especially because public authorities may well use instruments of a typically private law character, e.g. contracts. Some guidance has been provided by the Court of Justice in its holding that the Convention is not to be applicable where a public authority is acting in the "exercise of its public powers". In practice this will imply at least that the Convention will not apply to situations in which an authority within public administration has made decisions (administrative decisions) in the course of its statutory area of competence. In an attempt to illustrate the area of application Art. 1(1), 2nd clause, sets forth that – in particular – the Convention shall not apply to revenue, customs and administrative matters.

Art. 1(2) excludes a number of specific areas from the area of application despite the traditional conception of some of them as private law matters. The exclusions relate to matters concerning the status or legal capacity of natural persons, rights in property arising between spouses, on succession or by wills, which implies that the most important parts of family law, law of persons, and succession law are outside the ambit of the Convention. Other exclusions are matters in relation to bankruptcy, composition and similar schemes, i.e. central areas of insolvency law. Finally the Convention will not apply to social security matters and arbitration.

The Convention is applied by the courts in the Member States. To ensure that the application – including in particular the interpretation of the Convention – is uniform in the various Member States, the above-mentioned Protocol of 3 June 1971 authorises the Court of Justice to interpret the Convention with binding effect for the national courts. The procedure is on more or less the same lines as where the Court of Justice makes opinions in preliminary rulings on the interpretation of community law: The highest courts in the Member States and courts otherwise making appellate decisions *may* refer interpretation issues concerning the Convention to the European Court and they are bound to do so if they find it necessary in order to be able to pronounce a judgment, cf. Chapter 3, Sections 3.6 and 4.6.3.

The Convention starts out with defining a general jurisdiction based on domicil to the effect that defendants who are domiciled in a EU state must be sued at the courts of that state. This starting point may be derogated from partly by means of a great number of special jurisdiction rules (Arts. 5-16), partly by an adoption of venue agreements etc. (Arts. 17-18). Compared to the jurisdiction rules under the Danish Administration of Justice Act, in particular Parts 21-22, the Convention rules hold little surprise. Since the Convention to a certain extent only aims at establishing the jurisdiction in the relationship between the courts in several countries such cases will necessitate – once it has been established that the case must or may be brought in Denmark – that the Danish rules are used on supplementary basis to establish which Danish court is to be competent court.

Courts which do not possess competence under the Convention must refuse to take jurisdiction if a case is brought before them despite the Convention rules and the competence rules also imply that the same parties may not conduct the same case before the courts of various countries, cf. Arts. 19-23.

8.1.2. The ordinary competence rule of the Convention

Under Art. 2(1) defendants domiciled in one of the Member States shall be sued before the courts of that state irrespective of the nationality of the defendant in question. The court which is to hear the case is determined under the national rules of the Member States in question, thus in Denmark the rules of the Administration of Justice Act govern factual and geographical jurisdiction (ss. 224 et seq) of the Administration of Justice Act). The seat of a company and other legal person will be equivalent to that of a natural person's domicil, cf. Art. 53(1).

The Convention does not define the domicil concept. In determining whether a party is domiciled in the state in which proceedings have been brought the courts of that state are to apply their national rules, cf. Art. 52(1).

The starting point in Art. 2(1) may be deviated from where the legal relationship in question is connected in various ways to a Member State other than the domicil state, cf. the two following Sections, and where the parties have agreed on a valid venue clause, cf. Section 8.1.5.

8.1.3. Competence rules in Arts. 5-15

Arts. 5-6 of the Convention contain various competence rules characterised by the possibility for the plaintiff to *choose* whether he will institute proceedings *either* in accordance with the ordinary rule in Art. 2 *or* before the courts of another member state in view of the special attachment of the legal relationship to that other state. In the latter case, the factual competence of the courts depends on the national rules of the individual member state in this respect. The most important competence rule in practice of this character relates to contractual obligations, disputes relating to damages in tort, disputes arising out of operations of a branch or other establishment, and cases involving several defendants.

Under Art. 5, no. 1, cases concerning *contractual matters* may be brought before the courts at the place of performance of the obligation in question, cf. the comparable rule under national law regarding exceptional venue in s. 242 of the Administration of Justice Act. The provision will also comprise money obligations. The place of performance is determined where necessary by the court before which the case has been brought with the modification expressed in the provision that the place of performance in a case regarding individual contracts of employment is the place at which the employee habitually performs his work. Art. 5(3) uses a similar approach in that cases in respect of *tort damages* may be brought before the court at the place at which the harmful act occurred, cf. for national law the "delict venue" in s. 243 of the Administration of Justice Act. Where the case relates to the *operations of a branch,* agency or similar establishment Art. 5, no. 5, sets forth that it may be brought before the courts at the place at which the establishment is situated though practice has developed a condition whereby the establishment must have its seat within the EU. Finally, where *several defendants* appear in a case e.g. in debt obligations involving a number of co-debtors, the case may under Art. 6, no 1, be brought before the courts at the place where any one of them is domiciled.

Title III of the Convention (Arts. 7-12a) and IV (Arts. 13-15) contain special competence rules as regards *insurance matters and consumer matters.* On the presumption that the insured and the consumer is the weaker party in relation to their contract partners, cf. below Chapter 15, the main view of the Convention is here that the insured/the consumer may sue the insurer/the trader contract partner not only at the courts in the Member States of the contract partner's residence but also at the courts of the insured's or consumer's own Member State (Articles 8 and 14). Where liability insurance or insurance of real property is concerned the insurer may further be sued in the courts of the place where the harmful act occurred (Art. 9). As regards consumer cases the solution corresponds to some extent to the special venue rule in respect of certain consumer cases in s. 244 of the Administration of Justice Act.

8.1.4. Exclusive jurisdiction rules in Art. 16

Other deviations from the general competence rule in Art. 2 follow from the provision in Art. 16 of the Convention. The contrast between this rule and the rules referred to in the preceding Section is that Art. 16 allocates *exclusive jurisdiction* to the courts in individual member states in a number of cases (and only those). Where one of the situations described in the provision occur and such situation refers to the main issue of the case all other jurisdiction rules are superseded including Art. 2 which means that the case must be brought at the court indicated by Art. 16. It is expressly said that the exclusive jurisdiction shall apply regardless of domicil.

The most important s.-16 situation in practice relates to proceedings concerning real *property rights* and tenancies or leases in such real property (no. 1). Jurisdiction here lies with the courts of the Member State in which the property is situate, cf. the exception venue under s. 241 of the Administration of Justice Act.

Exclusive jurisdiction will also lie in a number of matters relating to companies, intellectual property and to the validity of entries into public registries (e.g. land registries) and to enforcement of court decisions.

Art. 16 only relates to international competence. The issue as to which national court will be competent is determined by national law in the country upon whose courts jurisdiction has been conferred under Art. 16.

8.1.5. Jurisdiction agreements

To a certain extent the parties may agree that their disputes are to be settled by a specified court in one of the member states or – more generally – by the courts of such state so that the competence rules mentioned above will be deviated from. Such agreements are treated in Art. 17.

In order to give efficacy to such jurisdiction agreements it is a requirement, that the agreement has been concluded between parties of whom at least one is domiciled in an EU-state, that the parties have agreed that jurisdiction shall lie with a court or the courts in an EU-state, and that legal issue relates to several states.

Next, the Convention sets up a number of *validity requirements* governing the jurisdiction agreements within the ambit of the Convention, cf. Art 17(1) and (4).

The Convention does not regulate the issue of the possible invalidity of jurisdiction agreements under ordinary invalidity rules (duress, fraud, undue influence etc.). Where such issue is raised at a Danish court and it only pertains to the validity of the jurisdiction agreement Danish law will be applied to determine the issue i.e. in particular the rules in the Contracts Act.

The effect of a valid jurisdiction agreement is, under Art. 17(1), that the court(s) appointed in the agreement is deemed to have exclusive jurisdiction. However, Art. 17(5) provides a modification. Where the agreement has been concluded in favour of only one party such party will retain the right to bring proceedings at any other court competent under the Convention.

8.1.6. Special note on preliminary remedies

Under Art. 24 of the Convention application may be made to the courts of another Member Sate which does not have jurisdiction under the Convention in respect of the substance of the main proceedings for any preliminary remedies which may be available under the statutory rules of that state.

The preliminary remedies under Danish law are *attachment* (provisional seizure of goods) and *injunction*. The international jurisdiction of the bailiffs' courts in such proceedings are contained in ss. 631 and 646 of the Administration of Justice Act, both in conjunction with s. 487. Of particular interest in international context is s. 487(2) which, for debtors whose home court is outside Denmark confers jurisdiction on the bailiff's court at the place where the debtor is staying or where he holds assets.

Where attachment has been made or injunction laid down the creditor must bring proceedings in respect of the claim or other cause of action for which the remedy is used unless the debtor waives pursuit. During the action a separate claim for ratification of the interim remedy (attachment/injunction) must be made, cf. ss. 634 and 648 of the Administration of Justice Act. The timelimit for bringing the action in Denmark is 1 week after the attachment was made and two weeks for injunctions. If the proceedings on the main action (the claim etc.) are to be brought at the court in another EU country the timelimit is in all events two weeks, cf. the Administration of Justice Act ss. 634(4) and 648(1). Separate proceedings in ratification of the attachment/injunction must be brought in Denmark within the same timelimits.

8.2. Outside the ambit of the Convention

8.2.1. The main rule

Outside the ambit of the Judgments Convention the international jurisdiction of Danish courts is based on a number of provisions in the Administration of Justice Act. The starting point is that the defendant must have home court in Denmark, ss. 235, 236, and 238(1).

For natural persons a home court will lie when the defendant

1. is *resident* in Denmark even if he is also resident abroad, s. 235(2)
2. is *staying* in Denmark without residence elsewhere, s. 235(3),
3. has had his *latest residence* or *place of sojourn* in Denmark without permanent address or known place of sojourn elsewhere, s. 253(4),
4. is a *Danish citizen* and *resident abroad* without being subject to the jurisdiction of the country of residence, s. 236. In such case, home court is deemed to be Copenhagen.

Under s. 238(1) *legal persons* (companies etc.) have home court at the place of the main office (the "seat" of the company). Where such seat is not to be identified home court will be deemed to be at the place where one of the members of the board or management is resident.

8.2.2. *Exceptional jurisdiction*

Where home court is not applied under the rules mentioned, Danish courts may still have jurisdiction when the proceedings have a specified relationship to Denmark. This applies for one thing in a number of cases of which some resemble those described in the Convention Arts. 5-6 and 13-15, cf. regarding other deviations from the main rule in the two following Sections.

Under the Administration of Justice Act s. 246(1), ss. 237 and 238(2) proceedings may be instituted in Denmark when the defendant is a *trader* in Denmark and procedures relate to his business activities.Proceedings are instituted at the place where the business operations are effected. Further, proceedings may be instituted in Denmark if the case relates to performance of a *contractual obligation* and in that case before the court at the place of performance, s. 246(1) cf. s. 242. As a main rule, performance of purely pecuniary obligations are disregarded. Further proceedings on liability in respect of *legal wrongs* – especially damages claims – may be brought in the court at the place where such wrong has occurred, s. 246(1), cf. s. 243. Finally, a consumer may in cases concerning *consumer agreements* under s. 246(1), 2nd clause, institute proceedings at his home court against trader companies or persons who have no home court in Denmark. It is a requirement that special offer or advertising in Denmark has preceded the conclusion of the contract and that the consumer has made the dispositions necessary for the conclusion of the contract in this country.

Proceedings in relation to *rights in real property* in Denmark may in all circumstances be instituted in the court at the place where the property is situate, cf. Administration of Justice Act s. 241.

8.2.3. *Jurisdiction agreements*

The international jurisdiction of the Danish courts may also derive from a (valid) jurisdiction agreement whereby jurisdiction is conferred on Danish courts for situations in which they would otherwise not be competent, cf. s. 246 of the Administration of Justice Act, combined with s. 245. Conversely, the parties may, prima facie, agree to deprive Danish courts of a jurisdiction following from the rules in the Administration of Justice Act. In consumer cases a preceding jurisdiction agreement is not binding on the consumer. Danish law does not set up form requirements for jurisdiction agreements.

8.2.4. *Sojourn and goods jurisdiction*

Where jurisdiction in Denmark is precluded under the rules mentioned above Danish courts will have international jurisdiction in the following situations:

1. When proceedings relate to *property rights* and the defendant is a *natural* person who has no home court in Denmark. Proceedings may be instituted

at the place where the defendant *stays* at the time of service of the writ of summons, cf. s. 246(2) of the Administration of Justice Act.

2. In proceedings of like nature where the defendant (irrespective of status as a natural or legal person) has no home court in Denmark. Proceedings may be instituted at the place where the defendant had *goods* at the time proceedings were brought, cf. s. 246(3) of the Administration of Justice Act.

Of the two rules conferring under the circumstances international jurisdiction to Danish courts on a very slender basis s. 246(3) is by far the most important in practice. "Goods" are defined as any asset of *economic value* belonging to the defendant at the time proceedings are brought. Basically it is irrelevant whether the asset in question – e.g. a car registered abroad – is only in Denmark on a temporary basis. Rights under a claim are comprised though there will be a requirement, in practice, that such claim is of a reasonable clarity and certainty.

Under the express reference in Art. 3(2) the rules in s. 246(2-3) may not be relied upon where the Convention applies.

9. Recognition and enforcement of foreign judgments

9.1. Introduction

Recognition of a decision made by a foreign court will imply in particular that the decision is relied upon or recognized in the sense that new proceedings between the same parties on the issue decided will be dismissed. The *enforcement problem* relates to the possibilities of activating the authorities of compulsion – the bailiff's courts – on the basis of the foreign judgment with a view to performance of such judgment in part by a levy of execution and subsequent forced sale. In both respects it is of vital importance where the original judgment was pronounced.

9.2. The EU-area

As between the rest of the 14 EU states the Judgments Convention was replaced from 1 March 2002 by Council Regualtion 44/2001 on the courts' competence and on recognition and enforcment of court decisions in the civil and commercial law area (the Judgments Regulation). In the relationship between Denmark and the other EU states the EU Judgments Convention is still applicable, cf. Section 8.1.1 above.

9.2.1. Recognition

In Arts. 26-30 the Judgments Convention contains rules on recognition of judgments originating from the courts of the EU Member States. In principle the exact designation of the judgment is irrelevant, cf. Art. 25. It is a condition that the decision is within the Convention's substance area of application (civil matters etc., cf. above Section 2.1.1). But it is no condition that the decision has been made under the international jurisdiction rules of the Convention. All decisions within the area mentioned are comprised including decisions made in purely national cases.

The conditions of recognition are stated in Arts. 27-29. Among the factors considered are whether – in judgments given in default of appearance – the defendant had a reasonable access to safeguard his interests (Art. 27, no. 2), and wether the decision is possibly incompatible with any decision pronounced between the same parties in the state in which recognition is sought (Art. 27(3). In no circumstances may the foreign decision be reviewed as to its substance (Art 29) and as a main rule no review of the jurisdiction of the court in the state of judgment is to be made (Art. 28(3)).

9.2.2. Enforcement

A fundamental requirement of enforcement of a decision made by a court in one of the other member states is that the recognition conditions are satisfied, cf. Art. 34(2) of the Convention. Further, it must be shown that the judgment is enforceable in the state in which it was given, cf. Art. 31. The procedure in enforcements is the same as for purely Danish decisions.

Court settlements from another EU state enforceable in that state are treated in the same way as judgments, cf. Art. 51 of the Convention.

9.3. Nordic decisions

As between the five Nordic countries a Convention of 5 october 1977 regarding recognition and enforcement of judgments etc. is applicable. Under Art. 1 of the Convention judgments and settlements in respect of *private law claims* pronounced or made in one of the states shall be recognised and enforced in the other states in accordance with the national law of each state. Denmark provided more detailed rules for the performance of the Convention obligations in Consolidated Act No. 635 of 15 September 1986. In most respects the importance of the Convention has gone with the Danish accession to the Lugano Convention, cf. above in Section 8.1.1.

9.4. Other decisions

Outside the areas mentioned above the starting point is that foreign decisions are not recognised and that they are therefore inapplicable as a basis for enforcement. Thus, the power conferred under ss. 223a and 479 of the Administration of Justice Act on the Minister of Justice to lay down rules whereby decisions from foreign courts and authorities regarding claims in civil matters and foreign public settlements on such claims shall have binding effect in Denmark and be enforceable in this country has not been used with a view to laying down general rules.

10. International arbitration

10.1. The arbitration concept. Legal basis

The national legal basis in relation to arbitration consists first and foremost of Act No. 181 of 24 May 1972 (the Arbitration Act) and Consolidated Act No. 117 of 7 March 1973 regarding recognition of foreign arbitration awards etc. (Consolidated Act on arbitration). In international context Denmark has acceded to a number of conventions. Most important among these is the New York Convention of 10 June 1958 on Recognition and Enforcement of Arbitral Awards and the Geneva Convention of 21 April 1961 on international commercial arbitration. A complete set of recommended guidelines in respect of arbitration procedure of great practical importance – especially to ad hoc arbitration – is available in the form of the "Arbitration rules" drafted by the UNCITRAL (United Nations Commission on International Trade Law). The same institution has also prepared a "Model Law of International Commercial Arbitration".

10.2. Territorial identification of the arbitration: national and international arbitration

Under s. 9 of the Arbitration Act a Danish award is enforceable under the provisions of the Administration of Justice Act on enforcement of judgments. Foreign awards on the other hand are subject to the provisions of the Consolidated Act on Arbitration, cf. below Section 4.5. In addition Danish courts may give assistance to Danish arbitration courts, cf. the Arbitration Act, ss. 3 (establishment), 4 (challenges against capacity) and 6 (determination of fee).

The parties may agree that the original forum is Danish and that accordingly the arbitration is deemed to be Danish. Their choice of a national arbitration institution will normally be construed to that effect. In the absence of agreement, the issue must be determined under the socalled "individualising method" i.e. the relationships of the arbitration and of the case are considered in such respects as may be deemed relevant and on this basis a total balancing is made.

10.3. The arbitration agreement

In the absence of agreement on choice of law the validity issue under Danish law is to be determined by reference to the law of the country where arbitral award is to be given, or where such place cannot be identified, under the rules following from Danish private international law, cf. s. 11(2) of the Consolidated Act on Arbitration.

Arbitration agreements on legal relationships which the parties cannot fully control, e.g. a number of central matters within family law and law of persons, will be invalid. The same applies if the agreement provides for a combination of arbitration courts or a procedure which may be considered prejudicial to the parties' – or one party's – best interests.

Danish law does not set up form requirements in respect of arbitration agreements. Thus, oral agreements will be valid if they can be shown to exist. However, it is self-evident that the agreement will normally be in writing.

10.4. Choice of law

The parties to the arbitration case may agree which country's law is to be applicable by the court for their dispute. Where no agreement has been made the court must address the issue itself. The parties may agree that the issue shall be decided upon "equitable" considerations (reasonableness criteria).

10.5. Recognition and enforcement of foreign arbitration awards

Under s. 1 of the Consolidated Act on Arbitration foreign arbitration awards are prima facie binding in Denmark. However, recognition may be refused, upon application, on various grounds cf. s. 3.

As regards enforcement s. 2 of the Consolidated Act sets forth that awards in disputes concerning commercial matters which have binding effect in Denmark, cf. above, and were made in a country which has acceded to the New York Convention, cf. above Section 4.1. are enforceable in Denmark. Where the arbitration award is not comprised by the New York Convention it will be incapable of immediate enforcement in Denmark.

10.6. International Commercial arbitration

Ss. 4-14 of the Consolidated Act on Arbitration relate to arbitration in commercial matters between parties who, at the conclusion of the arbitration agreement, had their residence or seat in different countries which are parties to the Geneva Convention.

The Consolidated Act contains rules on the form of the agreement (s. 4(2) – prima facie, it must be in writing – on the establishment of the arbitration court (ss. 5-10), on choice of law (ss. 11-12), and on the grounds of the decision (s. 13).

CHAPTER 23

Environmental law

by Morten Wegener

1. The external environment as an area of legal regulation

Not until recently have the matters which are commonly comprised in Denmark under the designation of "the environment" become the object of an independent area of legislation. The emergence of this area and its heavily increasing practical and political importance is first and foremost connected to various aspects of the techno-economic and social development which has taken place throughout the industrialised part of the world in the period from the end of the second World War, accelerating especially from the 1960s: abuse of natural resources, rapidly increasing pollution of nature stemming from substantially increased and differentiated production and consumption as well as from other radically changed living conditions for large sections of the population, especially in that they, on the one hand, are concentrated in large urban areas, but on the other, through the proliferation of motor vehicles, have become much more mobile. Especially the former of these matters immediately presents major possible hazards, not only to nature if looked upon as a separate unit, but also to people and their present and future living conditions.

Regardless of which criteria are applied, it causes considerable – not to say almost insurmountable – difficulties to characterise in a fairly accurate and overall way the catalogue of legislation, commonly referred to as "environmental legislation" (or as the subject of a special teaching and research discipline labelled "environmental law"). It is indisputable, however, that the object is certain measures pertaining to matters in *the external environment*, i.e. the physical surroundings of human beings, especially "nature". What is termed the interhuman or social environment – e.g. the working environment – thus falls outside the ambit of environmental legislation/environmental law. Apart from this, it is hardly possible to go further than to establishing that environmental legislation has a certain core field and otherwise altogether diffuse demarcation lines to a number of other areas of legislation/law. The core field consists of legislation which, for the purposes of protecting the external environment, controls human behaviour towards this environment, especially in respect of pollution, any other unacceptable use and exploitation of resources, and as regards keeping especially natural resources clear of human interference or specific types of such interference. The need for protection may, to a varying extent and with varying degrees of strength, affect legislation falling outside the core field, but will, in this connection, most often be accompanied by other needs, e.g. – as is seen within agricultural and fisheries legislation – of industrial policy nature, hence the diffuse demarcation lines.

The legislation existing within the core field may – as already suggested – be divided into three different basic categories according to subject of legislation. The first of these is concerned with *the prevention and control of pollution*. The principal Act is Consolidation Act no. 658 of 22 September 1998 on Environmental Protection which for the purposes of an overall view should also be considered the principal Act within environmental legislation, cf. Section 2 (below) treating the Act in outline. The second deals with *the regulation of the location and fitting of buildings*. To this end, the principal Acts are Consolidation Act no. 452 of 24 June 1998 on Planning and Consolidation Act no. 551 of 28 June 1999 on Building. The third category contains legislation which – especially in the form of preservation – *protects natural resources from human interference*. The principal regulation within this area is found in the Nature Protection Act (no. 835 of 11 January 1997 as amended). As the titles of the above principal Acts indicate, environmental legislation is, to a considerable extent, directed towards the use of real property. The measures are more or less exclusively of public law nature and largely take the form of general or specific restrictions for which criminal sanctions are imposed, although there are examples of attempts by means of subsidy schemes or – especially within the last few years – by the levying of duties, e.g. on polluting activities, to meet the needs for protection with which the legislation is generally concerned.

Since environmental problems, especially in respect of pollution and abuse of resources, know no borders, it is evident that the field of environment to a large extent invites far-reaching international cooperation. In Europe, such cooperation mainly takes place in particular under the auspices of the EU, and based on the provisions on environment contained in the EC Treaty (Arts. 174-176). Important parts of Danish environmental legislation, first and foremost in the field of environmental protection, are thus rooted in EU legislation. On a global scale, cooperation mainly takes place under the auspices of, or otherwise in connection with, the UN in respect of the formulation of treaties within certain limited areas or of more comprehensive environmental action programmes.

2. The Environmental Protection Act in outline

2.1. Purpose and basic principles

Pursuant to s. 1(1) of the Environmental Protection Act, the Act shall contribute to the protection of the country's nature and environment in order that social development can take place on a sustainable foundation, respecting the living conditions of people and the preservation of fauna and flora. The provision represents a very widely formulated – and per se non-operational – programme in respect of the efforts requested by virtue of the Act. "A sustainable foundation" is taken to mean that social development should take place in such a way that human needs of the present are met, without compromising the ability of future generations to meet their own needs. By juxtaposing "living conditions of people" and "the preservation of fauna and flora", it is indicated, in principle, that also strictly tangible assets shall qualify for protection.

S. 1(2) contains somewhat more specific indications of purpose. Under this provision, the Act is especially directed towards *the* prevention and control of pollution of air, water, soil and subsoil as well as of vibration and noise nuisances, *the* formulation of rules, justifiable on sanitary grounds, on importance to the environment and to people, *the* restriction of use and waste of raw materials and other resources, *the* promotion of application of cleaner technology, and *the* promotion of recycling and minimisation of problems in connection with waste disposal. All in all, the provision may be seen as the overall result of the fact that the Act is based upon a *preventive action principle*: the all-important issue is, in every respect, the prevention of pollution, waste of resources, etc., and not the subsequent control and rectification thereof.

In addition, a special version of the preventive action principle is emphazised in s. 3(1) of the Environmental Protection Act as a guiding principle in connection with the administration of the Act, i.e. both at the drafting by the authorities of general rules, and at the specific decision making. Under this provision, importance must be attached to what is attainable by the application of the least polluting technology, including less polluting raw materials, processes and plants, and the best possible anti-pollution measures. It is an overall priority in respect hereof that preventive efforts through the application of cleaner technology should weigh *particularly* heavy at the assessment. From the travaux préparatoires of the Act, this *principle of cleaner technology* in general does not imply that certain requirements can be imposed in respect of application of a certain type of technology. On the contrary, threshold limit values should be fixed – i.e. certain levels of pollution – in order to constantly encourage business enterprises to develop and apply technologies which pollute to an ever decreasing degree.

For the purposes of assessment of the extent and nature of measures for prevention and control of pollution, s. 3(2) sets forth that importance must be attached to the nature of the external surroundings and the possible effects of the pollution on these surroundings as well as on the entire cycle which substances and materials go through, in order that waste of resources be kept at a minimum. With such reference to "possible effects", a *precautionary principle* has been formulated, which under the travaux préparatoires of the Act purports that absence of full scientific proof shall not justify that the authorities refrain from intervening by fixing general rules and guidelines to the extent that risks of serious and irreversible environmental damage exist. The travaux préparatoirs further provide – somewhat self-evidently – that the administration of the Act is subject to the socalled common administrative law *principle of proportionality* commonly applied in administrative law, i.e. a requirement that a reasonable balance between ends and means be maintained, which could be of importance, e.g. in cases where the environmental advantages must be considered marginal and thus only attainable by means of disproportionate investments. S. 4 of the Act provides a number of other important principles. Under subs. 1 of the provision, any person contemplating to start an activity which could be the cause of pollution shall choose such a place for the exercise of the activity that the danger of pollution is kept at a minimum. Subs. 2 describes a number of interests which should be taken into account (the nature of the area, the present and contemplated future use, etc.). This *location principle* implies that any polluting activity shall be located in surroundings which must be considered able to carry the burden of the pollution, and that areas which are found to be of a particular sensitive nature, should be kept free of such polluting activities or at least of certain types of activity. In pursuance of s. 4(3) of the Environmental Protection Act, it is further provided that both new and existing business enterprises shall take the precautionary steps necessary in order to prevent and control pollution, and organise the fitting up and operation of their business in such a way that pollution is kept at a minimum. In respect of this *minimisation principle* it is further provided by the provision that when fitting up the business equipment and when organising the operation – including the selection of manufacturing processes, raw materials and intermediary products – it must be secured that application of resources, pollution and waste disposal are kept at a minimum. In accordance with what is commonly referred to as the *pollutor pays principle*, any costs incurred in respect hereof are thus borne by the undertaking. Under s. 4(4), this principle shall further apply to the extent that pollution has occurred or a pollution risk has arisen. Any person causing such matters ("the responsible party") shall take the precautionary steps necessary in the attempt to efficiently prevent or correct the results of the pollution, and attempts to restore the previous state of affairs must also be made, cf. Section 2.8.2 for further reference on liability in damages in this respect.

2.2. Administration

The administration of the Environmental Protection Act is undertaken at central level by the *Ministry of Environment* (currently the Ministry of Environment and Energy) and by the *National Agency of Environmental Protection* set up by the Ministry. The overall distribution of responsibility is such that the Ministry is mainly in charge of the general regulation, including the drafting of ministerial orders under the large number of powers vested by virtue of the Act, cf. below. Upon delegation from the Ministry, cf. s. 80, the Agency draws up guidelines within the scope of the Act and deals with cases of more specific character, e.g. cases in which the Act provides that decisions in respect hereof should be made centrally, including certain appeal cases.

The day-to-day administration is otherwise, especially in connection with the hearing of specific cases (issuing injunctions/orders, granting authorisations/ approvals, supervising) carried out by the local authority *district council* or by the *county council* in the local authority/county in which the activities in question are undertaken. The more specific distribution of responsibilities between the two local authorities is provided by the individual provisions of the Act. Particularly in connection with especially polluting activities (listed undertakings, cf. Section 2.5), the starting point is that the county council shall treat cases concerning large geographical areas or which in terms of pollution are particularly complicated, while the local authority district council shall handle all other cases of such nature.

The appeals rules contained in the Act are treated in Section 2.7.

2.3. Regulation technique

The regulation technique applied in respect of the Environmental Protection Act differs from the techniques generally applied in connection with most other Acts in that to a large extent the general provisions on purpose and underlying principles, cf. Section 2.1, are not accompanied in the Act by detailed regulation, converting such purposes and principles into more specific prohibitory and instructive rules, e.g. in respect of certain threshold limit values. Instead, detailed regulation is to a considerable degree left to the Minister of the Environment, empowered by the Act to make such delegated legislation. It is thus not possible in all cases to consult the Act to see what rules apply to a certain area of law. The reason for choosing this technique is especially founded on the following: the field of pollution contains such special and serious hazards, complicated connections, rapidly changing needs and recognitions that regulation which is far more flexible than ordinary legislation is considered more expedient. The Environmental Protection Act is thus an example of so-called *framework legislation.*

The authorities conferred by the Act have been implemented in a large number of ministerial orders issued by the Ministry of Environment in respect of a variety of matters, cf. Section 2.5. In addition, several guidelines have been drawn up by the National Agency of Environmental Protection concerning the application of the Act in certain respects. Although the guidelines, as opposed to the orders, in principle are only subordinate sources of law and do not have binding effect on the local authorities, they are in practice relied upon by such authorities to a large extent. From the point of view of a business enterprise, the overall regulation, including the Environmental Protection Act, the ministerial orders and the guidelines, will thus ordinarily seem quite complex and in large part diffuse.

A special – albeit hardly very practical – means of regulation is treated in s. 10 of the Act. Under subsection 1 of this provision, the Minister of the Environment shall, for the purposes of limiting the total level of pollution, i.e. pollution which in national or international terms presents a major environmental problem, be empowered to set binding objectives in respect of reducing the application, the discharge or disposal of specified products, substances or materials. In order to achieve these objectives, the Minister may (subs. 2) make *agreements* with business enterprises or associations of enterprises. The object of such agreements is to determine which environmental improvements are attainable, and which means should be applied for the performance of the individual agreements. The Minister may draw up rules as regards the basis of the agreement and the general terms and conditions in respect hereof. The imbalance thus created between public authorities and the enterprises the prime reason why regulation of this nature is not comparable with the form of self-regulation undertaken by the parties to an ordinary contract under contract and property law.

2.4. Scope of the Act

The scope of the Act is stated in s. 2. Under subs. 1 of this provision, the Act shall apply, first, to any activity which through the discharge of solid, liquid or gaseous substances, or of micro-organisms which could harm the environment and health, or which by the generation of waste could cause pollution of air, water, soil and subsoil (no. 1). Further the listing includes vibrations and noise (no. 2), products or goods which in connection with their manufacture, storage, application, transportation or disposal may cause pollution (no. 3), means of transport and other mobile machinery which may cause pollution (no. 4) as well as certain sanitary matters related to animal husbandry and vermin (no. 5). S. 2(2) establishes that the Act also applies to any activity concerning risk-involving processes and to the storage of substances with dangerous qualities, to the extent that disturbances of such activities or an accident may cause immediate danger of pollution.

The definition of activity applied is extremely wide meaning *any form of display of activity*, irrespective of whether such activity is business-related, private or public, stationary (connected to real property) or mobile. The list contained in s. 2(1) of solid, liquid or gaseous substances, etc. mainly implies that effects in the form of impressions of light and visual impressions as well as esthetic matters fall outside the scope of the Act.

2.5. Substance of the regulation

As mentioned above, the statutory powers vested in the Minister of the Environment, especially by Part 3 (ss. 7-18) of the Act, are converted into a large number of ministerial orders. These orders contain more specific rules and related general prohibitions and orders, approval and authorisation schemes, etc. in respect of a variety of highly dissimilar activities. By way of illustrating the span and intensity of the regulation, it may be mentioned, e.g. that the Minister is empowered to lay down rules in pursuance of s. 7(1) on pollution from business undertakings, equipment, machinery, tools, heating systems and means of transport (no. 1) and on pollution from sewage disposal plants, water purifying plants, refuse disposal plants, and discharging plants as well as from the fitting and operation of such plants (no. 3). For these purposes, a number of ministerial orders have, inter alia, been designed in respect of a variety of matters ranging from setting up and operating garages, noise from wind turbines, application of sludge, waste water, and compost for agricultural purposes, to surface treatment of ships, salt-water-based fish farms, threshold limit values for discharge of different substances and for refuse incineration plants.

In some instances, however, the immediate powers in respect of the measures instituted by the authorities are vested in full or in part by the Act itself. Firstly, this is the case in connection with the protection of soil, subsoil water and surface water (Parts 3 and 4 (ss. 19-32) of the Act) and in respect of waste disposal (Part 6 (ss. 43-48)). Furthermore, various special rules apply under Part 5 (ss. 33-41) of the Act to certain enterprises which are especially polluting. These enterprises are recorded on an exhaustive list prepared by the Minister of the Environment (hence the term "listed enterprise"), cf. s. 35 of the Environment Protection Act and Schedule 1 of the Consolidation Act no. 794 of 9 December 1991 as amended. The list which is presumed to include some 7000 Danish business enterprises, both of private and public description, has been divided into 10 main categories according to nature of activity (e.g. the processing of animal raw material, and power and heat production). For every category there is a detailed description of the type of activity likely to be included (e.g. ironworks, steelworks, metalworks, and strip mills). Any activity falling within the description of the list shall under s. 33 of the Act be prohibited from being constructed or started, until approval of such construction, etc. has been granted, and the enterprise shall also be debarred from making, without approval, enlargements or alterations to the buildings or other operations in such a way that pollution is increased. Such approval, which of course is conditional upon a thorough examination of the environmental conditions of the enterprise, must include terms for the establishment and operation of the activity, cf. s. 34, and a fee is payable depending on the nature of the activity undertaken. Such terms will normally be formulated in accordance with the guidelines prepared by the National Agency of Environmental Protection, cf. Section 2.3. Certain types of listed enterprises, e.g. breaking-up plants, shall in addition provide security under s. 39a to the approval authority for the covering of any future expenses incurred by such authority in respect of accumulated waste. The grant of approval provides a certain kind of protection in return for the issue within a certain period of time, usually eight years, of an order or injunction in respect of the pollution of the business. To these ends, s. 41(4) lays down that during this period of time, the approved enterprises shall not be subject to any additional orders or injunctions, unless new information on the hazardous effects of the pollution has been discovered, or the pollution results in environmentally damaging effects which could not have been foreseen at the time of the grant of approval, or unless such pollution otherwise damages what was the basis of the approval at the material time of the grant.

Part 5 of the Act contains one important provision in respect of pollution from business enterprises which are not included in the list referred to. In pursuance of s. 42, orders may be issued, especially for the reduction of pollution, provided that such undertakings cause insanitary conditions/material pollution or significantly more pollution than necessary by application of the least polluting technology. If the nuisances cannot be remedied, the undertaking shall be subject to prohibition. The guidelines issued by the National Agency of Environmental Protection are also in this connection of great importance.

2.6. Supervision

Efficient supervision is a necessary precondition for the Environmental Protection Act to have the intended effect. Under ss. 65-66 of the Act, the duty of supervision is, in most cases, incumbent upon the local authority district council, although the county council will supervise part of the listed enterprises as well as enterprises operated by the district authorities. The county council will also undertake a more general supervision obligation (in respect of "the environmental state of the surroundings"). The supervision task does not cease when the operations of a business discontinue, i.e. the authorities must also supervise the pollution or risk of pollution from closed business enterprises. In the event that an unlawful practice is discovered, the supervisory authority must, except from in cases of minor importance, demand that the unlawful practice be terminated by issuing a socalled "enforcement notice". In this connection, the continued operation may i.a. be prohibited, the undertaking may be ordered to bring back to *status quo* the state of affairs, and – in case of non-compliance with the notice within the time specified – the authorities may institute that the ordered measures be performed for the account of the responsible person ("self-help acts"), cf. ss. 68-69 and also s. 70(2) on the right to immediate recovery of expenses in respect hereof. In case of emergency, e.g. where immediate intervention is called for in order that material pollution be prevented, the supervisory authorities can in pursuance of s. 70(1) of the Act take the necessary steps without notice and for the account of the culprit (with possibility of recovery as above). Further, the person responsible has a duty to notify the supervisory authority immediately and without delay of any operation disturbances or accidents causing material pollution or involving danger of such pollution, cf. s. 71. A large number of enterprises – some 100,000 in total within industry and agriculture – are charged a fee for supervision proportionate to the nature of the activity and the workload which the supervision entails.

It is of particular importance to the supervision tasks, for one thing, that a large number of – typically small – business undertakings are to register with the district council prior to commencing operation, and for another, that the environmental authorities are granted access, by virtue of s. 87 of the Act, to the extent it is necessary, at any time and without a warrant, to enter public and private property and premises in order to exercise the powers vested by the Act, including making investigations. Police assistance will be available to the extent necessary for such purpose.

2.7. Appeals, etc.

Decisions under the Environmental Protection Act are normally to be communicated in writing to the person or persons, undertakings or others to whom the decision is directed ("the addressee"), cf. s. 74(1). If the decision is subject to appeal, it must further – e.g. by means of public announcement – be communicated to other possible appellants, cf. below. Under s. 74(2), approval of listed enterprises must always be publicly announced.

Apart from certain cases of minor environmental importance, e.g. concerning rats and animal husbandry and the above-mentioned "enforcement notices", decisions made by district or county councils may be appealed to the National Agency of Environmental Protection, cf. s. 91. Appeals must be filed within four weeks from the day the decision was communicated. Prima facie, appeals in writing will act as a stay of proceedings in respect of any orders or injunctions, while the opposite applies to appeals in respect of authorisation, approval or exemption, cf ss. 93-96. Pursuant to s. 98, the group of appellants is more extensive than in connection with most other administrative decisions. In addition to the addressee and any other persons with an individual, material interest in the outcome of the case – for instance and in particular neighbours – the district council has appeals authority in respect of county council decisions and a corresponding access lies with the county council for district council decisions. Other specified appellants include the medical officer of health and a number of national organisations, e.g. the Danish Society for Nature Preservation, the Labour Movement Commercial Council, and the Consumer Council. Right of appeal is finally granted on certain terms to certain local societies who have as their primary objective the preservation of nature.

Various decisions may be appealed to the *Environmental Appeals Board*, cf. ss. 102-109 of the Act. This applies, first, to cases in which decision in first instance (exceptionally) has been made by the National Agency of Environmental Protection, cf. s. 103(1)(1) and cf. ss. 25 and 82. Further, appeals are available in respect of important or leading decisions by the Agency made in its capacity of appeals body, to the extent that such decisions concern listed enterprises or certain sewage disposal plants, cf s. 103(1)(2). The time limit for appeals to the above Board is the same as for appeals to the National Agency for Environmental Protection. Appellants are the same persons, organisations, etc. as listed above save the national officer of health as well as the authority who made the first instance decision.

Where the decisions of the environmental authorities made under the Environmemtal Protection Act or under the rules laid down in pursuance thereof are to be subjected to judicial review proceedings must be commenced within six months after the finding or decision has been made or otherwise publicly announced, cf. s. 101(1).

2.8. Enforcement

2.8.1. Criminal liability

Infringements of the Environmental Portection Act and of the body of rules attached thereto is punishable by criminal law sanction in a number of instances. The same applies to infringement of or non-compliance with certain types of specific decisions made by the environmental authorities, e.g. injunctions or orders or terms in respect of authorisations or approvals, cf. s. 110 of the Act.

The starting point is that infringements are punishable by penalty. However, a sentence of simple detention or imprisonment of up to two years may be attracted for offences involving intent or gross negligence and the offence caused harm to the environment or produced a danger of such harm, or where a financial gain had been obtained or aimed at – including as a result of costs-saving – by the infringing person or others. If the criminal conduct was instigated by a company, a penalty may be imposed on such company. The same applies to any infringement by the Government, county or district councils, or other local authority associations. Any gain resulting from the infringement is subject to confiscation. If such confiscation is not carried out, the court shall, when fixing the penalty, pay special attention to the size of any financial gain obtained or intentionally sought. The level of sanctions has long been subject to criticism, the opinion from political quarters being that the sanctions imposed in general are far too lenient. The size of the penalties imposed has, however, been increasing over the past few years and a few decisions of these years have in fact involved custodial sentences.

2.8.2. Civil liability

If damage is caused to the person or property of others by conduct contrary to the Environmental Protection Act, the question of civil liability shall in general be assessed under the general Danish law of damages (the principle of fault ("culpa")), cf. Chapter 7.

Pursuant to Act no. 225 of 6 April 1994 on compensation for environmental damage (the Compensation for Environmental Damage Act), more stringent rules shall apply in respect of damage caused in connection with a number of especially hazardous or polluting enterprises. The Act, which came into effect on 1 July 1994, concerns damage caused after that date, i.e. it will not suffice that the damaging effects appeared after the commencement date if the wrongful act or omission was prior to this date. Under s. 1, the Act shall apply to damage caused by pollution of air, water, soil, or subsoil as part of such commercial or public activity listed in a Schedule to the Act, and in addition it shall apply to nuisances in the form of noise, vibrations, or the like. As regards the pollution concept, the definition is thus largely similar to the one contained in s. 2 of the Environmental Protection Act, cf. Section 2.4 (above). The Schedule mentioned is also very similar in structure and substance to the Schedule referred to in Section 2.5 in respect of listed enterprises. They are, however, not completely identical in that the Act – in addition to the listed enterprises – also applies to garages, certain sewage disposal plants, and agricultural properties as well as to undertakings making use of large underground oil tanks, including leased premises.

The very stringent rules on liability for damages contained in s. 3(1) of the Act are to be seen as far-reaching implementation of the "pollutor pays principle", cf. Section 2.1 (above). If pollution is caused as part of any commercial or public activity included in the above Schedule, compensation must be paid for the damage caused by the pollution. The wrongdoer thus incurs strict liability, regardless of whether he and/or his employees were at fault, provided, of course, that the damage was the direct cause of the especially hazardous or polluting activity. If the damage was caused by the fact that the activity was carried out by virtue of mandatory rules provided by a public authority – e.g. terms in an environmental approval – no liability in damages will lie, cf. s. 3(2). Where the injured party has contributed to the harm intentionally or negligently – with personal injury and loss of breadwinner the level is increased to gross negligence – the compensation may lapse or be subject to reduction, cf. s. 4.

Under s. 2 of the Act, "damage" is defined as covering any personal injury or loss of breadwinner, damage to property, other loss of property and reasonable costs for avoiding or preventing such damage or for restoring measures of the environment. It thus follows that the substance of the definition is traditional in every respect in that – as is the case with the general law of damages – first, the definition only covers financial damage. The latter category of damage also comprises expenses incurred by the environmental authorities through self-help acts, cf. Section 2.6 (above). Second, it is a precondition that an individual injured party can be identified which could prove difficult in a number of environmental damage cases. Since environmental organisations, etc. in general cannot be considered injured parties, such organisations are barred from claiming damages.

Under s. 5(1), the Compensation for Environmental Damage Act shall be mandatory to the effect that agreements made prior to the damage, dispensing with the provisions contained in the Act – i.e. before any certain signs of the effects of the damage have emerged – are to be void if such derogation is to the detriment of the injured party. However, the mandatory character does not apply, under s. 5(2), to agreements made between the party liable for the damage and the government, a district council or any other public sector body, or with a trader acting in the course of his business. Thus, in connection with transfers of an environmentally hazardous entreprise as a going concern, agreement may e.g. be validly made between the transferor and the transferee – although subject to privity of contract principles – for the purposes of limiting the liability of the vendor for pollution damage.

Under s. 6(1), claims for damages under the Act shall be statute-barred five years after the day on which the injured party became cognisant of or ought to have become cognisant of the damage, the wrongdoer, and the whereabouts of such wrongdoer, i.e. limitation will prima facie set in in accordance with the general rules for damages claims in the Limitation Act of 1908, cf. Chapter 17. The provisions on interruption and suspension of the limitation period contained in clause 2 of s. 2, and s. 3 of the 1908 Act will apply correspondingly. Since a very long period of time may pass in practice before the damage occurs, s. 6(2) lays down that to the extent a claim has not become statute-barred in pursuance of s. 6(1), the claim shall lapse no later than 30 years after the event causing the damage. For the purpose of interruption of this period, clause 2 of s. 2 of the 1908 Act shall apply. The period may thus only be interrupted by the acknowledgement of fault by the wrongdoer or by the institution of legal proceedings against him.

The Compensation for Environmental Damage Act is non-exclusive in the sense that the injured party shall not be debarred from claiming damages on other grounds. Under s. 7(1) of the Act, the injured party may thus bring an action for damages under the general rules pertaining hereto or in pursuance of other statutory rules. The injured party is thus free to choose the cause of action most beneficial from his point of view.

Index

V

W